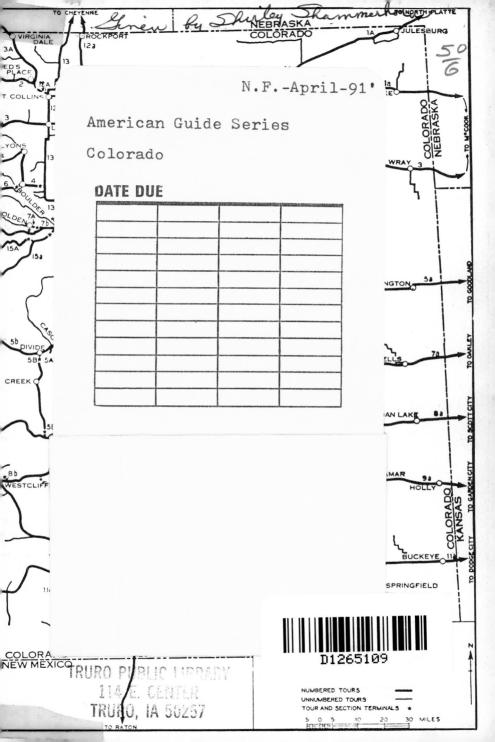

N.F.-April-91'

American Guide Series

Colorado

DATE DUE

D1265109

NUMBERED TOURS
UNNUMBERED TOURS
TOUR AND SECTION TERMINALS ✱

5 0 5 10 20 30 MILES

COLORADO

A Guide to the Highest State

COLORADO

A Guide to the Highest State

NEW REVISED EDITION
HARRY HANSEN, *Editor*

*Originally Compiled by the Federal Writers' Program
of the Work Projects Administration
of the State of Colorado*

AMERICAN GUIDE SERIES

ILLUSTRATED

HASTINGS HOUSE • *Publishers* • *New York*

First Published in 1941
Second Printing, 1943
Third Printing, 1945
Fourth Printing, 1946
Fifth Printing, 1948
Sixth Printing, 1951
Seventh Printing, 1959
Completely Revised Edition, September 1970

ISBN: 8038–1145–4
Library of Congress Catalog Card Number: 75–132150
Copyright © 1970, by Hastings House, Publishers, Inc.
Copyright 1941, by the State Planning Commission
Printed in the U.S.A.

A Note About the New Edition

This revision of *Colorado, A Guide to the Highest State,* brings abundant proof that even a state solidly anchored on the eternal hills can be subject to continuing change. Since the original edition of this *Guide* was prepared by the Federal Writers of the Work Projects Administration, vast areas of barren land have been reclaimed for productive fields, plunging rivers have been channelled for flood control, irrigation and power, and the earth has yielded mineral wealth of a kind unsuspected by the goldseekers. Thousands of miles of new roads link producer and market, and in the air swift-moving vehicles bring the snowclad slopes nearer for recreation. Only the railroads have shrunk.

The original *Guide* was sponsored by the Colorado State Planning Commission and produced "as part of a nation-wide plan to give employment to professionally trained writers, journalists, and research workers." Many legends and traditions were hunted down and the activities of big cities and little towns were described. Harry Simonson, State Supervisor, noted especially the help given by librarians, educators, historians, art directors and State officials. The general plan of the American Guide Series was devised by Henry G. Alsberg. Editors of the Colorado *Guide* were Mary F. Adams, Morris W. Cleavenger, and George F. Willison, with Thomas Hornsby Ferril as consultant. The fine essays on Colorado's past have been retained in this edition, but cities, towns, and tours, have been thoroughly revised, and much useful information has been added to these pages.

Contents

Part I. Colorado and Coloradoans

Part II. The Urban Scene

Part III. Up and Down and All Around

Page

Page

Part IV. Appendices

Illustrations

EDUCATION

SPORTS AND RECREATION

Maps

Population

U. S. Department of Commerce, Bureau of the Census

Preliminary 1970 census counts from Colorado show the State's population to be 2,195,887. The final official total in the 1960 census was 1,753,947.

Preliminary counts show also that Denver continues as the largest city in Colorado. The 1970 count for the city is 512,691 compared with a final official total of 493,887 in 1960. The count in the State's most populous county, Denver, rose to 512,691 from 493,887 in 1960.

The count for Lakewood, 93,403, makes it the fourth largest city in Colorado.

The 1970 population figures for the first six cities are:

	1970	1960
Denver	512,691	493,887
Colorado Springs	124,805	70,194
Pueblo	96,728	91,181
Lakewood	93,403	19,338
Aurora	74,425	48,548
Boulder	65,977	37,718

General Information

Highways: It is possible to cross Colorado in all directions on wide, well-maintained roads the year around. As of January 1, 1969, the Federal Government had completed 974.84 *m.* of Interstate Highways. There were 3,239.52 *m.* of U. S. Highways, and 4,735.05 *m.* of State Highways, a total of 8,949.41.

In addition the Counties maintained 66,745 *m.* of roads with various kinds of surfacing, and there were 5,999 *m.* of city streets. The Highway Department reported that the total mileage was 81,694.05.

The important Interstate roads are the east-west 80S, entering the State from Nebraska at Julesburg, and the east-west 70, coming from Kansas to Burlington. Both go to Denver, where 80S stops. Interstate 70 proceeds west and crosses the State into Utah via Grand Junction. The main north-south artery is Interstate 25, which was joined by Interstate 80 at Cheyenne and moves down Colorado, through Fort Collins, Denver, Colorado Springs, Pueblo, and Trinidad into New Mexico.

The Navajo Trail: The trail enters Colorado from Kansas on US 50 east of Holly, proceeds west through Lamar, Las Animas, and La Junta, where it moves southwest on State 10 to Walsenburg, then takes US 160 to Alamosa, Monte Vista, Del Norte, Pagosa Springs, Bayfield, Durango, Cortez. At Cortez the trail is followed by US 164, leaving Colorado at Four Corners. From Lamar to Four Corners the mileage is 435. In Arizona the trail is followed by US 164 and US 89.

Mountain Passes: There are 29 mountain passes in Colorado. The highest spot on a road is Trail Ridge High Point on US 34 in Larimer County, 12,183 ft. The highest mountain pass is Berthoud on US 40 in Clear Creek and Grand Counties, 11,314 ft.

Most of the mountain passes are kept open during the winter; only seven are closed. Those open are Berthoud (US 40), Douglas (State 139), Fremont (State 91), Gore (State 84), Hoosier (State 9), Kenosha (US 285), Lizard Head (State 145), Loveland (US 6), Molas Divide (US 550), Monarch (US 50), Muddy (US 40), North La Veta (US 160), North Pass (State 114), Poncha (US 285), Rabbit Ears (US 40), Red Hill (US 285), Red Mountain (US 550), Squaw (State 103), Tennessee (US 24), Trout Creek (US 24, 285), Ute (US 24), Vail (US 6), Wilkerson (US 24), Willow Creek (State 125) and Wolf

Creek (US 160). Passes closed in winter are Cucharas (State 111), Cumbres (State 17), Independence (State 82), La Manga (State 17), McClure (State 133), and Trail Ridge High Point (US 34).

Driving Regulations: On narrow, winding mountain roads and blind curves, 20 mph.; on open mountain roads, 40 mph.; on open, surfaced roads, 60 mph. A speed limit of 70 mph. is permitted on surfaced four-lane highways; special situations are covered by black-and-yellow signs. A motorist traveling in either direction must stop before reaching a school bus flashing red lights when stopping. On a four-lane highway a motorist must stop for the flashing bus lights only when traveling in the same direction. Accidents must be reported to State Patrol, County sheriff, or city police. For travel on remote and unimproved roads previous inquiry about conditions is recommended; during winter extra food, water, blankets are advised, and possibly tire chains or snow tires.

Officers of the Colorado State Patrol are on duty to supervise traffic, help when needed, inspect vehicles, visit tourist camps, report thefts. Hq of the Board is in Denver and there are 411 officers and employees.

Driver's Licenses: Any person who is employed in Colorado, owns or operates a business there, or has lived there for 90 days is considered a resident and must have a driver's license. Anyone who moves to Colorado and had a license in his former state has 30 days grace in which to obtain a license. Any non-resident who is at least 16 and has a license from his home state may drive continuously for 120 days without a Colorado license. Any member of the Armed Forces may drive a vehicle for the Armed Forces. Any non-resident in active duty with the Armed Forces and his dependents over 16 who have a license from their home state are exempt from a Colorado license. A non-resident with a driver's license from home who is temporarily a student in Colorado is also exempt. Detailed information about the regulations governing licenses for chaffeurs and motorcycle operators are published by the State Motor Vehicle Division, State Dept. of Highways, Denver.

Federal Fees and Regulations: The Golden Eagle Passport admits the holder to all Federal recreation areas where a fee is charged. It costs $7 and is valid for one year. It also will admit to such areas all persons who accompany the holder in a private noncommercial vehicle. It does not exempt the holder from such fees as are charged for camping, bathhouses, firewood, guided tours, and similar services. It permits the use of a trailer that is towed, not operated. Anyone wishing only a single day permit pays $1, which includes occupants of his car. Visitors also may get short-term single area carload permits for $3 to $5, depending on length of stay. The passport does not cover hunting or fishing licenses. Persons under 16 and groups entering Federal areas for purposes not connected with recreation, such as school study classes are not charged a fee. The Golden Eagle Passport may be obtained at the entrances to Federal recreation areas, at the Bureau of Federal Recreation, Bldg. 41, Denver Federal Center; at County offices of the Department of Agriculture's Stabilization and Conservation Service; at the Bureau of Indian Affairs of the Department of the Interior; at the American Automobile Assn. offices; at the Corps of Engineers, USA; or address Operation Golden Eagle, Bureau of Outdoor Recreation, Box 7763, Washington, D. C., 20044—not forgetting to enclose the $7 fee.

Campgrounds: Everywhere in Colorado there is provision for outdoor recreation. Federal, State, and private campgrounds give the visitor a wide choice of scenery, lakes for fishing, swimming, boating, and woods in which to raise a tent under the allurement of the pines. Most of the campgrounds have facilities for overnight parking. They have fire grates, garbag containers, picnic tables, sanitation facilities, and room for tents. Trailers may not be longer than 22 ft. Unless specially stated there are no laundromats, shower baths or trailer connections except in the private campgrounds. The Colorado Game, Fish & Parks Dept., 6060 Broadway, Denver, publishes the *Colorado Campground Guide* for free distribution.

Campground fees: A fee of $1 a day in the form of a windshield sticker is charged per car and covers all occupants until 5 P.M. next day. A year's permit is $5. Replacement of sticker costs $2. These fees are charged by the 24 State Campgrounds.

National Recreation Areas: For specific information about National Parks, Forests, Historic Sites and other Federal areas in Colorado, address the Superintendent at the following places:

Arapaho National Forest, 1010 Tenth St., Golden 80401
Bent's Old Fort National Historic Site, Box 581, La Junta 81050
Black Canyon of the Gunnison National Monument, c/o Curecanti National Recreation Area, Montrose 81401
Colorado National Monument, c/o Curecanti National Recreation Area, Montrose 81401
Curecanti Recreation Area, Montrose 81401
Dinosaur National Monument, Dinosaur 81610
Grand Mesa-Uncompahgre National Forests, Post Office Building, Delta 81416
Great Sand Dunes National Monument, Box 60, Alamosa 81101
Gunnison National Forest, 216 N. Colorado, Columbine Hotel, Gunnison 81230

Hovenweep National Monument, c/o Mesa Verde National Park 81330
Mesa Verde National Park, Mesa Verde 81330
Pike National Forest, 320 W. Fillmore, Colorado Springs 80907
Rio Grande National Forest, Fassett Building, Monte Vista 81144
Rocky Mountain National Park, Box 1080, Estes Park 80517
Roosevelt National Forest, 211 Canyon, Fort Collins 80521
Routt National Forest, Hunt Building, Steamboat Springs 80477
San Isabel National Forest, Post Office Building, Pueblo 81002
San Juan National Forest, Box 341, West Building, Durango 81301
Shadow Mountain Recreation Area, c/o Rocky Mountain National Park, Box 1080, Estes Park 80517
White River National Forest, Old Post Office Building, Glenwood Springs 81601

Climate and Equipment: Because of topography, Colorado's climate varies to a marked degree in different localities. In general winters are mild and summers are comfortably warm, with cool evenings and nights. Visitors should provide themselves with light wraps for summer evenings. Hikers and campers in mountain regions should have sweaters and jackets and should wear thick-soled shoes or boots. Hats with broad brims are recommended to guard against sunburn. Winter sports equipment can be rented at the larger resorts.

Poisonous Reptiles, Insects, and Plants: Rattlesnakes are frequently found in arid sections of plains and foothills; in infested areas, wear boots for protection. The wood tick, carrier of Rocky Mountain spotted fever, is common to many mountainous sections in early spring, especially where sheep have been pastured. Not all ticks are fever carriers, and there is no considerable danger from them if proper precautions are taken. Poison ivy, found chiefly at low elevations, is not common in the State. Visitors are cautioned not to eat berries of mountain shrubs, as they may be poisonous.

Sale of Liquor: Sale to minors is prohibited. Bottled liquor is sold only in licensed liquor stores and drug stores from 8 A.M. to 12 midnight, and cannot be consumed on the premises. Sale of bottled liquor is prohibited on Sundays, Christmas, and on elections days until after polling hours. Alcohol is sold by the drink 8 A.M. to 12 midnight (except in cities of more than 50,000, where hours are 8 A.M. to 2 A.M.), and on Sundays 8 A.M. to 8 P.M.

Historical Museums: The State Historical Society of Colorado maintains nine museums in seven cities, and two historical sites, all free, as follows: Baca House and Pioneer Museum, Trinidad; Bloom House (Victorian, 1880), Trinidad; Colorado State Museum, 200 14th Ave., Denver, 9–5 Monday through Friday, 10–5 weekends, holidays; Dexter Cabin, Leadville; El Pueblo Museum, 905 Prairie Ave., Pueblo; 9–5 Tuesday through Friday, 10–5 weekends, holidays; Fort Vasquez, Platteville (fur trade post, 1830s); Healy House, Leadville; Old Fort Garland, 1858–1883, Fort Garland; Ute Indian Museum, Montrose. Also Georgetown Loop mining area, between Georgetown and Silver Plume; Pike's Stockade, 1807, replica, near La Jara. Other museums with pioneer, Indian, archaeological exhibits are at Boulder, Colorado Springs, Cortez, Cripple Creek, Fairplay, Florissant, Fort Collins, Fort Morgan, Golden, Grand Junction, Greeley, Gunnison, Hot Sulphur Springs, Julesburg, La Veta, Littleton, Longmont, Loveland, Ouray, Rocky Ford, Saguache, Salida, Silverton, Steamboat Springs, Sterling, and Victor. Leaflets describing some of the historic sites are published by the State Historical Society of Colorado.

Mineral Hot Springs are located in or near Canon City, Del Norte, Durango, Eldorado Springs, Glenwood Springs, Hooper, Hot Sulphur Springs, Idaho Springs, Lay, Mineral Hot Springs, Mt. Princeton Hot Springs, Ouray, Pagosa Springs, Poncha Springs, Powderhorn, Redstone, Steamboat Springs, and Waunita Hot Springs.

Calendar of Annual Events

Colorado has a large roster of civic, competitive, sporting, recreational and cultural events, so that there is hardly a community that does not offer activities to enrich the lives of residents and visitors, winter and summer. Rodeos in summer, skiing in winter, appeal to spectators and participants. The State several times a year publishes pamphlets that tell where unusual events are taking place. These are issued by the Travel Development Section of the Division of Commerce & Development, 602 State Capitol Annex, Denver, Colorado, 80203. Consult also the Colorado Visitors Bureau, 225 West Colfax Ave., Denver, the State Department of Highways, 4201 East Arkansas Dr., Denver, 80222, and the Chambers of Commerce of the separate cities.

Dates of events may vary, but they usually come in approximately the same weeks, as indicated below.

JANUARY

First Week—Snowmass Snowmobile regatta, Aspen. Snowmobile safari, Creede to Lake City, Monte Vista. Twelfth Night festival, Boulder.

Second Week—Denver Univ. Winter Carnival, Winter Park. National Western Stock show, Denver (runs nine days). Winterskol, Aspen.

Third Week—Blue Mesa Snowmobile races, Gunnison.

Fourth Week—Ski Spree, with selection of Queen, Glenwood Springs (into February).

FEBRUARY

First Week—Agricultural Institute, Brighton. Winter Carnival, Steamboat Springs. Cup races, Loveland.

Second Week—Rock Cup championship contests, Aspen. Western State Winter Carnival, Crested Butte.

Third Week—Winter Carnival, Leadville. Figure Skating championships, Colorado Springs.

MARCH

First Week—Colorado Cup races, Winter Park. American International Team races, Vail. National Cross Country Ski week, Durango. WCHA Hockey League, Denver University.

Second Week—NCAA National Hockey Championships, Colorado Springs.

Third Week—NCAA National Ski Championships, Steamboat Springs. Carnival, Monarch Ski area, Salida.

APRIL

First Week—Easter Sunrise services at Aspen; Colorado National Monument, Grand Junction; Garden of the Gods, Colorado Springs; Red Rocks, Morrison; Auditorium, Denver. Greyhound racing, Loveland. National Intercollegiate Flower Contest, Fort Collins. Rocky Ridge Spring concert, Estes Park.

Second Week—Gateway Downs racing, Holly. Airline Ski picnic, Vail.

Third Week—Hobby show, Estes Park. Community Concert, Rocky Ford. Denver Bears, Mile High Stadium. Horse racing, Pikes Peak Meadows, Colorado Springs.

MAY

First Week—May festival, Estes Park. CSU College Days, Fort Collins. Mineral Pools open, Steamboat Springs. Buffalo Downs horse racing, Cheyenne Wells. Music and Blossom festival, Canon City. Skyline Stampede rodeo, Fort Collins. Brush & Palette exhibit, Grand Junction. International Art exhibit, Pueblo. May Day Slalom, Arapahoe Ski, Dillon.

Second Week—Top of the Nation rodeo, Monte Vista. Continental Divide raceways, Castle Rock. Arapahoe Gun Show, Littleton. Rocky Ridge Music center, Estes Park. German Hofbrau celebration, Steamboat Springs. Art show, Rocky Ford. Denver Bears, baseball (*to September*). Southern Ute Bear Dance, Ignacio.

Third Week—FFA Rodeo, Rifle. Nomad Players, U. of Colorado. Broomfield Days, Broomfield. Lamar Days, Lamar. Dolores River races, Cortez. Gateway to the Rockies, Arvada.

Fourth Week—Elitch Gardens open, Denver. Lakeside Amusement Park opens, Denver. Trail Ridge Road opens, Estes Park to Grand Lake. NJCAA Baseball tournament, Grand Junction. FFA Rodeo, Greeley. U. S. Air Force Academy, graduation exercises. Sunrise Slalom, Grand Lake.

JUNE

First Week—Silverton narrow gauge railroad opens, Durango (*daily to October*). Uranium Downs, racing, 2 weeks, Grand Junction. Kowboy Karnival and Little Britches rodeo, Hotchkiss. Ski Golf Team tournament, Vail. Last Chance melodrama, Gunnison (*through August*).

Second Week—Rangely Days rodeo, Rangely. Sidewalk Art show, Central City. Kennel Club Dog show, Colorado Springs. Gem and Mineral show, Grand Junction. Creative Youth Symphony workshop, Ouray. Craig Appaloose show, Craig. Southern Colorado Kennel Club show, Pueblo. Chautauqua, Boulder (*to September*). Greyhound racing, Kennel Club, Pueblo (*into August*). Greyhound racing, Mile High Kennel Club, Denver. Horse show, Grand Junction. 4-H Horse show, Cahone.

Third Week—Ute Mountain Roundup rodeo, Cortez. Institute of Humanistic Studies opens, Aspen (*through August*). Rock Climbing demonstration, Cheyenne Canyon, Colorado Springs (*to September*). Square Dance festival, Central City. Imperial Hotel melodrama, Cripple Creek (*to September*). Diamond Circle melodrama, Durango (*until late September*). Iron Springs melodrama, Manitou Springs (*to September*). Evening nature talks, City Park, Steamboat Springs. Rio Grande River Raft races, Monte Vista. Sports Car rally, Glenwood Springs. Annual rodeo, Walsenburg. Central City Opera opens, Central City (*through July*). Music in the Mountains, Rocky Ridge, Estes Park. Town & Country Days,

Steamboat Springs. Invitational Scotch Foursome golf, Grand Lake. Huerfano County Annual Soil Conservation tour, Walsenburg.

Fourth Week—Aspen Music Festival opens at Amphitheater in the Meadows (*through August*). Melodrama nightly, Vail (*through September*). Summer Theater, Broadway plays, Salida. Flight Days rodeo, Eagle. Rock Hounds Gem and Minerals show, Fort Collins. Pikes Peak Auto Hill Climb, Colorado Springs. Perry Mansfield Camp dance and Drama Festival, Steamboat Springs. Stampede Rodeo, Grand Junction. Little Britches rodeo, Pikes Peak Stockmen's Center, Colorado Springs. Bookcliff Rifle match, Rifle. Jackpot Roping, Estes Park. Centennial Park horse races, Littleton (*until October*). Chautauqua opens, Rye (*through August*). Edgar Mine, guided tours, Idaho Springs (*until September*). South Fork Raft Races, Creede. Soapbox Derby and Parade, Pueblo. The Troupe summer theater opens, Grand Lake, Donkey Derby Days, Sterling.

JULY

First Week—Independence Day is observed in many communities with parades and fireworks. Broadmoor Women's Invitational golf, Colorado Springs. Old-fashioned Days, Arvada. Rotary Club fireworks, Mountaineer Bowl, Gunnison. Safco 4th of July Tennis tournament, Pueblo. National AAU Swim, Aurora. Go West with Greeley rodeo, Greeley. Broadmoor International Theatre, Colorado Springs (*through August*). Sailing regatta, weekends, Dillon Reservoir. Arabian Horse Show, Estes Park. Little Theatre of the Rockies, Greeley. University Band concerts, Boulder. *Rocky Mountain News* Showagon, Denver. Pioneer Celebration, Crested Butte. Pick 'n Hoe Celebration, Dove Creek. Mountain Cycle race, Glenwood Springs. Buffalo Barbecue, Idaho Springs. Range Call Rodeo and Meeker Massacre pageant, Meeker. Jeep Flare parade, Ouray. Red Ryder Roundup, Pagosa Springs. Cherry Day, July 4, Paonia. Indian Dances, Salida. Roundup Rodeo, Steamboat Springs. Old-fashioned Mountain Fourth, Telluride. Huck Finn Day, Walsenburg. Championship Trap Shoot, Craig.

Second Week—Men's Garden Club of America show, Fort Collins. Train Robbery spectacle, Idaho Springs. Pack Burro race, Leadville-Fairplay. Koshare Interpretative Indian Dancers, Boy Scouts, La Junta (*Wednesdays and Saturdays during July*). Band Concerts, City Park, Denver (*through August*). Open Golf tourney, Craig. Morgan Horse Show, Estes Park. Philharmonic Alpine Festival, Evergreen (*through August*). Pine Cone Theatre, Grand Lake (*through August*). Royal Gorge Roundup, Canon City. Miss Colorado Pageant, Sterling.

Third Week—Whitewater Boat races on the Arkansas, Salida-Cotopaxi. National Omok'xe (games on horses) Greeley. Pike's Peak Range Riders Street Breakfast, Colorado Springs. Rooftop rodeo, Estes Park. Cattlemen's Days rodeo, Gunnison. Ride 'n Tie rodeo, Craig. Little Britches rodeo, Steamboat Springs. Ute Train Stampede rodeo, Woodland Park. Mormon Pioneer days, Manassa. Chamber of Commerce Barbecue, Aurora.

Fourth Week—Quarter Horse races, Monte Vista. Deltarado Days, RCA rodeo, Delta. Ski-Hi Stampede rodeo, Monte Vista (*into August*).

AUGUST

First Week—Buffalo Bill Days at Golden, usually Aug. 1 and 2. First day, games, street dancing, pancake supper. Second day, Saddle Club ride up Lookout Mtn. to ceremonies at grave at noon; parade in Golden; reception to Governor at Foothills Art Center; band concert, dinner, square dance at Golden Recreation Center. Colorado University Shakespeare Festival at Boulder (two weeks) ; also C. U. excursion to Mt. Alice. Bronc Day, barbecue, Green Mountain Falls. Western Colorado Golf meet, Montrose. Alpine Tunnel Days, Pitkin. Pikes Peak Marathon, Colorado Springs. Firemen's Day, Colorado Springs. Colorado Day, Central City. Montelores Junior Fair, Cortez. RCA rodeo, Evergeen. Northwest Colorado Horse Show, Steamboat Springs.

Second Week—Kit Carson County Fair, Burlington. Pikes Peak or Bust roadeo, Colorado Springs. Outdoor Choral concerts, Gunnison. FFA and Tricounty 4-H fair, Monte Vista. Excursion to James Peak, Boulder. El Paso County fair, Calhan. 4-H Farm fair, Walsenburg. Navajo Trails Fiesta, Durango. San Miguel Basin rodeo, Norwood. Animal Shoot for Archers, Monte Vista. Snowmass Chess tournament, Aspen. Arapahoe Glacier hike, Boulder. Mt. Evans Bicycle climb, Idaho Springs. 4-H Club exhibits, Craig. Western Welcome week and Sidewalk Art show, Littleton. Sidewalk Bazaar, Glenwood Springs. Hilton Square Dance Festival, Denver.

Third Week—Excursion up Mt. Princeton, Boulder. Lipton Cup Yacht regatta, Grand Lake. Open Golf tournament, Rocky Ford. ATA Handicap sheet, Craig. Little Britches rodeo, Littleton. Latimer County fair, Loveland. Artists Alpine Holidays, exhibits, Ouray. Four Wheelers trip, Gunnison. Aspen Rodeo, Aspen. Sand and Sage Roundup, Lamar. Moffat County fair, Craig. Arkansas Valley fair, rodeo, and Watermelon Day, Rocky Ford. Logan County Fair & Rodeo, Sterling.

Fourth Week—Broadmoor Ice Review, Colorado Springs. Delta County fair, Hotchkiss. Sheriff's Posse rodeo, Montrose. Water Pageant, Loveland. International Golf, Colorado Springs. Rocky Mountain Kennel Club, dog races, Colorado Springs. Colorado State Fair and Industrial Exhibition, Pueblo. Garfield County fair, rodeo, Rifle. Buffalo Barbecue, Manitou Springs. Skin Diving meet, Grand Lake. Larimer County Fair, rodeo, Loveland. Weld County Harvest Fair, Greeley. Las Animas County Roundup Rodeo, Trinidad, names Miss Rodeo Colorado.

SEPTEMBER

First Week—Labor Day is observed locally with exercises or parades in many Colorado communities. It is often the closing day or weekend of county fairs, as at Ouray. It also marks the closing of summer activities, Chautauqa at Boulder, Chuck Wagon Dinners in the Colorado Springs area, Melodrama at Cripple Creek, Manitou Springs, Gunnison.

Other September Events—Jackpot Roping and Racing, Estes Park. Roundup, Trinidad. Ten High Rodeo, Leadville. Four-wheel Drive Rally, Walsenburg. Continental Divide Raceways, Castle Rock. Photographic Contest, Fall Color week, Ouray. Corn Festival, Haxtun. Fall Jeep tour, Salida. Centennial Raceways, Rocky Mountain Quarter racing, Littleton. Stone Age fair, Loveland. Pioneer Day, Norwood. Aspencade barbecue, Rye. Trips to High Country, Gunnison.

Spectator sports start at all the colleges in September.

OCTOBER

October and early November have some harvest celebrations, but most of the fairs have been held by this time. Carbondale celebrates Potato Day with a barbecue and rodeo on the eve of the hunting season. There are special duck hunting programs at the National Wildlife Refuge, Monte Vista. October marks the opening of musical and dramatic events that continue to March, May, and June. These include the University Theatre series, and Nomad Players in

Boulder; the Civic Players in Colorado Springs; the Bonfils Theatre, Trident Theatre, University of Denver Theatre, Denver; the Denver Symphony Orchestra concerts, Denver; the Artists' Series, College Center, Greeley, etc.

The big game season normally opens the third week in October.

NOVEMBER

First Week—Ski season opens. Olaeta Basque festival, Gunnison. Little Western Stock Show, Fort Collins.

Second Week—Veterans Day observances, Walsenburg and elsewhere. Basque Festival, Grand Junction. Big Horn Camper Caravan, Grand Lake. Greeley Concert Assn. programs open, Greeley. Colorado State University Theatre, Fort Collins.

Final Weeks—Ski Holiday Fashion show, Snowmass, Aspen. Norwood Puppet Theatre opens, Denver. Christmas in the Hills lighting ceremony, Estes Park.

DECEMBER

December is the month when the Ski Season is in full swing and airplane and bus schedules are adjusted to take skiers to the 33 areas where inns and hotels await visitors. Snowmobile contests are staged in several places. The Alpine Holiday Ski Race takes place at Snowmass, Aspen, about the third week. The Two-Shot Goose Hunt is a mid-December event in Lamar. Broadmoor Invitational Ice Hockey tournament is held at Colorado Springs during the third week. The Koshare Winter Ceremonials take place at La Junta the fourth week. The Yule Log ceremony at Palmer Lake takes place the Sunday before Christmas. The Beulah Yule Log hunt takes place at Pueblo.

In anticipation of the holidays the metropolitan areas start Christmas decorations early. Denver has a special Christmas display at its Civic Center beginning about December 18 and lasting one month. Ad-A-Man Fireworks on Pikes Peak, is a regular New Year's Eve feature of Manitou Springs.

Outdoor Recreation

Hunting and fishing for years have drawn many thousands of sportsmen from outside the State to Colorado. Their numbers, when combined with those of residents, runs from 700,000 to 1,000,000 annually. Their expenditures have become a source of large income to the State. In order to provide sufficient game for their efforts, and at the same time protect the wild species from extermination, the Department of Game, Fish and Parks supervises and regulates the sport.

FISHING

Fishing is practically an industry, in which the State plays a big part by subsidizing hatching and stocking of more than 600 tons of trout a year. More than 500,000 fishing licenses are sold annually, and possibly 25,000,000 fish are caught by men who have patience and leisure time. The most popular fish is the trout, and the harder it fights, the better the sportsmen like it. About two-thirds more trout are introduced into Colorado's waters than any other variety. A special division of the Department of Game, Fish and Parks studies methods beneficial to the fish and acquires new areas for public use. The Department operates 22 trout stations and regulates fish and wildlife resources at 13 reservoirs. The Federal Bureau of Sports Fisheries and Wildlife has two stations in Colorado and contributes fish to the streams. The Bureau administers federal aid in Fish and Wildlife Restoration Acts paying the State 75 percent of the cost of projects benefiting the fish. Funds for the wildlife program come from an 11 percent tax on certain types of firearms and ammunition; for fish there is a 10 percent tax on sport fishing tackle. The Leadville National Fish Hatchery produces about 100,000 pounds of trout a year. The Creede National Fish Hatchery produces trout for stocking the national forests.

Licenses and Regulations: The State defines a resident as a person who has had permanent domicile in the State for six months immediately prior to his application for a license. A resident combination fishing and small game hunting license is $7.50. A resident fishing license costs $6: a nonresident annual fishing license, $10; a nonresident 10-day fishing license, $5. A member of the Armed Forces stationed in the State is considered a resident. A member of the Armed Forces who is a patient at an army hospital in the State may have a fishing license free. A juvenile under 15 needs no license but cannot possess more than one-half of the regular daily bag; if he wants the full bag he needs a license. Bait is not permitted.

There are regulations governing the use of artificial flies and lures, bow and arrow, spear, spear guns and gigs, and places where they may be used. Regulations also specify open seasons, experimental waters, limitations on the size of bags, and size of fish taken. As these rules vary in different waters and for different species, fishermen should obtain a copy of the regulations from the Colorado Game, Fish, and Parks division or the local authorities (*free*).

Fish Hatcheries are located in or near Bellvue, Cedaredge, Chalk Cliff, Chipeta, Crystal River, Dolores, Durango, Estes Park, Finger Rock, Glenwood Springs, La Jara, Las Animas, Mount Shavano, North Fork Gunnison, North Fork Thompson, Pitkin, Poudre Ponds, Rifle Falls, Roaring Judy, Watson Lakes, and Wray.

HUNTING

Colorado is the most favored State for big game hunting in the whole Rocky Mountain region. Sportsmen come from the entire country because hunting is carefully regulated, forays bring results, and accommodations are plentiful. For the State hunting is a source of large income. Not only does the sale of licenses yield several million dollars, but the amounts that visitors spend are substantial and applied in bus and plane fares, purchase of supplies, hotel accommodations, and the services of guides and instructors. Out of its earnings the State maintains its superior supervision.

The Division of Game, Fish and Parks summarized the total income and number of animals taken during the 1968 seasons thus:

Licenses sold, 415,329; revenue, $6,611,977.

Species hunted, 19; animals killed, 1,201,340.

Fees: Resident sportsman's license (deer, elk, bear, mountain lion, small game, fish) $30; non-resident, $135. First deer, resident, $10; non-resident, $50. Second deer, resident, $7.50; non-resident, $10. Elk, resident, $12.50; non-resident, $75. Bear, resident, $5; non-resident, $25. Mountain lion, resident, $25; non-resident, $50. Archery fees: deer, $7.50 and $25; elk, $10 and $25.

The minimum age for big game hunting is 18, but youngsters 14 to 18 may hunt with an adult provided they have paid the license fees.

Game may not be enticed by lights, electrical devices, poisonous agents, nor may dogs be used unless permitted by regulations for taking bear and mountain lion. Turkey may be taken by shotgun under 10-gauge and above 20-gauge, and by longbows. A hunter may not shoot from an aircraft or motor car or fly a plane below 500 ft. altitude. There are many other regulations regarding seasons, kind of weapons (size of arrows, for instance), bags, and other limitations.

Rifle hunters are required to wear a head covering and an outer garment containing 500 square inches of daylight fluorescent orange color. All persons born on or after January 1, 1949, will be required to complete a hunter safety training course before buying a hunting license. A certificate attesting to this will be demanded. Juveniles also will have to carry such a certificate. Certificates from other states will be honored by Colorado.

The Buckskin Network: As a service to hunters radio stations in Denver and in cities and towns of the hunting area will broadcast emergency messages at about 6 A.M., noon, and 6 P.M. during the season to inform hunters of any calamities (death or illness) at home. The Grand Junction office of the Colorado State Patrol will act as the clearing house. Hunters may leave instructions at home on how they can be reached.

Hunting Proceeds for a Typical Year, 1968
Source: *Colorado Department of Game, Fish & Parks*

Licenses Sold		Proceeds	Species Hunted	Animals Killed
Antelope	6,795	$70,700	Antelope	5,493
Bear	1,530	14,850	Bear	671
Buffalo	7	1,400	Buffalo	7
Deer	171,747	3,347,396	Deer	83,634
Elk	60,074	1,486,298	Elk	15,393
Mountain Goat	20	800	Goat	15
Mountain Lion	25	1,125	Bighorn Sheep	32
Bighorn Sheep	131	5,240	Turkey	419
Turkey	1,227	6,225	Squirrels	5,067
Small game	41,110	194,575	Rabbits	345,669
Combination			Ducks	168,532
small game,			Doves	308,881
fish	124,105	930,788	Geese	19,379
Sportsman's	8,558	552,630	Blue Grouse	27,251
			Sage Grouse	13,107
	415,329	$6,611,977	Chukar Partridge	4,469
			Pheasants	146,563
			Quail	53,376
			Ptarmigan	3,382
				1,201,340

WINTER RECREATION

Skiing has become one of the major industries of Colorado. It has brought into profitable use an immense area in the Rocky Mountains formerly considered inaccessible when snow fell. Today the light, powdery snow that covers peaks and valleys in the north central part of the State is so highly esteemed by followers of the sport that thousands of people from outside the State converge on this area. More than 1,000,000 visitors use the ski slopes in a winter recreation area that covers up to 50,000 sq. mi. An increase of 15 to 20 per cent a year has been seen by business analysts. The State and employment services have risen to the opportunities presented. Numerous sites now have ski centers with full equipment in chair lifts, T-bars, runs for beginners, lodges and rest points en route, ski schools, ski patrols, ambulances, and trails. Hotel, motels, cabins, restaurants and snack bars are everywhere; inns advertise wood-burning fireplaces, indoor pools, accommodations for families, even baby-sitters. Highways are kept open; airplane and helicopter facilities connect local and metropolitan points. And information services never have been better.

Colorado Ski Country, USA, is the way the Rocky Mountain Ski Area Operators Assn. promotes its projects. The State works through the Division of Commerce and Development and the Colorado Ski Information Center, of the Colorado Visitors Bureau, 225 West Colfax Ave., Denver. The Center mails biweekly reports of conditions in the ski areas to newspapers, television and radio stations, travel agents, clubs and shops. It publishes a pamphlet, *Colorado Skiing,* with information about ski locations, resorts, accommodations, and rates. The Rocky Mountain A. A. A. also publishes ski information in *Where to Vacation in Colorado.*

The Rocky Mountain Division of the United States Ski Assn. is a nonprofit organization that supports recreational skiing, sets standards for competitive events, and aids ski development. It is the successor of a number of organizations that started in the late 1920's. It cooperates with the National Ski Patrol System Inc., which trains patrolmen in giving first aid, promoting safety, and helping Civilian Defense and the Red Cross. The Division has its hq in the Boston Bldg., Denver, 80202.

While the object of most visitors is skiing, many bring their families to enjoy the clear air in the winter sunshine. Communities have been quick to see the advantages to resorts if they have diversity of entertainment. For this reason they have all sorts of winter sports, and special accommodations for women and children. They arrange daily tours to scenic and wild areas; snowmobiling, sledding, tobogganing, tubing, sleigh rides, dog sledding, snowshoeing, skibobing. Frozen lakes are available for ice skating. A winter sports map is available from the Colorado Visitors Bureau, Denver.

Areas best equipped and supplied with the largest number of hotels, motels and restaurants are the Aspen, Vail, and Winter Park localities. Aspen is 40 *m.* from Glenwood Springs via State 82, 210 *m.* from Denver and 130 *m.* from Grand Junction via Interstate 70, US 6, and State 82. Aspen & Vail Airways to Sardy Field, 3 *m.* from Aspen. Continental Trailways daily express between Stapleton Airport, Denver, and Aspen. D. & R. G. W. to Glenwood Springs, bus to Aspen. The slopes:

Aspen Mountain. Seven chairlifts carry 5,775 per hr. to 45 runs up to 2 *m.* long. Ski School.

Aspen Highlands. Eight lifts, take 5,700 per hr. Thirty runs 250 to 5 *m.* long.

Buttermilk-Tiehack. Chairlifts, T-bars, accommodate 4,000 per hr. Has 22 runs, total 35 *m.*

Snowmass-at-Aspen. Is 9 *m.* sw of Aspen, has 5 double chairlifts, carrying 5,200 per hr., over 50 *m.* of runs up to 3 *m.* long. Night skiing. Guided tours from top of No. 4 lift into Moraine Valley and East Alpine.

Vail has had a sensational rise in popularity within the 1960's, based on its superb ski area and its excellent accommodations and restaurants. Although 110 *m.* west of Denver on Interstate 70, US 6, its three times daily service on Continental Trailways (2½ hrs.) from Stapleton Airport has made it easily accessible. There is a similar service from Grand Junction. Rocky Mountain Airways makes several scheduled flights daily between Denver and Eagle Airport, 35 *m.* west of Vail.

The ski slopes are on both the north and south sides of Vail Mtn., 11,250 ft. tall. There are 45 runs, 1 *m.* to 6 *m.* long; beginning, medium and expert areas, including Prima, a "super-expert" run in Northeast Bowl. One gondola lift, (63 gondolas), 6 double chairlifts, 2 pomalifts, capacity 8,400 per hr.

Winter Park is another growing ski area and has the advantage of being only 67 *m.* from Denver on State 40. Has regular service by Continental Trailways and a weekend ski train on the D. & R. G. W. Four chairlifts and 4 T-bars carry 7,700 per hr. to 32 runs. Snoasis warming house and restaurant at Midway. *Ski Idlewild* is the Winter Park area solely for beginners with 5 slopes, 5 trails.

Other ski resorts:

Arapahoe Basin. Is 11 *m.* east of Dillon and 66 *m.* from Denver via Interstate 70, on Continental Trailways. Capacity 6,000 per hr. with 3 double chairlifts, 5 pomas; has 20 runs, longest 16,000 ft. Snow Plume refuge atop Norway Mtn., 12,500 ft. Willy Schaefer ski school.

Breckenridge. Denver 81 *m.* via Interstate 70. Continental Trailways to Frisco, 9 *m.* north. Colorado Springs 105 *m.* via State 9. Capacity 6,400 skiers per hr., 35 runs. Ski school.

Ski Broadmoor. Located 4 *m.* south of Colorado Springs. Two ski slopes, lifts 700 skiers per hr. Night skiing. Indoor ice skating. Continental Trailways and 3 scheduled airlines. Ski school.

Crested Butte. Gondola, 7,500 ft., double chairlift, T-bar, J-bar, 15 runs. Summit, 11,300 ft. Located 28 *m.* from Gunnison via State 135. Frontier Airlines, Continental Trailways to Gunnison, cab service to Crested Butte.

Fun Valley. Is 30 min. from Denver via 6th Ave., 6 *m.* from Columbine Air Park, Littleton. One chairlift, 8 runs.

Geneva Basin. Four lifts, 11 runs. From Denver, 65 *m.* via US 285. Continental Trailways to Grant. Ski school.

Hidden Valley. Ski runs, ice skating, tube sliding, snowshoeing. Ten miles from Estes Park on US 34. Ski school.

Lake Eldora. Four lifts, 21 trails; beginners area; 5 *m.* west of Nederland. One hour from Denver via Denver-Boulder Turnpike and State 119. Ski school.

Loveland Basin and Loveland Valley. Four double chairlifts, rope tow, pomalift, capacity 7,000 per hr.; 22 runs, huge open bowls. Summit, 12,230 ft. Accommodations, Georgetown and Idaho Springs. On Interstate 70, Denver 56*m.* Continental Trailways. Ski school.

Meadow Mountain Ski Area. One double chairlift, 1 pomalift, 6 runs; 4 *m.* from Vail at junction Interstate 70, US 24. Ski school.

Monarch. Two double chairlifts, 1 pomalift, 17 runs. Salida, 21 *m.* west via US 50. Continental Trailways to Salida. Ski school.

Powderhorn. One double chairlift, 1 pomalift. Mesa, 8 *m.,* Grand Junction, 43 *m.,* Interstate 70. Airport at Grand Junction for Frontier and United Airlines. Continental Trailways and D. & R. G. W. to Grand Junction. Ski school.

Purgatory. Has 13 *m.* of trails. Durango 25 *m.* via US 550. Frontier Airlines to Durango Municipal Airport.

Sunlight. Two chairlifts, 1 pomalift, 18 runs; 10 *m.* south of Glenwood Springs, on Interstate 70. Continental Trailways, D. & R. G. W. Ski school.

Mt. Werner. Has 3 double chairlifts, 2 pomalifts, 26 runs; capacity 5,500 per hr. Bus service to Steamboat Springs and Yampa Valley Airport.

PART I

Colorado and Coloradoans

The Land

COLORADO is a rectangle a little west of center in the western half of the United States, endowed with a generous slice of the Great Plains and a huge segment of the Rocky Mountains, through which runs the Continental Divide. It exists on a plateau that at its lowest is 3,350 ft. above sea level, from which fifty-three mountains rise higher than 14,000 ft. There are thirteen peaks taller than Colorado's tallest—Mount Elbert, 14,431 ft.—one in California and twelve in Alaska, but the Colorado average of 6,800 ft. qualifies it for the title of the Highest State. Officially it is the Centennial State, commemorating its admission to the Union, August 1, 1876, 100 years after the Declaration of Independence of 1776.

Colorado is the eighth largest state in area, 104,247 sq. mi., with 450 sq. mi. of water. It is about 387 miles from east to west, and 276 miles from north to south. It is bounded on the east by Nebraska and Kansas, on the north by Nebraska and Wyoming, on the west by Utah, and on the south by Oklahoma and New Mexico. The 1960 national census found it had 1,753,947 people and was the 33rd state in population in the United States, with a density of only 16.9 persons per square mile. Estimates by local authorities in the late 1960's placed the population as slightly under 2,000,000.

The snow-capped mountains are the source of six large river systems, one of which, the Colorado, speeds its water southwestward to the Gulf of California and thence to the Pacific Ocean; the other five are the Arkansas, North Platte, South Platte, Republic, and Rio Grande, and reach the Missouri River, the Mississippi River, or the Gulf of Mexico. The rivers are diverted by dams and reservoirs to irrigate the farms, turn turbines for producing electric power and light, and provide lakes that have opened large areas for recreation.

The intangible element that makes Colorado great is climate. You can't touch it, but you can feel it. Many Coloradoans are unaware how wonderful it is until they move beyond the bounds of their State and encounter the kind of weather other folks have to endure. The basic quality is its lack of humidity. Its high elevation removes it from low areas with large bodies of water; the streams of cold water rushing down the mountainsides help keep heat and humidity down. There is little discomfort in extremes of temperature. The average yearly precipi-

3

tation is 16.62 inches, but some of the high plains in the eastern part of the State are semi-arid. The great backbone of the Rocky Mountains is a barrier to winter storms from the Pacific coast and diverts them. Although Denver is one mile above sea level, it has a higher average maximum temperature in January than any point in its latitude all the way to Atlantic City on the east coast.

The Great Seal of Colorado was originally adopted by the First Territorial Assembly, 1861. The present seal carries the date 1876, the year Colorado became a state, the legend *Nil Sine Lumine,* or Nothing Without Providence, the eye of God in a triangle, the Roman fasces, and a shield with three mountain peaks and a miner's pick and hammer. The State flag, adopted June 5, 1911, has three horizontal stripes of blue, white, blue, on which is superimposed a large red C in the form of an open circle, with a gold center. The State flower, adopted April 4, 1899, is the white and lavender-blue Rocky Mountain columbine, *aquilegia caerules.* The State bird is the lark bunting, designated April 29, 1931. The State tree is the Colorado blue spruce, *picea pungens,* adopted 1939. The State song is *Where the Columbines Grow,* by A. J. Fynn, adopted 1915.

Up the watercourses came Spanish, French, and American explorers. After them came the Mountain Men—Jim Bridger, Kit Carson, Jim Beckwourth, Jim Baker, "Broken Hand" Fitzpatrick, "Uncle Dick" Wootton, and many another trapper and trader of almost legendary fame. All these kept close to the streams, tracing them to their sources in search of beaver and other peltry so that milord in London—and in Paris and New York, too—might appear resplendent in a white beaver topper. With the decline of this curious trade linking the farthest frontier with the distant world of fashion, gold stimulated a human flood that swept across the plains and into the mountains. Gold-hunters, too, kept close to the streams, for without water they could not wash "pay dirt" in pans and sluices, could not operate stamp mills and smelters. And water, like a magic fountain, has ever run through the day dreams—and at times through the nightmares—of cowmen, sheepmen, beet growers, hay ranchers, truck gardeners, and general farmers.

Down the middle of the State winds the Continental Divide, splitting it in two roughly equal sections, the Eastern and the Western Slope, geographically and even economically distinct. South from Wyoming the Divide follows the crest of the Park Range, turns sharply eastward along the Rabbit Ears for fifty miles, then turns as sharply southward along the Front or Rampart Range through Rocky Mountain National Park and the glacier country. Angling southwestward to the high Mosquitoes, "that highway of frozen death" in boom days, the Divide boxes in the headwaters of the Arkansas and follows the towering Sawatch and Collegiate Ranges to the lower Cochetopa Hills, the watershed between the basins of the Pacific-bound Colorado River and the Gulf-bound Rio Grande. Again ascending, it runs up and over the precipitous San Juans to descend along its lesser ridges into New Mexico. Pikes Peak and Longs Peak, as well as Evans, Blanca, La Plata, Shavano, and many other of Colorado's highest summits, stand apart from the Divide.

But Colorado, contrary to popular belief, is not entirely mountainous. Broken only by occasional sand hills and isolated buttes, vast stretches of it are as smooth and level as a tidal flat, which is what they were, in fact, in the far distant past. Emerging gradually from the true prairies of Kansas and Nebraska, the high plains slope gently upward some two hundred miles to the base of the foothills. Northeast across these plains angles the South Platte; southeast, the Arkansas. Between their fertile and intensively cultivated valleys, bright green ribbons threading a brown expanse, lies a huge dry farming area, crisscrossed by thousands of miles of barbed wire, checkered with farms, dotted here and there with the green oasis of a prairie hamlet shading itself from the blistering sun under trees as carefully transplanted and lovingly tended as garden flowers. Rainfall here is scant, seldom attaining the annual State average of 16.62 inches. Winds are high in spring, and now and again a tornado has whirled its terrifying course across these plains homesteaded by sturdy hopefuls two or three generations ago. Nature in one of her more amiable moods favored them for a time; in recent years, however, they and their descendants have suffered the ravages of severe drought. But these weather-beaten plainsmen, bred to the earth, continue to grow crops and graze beeves in spite of drought, wind, insect plagues, occasional devastating hailstorms, and the now lessening menace of dust—"black snow"—to their fields.

A marked change occurs where plain meets mountain. The terrain abruptly begins to roll and swell upward. Dark evergreen forests, with some cedar here and there, creep down the slopes to terminate in a sharp line at the plains. Here along the base of the foothills, within a band some thirty miles wide extending from Wyoming to New Mexico, live two-thirds of all Coloradoans. With the exception of Grand Junction, far down the Western Slope near the Utah boundary, this narrow strip contains all of the State's cities of 10,000 or more— Fort Collins, Greeley, Boulder, Denver, Lakewood, Colorado Springs, Pueblo, and Trinidad, and many thriving smaller places between. Denver alone shelters more than a fourth of Colorado's people, and with Colorado Springs and Pueblo, considerably more than a third.

Within this band is concentrated the State's commercial and industrial activity: vegetable canning plants, meat packing plants, coal mines, steel mills and forges, stockyards, large wholesale and retail houses, factories of many kinds, and most of Colorado's busy beet sugar refineries. This north-south population band is curious, for main lines of traffic and travel have always followed an east-west course and still do. The explanation again is—water. These communities along the foothills are strategically placed to tap the larger mountain streams as they debouch upon the plains, and the valleys of these streams provided the easiest routes in early days for the highly profitable distribution of supplies to boom camps in the mountains.

Down the middle of the State, behind the front ranges, stretches a chain of four large parks, great level expanses rimmed by snow-capped peaks. In North Park, a circular basin opening into Wyoming in the north-central part of the State, are the headwaters of the North Platte. Directly south, across the Continental Divide, is Middle Park, through which the Colorado, the State's largest river, flows westward toward the Pacific. Farther south, again across the Divide on the Eastern Slope, lies South Park, the *Bayou Salado* of the Mountain Men, a favorite hunting ground of the Ute, a broad and beautiful mountain meadow at the source of the South Platte. These grassy basins, with little or no timber, have been cut up into farms and ranches for the most part, and life here is rather in the plains than the mountain mode.

Midway along the southern boundary, traced by the Rio Grande as it flows sluggishly toward New Mexico, is a large triangular park known as the San Luis Valley, once the bed of an inland sea, a naturally arid but widely irrigated section, its adobe villages and scattered *jascals* the center of Spanish-American culture in the State. These villagers are descendants of the free Spanish settlers who followed the triumphal march of the Conquistadores, or of the retainers brought along by the *haciendados* who divided up the Southwest in princely demesnes under the seal of the Spanish and Mexican governors at Santa Fe.

West of the chain of parks the mountains shelve off into the mesa country that stretches away toward the purple sage flats along the Utah boundary, a beautiful but often sterile land inhospitable to man and beast. Through the mesa country flows the Colorado and its chief tributary, the Gunnison, both lined with fields and orchards on their lower reaches. Between them, almost at the point of their confluence in Grand Junction, looms the huge mass of Grand Mesa, rising 10,000 feet to a vast table top, the largest in Colorado. The lower surrounding mesas are heavily forested, for the most part, and on these and in the more remote valleys between them are the last strongholds of the cattle barons in Colorado. Down the roads, in place of bouncing buckboards behind a plunging span of cayuses restive in harness, roar the farm trucks with their heavy tires, as brown as the sun- and wind-burned faces of the cowmen in boots, spurs, Levi's, and ten-gallon Stetsons.

In the northwestern corner of the State are two great and still almost inaccessible river gorges, along the Yampa and the Green, tributaries of the Colorado. Here, in wild and fascinating country row included within the Dinosaur National Monument, is Brown's Hole, a favorite rendezvous of the Mountain Men when beaver was king, later the hideout of cattle rustlers, highwaymen, and bank robbers.

The southwestern corner of Colorado, ringed by the high and precipitous walls of the San Juans, San Miguels, and La Platas, is occasionally cut off from other parts of the State for days at a time during winter months when heavy snows pile up in drifts thirty feet high in the steep narrow passes. In this corner is the breath-taking mesa country once peopled by the Cliff Dwellers, those accomplished Indians of an early pueblo culture who suddenly and mysteriously vanished some seven centuries ago. Their elaborate and often quite beautiful "apartment houses," built in natural caves high up on sheer canyon walls, dot the region and extend into neighboring states. The more important ruins in Colorado are now preserved and protected in Mesa Verde National Park, Yucca House National Monument, and Hovenweep National Monument on the Utah boundary. This is still Indian country, for here are the Ute Mountain Indian Reservation and the Southern Ute Indian Reservation, a narrow arid strip inhabited by the 4,000 or more descendants of Colorado's once most numerous tribe, which held the whole mountain country as its range.

Tucked away in mountain pockets throughout the State are many old mining towns, all much shriveled since their lusty youthful days. Many are true ghost towns, long since abandoned. Yet the lure of gold is as strong as ever in the decaying camps, for old sourdoughs have never lost faith in the mountains, knowing well that their manifold hidden treasures have scarcely been touched.

And there is more than gold, or silver, or coal and oil, or zinc and molybdénum, in "them thar hills." There are crystalline streams with a sparkle brighter than the brightest ores, stocked with flashing rainbow trout, and Eastern brook, Loch Leven, cutthroats, and German Browns. There are great silent forests of lodgepole and yellow pine, piñon, Douglas fir, and blue spruce, for along the mountains runs the broad timber belt of Colorado. Most of it is now set aside in State and national forest reserves; national forests alone cover almost a fifth of the State. Here in this forested mountain country, much of it still a primitive wilderness of magnificent beauty, are the renowned playgrounds of Colorado, enjoyed alike by "natives" and their many guests, who in season all but outnumber their hosts. This yearly invasion of their haunts does not much bother old-timers in weathered mining camps and on remote mountain ranches, although occasionally they can be heard grumbling among themselves at the intrusion as they reminisce about the days "when Colorado meant gold, silver, and cattle, instead of tourist camps, dude ranches, and irrigated farms."

Along with this love of the glamorous old order, their children have inherited "the look of eagles"; they walk with the free stride of the mountain-born; they are a proud and self-sufficient lot; they ask no favors—and seldom receive them. But they are a hospitable folk, for their hospitality has been handed down as a tradition from the days when the only cardinal sin in the mountains was to refuse a stranger welcome.

MAKING OF MOUNTAINS AND PLAINS

Colorado has not always been a sharply serrated mass of prairies, plateaus, and soaring peaks. For millions of years in its distant past it was a level plain in its entire extent. In time it became a series of vast plateaus, later broken by cataclysmic upheavals that leveled some to prairies, buckled others into tower ranges. At least four times Colorado has been wholly or partially submerged by invasions of the sea that reduced it to a waste of shifting islands and muddy ocean bottoms. A score of times the land broke under the pressure of vast crustal warpings or was split by volcanic explosions. Droughts turned new land into deserts; fern forests overran the deserts and perished in turn under new droughts or marine invasions. When the seas subsided for the last time, dense subtropical jungles covered what are today grassy plains and snow-capped peaks. Ice sheets crept down from the north and then retreated. Meantime, through all these changing scences, animal and plant life inexorably continued to evolve slowly from simpler to more complex forms.

At the beginning of the Paleozoic era, some five hundred million years ago, Colorado was a uniform plain leveled by the long erosive processes of the preceding Algonkian era, as was true of the entire Continent. From time to time vast sheets of water swept over the levels, and the geological history of the State during the three hundred and thirty million years of the Paleozoic era is largely a record of the changing relations of land and water. As the seas rose over the old continental shore lines, they invaded Colorado, first from the northwest, then from the southwest, while decayed mantle rock spread as mud along the retreating or advancing coasts. When the area emerged as dry land, sluggish rivers meandered across great flats, carrying sediment to salt-water basins or fresh-water lakes, ultimately carving the flats into low hills and valleys very similar to those now found on the eastern prairies.

The climate became arid toward the close of the era, and those parts of the State that remained above water became deserts of shifting sands. These in time were stratified by constantly changing water levels into numerous grades of calcareous clays and sandstone. Rocks dating from this period are predominantly red, with occasional greenish and gray tints and even streaks of white. The upturned sedimentary red rocks along the eastern front of the Rocky Mountains, as seen in the Garden of the Gods at Colorado Springs and the Park of the Red Rocks west of Denver, are largely of late Paleozoic origin. The era closed with the crustal warping known as the Appalachian revolution, which raised the mountain chain of that name and spilled back the seas from Colorado.

The Paleozoic era was important in the evolution of plant and animal life. When the seas first advanced into Colorado, they brought sponges, marine worms, jellyfish, clams, snails, and other invertebrates. Before the first waters receded, some of these life forms had reached the height of their development and were beginning to decline. The second great advance of the Paleozoic seas occurred during the Devonian period, or Age of Fishes; there was a marked development of marine vertebrates, but fantastic trilobites, sea scorpions, and other invertebrates continued to flourish. Centipedes and spiders now crept along the rocks, and giant dragon flies—some with a wing spread of more than two feet—hovered over the marshes. Even before the Appalachian revolution amphibians had become the dominant form of animal life, and the progenitors of the reptile had appeared. Fossils of a primitive fish, believed to be one of the oldest vertebrates yet discovered, have been unearthed in late Paleozoic rock near Canon City.

While the skeletons of primitive fauna were being embedded as fossils in the rock museums at the bottom of the seas, the record of plant life was seriously damaged by erosion. The Paleozoic era probably opened with a luxurious growth of seaweeds throughout Colorado, but fossil evidence is lacking. During those periods when the land rose above the waters, it was a barren waste, without trees or vegetation. Millions of years later the State was covered with dense fern forests, in which grew primitive unisexual flowers; some trees, ferns, and club mosses attained heights of sixty to one hundred feet. As these and similar plants fell and decayed, they formed thick beds of peat, which later hardened into rich anthracite beds as in Pennsylvania; where conditions were favorable, a few such beds were created in Colorado.

Colorado entered the Mesozoic era, approximately one hundred and ten million years long, with a gigantic upheaval. Later, during the

Jurassic period, the rise of the Colorado plateau was interrupted by a sudden brief return of the sea, followed by the creation of hundreds of large fresh-water basins in which were laid thin strata of varicolored rocks, chiefly limestones, sandstones, and marly shales. The Jurassic deposits east of the Continental Divide are known as the Morrison formation, those west of the Divide as the McElmo. The former underlies most of Colorado's eastern plains and appears here and there as outcrops along the frontal mountains from Wyoming to New Mexico.

Late in the Mesozoic era, during the Cretaceous period, an extension of the Gulf of Mexico invaded Colorado and joined a southward advancing arm of the Arctic Ocean. The entire State was again submerged, this time in a shallow mediterranean sea, a settling ground for gravel, sand, and mud containing millions of marine fossils. Gradually the gravel consolidated into conglomerate; the sand, into sandstone; and the mud, into shale—and all were cemented together by the weight of the surface layers above. Jurassic and Cretaceous rocks contain some of the most interesting fossils yet discovered in Colorado. Cretaceous rocks range in thickness from two thousand feet near the borders of the State to approximately ten thousand feet in the vicinity of Denver. The lower marine deposits contain numerous small oil reservoirs, while in the upper layers are valuable coal beds, laid down in fresh-water swamps and lagoons. The general emergence of the land during the era was accompanied by a marked improvement in climatic conditions, which in time transformed the Colorado desert into a garden.

Although great mountain-making movements, accompanied by igneous activity, recurred during later geological ages, the basic mountain structure of the region was formed about eighty million years ago, near the close of the Mesozoic era. A great warping and faulting movement gradually elevated the entire area above the surrounding plains, folding and tilting granite and sedimentary strata into jagged sky-scraping ranges. From gaping cracks in the upturned rocks poured molten lava, some of which congealed in crevices and subterranean reservoirs, but most of it burst from volcanic vents to tear immense holes in the mountain block. Avalanches of debris tumbled into the lowlands, and volcanic ash was so thickly scattered that it formed thick sedimentary layers over large areas. Erosion by wind, water, and glaciers through the ages has sculptured the mountain masses to their present contours, and has left such geological monuments as the Black Canyon of the Gunnison, the Royal Gorge of the Arkansas, Lodore Canyon of the Green, and Yampa Canyon.

The Mesozoic era was the age of reptiles; these creatures ruled land, sea, and air. Although turtles, crocodiles, lizards, and sea serpents reared powerful dynasties, the dinosaurs were easily supreme. These fantastic creatures ranged from one foot to eighty feet long, from a few inches to twenty feet high, and from a few pounds to scores of tons in weight. They were both herbivorous and carnivorous, and some species were heavily armored. Yet, before the close of the Mesozoic era, most of them had vanished, leaving only an insignificant posterity. Reptilian birds and more modest mammals appeared on the evolutionary horizon.

Skeletons of the grotesque monsters that once inhabited Colorado have been excavated from the Morrison formation near Denver; a Colorado diplodocus more than seventy-five feet long is on display, with many other paleontological treasures, at the Colorado Museum of Natural History, Denver. Near Canon City scientists have uncovered a dinosaur with feet three feet long and two and a half feet wide. Exposed rock strata along the hogbacks west of Denver contain thousands of ancient invertebrates of the Cretaceous period. Specimens of dinosaur remains have been unearthed on the Utah border and are on exhibition at Dinosaur National Monument.

Mesozoic plant life emerged with great difficulty from the Colorado desert. Thickets of ferns, palms, cyceads, horsetails, and ginkgos first made their appearance; then conifer forests sprang up on the low subtropical hills. Yews, cypresses, cedars, and pines advanced rapidly toward modern types. Towards the close of the era appeared figs, magnolias, tulip trees, laurels, cinnamon trees, holly, oleanders, maples, birches, sycamores, oaks, beeches, and walnuts. Flowering plants flourished throughout the State. Today fossil palm leaves are found in many of Colorado's rock formations, particularly near Golden and Boulder. Valuable leaf imprints of the Cretaceous period come from the Green River formation, from rock beds near Chandler, and occasionally from deposits near Denver and at Florissant.

As the seas never returned to Colorado, the Cenozoic era—the most recent sixty million years of geological history—has left only a scanty record of itself in fresh water and saline lake deposits. The rocks of the Tertiary period, first of the chief subdivisions of the era, were laid down in shallow basins or on the flood plains of ill-defined and shifting rivers. Recent deposits in the State consist largely of windblows and sand dunes on the level plains, swamp muck in the higher mountain valleys, and alluvial gravel, sands, and loams along the streams.

Volcanic eruptions and crustal warpings continued until comparatively late in the Tertiary period, at which time the evolution of the Rocky Mountains and the Colorado plateau to their present form was completed. Colorado's metallic ore deposits apparently came from deep within the earth, forced up by volcanic activity, the chemical action of vapors, and rising water solutions, and were deposited in concentrated masses in the veins and faults of surface rocks. Evidence of this has been found in the mining camps of Cripple Creek, Alma, Breckenridge,

Central City, and others where signs of former volcanic activity are manifest.

To some extent minerals are still being deposited, as is evidenced by the large number of hot mineral springs within the State. Although these thermal springs are undoubtedly much smaller than those of earlier geological periods, Big Pagosa Springs—the largest in the State—has an average flow of seven hundred gallons a minute, and those at Glenwood Springs discharge some three thousand gallons a minute.

Minerals necessary for fertile soils have been supplied in abundance in Colorado. For the most part, its soils are sandy or gravelly loams, composed chiefly of fine grains of quartz, feldspar, and clay, with some mica. Colorado prairie soils have an extremely wide range in both color and texture, and vary in appearance from light brown and almost chalky white to dark red, chocolate, and black. In texture they range from very fine sands to refractory adobes and clays.

The great ice sheet that scoured large sections of North America between twenty-five and sixty thousand years ago, did not touch Colorado. But exposed masses of glacial rock, isolated boulders, and terminal moraines indicate the presence of smaller alpine glaciers on many Colorado mountains. Remnants of these ice sheets still exist in Rocky Mountain National Park and in the mountains west of Boulder. Beautiful cirques and U-shaped valleys at the eastern approach to Berthoud Pass are other reminders of this period.

While the turbulent end of the Mesozoic era was accompanied by conditions hazardous to plant and animal life, both flora and fauna evolved rapidly toward modern forms during the comparatively brief Cenozoic era. Birds cast off their reptilian characteristics and established a dynasty of their own. Mammals became the dominant type. Colorado fossils present a clear record of the evolution of the horse and the rhinoceros from primitive five-toed ancestors no larger than a dog. The evolution of the dog, cat, and bear families has been similarly traced in finds made within the State. The plains of northeastern Colorado have yielded remains of ancient turtles of gigantic size, as well as skeletons of the mammoth, giant pig, rhinoceros, and saber-toothed tiger. One of Colorado's paleontological prizes is the skull of a vintacolotherium, discovered in 1924 in the Eocene beds of Moffat County. This land animal approximated a small elephant in size, and had six horns, two huge fighting tusks, and a brain approximately as large as a sheep's.

Subtropical flora covered Colorado land surfaces during the early Tertiary period. Palm trees with broom-shaped leaves four feet long grew in the forests. Myrtles, sycamores, buckthorns, dogwoods, hawthorns, figs, sweet gums, cinnamons, and water lilies flourished; grasses took possession of all open spaces. Less favorable conditions prevailed after a new continental elevation, but with the retreat of the glaciers the climate again became temperate and modern forms of plant life proliferated.

During the prolonged construction and modification of the region now included within the State, nature played strange geological pranks. Among the resulting marvels is the Colorado National Monument in Mesa County near Grand Junction; huge caves and passages honeycomb the region, which is seamed with numerous canyons in which stand hundreds of monoliths like naked sentinels; names such as Steamboat Rock, Battle Rock, Double Balance Rock, Umbrella Rock, Devil's Kitchen, and Cold Shivers Point suggest the topography of the region. Erratic erosion has produced the fantastic volcanic formations of Rio Grande National Forest in the southern part of the State; here innumerable cones, massive plugs, and red pinnacles tower above majestic gorges. At Manitou Springs, near Colorado Springs, is the Garden of the Gods, a mass of upturned red rocks sculptured into weird formations; equally interesting is Red Rocks Park, west of Denver. The great shifting sand dunes in the San Luis Valley are the last remnants of a once vast prehistoric desert.

PLANT AND ANIMAL LIFE

Colorado's great diversity of flowers, shrubs, and trees is attributable to the climatic conditions that prevail at widely different altitudes. Each thousand feet in altitude represents an approximate difference of three degrees in temperature; the range in temperature found in a thirty-mile journey from the plains to the top of the Continental Divide is greater than that ordinarily experienced in traveling a thousand miles from north to south. For this reason few parts of the world are more interesting biologically than the Rocky Mountains.

To the amateur botanist Colorado offers exciting exploration in regions where new species are constantly being discovered; the professional student finds here an almost limitless opportunity for intensive study and research. To the wayfarer unacquainted with technical names or scientific data but appreciative of stately trees and beautiful flowers, the landscape presents colorful and beautiful scenes with the changing seasons.

The first professional to "botanize" in what is now Colorado was Edwin James, historian and naturalist of Major Long's expedition of 1819–20, which traveled southward from the South Platte Valley along the mountains. The wild mock orange has been named *Jamesia,* or *Edwinia,* in his honor. Frémont's expeditions in 1842–45 were accompanied by botanists John Torrey and Asa Gray; the latter's papers appeared in official documents and in the *American Journal of Science.*

Between 1860 and 1870 local specimens were collected by Charles C. Parry, for whom the Parry primrose was named. Among other naturalists of this period was George Engelmann of St. Louis, for whom the Engelmann spruce was named.

Colorado flora, according to the best authority, is distributed among five zones, each with its more or less distinct characteristics. The semiarid plains zone ends at an altitude of 6,000 feet; the foothill zone lies between 6,000 and 8,000 feet; the montane zone extends to 10,000 feet, and the subalpine to 11,500 feet, with the true alpine zone above it.

Although at first sight the plains seem to be merely a brown or tawny expanse of buffalo and grama grass, closer observation reveals a surprising variety of plant forms, usually low and sparse, but intensely colorful. Scientists have recorded 2,989 different varieties of wild flowers in and near the foothills, 500 of which are peculiar to the plains alone. Climatic conditions in this section have made the cultivation of seed flowers an important enterprise in the river bottoms.

In the spring, before sun and wind have dried the soil, prairie flowers are numerous—the early-blooming sand lily, the evening primrose with blossoms shading from cream to rose pink, strong-scented yarrow, coral-colored wild geranium, yellow and orange buttercups, Colorado bee plant, and the white star flower that blooms at dusk. At times the plains are covered with a mantle of wild dwarf marigolds. By midsummer, most of these flowers are gone, but a few linger in the river bottoms with wild iris and graceful cattails. Only the yellow sunflower and the purple-tasseled Scotch thistle flourish with undiminished vigor through the summer amid pigweed, shepherd's-purse, and Russian thistle, or tumbleweed. Another hardy plant is the devil's claw, the seeds of which are distributed by pronged seed pods which cling to every moving object that touches them. The ubiquitous loco weed, with violet, cream, or white flowers, is bitterly hated by cattlemen for its poisonous effect upon livestock.

In drier regions the plains are carpeted with biennial burdock or cocklebur, Mexican sandbur with delicate yellow blossoms and villainous triangular thorns, prairie sandbur, silvery sage, and the mesquite shrub with its fragrant blooms and sugar-filled pods. Some plants in the arid regions, like the rose mallow and the purple-flowering bush morning glory, project their roots six to ten feet deep in search of water. Both on the eastern prairies and in the western mesa country grows the yucca, popularly known as soap weed, or Spanish bayonet, its great spike of creamy flowers projecting from a barricade of dagger-tipped leaves. With its deep-growing fibrous roots it flourishes on arid land. The four varieties native to the State were long used by Indians for many purposes; its tough leaf fibers were made into rope; the pods were ground into a flour; the roots, which lather freely in water, were used as a soap.

Colorado has twenty-four varieties of cacti, most of which can be seen at the Colorado Museum of Natural History, Denver. The opuntia, or jointed cactus, assumes forms ranging from the flat-lobed prickly pear, blending all too well with the prairie sod, to the giant tree cactus, which attains a height of ten feet in Furnace and Blacksmith Canyons in the southern part of the State. The blossoms of the prairie cacti are usually yellow, although some are a deep silky red or hybrid orange. Southern Colorado produces a round-lobed pincushion cactus bearing pink, yellow, and deep wine-colored flowers. Peculiar to the Western Slope is the rose-colored prickly pear. The pods of the cactus are often fried, and its leaves are sometimes used in the manufacture of candy.

Buffalo bush, with silvery foliage and edible berries, nuttals, and round-leaf saltbush are among the chief shrubs of the plains. Rabbit-wood, a kind of sandalwood with greenish flowers and pulpy fruit, is common, as is the creosote bush, so named because its resinous foliage has a strong odor of creosote. Gray saltbush, or chico-brush—better known as greasewood—grows in alkaline soil and in the shale beds of the lower foothills. Thirty species of shrub willows border lowland streams and grow in marshy areas; many are highly ornamental and are sought in the spring for their silver catkins.

Native cottonwoods, esteemed by early settlers on the hot plains, have been largely replaced in the more populous areas with more desirable poplars, elms, maples, birches, and locusts, all transplanted. Often mistaken for a willow, the narrow-leaf cottonwood usually grows along the rivers at low altitudes. The lance-leaf variety is occasionally found near Colorado Springs and Fort Collins, and across the Divide at Montrose. As the plains rise toward the foothills, beaked hazel nut, mountain ash, green ash, Rocky Mountain maple, and boxelder become common; mountain and scrub oak grow along the streams, and dog birch flourishes in the marshes.

The Colorado oak occurs on both sides of the Continental Divide but prefers the rocky hillsides in the southern part of the State, as does the Norman tea fir with its slender loose-spreading limbs. The southern foothills are also noted for their thick growths of Rocky Mountain cedar, which grows in stunted shrub-like masses on otherwise almost sterile ridges. Desert juniper, rock pine, and manzanita are ubiquitous in southern Colorado, giving way to scrub juniper and trailing cedar in the north. Dense knotty piñon pines with low spreading dark branches are found from the Wyoming border to Mesa Verde National Park.

The foothill region is matted with berry shrubs: hackberry, Fendler's barberry, Frémont's barberry, snowberry, wolfberry, thimbleberry, Western buckberry, billberry, and coralberry. Currants, gooseberries, wild grapes, plums, strawberries, elderberries, Western chokeberries, and other edible wild fruits ripen in ravines and canyons. Turret plant, or deer's tongue; Oregon grape, an evergreen shrub with blue berries, often used in place of holly during the Christmas season; kinnikinnick, known as bearberry in other parts of the country and used by the Western Indians as a substitute for tobacco, bearing delicate ivory-colored flowers in early spring and bright scarlet berries later—all grow thickly on the higher foothills. Yellow Johnny-jump-ups gleam in mossy crevices, and the hairy-stalked pasque flower raises its purple spikes from plains to alpine meadows.

Colorado lichens, often mistaken for moss, are among the most familiar flora of hill and mountain country. Lichens often encrust tree trunks and limbs but more generally cling to rocks in patches of pale green, yellow, gray, and brown. Dry air and scant moisture are unsuited to fern life, but thirty varieties of this plant have been collected within the State, chiefly from shadowed canyons and rocky crevices in the subalpine zone; the most common are the bracken, the lady fern, and the male fern.

The columbine, Colorado's official flower, reaches perfection in the cool shade of tall aspens but is found from the lower foothills to timberline. Its specific name *coerulea* means blue, but its sepals are sometimes purple, pale lavender, and even white. A companion flower, the wild yellow pea, often grows among columbine clusters.

Wild roses, ranging in color from almost pure white to deep red, scent the air of foothills and mountains during June and July. On the higher slopes bloom pale lavender Mariposa lilies, one of the best known of Colorado's wild flowers; here also occur mountain lilies, orange-red wood lilies, and maroon-centered gaillardia, intermingled with dwarf cornel, mountain rue, and wild four o'clock. Midsummer is the blooming season for rose and cream meadow lotus, azure-fringed gentians, and pink-and-white wood mint. Fragile Dutchman's pipe, the yellow dog's tooth violet, even occasionally the rare pink variety of the latter, mingle with purple woods violets and blue bells in secluded hollows, while the forest floor is dotted with yellow butterweed, tall bitter cress, purple monkshood, and chiming bells. Brown-eyed Susan, gay-plumed Indian paint brush, coral fox glove, delicate blue harebells, mountain forget-me-not, and mountain daisy spill over the slopes in a riot of color intensified later by pink eight-petaled dryads, asters, golden rod, and the single-and twin-flowered wintergreen.

The orchid family is represented by the golden lady slipper, the delicate little calypso, lady's tresses, and spiranthes, growing in mountain meadows and along streams. The coral-root orchid is frequently found in the woods, as are the peculiar pine drops of the Indian pipe family. In shaded marshes blossoms the little red elephant, originally discovered in Greenland; each flower on its spike resembles the head and trunk of a miniature elephant.

High in the mountains the white marsh marigold, yellow globe flowers, and the purple anemone, or wild crocus, push through the snowbanks in early spring and summer. Along streams fed by melting snows are the alpine primrose, the topaz monkey flower, the kings crown, and the rose crown. The alpine gold-flower is perhaps the most striking, and throughout July it carpets high mountain meadows with its vivid yellow. Dense matted clusters of fragrant brilliant-hued alpine flowers, seldom more than two inches high, bloom in profusion on the grasslands, or tundras, of the highest peaks.

Many ornamental shrubs, some of which withstand transplanting to urban environment, lend color and fragrance to the mountain area. In early spring, flowering currants gleam in masses of pale gold, and the thimbleberry is white with flowers resembling a single rose. The yellow flowers of the fly honeysuckle are surrounded by reddish leaves, and the wax flower blooms ivory white against deep emerald backgrounds. Glossy mountain laurel with rosy flowers—often called calico bush—mountain balm or ivy, native hawthorn, shrubby purple cinquefoil, mountain mahogany, and poison ivy form wild tangles that cover slopes and canyon floors. Three-leafed sumac and mountain sumac color the higher slopes with their massed scarlet foliage and dark red fruit clusters, while festoons of matrimony vine, woodbine, and red ozier, or dogwood, add their colors to the autumn foliage. On the slopes of the southern mountains the mock orange lifts its stiff branches and snowy blossoms.

Most of Colorado's mountain trees are coniferous and play an important part in minimizing erosion and helping to conserve water for lowland irrigation. Massed conifers act as giant reservoirs, storing up heavy snows so that they melt slowly. To protect these all-important watersheds, the Federal Government has set aside millions of acres of mountain land as national forests.

White firs, common on the lower slopes of central and southern Colorado, are dwarfed by dense forests of slender lodgepole pines farther north. The Douglas fir attains heights of 100 feet, soaring almost as high as the Alpine fir, and has a slender trunk, light spongy wood, and flat blunt leaves. The western yellow pine, often called bull pine, is considered Colorado's best timber tree, and is found everywhere in the higher mountain regions except in the northern part of the State. Ornamental bristle-cone pines grow on all the higher slopes.

Engelmann spruce and balsam fir, to be found up to timberline, grow in dense stands on cool exposures and are regarded as the best water conservers. The Douglas spruce frequents north slopes, and the majestic blue spruce, the unofficial State tree, is usually found near higher mountain streams. From the lower conifer belts to timberline grows the quaking aspen, known elsewhere as white poplar for its chalky white trunk. A broadleaf tree, it is especially beautiful in fall with its brilliant reds and yellows. It grows quickly from live roots and is the first to appear after forest fires.

Few Colorado trees are more striking than the sentinel timberline pines. Their dwarfed and gnarled limbs, appearing to writhe in torture, make them a favorite with painters and photographers. Known as "wind timber," they are living skeletons of the lumber, fox-tail, and bristle-cone pines which wage an unending fight with the cold fierce winds that sweep the alpine snow fields on the roof of the Continent.

As for animal life, early explorers found the Colorado mountains and plains abounding with herbivorous and predatory wild beasts, the chief food supply of the Indians. Slaughter by trappers and hunters, and encroachment of settlers upon their natural habitats, have tremendously reduced their numbers—in some instances, almost to extinction.

Before the coming of the white man, it has been estimated, some thirty million bison—described by Coronado as "large humped cattle, maned like lions"—roamed the plains and the level expanses of mountain parks; today, there remain only a few small protected herds. The antelope, once so numerous that hunters sold their carcasses by the wagon load, are certainly doomed unless adequate compensation is made for the rapidly diminishing open range. Only a few of these small, tawny, prong-horned animals now remain on the plains and lower foothills, so timid and fleet of foot that they are rarely glimpsed. The gray prairie wolf, enemy of buffalo and cattle alike, is virtually extinct; but its cousin, the coyote, seems to thrive in spite of all attempts to exterminate it.

Although agricultural and industrial expansion has swept the larger animals far back into mountain fastnesses, the plains and foothills are populated with a variety of interesting smaller creatures. Skunks of several kinds are to be seen—and avoided—from prairie to upper hills. Badgers, gophers, moles, and shrews abound, and on the plains is another squirrel-like rodent, the spermophile. Rabbits, cottontails and "jacks," both white and black tailed, are plentiful, and prairie dog "towns" flourish in spite of poison campaigns.

The greatest scourge of the prairie land is the grasshopper. The small green variety is native to the State, but most of the larger species migrated to Colorado when the land was put under cultivation; they range from the bulky "lubber," occasionally two inches long, to the small "Carolina locust." The damage done by these pests is tremendous; recent poison campaigns have yielded as high as five bushels of "hoppers" an acre; swarms of them now and again invade the cities like another Egyptian plague.

The official State bird, the black-and-white lark bunting, nests in the tall grass and yucca of the prairie and plateau lands. Desert horned lark and the highland plover, the latter far from the salt marshes and shore lines preferred by most of its kind, are common on the plains, as are the meadow lark, robin, and the sweet-voiced western mocking bird. Overhead soars the rough-leg hawk, and the prairie falcon, joined at times by the carrion-eating turkey buzzard; at dusk the western night hawk, or bullbat, wheels in the sky. Familiar to prairie travelers are the western horned owl and the white-rumped shrike, industriously catching grasshoppers and laying up a supply for future use by impaling them on thorns or the spikes of barbed-wire fences; the little burrowing owl bobs clownishly at the mouth of an abandoned prairie-dog hole, and the long-tailed magpie chatters shrilly among dusty cottonwoods.

Irrigation attracted a host of new birds, and as large areas of the plains are now cultivated fields, many varieties have migrated to these sections. Here are innumerable song sparrows, Western yellow throats, and both yellow-headed and red-winged black birds. In the marshlands are found at least eighteen species of wild duck, two of wild geese, and many varieties of wading birds. The grebe, or helldiver, appears in summer, and the loon is a winter visitor. The mourning or turtle dove, several kinds of swallows, and large numbers of a resplendent ringnecked pheasant, introduced from China, find Colorado an ideal home.

In the foothills are dusky grouse and dignified sage hens; in the seclusion of ravines the blue bird, the brilliant tanager, a variety of woodpeckers, and dozens of other birds brighten the shadows with flashing color. On the higher slopes lives the camp-robber, or Rocky Mountain jay; here also are the Rocky Mountain grosbeak, the hermit thrush, rosy finch, crossbill, and the boisterous brown nuthatch, said to be the only bird that descends a tree trunk head foremost. Broad-tailed and rufous humming birds are common; the latter, not much larger than an insect, winters in the tropics, spends a few weeks in the Colorado hills, and summers in Alaska. The gray dipper, or water ouzel, builds its oven-like nest among the spray-drenched rocks along mountain streams and plunges boldly into the water to catch fish. The white-tailed ptarmigan is the highest ranging of all Colorado birds, and white-throated swifts and the demure canyon wren also frequent the loftier ranges.

Bald or white-headed eagles are frequently sighted wheeling in the sky, but the graceful golden eagle, nesting on inaccessible crags, is more common. In the mesa country of the Western Slope the long-tailed crested road runner, or chaparral-cock, is often seen racing along the highway or engaging in deadly combat with its ancient enemy, the rattlesnake, which it kills just for the sport of it, apparently.

The larger carnivores of the mountain area, the mountain lion and the grizzly bear, once very numerous, have been all but exterminated by systematic hunting encouraged by large bounties. Forest rangers estimate that less than half a dozen grizzlies remain in the State. Black and brown bears are still rather numerous; the lynx, or bobcat, still prowls the hills. The western red fox is found along timberline, but the mountain wolf, like the prairie lobo, is virtually extinct. The black-footed ferret, the Rocky Mountain weasel, and the dwarf weasel, the smallest true carnivore in Colorado, are found in scattered areas.

Through the aspen thickets in remote regions range herds of black-tailed or mule deer, frequently to be surprised close to mountain highways. Higher in the mountains, where snows are deep and fodder is scarce, elk thrive in an alien environment. Near timberline is the habitat of the protected and rarely glimpsed bighorn sheep.

Martens and porcupines live on the mountain slopes, while along streams and lakes are western mink, muskrat, and a few otter; partially submerged beaver "houses" dot less frequented watercourses. Rabbits of several varieties, notably Baird's snowshow rabbit, live on the higher slopes.

Bats are found throughout the State; the little brown bat and the grayish big-eared bat are the most common. Rats and mice, nocturnal by habit, are seldom seen during the day; but hollow logs and stumps, crevices in rock piles, ditches, weed borders, and marshes harbor myriads of them. Perhaps the most interesting of the small mammals is the diminutive cony, or pika, an odd rabbit-like creature found only in rock slides above timberline and unknown outside the State. For its practice of curing and storing hay in small stacks for winter use, it is known as the "Haymaker of the Heights." Black, gray, and brown squirrels disport themselves in the conifer forests; the ground squirrel, familiarly known as the chipmunk, is extremely tame and approaches close to mountain camps to pick up whatever choice bits can be found.

Colorado has its share of reptiles and amphibians, confined largely to the plains, foothill, and plateau country. Of the numerous varieties of lizards that slither over sun-warmed stones on hillside and in canyon, the most interesting is the horned lizard, miscalled the horned toad, sold in many curio shops, either mounted or alive. Many lakes near Denver and Boulder harbor painted turtles; the soft-shell and the yellow-necked mud turtle are found in the eastern rivers; and the land tortoise is common on the plains. Of native snakes only the prairie rattler, which occasionally strays into the foothills and lower mountains, is poisonous, although a few specimens of the deadly western diamond-back have been found in the southern part of the State.

In all sections of the State are bugs and beetles, varying in size from the two-inch dark-shelled cockroach to the small round ladybird decked in her bright colors. Many beetles, armed with needle-like antennae, seriously damage trees and standing fields of grain. At least 243 species of parasitic plant lice and many different scale insects have been listed as unwelcome Colorado guests; regiments of energetic ants build their labyrinthian tunnels in sandy soil, under rocks, and around dead trees. The peculiar stick insect, resembling a miniature bamboo fishing pole with legs, is found in widely scattered sections. Myriads of gnats and mosquitoes emerge each summer from swamps and stagnant water on the prairies and in the high mountain parks. Mosquitoes of the *Culicidae* family, which carry malaria, are rare in Colorado, but the wood tick lurks in old fence posts, fallen timber, and shrubby undergrowths, and is to be guarded against as a carrier of spotted fever.

Of the fifteen varieties of spiders, the crab spider, the jumping spider, and the wolf spider are common types; the venomous black widow is not a rarity. The giant tarantula of the plains, popularly believed to be poisonous, is harmless, as are all smaller members of its family. The many-legged centipede, which often—too often—secludes itself in boots or other unexpected places, lives along the eastern base of the foothills; in the Arkansas Valley specimens five inches long have been caught.

Butterflies, moths, and flies of many colors and varieties occur throughout the State. The more common butterflies are the mourning cloak, painted lady, milkweed, tortoise shell, and numerous swallowtails. Lightning bugs hover over the prairie meadows, and Colorado's dry sunny climate and abundance of flowers find favor with more than seven hundred kinds of bees.

Rivers and lakes throughout the State contain a great variety of fish. In lakes, reservoirs, and sluggish prairie streams are channel cat, bullheads, sucker, carp, and minnows. Colder mountain streams and lakes, fed by melting snows, are preferred by such hardy swimmers as perch, flat sunfish, sebago or landlocked salmon, and many varieties of silver or blue bass. And the pride of Colorado flash through these same waters—cutthroats, steelheads, speckled, Eastern brook, Loch Leven, and famed rainbow trout—names that bring a sparkle to every angler's eye. State and Federal hatcheries annually release many millions of fingerlings in Colorado waters.

NATURAL RESOURCES

A primary sources of wealth is farm land comprising not quite three-fourths of the acreage of the State. Approximately 32,000,000 acres are suitable for grazing, most of which are in use; some 13,000,000 acres can be farmed, but little more than half are under cultivation. A wide variety of fertile soils, usually rich in mineral matter but deficient in humus, and ranging in texture from sandy loams to refractory clays and adobes, characterizes the arable lands. The climate, one of the State's chief attractions, is generally mild and sunny, but varies considerably from one section to another, influenced in large part by wide differences in altitude. From the State mean of 44.9 degrees, local average temperatures range upward to 54.4 degrees at Lamar in the lower Arkansas Valley and downward below the freezing point on the Alpine meadows at the top of the Continental Divide. Agriculture on the lower Western Slope is favored by a growing season of 186 days, while at Pagosa Springs near the base of the San Juans only 76 days normally intervene between killing frosts. In Leadville, at the headwaters of the Arkansas, snow has fallen more than once on the Fourth of July. Annual precipitation ranges from as little as seven inches in the San Luis Valley to almost twenty-seven inches at Silverton in the towering San Juans; the State mean is 16.62 inches. As rainfall in most farm areas is deficient, elaborate irrigation systems are required to water almost all lands off the main watercourses. Fields irrigated with water drawn in ditches or flumes from running streams, lakes, reservoirs, and artesian wells aggregate more than a fourth of all farm lands in the State. Only California exceeds Colorado in irrigated area.

Colorado ranks high among the States in potential water power. Running streams can generate horse power the year round without mountain dams and reservoirs. Wind power, although too uncertain for industrial use, has been of great value in pumping water for livestock on the arid plains, and high wind velocities on mountain peaks may perhaps prove an abundant source of energy in the future.

Immense mineral deposits underlie widely scattered areas in central and western Colorado. Roughly, the largest metal mining region extends along the Continental Divide from the golden "Kingdom of Gilpin," in the mountains west of Denver, to the headwaters of the Rio Grande and into the San Juans in the southwestern corner of the State. The rich Cripple Creek gold fields lie isolated in the tiny crater of an extinct volcano behind Pikes Peak; also isolated are the vanadium and uranium beds in Paradox Valley along the Utah boundary. The extent of the metal reserves in the Colorado Rockies is unknown, for many veins have merely been tapped and others are constantly being discovered. As the mountain-making process cracked, broke, and telescoped rock strata throughout the mining area, leaving innumerable crevices, fissures, and reverse faults, prospecting has posed problems often less successfully solved by strictly scientific method than by the trial-and-error system necessarily employed in piecing together a baffling jig-saw puzzle. But in spite of all natural obstacles, Coloradoans have already dug and blasted billions of dollars worth of precious and industrial metals from the granite warehouses of the Rockies. More than 250 useful minerals have been discovered within the State, and 33 were extracted for market during the 1960s. Colorado stands first among the States in the extraction of molybdenum, tin and vanadium.

Colorado ranks first among the States in coal reserves, being credited by the United States Geological Survey with 417,982,149,000 short tons bedded in an area of 19,754 square miles; these are sufficient at the present rate of consumption to supply the entire nation for seven centuries. On the Western Slope are three large fields—one in Moffat County in the northwestern corner of the State, another about midway along the Utah border, and the third in the San Juan Basin to the southwest. The eastern coal beds stretch in a broken and irregular chain along the foothills from Wyoming to New Mexico. At their southern extremity, in and around Trinidad, are great bodies of iron ore, but these have proved more costly to work than deposits in neighboring states.

Productive and extensive oil and gas fields have been discovered in widely scattered parts of Colorado since petroleum was first found in the Arkansas Valley, near Florence, in 1862. More important, however, is the petroleum locked in the Federal Government's reserve of 952,239 acres of Tertiary oil shale in Mesa, Garfield, and Rio Blanco Counties on the Western Slope. The Federal Oil Conservation Board estimates that these shales contain many billions of barrels of recoverable oil, equivalent at the present rate of production to the country's entire output for half a century. Natural gas has been discovered over a wide area, and in the 1960s was being piped to many cities. Carbon dioxide gas has been found in Jackson County near by. Helium gas has been struck in Las Animas County on the southern plains, and in western and northern Colorado.

The quantity, quality, and infinite variety of Colorado stone— granites, marbles, limestones, sandstones, and lavas—are known to builders and architects throughout the world. Decorative marbles occur in Wet Mountain Valley and along the upper Arkansas on the Eastern Slope, and at Marble on the Western Slope. Large clay beds near Denver and elsewhere have given rise to many important manufactories of pottery, brick, tile, terra cotta, and similar products.

Colorado has eleven national forests entirely within the State and one extending across the western boundary into Utah. These forests embrace 13,712,352 acres. State nurseries replace losses from fires at the raté of several million trees a year. The annual growth of the forests approximates 500,000,000 board feet, of which little more than a tenth is cut yearly. But the forests with their plant and animal life serve a far more important purpose than timber production; they are of inestimable value in forwarding conservation, recreation, and the general health and welfare. They are the great natural reservoirs that store the water upon which Coloradoans so largely depend; they provide the summer playgrounds upon which are based the State's largest "industry," tourist travel.

The People

THE story of Coloradoans and their achievements does not begin with the great Pikes Peak Gold Rush of 1859 and the establishment of the contemporary cultural pattern. It stretches far back into the past, to the days more than ten thousand years ago when savage men roamed the plains, hunting the beasts of the time, warring among themselves, eventually vanishing as more advanced cultural groups appeared. Some two thousand years ago, approximately at the beginning of the Christian era, men skilled in weaving baskets came to live in the western mesa country. Other men distinguished for their skill in building cities of stone on mesa rims and in natural caves high up on sheer canyon walls later absorbed the Basket Makers and their culture; in turn they vanished to make way for warlike nomads, the forbears of the Indians whom steel-clad Spaniards encountered on their explorations northward from Mexico in search of fabulous cities of gold. French *voyageurs* later explored the northern streams of Colorado, to be hunters, trappers, and traders.

"Gold!"—always a magic cry—was the tocsin that signaled the great Pikes Peak rush of '59, one of the great mass migrations of American history. Men of almost every nationality, occupation, and station in life swarmed into the Colorado mountains, and in their wake followed farmers, largely of European stock, to settle in the fertile valleys. Up from the south, across the open grasslands, were driven tremendous herds of Texas Longhorns, once numbered in the millions, now almost extinct. Barbed wire abruptly terminated the era of the open range, and American, English, and Scottish cattle barons gave way to a new type of settler, the dry-land farmer, usually American-born of English, German, Scandinavian, or Irish stock. Men discouraged in their search for sudden riches in the hills came down to the plains to work in the fields and the growing industrial centers, where they rubbed shoulders with more recent immigrants—Italians, Hungarians, and Slavs. Orientals appeared—Chinese in the mines, Japanese on the farms. German-Russians were lured from the Volga by the introduction of sugar beet culture, which they knew well. Later, Spanish-Americans flooded in from the southern valleys and from Mexico to work the beet fields.

All these—and more—are Coloradoans, and their story is the history of the State.

MEN OF THE STONE AGE

Thousands of years ago, when the last of the great ice sheets was melting and slowly retreating northward, there roamed the plains in the eastern part of the State an unknown people—artisans in their own right—who remain a tantalizing mystery to archeologists and anthropologists. The latter have found no skeletal remains of these people, but numerous artifacts reveal their presence and in a measure indicate the grim struggle for existence in which they were engaged. Spearheads of these early hunters have been found with the bones of a prehistoric bison believed to have lived more than ten thousand years ago. At the Lindenmeier Site (*see Tour 13*) has been unearthed a campsite that was used by them, according to some authorities, at least 20,000 years ago.

Two types of stone artifacts were left in Colorado by this vanished race. The Folsom point, first found near Folsom, New Mexico, ranges from one and a half to four and a half inches long, and is characterized by a long wide groove along both sides from the base to the point. This groove was formed in a single operation by removing a long delicate flake of stone. The manner in which this spall was removed from each face of the blade is fairly clear to students, but they have not skill to perform the operation themselves. The ancient people who fashioned these points were highly accomplished workmen who knew the secret of flaking the hardest stone with great precision.

The second type is the Yuma point, named for the county in the northeastern corner of the State where many such artifacts have been found. The Yuma point is longer and narrower than the Folsom; it has no groove but is similarly distinguished by remarkable flaking. Long flakes of stone were sometimes removed straight across the blade, sometimes at an angle. Bows probably were unknown to the Folsom and Yuma men, but both types of points, when affixed to shafts, made highly effective projectiles. A Yuma point has been found with a square idented base, which may have been inserted in a wooden handle for use as a knife. Since 1930 great numbers of both points have been exposed in northeastern Colorado by wind erosion; in fact, two-thirds of all such artifacts have been found here. An unusually large collection is annually exhibited at the Stone Age Fair at Cornish (*see Tour 12a*), and another comprehensive collection is in the Colorado Museum of Natural History, Denver. While the exact age of the points cannot be definitely determined, evidence indicates that the Folsom and Yuma cultures were contemporaneous.

The next culture of record in Colorado is of comparatively recent date and had no historical relationship with the Folsom or Yuma culture. Between 100 B.C. and 100 A.D., there came into the mesa lands of southwestern Colorado, southeastern Utah, and northeastern Arizona, a long-headed race of Indians who planted corn and squash, dug granaries and pit houses, and fashioned excellent coiled baskets, as well as sandals, cord, and rope. This culture reached its height in the Modified Basket Maker period when these people began to build permanent habitations in the form of pit houses, with superstructures of poles, brush, and earth. Remains of hundreds of these structures have been found on Mesa Verde and throughout the San Juan Basin. The subsequent invention of true pottery by these people was marked by a decline in basket work. The bow and arrow appeared during this period, but it is not known whether the weapon was "invented" by the Basket Makers or introduced by invading Indian tribes.

About 800 A.D. a new type of people appeared in the Southwest, and through peaceful infiltration absorbed the Basket Maker and his culture, and in time evolved their own Pueblo culture. These newcomers, characterized by skulls deformed by hard cradle boards, learned to fashion better pottery, evolved more productive methods of agriculture, wove cotton into cloth, learned the art of masonry, and developed the crude pit dwellings of the Basket Maker into massive and complex pueblos constructed of stone and mud. These early Amerinds who farmed or rather gardened southwestern Colorado also built large temples, watch towers, and *kivas,* or ceremonial chambers. Later, when attacked by less civilized tribes, they built high upon the walls of Colorado canyons the famed cliff dwellings that served them as a refuge from their enemies. Circular receptacles, hollowed in the rock walls of the natural caves in which they constructed their dwellings, were used to store food and enabled the apartment-fortresses to withstand long siege.

The most noted ruins in Colorado are the cliff dwellings and pueblos in Mesa Verde National Park (*see Mesa Verde National Park*). On the border between Colorado and Utah are four groups of similar prehistoric dwellings in the Hovenweep National Monument (*see Tour 11D*). The Yucca House National Monument (*see Tour 11*), at the base of Sleeping Ute Mountain in the extreme southwestern part of the State, preserves the ruins of still another village. Recent explorations along the Yampa River in northwestern Colorado (*see Tour 7c*) indicate that the Pueblo peoples may also have entered this region.

The Pueblo culture flourished between 900 and 1200 A.D., in what is known as the Pueblo Classical Age; during these centuries most of the great cliff dwellings on Mesa Verde were constructed. Decline

History

ROUND TOWER AND SQUARE TOWER, CLIFF DWELLING, MESA VERDE

Fred Wang Photo, National Park Service
DWELLINGS UNDER OVERHANGING CLIFF, MESA VERDE

STORAGE PIT SOUTH
COURT, MESA VERDE

*Jack E. Boucher Photo.
National Park Service*

Stewart Bros.   *State Historical Society*
ZEBULON PIKE, EXPLORER   KIT CARSON, FRONTIERSMAN

SKETCH OF OLD FORT MASSACHUSETTS

U. S. Army Signal Corps

CHIEF OURAY AND OTHER UTE CHIEFS, PHOTOGRAPHED BY
WILLIAM H. JACKSON IN 1870

EARLY TELLURIDE; MAIN STREET

WAGON TRAIN CORRALING IN DENVER STREET, 1866

Central City Opera Assn.

BAR IN THE TELLER HOUSE, CENTRAL CIT

DINING ROOM
HOTEL DE PARIS, GEORGETOWN
Farm Security Administration

FIREPLACE
HEALY HOUSE, LEADVILLE
Adolph Horowitz

EARLY DAY STREET SCENE, CRIPPLE CREEK

PALACE THEATRE, DENVER

Joe Sturdevant

FIRST DENVER & RIO GRANDE TRAIN GREETED BY MINERS
AT CREEDE, 1891

NARROW-GAUGE DENVER & RIO GRANDE AT MARSHALL PASS
NEAR GUNNISON

was sudden and dramatic. Chronology based upon a study of tree rings indicates that the Cliff Dwellers suffered a great drought between 1276 and 1299. Either as a result of this disaster or of an attack by marauding Indian normads, the Cliff Dwellers abandoned their habitations and drifted southward, leaving no trace, although competent authorities believe that they may have been absorbed by other pueblo people who still live in the Southwest.

INDIAN NOMADS

The first whites to explore what is now Colorado found most of it occupied by branches of two large Indian linguistic groups—the Shoshonean, who claimed the mountain country and a portion of the southern plains, and the Algonkian tribes who held the northeastern plains section. How many they numbered, all told, is uncertain. Existing records are vague and contradictory through want of understanding of Indian tribal divisions, fluctuations in population caused by unremitting warfare, and the predilection of the military to exaggerate the numbers of the foe. The Indians in the State never totaled more than 10,000 persons, according to some historians, but other estimates run twice as high.

The chief tribes on the plains were the Cheyenne, Arapaho, Comanche, and Kiowa. Before the advent of the white men these tribes were bitter enemies, almost constantly at war, with the Cheyenne and Arapaho allied against the Comanche and Kiowa. Less permanent residents of the plains were the Pawnee of Caddoan stock, the Sioux, the Kiowa-Apache, and the Plains Apache, or Lipan. Crow and Blackfoot war parties occasionally penetrated from the north as far as the South Platte River, and in the sixteenth century the Spanish found Navaho along the banks of the Rio San Juan in southwestern Colorado. The Mountain Apache, or Jicarilla, frequently came into Colorado from New Mexico and Arizona to make raids on the plains tribes and to trade with their friends, the Ute.

The mountain-dwelling Ute, Colorado's chief representatives of Shoshonean stock, appear to have been the only indigenous tribe of Colorado; all others were migrants who came in a series of waves set in motion by the pressure of stronger peoples behind them. The seven tribes of Ute in the State were grouped in four major divisions—the Southern Ute, which included the Capote, Moache, and Wiminuche bands; the White River Ute, made up of the Yampa and Grand River tribes; the Tabeguache Ute, comprising the Tabeguache proper and the Uncompahgre; and the Uintah Ute, embracing a number of tribes largely resident in Utah although a few lived in the extreme northwestern corner of Colorado. The Ute tribes were in turn subdivided into smaller bands, each with its own name and civil organization. Great differences in dialect and culture characterized these divisions, as was to be expected in a tribe so widely scattered and inhabiting territory as diverse as the mountain fastnesses in the central part of the State and the semiarid plateaus to the west and south. The Ute held the entire mountain region, guarding the low passes against the plains Indians with whom they were constantly at war. This unremitting warfare proved a source of irritation and alarm to white communities near the foothills, for war parties on raid and counterraid constantly threatened the new settlements. On one occasion a party of Arapaho, after an unsuccessful attack upon the Ute, sought refuge in the very heart of Denver, to the anger and dismay of the inhabitants, who knew that the pursuing Ute would not distinguish between their hereditary enemies and the whites who ostensibly were offering them shelter. Fortunately, the mountain warriors turned back before they reached Denver.

The Ute were never really conquered; in the end, they were turned to the ways of peace by their chiefs—notably, the great Ouray, always a friend of the whites. As early as 1705 the Ute joined a conspiracy of the Navaho and other tribes against the Spanish; later, they frequently raided the Spanish settlements in New Mexico for horses, scalps, and plunder. Governor Cossio of New Mexico led a punitive expedition against them in 1719, but the mountain warriors eluded him and the raids upon the Spanish settlements continued. On Christmas Day 1854, a band of Ute under Tierra Blanca captured old Fort Pueblo (*see Pueblo*) and massacred all but a Mexican woman and two children. The woman was later killed, but the children were finally returned to their people. In 1855 the Tabeguache band under Kanakache attacked the Spanish colony at Guadalupe but were decisively defeated (*see Tour 15c*). A second expedition from New Mexico took the trail of the hostiles, and defeated them in several engagements with heavy losses. The Ute finally sued for peace, returning hostages and much plunder. Subsequently, the attitude of the Ute toward the white settlers who were gradually encroaching upon their hunting grounds was far from friendly, but was rarely openly hostile. Ranchers were occasionally killed, and from time to time prospecting parties were wiped out, but no serious outbreak occurred until 1879 when the increasing resentment of the Ute culminated in the Meeker Massacre (*see Tour 17*).

Earlier, by a treaty in 1868, the Federal Government had assigned the Ute a large part of southwestern Colorado, but with the discovery of rich mineral deposits in this region steps were taken to recover it. In 1873, largely through the counsel of Ouray, the Ute ceded the mineralized San Juan district. As late as 1874, however, they retained title to 15,500,000 acres on the Western Slope and occupied most of the territory west of the Continental Divide. In 1881 the Northern Ute who had participated in the Meeker Massacre were removed to a reservation at Uintah, Utah. One last abortive attempt to reclaim their old lands was made by a band under Colorow; after this failure the Ute made no further resistance. The Southern Ute were subsequently placed on a small reservation in the barren southwestern corner of the State (*see Tours 11D and 11E*). Intermarriage between the Ute and the Jicarilla Apache was common. The celebrated Ouray—or more correctly, Ure—was born of such a union, his mother being a Jicarilla; Chief Colorow was likewise of mixed Ute and Apache blood.

The Comanche, first of the plains tribes to appear in Colorado, were driven from their home in the Black Hills by the Sioux; they moved southward, pushed by the war-like Kiowa, whose allies they later became. As the Comanche were of Shoshonean stock, they were friendly for a time with their kinsmen, the Ute; later estranged for some unknown cause, the two tribes became bitter enemies. After their arrival in Colorado, where they ranged the extreme southern part of the State, they became a nation of fierce and ruthless fighters, the scourge of the settlements in New Mexico and Texas; they extended their depredations deep into old Mexico, where they were hated and feared above all other tribes. The Comanche were accomplished horse thieves and raiders, and grew tremendously rich in horses, general plunder and hostages; they carried off white women and children and held them for ransom, which was usually paid in the form of ammunition, whisky, and supplies. Women captives were frequently taken as legal wives by chiefs and warriors, and some of these women refused to leave their husbands when their ransom was paid. Quanah Parker, the great Comanche chief, was born of such a union; his mother, Cynthia Parker, had been stolen by Comanche raiders when a child and refused to return to her people.

Next to arrive in Colorado were the Kiowa, or *Ka-i-gwa*, "principal people." Of unknown origin, they are classed as a separate linguistic unit, for little similarity exists between their tongue and that of any other tribe. Although few in number, they were regarded as the most predatory and bloodthirsty of all the plains Indians, and are said to have killed more whites in proportion to their number than any other tribe. They took possession of a region south of the Arkansas River, and after fighting the Comanche for years, made an alliance with them, sharing a large territory as hunting grounds, harrying white settlements in every direction. The Kiowa played an important part in the Indian wars between 1861 and 1869, and also in the "Buffalo War" of 1873-74, when the allied Cheyenne, Arapaho, Comanche, and Kiowa made a last desperate stand against white hunters who were destroying the few remaining large buffalo herds in Oklahoma and Texas.

On the heels of the Kiowa came the allied Cheyenne and Arapaho. The war-like Cheyenne took the lead in almost all policies of war and peace, and the Arapaho usually followed their tempestuous allies. The Cheyenne called themselves *Tsis-tsis-tas*, variously translated as "similarly bred," or "the slashed people"; the tribal sign signified "cut" or "slashed." The name by which they are commonly known is a corruption of the Siouan word *Sha-hei-la*, "people of alien speech." Originally an agricultural people, the Cheyenne had long since become buffalo hunters as they were relentlessly forced west and south by the Sioux. At some unidentified period during this slow migration they formed their lasting friendship with the Arapaho. Entering Colorado, they drove the Kiowa southward to crowd the belligerent Comanche and precipitate a flurry of intertribal wars. From these conflicts the Cheyenne and Arapaho finally emerged triumphant in undisputed possession of the territory north of the Arkansas and east of the mountains.

After the construction of Bent's Fort on the Arkansas River in 1832 (*see Tour 9A*), the Cheyenne tribes divided. One part migrated to the Arkansas Valley and became known as *Sowonia*, or "Southerners," while the other part remained about the headwaters of the North Platte and the Yellowstone Rivers. This split, designed to facilitate trading with the trappers who came to Bent's Fort, weakened them and hastened the destruction of their tribal organization.

The plains Indians were not easily subdued. In 1840 a great council had been held on the banks of the Arkansas River, at which Cheyenne, Arapaho, Kiowa, and Comanche settled their differences and formed an offensive and defensive alliance against other tribes and the increasing menace of white immigration. This treaty was never broken, and the alliance of the Four Nations had far-reaching effects upon the history of the West. Presenting a united front against invaders of their buffalo lands, these fierce and implacable tribes made a determined stand in defense of their homes.

From their first contact with the whites, the Arapaho and Cheyenne were alternately hostile and friendly, often changing for no apparent reason. The earliest pioneers found them almost universally opposed to white invasion, although they were friendly enough toward Bent and other traders. They were continuously hostile between 1855 and 1857, when the military took the field against them and defeated them with considerable losses. In 1861 the two tribes concluded a treaty with the Federal Government by which they relinquished all claim to the greater part of their Colorado lands. A temporary peace followed, but failure to fulfill promises made to them in regard to annuities and other matters brought renewed raiding; this in turn led to the Sand Creek Massacre (*see Tour 8a*), in which the Southern Cheyenne received a stunning blow. Ten years of almost continuous warfare followed this ill-advised affair. Northeastern Colorado, Nebraska, and Kansas were ravaged, with inestimable losses in life and property. Julesburg and most of the stage stations in the South Platte Valley were destroyed; wagon trains were burned, and all trails were virtually closed.

Gradually the tide of warfare turned against the Indians. In 1868, at Beecher Island on the Arickaree River (*see Tour 3*), the Cheyenne lost one of their greatest leaders, Roman Nose, and their failure here to defeat a foe numerically so much weaker did much to shake their morale. That winter, in Nebraska, Chief Black Kettle's village on the Washita River was destroyed, and in the summer of 1869 Tall Bull was defeated at Summit Springs (*see Tour 1a*). The "hostiles" were continuously harried until the last of the Southern Cheyenne surrendered in 1874 and were settled on a reservation in western Oklahoma. The Northern Cheyenne, still irreconcilable, joined Sitting Bull in the Sioux War of 1876, participating in the Custer Massacre and in Brook's Battle on the Rosebud. In the winter of 1878–79 the larger bands of hostile Cheyenne under Chiefs Dull Knife, Wild Hog, and Little Wolf surrendered and were removed to Fort Reno, Oklahoma, to be settled with the southern unit of the tribe. After considerable friction generated by their not un-natural dislike of a strange land so different from their home, they were assigned to the present reservation in Montana. Little Wolf and his people, after their final capitulation, became scouts for the Army and saw active service against the still hostile Sioux.

The Arapaho roamed a narrow strip of plains country along the front range of the Rockies, between the Cache la Poudre and Arkansas Rivers. Like the Cheyenne, they divided into a northern and a southern branch; the former held the country north of the South Platte River, while the latter occupied the valley of the Arkansas, along with the Southern Cheyenne, with whom they fought side by side during the wars of the 1850's and 1860's, and with whom they shared land in the Oklahoma reservation. The Arapaho, although a milder people than their allies, were savage fighters when aroused and bore an enviable record for prowess. There was a strong infusion of Arapaho blood among the Cheyenne, but the tribal stock of the former remained almost pure; Cheyenne men frequently married Arapaho women, but, curiously, there is no recorded instance of a marriage between an Arapaho brave and a Cheyenne girl. Arapaho, although sometimes translated as "tattooed people," is a corruption of the Pawnee word *Lirapahu,* "traders." Their own name for themselves was *Inuniana,* "our people."

The last tribe to enter Colorado and claim hunting grounds were the Pawnee. They came from far to the south, and the record of their journey to the West is unknown. They first made their headquarters on the Republican River some three hundred miles east of the Rockies, and in Colorado their territory embraced only the extreme northeastern corner of the State. Bitter enemies of almost every other tribe, they were notable fighters individually, but as a group they were relatively weak and on the eve of white settlement they held their semiarid hunting grounds largely on the sufferance of stronger neighbors who sought more desirable territory. Of all Colorado tribes the Pawnee alone were consistently friendly to the whites, seldom resorting to war, waiting patiently for the Federal Government to right any wrongs they had suffered; many Pawnee served with the Army against the "hostiles." A semisedentary people, the Pawnee crudely cultivated small gardens and lived during the summer months in makeshift dwellings of logs, sod, and bark. The remainder of the year they roamed the plains on hunting expeditions, living in skin lodges, supplementing their limited vegetable diet with meat. When the Indian wars were over, the Pawnee, too, were settled on reservations in Oklahoma and Texas.

CONQUISTADORES AND VOYAGEURS

Coronado, while searching for the fabulous Quivera and Seven Cities of Cibola, was the first white man to set foot in what is now Colorado, so it is popularly believed. But historians will only concede that he may "just possibly" have touched the southeastern corner of the State on his return march to Mexico in 1541. In any case, the Spanish were the first Europeans to explore the region. As early as 1650, mine owners in New Mexico were pursuing runaway Indian slaves toward a section of the Arkansas Valley known as El Quartelejo, probably in eastern Colorado or western Kansas. Juan de Uribarri, leader of such an expedition in 1706, became alarmed at evidences of French penetration from the Mississippi and took formal possession of the country in the name of King Philip V, naming it Santo Domingo.

Throughout the eighteenth century Spain and France contended for possession of the great plains west of the Mississippi. If the French knew of Uribarri's act of annexation, they ignored it, and their traders and trappers continued to push westward toward the mountains. To check these *voyageurs,* Spanish authorities sent military expeditions northward through Colorado in 1719 and again in 1720; the latter, under the command of Pedro de Villasur, was trapped and annihilated by Indians. The French based their claim to this region upon La Salle's magnificent verbal appropriation in 1682 of all territory between the Alleghenies and the Rockies, but their knowledge of the country was extremely vague. It adjoined the Orient, so they believed, and in passing through eastern Colorado on their way to Santa Fe in 1739, the Mallet brothers were convinced that they had trod Chinese soil. Eager to tap the fabled wealth of the Celestial Empire, the French governor at New Orleans made every effort to hold the intervening plains that presumably gave easy access to it. French influence was brief, however, and appears today only in a few such river names as the Platte (Rivière la Platte) and the Cache la Poudre.

Spain's assertion of ownership continued to be strengthened by exploration and occupation. Juan Maria Rivera and others undertook sporadic searches for gold in the San Juan and Sangre de Cristo ranges in 1765, and in 1776 the Franciscan friars, Silvestre Velez de Escalante and Francisco Antanasio Dominguez, made their way northward from Santa Fe into the White River country in northwestern Colorado while seeking a shorter route from the New Mexico to the California missions. These early Spanish explorers left their own memorial in the beautiful mouth-filling names they bestowed upon mountains, rivers, and places throughout southern Colorado—among others, the Rio Grande del Norte, the Sangre de Cristo and San Juan mountains, and El Rio de Las Animas Perdidas en Purgatorio, or River of Souls Lost in Purgatory, later given the French form of Puragtoire by Gallic trappers and later corrupted to Picketwire by American cowmen.

But exploration had far less weight than imperial politics in determining the ownership of the region. At the close of the Seven Years' War in 1762, France was forced to cede to Britain all territory east of the Mississippi, except New Orleans, and at the same time it was revealed that by a previous agreement France had ceded to Spain all territory west of the Mississippi, together with New Orleans. Brooding over the loss of their vast empire in the New World, the French found an opportunity in 1801 to force Spain to relinquish its share of the loot in exchange for the Duchy of Tuscany, Italy. Two years later, hard pressed by his enemies, Napoleon sold the vast Louisiana Territory to the United States for $15,000,000. It was purchased almost sight unseen, and President Jefferson was bitterly criticized and ridiculed for buying a pig in a poke, not worth half the price.

PLAINSMEN AND MOUNTAIN MEN

In part to determine the southwestern boundary of the Louisiana Purchase, then held to be the Red River, Lieutenant Zebulon M. Pike was officially dispatched with a small party to explore the region. The expedition reached the present site of Pueblo on November 23, 1806, and Pike and a few men set out to climb the great peak that bears his name. For days it had been seen hanging like a white cloud on the horizon to the north, and the clarity of the atmosphere made it appear deceptively close. Lightly clothed and with little food, having to battle their way upward through a blizzard, Pike and his men failed to reach the summit, and in his journal Pike noted his opinion that the peak could not be scaled. He then moved westward up the Arkansas River to its source, retraced his steps some distance, and crossed the Sangre de Cristo into the San Luis Valley, proceeding westward to the Rio Grande, which he mistook for the Red River. Five miles up the Conejos, a tributary of the Rio Grande, the party encamped and built a fortified stockade. In February 1807, Pike learned that he was on foreign soil when Spanish soldiers appeared and placed him and his command under nominal arrest. Taken to Santa Fe, later to Mexico, he was subsequently released and died in battle during the War of 1812.

The southwestern boundary of the Louisiana Purchase was not determined until 1819 when it was agreed that it should run along the Arkansas River into the mountains and thence northward along the Continental Divide. At the same time President Monroe sent Major Stephen H. Long and a party to explore the region along the new boundary. Entering Colorado in 1820 by way of the South Platte River, the party moved south along the mountains to the Arkansas River, which a few of Long's men ascended as far as the Royal Gorge. Long conceived a poor opinion of the plains section of Colorado, dismissing it as "the Great American Desert" upon which nothing would ever grow. During this expedition the first recorded ascent of Pike's "unscalable" peak was led by Dr. Edwin James, scientist and historian of the party, whose reports served to acquaint the country with the western frontier, stirring the imagination of bolder and more restless spirits.

Plainsmen and Mountain Men were soon courageously pushing into this wilderness, penetrating every corner of it, following the streams high into the mountains in search of beaver and other prized fur-bearing animals. Trading posts sprang up at strategic points along the base of the foothills. The most celebrated of these first mercantile establishments and social centers of Colorado was that built near the present site of La Junta by the Bent and St. Vrain Company, a subsidiary of the American Fur Company. This adobe fortress, begun in 1828 and completed four years later, the largest in Colorado (*see Tour 9A*), was managed by William Bent, his three brothers, and their partner Ceran St. Vrain, reputedly a French nobleman. The Cheyenne, Arapaho, Kiowa, and Comanche came to trade at the post, and here was held the great council of 1840 at which these ancient enemies buried the hatchet and effected a permanent alliance. Here, too, at one time or another, came virtually every hero of actual or mythical prowess in the Old West—Jim Bridger, perhaps the greatest of the Mountain Men; Jim Baker and Tom ("Broken Hand") Fitzpatrick; "Uncle Dick" Wootton, with his bristling black hair and his shrewd eye for a good "swap" or other forms of profitable enterprise; and Jim Beckwourth, the mulatto who became a war chief of the Crow; the tribe became so enamored of him and so dependent upon his courage and skill, so Beckwourth said, that they sought to prevent his departure by poisoning him so that they might "keep him with them always."

Kit Carson, trapper, scout, and Indian agent, was a hunter at the post from 1831 to 1842, living much of his life in the vicinity, dying in 1868 at Fort Lyon, forty miles to the east. Traders and trappers brought their wives, either Mexican women from Santa Fe or Taos, or Indian squaws from almost every tribe west of the Mississippi, and their half-breed children romped and tumbled about the fort. Indian wives were frequently changed, and several or more squaws graced many a trapper's household. They were usually well-treated, however, and were "as happy as red paint and 'froo-foo-raw' could make them." Thomas J. Farnham visited the fort in 1839 and has left a fascinating record of life there in his *Western Travels,* as has Francis Parkman in his *Oregon Trail.*

The post, a resting point for Kearney's Army of the West in 1846 and for Price's forces en route to Santa Fe in 1847, was abandoned in 1852 with the decline of the Indian trade; William Bent tried to sell the fort to the Federal Government as a military station, and when he failed, blew it up rather than have it occupied without payment. Down the Arkansas he built another post near the present site of Fort Lyon, where this greatest of Plainsmen continued in business until 1862, dying seven years later on a ranch near the Purgatoire River.

The Bents' most active rival was Louis Vasquez; in 1836 he and Andrew Sublette built a trading post for the Rocky Mountain Fur Company on the South Platte just north of the present site of Denver. Fort Vasquez was likewise a rendezvous of Plainsmen and Mountain Men; although Vasquez was not as well liked as the Bents, he did a thriving business with the Northern Cheyenne and Arapaho, and with white trappers and hunters from the Ute country. In 1840 the post was sold to Locke and Randolph, and in 1842 it was captured and looted by Arapaho raiders. This post has recently been reconstructed. The trade in beaver pelts began to decline about 1840, and the posts, one by one, were abandoned. Their protective functions were assumed by military forts, the first of which, Fort Massachusetts, was built in 1852 for the protection of settlers in the San Luis Valley; it was soon abandoned for a better site at Fort Garland near by.

Between 1842 and 1853 Lieutenant John C. Frémont led five exploring expeditions into the Rocky Mountain region, the first three under the auspices of the Federal Government. On his expedition in 1842 Frémont followed the South Platte to Fort St. Vrain, struck northward to Fort Laramie, and returned east along the North Platte. The next year he crossed Colorado twice on his way to and from the Pacific. In 1848, while attempting to find a feasible railroad route through the Rockies, he and his men became snow-bound high in the La Garita Mountains of southern Colorado. After fearful privations Frémont and a few men succeeded in reaching Taos, New Mexico. The fifth expedition in 1853 took him through the San Luis Valley, over Cochetopa Pass, and into the basin of the Gunnison River, along much the same route followed earlier that year by Captain John W. Gunnison.

During this pre-settlement period the political status of Colorado changed frequently. As the Louisiana Territory was apportioned, the plains section north of the Arkansas was assigned in turn to Louisiana, Missouri, Nebraska, and Kansas. The remaining two-thirds of the State, south of the Arkansas and west of the Continental Divide, fell to Mexico when it achieved its independence from Spain in 1821. Later, when the Republic of Texas won its freedom from Mexico in 1836, the former laid claim to a strip of land extending north along the mountains to the 42nd parallel. The quarrel between the two southern republics over this territory continued after Texas had been admitted to the Union and did much to precipitate war between the United States and Mexico. By the Treaty of Guadalupe Hidalgo the United States acquired all of what is now Colorado, dividing its southern and western sections between New Mexico and Utah.

By the treaty the United States agreed to respect the property rights of all who had settled in the territory, for Mexico had made desperate attempts to preserve her northern possessions by colonizing them, awarding huge land grants to favored individuals, creating within the present State the princely demesnes of Maxwell, Nolan, Baca, and Sangre de Cristo. On this last grant the first permanent settlement in Colorado was made in 1853, near the present town of San Luis in the San Luis Valley. But settlers here or elsewhere in the region were few, for the traders and trappers who had tried ranching after the decline of the fur trade had not prospered, and only a handful remained on the plains or in the mountains by 1855. Colorado was still a wilderness, although destined to remain so but a short time.

"PIKES PEAK OR BUST"

The discovery of gold in Colorado in 1858 ushered in a turbulent era. A few fortune hunters, almost a decade before, had paused on their way to the California gold fields to pan gravel along the Rocky Mountain streams. Among them was Green Russell, a miner from the Georgia gold fields, accompanied by his brothers, Oliver and Levi. They "raised color" on Cherry Creek, within the present confines of Denver, and on the Cache la Poudre, forty miles to the north. On his return from California, Russell was reminded of this when he heard from his Cherokee wife that a party of her people also had found traces of gold along the Rockies. In 1858 Russell organized a party, which included many Cherokee, and set out for the mountains, searching along their base to the mouth of Cherry Creek. The gold they panned was negligible, but exaggerated reports of their activities drifted eastward to fall upon the ears of the credulous who instantly recalled the fabulous California discoveries of '49. By Christmas 1858, several hundred impatient fortune-seekers were gathered in two small settlements on opposite banks of Cherry Creek close to its junction with the South Platte.

Mining operations were impeded during the winter, but this only increased the excitement. Some gold-hunters returned to the Missouri Valley to purchase supplies, and took with them minute samples of Pikes Peak "dust" to be shown in stores, saloons, and newspaper offices. Stories and rumors spread, becoming steadily more glowing; emigrant companies were organized in many communities and spent the winter preparing for the race to the Rockies in the spring.

All kinds of conveyances took to the Overland and Santa Fe trails as early as February 1859; the more impatient and reckless blazed a new and shorter route, the Smoky Hill Trail, across central Kansas. By March the rush was well under way. Many in this frantic migration had left home with sanguine expectations of finding creeks bedded with golden sands and mines studded with nuggets. Within a few weeks at most, so they believed, they would be rich and on their way home. Disappointment overwhelmed them when they found no pot of gold at the end of the rainbow in the hodge-podge of mud-plastered huts along Cherry Creek. They were increasingly alarmed to find that even pots of pork and beans were scarce. Outraged and disgusted, weary of sleeping in wet blankets through freezing storms of snow and hail, their spirits at low ebb after having fruitlessly urged their starved and weary cattle over the immense barren plains—those same plains so unflatteringly described by Major Long forty years before—hundreds of Fifty-niners abruptly faced about and began an equally reckless stampede back to "The States." Along the way they met westbound travelers, many of whom, having heard their disillusioned and often angry tales, joined the retreat without having come within sight of the mountains. Yet enough pushed on to overcrowd the adjoining camps of Denver City and Auraria, which continued to grow at a lively pace, peopled by men who desperately wanted to find gold but had not the slightest idea where to look for it.

Into this scene of restless inactivity rode a horseman with a report of rich new diggings on Clear Creek, some 40 miles west in the mountains. George Jackson had found gold-bearing sands on Chicago Creek early in January, and on May 6, 1859, John Gregory had made his great strike at what soon became the booming camp of Central City. Horace Greeley, editor of the New York *Tribune,* who had come to inspect "the Kansas gold fields," dashed up to Gregory Gulch and a month later described the scene for his readers: "As yet the entire population of the valley—which cannot number less than 4,000, including five white women and seven squaws living with white men—sleep in tents or under booths of pine boughs, cooking and eating in the open air. I doubt that there is as yet a table or chair in these diggings. . . . The food, like that of the plains, is restricted to a few staples—pork, hot bread, beans, and coffee forming the almost exclusive diet of the mountains; but a meat shop has just been established, on whose altar are offered up the ill-fed and well-whipped oxen who are just in from a 50-day journey across the plains." Greeley added that less than half of the 4,000 inhabitants had been there a week, with 500 arriving daily.

Greeley's report on the gold camp further stimulated the rush, and the Clear Creek fields were soon staked out. With picks and shovels scarring the hillsides in all directions other strikes were made, notably in South Park and along Boulder Creek. In isolated mountain valleys and gulches lusty new camps appeared. Tarryall, Hamilton, Buckskin Joe, Fairplay, Golden, Gold Hill, Boulder, Colorado City, and other towns were established in the frantic year of '59.

Pioneer merchants with wagonloads of supplies from the Missouri River and New Mexico followed close upon the heels of gold-hunters. Tent stores and log saloons did a brisk business along the muddy streets of raw new towns. Barrels served as counters over which storekeepers, with cheerful impartiality, dispensed salt, sugar, picks, coffee, nails, gold pans, potatoes, onions, rice, flour, shoes, and a particularly villainous brand of whisky known as "Taos Lightning"; prices rose sharply until flour sold at $40 a hundred pounds. As the winter of 1859 approached, many miners returned home to bring back their families in the spring, after which the camps began to assume an air of permanence. Some 10,000 persons, it was estimated at the time, stayed through the second winter.

Late in 1859 the first school in the gold fields was established by "Professor" O. J. Goldrick, who had come thundering down Cherry Creek cracking a bull whip at a plunging ox team. Goldrick looked the part of the "professor," having arrived in silk hat, yellow kid gloves, and broadcloth frock coat, the pockets of which contained a B.A. from the University of Dublin, an M.A. from Columbia University, and cash to the sum of 50 cents. His salary insured by passing the hat, which netted him $250, Goldrick opened the Union School in a one-room, mud-roofed log cabin on Blake Street, Auraria, on October 3, 1859. A small unglazed hole in the gable provided light, and a strip of canvas from a wagon top covered the slightly larger opening that answered for a door. Thirteen pupils were in attendance that first day, "two Indian, two Mexican, and the rest white, and from Missouri." Goldrick wrote to inform John D. Philbrick, superintendent of schools at Boston, of the momentous event, and the latter sent warm greetings "from the cradle of the free school on the Atlantic shores . . . to your Union School on the frontier of civilization at the foot of the Rocky Mountains." Twenty-three years later, after an inspection of Denver schools, Philbrick reported that "the creation of a system of schools on so large a scale, of such exceptional merits, and in so brief a space of time, is a phenomenon to which the history of education affords no parallel."

Settlers were so proud of their initial institution of learning that they met every wagon train with the cry, "We've got a school," urging immigrants with families to tarry. Enrollment increased rapidly; two more private schools were established at Denver within the year; schools were opened in Central City, Blackhawk, and Georgetown. At Boulder, a community of some twenty log cabins, the first schoolhouse in the State was built in 1860 with funds raised by Abner R. Brown, a schoolmaster of New York and Iowa, who had come West to prospect for gold; finding none, he resumed his teaching. That same year Goldrick organized and became secretary of the first library association, with one book on its shelves, probably the Bible.

The gold fields had a newspaper soon after the arrival early in 1859 of William Newton Byers, a sometime surveyor, who had come from Omaha "with his shirt tail full of type," accompanied by Dr. George C. Monell, a fellow-townsman, and Thomas Gibson, a printer of Fontanelle, Nebraska. Four days before they had hauled in their Washington hand press, John Merrick had arrived from Leavenworth, Kansas, with a press that had been fished out of the Missouri River. Thrown into the river after it had been used by Mormons at Independence, Missouri, the press had been rehabilitated and employed to print the St. Joseph *Gazette* for some years before it passed into Merrick's hands. The spirited race to publish the first newspaper at the diggings was won by Byers, who got his *Rocky Mountain News* on the streets of Denver City and Auraria twenty minutes before Merrick's *Cherry Creek Pioneer* made its first and last appearance, for Merrick immediately sold out to his rivals for a $30 grubstake and departed for the boom camps in the mountains.

The *Rocky Mountain News* has since been continuously published, and on June 11, 1859, issued its first "extry," printed on brown wrapping paper, to headline Horace Greeley's enthusiastic report on the previously discredited gold fields. General news was obtained by pony relay from Fort Laramie, Wyoming, the nearest post office 20 miles to the north. This expensive procedure necessitated a charge of 25¢ a copy, or $25 a year, payable either in coin or in gold dust, the general medium of exchange. Occasional issues sold at $1.25 a copy, and the scarcity of news was such in the isolated camps that readers were never wanting. Thomas Gibson, Byers' partner, soon withdrew and on May 1, 1860, established the *Rocky Mountain Herald,* Colorado's first daily (now a weekly), which forced the *News* to begin daily publication.

The Merrick press, with the demise of the *Cherry Creek Pioneer,* began another phase of its already remarkable career, being carted here and there throughout the mountains to print newspapers in one boom camp after another. Upon it Thomas Gibson ran off the short-lived *Gold Reporter* at Gregory Gulch (Central City) in August 1859, the pioneer journal in the golden "Kingdom of Gilpin." The press was then removed to the town of Golden to print the *Western Mountaineer* during 1860. With the demise of this journal, Merrick's press was hauled to southern Colorado in 1861 to print its pioneer newspaper, the Canon City *Times.* The next spring it journeyed to the boisterous camp of Buckskin Joe in South Park to compete with the *Miner's Record* of Tarryall near by. Again the valiant hand press was carted through the hills, to Valmont, where it gave birth to the *Boulder Valley News.* But within a few weeks the Valmont editor was plied with strong drink by citizens of Boulder, who kidnapped him, his press, and type cases, and carried them home in triumph to establish the Boulder *News.* The Colorado career of the press terminated when it was sold to a publisher at Elizabeth, New Mexico.

It was an era of personal journalism, and it left its mark upon the Colorado press. Editors indulged in lively personalities with one another and with all-comers. "The Black Hawk (sic) *Journal* appears diurnally now, printed on half a sheet of cartridge paper," remarked the *Rocky Mountain News* in 1868. "Its editor dislikes to use that kind of paper for what it was intended, so he makes it do service to fulminate his daily lies." A six-shooter in the hands of an irate reader was the only libel law, and many a frontier editor faced such a "suit." Byers edited the *News* with several revolvers within easy reach; on one occasion desperadoes attacked his office for uncomplimentary remarks published about them, and a spirited fusillade ensued as his printers snatched up the rifles always stacked near the cases. A few days later Byers was kidnapped by the gang and escaped with his life only because their leader was a fellow lodge member.

TERRITORIAL DAYS

The Argonauts, as the first-comers christened themselves, were ambitious for self-government, perhaps somewhat prematurely. On November 6, 1858, when there were not two hundred men within a radius of two hundred miles, a score or more met and solemnly organized the gold fields as Arapahoe County, Kansas Territory. Delegates were as solemnly elected to sit in the Territorial legislature and in the Congress at Washington. These Arapahoe County officials were recognized by Kansas, but the gold fields were so remote that pioneers were forced to organize their own local governing units, especially in the mining camps where personal clashes and violent disputes over claims were frequent. Thus the Peoples' and the Miners' Courts were born; the former usually adjudicated criminal cases, while the latter fixed the limits of mining districts and formulated mining codes. The first Miners' Court was formed at Gregory Gulch on May 9, 1859, and it soon evolved a highly workable code that was adopted by other mining districts. Plains towns such as Denver were governed by Peoples' Courts, which were notably orderly and fair. These improvisations were effective in handling local problems, but the need of uniform laws for the entire region made itself increasingly felt.

After a mass meeting in Auraria, April 11, 1859, a State constitution was drafted. It was rejected by popular vote in September, however, for a majority believed that Colorado was not yet ready for statehood and rightly suspected the motive of those promoting the agitation. Advocates of statehood then moved in a more popular direction. A delegate was elected to memorialize the Congress to establish a new territory in the mountain region, and a committee was appointed to draft the "Organic Act of the Jefferson Territory," under which the region was to be governed "until such time as the Congress of the United States shall provide a government for us." Without sanction of the Congress, an election was held late in October, and Robert W. Steele was chosen as governor of the provisional Territory, inaugurating a confused period when authority in the gold camps and the plains towns was shared by provisional officials, Arapahoe County officers, and the Peoples' and the Miners' Courts. The efforts of the delegate sent to Washington were not immediately successful, for the attention of the Congress was fully concentrated on the rising storm soon to break in the Civil War, but a bill to establish a territory within the boundaries of the present State was passed at length on February 28, 1861. The first official delegate, Hiram P. Bennett of Denver, took his seat nine months later.

William Gilpin, who had played a prominent role in the conquest of New Mexico during the Mexican War, was appointed first Governor of Colorado Territory, so named at his suggestion because it was the source of the Colorado River. On his arrival in May 1861, Gilpin ordered the taking of a census, which revealed a population of 25,371 in the Territory—20,798 white males, 4,484 white females, and 89 Negroes. Although this was not the true total, as many men were off prospecting in the mountains, it nevertheless indicated a sharp decline within a year, for the 1860 Federal Census had recorded a total of 34,277 persons—32,654 white males, but merely 1,577 white females, together with 46 free Negroes. The differences between the two census totals are significant. Thousands of men had abandoned the gold fields, it appears, but those who remained evidently planned to settle permanently and had sent home for their wives and families, which undoubtedly accounts for the 300 per cent rise in "white females."

In July 1861 a supreme court was organized, and a delegate to the Congress was chosen. Elected in August, the first assembly convened in Denver the following month; one of its first acts was to create seventeen counties: Arapahoe, Boulder, Clear Creek, Costilla, Douglas, El Paso, Fremont, Gilpin, Guadalupe (renamed Conejos), Huerfano, Jefferson, Lake, Larimer, Park, Pueblo, Summit, and Weld. Bitter strife among several towns in their rivalry to become the Territorial capital harassed the legislators. The first legislature, sitting in Denver, selected Colorado City as the capital, but the second legislature was in session there only a few days in 1862 when it adjourned to Denver. That same year Golden was chosen as the capital when it offered the use of a frame building, with free firewood to heat it. The assembly met both in Golden and Denver up to 1867 when Denver was named the permanent seat of the Territory.

At the outbreak of the Civil War, Colorado was quick to pledge loyalty to the Union, but when the call for troops came, almost as many left to enlist under the Confederate as the Union flag. Governor Gilpin, an ardent Unionist, quickly raised eleven companies on his own initiative, and in his zeal to equip them, issued $375,000 in drafts against the Federal Government without authorization. These drafts, at first repudiated by Washington, caused a financial panic in the region, which led to Gilpin's removal from office in 1862. But the troops thus organized performed valiant service in the West during the war, constituting part of the force that defeated a Confederate army under General Henry H. Sibley at La Glorieta Pass, New Mexico, averting the loss of the gold fields to the South.

Nearer home and of much greater moment to the settlers were the Indian wars that wrote a bloody chapter in Colorado's history. The outbreak of the Civil War necessitated the recall of many troops from the plains, and in 1862 signs of restlessness among the plains Indians multiplied. Early the next year they began to raid outlying ranches and small wagon trains. Conditions grew worse in 1864 when the overland trails were periodically closed. Governor John Evans, Gilpin's successor, summoned a council of the tribes to effect a settlement, but little came of the negotiations.

On November 29, 1864, Colonel John M. Chivington of the Third Colorado, eager to strike a paralyzing blow at the Arapahoe and Cheyenne, led a large force to Sand Creek (*see Tour 8a*), where some seven hundred Indians were encamped under the protection of military authorities. Hundreds of Indian women and children were killed during the action, which aroused much protest throughout the country, and far from terrorizing the Indians, aroused them to fury. In 1865 the united plains tribes spread terror along the mountains. Overland communications were interrupted for weeks at a time; the Territory often suffered from want of supplies; ranches, farms, emigrant trains, and stagecoaches were captured, plundered, and burned. With the termination of the Civil War, troops were released for duty on the frontier, and by 1867 the Federal Government had succeeded in removing the Cheyenne and Arapaho to reservations in Oklahoma. The Cheyenne and their allies went on the war path once more in 1868 but were decisively defeated on the Arickaree River at the Battle of Beecher Island (*see Tour 3*). In 1869 the plains tribes in Colorado were finally subdued.

There were times during the 1860's when destructive forces seemed to be in league against the settlers. Within a year fire and flood threatened to obliterate Denver; the plant of the *Rocky Mountain News,* which had been erected on piles in the center of Cherry Creek so that it might be equally welcome in the bitterly jealous camps of Auraria and Denver City on opposite banks of the stream, was completely wrecked by a devastating flood that also swept away the city hall, drowning many prisoners in the jail. Clouds of grasshoppers descended upon farmers' fields and stripped them bare within a few hours. Placer mining declined alarmingly as the richer diggings were washed out; hard-rock mining was still awaiting a successful solution of the baffling problem of treating refractory gold and silver ores. Many mining companies had been dishonestly capitalized, and after the first excitement capital was difficult to obtain.

"I meet no manager of a mine here," wrote a visitor in 1865, "whether an old miner or an agent from the home capitalists, who does not condemn as foolish in itself, a fraud upon the public, and a damage to the whole mining interest, this practice of making the nominal capitals from two to ten times the actual, in the generally vain hope of gulling the flats in Wall Street or in New England country towns." Coloradoans were at times hard pressed to make a living; the 1870 census revealed a population of 39,864, an increase of merely 5,000 since 1860 and certainly a decrease from the population of the Territory during some of the intervening years.

But the tide of fortune now began to turn. A network of communications had been developed since the stringing of the first telepgraph line into Denver in 1863; roads and bridges were built to link plains towns and mining camps. Although hopes of a transcontinental railroad were dashed when the Union Pacific was routed through the lower mountain passes in Wyoming to the north, resolute Coloradoans overcame their comparative isolation in 1870 by constructing the Denver Pacific Railroad to connect with it at Cheyenne. By 1872, General William J. Palmer had built his Denver & Rio Grande Railroad south to Pueblo and was soon laying track westward toward Canon City. These railroads and others worked a marvelous transformation in the young Territory.

Great cattle ranches spread out over the plains, many owned by English and Scottish investors. Enormous herds of Longhorns were driven north from Texas to be shipped from Colorado railroads, having grown fat from rich pastures of buffalo grass along the way. These colorful days of kingdom-like ranches and great annual round-ups were short, but the cowman has left his imprint upon Colorado. From the ranches came such terms as lariat, latigo, rodeo, corral, chaps, bronco, and mustang, largely of Spanish derivation, and such expressions as "gone West" or "Crossed the Great Divide." Only the cowman could have christened towns with such names as Loco, Wildhorse, Cowdrey, Mustang, and Horsefly; it was he who named Cow Creek, Horsetail Creek, and Cripple Creek. He, too, was responsible for much horse lore, cow lore, and snake lore, some of which still persists. A "lineback" buckskin, it is said, is the toughest of all horses, and no rattlesnake— at least, none acquainted with the lore—ever crossed a hair lariat. The cowboy's mournful ballads are still sung, and his persisting influence is reflected throughout the State in scores of dude ranches, which perpetuate, in a nice way, the free and rollicking life of the range.

Farming began to flourish at the same time. Thousands followed the railroads and laid out fields along the tracks. Cooperative agricultural enterprises were established, notably the Union Colony founded at Greeley in 1870 under the leadership of Nathan Meeker, agricultural editor of Horace Greeley's New York *Tribune.* The community constructed the first large irrigation project in Colorado and soon had its own *Tribune;* using the newly perfected electrotyping process, its name was printed in the handwriting of Greeley, whose script Abraham Lincoln had repeatedly complained he simply could not read. Colorado Spring's first newspaper, *Out West,* now the *Gazette,* began publication in 1872; the Longmont *Sentinel* and the Trinidad *Enterprise* had been established a year earlier. Pueblo read the *Colorado Chieftain,* founded in 1868, being the only newspaper between Denver and Santa Fe at the time.

Nathaniel P. Hill, metallurgist of Brown University, erected Colorado's first successful smelter at Blackhawk in 1868 and laid the foundation of a large personal fortune. Processes for treating refractory gold and silver ores were further perfected during the 1870's, which stimulated a revival of mining. Rich gold and silver strikes were made in the remote San Juan country in southwestern Colorado, a wild section assigned to the Ute by treaty in 1868. The Indians were now dispossessed, and in 1873 the region was thrown open to settlement. Within a few months the towns of Del Norte, Silverton, Ouray, and Telluride were booming on sites recently occupied by Ute tepees.

In 1874, Colorado College was founded at Colorado Springs by local Congregationalists, ten years after the Methodists of the State had established Colorado Seminary, now the University of Denver. A start had been made toward an adequate system of free public education, but school superintendents had a disconcerting way of leasing or selling school lands and pocketing the proceeds. As population rapidly increased, stimulated by the advent of the railroads, the legislature created the office of Superintendent of Public School Instruction, with a salary of $1,000 annually. The Territory soon had 60 school districts, 120 schools, and 80 schoolhouses, the largest of which was in Central City. Denver had three schools, but the first public school building was not completed until 1873, when 1,590 pupils were enrolled, four being "children of artists." Boulder graduated the first high school class in the State in 1876, and the East Denver High School graduated a class of seven the next year.

Colorado was rapidly coming of age and becoming more and more insistent on being admitted to statehood.

STATEHOOD: THE FIRST YEARS

In 1863, two years after Colorado had become a Territory, its delegate in the Congress somewhat rashly introduced a bill to authorize its entrance into the Union as a State. The measure died in committee, but in March 1864 the Congress passed an enabling act for the purpose. A constitution was drafted and accepted by a small majority of voters, and in May 1866 the Congress passed a measure admitting Colorado to statehood. President Andrew Johnson vetoed this measure and a similar one passed the following year. But by the middle 1870's Colorado's claims could not longer be ignored. A convention met in Denver on December 20, 1875, to draft another constitution. This was ratified by the people, and at last Colorado was admitted to the Union as the thirty-eighth State on August 1, 1876, the centenary of the country's independence—hence its title, the Centennial State. Territorial Governor John L. Routt was continued in office as the first chief executive of the State.

The constitution, under which the State is still governed, is notable for the detailed manner in which it vests all political power in the people and enumerates the particular rights of the individual. In this it reflected the spirit of the Miners' and the Peoples' Courts of the early

1860's. But the regard of the framers of the constitution for such rights was responsible for the chief defect of the document, which contained, along with purely constitutional provisions, a great mass of statutory matter. This, in the opinion of many authorities, has served to thwart progressive legislation. Social and economic readjustments have necessitated many changes in the constitution, and the clumsy and unwieldy process of amendment has been resorted to no less than fourty-four times.

Many of the statutory inclusions were born of the needs and conditions of the times. Provisions abrogating the law of riparian rights along streams by stipulating that water shall be prorated among users on the basis of priority of rights, as established by their diversion, and beneficial use of such water, may properly have no place in the constitution, but no one familiar with the history of irrigation in the West has seriously questioned the soundness of the legislation itself.

The governmental structure has the usual executive, legislative, and judicial branches. The executive consists of the governor, secretary of state, treasurer, auditor, attorney general, and superintendent of public instruction, each elected for a two-year term. Although nominally the chief executive, the governor has little real authority over other elected officials. The bicameral legislature holds regular sessions at the beginning of each odd-numbered year. Both statutory laws and constitutional amendments may be initiated by the people. Heading the judicial branch of government is the supreme court of seven members. Under it are fourteen judicial districts, with twenty-six district courts, sixty-three county courts, and numerous justices of the peace. Virtually all State employees in Colorado are protected by civil service.

With the statehood came a period of great prosperity and phenomenal growth. Businesses of all kinds flourished. Agriculture had become so profitable that farmers began cultivating the semiarid plains, experimenting with new methods of dry-land farming. Between 1870 and 1880 population increased almost five fold to a total of 194,327, stimulated in large part by fabulous silver strikes at Leadville, Aspen, and other camps. Railroad construction boomed; in mountain canyons and in the courts, the Denver & Rio Grande and the Santa Fe railroads waged war for disputed rights-of-way, with Leadville's bounty as the prize. The Denver & South Park Railroad between Denver and Leadville was one of the most profitable carriers in the world in the days of the silver boom. The fuel needs of railroads, smelters, and steel plants led to intensive development of large coal fields, which in turn created new industries and new mining camps. Much of the wealth of the mountains flowed down into the larger cities on the plains. Denver, Pueblo, and newly founded Colorado Springs grew amazingly. So rapid was the spread of population at this time that twenty-four new counties were created, eight of them in the plains farming area, to which homesteaders came in ever increasing numbers. The valleys on the Western Slope were filling up; the Grand Junction *Democrat,* founded in 1883, was absorbed by the *Star,* which in turn was succeeded by the *Daily Sentinel,* the most influential newspaper in the mesa country.

Higher education at last received adequate public support. Although authorized by the first Territorial legislature in 1861, the University of Colorado did not open its doors until 1877. Meantime, in 1874, the legislature had appropriated $45,000 for.the School of Mines at Golden. That same year the Territorial Assembly had established the Colorado School for the Deaf and Blind at Colorado Springs. In 1879 Fort Collins citizens instituted a movement to establish an agricultural school, a "radical" proposal agreed to by the legislature only after long debate; it became the College of Agriculture and Mechanic Arts, and is now Colorado State University. The State Normal School, established in Greeley in 1890, became the Colorado State College of Education in 1935 and Colorado State College in 1957.

The last decade of the nineteenth century began auspiciously. The 1890 census revealed a population of 413,249, an increase of more than 100 per cent since 1880. A rich silver strike at Creede in 1890 rivaled those made earlier at Leadville and Aspen. With the Federal Government buying 4,500,000 ounces of silver bullion a month under the Sherman Act, the price of silver rose to more than $1.00 an ounce, and Colorado mines were producing 58 per cent of the country's supply. Construction of a monumental granite State Capitol at Denver was begun; the cornerstone was laid in July 1890, and the building completed in 1896.

But neither the Sherman Act nor the Creede bonanza could stay the forces hurrying the State and the Nation into panic and depression. Notwithstanding augmented silver purchases by the Federal Government, the white metal was being produced far in excess of demand. When the silver market tumbled, one of Colorado's great economic props collapsed. Remonetization of silver became a national as well as a local issue. The two major political parties of the country were torn internally by it, and the Populist Party, which demanded a return to bimetalism, was born of a fusion of partisans of both camps. Feeling ran especially high in Colorado, and in the election of 1892 the entire Populist ticket was swept into office, with Davis H. Waite as governor. Matters were at a crisis with many banks closed; real estate was almost valueless; scores of business houses were bankrupt; a three-year drought had taken its toll, and in the dry farming areas whole counties were almost deserted as discouraged men abandoned mortgaged farms, leaving unpaid-for tools and machinery to rust in the fields.

Silver prices were already low when news came that the mints in India, the most important remaining market for silver, had ceased coinage. Even more shattering, the Sherman Act was repealed at a special session of the Congress in November 1893. Colorado staggered under the repeated blows. Leadville, Aspen, Creede, and all of the silver camps lay paralyzed. Mines ceased operations; the fires in the smelters went out; jobless mine workers and their families crowded into Denver, creating unemployment problems so critical that an extra session of the legislature was called to enact emergency relief measures. Recurrent labor disputes perplexed the State, and politics remained in a confused state, with all parties divided on the silver question. The one bright gleam through the dark decade was the discovery in 1890 of the Cripple Creek gold field, destined to be the State's greatest, which by the end of the century was yielding more than $20,000,000 in precious metals annually.

In 1893, in the midst of its perplexities, Colorado extended suffrage to women, being the second State to do so. Education and the press expanded. Born of several mergers, the Boulder *Camera* was first published in 1890 by Colonel L. C. Paddock. In this decade, too, was founded the Denver *Post,* which soon had a wide circulation and influence in the Rocky Mountain region. *'Tis a Privilege to Live in Colorado* reads a banner head on its front page, quoted as often and more seriously than the inscription that runs in large letters across the facade of its plant, *O Justice, When Expelled From Other Habitations, Make This Thy Dwelling Place.* Established in 1892, the *Post* was bought three years later by Frederick G. Bonfils and Harry H. Tammen, whose prowess in many fields brought "Bon" and "Tam" a national reputation; both have been sharply characterized in *Timberline* by Gene Fowler, novelist and scenarist, once a luminary on their always capable staff. Tammen, as Fowler saw him, was "a dreamer, bubbling with acrobatic phrases, a puck with both hands full of firecrackers," while Bonfils was "austere, . . . believing that money meant Power, . . . a brooding Sphinx." Meantime, the *Rocky Mountain News* had passed from Byers to U. S. Senator Thomas M. Patterson, an ardent campaigner against the "money trusts," who clashed bitterly with his rivals on the *Post.* Their mutual accusations and recriminations were scorching, for the era of personal journalism was not yet over. Cited for characterizing the Supreme Court as "the Great Judicial Slaughter House and Mausoleum," Patterson defended himself by saying that he had simply spoken the truth; the court fined him $1,000 for contempt, which, retorted Patterson, expressed his sentiments exactly.

TWENTIETH CENTURY

As the nineteenth century waned, Colorado discovered that its greatest source of wealth lay not in its mines but its farms. The drought years of the early 1890's came to be only a painful memory as more homesteads were taken up each spring by farmers from the Midwest and the north-central States—hardy men of every descent—English, Irish, Scandinavians, Germans, Hungarians, and Italians, among others. Sugar beet culture spread rapidly in the valleys of the Colorado, South Platte, and Arkansas Rivers, attracting many German-Russians from the Volga, where they had long practiced such culture. As these acquired larger and larger farms, Spanish-Americans came from the Southwest in augmented numbers to cultivate their spreading acres. Thousands of workers of all European stocks found employment in the beet sugar refineries. The demand of beet growers for water led in turn to the development of even larger irrigation projects, and legislation during the early years of the century was largely concerned with laws governing water rights and appropriations for reservoirs and water diversion tunnels. Two large reclamation projects, the Uncompahgre in 1904 and the Grand Valley in 1912, were authorized, to provide farmers on the Western Slope with water.

While the agricultural sections made tremendous gains, the mining districts remained strangely quiet. In 1899 Teller County, with its Cripple Creek gold fields, had a population in excess of 30,000, but within a few years it had a mere 14,000. Between 1900 and 1910, with prices ranging from 52¢ to 68¢ an ounce, silver mining languished. The days of wild booms and of fortunes made overnight and often spent as quickly were quite definitely ended, and large numbers of people turned to other pursuits. As a result, many small commercial enterprises and mechanical industries sprang up to serve the needs of an increasingly complex social and economic order.

In 1902 a "home rule" amendment to the State constitution freed communities of 2,000 population or more from certain hampering restrictions, permitting them for the first time to choose and hold accountable all of their administrative officers. A normal school, now Western State College, was founded at Gunnison in 1909. Civic associations were organized to promote many kinds of reforms and elevate the "moral tone" of Colorado. The Citizens' Protective League of Denver, founded to "squelch the knocking and blackmailing newspapers in our beautiful but benighted city," demanded that no news story, editorial, or advertisement unfit for fifteen-year-olds to read should be published, and that "the petty quarrels and constant warfare between newspapers be permanently discontinued," evidence that the sands were running out on personal journalism.

Labor troubles continued to smolder. In 1903 and 1904 ill feeling between mine owners and miners' unions flared up violently in the Cripple Creek district. Labor disputes in the coal fields came to a head in 1914, when striking miners at Ludlow engaged in a sanguinary battle with a detachment of militia sent to patrol the strike area. From these troubles came the passage in 1915 of workmen's compensation measures and an act establishing the State Industrial Commission to compose differences between employers and employees.

The State had settled down to orderly progress by 1910, at which time the census revealed 799,024 residents, a gain of 259,324 since 1900. Development was greatly influenced by increased use of the automobile; better highways were built, making much of the mountain country easily accessible for the first time, and Colorado began to prosper from a new "industry" of almost undreamed-of potentialities, tourist travel. Colorado became a summer playground for the South and Middle West. The Federal Government recognized the need of preserving the natural beauty and historic interest of certain regions by creating two national parks, the Mesa Verde in 1906, the Rocky Mountain in 1915, and later set aside four national monuments. Steps had previously been taken to protect forests and watersheds. The White River National Forest, established in 1891, was the first of eleven such forest reserves in the State, which now embrace 13,712,352 acres.

An analysis of the Census of 1960 showed that Colorado had 1,753,-947 people, had increased 32.4 percent since 1950, averaged 16.9 persons per square mile, and ranked 33d in population among the States. Taking the round numbers, 1,700,000, as a base, the Census Bureau reported that Colorado had 843,575 white males and 857,125 white females, and 26,892 nonwhite males, and 26,353 nonwhite females. There were 39,792 Negroes, 4,288 Indians. As in California the Indians had increased; in 1950 Colorado had only 1,587.

The report on the foreign-born residents of the United States made by the Census of 1960 showed that Colorado had 59,874 foreign-born. Of this number 5,269 came from England, 8,522 from Germany, 1,047 from Hungary, 894 from Ireland, 4,797 from Italy, 2,032 from Poland, 2,468 from Sweden, 7,583 from Russia, 1,628 from Yugoslavia, and 4,882 from Mexico. However, there are many second and third generation citizens who perpetuate some of the traits of their ancestors, and of these the Americans of Spanish-Mexican origin are the largest. Many Spanish speaking farmers live near the southern border, especially in the San Luis Valley.

A survey of how Coloradoans carry on their daily tasks shows that most of them are neither farmers nor miners. The State that stirred the pulsebeats of the continent with its tales of fortunes dug out of the rock and cowboys riding the range has more white-collar boys behind desks and girls behind store counters than hardy adventurers prospecting the hills. About 800,000 Coloradoans make their living no differently from the people of Boston, St. Louis, and Seattle. Of this number only about 40,000 are engaged in agriculture, and only 12,500 in mining, which includes coal and petroleum, and some of the latter are behind desks.

The Colorado Department of Labor and Employment, which adds up its figures in the shadow of the Capitol, explains that the biggest group of employed persons is on the public payroll. In March, 1969, for instance, the largest segment was under Government—172,600, of which number the Federal Government paid 44,500. The State paid 39,600, but this included 23,300 engaged in teaching, while cities, towns and other communities employed 88,500, of whom 56,700 were teaching. In a typical year the five-county area that the Bureau of the Census recognizes as the Metropolitan Area of Denver (SMSA) has 500,000 employed, about 440,000 in what the Division of Employment calls the non-agricultural wage and salary classification. Most of these people are not in manufacturing but selling goods.

Colorado has a Labor Peace Act that is similar in many provisions to the National Labor Relations Act, but more restrictive in the conditions concerning the union shop. It stipulates that 75 percent of the employees in the bargaining unit who vote must vote for a union shop before an agreement can be entered into requiring union membership as a condition of continued employment.

Unemployment rarely rises to 3 percent of the work force. About 20,000 to 22,000 are unemployed, varying with seasonal conditions. Colorado has an Employment Security Program, which includes job placement, testing and counseling services, and unemployment insurance, to which employers contribute. The benefits of unemployment insurance are not high enough nor continued long enough to destroy the incentive to work. If the employer is responsible for the unemployment, a full award is granted to the worker; if employer and worker both contribute to the unemployment a 50 percent award is made. No award is made if the employee is solely responsible. The maximum duration of insurance is twenty-six weeks, and the maximum weekly benefit $54, subject to review every six months based on prevailing wage rates. A worker is not eligible if he engages in a strike or labor dispute, or is on a disciplinary suspension, or takes a voluntary leave of absence. Not all workers are insured under the act; excluded are State and Federal employees, newsboys, domestic servants, real estate, insurance and security salesmen and barbers paid by commission, and a number of others.

Property in Colorado is assessed at 30 percent of its actual value. Corporations are taxed 5 percent of net income from sources within the State. Individual taxes range from 3 percent on the first $1,000 of net taxable income to 8 percent on net over $10,000. Resident individuals with income from intangibles pay a 2 percent surtax on the gross amount after a $5,000 exemption. A $750 exemption per dependent is allowed, plus the full amount of Federal taxes.

RELIGION AND EDUCATION

Both the Protestant and the Roman Catholic denominations of the Christian faith were represented in the explorers and discoverers who first crossed what is now Colorado. The Spanish-speaking farmers who took up land claims on the southern boundaries were adherents of the Roman Catholic Church, as their descendants are today. The settlers who crossed the plains from Nebraska and Kansas were mostly Baptists, Methodists, Lutherans, and members of other evangelical bodies. Priests arrived early to work among the Indians, and itinerant preachers tried to introduce a spiritual note in mining camps that were tough and inhospitable. There are, however, numerous tales of revival meetings and efforts to rout gin and the devil. Here and there a ghost town has a house with an attempt at a steeple, where the miners once joined in the traditional hymns.

Colorado today has about 100 recognized Protestant groups and a number of others without affiliations, and from 65 to 70 percent of the people are Protestants. In 1968 there were 381,433 Roman Catholics, and about 35,000 Jews. The Methodists established the University of Denver in 1863 and the Baptists founded Colorado Woman's College, now Temple Buell College, in 1888. Regis College for men, and Loretto Heights College for women, both in Denver, are Roman Catholic institutions. There are 10 two-year colleges and 17 four-year colleges and universities in Colorado, with an attendance in 1968 of 99,920. The last two decades have seen a great deal of new construction on college campuses, also an expansion of curricula. Many communities are making efforts to add a junior college to their local systems of public education, with especial facilities for vocational and preparatory science courses (*see Manufacturing*).

The Economic Base

W HEN the Atomic Energy Commission announced that a new power reactor, to be called the Fort St. Vrain Nuclear Generating Station, had been authorized, Colorado industry had another opportunity to apply new forms of energy. The AEC, the Gulf General Atomic, Inc., and the Public Service Co. of Colorado had cooperated to make possible the construction of a high temperature, gas-cooled reactor facility providing 330,000 electrical kilowatts. This was to be the largest plant of its type, and its net thermal efficiency of about 40 percent would be the highest of any nuclear power plant operating in the United States. The AEC would contribute $47,800,000 to the total estimated cost of $73,500,000.

This was far from the first act of the AEC to bring Colorado industry into the Atomic Age. At this time it also had contracts for laboratory research and other atomic work with the University of Colorado in Boulder, the Rocky Flats Plant of the Dow Chemical Co. of Boulder, and a Grand Junction contractor for uranium handling. Dow Chemical in 1969 was the major ordnance plant in Colorado; it reported $121,700,000 already had been used in building operations that would total $199,600,000. The concentration of scientific laboratories in Boulder gives the State a place in the front rank of research dealing with space physics, nuclear physics, nuclear spectroscopy, solar science, and aeronomy. Also study and use of radioisotopes was taking place there and in other institutions of higher education and medicine in the State.

The United States Government repeatedly has found the quality and stability of the labor force of Colorado useful for defense plants. One that contributes to the earnings of the State is the Martin missile plant in Jefferson County. Cutbacks in defense contracts, however, have a depressing effect on the economy; the Denver Business Activity Index reported that manufacturing employment in Denver declined from 70,800 in October, 1963, to 59,400 in February, 1965, when 20 to 25 percent of its labor force was employed in defense-related industries.

Manufacturing commands the largest employment in Colorado. In former years food processing was the largest segment of manufacturing, but in recent years electrical machinery has moved ahead. Since 1960 the number of electronics firms in the State has risen from 40 to over

100. Their products include electrical components and accessories, communication equipment, electronic control equipment, electrical measuring instruments and aerospace electronics. Food processing, however, will always command a major market, based on the increasing consumer population. With 38,000,000 acres of land in farms and ranches, the State supply is more than adequate. Weld County ranks ninth in the nation in value of all farm products sold.

The Denver division of the Martin Marietta Company builds the Titan group of intercontinental ballistic missiles. It has a contract to build two of the spacecraft for landing on Mars. Beech Aircraft Corp. provided cryogenic loading systems for the Gemini flights and was associated with the Apollo program. Ball Bros. Research Corp. in Boulder had a part in building the Orbiting Solar Observatory. At Colorado Springs defense and other Federal contracts were carried out by the Nuclear Division of Kaman Aircraft Corp., Burroughs, and Philco Corp. The North American Defense Command there follows the orbits of every man-made object in space. Programs related to NASA and space projects of the Dept. of Defense are carried on by the University of Colorado, Colorado State University (Fort Collins) and the University of Denver.

MINERALS AND MINERAL FUELS

Gold mining began in 1858 with small placer operations in what is now Denver. The following year George A. Jackson discovered a valuable deposit on Chicago Creek in the mountains thirty miles to the west, and four months later, on May 6, 1859, John H. Gregory of Georgia made his celebrated strike near by on the North Fork of Clear Creek. Here boomed the camps of Blackhawk and Central City, which led the State in gold production for more than a quarter of a century, being surpassed only when Cripple Creek achieved its phenomenal production in the 1890's.

Operations during the gold rush spread rapidly into South Park, which proved so rich in "pay dirt" that it was described as "one big placer." Tarryall, Fairplay, Buckskin Joe, and Montgomery were added to the roster of roaring camps. By April 1860 venturesome prospectors had pushed their way up the Arkansas River to California Gulch, which within two years produced an estimated $1,000,000 of "dust." Meanwhile, the search for yellow treasure took men northward to the Blue River and as far South as Rosita in the Wet Mountain Valley. Several prospectors even blazed trails across the Continental Divide to the headwaters of the Yampa and into the Gunnison River country and the remote ranges of the San Juans.

By 1874, with the richest placer deposits exhausted, gold mining had reached a low ebb, annually producing less than $2,000,000. Silver became the State's leading mineral, forging far to the front after 1878 when carbonate ores rich in lead and silver were discovered along California Gulch. Thus from an abandoned gold camp sprang Leadville, the most important silver camp in the State and one of the greatest in the world; almost overnight it became a rip-roaring town of 30,000, where great fortunes were made in a day and spent as quickly in a lurid scene of organized vice, shooting scrapes, and grand opera. But, above all, Leadville was the hub of a large industrial empire where practical men turned speculative hard-rock mining into a profitable business. The silver boom brought profound changes in the mining industry. Up to 1878 the production of all metal mines in the State had never exceeded $8,000,000 annually. Rising steadily, silver reached a peak production of $23,000,000 in 1892, when the silver mines yielded an additional $5,000,000 of lead and almost $1,000,000 of copper. Not until 1892, when operations at Cripple Creek were well under way, did the annual production of gold total $5,000,000.

The day of the individual small mine operator soon passed. During the initial boom, ore had to be "picture rock" to attract prospectors and investors; it had to be amenable to treatment by simple processes; if gold and silver could not be seen with the naked eye, there was little enthusiasm for the "diggings" from which it came. With the depletion of "grass root" deposits, mining operations necessitated vast capital investments. Mining companies were organized to finance the construction of deep shafts and miles of tunnels, drifts, cross-cuts, and elaborate underground railroads. Pumping, drainage, and ventilating systems were installed; large mills and smelters were constructed to process ores.

The improvement of milling and smelting was a long and costly process. The first smelter was constructed in 1868 at Blackhawk, but for some time ore was still shipped to larger smelting centers where coal was cheap. By the 1890's smelting in Colorado had greatly expanded and was centralized in Leadville, Colorado City, Denver, Pueblo, and Durango. The cruder phases of ore reduction were performed at the mines because of high transportation costs in remote mountain areas; millions of dollars were spent on various types of mills for this purpose, but technological development was so rapid that many mills became obsolete within a few months. Yet the wealth of the mines was such that money for new ventures constantly poured into the State.

Prospectors pushed across the Continental Divide and in the last quarter of the nineteenth century made rich silver strikes at Ouray, Silverton, Telluride, Rico, and Creede. The pioneers who developed these new regions were forced to surmount great obstacles. Transportation was so difficult that only the highest grades of ore could be worked; for many years the more remote districts were accessible only by plodding burro. Creede, founded in 1890 when N. C. Creede staked the Holy Moses Mine in the rich district soon known as "King Solomon's Mines," was for a brief period one of the most prosperous camps in the State.

The demonetization of silver and the panic of 1893 dealt a hard blow to the white metal camps. As silver had long been the main source of wealth in these areas, ore samples were tested only for their silver and lead content. In 1895, Thomas F. Walsh, owner of a pyrite smelter at Silverton, sampled the dumps of the Camp Bird Mine, which had been worked for low-grade lead and zinc sulphides carrying some silver, and discovered that they contained tellurium compounds rich in gold. The Camp Bird soon became the second richest gold property in the State, yielding $25,000,000 during the next twenty years. The gold fever spread to other white metal areas. In 1898 Leadville again became a gold camp, and for nine years poured forth immense treasure from deep-lying quartz veins overlooked for almost a half century.

Meanwhile, Bob Womack, a cowboy, had discovered rich gold-bearing quartz on a great cattle ranch at Cripple Creek. This celebrated mining district lay on a sedimentary plateau about six miles square in the crater of an extinct volcano, piled with immense masses of lava and granite containing dry quartz impregnated with pure gold. Cripple Creek, in its day one of the richest gold camps in the world, was known far and wide for the Portland, the Creeson, the Independence the Mary McKinney, and other celebrated mines. Between 1892 and 1900 annual production of gold in Colorado mounted from $5,000,-000 to $28,000,000; in the latter years almost two-thirds came from the Cripple Creek district. This flood of gold assisted the State in weathering the storms of economic depression that followed 1893.

Gold production in Colorado reached 31,915 troy ounces, valued at $1,117,000 in 1966, according to the report of the U. S. Bureau of Mines. Both lode and placer mining still continues; there were 43 lode mines and 14 placer mines. Placer mining yielded only 1,374 troy ounces, less than 4 percent of the total. Less than 25 troy ounces was recovered from cleaning up at mills, an assay office, and railroad cars that had carried lead and zinc concentrates. Eight of the placer operations were recovering gold from sand and gravel. The Idarado mine of Idarado Mining Co. in Ouray and San Miguel Counties produced about three-fourths of the State output, and with two others produced more than 1,000 troy ounces each. Silver from lode and placer mining was 2,085,000 troy ounces worth $2,657,000. The Idarado mine also produced two-thirds of the State's copper output and 44 percent of the lead. Zinc had a value of $15,900,000, exceeding that of copper and lead; the Eagle Mine of the New Jersey Zinc Co. was the largest producer, and the Idarado produced more than 1,000 tons.

After the decline of gold and silver production coal became the most profitable mineral. It has since been surpassed by molybdenum, petroleum and natural gas. Colorado uses all but one-fifth of the coal it produces, much of it supplying the generation of electricity, and some of it used in the making of coke. The State ranks first in the United States in bituminous coal reserves and third for both sub-bituminous and anthracite reserves. Nearly one-fourth of the State is underlaid by coal deposits. Much of the coal is obtained by strip mining, which in 1966 accounted for 1,600,000 tons or 31 percent of the 5,200,000 tons produced. Underground mines produced 3,600,000 tons, or 68 percent. Strip mines in Montrose and Routt Counties, and underground mines in Las Animas, Mesa, and Weld Counties, are the principal sources of coal for generating power. The largest generating plant in the Rocky Mountain region is the Cherokee Steam Electric plant of the Public Service Co. of Denver. It has been consuming 800,000 tons of coal a year and will greatly increase its needs when a new 350,000 kilowatt unit is added to its facilities, making the capacity of its plant 750,000 kilowatts.

The first coal mining operations were started in 1864 in the northern and southern parts of the State. From decade to decade coal became an increasingly important element in Colorado's economy until at length it achieved first rank among mineral products, a position it maintained for many years. In 1913 more than 12,000 men were employed in and around the coal mines, but improved methods in mining have since increased production and reduced the number of workers approximately 25 per cent. Up to 1938 output had totaled 395,718,000 tons, valued at $819,154,000. Colorado coal ranges in quality from black lignite and sub-bituminous varieties to true anthracite. Vast coal deposits underlie the eastern base of the mountains in a wide strip from New Mexico to Wyoming, and are found in Routt County and elsewhere on the Western Slope. The coal beds, it has been estimated, contain reserves sufficient to supply the entire country for centuries.

Labor troubles accompanied the development of the industry. In 1900 forty-one "wildcat" strikes occurred in the coal fields. In 1903, with the hard-rock miners on strike in almost all camps, coal miners in the State laid down their tools, demanding an eight-hour day and better working conditions. The miners in the northern fields soon won their demands, but the issue remained unsettled in the southern fields where large operators refused to negotiate with the United Mine Workers Union, established in the State in 1899.

In the summer of 1913 the union sent organizers into the southern fields and on September 23rd called a strike. The miners sought recognition of the union and a written contract providing an eight-hour day, strict enforcement of the State mining laws, a check weighman elected by themselves, and the right to board and buy goods where they pleased;

almost all miners' communities were on company property. On the day of the strike 8,000 to 10,000 miners packed their belongings on carts and wagons and, with their women and children, moved down the canyons through snow, sleet, and drenching rain to the tent colonies established by the union. Clashes between the strikers and mine guards were frequent, and scarcely a week passed without fatalities. The militia was ordered into the strike districts, and on April 20, 1914, an armed clash occurred between a militia company and strikers in a tent colony at Ludlow, near Trinidad. The tents caught fire, and two women and eleven children died. Altogther, the engagement cost twenty-one lives, including that of a militiaman. Enraged strikers took possession of the coal fields from Walsenburg to Trinidad; two counties were virtually under their control. On June 1st Federal troops marched in and fighting ceased. The Ludlow "massacre" brought the Rockefeller interests to Colorado to institute in their companies an employee representation plan designed to afford miners easy access of company officials for redress of grievances. The plan was praised and copied by others, but in 1938 was outlawed as a company union by the National Labor Relations Board.

The 1930's once more brought unsettled conditions to the coal fields. Miners received two wage cuts in 1925; two years later a strike of all coal miners in the State was called for a six-hour day, a five-day week, and a basic day wage of $7.75. In the southern fields the strike met with varied success, but in the northern fields all mines but one were closed. In an armed clash at the open mine November 21, 1927, six men were killed and about 60 people injured, including many women and children. Martial law was immediately declared. The strike continued until February 1928, by which time almost all companies had granted an increase of 50¢ a day in basic wage rates as recommended by the Colorado Industrial Commission. The mine at which the fatal clash occurred soon passed into the control of Miss Josephine Roche, later Assistant Secretary of the Treasury in President Franklin D. Roosevelt's cabinet, who recognized the United Mine Workers and signed a written contract for a basic wage of $7 a day. The company inaugurated measures to promote social welfare and facilitate collective bargaining; farm lands were developed for the use of employees and an effort was made to stabilize employment.

OIL, GAS, MOLYBDENUM

In the spectacular past Coloradoans lined their pockets with gold and silver; today's mineral wealth comes primarily from petroleum, natural gas, and molybdenum. Crude petroleum has become the most valuable mineral fuel produced in Colorado, and although inflation drives values up even when output declines, the product has held first place in recent years. In 1966 the production of 37,111,000 42-gallon bbl. was worth more than $97,000,000 to the economy and comprised 28 percent of the total valuation. There were 2,371 producing wells, and at year-end 42 were flowing, 1,649 were pumping, and 480 were shut in. A total of 48 percent of the State output came from the Rangely-Weber and Wilson Creek fields in Rio Blanco County; other leading fields were in Washington, Logan, Morgan, Montezuma, and Weld Counties. *Colorado Oil and Gas Statistics* disclosed that cumulative production to January 1, 1967, at Rangely reached 385,128,580 bbl. of oil. Drilling continued in 30 counties and 35 new wells were developed in Rio Blanco County during the year. Three crude-oil refineries processed 13,100,000 bbl. of oil in one year, but 11,900,000 came from outside the State. Two of the refineries were the Continental and the Tenneco in Denver.

Molybdenum has the second highest valuation—$88,851,000, in 1966 is typical. Colorado has the largest output in the country, all produced by Climax Molybdenum Company Division of American Metal Climax, Inc. A new plant at Climax, near Leadville, and new operations at the Urad mine have added to production, which sometimes reaches 42,300 tons daily. Climax also recovers monazite, a combination of rare earth phosphates. Colorado produces 72 percent of the vanadium in the United States. The largest source is the Rifle mine in Garfield County; it is also processed at Grand Junction and Uravan.

Production of uranium ore continues with varying quantities and prices, the U. S. Bureau of Mines reporting 633,113 short tons worth $10,530,000 in 1966, as compared with 574,795 short tons worth $10,-651,000 in 1965. Montrose County, where value of all minerals produced is usually more than $12,000,000, accounted for 47 percent of the State output. Of 69 operators three mine about 90 percent of the State total—Union Carbide Corp., Climax Uranium Co., Climax Molybdenum Co., and Vanadium Corp. of America.

A shipment of Colorado uranium, or pitchblende, from Gilpin County, and of yellow carnotite, a uranium-vanadium compound from Paradox Valley, was used by M. and Mme. Curie of Paris in their famous experiments that led to the extraction of radium. For some ten years Colorado dominated the world market for radioactive ores, but after 1923 the production of new mines in the Belgian Congo cut the price of radium.

Colorado is supposed to have natural gas reserves of 1.5 trillion cu. ft., a quantity difficult to comprehend; more comprehensible is the report that production reached 139.9 billion cu. ft. in 1967 and that the State had lost 66.2 billion cu. ft. in the year. Exploration for new fields continues, but results are not sufficient to offset the decrease in reserves. Gas comes principally from La Plata, Moffat, and Rio Blanco

Counties. In order to release gas held in the Cretaceous sands of western Colorado it is sometimes necessary to use nuclear explosives. Much of the natural gas in use is transported by the Colorado Interstate Gas Co. from the Texas Panhandle, western Oklahoma, Wyoming, and Kansas. This company has recently transformed the depleted Fort Morgan gas field into a huge underground storage basin at a cost of $3,000,000, on which it draws for serving the Denver metropolitan area. The ultimate storage capacity in this field is 17 billion cu. ft. A new 16-inch pipeline carries an extra supply of 125,000,000 cu. ft. of natural gas from Fort Morgan to Denver. Another storage basin is an abandoned coal mine near Denver, which holds 2.3 billion cu. ft.

Oil shale is one of the great unexploited resources of Colorado and studies of ways to recover and market the oil continue to be made by the Federal Government, the State, and private corporations. Six oil companies spent millions in 1964 for experimental work at the facilities in Rifle leased by the Government to the Colorado School of Mines Research Foundation. Drilling in Rio Blanco County has disclosed oil shale 3,050 ft. thick. When it was announced that the shale contained dawsonite, a mineral containing aluminum and sodium, as well as nahcolite, a sodium mineral, there was a rush of applications for sodium leases, but considerable confusion when the Government refused to let mining shale for sodium include retention of the oil. The deposits of shale occur chiefly in an area of about 1,500 sq. m. in Rio Blanco and Garfield Counties.

The importance of this huge supply to the economy of Colorado has resulted in a number of studies to determine how the oil is to be recovered and how the byproducts are to be used. Conferences on a uniform policy for oil shale development in Colorado, Utah, and Wyoming, have been resumed by State officials and the U. S. Dept. of the Interior. The slow progress in clearing title to mining claims on public lands as well as the disposition of oil shale byproducts have held up decisions. Useful to an understanding of the subject are *Status and Problems of Colorado Oil Shale Development,* authorized by the State Dept. of Natural Resources, 1963, and *Regional Economic Impact of a U. S. Oil Shale Industry,* by the Denver Research Institute, affiliated with the University of Denver, 1966.

Other important minerals of the State are cement, feldspar, mica, gypsum, barite, and lime. Quarrying has increased in importance as granite, marble, limestone, sandstone, lava, and other Colorado building stones have become better known to architects. Good granite is found in widely scattered parts of the State, notably at Gunnison, Silver Plume, Cotopaxi, and in South Platte Canyon. Marble is quarried in the vicinity of Salida, Marble, and in Wet Mountain Valley. Travertine, olivine, and dolomite have been shipped from Colorado quarries to many States. Near Livermore are the only developed beds of alabaster in North America.

RANCHING

Although farming preceded ranching in Colorado and has long since surpassed it in importance, the great cattle ranches of the seventies and eighties first gave agriculture any considerable weight in the State's economy. Stock raising began in the fall of 1858 when a prospector turned his oxen loose to shift for themselves on the grassy flats now occupied by Denver. When the animals were rounded up in the spring, he found that they had grown sleek and fat. With the discovery that cattle could be pastured on the plains, great herds of Texas Longhorns were driven northward into the lower Arkansas Valley and other sections of the plains. The penetration of transcontinental railroads soon opened up new cattle country in the mountain parks and on the Western Slope. Thousands of cattle were loaded for eastern markets at Antonito, Lamar, Julesburg, Sterling, Brush, Walden, and other Colorado shipping centers.

As there were no fences in early days, cattle sometimes strayed as far as two hundred miles from their home ranges. Cowboys were hired to guard the herds and keep them on the richest available pastures. Every spring the calves were rounded up and branded; every fall the fattened steers were rounded up for market. The round-up, a community enterprise, brought together cowboys and stockmen from dozens of ranches. Organized gangs of thieves preyed upon the cattle and sometimes stole entire herds. Cowmen waged a relentless war against these rustlers and finally succeeded in breaking up the larger gangs.

By 1879 cowboys were riding herd on 855,000 head of cattle in Colorado, chiefly on great open ranges, part of the public domain. At this period the cattle industry was concentrated in the hands of large ranchers whose herds numbered from ten to fifty thousand head. Their ranches were of corresponding dimensions; the "JJ" ranch of the Prairie Cattle Company in the lower Arkansas Valley extended fifty miles east from La Junta and seventy miles south into New Mexico and Oklahoma, embracing 2,240,000 acres. English and Scottish interests controlled many of the larger properties.

Until the Leadville boom of 1879–80 cowboys were the only large body of wage earners in the State. Isolated in small groups during the greater part of the year and sharing with their employers the hazards of frontier life, they usually regarded the ranch as in part their own, as it often was, for many cowboys owned small herds of cattle and horses that grazed on the open range along with the stock of their employer.

The reign of the powerful cattle barons was comparatively brief, for the ranges were soon overstocked. In the hard winter of 1886–7 fully half of their stock perished and the succeeding drought took a heavy toll. Meanwhile, homesteaders had been taking up more and more claims, drastically reducing the extent of the open range, and by the close of the century cattle raising had become a scattered and usually small-scale enterprise. Shorthorns, Herefords, and other breeds of better beef stock replaced the hardy but scrawny Texas Longhorns. Today, a few large ranchers still own immense tracts of land but more of them lease pasture from farmers and the Federal Government.

Livestock adds materially to the prosperity of Colorado and the food resources of the nation. While miners' gold provides the glow of wealth on the dome of the Capitol, farm and ranch products build substantial fortunes year after year in the country's highest State. The value of livestock and poultry on Colorado farms is subject to the fluctuations that affect all markets, but generally it points upward, and may be expected to increase both in volume and income. Production of meat animals is around 1.5 billion pounds annually; cash receipts have been more than $600,000,000 in recent years, reflecting higher prices paid for cattle and hogs, and a larger production of hogs. The Department of Agriculture reported that the value of livestock and poultry on January 1, 1968, showed an increase of 8 percent over that of a year earlier.

Colorado regularly has more sheep on feed than any other state. It had seventh place in the number of sheep and lambs, and seventh in cattle and calves on feed lots on January 1, 1969; seventh in the number of beef cows 2 years old and older. It is twelfth in the total of cattle and calves, eighteenth in turkeys, twentysixth in hogs, and thirtysixth in the number of chickens. There were 3,119,000 head of cattle and calves on January 1, 1969, compared with 3,060,000 a year earlier. Total inventory value of cattle and calves on farms was $474,000,000, a rise of 8 percent. The value per head of cattle was $152, as against $143 in 1968. Both the number of milk cows and milk production were up.

The number of sheep and lambs has suffered a slight decline but the value of stock sheep is up 8 percent. There also are fewer lambs. Open weather late in the year gave opportunity for sheep and lambs to clean up corn fields, sorghum stubble, and beet tops, but wheat pasture was limited because of dry soil.

Colorado is a big wool market. A total of 1,182,000 head of sheep and lambs was shorn in 1968, but wool production, 10,455,000 pounds, was down about 9 percent. Incentive payments are made to wool, lamb and mohair producers under the National Wool Act to keep the national average price of wool to a basic figure. Hogs and pigs have held their own, with an increase of about 11 percent recently, and average value of a hog to $28.20, up from $26.40 in a year. The inventory of chickens has also increased. At the beginning of 1969 there were 76,000 turkeys in Colorado, up from 65,000 the year before, and the value rose in kind.

Horses also are a product of Colorado ranches. In 1964 the State counted 48,556 horses, of which 36,897 were saddle horses and cow ponies. Mules and burros numbered 1,116.

The *Colorado Year Book, 1962–1964,* published by the State Planning Commission, reported that the livestock industry was changing rapidly. Production was being increasingly specialized to serve new food retailing outlets. The Union Stock Yard Co. had added auction selling of cattle and sheep to private treaty trading. Commodity marketing principles were being adapted to livestock trading. Modernization of packing plants, to make use of the advantages of automated processing equipment, was recommended. But "it is expected that livestock will continue to produce more dollars for the economy of Colorado than any other industry."

FARMING AND IRRIGATION

Agriculture continues to be a source of major income in the Colorado economy, profiting by irrigation but subjected to the vagaries of the weather. The lack of rain, suffered in the Eastern Plains in 1967, was an obstacle hard to overcome, but cutworms and brown wheat mites could be fought by spraying in the northeast where moisture was more available. Early frosts are injurious to fall potatoes and dry beans in southeastern Colorado. Yet the 1969 issue of *Colorado Annual Statistics,* compiled by the Colorado Crop and Livestock Reporting Service, was able to show that a preliminary estimate of the value of crops in 1968, $299,000,000, was practically the same as in 1967, while corn, for grain and silage, set a new high record for the sixth year; corn for grain had the fourth largest crop of record and dry bean output was the largest since 1963. These were offset by the lowest alfalfa seed production since 1928, and by losses in sorghum grain and potato crops.

Farms have been decreasing in numbers in Colorado, as in the United States generally but have been growing in size. Despite the movement of farmhands to urban occupations the owner has been able to cover more ground by mechanization. In 1960 the United States had 3,962,000 farms and the average size was 297 acres; in 1968 the number had dropped to 3,054,000 but the size had expanded to 369 acres. Since farms vary considerably in size it is easier to say that farm land dropped by slightly over 53,000,000 acres. Colorado in 1960 had 37,000 farms of 40,300,000 acres; and the average farm had 1,080 acres; in 1968 it had 31,000 farms of 39,500,000 acres, and the average size had risen to 1,295 acres.

The Colorado Department of Agriculture reported that realized net farm income to farm and ranch operators in 1967 was $137,900,000,

15 percent less than in 1966. Farm production expenses were up 12 percent, higher than in any previous year. Cash receipts totaled $885,-283,000, up 8 percent. Lower receipts from crops were offset by higher cash receipts from livestock and livestock products. In addition the U. S. Government paid the farmers $57,606,000, but this was below the $62,-470,000 paid the year before. Preliminary reports for 1968 indicated that all receipts would be higher by 7 and 8 percent. Prices in 1968 were higher for cattle, calves, turkeys, milk, wool, broomcorn, cabbage, lettuce, and tomatoes.

While gross farm income increases, production expenses keep pace with it, and the realized net farm income gets no advantages. A comparison of expenses from 1963 to 1967 shows that the cost of feed in millions of dollars rose from $123.8 to $155.4; that livestock costs rose from $168. to $257.9; that hired labor rose from $492. to $665. Taxes are up, $31.9 to $37.9, and interest on farm mortgages went from $17. to $29.5.

In 1968 Colorado farmers harvested 5,281,000 acres of crops, slightly more than the year preceding. In 1967 the farm value of wheat totaled $50,462,000; in 1968 the total value was $51,832,000. In 1967 production of winter wheat was 37,362,000 bu., valued at $46,329,000. Out of the total of 1,916,000 acres harvested, 107,000 were irrigated land, which had a yield of 33 bu. per acre, whereas the non-irrigated land yielded only 18.7 bu. per acre. The effect of irrigation on sorghum grains is comparable; in the same year irrigated acreage yielded an average of 70 bushels per acre; dryland yields averaged 19.7 bushels. Production was 10,295,000 bushels in 1968, worth nearly $10,000,000.

Sixteen varieties of winter wheat are being planted, but three varieties were used in 83 percent of the planting. The test of a brand is in its yield per acre, and farmers are quick to transfer their favor to the seed that gives best results. Resistance to diseases is also a factor. The Wichita variety, which was planted almost universally up to 1959, has been losing ground to Scout, which is being adopted for its high yield and good milling and baking qualities. While Wichita retained its popularity in the 1960s, grown in 34 percent of the seeded acreage, it was damaged by adverse weather conditions in eastern Colorado. Scout is being planted in 30 percent of the wheatlands, and Warrior has become the third leading variety, foremost in yield per acre. The average yield of the State in 1968 was 20.9 bu. per acre, with the northeastern district attaining 24.4 bu. per acre. Of new varieties that have been developed, Lancer combats stem rust, and Delmar, planted chiefly in the northwestern section, resists dwarf bunt. More than 20,000,000 bu. of corn for grain are raised annually, valued at over $23,000,000.

Colorado is the third largest producer of sugar beets, with 2,621,000 tons in 1968, nearly as much as Idaho, 3,323,000 tons, but below California, which produced 5,969,000 tons. Sugar beets thrive in the northeastern and east central sections of Colorado, where Weld County, with about 60,000 acres in beets, is currently producing up to 900,000 tons and has produced over 1,200,000 a year. Larimer, Morgan, Logan, Yuma, and Kit Carson Counties are major sugar beet growers, but there are profitable yields also in the southeast and in the western counties of Mesa, Delta and Montrose. In 1967 Colorado produced 2,610,000 tons paying the farmer $29,680,000. Planters of sugar beets are paid benefits under the U. S. Sugar Act of 1948, the object of which is to protect the domestic sugar industry. About 4,000 Colorado growers received support in excess of $7,216,000 under this act in 1963. The largest processors are the American Crystal, Holly, National and Great Western companies.

Since World War II Colorado, with the help of the Federal Government, has made immense progress in utilizing the waters of its rivers for irrigation of thousands of acres, supplying the water needs of its cities, and providing hydroelectric power. The six major rivers are the Colorado, which drains the Rocky Mountain area with its tributaries, the Yampa, White, Gunnison, Dolores and San Juan; the Rio Grande, which flows in the south central part of the State; the Arkansas, which starts near Leadville and moves through Pueblo, La Junta, and southeast; the North Platte, in north central Colorado; the South Platte in the northeast, and the Republican, in the northeast.

The snows of the mountains provide the waters of western Colorado, which has 37 percent of the State's land area and 69 percent of the surface water. Diversion of this water to the east slope and to the less well-supplied areas of the eastern plains has been accomplished with the help of the Bureau of Reclamation of the U. S. Department of the Interior, and the Corps of Engineers, USA. About 1,900 reservoirs now store water for irrigation and a large number provide electric power.

One of the largest undertakings was the Colorado-Big Thompson Project of the Bureau of Reclamation, (1938–1959), which made possible the transport of more than 300,000 acre-ft. of water from the western slope, supplying water to about 720,000 acres in north central Colorado, and using tunnels, canals and pipelines in a system covering 250 miles. It takes water from east of Grand Lake on the Colorado River and lifts some of it through the Alva B. Adams Tunnel, 13.1 *m.*, to the Big Thompson River. The largest reservoir in its system is Lake Granby, which stores 539,800 acre-ft. The John Martin Dam and Reservoir completed in 1948 by the Corps of Engineers, 18 *m.* west of Lamar on the Arkansas River, covers 17,500 acres and contains 655,000 acre-ft. of water.

A major undertaking begun in 1964 is the Fryingpan-Arkansas Project, which will cost more than $200,000,000. Starting with Ruedi Dam on the Fryingpan near Basalt, which will impound 100,000 acre-ft., water also will be collected at the 10,000 ft. level by a group of tunnels and carried to the east slope by the Divide Tunnel, 5.3 *m.* long. It will be used in a number of power plants, provide water for Colorado Springs, Canon City, Pueblo and several other cities, and irrigate 286,000 acres in the Arkansas Valley, almost to the Kansas line.

The Silt Project, begun in 1964, near the towns of Rifle and Silt, will take water from Rifle Creek and the Colorado River for irrigation. The Curecanti Project makes use of the water of the Gunnison River and comprises three large dams, one of which, the Blue Mesa, will compound a lake of 915,000 acre-ft.

Water policies and projects are supervised by the Colorado Water Conservation Board, while administration of distribution and transfer of water is conducted by the Office of State Engineer of the Division of Water Resources. Water Commissioners and Deputy Commissioners, one of each from the 70 Water Districts, are part of the State Engineer's Office. There also are the Irrigation District Commission, Irrigation Division Engineers, and the Ground Water Commission, which administers the allocation and supplies of ground water.

The irrigated sections of Colorado grow wheat, rye, and other cash grains. Corn, oats, barley, and grain sorghums are raised primarily as feed crops on both irrigated and dry farms. Hay, the State's leading crop, is not entirely grown in irrigated regions; a considerable part is cut from natural meadows in the mountains and on certain sections of the plains; alfalfa, clover, timothy, sweet sorghum, forage, and wild hay are the principal varieties. Potatoes, Colorado's chief vegetable crop, are grown in all but five counties, although production is largely limited to the San Luis and South Platte Valleys; sharp price fluctuations in recent years have made income from this crop uncertain. Pinto beans are an important cash crop on the plains, particularly in sections where water is scarce or unavailable. Some broomcorn is grown in the southeastern corner of the State.

Many of the irrigated sections are well suited to horticulture. Refrigerated motor trucks and airplanes have greatly widened the market for this produce, making it possible for a family in London to have Colorado fruit within days after it has been picked. Apples are grown in Delta and adjoining counties on the Western Slope, in Fremont County, in some lower sections of the Arkansas Valley, and in Larimer, Jefferson, and Boulder Counties along the South Platte. In 1967 about 500,000 bu. were picked. Peaches and pears are grown in the Arkansas Valley, and on the lower mesas, deltas, and flood plains of the Colorado and Gunnison Rivers, where water for irrigation is plentiful, the climate mild, and the growing season longer than in other sections of the State. Colorado cherries are largely of the sour variety, although some sweet cherries are grown on the Western Slope in the Delta and Grand Junction areas. Two-thirds of the State's cherries are harvested in Larimer County, with Fremont, Mesa, Jefferson, and Delta Counties ranking next in order. Small quantities of grapes, apricots, and plums are raised in the orchard country along the lower valleys of the Colorado and Gunnison Rivers; grapes and plums flourish along the Arkansas.

Jefferson County and other areas in the vicinity of Denver are the berry patch of Colorado and furnish the local market for a brief period each summer. Berries are also grown in most of the fruit areas of the State, especially along the Grand Mesa in Garfield County. Glenwood Springs on the upper Colorado River is widely known for its wild mountain strawberries.

Truck farming has become an important enterprise in the irrigated farm regions, but violent price fluctuations have made it a hazardous occupation. The Rocky Ford cantaloupe is celebrated throughout the country, and in recent years honeydew melons and winter watermelons have become increasingly important in the Arkansas Valley; these melons are now vine-ripened and pre-cooled before shipment. Another important garden crop is crisp head lettuce, which grows in high mountain meadows and matures late in the season when supplies elsewhere are depleted. Green peas, cabbage, tomatoes, onions, snap beans, cauliflower, and mushrooms are also grown. Colorado giant and short-strain pascal celery is probably the State's most widely praised vegetable; a large part of the crop is grown immediately west and north of Denver, but small crops are grown along the Arkansas in the vicinity of Canon City and Pueblo. Most of this celery is wrapped with paper to bleach it in the field, and is then stored in trenches for further bleaching for the Thanksgiving and Christmas markets; shipments are usually made by truck or in small gift packages by express. The growing of carnations has become a major business and Colorado is often called the Carnation State. It also grows orchids, Easter lilies, chrysanthemums, roses, gladioli, baby'sbreath, bedding plants, potted plants, and delivers large quantities of cut flowers to the East by air express.

Although most of Colorado farm produce is grown on irrigated tracts, the vast bulk of the State's cultivated land is without water. Dry farming on a large scale began about 1880, by which time all land in well-watered river bottoms had been preempted and land-hungry homesteaders began to checker the arid plains with rectangles of barbed wire. But enthusiasm for this "rain belt," as it was in fact during the favorable 1880's, wilted during the bitter years of drought and depression in the early nineties. Many farmers were ruined; entire communities were abandoned, and the plight of eastern Colorado was so serious that it was ten years before recovery began. This trying period pointed the need of establishing experiment stations; in time these succeeded in placing dry farming upon a scientific basis by developing special drought-resisting seed and such drought-resisting crops as dwarf cane, higary, federita, grama, and Sudan grass. New methods of cultivation designed to preserve moisture were also introduced, and $2 wheat during the first World War brought farmers hurrying to plow up the plains.

In recent years the Federal Government has assisted in alleviating the worst evils of the post war era by stablizing production and marketing. Today, hundreds of successful farmers in the plains counties grow a diversity of drought-resisting crops and seldom have a complete failure. In addition, they have introduced dairy farming and poultry raising as subsidiary sources of income to protect them against total loss during dry years. The plains towns of eastern Colorado are shipping points for wheat, corn, hogs, cattle, sheep, eggs, poultry, butterfat, and a wide variety of similar produce.

Colorado has many agencies for protecting agriculture, stopping soil depletion, building watersheds, controlling floods, providing loans, and cooperating with the Federal Government in price support. The U. S. Dept. of Agriculture conducts price support through the Commodity Credit Corp. Support for cotton, corn, wheat, rice, tobacco and peanuts is mandatory. The Federal Government stores commodities when private facilities are full and in 1963 had 600,000 bu. stored. Extensive studies are supervised by the Colorado Agricultural Experiment Station at Colorado State College in Fort Collins. It has eight branch stations that do research into every phase of developing crops and livestock.

Today farmers throughout the State of Colorado are strongly organized for mutual improvement of methods, markets, and growth. Every agricultural county has an agricultural planning committee that coordinates information received from various agencies and reports to the Colorado State Agricultural Planning Committee. Planning in counties is carried on by an agricultural council, a home demonstration council, a 4-H Club council, and a young farmer-homemarker council, involving about 15,000 people. The National Farmers Union and the American National Cattlemen's Assn. have their headquarters in Colorado. Farm operators also make use of cooperatives under the Cooperative Marketing Act.

STAGECOACH TO AIRLINER

The development of transportation in Colorado is a story of high courage and eventful daring. More than half of its terrain is rough and mountainous, but builders of railroads and highways have blasted and tunneled their way across this wilderness of peaks and canyons into the remotest sections of the State. Remarkable engineering feats have attended this work at every step—Hanging Bridge in the Royal Gorge, by which tracks are suspended above the roaring waters of the Arkansas River; the Carleton Tunnel, the Moffat Tunnel, and the Trail Ridge Road.

The first routes of the white man into and across the State naturally followed the trails and passes used for centuries by the Indians. Such was the branch of the Overland Trail up the South Platte River; such, too, was the Mountain Division of the Santa Fe Trail, which left the Arkansas River at Fort Bent and struck southwestward through what is now Trinidad to enter New Mexico over Raton Pass; the Ute Pass Trail along the northern base of Pikes Peak into South Park was named for the Indians who habitually used it. The watercourse routes provided practicable avenues of travel and assured wayfarers of fuel, water, and forage. During the feverish gold rush of 1859, however, fortune-hunters were willing to face almost any danger and endure any hardship if only they could make better speed, and they blazed a more direct but more hazardous route, the Smoky Hill Trail, which followed the Smoky Hill River through west central Kansas and proceeded across the high dry plains to Denver, a route roughly paralleled by present highway US 40. These early trails were little more than many pairs of ruts made by the wheels of heavy wagons. When a pair had been worn too deep for use, wagons straddled the old ruts and created new ones. On the prairies of eastern Colorado the grass-grown scars of these emigrant and trade routes are still to be seen here and there. In addition to rough roads, early travelers faced the hazards of bogs and swollen rivers, as well as the danger of attack by Indians and outlaws.

One of the earliest vehicles used by trappers and traders was the two-wheeled Red River cart, ordinarily used in conjunction with trains of pack mules. As trade developed with New Mexico, the cumbersome Spanish *caretta* with its two great wooden wheels came creaking along the Santa Fe Trail. The ox-drawn prairie schooner characterized the gold rush period, although in the feverish year of 1859 every kind of burden-bearing animal and conveyance was pressed into service. In their anxiety to reach the new Eldorado many gold-hunters started on foot in patent-leather boots and high stove-pipe hats, with merely the supplies that could be carried in a carpetbag or wheelbarrow. Many of the disappointed prospectors attempted to return to "America" by navigating the South Platte, ventures that usually ended in disaster.

Transportation companies were soon organized to serve the gold fields; one of the first was the Leavenworth and Pikes Peak Express, which in 1859 began carrying mail and freight from the Missouri River to Denver and Auraria. Five years later the Butterfield Overland Dispatch, better known as the B. O. D., inaugurated a fast freight and passenger line along the Smoky Hill route. In 1866 the Wells Fargo Company acquired both lines. Until supplanted by railroads and motor buses, the stagecoach lines were extended to serve even the most isolated communities. On some of the crude mountain roads grades were so steep that the drivers had to drag huge logs as brakes, and travel was literally hair-raising.

From the first, Coloradoans were aware of the transportation handicap imposed by the Rockies and bent every effort to have a transcontinental railroad constructed through the State. They sponsored costly surveys in an attempt to persuade Union Pacific officials to build their line through the mountains west from Denver, but the easy grade of Sherman Hill in Wyoming proved more persuasive. The first railroad in the State, completed in June 1870, linked Denver with the Union Pacific at Cheyenne. Connections with Kansas City and St. Louis were established later that year with the completion of the Kansas Pacific Railroad, now part of the Union Pacific System.

In 1871, General William J. Palmer and his associates began construction of the Denver & Rio Grande, a daring and elaborately conceived system. The D. & R. B. reached Pueblo the following summer and pushed westward up the Arkansas to Florence. In February 1878 the Santa Fe Railway, which had entered Colorado along the Arkansas Valley from the east, outwitted Palmer and secured control of Raton Pass on the route southward into New Mexico. Two months later, however, the Denver & Rio Grande won a spectacular war with the Santa Fe for possession of the right-of-way through the Royal Gorge of the Arkansas, which enabled it to push on and across the Continental Divide at Marshall Pass (10,856 alt.), then and now the highest transcontinental railroad traverse in North America; this narrow-gauge line was completed to Utah late in 1882. By July 1880, rails had been laid north to Leadville, but Rio Grande's standard gauge main line from Denver to Ogden over Tennessee Pass was not completed until 1890. Many of the independent local railroads constructed during this early period have since been abandoned or absorbed by the seven major trunk lines entering the State.

Denver's recurring dream of a transcontinental railroad seemed to be on the point of fulfillment in 1902 when David H. Moffat and associates built the Denver, Pacific & Northwestern Railway, later renamed the Denver & Salt Lake (Moffat) Railway, financed with local capital. Moffat and his partners sank their fortunes in the venture but could not proceed with construction beyond Craig, Colorado. The construction of the Moffat Tunnel (1922-27), built with public funds, and the completion in 1934 of the Dotsero Cutoff, linking the Denver & Salt Lake with the main line of the Denver & Rio Grande, placed Denver for the first time directly on a main transcontinental route.

The early railroads in the mountains were narrow gauge. Light rails laid three feet apart carried small but powerful locomotives drawing freight cars and passenger coaches of proportionate size. The Denver & Rio Grande, first to employ the narrow gauge, was dubbed the "baby railroad," but its diminutive trains were soon winding their way up narrow canyons into almost inaccessible districts. A narrow gauge line, it was said, "could curve on the brim of a sombrero," and in many places virtually had to do so; the early boom camps were served almost exclusively by such narrow gauge systems.

Transporting the huge output of farm and factory to market and the ultimate consumer uses the energy of a large segment of the labor force. About 300,000 trucks, light and heavy, farm and inter-city carrier, roll over approx. 75,000 miles of roads and highways of all kinds of construction, paying gasoline taxes, road use and license fees, and contributing mightily to government and business income. While most of this haulage is intrastate, there are a number of interstate carriers. The *Colorado Year Book* says: "More than 800 Colorado communities are served by no other form of transportation and are dependent upon trucks for all the daily necessities of life. Virtually every item in the home or on the shelf at the store traveled at least part way by truck."

Although the seven major railroads of Colorado have lost much of their passenger business and removed unused track, they remain most important for long-haul freight and have a large payroll in Colorado. The principal lines are the Denver & Rio Grande Western, Union Pacific, Santa Fe, Burlington, Colorado & Southern, Rock Island, and Missouri Pacific. Total mileage of these and six smaller lines inside the State is around 3,600; in 1930 it was just under 5,000. The Denver & Rio Grande Western has more than 1,000 miles of track; the rest taper down to five with less than 100 miles, and the Southern San Luis Railroad with 1.3 miles. The short-haul lines inside the State include the Great Western, 63 miles, and the Colorado & Wyoming, 32 miles. Several of the larger railroads have erected multilevel loading platforms to accommodate piggyback shipments of automobiles.

The phenomenal rise in air travel has most of the airports figuring on expansion. Even Stapleton, at Denver, which is considered meeting all current requirements, wants a slice of the Rocky Mountain Arsenal for longer and better runways. Colorado is served by eight scheduled airlines, 35 local and unscheduled companies, and a number of helicopters. Direct service to Europe was instituted by Trans World Airlines in 1963. There are more than 180 public and private airports. United Air Lines carries the largest number of passengers, air mail, and air freight reaching Stapleton at Denver. Braniff International Airways, Trans-Central Airlines, Continental Airlines, Ozark Airlines, Frontier Airlines, Western Airlines, and Aspen Airways are the other scheduled carriers. Frontier, which began as a service between Denver and Durango in 1946 has expanded into midwestern states and is especially useful to

Colorado Springs, Pueblo, Alamosa, Grand Junction and other Colorado cities. Aspen Airways, the newest of the services, has developed flights to Aspen and the recreation area of the Rockies, especially to the ski slopes in winter. United maintains an Air Flight Training Center at Stapleton.

MANUFACTURING

Long before Colorado became a State, the tumultuous progress of hard-rock mining had given rise to milling, smelting, and manufacturing enterprises. An *arastra,* a primitive ore crusher of Spanish origin, was at work in Gregory Gulch early in the summer of 1859, pulverizing "blossom rock" and other soft ores from decomposed surface veins. The mule-driven *arastra* soon gave way to stamp mills powered first with water, later with steam. Harnessing small but swift mountain streams, miners built scores of water wheels to turn cam shafts that lifted heavy stamps, huge blocks of iron, with which ore was pounded to dust. As more refractory ores were encountered, such crude methods proved increasingly inefficient, recovering less than half the precious metals contained.

After much experimentation smelting solved the major problems posed by Colorado's peculiarly difficult ores. Nathaniel P. Hill, metallurgist of Brown University, organized the Boston and Colorado Smelter Company and in 1868 erected the State's first smelter at Blackhawk in Gregory Gulch. For several years this plant and the others reduced crushed ores by concentrating gold and silver on a copper matte; these plates were shipped to refineries in Swansea, Wales, and other points abroad. The Boston and Colorado Smelting Company built its own separating works in 1873, and five years later erected its Argo plant in Denver where coal was cheaper. Other notable smelters in Colorado were the Leadville Smelter (1877), the Grant Smelter (1878) in Denver, the Arkansas Valley Smelter (1879) in Leadville, the Durango Smelter (1872), the Globe Smelter (1886) in Denver, and the Philadelphia Smelter (1888) in Pueblo. In 1899 the larger smelting interests in the State were merged as the American Smelting and Refining Company by the Guggenheim brothers, who had founded their family fortune on the mines and smelters of Leadville. As more complex ores were encountered, new processes were introduced to extract the five basic metals—gold, silver, copper, lead, and zinc—and to separate these from one another. In 1896 a chlorination mill had been erected at Cripple Creek to concentrate ores for shipment to the smelters. The cyanide process, however, proved more satisfactory. Colorado mining engineers pioneered the introduction of the cyanide process and have invented many important devices for the treatment of low-grade ores.

The biggest change that has come to Colorado industries since World

War II is the expansion of electronic plants and the successful operation of research laboratories. The results have been so satisfying that numerous national electronic companies have opened branches in the State. Fifty years ago agriculture was still the largest producer and food processing was the largest industry. Then heavy manufacturing grew, supported by such solid establishments as C. F. I. & Steel Corporation, Gates Rubber Company, and Samsonite Corporation. From 1954 to 1963 the growth of employment in manufacturing was five times the national average. Electrical machinery zoomed ahead; stone, clay and glass products were second, fabricated metal products were third, food and kindred products fourth, in value added by manufacturing. In the number of men employed, food and kindred products was second. The major food processing was of sugar refining, meat packing, canning and beverages.

According to an official State report, *Industrial Colorado,* by the Colorado Division of Commerce and Development, electrical machinery accounts for the most recent upswing. This includes electrical components and accessories, communication equipment, industrial electronic and control equipment, electrical measuring instruments, electrical industrial apparatus, and aerospace electronics. In 1967 the State Division of Employment and the Bureau of Labor Statistics, U. S. Dept. of Labor, showed that 20,700 were employed in machinery, including electric; 19,000 in food and kindred products, 8,800 in ordance, 8,700 in paper, printing and publishing, 6,200 in textiles, apparel and leather, and 5,300 in rubber and plastic products.

Despite its huge area devoted to forests Colorado has not developed a substantial industry in plywood and hardboards. It has done better in furniture and fixtures. About one-third of Colorado is covered with forests, and out of the total 12,000,000 acres are open for commercial use. Although aspen is popular for paneling and plywood, there were in 1968 but one plywood mill and one paneling plant exploiting this product. Engelmann spruce takes first place in lumber, followed by lodgepole pine, ponderosa pine, Douglas fir and aspen.

Chemicals are not as big as electrical machinery, but the industry annually adds more than $50,000,000 in value to the economy, producing 33 basic chemicals used in fertilizers, pesticides, medicines, pharmaceuticals, and even explosives.

Ordnance and accessories is a category that was practically nonexistent in 1950. Since that time the two major installations—the Denver Division of the Marietta Martin Co. and the Rocky Flats facility of Dow Chemical Corp. have made this important.

Colorado industry has benefited especially by the large number of scientists, engineers, and technically trained persons resident in the State. This is partly because of the great variety of courses offered in the universities and colleges. Four universities offer graduate programs in technical fields. The University of Colorado offers degrees in all areas of science, engineering, and mathematics. Doctoral programs of the University of Denver include chemical engineering, chemistry, electrical engineering, metallurgy, and physics. Colorado State University has twenty-four departments in mathematics, engineering, and the physical and biological sciences. The Colorado School of Mines offers courses in geology, geophysics, mining, metallurgical and chemical engineering. The engineering schools also have courses designed to continue the education of employed engineers and scientists. These courses include aerospace engineering, and electrical engineering at the University of Colorado, civil, mechanical and electrical engineering at the University of Denver; metallurgical and geological engineering at the Colorado School of Mines, and electrical and mechanical engineering at Colorado State University, the last-named also providing video tape television to industrial plants for some of its courses. The junior community colleges often lay the foundation for higher vocational and technical training.

A study of Colorado's advantages as a location for research and development laboratories was made by the Denver Research Institute and became the basis for the State's summary of the national companies that had established major branches in Colorado in recent years. They included IBM in Boulder, Hewlett Packard at Loveland and Colorado Springs, Martin Marietta in Denver, Western Electric in Aurora, Ampex in Colorado Springs, Colorado Hickok in Grand Junction, Beech Aircraft in Boulder, Honeywell in Denver, TRW in Loveland, Sparton in Grand Junction, Dow Chemical in Golden, Amphenol in Longmont, Marathon Oil Co. research center in Denver, Ball Brothers research in Boulder, and Sundstrand in Denver. Eastman Kodak has arranged for a large plant in Windsor, Eagle-Picher in Colorado Springs, Dura Business Machines in Greeley, and the Grover Company division of Powers Regulator in Denver.

Most impressive is the roster of Federal laboratories, nonprofit foundations and private research agencies. The National Bureau of Standards Laboratories at Boulder employs 700 people, 400 of them scientists and engineers, doing research in cryogenics, astrophysics, and standards for electronic measurements. The Environmental Science Services Administration formed in 1965 from a group of agencies including the U. S. Weather Bureau and the Coast & Geodetic Survey, made Boulder its center for exploration of the earth's environment, with a staff of 700. The U. S. Geological Survey has facilities in Denver that employ 1,400, 500 of them engaged in research. The National Center for Atmospheric Research in Boulder is a private nonprofit corporation of twenty-four universities sponsored by the National Science Foundation, and employing 400. Extensive laboratories and other facilities maintained in Denver by the Bureau of Reclamation of the Department of the Interior for water resources development employ 1,400.

Other representative corporations that contribute mightily to the well being of the State's economy and are mentioned elsewhere in this *Guide* include Adolph Coors Co., American Crystal Sugar Co., Great Western Sugar Co., Holly Sugar Co., C.F.I. & Steel Corp., Climax Molybdenum Co., Ideal Cement Co., Coors Porcelain Co., Dixson, Inc., Forney Industries, Stanley Aviation Co., Sterling Colorado Beef Co., Ampex Corp., Beech Aircraft Corp., E. I. DuPont de Nemours, Kaman Nuclear Division of Kaman Aircraft Co., Shell Chemical Co., Union Carbide Corp., and Westinghouse Georesearch Laboratory.

Promotion of industrial sites and facilities has become a prominent feature of business activities. Instead of waiting for a national corporation to determine where to place a regional division, municipalities now unite all civic forces to make attractive offers to the corporation. While competition in identical lines is not encouraged, all concerned now recognize that the good of the whole depends on the healthy operation of all the constituent parts. Colorado has so much to offer in space, highways, easy access to the whole mountain section of the United States, and a labor force with a satisfactory wage structure and few stoppages, that it starts with a strong base for operations. As an instance of civic alertness there is Pueblo, which has three far-seeing agencies working for it. The Pueblo Industrial Development, founded 1963, is a non-profit organization that negotiates long-term leases on more than 800 acres of industrial sites at Pueblo Memorial Airport, all on land owned by the city. The Pueblo Development Foundation, founded 1964, exploits opportunities in business and industry over the whole area. The wide-ranging Southern Colorado Economic Development District, with main offices in Pueblo, keeps the prosperity of fifteen counties in view, and concerns itself with possibilities of new use of resources, attractions for tourism, and vocational and technical education. In the latter part of 1968, 130 organizations with similar objectives were at work, quite apart from the numerous chambers of commerce that were furthering the business life of their communities.

The Arts

IN ARCHITECTURE, public and private design was still largely following the eclectic practices of the 1930's when the original edition of this *Guide* was published. There had been little incentive to risk investment in any but conventional structures prior to the coming of World War II. After the war stability was reestablished in the markets, new funds were appropriated by state and national agencies, and the pent-up need for new buildings started a resurgence of construction. As after every war, the old order lost its authority, there was a break with conventional practices, and new forms received a welcome.

At the start of the century churches were still modifications of the classical designs and a congregation rarely considered its house of worship complete without a belfry. Whereas Protestant designs were often adapted from the English Gothic, Roman Catholics seemed to favor the French. Denver has examples of both styles in St. John's Episcopal Cathedral (1911) and the Cathedral of the Immaculate Conception (1912). There is also a church designed by Ralph Adams Cram, the great advocate of pure Gothic, St. Andrew's Episcopal Church. Educational institutions, like churches, sometimes chose the Romanesque; there is a good example at Loretto Heights College.

The impulse to experiment with new designs seems to have come from several sources. The European magazines were filled with new concepts. Because construction was costly, there was a tendency to eliminate extraneous ornament; prefabrication fitted with uniformity, and aluminum and concrete were used more generally. In office structures there was a preference for the functional; in twenty years Colorado cities were dotted with tall pyramids that had windows on four sides and with solitary aloofness reached into the sky. Inside they recognized the needs of the time by providing garages for vehicles.

In *Architecture Colorado* Olga Jackson has described the changes with text and pictures (Thorson, Carlson & Jackson, 1966). She shows how modern churches are departing from the traditional patterns. Grace Methodist Church in Denver, 1963, has wood shingles and a circular altar. Calvary Temple, enlarged in 1962, has a shed roof that can shelter 2,000 worshipers. Peace Lutheran Church in Arvada (1966) emphasizes its gables. Innovations were practiced in other public structures. St. Joseph's Hospital, Denver, added circular units in 1965.

It is in downtown Denver that simplicity and functional elements are most marked. The Denver-Hilton, one block long, twenty-two stories tall, and an interior garage, rises like a huge concrete wall perforated with nearly 800 windows for its 884 rooms. It is connected by a bridge over Court Pl. with the May D. & F. building, completed in 1958. A section of the store is in the form of a hyperbolic paraboloid, best described as a huge metal tent, with anchors at four corners. Despite its ponderous roof it gives the impression of having an easily accessible interior. The newest uses of materials and modern design may be seen in the Convention Center, the General Hospital, the Art Museum, and the Museum of Natural History, all in Denver. *For mention of new office buildings see* DENVER.

Clay, stone, wood, sod, and other structural materials are plentiful in Colorado, and all have been ingeniously employed within its boundaries for centuries. A thousand years ago the Cliff Dwellers used stone in building their fortress-like and curiously modern "apartment houses" in great natural caves and crevices high on the canyon walls at Mesa Verde and Hovenweep.

The structural use of Colorado clay in the form of adobe, practicable only in arid climates, has been traced back some two thousand years to the Basket Makers, who covered their pit dwellings with dome-shaped roofs fashioned of interlaced willow bows and plastered with adobe mud. Spanish priests early taught the Indians to use adobe in the form of precast bricks, a superior type of construction to the aboriginal method of puddling. The traditional form of adobe dwellings antedates the Spanish, however, and was adopted by them from the design of the pueblos of the mesa country and the dwellings of the common folk among the Aztecs and other peoples of Mexico. The first Spanish-speaking settlers in the southern valleys of Colorado found adobe clay in quantity and naturally built such houses as they had known farther south. Adobe structures are beautiful in an appropriate setting of cliff wall and mesa, for their simple lines and soft coloring harmonize well with their background.

The true adobe house is simple in design, usually consisting of a single room, with walls of sun-dried bricks about a foot long, six inches wide, and three inches thick, made of adobe and straw. The flat roof is also of adobe, supported by rafters called *vagas,* hewn from long logs; these are usually allowed to project beyond the walls at each end of the house. West of Trinidad, at Tijeras and Cordova Plazas, some of the old single-room houses erected in the 1870's have been converted into large communal dwellings by adding bays of rooms or additional apartments to the sides of the original building as members of the family have married. Although adobe construction has declined, its influence is apparent in the lines of "modern pueblo" houses built by some who have become rather bored with the usual bungalow, early Tudor, Spanish villa, and Georgian Colonial styles that prevail in the better residential section of the cities.

From the beginning of settlement, construction and design were influenced at once by climate and the character of available materials. Each region early developed types of houses and buildings best suited to the local scene and the means at hand; these types have in part persisted although ease of transportation has brought a measure of uniformity and standardization by making readily available in widely separated communities all kinds of structural materials—brick has been shipped into granite-bottomed mountain towns, dressed lumber into the treeless plains.

The early settler, faced with the all-engrossing problems of survival, had little time or energy for embellishing his house; its primary purpose was to shelter him and his family from sun and storm. The first settlers on the plains—cattlemen and buffalo hunters who came in the 1860's and 1870's—found no stone and no timber, not even the useful adobe. Their first habitations were therefore crude dugouts with roofs of brush and dirt, a type still to be seen in parts of the dry mesa country in southwestern Colorado. The farmers who followed the cattlemen improved upon this construction by plowing up narrow slabs of sod, which were used to build walls and roofs; flowers often continued to sprout and bloom on the sod houses, transforming them into curious gardens. Cool in summer, warm in winter, these sod houses, few of which survive, were in many respects more serviceable than the flimsy frame structure that succeeded them.

The mining camps in the mountains were initially marked by structural forms as simple as those of the plains or mesa country. Here again use was made of the material at hand. As thick stands of pine covered the mountains, the first structures in the camps were of logs, either unpeeled or roughly squared. Soon portable sawmills were cutting slabs of green pine lumber, and frame construction began. Use of masonry in the camps was usually deferred until a reasonable degree of permanency seemed assured, but the miners' chronic optimism often induced disastrous illusions. This was the day of false-fronts, when rows of one-story buildings in every town were camouflaged to give an impression of far greater size. False-front buildings still characterize many mountain towns and plains villages. Log houses have never gone out of fashion in the mountains, and such construction has reached elaborate proportions in "rustic" hotels and lodges.

The discovery near Denver in the 1860's of fine brick clay profoundly influenced the trend of architectural design. Bonanza kings and merchant princes saw in the product of the kilns a material well suited to give expression to their conceptions of elegance and grandeur.

It became a mark of distinction, a matter of prestige, to build with brick, especially where it was most expensive; tons and tons of brick were shipped at great cost to Leadville and other boom camps in the mountains to build cottages, business buildings, and opera houses. The more pretentious structures were usually "jigsaw" in a late Victorian manner, being heavily ornamented with wooden scrollwork; a number of these "jigsaw" houses remain in Central City, one of the more notable being the Frederick Kruse House, built in 1874. Later, brick exteriors were embellished with cast iron trim. Among the better brick structures of this period are the Teller House at Central City and the ornate Hotel de Paris at Georgetown. The Tabor Opera House at Denver, erected in 1880 and recently demolished, reflected the then-budding Romanesque revival. A notable exception to the use of brick is the Central City Opera House, completed in 1878, built of granite from the surrounding hills.

A change of fashion among the wealthier was heralded by Glen Eyrie, built early in the 1870's a few miles northwest of Colorado Springs by General William J. Palmer, railroad promoter. Believing that a man's house literally should be his castle, the General built a remarkable one, with towers, turrets, and other obsolete military appurtenances. The neighborhood was searched for flat weathered stones to impart an aspect of great age to the building. As the roof looked too new, the General had it torn off and rebuilt with tiles from an old English church; antipathetic to chimneys, he had a tunnel dug into and up the mountainside to carry off smoke. Glen Eyrie now shelters The Navigators of Colorado Springs.

The Romanesque revival that swept the country during the 1880's and 1890's influenced the design both of business and private houses, and several of the old mansions still standing on Capitol Hill in Denver are as fine examples of this style as any in America. The house built in Denver by Walter Cheesman was bought by Claude Boettcher in 1961, and later presented by the Boettcher Foundation to the State for an Executive Mansion. It stands in the Capitol Hill area between East 7th and East 8th Avenues and Logan and Randolph Sts. High-rise apartment buildings are giving a new skyline to the Capitol Hill district. The Hampshire House apartment hotel of 1963 is eighteen stories tall with indented balconies. Another new structure of this kind is Penn VII, at 700 Pennsylvania Ave.

As designers have struggled for greater freedom of expression, encouraging advances have been made in the field of public buildings and monumental architecture. The design of the new Denver Federal Reserve Bank is an example. Similarly, the Denver City and County Building, the work of the Allied Architects of Denver, has given an impetus to dignity and simplicity in its environs. Probably the finest achievements, however, have been made in the design of educational institutions, for here the architect has been allowed the greatest latitude in demonstrating that the useful and the beautiful can be one. The adaptation of a rural Italian style, so well suited to the mountainous setting of Boulder and the richly colored stone quarried near by, spared the University of Colorado campus the monotony of the usual Collegiate Gothic. This work by Charles Zeller Klauder and Frank Miles Day of Philadelphia makes the university one of the most attractive in the country.

The United States Air Force Academy, north of Colorado Springs, is already famous for its Chapel of all faiths, a tetrahedron of aluminum, remarkable for its seventeen spires. Its principal designer was Walter A. Netsch. The other buildings of the Academy, modern in their reach for maximum light, air and general usefulness, are by Skidmore, Owings & Merrill. The Broadmoor International Center in Colorado Springs, built in 1961, is described as a hyperbolic parabaloid, differing in some details from the May D. & F. construction in Denver. In 1962 the Broadmoor Hotel added a nine-story extension conforming to the Italianate character of the original, erected in 1922.

PAINT AND STONE

Little is known of the earliest aboriginal art in Colorado. Few traces remain of the Basket Maker culture. The Cliff Dwellers were accomplished in the ceramic arts, but decoration of pottery appears to have been developed by them only a short time before their mysterious disappearance. Their painting was purely ceremonial, and the few examples of their petroglyphs that have been found are so highly stylized that in most instances the subjects can only be conjectured. The Indian nomads of plains and mountains painted on leather, both for decorative purposes and to record historical events, using highly developed geometric designs as well as human and animal figures; the latter were often strongly and imaginatively conceived.

The first pictorial representations of the State, it appears, were by Samuel Seymour, a draughtsman member of Major Stephen H. Long's expedition in 1820; his work appeared as illustrations of the published account of the expedition. In 1832 George Catlin, a Philadelphia law student, came west to live among the Indians and paint them; much of his work is preserved in the Smithsonian Institution, Washington, D. C. Another early artist was J. M. Stanley, who came in the 1840's to paint Indian and pioneer life; his work, for the most part, appeared only in the annals of the Smithsonian. John C. Frémont, a better engineer and soldier than artist, made sketches of the mountains on his expedition of 1842. Others of the pioneer period were Walter Carey, illustrator, and John Howland, staff artist on *Harper's Weekly,* who began painting western scenes in 1857. Howland later studied in France and attained some recognition as a sculptor; his *Soldiers' Monument* (1907) stands on the lawn of the Capitol at Denver. These artists, largely self-taught, were followed by painters with formal European training—among others, Albert Bierstadt, who, brought to America as a child, returned to his native Dusseldorf, Germany, to study in the genre school of Auchenbach. Returning to America in 1858, he joined the Landers surveying expedition to the Colorado Rockies, where he found inspiration for most of his better-known works. On this first visit he executed *Morning in the Rocky Mountains,* as well as *Rocky Mountains—Landers Peak,* now in the Metropolitan Museum, New York City. He painted prolifically on his many Western trips, and as art proved to be an excellent medium for selling stocks and bonds abroad to finance construction of railroads on the frontier, Bierstadt accumulated a larger bank balance than most painters, for his canvases caught the fancy of the wealthy, the Federal Government, and many foreign governments. The Congress appropriated $20,000 for one work, and the eccentric Earl of Dunraven paid $15,000 for his *Park in Colorado.* Among his better-known canvases are *Storm in the Rocky Mountains* and *The Last of the Buffalo,* both painted in 1863. Examples of his work hang in museums at New York and Chicago, in the Corcoran Gallery, Washington, D. C., and in the Royal Academy, London.

Thomas Moran, equally a representative of the "heroic school" of landscape painting, was less well known than Bierstadt but perhaps technically superior. Trained in Europe, Moran came west in 1873 and made woodblocks for the U. S. Geological Survey, which possess great historical as well as artistic value. From time to time he essayed larger works in oil and also did illustrations for *Harper's* and the advertising literature of the Denver & Rio Grande Railroad. Although his work was as grandiose in a way as Bierstadt's, Moran was not as facile and was less prized by galleries and patrons. Perhaps his best known painting is *Mount of the Holy Cross.*

Another well-known artist of this period was Fitz-Hugh Ludlow, who accompanied Bierstadt on his second visit in 1863 and painted scenes in the Rockies, the Sierras, and the mountains of the Pacific Northwest for use in railroad brochures. Worthington Whittrege came on a sketching tour with General J. Pope in 1865 and painted many landscapes—*The Plains at the Base of the Rocky Mountains, Sangre de Cristo Mountains,* and *The Platte River;* the latter two were exhibited at the Paris Exposition of 1878. Emanuel Leutze, whose *Washington Crossing the Delaware* is known to all, and whose *Westward The Course of the Empire* appears in the Capitol at Washington, visited

Colorado in 1859 and painted several small water colors, one of which, *Central City, Kansas Territory,* is in the Denver Public Library. Harvey Young, native of Vermont, traveled through the Rockies for several years with burro, pick, shovel, gold pan, and sketch box; later, the Denver & Rio Grande Railroad fitted him up with a studio car in which he painted many scenes reproduced in its "literature." Young, probably the first impressionist in the region, perfected a varnish process that gave his water colors the appearance of oil paintings.

In early days, with "practical" men busy mining or fighting Indians, art was regarded as a pastime for idlers and dreamers; instruction was available only when some established artist came to regain his health. But shortly after the founding of Colorado Springs in 1871 a pioneer art colony was established there by Eliza Greatorex, first woman member of the National Academy. Others in the group were Walter Parrish, Thomas Parrish, and the latter's wife; some of their work has been preserved in the El Paso Club and older residences in the city. An English landscapist, Walter Paris, and Hamilton Hamilton, portrait painter and instructor, exercised considerable influence in Colorado art circles at this time. Charles Craig, resident of Colorado Springs in the early 1880's, spent much of his time among the Ute, and his portraits of them appear in many collections. Other early artists of the city were W. H. Bancroft, largely self-taught, who had carried Thomas Moran's elaborate apparatus during the latter's visit in 1860 and was much influenced by him; Leslie J. Skelton, a prolific landscapist, who sold 5,000,000 postcard reproductions of his works; Carl G. Lotave, pupil of Zorn, known for his landscapes and murals; and John J. McClymont, whose portraits of Colorado business and political leaders brought him a reputation toward the close of the century.

The Broadmoor Art Academy, founded in 1919 under the sponsorship of Eliza Greatorex, had as its first instructor Robert Reid, N.A., who is represented by murals in the Library of Congress and other public buildings. The academy, now the Colorado Springs Fine Arts Center, has had on its staff such distinguished artists as Henry Varnum Poor, George Biddle, Pepino Mangravite, John Ward Lockwood, Arnold Blanch, and Willard Nash. One of its directors was Boardman Robinson. An art appreciation department established a half century ago at Colorado College by Marie Sahm became the Fine Arts Department of the institution. A distinctive contribution to Colorado art was made in 1902 when Artus Van Briggle established a pottery at Colorado Springs and from local clays fashioned pieces of striking and varied design, often making use of aboriginal motifs. His wife, Anne Gregory (Ritter), became one of the State's better-known painters. Today the Pottery at 400 S. 21st St., is open daily to visitors.

Although organized in 1880 the Denver School of Fine Arts did not offer instruction until 1892 and in the same year established a museum. On its faculty was Preston Powers, who enjoyed an international reputation as a sculptor; his bust of Chief Justice Henry Thatcher appears on the walls of the Supreme Court Chambers in the State Capitol, and his bronze Indian figure, *The Closing Era,* stands on the east lawn. After many difficulties, of which the want of public interest and support was chiefest, the Denver School of Fine Arts in 1924 became the Chappell School of Art, affiliated with the University of Denver. John E. Thompson (1882–1945), one of the first to bring a knowledge of the Post-Impressionist school to Colorado, exercised great influence throughout the State, where some of his finest murals were painted.

The first exhibition of the Denver Artists Club was held in 1894 with a display of oils, water colors, sculptures, and etchings by artists of the city and vicinity. From the club grew the Denver Art Association, which enrolled painters, workers in other media, and serious students and patrons of the arts; this group founded the present Denver Art Museum in the Civic Center. The association's first director was Reginald Poland; he was succeeded first by George William Eggers of the Chicago Art Institute and then by Arnold Ronnebeck, pupil of Maillot and Bourdelle, whose sculpture, lithographs, and other works are well known in America and abroad. In 1922 the Chappell residence was donated to the association as a gallery. The institution has been aided by gifts and loans of numerous private collections of pictures, furniture, and ceramics. Its present expansion adds an imposing new structure to the Civic Center.

Henry Read, an Englishman who came to Denver in 1891, fathered what was probably the first municipal art commission in America, established by charter in 1904. As its first undertaking it planned the Civic Center, which is today embellished with two bronzes—*The Broncho Buster* and *On the Warpath*—by Alexander Phimister Proctor, widely known for his animal figures.

Among prominent contemporary Colorado mural painters is Frank Mechau, three times winner of a Guggenheim Fellowship, formerly associated with the Fine Arts Center at Colorado Springs, later director of the School of Art, Columbia University. Mechau is represented in the Museum of Modern Art, New York City, and by murals in the post offices at Colorado Springs, Glenwood Springs, and Washington, D. C., and by a painting in the Denver Art Museum. The works of another muralist, Allen Tupper True, breathe a refreshingly authentic western atmosphere. Born in Colorado Springs, True studied under Howard Pyle and Frank Brangwyn, and has murals in many Denver buildings and in the Missouri State Capitol. Perhaps the most interesting and germinal of his later work has been his use of Indian motifs in color and decorative designs for large industrial plants; his treatment of

the 11-story hydroelectric plant at Boulder Dam has been highly praised.
Dean Babcock, of Denver and Estes Park, achieved recognition
for his mountain landscapes and magazine illustrations. George Elbert
Burr, nationally known for his etchings and pastels of mountains and
deserts, is represented in the permanent collections of museums throughout the country. Marvin Martin and Gladys Caldwell Fisher are Colorado sculptors.

The Fine Arts departments of the universities have done much to
encourage and train young Coloradoans working in the graphic and
plastic arts. In the 1930's they were associated with Colorado unit of
the Federal art program. The work of this group reflected the current
trend among Western artists toward the use of primitive indigenous art
forms; both the painting and sculpture of the younger school was
strongly influenced by the highly stylized manner of the Indian, particularly that of the modern Pueblo Indians. Of the mural painters in this
group, Pascal Quackenbush has decorative panels in St. Martin's Chapel,
St. John's Episcopal Church, Denver, and at the University of Colorado,
Boulder. The State unit of the Index of American Design has contributed
many fine water-color reproductions of the New Mexican *santos* and
bultos in the fine Anne Evans collection.

Along a parallel line was the results achieved by the Adult Education unit of the WPA in reviving the rapidly dying handicrafts—
weaving, embroidery, wood carving, and leather work—of the Spanish-
American people in the southern part of the State.

Interest in contemporary painting and sculpture continues active in
Colorado cities, especially in Denver and Colorado Springs, and in the
universities. Both the Colorado Springs Fine Arts Center and the Denver
Art Museum have work by Colorado artists in their permanent collections. Among the artists represented at the Fine Arts Center are Bernard Arnest, Lawrence Barrett, Helen Barchilon, Watson Bidwell
(1904–1964), Edgar Britton, Jean Charlot, Mary Chenoweth, Ken
Goehring, Vance Kirkland, Edward Marecek, Gene Matthews, Herman Raymond, Robert Reid (1862–1929), Boardman Robinson (1876–
1952), Joseph Russo, Frank Sampson, Francis D. Smith (1874–1956),
John Edward Thompson (1882–1945), and George vander Sluis.

Boardman Robinson was head of the Fine Arts Center School up to
1946. Edgar Britton is a widely known Denver sculptor, particularly in
architectural work. Jean Charlot, who taught at the Fine Arts Center, is
now living in Honolulu. Miss Chenoweth, wellknown for her prints,
teaches at the Center. Kirkland was formerly head of the art department of the University of Denver. Marecek is a teacher in the Denver
Public Schools. Miss Barchilon, Matthews, and Sampson teach at the
University of Colorado in Boulder. Vander Sluis, former teacher at the
Center, is now associated with Syracuse University.

Among the Colorado artists represented in the permanent collections of the Denver Art Museum are the following living painters: Herbert Bayer, Roland Detre, Angelo di Benedetto, Vance Kirkland, Eugene Matthews, Frank Mechau, Enrique Montenegro, William Sanderson, A. T. Schomberg, Paul K. Smith, John Ulbricht, and Clarence van Duzer. Deceased painters are Albert Bancroft, Watson Bidwell, Nel Silverman, John D. Howland, and John Edward Thompson. The Denver Art Museum has recently acquired paintings by Schomberg, Kirkland, and Benedetto. Colorado sculptors represented at the Museum include Edgar Britton and Robert Mangold, and the late Marguerite Kassler, Arnold Ronnebeck, and Wilbert Verhelst. The Museum has acquired a new sculpture by Mangold.

FRONTIER ENTERTAINMENT

Denver sat through its first concert in 1864 when selections from Mozart's *L'Enchantress* were rendered as a solo on the cornet by Alex Sutherland, who as a boy had sounded the bugle for the storied charge of the Light Brigate of Balaklava. A few more cultivated settlers had transported pianos to the Colorado frontier, but respectable Denver depended in large part for its music upon Sutherland and the St. John's Episcopal Choir until 1866 when the first choral society, the Denver Musical Union, was organized. In 1869 the first shop exclusively for the sale of music and instruments was established, and German residents organized the Denver Maennerchor the next year. In 1872 the Denver Choral Union sang Handel's *Esther,* reputedly the first cantata to be sung west of the Mississippi. Joseph Wieniawski, Polish pianist, appeared late in the 1870's and inaugurated a new era by demonstrating that "an artist could visit the West without being scalped by Indians or buried in a dust storm."

In 1877 the first company of Colorado amateurs presented *The Bohemian Girl* in Denver, and Welsh miners in the mountains were soon forming choral societies to sing their traditional airs. In 1881 the Denver Opera Club was organized and presented the works of Gilbert and Sullivan in several Colorado towns. The next year *Pinafore* was played in Denver at a benefit for the Ladies' Relief Association, with all expenses borne by the Carbonate King, H. A. W. ("Haw") Tabor (*see Leadville*). But all this "levity" aroused the wrath of the churches; every pulpit rang with violent denunciations of opera and opera singers; amateur performers, most of whom were church members, hastily deserted their public, and operatic scores gathered dust as Haydn, Gounod, Mendelssohn, and Handel (his *Messiah,* particularly) were offered to suddenly chastened audiences. But light opera had become popular, and in

1882 Colorado's first "native" opera, *Brittle Silver,* had its première in Denver.

Dr. Leopold Damrosch, father of Walter Damrosch who later directed the Metropolitan Opera in New York City, brought his orchestra to Denver in 1882, as did the renowned Theodore Thomas of Chicago; for a week, with season tickets priced at $25, Denverites and other Coloradoans who could afford it "sat quiet and gave themselves up to the full enjoyment of an unparalleled treat." At the same time the orchestras of the Tabor Grand Opera House and Ed Chase's noted and rather notorious Palace Theater, a complete pleasure resort, joined with members of the Ladies Orchestra in giving recitals of "good music" under the direction of Frank Damrosch, another son of Dr. Damrosch.

Well-known musicians born in Colorado or resident in the State for many years include John H. Gower (1855–1922), organist, and composer of the music for Kipling's "Recessional"; Jean Allard Jeancon (1874–1936), authority on Indian music; and Paul Whiteman (1891–1967), Denver-born "King of Jazz"; Henry Houseley (1851–1925), English composer of operas, cantatas, and works for orchestra, string quartet, and organ; a founder of the American Guild of Organists, Houseley was for 37 years organist at St. John's Cathedral, Denver. Monsignor Joseph Bosetti, composer of numerous masses and motets, once organist at St. Peter's in Rome, trained a Denver male choir in the Gregorian tradition. Charles Wakefield Cadman, although he lived but a few years in the State, completed his opera *The Land of Misty Water* in Estes Park, and his operatic cantata *Sunset Trail* had its première in Denver in 1924. A Denver musician, Edwin McArthur accompanist of Kirsten Flagstad, directed the Philadelphia Symphony Orchestra as it accompanied the great Norwegian singer in a series of concerts in New York City early in 1940.

DRAMA AND MELODRAMA

As music in the Pikes Peak country was cradled in the larger and more lavish saloons, gambling halls, and other pleasure houses, so drama in the region was born of Venus Meretrix and Bacchus, better known on the Frontier as John Barleycorn. The early theaters were, for the most part, crude variety houses conducted as integral units of such pleasure resorts; the artistry of performers, who were almost entirely female, was judged by the turn of their figures and by their seductive charms in inducing members of the audience to buy drinks at the bar between acts, and during them as well.

Colorado's first stage performance was offered at Denver City on October 3, 1859. Here in Apollo Hall, an unplastered candle-lighted room above a noisy Larimer Street saloon, three hundred men paid $1 each—for the most part, in gold dust weighed on box office scales—for a seat on crowded wooden benches to see "Colonel" C. R. Thorpe and his troupe of barnstormers from Leavenworth, Kansas, present *The Cross of Gold* and *The Two Gregories,* a double bill enlivened with songs and dances by "Miss" Flora Wakely and "Mademoiselle" Haydee. Thorne soon departed with no great burden of "dust," but "Mademoiselle" and others in the troupe remained. Recruiting the "inimitable Mike" Dougherty, a habitually inebriated miner from Gregory Gulch with a flair for the comic, they performed three nights a week to appreciative audiences whose enthusiasm on occasion reached such heights that the entire cast was loudly and publicly invited downstairs to have a drink. Later, the company journeyed to Central City, where, on the second floor of the Hadley log cabin, the gold camp enjoyed its first taste of more or less serious drama.

On December 12, 1859, A. B. Steinberger, Denver's first dramatist, wrote and directed the production of *Skatara, The Mountain Chieftain* at Apollo Hall, to celebrate the creation of the short-lived Territory of Jefferson. A few months later amateurs produced a play on the evils of strong drink, and a certain Mr. Wyncoop, cast as the horrid example, was warmly praised by the *Rocky Mountain News* for playing his role "with a most thrilling effect, particularly in his delirium-tremens scene." In 1861 the Denver Amateur Dramatic Association made its bow at the Apollo with a series of benefit performances; *Pizarra,* the opening play, netted $124 for Denver's first community chest.

The Colorado theater began to assume a less ephemeral form in September 1860 when Jack Langrishe brought his company to Denver by mule team from Fort Laramie, Wyoming. A genial Irishman, one of the great troupers of the early West, Langrishe "convulsed his audiences in comedy roles, principally because of his enormous nose and powerful voice"; he and Mike Dougherty soon combined their talents and organized a barnstorming circuit in the mountains, playing at Central City, Georgia Gulch, Delaware Flats, Montgomery, French Gulch, Buckskin Joe, and other boom camps; Central City was favored with a six-weeks' season of varied fare presented in the Hadley cabin, now christened the Montana Theater. Returning to Denver, Langrishe and Dougherty took over the Platte Valley Theater, the first to be built for the purpose, which had opened in October 1861 with *Richard III* and *The Devil's In The Room,* a comedy spiced with variety acts; as an additional attraction, the manager of the theater had appeared "in dress suit and white kid gloves," to recite a serious poem.

Renaming this theater the Denver, Langrishe and his partner opened with *The Mistletoe Bough* and during the season presented everything from high tragedy to the lowest burlesque, with occasional concerts and stereopticon shows. One playbill announced an unusual musical program, which mounted to a smashing climax that literally shook the house when, as the musicians swung into "The Battle of Charleston," a spirited overture, a salvo of cannon was fired from a battery kindly loaned for the occasion by a certain Captain Hawley; this was followed by the "Anvil Chorus," which proved something of an anticlimax, even though it was most realistically pounded out on six anvils loaned for the occasion with equal kindness by blacksmith Meyers. The Denver Theater changed hand and names many times until, as the Wigwam, it burned in 1873. During the intervening years there had appeared upon its stage many traveling companies and such noted lecturers as Artemus Ward, George Francis Train, P. T. Barnum, and Cassius Clay.

In the 1870's the remodeled city armory in Denver became the Forrester Opera House, visited by the elder Sothern, Tom Keene, Lawrence Barrett, Edwin Booth, Joe Jefferson, Mrs. Scott Siddons, and other headliners of the day. In 1873, Ed Chase, who in the gold rush days had established the renowned Progressive gambling saloon in Denver, built the Palace Theater on Blake Street. Here, under a genial master of ceremonies, chorus girls sang and danced when not serving drinks to the audience or to those courting Lady Luck in the gambling rooms upstairs; comedians in blackface added a minstrel touch, and a large orchestra furnished music for entertainment and dancing. Conducted with decorum, the Palace was nevertheless loudly denounced by the religious as "a death-trap to young men, a foul den of vice and corruption." But for many years Chase continued to entertain here, with wine, women, song, dance, and the click of poker chips, all local and transient celebrities, including Eugene Field, managing editor and dramatic critic of the Denver *Tribune* for several years.

Between 1868 and 1880 substantial brick and stone opera houses, far superior to the theaters in Denver, were constructed in Aspen, Fairplay, Central City, Leadville, and other mining towns, thanks to the lordly munificence of bonanza kings, although miners paid through the box office their fair share of the expense of bringing in distinguished and often exotic "talent." In its heyday Leadville had a dozen theaters, legitimate and illegitimate. At the head of notorious State Street stood the Grand Central, built in 1878, which proclaimed itself "the largest and most elegantly appointed playhouse west of Chicago." Behind its kerosene footlights was presented lusty and often bawdy entertainment of every kind, from *Around The World in 80 Days,* with "real elephants and camels," to *Nana, The Lovely Blonde,* "four hours of Elegant Pleasures Blended with a Voluptuous Feast without Coarseness." On rare occasions the management gave a ladies' matinee, closing the bar, prohibiting smoking and drinking in the auditorium, extending positive assurance to the hesi-

Cattle, Sheep, Irrigation

PASTURAGE IN THE VALLEYS, EASTERN SLOPE

CATTLE BUYER INSPECTING CATTLE AT TERMINAL MARKET

U. S. Dept. of Agriculture

COLORADO FEEDER LOT SYSTEM, EAST LAKE

HEREFORD CATTLE IN FARR FARMS FEED LOTS, GREELEY

U. S. Dept. of Agriculture

IRRIGATED PASTURE, SHAVANO SOIL CONSERVATION DISTRICT

SPRAYING CATTLE FOR FLY CONTROL

SHEEP ON CRYSTAL RIVER RANCH, NEAR CARBONDALE

INSPECTING SHEEP FOR SKIN DISEASES

BIGHORN SHEEP NEAR SHEEP LAKE, ROCKY MOUNTAIN
NATIONAL PARK

FEDERAL OFFICIAL INSPECTING LIVESTOCK

FEEDING CATTLE IN HOLDING PENS

GRADING A LAMB AT A TERMINAL MARKET

TAPPING THE COLORADO RIVER FOR IRRIGATION OF GRAND VALLEY

IRRIGATION BY 8-INCH SIPHON TUBES, SAGUACHE COUNTY, NEAR CENTER

CONCRETE DITCH LINING CANAL, MORGAN COUNTY

tant that "no feature of the entertainment can be objected to by the most refined society." At this house, just before his death early in 1880, appeared Charles Algernon Sidney Vivian, the English actor who in 1867 had founded the Jolly Corks, subsequently reorganized as the Benevolent Protective Order of Elks.

Most of Leadville's temples to Thespis were "wine theaters" of questionable repute. A few did not charge admission, but patrons were brusquely admonished, "You Must Patronize the Bar"—not that such an argument *ad hominem* was often needed. The Gaiety, the New, the Theatre Comique, and most other houses were concentrated along State Street, which was a bedlam from dark to dawn. Every evening each theater sent its large band into the street to blare for a time and then to parade the town with banners advertising *Shot in the Eye, Who Stole Keyser's Dog, Female Bathers,* and similar attractions. One house offered "30 Acts in Lightning Succession—No Long Waits." Curtains went up at nine, and lights did not go out until the last roistering miner, smelter hand, or Carbonate King had been pushed out the door at four or five in the morning. Tabor and other Carbonate Kings had private boxes in these theaters where the loudest applause was reserved for the personable coryphees who closest approached or actually achieved nudity. Minstrel shows were always popular; Uncle Tom's Cabin was a perennial favorite, and zest was added when "ferocious" bloodhounds were introduced to chase Eliza across the ice; to keep the general excitement within reasonable bounds, programs bore a note that the hounds would not be "allowed to hurt the audience."

Late in 1879 the Tabor Opera House opened in Leadville with the old trouper Jack Langrishe treading the boards in such sure-fire melodramas as *Life and Trials of a Factory Girl, Flower Girls of Paris, Naval Engagements, West Point Cadet, No One's Darling,* and *Ireland As It Was,* "with Mr. and Mrs. Langrishe in the great characters of Ragged Pat and Judy O'Trot." *Othello* was presented early the next year, but it was thought necessary to append *The Artful Dodger,* a "riotous" farce. Later came Oscar Wilde, who appeared in "flossy" white silk neck-handkerchief, silk knee breeches, silk stockings, and patent-leather pumps, all lighted by a huge diamond solitaire, to lecture miners on art, dress, and personal ornament. Upon his return to England, Wilde solemnly told gaping English audiences that a few hours before his appearance at the Tabor Opera House, two desperadoes had been seized, hauled upon the stage, tried for their lives, convicted, and there promptly hanged—which indicates that the tall tales of the miners made a far deeper impression upon Wilde than his pale and bizarre aesthetics upon them. Meantime, Leadville had had its first and last taste of grand opera, and frankly confessed its disappointment. Of the six operas presented by the Emma Abbott English Grand Opera Company, *Fra Diavolo* was most appreciated, but local critics complained that even in this there was little blood and thunder—only one or two corpses were laid out for the theatrical undertakers—and then, too, "the bed scene in the second act wasn't all it was cracked up to be because of Miss Abbott's prudent and prudish rendition of this little episode."

In 1878 the Central City Opera House opened with "a dazzling social display" as "the intelligence of this section of the mountains" sat at the feet of Henry Ward Beecher to hear him lecture on *Hard Times,* a curious choice of subject for that opulent gold camp. For many years the opera house remained one of the leading theaters in the State, and Edwin Booth, Lotta Crabtree, Januscheck, Modjeska, and almost every noted player of the time trod its boards. The earliest Aspen Opera House, while well known in its day, never achieved the renown of its contemporaries in rival camps. By the 1880's Colorado Springs had its Old Opera House, later replaced with the Burns Theater. Pueblo converted a roller skating rink into a theater in 1886, and four years later erected its Grand Opera House.

On transferring his allegiance to Denver, Tabor felt that he could do no less for the State capital than he had for Leadville, and erected the Tabor Grand Opera House, notable for its lavish decorations and furnishings, its large stage some seventy feet wide and fifty feet deep, and its great curtain picturing an ancient Roman city falling to ruin. The Tabor Grand, as it was always known, was popular with strolling players as the only theater west of Chicago with hot running water in the dressing rooms. The building lasted until a few years ago.

Because of the theater's capacity and Denver's merited reputation as an excellent "show town," a large number of the distinguished players of the 1880's and 1890's appeared at the Tabor Grand—among others, Mary Anderson, Maggie Mitchell, Lily Langtry, Richard Mansfield, Helene Modjeska, Sarah Bernhardt, and young Minnie Maddern, later renowned as Mrs. Fiske.

Tabor's playhouse faced serious competition in 1889 with the building of the People's Theater, a castle-like structure later destroyed by fire. The popular theater of the 1890's, however, was the Broadway, a playhouse of ornate East Indian design, which opened auspiciously in the summer of 1890 when the Emma Juch Grand Opera Company, with one hundred and fifty voices, presented *Carmen.* This theater soon supplanted the Tabor and was itself eclipsed in 1913 by the Denham, which later turned to repertory and, like its predecessors, eventually succumbed to motion pictures.

Denver has had several successful stock companies in the past half century. The Manhattan Beach Theater supported a summer company which presented light opera and musical comedies during the early 1900's; for some time Lakeside Park also maintained a theater. The Denham supported a year-round stock company for many years, with Otis Skinner, Tom Powers, Ernest Glendenning, and Gladys George among the principal players. In 1909, under a program initiated by Mayor Robert Speer, the Denver Auditorium became one of the first municipal theaters in the United States; for some years leading road companies presented drama here at prices ranging from 25¢ to $1. In 1936 the Colorado unit of the Federal Theater Project took over an abandoned playhouse in Denver and for three years presented at popular prices a series of plays that included *Night Must Fall, Boy Meets Girl, Animal Kingdom,* and *Blind Alley.*

Denver's most noted playhouse, known in the profession from coast to coast, is the Elitch Gardens Theater, which made its debut in 1890 as a rather minor part of the entertainment at the Gardens and was successfully managed for a quarter of a century by Mary Elitch Long, the beloved "Lady of the Gardens." The house opened with "a select bill of high class vaudeville"; the first drama, *Helene,* was presented in 1894 under the direction of George R. Edison. Other successful plays followed with casts headed by "names" of the day; later, a symphony-orchestra was organized and gave concerts at the theater. During its half century of existence many ruling favorites of the stage have appeared at the theater—among others, Mrs. Fiske, Blanche Bates, Eleanor Robson, David Warfield, and Theodore Roberts; Sarah Bernhardt here presented *Camille* and *La Sorcerie* in a single day, an unprecedented performance for the temperamental French star. Elitch's has served as a training school for such actors of stage and screen as Fredric March, Florence Eldredge (Mrs. Fredric March), Loretta Young, Sylvia Sidney, Harold Lloyd, Helen Mencken, and Edward G. Robinson, as well as Douglas Fairbanks Sr., Ernest Truex, and Antoinette Perry, all Colorado-born.

Other players born in the State include Fred Stone, Edward Elsner, Walker Whiteside, and Ted Shawn, the dancer, as well as Jobyna Howland, known as the original Gibson Girl, and Maude Durbin, Otis Skinner's wife and leading lady. Still other Coloradoans have won a name for themselves in Hollywood. Eugene Walter, author of *Paid In Full* and *The Easiest Way,* and Burns Mantle, who wrote under the *nom de plume* of R. M. Burns, were dramatic critics on Denver newspapers. Bide Dudley, later conducting a syndicated theatrical column in New York City, began his career on the *Denver Post,* as did Gene Fowler, scenarist and novelist.

The little theater movement early found support in the State. Outstanding organizations of this type were the Civic Theater, associated with the University of Denver; the Experimental Theater of the University of Colorado, Boulder; the Little Theater of the Rockies, Greeley; the Mesa College Playmakers, Grand Junction; and the Koshure Club of Colorado College, Colorado Springs. Almost every accredited high school in the State formed its dramatic club. Technical assistance was extended to many of these groups by the adult education unit of the Work Projects Administration, which sponsored the Community Players and the Colorado Playmakers. An unusual Denver undertaking was the Bungalow Theater; its amateur company, organized in 1911 by George S. Swartz exclusively for Shakespearian productions, gave more than 1,000 performances up to its decease in 1931, and is said to have been one of the few theaters in the world to have presented all of Shakespeare.

Undoubtedly the most publicized dramatic event in Colorado is the annual Central City Play Festival, which is held four weeks each summer. In 1932 the historic old Central City Opera House, which had been boarded up for years, was presented to the University of Denver, and has been authentically restored by the Central City Opera House Association with funds raised by the sale of memorial chairs bearing the names of celebrities of early days. When it was announced in 1932 that Lillian Gish would appear in *Camille* under the direction of Robert Edmond Jones, many scoffed, arguing that the town was too isolated to ensure the success of the festival; a few old-timers screamed sacrilege. But even the most sceptical were silenced the next year when *The Merry Widow,* played by Gladys Swarthout, Richard Bonelli, and a fine Metropolitan cast, attracted a record attendance. Later, Walter Huston appeared in *Othello* and Ruth Gordon in *The Doll's House.* Several Gilbert and Sullivan operas have been presented, but by far the most successful production was the fourth, *Central City Nights,* which revived many favorite musical and dramatic acts of the days when the old opera house was in its glory.

The theater remains a viable cultural element in Colorado. Many performances take place in the summer and run all the way from the classics to melodrama. Melodrama is especially popular with tourists who enter heartily into the spirit of plots that involve a handsome lover, a wronged virgin, a designing scoundrel and an irascible father. Symphonic music also finds large, appreciative audiences. The universities and colleges encourage the performing arts. There are symphony orchestras in Denver, Boulder, Fort Collins, Golden, Greeley, and Pueblo. Opera is presented in Denver, Colorado Springs, Aspen, Central City, and Estes Park.

The Colorado Council on the Arts and Humanities is a State organization of recent origin that initiates and supports cultural programs and demonstrates how important these matters are to the people.

The Denver metropolitan area regularly offers a rich program of opera, plays, and music. The most impressive auditorium, unique in the world, is at the Park of the Red Rocks, about 14 miles from downtown Denver, where nature has provided perfect acoustics and thousands convene in the cool mountain air on summer evenings. Period plays are given in the Theatre in the Square of the restored Larimer Square in Denver. In summer there are performances by a stock company at the Elitch Gardens and the Denver Post Opera in Cheesman Park. Shakespeare under the Stars is an annual festival at the University of Colorado in Boulder. The Little Theater of the Rockies is located at Colorado State College in Greeley. The Arvada Festival Playhouse is active near Denver, the Broadmoor International Theater at Colorado Springs. The Sheridan Opera House at Telluride reopened in 1964.

A flourishing branch of entertainment is melodrama, performed usually in the summer. This is another phase of reconstruction of Colorado's pioneer days. Miners with sacks of "dust" were ready to pay for the appearance of famous stars, but melodrama was more relished by the tough prospectors who had no concern with Shakespeare. Melodrama was produced by home talent and every fair-sized town had it. In the repertory Dion Boucicault led all the rest. Grimy miners wept real tears when the stern father turned his erring daughter out of the house, usually during a snowstorm. They hissed the villain not because that was expected—as it is today—but from pentup anger.

Today dozens of companies perform plays that are both historic and original. There has been some effort to write new plays in the old manner, but no writer has become famous in this medium. The Imperial Players perform daily except Sunday in the Gold Bar Room Theater in the Imperial Hotel at Cripple Creek. The *Count of Monte Cristo* has been one of their recent successes. The Diamond Circle is of recent construction adjoining the Strater Hotel in Durango. Its performances include Boucicault's *Foul Play* and George M. Cohan's *The Tavern*. *East Lynne* has been revived in Breckenridge. The Dark Horse Players of Estes Park revived Bret Harte's *M'liss;* they have been succeeded by the Back Room Theater. The Iron Springs Chateau at Manitou Springs has performed *The Drunkard, Billy the Kid,* and *For Whom the Belle Told.* Boucicault's *Poor, Pure and Proud* was one of the plays given at the Colorado Hotel in Glenwood Springs. The Nomad Players appear in Boulder. The Troupe of American College Players performs at the Pine Cone Lodge in Grand Lake. The Arena Players of Colorado Springs have performed *The Actress and the Gambling Man,* which Lillian de la Torre based upon a historic abduction of 1860, and *The Jolly Cathleen Claim.*

BOOKS AND WRITERS

In its free and easy way romantic fiction made use of many solid and substantial works of an earlier day. In his *Arkansas Journal* (1811), which may be described as the first guide-work to the region, Lieutenant Zebulon Pike recorded his explorations up the Arkansas River and into the Colorado Rockies. A straightforward scientific account of Major Long's expedition of 1819–20, written by Dr. Edwin James, naturalist of the party, increased knowledge of the territory and stimulated interest in it. A work subsequently of great use to romancers was John Dunn Hunter's semi-autobiographical *Manners and Customs of Several Indian Tribes Located West of the Mississippi*, published at Philadelphia in 1823, which purportedly chronicled the writer's life among the Indians in the valleys of the Arkansas and the Platte. Far more authentic were the two volumes of letters and notes published in 1841 by George Catlin, painter, one of the few whites who had a good word to say for the Comanche and the Kiowa who roamed the southern Colorado plains. Although filled with errors of time, place, distance, and ethnology, Lieutenant John C. Frémont's journals of 1842 furnished additional raw material for home-loving romancers east of the Alleghenies. Thomas J. Farnham's *Travels in the Great Western Prairies* (1843), George Frederick Ruxton's *Adventures in Mexico and the Rock Mountains* (1847), and Francis Parkman's *The Oregon Trail* (1849) were narrative reconstructions of frontier life and hardships, and all had scenes laid in Colorado.

Real gold was discovered at last, and more reliable reports of the "diggins" were published by a number of visiting journalists and writers. Horace Greeley, editor of the New York *Tribune,* arrived in 1859 on one of the first stagecoaches from Leavenworth, Kansas, and in *An Overland Journey* (1860) painted a lively picture of "the Kansas gold fields," as they were known. With him came Albert D. Richardson, who published his adventures in *Beyond the Mississippi* (1867), and Henry Villard, later a railroad king of the Northwest, whose *Past and Present of the Pikes Peak Gold Region* appeared in 1860. All three works had many readers and are still of interest.

More distinctly Coloradoan were those who for longer or shorter periods lived in the State and wrote about it—notably, Helen Hunt Jackson, with her *Bits of Travel at Home* (1878) and *Nelly's Silver Mine* (1878); and Hamlin Garland, whose ten books on Colorado include *They of the High Trails* (1916). Among many others, this group embraces "Father" John Lewis Dyer, a miner-postman-preacher, whose *Snow-Shoe Itinerant* (1890) is an engaging story of the hardships and indomitable zeal of pioneer preachers; David Cook, chief of police of Denver, later major-general of militia, who dramatically recounted his encounters with frontier desperadoes in *Hands Up: A Pioneer Detective in Colorado,* now a collector's item; and M. H. Foote, wife of a Leadville mining engineer, whose *Led-Horse Claim* was the first novel to use a Colorado boom camp as locale.

Many of the pioneers kept diaries, and in later years many more wrote or dictated reminiscences of their experiences on the frontier.

Scores of interesting and significant personal histories, rich in flavor, simple and unaffected in style, have been preserved in the *Colorado Magazine,* published every two months by the Colorado State Historical Society, and in *The Trail,* which began publication as the *Sons of Colorado* in 1906 and suspended in 1929. Among published volumes of reminiscences are *Olden Times in Colorado* (1916) by C. C. Davis, editor-owner of the Leadville *Chronicle* during the feverish days of the boom; *The Log of a Cowboy* (1903) by Andy Adams, a western classic; and *Bright Yellow Gold* (1935) by Horace Bennett, on whose ranch in the Cripple Creek district dramatically occurred one of the great gold strikes of history. Dealing with a later generation, Anne Ellis's *Life of an Ordinary Woman* (1929) and Agnes Smedley's *Daughter of Earth* (1929), two of the finest American autobiographies, have Colorado backgrounds.

In the related field of biography stand T. F. Dawson's *Life of Edward Oliver Wolcott* (1911); Frank Water's *Midas of the Rockies* (1937), a story of Winfield Scott Stratton and the Cripple Creek gold discoveries; L. C. Gandy's *The Tabors* (1934); and Evalyn Walsh McLean's *Father Struck It Rich* (1936). *Here They Dug the Gold* (1931) by George F. Willison, Colorado-born, is virtually a biography of the early boom camps, a factual and fascinating chronicle of the almost incredible goings-on there and the curious *mores* of the bonanza kings.

Helen Stuart Williams' *Windy Creek* (1899) is a story of the Colorado prairie country; Randall Parrish's *Beth Norvell* (1907) depicts Spanish-American life in southern Colorado; *Second Hoeing* (1923) by Hope W. Sykes, in a vivid delineation of life and labor in the beet fields. Two of Willa Cather's novels have major scenes laid in Colorado—*Lost Lady* (1923) and *Song of the Lark* (1932). Upton Sinclair's *Mountain City* (1930) purports to be a story of Denver, and the journalistic ethics of the local press are pointedly castigated in *The Brass Check* (1919). *Salute to Yesterday* (1937) by Gene Fowler, for many years on the staff of the Denver *Post,* now prominent among Hollywood scenarists, also purports to be a story of Denver; at least, the scene of this quite mad extravaganza is laid there, and many local celebrities of yesterday and today are recognizable in the composite portraits he paints. His *Timberline* (1933) is a sensational story of his former employers, the renowned "Bon" and "Tam" of the Denver *Post.* Other graduates of the Colorado press who have won a wide public as novelists are —Courtney Ryley Cooper, with his *High Country* (1926) and many circus stories, and Clyde Brion Davis with *The Anointed* (1937) and *The Great American Novel* (1938), in both of which are characteristic local scenes.

Leadville appears in Will Irwin's *Columbine Time* (1921) and

Youth Rides West (1925), and also in *The Days of Her Life* (1930) by his brother Wallace, both of whom were born in the town. In 1933 Easley S. Jones published *Colorado: Two Generations,* and Dorothy Gardiner has written of her native State in two novels, *Golden Lady* (1936) and *Snow Water* (1939). Of the many resident writers of the "Wild West" school, the most widely read have been Cy Warman, William McLeod Raine, Robert Ames Bennet, Edwin Legran Sabin, and Clem Yore, none of whom has confined himself wholly to the Colorado scene.

Colorado pioneers have not only inspired but have themselves penned reams of verse—and worse. Arthur Chapman won acclaim with his "Out Where The West Begins," first published in the Denver *Republican.* Of Helen Hunt Jackson's many poems inspired by her life in Colorado Springs, probably the best known is "Cheyenne Mountain." Walt Whitman's "Spirit That Formed This Scene," Nellie Budget Miller's "Drought," and Lillian White Spencer's "Wild-Cat Lodge" are authentic in atmosphere and feeling.

Cy Warman, in addition to his early railroad yarns, wrote many light lyrics and achieved a national reputation when his "Sweet Marie" was set to music. Eugene Field, managing editor of the Denver *Tribune* from 1881 to 1883, penned numerous verses and pertinent paragraphs that appeared in his sprightly column, "Odds and Ends." In *A Little Book of Verse* (1889) he included a number of poems inspired by life in Blue Horizon Camp, as he called the old mining camp of Gold Hill.

Alfred Damon Runyon's two volumes of verse, *Tents of Trouble* (1911) and *Rhymes of the Firing Line* (1912), both in the Robert Service tradition, were written while he was on the staff of the Denver *Post.* Very different in substance and manner are the poems of Jamie Sexton Holme (Mrs. Peter Haynes Holme), collected in *The Star Gatherer* (1926).

RECENT BOOKS BY COLORADO AUTHORS

Colorado honors its authors and keeps record of those lucky enough to be born in the State, and of those who had the good sense to locate there. It has a special place for Thomas Hornsby Ferril, poet and essayist, who was born in Denver and has been associated with State activities, and won national distinction as well. His lines extolling the use of water embellish the Allen True murals in the State Capitol. Ferril is owner of and chief contributor to the *Rocky Mountain Herald* and edited the *Rocky Mountain Herald Reader* in 1966. He won the Robert Frost ($1,000) Award of the Poetry Society of America in 1960, and the Denver Post Award ($10,000) for a verse play, *And Perhaps*

Happiness, in 1958. A collection of his poems appeared in 1952, and *Words for Denver and Other Poems* in 1966.

Colorado also finds satisfaction in the warm, nostalgic glow in Hal Borland's writings, especially *High, Wide and Handsome* and *This Hill, This Valley,* although he now lives in the east. William McLeod Raine was living in Denver when he wrote some of his eighty-two novels. Gene Fowler remains a legendary character in Denver journalism; best known for *Good Night, Sweet Prince,* he drew on his newspaper experiences for *Timberline* and *A Solo in Tom Toms.* Mary Chase won renown and a Pulitzer Prize for writing the play *Harvey.* Andy Adams, whose *Log of a Cowboy* is still considered a capital introduction to a cowboy's life, lived in Colorado Springs and is the subject of a memorial collection in the Pioneer Museum there. A plaque in Pueblo commemorates Damon Runyon as Colorado's Kipling; he once worked on Pueblo and Denver newspapers. Similarly Cripple Creek honors Lowell Thomas, who learned in its schoolrooms how to become an orator and bag Lawrence of Arabia.

Many writers have drawn upon Colorado's past for nostalgic reminiscence and sound research. Dr. Leroy A. Hafen and Ann Woodbury Hafen produced *The Far West and the Rockies* in fifteen volumes (1954–1962). They also have written *Colorado and Its People* and *The Colorado Story,* now in its third edition; *The Colorado Gold Rush,* and, with C. C. Risler, *Western Reminiscences.* Richard Maxwell Pearl, of the faculty of Colorado College, specialist in geology and mineralogy, has written *Colorado Gem Trails and Mineral Guide* and in 1968 published *Seven Keys to the Rocky Mountains.* Robert G. Athearn has written the history of the Denver & Rio Grande Western Railway in *Rebel of the Rockies.* Henry Hough, director of research for the National Congress for American Indians Fund, published *Development of Indian Resources* in 1967. *Water—or Your Life* is an important contribution to conservation by Arthur Carhart, who has written many articles on landscape design, city planning, and recreation, and a number of novels.

While attention here is focussed on books about Colorado, there is a large amount of scholarly writing on matters not associated with the State by members of the faculties of Colorado colleges, as well as a storehouse of theses by candidates for higher degrees. For instance, Inez Hunt won the $500 Prize Award of the National League of American Penwomen for *Lightning in His Hand,* a biography of Nicola Tesla, written with the cooperation of Wanetta Draper. Margaret Cobb Shipley in 1966 published *Bright Future,* a history of the College of Engineering of the University of Colorado, written with Siegfried Mandel. Biographers seek their subjects everywhere. Etta Degering published *Gallandet, Friend of the Deaf,* in 1964 and *Christopher Jones, Captain of the Mayflower,* in 1965. Aylesa Forsee has written about Agassiz, Frank Lloyd Wright, and Artur Rubenstein; her *King of the Keyboard* came in 1969. Anne Spence Warner is the author of *Narcissa Whitman.*

Ralph Moody enriched Colorado lore by writing *Little Britches;* the name is now applied to a junior rodeo. His *Home Ranch* is based on personal experiences. Denver's lurid past provided Forbes Parkhill with themes for *The Wildest of the West.* Historic hotels are the basis for *No More Than Five in a Bed,* by Sandra Dallas, formerly on the staff of the *Denver Post.* Many books have been written about Col. William F. Cody, Buffalo Bill; one of the most recent is *Buffalo Bill and His Horse,* by Agnes Wright Spring. Louise Arp Ward, a librarian, wrote *High Country Names* with Elinor Eppich Kingery. A woman's memories of mining camps are given in *The Life of an Ordinary Woman,* by Anne Ellis, who also wrote *Plain Anne Ellis* and *Sunshine Preferred.* Marian Castle has used the mining days in Leadville in *Roxana,* and the 1890's in Creede, Ouray, and Denver in *Silver Arrow.* Marshall Sprague came to Denver for the climate and began writing about the past: *Massacre, the Tragedy at White River,* and *A Gallery of Dudes* are among his books. Allan Vaughan Elston, author of *Stage Road to Denver, Timberline Bonanza,* and other westerns lived on a ranch in his boyhood.

Alan Swallow is gratefully remembered in Colorado for his contributions as a "platten press publisher" of Americana and his Sage magazine and books. His collection of poetry is *The Remembered Land and the Nameless Sight, Poems, 1937–1956.* Swallow died on Thanksgiving Day, 1966, aged 51. There is a memoir in *Journal of the West* for July, 1969. William J. Baxter, columnist and humorist, founder of *Rocky Mountain Life* magazine, wrote *The Wayward West.*

Other historic subjects have been used by Maurice Frink, in *Fort Defiance and the Navajo Indians,* and Muriel Sibell in *The Bonanza Trail.* Her *Stampede to Timberline* was chosen by the committee of wives of United States Congressmen to be included in books for General Eisenhower's Gettysburg home. Ruth M. Underhill has written *Papago Indian Religion,* and more recently *Red Man's Religion.* Dorothy Gardner, granddaughter of a '59-er, has made the clash of settlers and Indians at Sand Creek the subject for *The Great Betrayal.* Walter Gann took another historic phase in *Trail of the Longhorns.* But one book not based on history no doubt stimulates a lively interest; it is Helen Ferril's *The Indoor Bird Watchers Manual,* written with Anne Folson in 1951.

Ghost towns have alerted a number of authors. Robert L. Brown opens new roads in *Jeep Trails to Colorado Ghost Towns;* Perry Eckhart is the author of *A Guide to the Colorado Ghost Towns and Mining Camps.* Ghost towns have a place in the writings of Caroline D. Bancroft. She wrote *The Unsinkable Mrs. Brown* in 1963, and in 1966

Mary Bennett Wills produced *The Unsinkable Molly Brown Cookbook*. Maurice Frink, former director of the State Historical Society of Colorado, has described the western cattle ranges in *When Grass Was King*. His *Photographer on an Army Mule* deals with life at Fort Keogh in the 1880's–1890's, when Christian Barthelmess photographed soldiers and Indians there.

Skiing is a new topic for Colorado writers, and although many articles about it are constantly appearing, little is available in books. *Ski Fever* and *Ski Racing* are recent publications by Curtis W. Casewit, who wrote *Mountaineering Handbook* with Dick Pownall in 1968. The late ski star, Buddy Werner, is remembered in *I Never Look Back*, by John R. Burroughs, who writes about his Steamboat Springs boyhood in *Headfirst in the Pickle Barrel*, and whose book about Brown's Park, Colorado, *Where the Old West Stayed Young*, won a Western Heritage Award.

Jesse Wendell Vaughn, a lawyer, is a historian of Indian wars and has written *The Reynolds Campaign on Powder River*, *The Battle of Platte Bridge*, and *Indian Fights*. Frank Waters, who wrote *The Colorado* for the Rivers of America series has told the story of Winfield Scott Stratton and Cripple Creek in *Midas of the Rockies;* he grew up in Cripple Creek. Clem Yore has drawn on the old mining camps for his lively westerns, *Ranger Bill, Trigger Justice, The Two-Gun Kid,* and *The Six-Gun Code*. John Edward Williams found the lore of the buffalo hunters useful for writing *Butcher's Crossing*.

Sandra Dallas has written *Gold and Gothic, the Story of Larimer Square*. Two books about Denver are *Denver in Slices,* by Louise Arp Ward, and *Denver's History Mansions,* by E. E. Kohl. Both are issued by Sage Press.

PART II

The Urban Scene

Boulder

Air Services: Municipal Airport, 2 *m.* northeast of city, for charter and private planes. Scheduled planes arrive at Stapleton International Airport, Denver; bus to Stapleton, 30 *m.,* $2.50.
Buses: Denver-Boulder Bus Co., 10 to 15 scheduled trips to Denver daily, 45 min., one way $1.10; round trip. $2. Depot, 1765 14th St.
Highways: Denver-Boulder Turnpike, US 36. Also US 36 and State 7 to Estes Park. State 119 to Roosevelt National Forest. Others, State 19, 93.
Railroads: Colorado & Southern, 2400 31st St., two passenger trains daily.

Information and Accommodations: Boulder Chamber of Commerce, Boulderado Hotel. *Boulder Daily Camera,* evenings, and Sunday a.m. Motels within easy access of Denver-Boulder Turnpike and other major highways. Boulder has 70 churches, 2 public hospitals besides the University Health Center.

Recreation: Boulder has 24 city and 4 mountain parks, 5,140 acres (get map at Chamber of Commerce). There are 3 18-hole and one 9-hole golf courses; of which Municipal Course is 2½ *m.* east on Arapahoe. ($1.50 week days, $2 Sundays). Also 3 private clubs. Swimming at Scott Carpenter Pool, 30th and Arapahoe, and Spruce Pool, 31st and Spruce. Band concerts in Central Park, summer evenings. Horseback riding, shuffleboard, softball, tennis, square dancing available. Kids fishing pool. Canyon Blvd., west of 9th. Fishing, Boulder Reservoir, 6 *m.* northeast, license $6. Circle trips (drives) in scenic mountain area are described on folder available at Chamber of Commerce. Arrange by phone for visits to Sommers-Bausch Observatory, National Bureau of Standards Environmental Sciences laboratory and National Center for Atmospheric Research.

Special Events: Independence Day celebration in University Stadium. Pow Wow Radio & Horse Show, last week in July. Annual hike to Arapahoe Glacier second Sunday in August.

BOULDER (5,430 alt., 56,000 pop. 1968, est., up from 37,718, 1960) fifth largest city, county seat, and seat of the University of Colorado, lies in a verdant basin under Flagstaff Mountain and near the Flatirons, 30 *m.* west of Denver on the Denver-Boulder Turnpike, opened 1952. Arapahoe Glacier, on the slope of the Continental Divide, provides its never-failing water supply, and Boulder Creek comes tumbling down the mountain-side past the University campus. The city covers 7,500 acres. Its remarkable business and industrial growth was stimulated by the coming of a number of scientific laboratories and research agencies, started in 1950 when the National Bureau of Standards, which employs more than 1,400, received a site of 200 acres donated by citizens. Others are Dow Chemical Co. (atomic energy research); Beech Aircraft Corp. (cryogenics research); Ball Bros. Research Corp. (solar observation satellites), and laboratories associated with the University.
The expanding prosperity has led to new municipal and business con-

struction, including a new Public Library, at 9th and Canyon Blvd., a new wing on the Municipal Bldg., new residential groups under Methodist and Presbyterian sponsorship, and the 40-acre Crossroads Shopping Center. Boulder is popular as a convention city, especially for scientific organizations, while the University furnishes the basis for numerous dramatic and musical programs as well as intercollegiate sports. The Philharmonic Symphony Orchestra is a well-supported organization.

When Captain Thomas Aikens, one of a party of Argonauts moving up the South Platte River in the fall of 1858, climbed the wall of old Fort St. Vrain and looked westward through a telescope, he saw "that the mountains looked right for gold, and the valleys looked rich for grazing." This prompted him to lead a small party from the main emigrant train and to settle on the site of Boulder. Arapaho Indians were encamped near by, and Chief Left Hand asked Captain Aikens if he remembered when the stars fell. When told it was in 1832, the chief said, "That is right, it was that year white men first came." Pointing to Donati's comet in the sky, Left Hand asked, so it is said, "Do you know what that star with the tail means? The tail points back to when the stars fell as thick as the tears of our women shall fall when you come to drive us away."

Left Hand then commanded the whites to leave within three days, and when they did not, came alone to the encampment and related a dream, saying that he had seen Boulder Creek flooded, the Indians engulfed, and the whites saved. The Indians did not immediately give up the site, remaining in the vicinity for two years, but rarely gave more trouble than hooking bacon slices from prospectors' frying pans with the end of their ramrods.

During the open winter of 1858–59, the settlers worked in their shirtsleeves, building cabins, hunting and fishing, laying out the new town, and even cutting hay. Game was so plentiful that the Wellman boys, three brothers from Pennsylvania, shot elk from the door of their cabin. The town was named Boulder City for the numerous large stones in the vicinity, and a town company was formed early in 1859; G. W. Gregg and T. W. Fisher were employed to plat the town, which hoped to become an important gold center.

The Wellman brothers, Henry, Luther, and Sylvanus, began to plow the day after their arrival in August 1859. They sowed an acre of turnips, which had grown to the size of a half dollar when George Nichols came into their cabin while they were eating. "Boys," said he, "did you ever see it rain grasshoppers?" And rain grasshoppers it did; they struck the end of the cabin and fell a foot deep on the ground. The turnips were "suddenly devoured . . . and so went the first crop ever planted in Boulder County."

Until late in 1859, according to a local historian, "there was not a foot of sawed lumber, nor a square of glass, nor a pound of nails in the town. The 70 log-houses were built along Pearl Street and around the public square, having doors and roofs of pine splints, with dirt floors. Bill Barney's hall had the first whip-sawed board floor, and this was duly dedicated by a dance . . . on Christmas Eve. There were 200 men in attendance, and all the ladies of the city, 17 in number." In want of stores, goods were sold from wagons.

Irrigation ditches were dug in 1859 and opened the following year, providing the persistent Wellman brothers with a fine crop of wheat, and Marinus Smith and William G. Pell with excellent vegetables. Successful irrigation was thus established in this area, and as late as 1910 old irrigation ditches still ran through the city.

Jonathan Tourtellote and Fred Squires came from New England in 1860, with their wives, Maria and Miranda, twin sisters. The men kept store in the front part of a double log house, selling groceries and mining supplies, while the back part became a hotel, kept by the women, who cut willows and made brooms for sweeping the dirt floor. They delighted in the sight of antelope coming down to the creek to drink, served meals on two boards brought from New England, and covered household goods with horse blankets when it rained through the splint roof. The first schoolhouse in Colorado was erected here this year; a post office was established, and the first frame house built.

The optimistic town founders held their lots for exorbitant prices, and when gold camps to the westward quickly declined, Boulder suffered likewise. But early mining days are still celebrated at the annual Pay Dirt Pow-Wow, with its rock-drilling contests, burro races, miners' dances, and Gold Camp Carnival.

The 1860's were lean years for Boulder City. Many discouraged people departed, and those who remained were sometimes reduced to a diet of parched corn. Some financial relief came in the winter of 1861–62 when Governor Gilpin sent agents here to buy horses and arms for the army. Indian uprisings in 1864 threw Boulder City into a panic; defense trenches were begun but abandoned after the scare had subsided. Martial law was proclaimed in 1865 when Indians blocked the South Platte road; Boulder City "raised, mounted, and blanketed" a company of volunteers to go against the Indians. The Boulder Valley and Central City Wagon Road, a toll enterprise, started in 1865, was finished two years later.

The prospect of obtaining a railroad and a university brought Boulder City to life in the 1870's. On its incorporation as a town in 1871 an immigration society was organized. The first schoolhouse was replaced with a more commodious structure in 1872. The following year two railroads reached the town, the Colorado Central and the Denver & Boulder Valley, both now part of the Burlington System. The Boulder County Industrial Association was organized in 1874 to sponsor county fairs, and the same year the legislature appropriated funds to build the University of Colorado. The Phoenix Hook and Ladder Company, with 50 red-shirted volunteer firemen, was formed in 1875, at which time the cornerstone of the first university building was "laid with Masonic ceremony." A brewery was established by Frank Weisenhorn and Charles Voegtle. Boulder High School, established in 1876, graduated the first high school class in Colorado. Boulder City was reincorporated and enlarged in 1878; it was several years before the "City" in its name was dropped "as a ludicrous superfluity." In 1878 the first freshman class, of twelve members, was enrolled at the university. From a few hundred in 1870 the population had increased to 3,060 by 1880.

POINTS OF INTEREST

The UNIVERSITY OF COLORADO is located on the southern edge of Boulder and consists of 135 buildings on 587 acres. It dates its operations from 1876; the legislature, which authorized it in 1861, failed to provide funds at that time. It has one of the most consistently attractive architectural styles in America, designed by Charles Zeller Klauder of Philadelphia, who adopted a modification of Italian rural structure with the use of the rose-tinted Colorado sandstone. Unsymmetrical in line, with red tile roofs sloping at various heights and angles, the buildings are of local sandstone taken from a quarry owned by the university. Well suited for construction, the sandstone splits easily into large sheets not more than five inches thick and has a rich variety of tone and color, which ranges from yellow to reddish-purple.

The University of Colorado was projected in 1861 as a mining school. Goldfield and neighboring mining camps were more interested in the plan than Boulder. Residents of Golden (see Tour 7A) were similarly ambitious and moved expeditiously toward their goal. The legislature created the University of Colorado on November 7, 1861, designating Boulder as its seat, and at the same time Golden was given the Colorado School of Mines. For more than ten years the university existed only on paper. In 1870 a board of trustees was named; the next year a site was donated to the State by Marinus G. Smith, George A. Andrews, and Anthony Arnott, pioneer residents. The legislature failed to provide funds to operate the university until 1874, when $15,000 was appropriated, but with the proviso that it had to be matched by the citizens of Boulder. Captain David Nichols, member of the legislature, rode all night to bring this news from Denver, and the money was forthwith subscribed.

In authorizing Colorado to take steps toward statehood in 1875, the Congress granted the university 72 sections of land. The cornerstone of Old Main, the first building, was laid September 20, 1875; classes met in it two years later. As none of the 44 students could meet the entrance requirements established by President Joseph A. Sewall, the university established a preparatory course. The first class of seven was graduated from the university in 1883.

The University has thirteen schools and colleges in the arts and sciences, one of which, the School of Dentistry, will not open until 1972. Medicine and nursing are located at the University Medical Center in Denver, where dentistry also will be taught (see Denver). In the 1968 year the University enrolled 26,250; of this total 7,007 were studying at the Denver Center for General Studies, and 2,318 at the Colorado Springs Center.

Building and expansion of facilities continue unabated at the main campus and elsewhere. In recent years the Engineering Center, with ten acres under one roof, and the first high-rise residence halls, reaching fifteen stories, have been completed. New buildings under construction in 1968–1969 were a School of Business Bldg., a Department of Psychology Bldg., and a Department of Physics Bldg., tradition, beloved of alumni, clings to older halls such as Old Main (1877), Macky Auditorium (1911), which seats 2,600, and the Simon Guggenheim Law Building, which exemplify older periods of architecture.

The NORLIN LIBRARY has one of the most attractive sites on the Boulder Campus. A recent inventory showed it had 805,959 volumes, exclusive of documents, records and microfilms. The library has built up strong sections of western Americana. In 1939 the University Museum and the Fine Arts Gallery moved into the Henderson Building.

A laboratory for upper air and space physics research is a new addition to the campus buildings, provided by the National Aeronautics & Space Administration. A separate building, the NUCLEAR PHYSICS LABORATORY houses the 30-million-electron-volt cyclotron, built by the staff with the financial support of the Atomic Energy Commission and placed in commission in 1962. Instruments for nuclear spectroscopy are also located here. The SOMMERS-BAUSCH OBSERVATORY, a 10½ inch refracting telescope donated by Bausch & Lomb Co. and Mrs. Elmer E. Sommers, is also used for high altitude observation at Climax.

The INSTITUTE OF ARCTIC AND ALPINE RESEARCH (INSTAAR) estab., 1951, hq in the Armory Bldg., was devoted to the ecology of the Colorado Rockies until 1967, when research was expanded to include dendrochronology, geomorphology, hydrology, permafrost, palynology. The foundation for a quarterly publication, *Journal of Arctic and Alpine Research,* was established. The major field activity is at the MOUNTAIN RESEARCH STATION, 9,600 ft. up on the Front Range, 25 *m.* west. A winterized laboratory was built in 1963 with the help of the National Science Foundation. Environmental measurement goes on all year at stations, the highest of which is on top of the Niwot Ridge, 12,300 ft. alt.

The NATIONAL CENTER FOR ATMOSPHERIC RESEARCH, estab. 1960, sponsored by the National Science Foundation, is a nonprofit corporation in which the University joins 24 other American universities. It uses the facilities of the High Altitude Observatory, adjacent to the Sommers-Bausch Observatory on the campus, and a laboratory on Table Mesa Drive in southwest Boulder.

The Federal Government has a large stake in scientific work asssociated with the University. The National Bureau of Standards has a Radio Standards Laboratory and a Cryogenics Division; the Environmental Science Services Admin. has six laboratories in Boulder, for Space Disturbance, Aeronomy, Wave Propagation, Atmospheric Physics and Chemistry, Telecommunication Sciences, and Earth Sciences. In a new building the Joint Institute for Laboratory Astrophysics, doing research in stellar atmospheres and spectroscopy, is supported by the National Bureau of Standards.

Old Main, once the center of the campus, is a three-story red brick building completed in 1877, the oldest of the university structures. During construction it threatened to collapse of its own weight, and "five tons of iron bolts, nuts, anchors, etc.," were needed before it was pronounced safe. A rope to the bell in the south tower is pulled joyously by freshmen to celebrate athletic victories.

White water lilies bloom throughout the summer on University Lake, to the north, reaching their greatest beauty during June and July.

Macky Auditorium, northeast of Old Main, a Collegiate Gothic edifice of light-colored sandstone, crowned with twin towers, was completed in 1911 and seats 2,600. Recitals on the four-manual Austin organ are given here during the summer school quarter. The auditorium was financed largely through bequests of Andrew J. Macky, Boulder banker.

East of the Field House is Norlin Stadium, seating 26,000, constructed in 1930 in a natural bowl and named for Dr. George Norlin, president of the university, 1918–1939.

CHAUTAUQUA PARK, entrance 11th and Baseline Sts., is the seat of the Colorado Chautauqua, founded in 1898 by a group of Texas vacationists. Park buildings include an auditorium, dining hall, community house, and 100 cottages, many for rent during the season. Entertainment consists of moving pictures, nature talks, travelogues, plays, lectures, exhibitions of magic, and concerts; automobile caravans are arranged to points of interest near Boulder.

The BOULDER COUNTY COURTHOUSE, Pearl and 10th Sts., designed by Glenn H. Huntington of Boulder and completed in 1934, is strikingly modernistic in line. The building is constructed of stone taken from the approaches of an abandoned railway bridge west of Boulder.

SCOTT CARPENTER PARK, named for the famous astronaut from Boulder, is one of the city's popular recreation areas, with an 18-hole grass-green golf course, fishing, boating, water skiing, horseback riding, and square dancing.

POINTS OF INTEREST IN ENVIRONS

Boulder Canyon, 1.3 *m.;* Roosevelt National Forest, 6.1 *m.;* Flagstaff Mountain, 7.2 *m.;* Gold Hill and Sunshine, early gold camps, 12.5 *m.;* Arapahoe Glacier, 33 *m.* (*see Tour 6*).

Colorado Springs

Air Services: Braniff, Continental, and Frontier Airlines, daily scheduled flights at city-owned Peterson Field, off US 24. There are 3 runways, 7,875 ft., 8,512 ft., 11,020 ft., with 1,000 ft. overruns. Commercial operators have light aircraft for sale and charter, air taxi service, flight instruction. Terminal Building, completed 1966, 21,000 ft., complete facilities with FAA control tower and U. S. Weather Bureau station.
Bus Lines: Continental Trailways, depot 202 E. Pikes Peak Ave., interstate buses via Denver, Pueblo and U. S. Air Force Academy; Greyhound Lines, depot, 227 E. Pikes Peak Ave., interstate services. Colorado Springs Coach Co. for metropolitan area.
Highways: Interstate 25 (Monument Valley Parkway), combining US 85, US 87, and State 1, is the major north-south route to Denver, 69 *m.*, and Pueblo, 43 *m.* US 24 to the east connects with Interstate 70. State 94 connects with north-south State 71. State 115 south through Fort Carson connects with US 50 near Florence. Other routes: State 4, 11, 27, 29, 38, 83, 94, 122.
Railroads: Freight service via the Rock Island, Denver & Rio Grande Western, Santa Fe, and Colorado & Southern (Burlington). Scenic routes are Pikes Peak Cog Railway, Mt. Manitou Incline, and miniature cog line from Broadmoor Hotel to Cheyenne Mountain Zoological Park.

Climate: The U. S. Weather Bureau in 1968 reported the 36-year average temperature as mean, 48.9°, maximum, 62.6°, minimum, 35.1°, and annual precipitation, 14.68 in. In 1967 temperatures were identical and only precipitation was greater, 19.28 in. Snowfall for 1967 was 31.7 in. compared with an average of 37.9 in. Humidity in 1967 averaged 37% at 11 a.m. and 39% at 5 p.m.

Information: Colorado Springs Chamber of Commerce, Holly Sugar Building, publishes an annual Statistical Digest. Commercial radio and television stations have all important channels; Colorado College operates an educational FM project. The *Free Press,* is issued daily and Sunday, 103 W. Colorado Ave.; the *Gazette-Telegraph,* evenings, Monday-Friday, mornings, Saturday-Sunday, 30 S. Prospect Ave. There are two legal publications, *Daily Transcript,* 22 N. Sierra Madre, and *Daily Record,* 1010 Sun Drive. Also 5 weeklies: *Labor News, Pike's Peak Journal* (Manitou Springs), *Security Advertiser & Fountain Valley News, Black Forest News* and *Regionnaire.*
Accommodations: Colorado Springs and environs are fully equipped with every form of hostelry, from luxury hotels to motels, lodges, cabins, trailer parks, and campgrounds. Restaurants likewise range all the way from those with a special cuisine to diners and chuck wagons. Besides consulting the standard travel guides visitors will find useful the annual travel directory, *Colorado,* prepared by Colorado Visitors Bureau, 225 W. Colfax Ave., Denver, Colo., 80202.

Recreation: Fishing is possible the year around except in a few restricted areas; consult regulations. Fees: non-resident 10-day license, $5, season, $10; resident, $5. *Hunting:* For small and big game hunting see regulations. Fees: non-resident first deer license, $50; second $10; elk, $75; bear, $25; small game and birds, $15. For resident, first deer license, $10, second $7.50. Annual Sportsman's License combining the privileges, non-resident, $135; resident, $30.

Skiing: There are more than 30 developed ski areas with over 120 lifts operating usually from Thanksgiving Day to April or May depending on snow. Pikes Peak Ski Area is open weekends, and Ski Broadmoor, on Cheyenne Mountain, every day except Monday. The Colorado Ski Information Center, 225 W. Colfax Ave., Denver, reports on snow conditions all hours during the season—phone 303–222–0671.

Sports and Games: There are 11 baseball diamonds and nightly games except Saturday and Sunday at Monument Valley Park; 14 softball diamonds and nightly games at Memorial Fields, 1300 East Pikes Peak Ave. Also 10 riding academies, 33 *m.* of park bridle paths and hiking trails; 7 bowling alleys with 155 lanes; 10 golf courses, 189 holes, in city and environs; 5 miniature golf courses, 2 driving ranges, 4 outdoor skating rinks. Municipal tennis courts for day and night playing at Monument Valley Park and Boulder Park; daytime courts at Thorndale Park, Bonney Park, and Unitah St.-Monument Creek Bridge. For shuffleboard 16 lighted courts are at Acacia Park. Swimming at Municipal outdoor Pool, Monument Valley Park and Prospect Lake, June-September; heated pool at Green Mountain Falls. Inside pools at Palmer, Wasson and Billy Mitchell High Schools open to public. Square Dancing Wednesday eve in Bancroft Park and Thursday eve in Acacia Park. Chuck Wagon dinners are served by the Jaycees in the Garden of the Gods Monday through Friday, approx. June 20 to Labor Day, and at Flying W Ranch, 2 *m.* north of the Garden, same time.

Special Events: Colorado Springs Kennel Club show, Ft. Carson Field House, June. Rock climbing exercises, Fort Carson Leadership Training School, bi-weekly, June-August. Pikes Peak Quarter Horse Show, Penrose Stadium, June. Pikes Peak Automobile Hill Climb, June 30. Broadmoor International Theater at International Center, July-August. Tennis Tournaments: Broadmoor Hotel, July 15–20; Colorado Springs Open, Monument Valley Park, July; Pikes Peak Open, August. Golf Tournaments: Broadmoor Women's Invitational, August; USGA National Amateur, at Broadmoor, August; Broadmoor Men's Invitational, July–August; Pikes Peak Invitational, 3d week in July; World Senior Golf Championship, August. Francis I. H. Brown International Team Matches, August. Pikes Peak or Bust Rodeo, Penrose Stadium, August. Colorado Junior Championship Rodeo, August. Greyhound racing at Rocky Mountain Kennel Club, Nevada Ave., August–October. Thoroughbred and Quarter Horse Racing, Pikes Peak Meadows, 20 *m.* south on Interstate 25, May-August. International Hockey, Broadmoor World Arena, December.

COLORADO SPRINGS (6,012 alt., 70,194 pop., 1960; 118,500,
1968 est.) seat of El Paso County (220,000 pop. est.), occupies a site of spectacular eminence below Pikes Peak (14,110 alt.) 69 *m.* south of Denver on Interstate 25. Although its industrial curve is steadily rising, it is nationally renowned for its salubrious climate, its access to scenic wonders, its opportunities for luxurious and plain living, and—quite recently—for its nearness to vital links in the U. S. military establishment. It is recorded locally that more than 2,500,000 visitors make the city their destination annually, that it comfortably accommodates more than one national convention a day, and that tourists, beribboned delegates, and sportsmen with fishing and hunting gear, annually drop more than $66,000,000 into its coffers, this being the 1966 figure. As of January 1, 1968, El Paso County, with a population of approx. 220,000, counted a labor force of 56,440, and only 1,610 unemployed, while the military personnel at Fort Carson, Ent Air Force Base, and the U. S. Air Force Academy, 10 *m.* north of the city, reached 33,266.

Although visitors who come to Colorado Springs for recreation stay only temporarily, the city annually adds a substantial number of permanent residents, which accounts for the continuing housing construction. In 1967 alone 3,881 new units were added, and 63 per cent of the families owned their own homes. Some mobility among householders is caused by the shifting military personnel, who usually stay four years. Seasonal residents have available at least 3,500 units in 150 motels that serve the community, while the eleven major hotels, led by the Broadmoor and the new Antlers Plaza, opened March 20, 1967, have 1,244 rooms.

Studies of the economy disclose a steady rise in retail sales, with food leading the categories, automotives second. A little over 30 per cent of the incomes are in the $5,000 to $8,000 bracket, with 16 per cent earning $10,000 and over.

The climatic conditions have drawn healthseekers to this area for generations. The International Typographical Union opened its home here in 1892, with special attention to sufferers from pulmonary diseases. There are six major hospitals with 855 beds for public use, besides centers for rehabilitation of crippled children, and treatment for cerebral palsy and mental disability. More than 500 beds are available in hospitals for military personnel.

The excellent highway system makes outlying parts easily accessible from the center of the city. This is located in the vicinity of Nevada and Pikes Peak Avenues, where the City Hall, the Post Office, the Library, the Auditorium, and the Antlers Plaza are to be found. Nevada Avenue is the fine north-south axis used by US 85 and US 87, but these highways and Interstate 25 also use the modern Monument Valley Parkway, which runs west of Fountain Creek and Monument Creek, into which Fountain flows. US 24 enters from the east on Lincoln Memorial Highway and departs over Midland Expressway to Manitou Springs and the Garden of the Gods.

Colorado City, known as "Old Town," and as West Colorado Springs, a narrow strip extending two miles along Fountain Creek, was founded as El Dorado City in 1859 by a party of gold hunters from Kansas. On the same site the year before the town of El Paso (Sp. the pass) had been laid out by other Kansas prospectors because it stood on an Indian trail through Ute Pass, offering access to the mines of South Park. The venture failed, and El Dorado City was renamed Colorado City. By 1861 more than 300 cabins had been erected along the river.

Very different was the founding and development of Colorado Springs proper. Its founders planned a community to attract and hold people of means and social standing, a citizenry of "good moral character and strict temperance habits." They made it clear that manufacturing establishments were not desired. Mills, smelters, saloons, and gambling houses were to be confined to boisterous Colorado City. General William J. Palmer, major promoter of the Denver & Rio Grande Railroad, who made and unmade towns by directing where tracks should be laid, was impressed with this site so near the mountains and the foothill canyons. His company purchased 10,000 acres for $10,000, and on

July 31, 1871, the first stake was driven at what is now the southeast corner of Pikes Peak and Cascade Avenues. Three months later the tracks of the Denver & Rio Grande Railroad, the first narrow-gauge line in the State, reached the prospective town from Denver.

During its first years it was known as Fountain Colony for its position on Fountain Creek; later, it was renamed Colorado Springs for the mineral springs at the near-by village of Manitou. Broad thoroughfares were laid out; many of those running north and south were named for mountain ranges, and principal cross streets were given Indian, French, and Spanish names. Lots were set aside for schools and churches; an extensive park system was projected; cash and twenty acres of land were donated for the founding of Colorado College. Written into all deeds was a clause prohibiting the manufacture or sale of intoxicating liquors on the premises, a restriction enforced until repeal of prohibition in 1933.

The first building served as Palmer's office, railroad station, and post office. Foundations of the Colorado Springs Hotel were laid in 1871. Thousands of cottonwoods were planted along streets and prospective parks; water from an irrigation canal ran in ditches along the streets; by the end of 1871 more than 150 structures had been built, many of them knockdown portable houses shipped from Chicago and put together on the ground within a few hours. A pioneer two-story business building was used as schoolhouse, courtroom, lecture hall, and church. A short-lived speakeasy of the day was equipped with a "Spiritual Wheel," a revolving contrivance upon which a customer placed a two-bit piece and received a glass of liquor from the barkeeper concealed behind a partition.

Within a year a passable road had been constructed to the springs at Manitou. Isabella A. Bird, British journalist, traveled over it that fall: "After fording a creek, I came upon a decayed looking cluster of houses bearing the arrogant name of Colorado City, and a few miles farther on I saw the bleak scattered houses of the ambitious watering-place of Colorado Springs. . . . A queer, embryo-looking place it is, out on the bare plains, yet rising and likely to rise, with some big hotels much resorted to. . . . I dismounted, put on a long skirt, and rode sidewise, though the settlement scarcely looked like a place where any deference to prejudices was necessary." The costume, which the traveler referred to as a "lady's mountain dress," consisted of a "half-fitting jacket, a skirt reaching to the ankles, and full Turkish trousers gathered with frills falling over the boots."

From the beginning the railroad publicized the region as a scenic wonderland and health resort. Pikes Peak was already a national landmark, and within a short time the Garden of the Gods, Seven Falls, Cheyenne Mountain, and the springs at Manitou were almost equally well known. Physicians extolled the dry air and bright sunshine, and several tubercular sanatoriums were established. The town grew rapidly. The irrigation ditches bordering every street were "in summer embossed with flowers. Ditch water was carried in tubs . . . for domestic purposes, and clear cold drinking water was peddled about the streets for twenty-five cents per barrel. . . . Cows wandered through the streets.

. . . Vegetables grew chiefly in cans, and stream-beds and cañons glittered with these omnipresent signs of civilization." Fresh meat was supplied to the local market by "Antelope Jim" Hamlin.

In winter, citizens had their Fortnightly clubs and afternoon teas, according to a contemporary, "with perhaps a Christmas ball at Glen Eyrie, and dances in some store building, where coffee and cakes were served on stoneware, and dim kerosene lamps lighted the charming Eastern costumes of the ladies. . . . The fashionable afternoon promenade was to the post office. . . . In summer, society played croquet on bare places of hard ground (grass was too expensive a luxury to be trodden under foot) . . . camped in the mountains, or took overland excursions in the parks, and all the year round every one rode or drove in a perpetual picnic under the blue, sunlit sky."

Droughts on the eastern plains and the grasshopper plagues of 1873–74 did not materially affect the community. The greatest excitement of the period was a threatened uprising of the Arapaho; all able-bodied citizens were called out, but it was a short-lived affair, marking the end of Indian troubles in the region. By 1873, when the town had supplanted Colorado City as the county seat, it was finding favor with artists and writers, some of whom made their homes here—among others, Helen Hunt Jackson, author of *Ramona*.

During the late 1870's many young Englishmen came to settle, and the town was often referred to as "Little Lunnon," a name perpetuated today in society columns. The newcomers introduced golf, cricket, polo, and fox hunting. As foxes were not often to be found, a piece of meat at the end of a rope provided a "scent" for the hounds to follow. Occasionally a coyote blundered upon the scene, and the pack went baying after the poor animal as he fled in terror, unaccustomed as he was to strange English ways.

The opening of the Antlers Hotel in 1882 was a gala occasion, but the new opera house got off to a poor start with *Camille*—a dismal choice, for a large proportion of the audience were health seekers. The Colorado Midland Railroad pushed westward from the city in 1885 to tap several prosperous silver camps; Colorado Springs was chosen as the western terminal of the Chicago, Rock Island & Pacific Railway in 1889. A cog railroad built to the summit of Pikes Peak in 1890 and the construction of street car lines to Manitou Springs brought many visitors. The silver panic in the 1890's was followed by rich gold strikes at Cripple Creek (*see Tour 5B*), just over the mountains to the west, discoveries that played an important part in the affairs of Colorado Springs and of Colorado City, which stirred with new life. This all-but-deserted town became a lively industrial center; several ore-reduction mills and railroad shops were built; mill workers, hard-rock miners in for supplies and amusement, promoters, gamblers, and ladies of the evening thronged to the streets. Almost every corner was occupied by a saloon, and the south side of Colorado Avenue between 25th and 26th Streets was solidly lined with barrooms and dance halls.

Colorado City had its share of labor troubles, the most important in 1903 when members of the Mill and Smeltermen's Union called a strike, alleging discrimination against union workers. For a time the town was an armed camp, loud with charges and countercharges of violence. The dispute brought about a sympathetic strike of miners in the Cripple Creek gold fields, but all strike objectives were lost.

Colorado City did the work, but the great gold fortunes went elsewhere. William D. (Big Bill) Haywood, labor leader, who described the community as a "forlorn little industrial town of tents, tin houses, huts, and hovels, bordered by some of the grandest scenery of nature," added that "none of the refined gold was left here—nothing but waste and slum." After 1912 the old mills were closed or torn down, to be replaced with the Golden Cycle Mill using a new and better reduction process. Population dwindled, and the town began slipping toward oblivion. In 1917, absorbed by its thriving rival to the east, Colorado City became West Colorado Springs and, while retaining marks of its identity, gradually conformed to the Palmer pattern of respectability.

Meanwhile, Colorado Springs had greatly profited from the Cripple Creek gold fields. Within a few months of the first strikes in 1891, five mining exchanges were operating day and night; soon a mining exchange building, the tallest structure in the city, was added to the skyline. Tradesmen, professional men, laborers, everybody traded in stocks and futures; hundreds of new mining companies were organized and their stock was sold throughout the country; promoters and investors rushed to the city to share in the prosperity. Bonanza kings invested part of their fortunes in substantial office structures and palatial houses. Wood Avenue, a short thoroughfare at the north end of town, named for the three Wood brothers, founders of Victor (see Tour 5B), was known as Millionaire Row. Here those who had made their fortunes from the Cripple Creek mines built elaborate mansions—all except "the Midas of the Rockies," Winfield Scott Stratton (see Tour 12b), who shocked the community by buying an old-fashioned frame house near the business district upon which he had worked as a carpenter years before. Between 1890 and 1900 the population increased from 11,000 to more than 23,-000; during the next decade Colorado Springs had claims to being the wealthiest city per capita in the United States.

With such a population the town never lacked patrons willing to contribute materially to its development. Among these, in addition to Palmer and Stratton, was the late Spencer Penrose, builder of the Pikes Peak Highway and founder of the Broadmoor Hotel development at the foot of Cheyenne Mountain. The mountain parks system, created in 1907, was increased when the Garden of the Gods was bequeathed to the city two years later. Agricultural development of eastern Colorado made the city a trading and supply center for a large new territory, later the regional headquarters of beet sugar companies. Coal and clay deposits in the vicinity led to the establishment of industrial plants.

POINTS OF INTEREST

The mellowed stone facade of Cutler Hall (1880) is one of the few reminders that COLORADO COLLEGE, located on N. Nevada Ave., goes back to 1874, when General William J. Palmer and the Congregational Church joined in its establishment. In 1907 it was secularized and now it is described as the only independent liberal arts college in an eight-state area. During the last twenty years it has been replacing its physical plant with modern construction, adding the CHARLES LEAMING TUTT LIBRARY, built by the El Pomar Foundation for $1,250,000, and the OLIN HALL OF SCIENCE, financed by the Olin Foundation, in 1962; Rastall Center (Student Union), 1959; Boettcher Health Center, 1964; Armstrong Hall of the Humanities, 1966, and new residential halls.

The College gives bachelor's degrees in the humanities, natural sciences and social sciences, offers pre-professional programs in dentistry, medicine, veterinary medicine, engineering and law. It has departments in dance, music and drama, and an experimental teacher education program, and offers the degree of master of arts in teaching. Special attention is given to its summer session. The studios of the College Department of Art are located in the Colorado Springs Fine Arts Center, at the edge of the campus. In 1968 the College enrolled 1,584 students and had a faculty of 149. It estimates the cost of tuition and extras at $1,500, and room and board at $900, a total of $2,400 annually.

UNIVERSITY OF COLORADO, Colorado Springs Center, is located in a group of buildings on an 80-acre site on Cragmore Road. There are classrooms, a library, a bookstore, and administrative offices. Here the University provides courses where students may earn credit toward graduate and undergraduate degrees in day and evening classes. Noncredit courses are also offered through the Extension Division. In 1967 there was an enrollment of 2,755, including 531 graduate students.

The BIBLE COLLEGE of the Church of the Nazarene on Chapman Drive opened its doors in the fall of 1967 to 118 students. The church has a 100-acre site and its original building cost $1,200,000.

SETON SCHOOL OF NURSING, at Penrose Hospital, has a three-year program leading to diploma and R. N. degree. There also are schools in x-ray, medical technology, and pathology. Penrose Practical Nurse School has a one-year program. Penrose Cancer Hospital has a three-year program in radio therapy. St. Francis Hospital has schools of medical technology and a Practical Nurse School. Beth-El School of Nursing is at Memorial Hospital.

COLORADO SPRINGS FINE ARTS CENTER, at 30 W. Dale St., was opened in 1936 in a building designed by John Gaw Meem and the gift of Alice Bemis Taylor, who also provided endowment. The Center was intended to deal with all the arts, especially exhibitions, music and theater, and to continue an art school. There are about thirty major exhibitions a year. Mrs. Taylor's interest in the art of the Southwest, especially religious folk art, led the Center to establish the TAYLOR MUSEUM, devoted to primitive and folk art, including Spanish American,

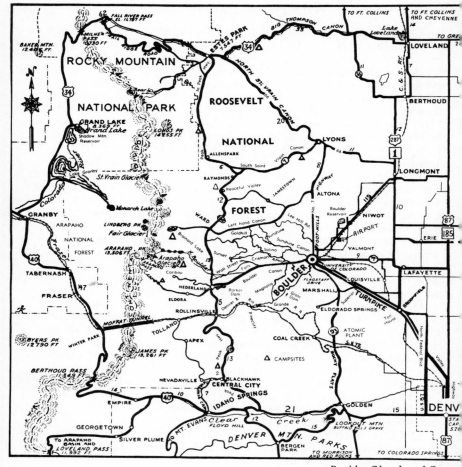

Boulder Chamber of Comm

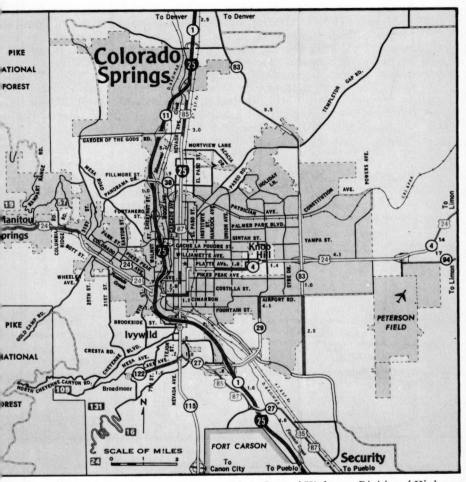

State Dept. of Highways, Division of Highways

Navajo and Pueblo textiles, replicas of Navajo sand paintings, folk art of Mexico and New Mexico, and of northwest coast Indians. In April, 1968, the Center opened the BEMIS ART SCHOOL FOR CHILDREN in a separate building of poured concrete in the same style as the main building. The Art School is closely associated with Colorado College. The Center stages numerous exhibitions; recent topics have been Artists West of the Mississippi, Artists of the Western Frontier, and Arroyo Hondo, the last dealing with religious folk art acquired by Taylor Museum. Films and plays, especially for young people, are regularly shown. The Children's Education project provides instruction after school and on Saturdays for city school children and provides transportation for bringing classes to the Center for exhibitions. It maintains an art library open to the public.

PENROSE PUBLIC LIBRARY, 20 N. Cascade Ave., was dedicated July 15, 1968. It embodies the newest technical devices for library use. It is the core of the Pikes Peak Regional Library District, which includes all of El Paso County except School District No. 3 and Manitou Springs. It is a gift to the community from the El Pomar Foundation, which donated $2,200,000 for land, building and equipment, and was named for Mr. and Mrs. Spencer Penrose, frequent donors to the needs of city and State. The Library has three branches: one in Palmer Lake, one in Cascade, Colo., and the West End Branch in Colorado Springs. It has three bookmobiles.

The original library building at 21 W. Kiowa St., has served the community since 1905. It is now known as the William J. Palmer Wing of the Penrose Public Library. It was built with a gift of $60,000 from Andrew Carnegie on land donated by General Palmer.

CHASE STONE CENTER, Pikes Peak Ave. and Cascade Ave., is a new business development of major proportions. Here are located the Antlers Plaza Hotel, opened 1967, where the London Grill and the Picadilly Bar convey an English atmosphere; the Holly Sugar Co. Building, in which is located the Chamber of Commerce and Visitor Information Center, and the May D. & F. Department Store. Adjacent to the Center the El Pomar Foundation chose a location for a $2,200,000 building for the Pikes Peak Regional District Library.

The BROADMOOR, one of the foremost resort hotels in the country and a sports center of national renown, is located in the unincorporated suburb of Broadmoor about 5 m. from the center of Colorado Springs. Visitors proceed south on Nevada Ave. to the city line, then turn southwest for about 1½ m. on Lake Ave. (State 122) to the hotel and Broadmoor Golf Club. The original eight-story core of the hotel was erected in 1918 by Spencer Penrose and Charles L. Tutt with the aim of making it "permanent and perfect." Not only has the hotel added new buildings and dining facilities but it has promoted recreational activities such as golf and skiing, and spectator sports in the Broadmoor World Arena. Bordering the lake are the main hotel and Broadmoor South, a nine-story structure that has in its top story the Penrose Room, consisting

Education

CHAPEL FOR ALL FAITHS, UNITED STATES AIR FORCE ACADEMY

THE LONG FACADE OF THE U. S. AIR FORCE ACADEMY

UNITED STATES AIR FORCE ACADEMY FROM THE AIR

University News Service

MEMORIAL CENTER, UNIVERSITY OF COLORADO, BOULDER

KITTREDGE RESIDENCE HALLS, UNIVERSITY OF COLORADO, BOULDER
University News Service

CAMPUS OF REGIS COLLEGE, DENVER

DAYTON MEMORIAL LIBRARY, REGIS COLLEGE, DENVER

College Information Office

HOUSTON FINE ARTS CENTER, TEMPLE BUELL COLLEGE, DENVER

WILLIAM E. MORGAN LIBRARY, COLORADO STATE UNIVERSITY,
FORT COLLINS

Office of Information, Colorado State University

Office of Information, Colorado State University

AUDITORIUM-GYMNASIUM COMPLEX, COLORADO STATE UNIVERSITY, FORT COLLINS

WHATELY CHAPEL, TEMPLE BUELL COLLEGE, DENVER

College Information Office

Photo Arts Studio, Durango

LESLIE J. SAVAGE LBRARY, WESTERN STATE COLLEGE OF COLORADO, DURANGO

ACADEMIC BUILDING, FORT LEWIS COLLEGE, DURANGO

Photo Arts Studio, Durango

DORMITORY IN DURWARD HALL COMPLEX, COLORADO STATE
UNIVERSITY, FORT COLLINS

of foyer, cocktail lounge and dining room, all decorated with old-world opulence.

The Lake Terrace Lounge on the mezzanine floor of the Main Building has on exhibit a collection of Chinese art gathered by the Penroses. The Golden Bee, an English pub of the early 19th century, has a priceless interior of carved mahogany brought over from England. It is installed in the Broadmoor International Center, an auditorium seating 2,400, and a summer theater. Recent additions include the Henry M. Beatty Hall, dormitory and center for figure skaters training at the World Arena, where there is a new annex with an ice surface 50 ft. wide and 150 ft. long. The Broadmoor Golf Club is the first 36-hole club in Colorado. The 18-hole Broadmoor West course was completed in 1965. The Spencer Penrose Stadium is a U-shaped arena that seats 10,000 under cover. The annual Pikes Peak or Bust Rodeo is held here in August.

Championship golf is played regularly at the Broadmoor Golf Club. Among its many events have been the International Curtis Cup match, the USGA Men's National Amateur, the Woman's National Amateur, the Women's Western Amateur, the Francis H. L. Brown International Team matches, the World Senior Golf matches and numerous others. There is a 155-stall riding stable and the US Equestrian Team event has been held here. Ice sports include figure skating championships, hockey games by Olympic teams, the International Hockey Tournament, and speed skating contests. The US speed skating team prepared for the 1964 winter Olympics at the World Arena and Broadmoor's Rosemont Reservoir, located behind Cheyenne Mountain, which has 200 acres of ice in winter and is a fisherman's paradise in summer.

The hotel maintains a complete winter sports area at Ski Broadmoor, on the slope of Cheyenne Mountain from Thanksgiving weekend to March. The chair lift serves 600 skiers an hour. The Winter House Restaurant and Lounge, ski instruction, a snow machine and floodlighting enhance the usefulness of the resort.

PIONEER MUSEUM, 25 W. Kiowa St. (*10–5 Tues.-Sat.; 2–5 Sunday*) has historical and archaeological objects, including Cliff Dweller pottery, and later Indian artifacts. Three rooms from the home of Helen Hunt Jackson, 228 E. Kiowa St., are incorporated in the museum. The author of *Ramona* was married here in 1875. She died in California in 1885 and was buried in Evergreen Cemetery here.

COLORADO SCHOOL FOR THE DEAF AND THE BLIND, S. Institute St., was established in 1874. In recent years the Legislature has appropriated funds for new structures, including a Vocational Training Bldg. Besides elementary and high school curricula the school has courses in driving, homemaking, baking, painting, industrial arts and physical training, and a college preparatory course. It publishes *The Colorado Index* for use of this and other institutions. Maintenance and operation cost about $700,000 annually; attendance is around 230.

The UNION PRINTERS HOME, E. Colorado Ave. and S. Union

Blvd., on a tract of 250 acres is maintained by the International Typographical Union as a hospital, tuberculosis sanitarium and home for aged members. It was founded in 1886 at the instance of G. W. Childs and A. J. Drexel of the Philadelphia Public Ledger and is supported by the dues of union members.

Colorado Springs and environs have a number of museums and collections of interest to students of history and specialists. The El Pomar Carriage House Museum, at the Broadmoor Hotel, displays carriages and vehicles of the 19th century in pristine condition, as well as accessories, harness and saddles. The McAllister House, 423 N. Cascade Ave., was built in 1873. Now completely furnished in the style of the period it shows how a well-to-do citizen lived. The May Natural History Museum of the Tropics is located 9 *m.* south of the city on State 115. The Cameron Doll and Carriage Museum is at 218 Beckers Lane, Manitou Springs.

The AMERICAN NUMISMATIC ASSN. makes its national hq at 818 North Cascade Ave., on a corner of the Colorado College campus, in a building completed in 1967. It is a one-story structure that contains a specialized library of 30,000 volumes and a museum. The association was organized in 1891.

ENT AIR FORCE BASE can be entered from Boulder, Union, Monument and Willamette Sts. It is the home of the North American Air Defense Command (NORAD), and a support base for hq of the USAF Aerospace Defense Command, the USA Air Defense Command, and the Royal Canadian AF Air Defense Command. The base was named for Major General U. G. Ent, commander of the 2nd AF in World War II. In March, 1963, all operations of the Air Defense Command were concentrated in the Chidlaw Bldg., 300,000 sq. ft., two blocks southeast of the base. On January 1, 1968, there were 6,568 military and 2,084 civilan personnel employed here. The NORAD Space Defense Center is operated by a squadron of the 9th Aerospace Defense Division in the Cheyenne Mountain complex. This division operates all missile and satellite detection and warning systems. The complex was dedicated in 1965. Dominating the skyline is a 275-ft. red and white micro-wave radio relay tower.

PETERSON FIELD, the municipal airport seven miles east on US 24, is operated in connection with Ent AFB. It was named for Lt. Edward J. Peterson, who crashed at the air field in 1942. A new Terminal Bldg. costing $1,400,000 was completed 1966, and in 1968 FAA installed a radar surveillance facility with a range of 60 *m.* distance and 30,000 ft. height. About 130,000 passengers enplane annually. Ent AFB housing, hangars, recreation center, shops, chapel, and dormitories are located on Peterson Field.

The UNITED STATES AIR FORCE ACADEMY, located on 17,900 acres at the foot of the Rampart Range, is approx. 10 *m.* north of the city limits on US 85 and 87 (Interstate 25). On January 1, 1968, it had a population of 10,712, including 5,185 military personnel, 5,527 dependents, and 2,562 civilian employees. The approx. 3,200 cadets will

be increased to 4,417 over four years, and added construction will cost
$40,000,000. There are now 31 buildings, and the VISITORS INFORMA-
TION CENTER (*open 8–5 daily*) is located at the southern entrance near
Colorado Springs. The architecture, called International Style, arouses
much interest, especially the CHAPEL, a combination of seventeen spires
rising 150 ft. and using much glass and metal. Also noteworthy are
MITCHELL HALL, the cadet dining hall seating 3,000; VANDENBERG
HALL, a cadet dormitory with 1,320 rooms, and the huge GYMNASIUM,
with a pool two-thirds the size of a football field. There are special quarters for visiting officers. The Cadet Wing forms and marches to lunch
every weekday at noon. The PLANETARIUM is open free on Saturday and
Sunday, September to June, and daily during the summer. A theater
shows academy films free. The golf course was named for General Eisenhower. The Frank J. Seiler Research Laboratory and the Air Force
Academy Preparatory School are also located here.

The Academy was established in 1954. From then to 1958 it was
located at Lowry AFB in Denver.

FORT CARSON, a military reservation of the United States Army,
is located at the southern edge of Colorado Springs and covers 141,333
acres. It is the home of the 5th U. S. Infantry Division (Mechanized)
and the Defense Communications Agency. The post has been operating
since 1942 and has an average of more than 21,500 military personnel
and 3,000 civilian employees. Its hospital has a capacity of 2,000 beds.

Denver

Air Services: Stapleton International Airport, 8100 E. 32nd Ave., for Aspen Airways, Braniff, Central, Continental, Frontier, Trans-World, United and Western scheduled flights; also Ozark, Trans Central, Vail. Helicopter Service. Connections with ski areas. Sky Ranch Airport, 7 *m.* east of Stapleton. Columbine Airport is southwest of limits in Jefferson County. Arapahoe County Airport, south of State 88, reached by Valley Highway.

Buses: Bus Center, 1730 Glenarm Pl., for Colorado Motorway, Denver-Boulder, Greyhound. Denver Union Bus Depot, 1805 Broadway, for Continental Trailways, Colorado Transportation, Rocky Mountain.

Highways: The Valley Highway, principal north-south artery, has Interstate 25, US 87, State 185. Denver-Boulder Turnpike, US 36, State 49, joins Valley Highway n. of city limits. Main east-west artery enters city at Colfax Ave., US 36, US 40, US 287, State 8, and Interstate 70, proceeds through city to Golden and beyond; branch of Interstate 70 curves northwest, State 72 runs parallel to Arvada. Major routes from northeast through Commerce City include Interstate 80S, US 85, US 8, State 3, 2, 265. Parts of Interstate routes under construction.

Railroads: Denver Union Station, 17th and Wynkoop Sts. Burlington Lines, Colorado & Southern, Denver & Rio Grande Western, Rock Island, Santa Fe, Union Pacific.

Information and Accommodations: The *Denver Post,* 650 15th St., daily and Sunday. *Rocky Mountain News,* 400 W. Colfax Ave., daily and Sunday. The *Daily Journal,* 1217 Welton St. *Record Stockman,* 3501 E. 46th Ave., weekly. Denver Chamber of Commerce, 1301 Welton St. Colorado Visitors Bureau, 225 W. Colfax Ave. (Colorado Hospitality Center, Colorado Ski Information Center, Colorado Convention & Visitors Bureau). Travel Development Section, Div. of Commerce & Development, 602 State Capitol Annex. The Colorado Visitors Bureau annually publishes a directory of hotels, motels, dude ranches, restaurants, etc. called *Colorado,* quoting prices. The *Denver Street Guide & Map* is published by Hotchkiss, Inc., 4055 Fox St.

Entertainment: Band concerts, City Park, July-August. Bonfils Theatre, plays. Denver Auditorium Theater, 14th and Curtis Sts., musicals, concerts Denver Post Opera, Cheesman Park, July. Elitch Theater, W. 38th Ave., and Tennyson, 10-week summer season. Denver Coliseum ice shows, fall and spring. Phipps Auditorium, plays, lectures, movies. Red Rocks Park, concerts, ballet, summer. Rocky Mountain News Showagon, variety by young people. University of Denver Little Theater. *Consult newspapers for dates.*

Museums: Colorado State Historical, E. 14th Ave. at Sherman. Clock Manor, Bergan Park, May–Oct. Colorado Photographic Arts Center, 1530 E. Colfax Ave. Denver Art Museum, 1343 Acoma. Denver Museum of Natural History, City Park. Denver Zoological Gardens, City Park. Governor's Mansion, 8th Ave. at Logan, tours Tuesdays. Larimer Square restoration, Larimer St. btw. 14th and 15th Sts. Wax Museum, 919 Bannock. Veteran Car Museum, 2030 S. Cherokee.

Spectator Sports: Denver Bears, Pacific Coast Baseball League; Denver Broncos, American Football League; Denver Rockets, American Basketball Assn., Denver Spurs, Western Hockey League. For intercollegiate competitions watch

newspapers. Racing, Horse: Centennial Turf Club, Littleton. Racing, Greyhound: Mile-High Kennel Club. Racing: Auto, Lakeside Amusement Park. Livestock Exhibition: National Western Stock Show, January.

Recreation: Many parks, inside and outside the city, have pools for swimming,
There are 18-hole municipal golf courses at these parks: City, Overland, Well-
shire, Willis Case, John F. Kennedy. Numerous tennis courts are available
throughout Denver. There are many lakes and reservoirs in the general area;
Sloans has docking for sail and power boats, water skiing, scuba diving. Cherry
Creek Reservoir, on State 83, has beach sports and some restrictions. Ice skating
is available in winter. For lists and information about permits and regulations
consult Colorado Hospitality Center, 225 W. Colfax Ave. Newspapers carry full
reports.

Climate: 12-month average is 64° max., 36° min., relative humidity 38%. Surges
of cold air from the west are usually moderated by descent down the east face
of the mountains, tempering the winter cold. Summer heat gets up to 87° in July.
Sunshine varies from 62 to 77 percent. Temperatures of 90° or over are reached
on an average of only 35 days a year and 100° is reached briefly once in 5
years. Air masses that influence Denver are polar air from Canada and the far
northwest; moist air from the Gulf of Mexico; warm dry air from Mexico and
the southwest, and Pacific air modified by its passage overland.

Miles to Denver: From Chicago, 1,013; Dallas, 784; Grand Canyon, 760; Houston, 1,026; Kansas City, Mo., 606; Las Vegas, 865; Los Angeles, 1,157; New
Orleans, 1,287; New York, 1,866; Omaha, 539; Phoenix, 937; Portland, O.,
1,205; Salt Lake City, 507; San Francisco, 1,264; Seattle, 1,356; Washington,
D. C., 1,710.

DENVER (5,280 alt.) capital of Colorado, the Centennial State (admitted to the Union in 1876), is known as the Queen City of the Plains,
and Mile High City, by virtue of its altitude, which is recorded on the
steps of the Capitol. One of the nation's great centers of trade, food distribution, and banking, and a key center for transportation, Denver today is a city where tall office structures rise beside vacant lots in midtown, testifying to confidence in the business prospects of coming decades.
In an atmosphere unusually salubrious and clear, where the golden dome
of the Capitol dominates a prospect that reaches to the Rockies on the
western horizon, Denver looks like a newly discovered oasis green with
verdure.

The City and County of Denver, covering 97 sq. m., are coextensive
and constitute a single governing unit. This is also the Second District
of the State Judiciary. Officials are chosen in nonpartisan elections and
serve four years: they include the mayor, auditor, two election commissioners, and nine councilmen.

An estimate of the population by the Bureau of the Census and the
Denver Regional Council of Governments gave the City and County of
Denver on January 1, 1969, 517,000 persons, and the Metropolitan Area
1, 167,000. In 1960 Denver had 493,887 (23d in the U. S.) and the
Metropolitan Area 929,383 (26th in the U. S.). The Denver Planning
Office in 1968 estimated the population of the minority groups at about 12
percent of the Metropolitan Area. Denver had 114,250, divided thus:
Persons with Spanish surnames, 57,750, or 11 percent; Negroes 50,000,

or 9.5 percent; orientals, 4,000; American Indians, 2,500. The Metropolitan Area had approximately 133,450 minority group members: 84,450 with Spanish surnames and 51,800 Negroes.

The traveler who comes to Denver by air alights at Stapleton International Airport and experiences a feeling of wellbeing induced by its spacious facilities and uncongested motor roads. Stapleton appears to have been built only yesterday, but already the authorities are planning extensive additions. Telephones are available with a direct line to hotels without charge. Coaches to the heart of town pass through miles of compact one-story cottages in neat gardens, many of recent construction. Highway lanes are divided by strips of grass kept green by a miniature sprinkler system.

The Capitol dome, visible from afar, is the distinguishing mark of the administrative center. Natives explain that the gold on the dome is not a coating of gilt such as is applied on other state capitols, but plates of gold mined from the auriferous earth, the original base of Colorado's wealth.

Denver is losing the uniform appearance caused by four to six-story business blocks and acquiring office buildings thirty to fifty stories high that stand in isolation like monumental pylons. These are banks, insurance offices, and hotels. They signify the end of the long frontier tradition, and they represent the financial power that is modern Denver. Not many years ago the Tabor Grand Opera House and the Windsor Hotel were the landmarks of a profligate era that all visitors came to see. They were tangible proofs of the legends of H. A. Tabor and the high living of the cattle barons, but today both are gone. Tradition may be invoked in the Brown Palace Hotel, but its rejuvenation is complete, and with several newcomers, including the 884-room Denver Hilton, it serves modern needs.

The air of Denver is clear and invigorating; the sky is a deep blue; a brisk wind dispels motor fumes. Traffic moves swiftly and there is evidence that regulations are strictly enforced, for pedestrians wait patiently for change in traffic lights, even when no motor car is in sight. Some vestiges of homely living cling to Denver; for instance, the newspapers report the daily entries on the police blotter—arrests for theft, disorderly conduct, assault—and the transactions of the courts, with long lists of culprits fined for bad driving.

The influence of Denver is not confined to the geographical limits of City and County but extends in all directions into five counties—Adams, Arapahoe, Boulder, Denver, and Jefferson. Some of its suburbs, populated by people who work in Denver, have their political obligations to a court house miles distant. At times there is feverish agitation to incorporate as a city, resulting in a situation such as that of June, 1969, when fewer than 10 percent of the residents of several western suburbs formed Jefferson City, and in November its city council voted to call it Lakewood, with an estimated population of more than 90,000. An account of this and other incorporations will be found under *The Denver Metropolitan Area*. Here it suffices to say that Denver is bounded on the north by Arvada (37,000 est.); Broomfield (6,600); Westminster (18,700); Thornton,.(14,500); Commerce City (18,000); Northglenn (23,000); on the east by Aurora (68,000); on the west by Wheat Ridge (34,000); Lakewood (90,000 est.); Bow-Mar (1,025). On the south are Englewood (37,400); Cherry Hills Village (3,200); Littleton (21,000). Like an enclave in the heart of Denver is Glendale (1,650).

Denver is a city where steady employment makes for contentment and stability. The reason is the large number of residents who draw pay from government work, meaning Federal, State, and municipal employment— 80,000. The Federal payroll provides for 26,100, but the other rosters are disproportionate because they include all teachers. District No. 1, the City and County of Denver, has approximately 4,000 teachers and 96,-000 pupils.

Denver has been transforming its midtown area by clearing out old structures, building skyward, and providing open spaces. One of the newest enterprises is Columbia Plaza, East 17th St. and Broadway, which was planned for 50 stories, 595 ft., to cost more than $30,000,000. It has a triangular site with five corner offices on each floor. The Broadway half of the Plaza was occupied for years by the Shirley-Plaza Hotel. The Columbia Savings & Loan Assn., one of the builders, takes the ground floor and a number of office floors. On the other side of 17th is the Denver U. S. National Bank, 25 stories, 293 ft. tall. The tallest structure before Columbia Plaza was planned was Brooks Towers, 1020 15th St., 42 stories and 420 ft. tall.

A number of buildings are notable for special features. The First National Bank Bldg., 621 17th St., 28 stories and 365 ft. tall, has a SKY DECK from which Denver and environs can be viewed. This bank has assets of nearly half a billion dollars. The Security Life Bldg., 384 ft. tall, at 16th St. and Glenarm Pl., offers visitors an opportunity to ride up 31 stories in an outside elevator, leading to the SPACE WALK and a panorama extending as far as the Rockies (*9 a.m.–10 p.m., May through December*). The Denver Club Bldg., 518 17th St., a 20-story building, has the EISENHOWER CHAPEL, built in commemoration of Dwight D. Eisenhower.

Denver authorities are engaged in long-range plans to replace unsightly factories, warehouses, and railroad facilities along ten miles of the South Platte River with parks, trails, and green banks. A development study (1967) estimated a program would cost $630,000,000 during twenty years, of which Federal, State and local units would provide 57 percent, city and county 13 percent, and private investors 30 percent. The Denver Parks and Recreation Department has cleared the land at the confluence of the Platte and Cherry Creek for a park, and to the City Transportation Museum was allocated the former Tramway Powerhouse at 1408 Platte St. The South Platte Area Development Council has helped curtail pollution in the waters, introduced fish, and planted trees. The city sold 13½ acres to Left Bank Hotels, Inc., for a hotel-motel complex. New park areas include Frontier Park, on the east side between West Yale and West Evans Aves., Ruby Hill Park, on the west side opposite the Overlook Park golf course, and Vanderbilt Park, on the west side between West Alameda and West Mississippi Aves. In December, 1968, the DENVER MILE-HIGH STADIUM, three blocks from the South Platte, was dedicated.

As the Denver Urban Renewal Authority (DURA) proceeds with its Skyline Project, some well known landmarks disappear from the scene. In the spring, 1969, the Daniels & Fisher store building, site of a popular tea room, was a victim, but its Tower, 375 ft., modelled after the Venetian Campanile, was retained as part of a new landscaping program. Also condemned were the Iron Bldg., 1031 17th St., the Cooper Bldg., 1009 17th St., and the old Federal Reserve Bank, 17th and Arapahoe Sts.

One of the projects given consideration by the Denver Planning Board is a Higher Education Center, to be located in the Auraria district, where Denver was founded, and to include a triangle bounded by West Colfax Ave., Speer Blvd., and the Platte River, and areas north of the Boulevard. The Colorado Commission on Higher Education authorized Dr. Frank C. Abbott, executive director, to study the possibilities. Lamar Kelsey and Associates of Colorado Springs reported the results of a survey in November, 1968. The project would bring about the close association of the University of Colorado Denver Center, located across Speer from the Auraria site; the Metropolitan State College, and the principal unit of Community College of Denver, a junior college that opened the first of three units in Adams County in 1968. Two elements of the Denver School System are within easy reach: the Emily Griffith Opportunity School, 1250 Welton St., and the West High School. The new Convention Center is one block east of Speer Blvd. The Metropolitan State College is a four-year State college giving both liberal arts and vocational training, which has leased its present facilities until 1973. A 145-acre site in Auraria has been approved for the college under the Urban Renewal program. The Federal Government has authorized $12,400,000 provided this sum is matched by the city and the State.

Denver has tapped the water resources of the Rockies to gain a supply that will serve double its present population. The principal units are Gross Creek Reservoir, Boulder County, holding 42,000 acre-ft.; Ralston Creek Reservoir, Jefferson County, 12,758 acre-ft.; Williams Ford Reservoir, Grand County, 14,930 acre-ft.; Dillon Reservoir, 1964, storing 252,000 acre-ft. and crossing the Continental Divide by means of the Harold D. Roberts Tunnel. From the South Platte area the water in Antero Reservoir, Park County, covers 58,000 acre-ft.; Eleven-Mile-Canyon, Park County, 81,917 acre-ft.; Cheesman, Jefferson County, 79,064 acre-ft. Just southeast of the Denver line in Arapahoe County the Cherry Creek Reservoir, built 1950 by the Corps of Engineers, USA, protects Denver from floods by Cherry Creek; it holds 95,000 acre-ft. of which 85,000 is reserved for flood control and 10,000 for silt control.

Denver's capacity for handling grain was increased considerably in 1963 when Cargill, Inc., completed an elevator in the North Yard with a capacity of 2,250,00 bu.

HISTORY

Louis Vasquez, a fur trader, built a post in the vicinity in 1832, but settlement did not begin until September, 1858, when a party from Lawrence, Kansas, who had spent the summer prospecting around Pikes Peak, were drawn north by reports that Green Russell's party of Georgians had discovered gold here along the South Platte. The Kansans built several log cabins on the eastern bank of the river at what is now West Evans Avenue, naming their settlement Montana City. The "City" was short-lived, for a number of the Lawrence men soon sought a more desirable site, joining forces with John Smith and William McGaa, two white traders living near the mouth of Cherry Creek and presumed to have influence with the Indians. This influence was important, for the local Arapaho and Cheyenne had been granted all of the surrounding territory "in perpetuity" by treaty with the Federal Government. Notwithstanding, the enterpreneurs platted the township of St. Charles on the eastern bank of Cherry Creek near its confluence with the Platte, and elected officers on September 28, 1858.

Believing there would be no great emigration to the Rocky Mountain region before spring, they set out for the Missouri River towns to advertise their paper city. This was a grievous error, for other expeditions of gold-seekers were making their way westward toward Cherry Creek and the Platte. Some of the Russell party, returning from the mountains, built cabins on the opposite bank of Cherry Creek. Smith and McGaa, apparently ready to ally themselves with each such venture, suddenly lost interest in the St. Charles project and joined the new arrivals in platting a second townsite, named Auraria for a mining town in Georgia. When word of this reached the St. Charles men on their way eastward, Charles Nichols returned in frantic haste to protect their claims. A third town company was organized with the arrival of another party of Kansans, led by General William Larimer and three Arapahoe County officials appointed by Territorial Governor James W. Denver of Kansas. Larimer's practiced eye recognized the potential value of the St. Charles site, which he and his associates proceeded to "jump," scorning the strenuous protests of Nichols. According to some historians, Nichols was threatened with violence unless he chose to acquiesce, which he reluctantly did. Later, the St. Charles promoters were compensated with shares in the new enterprise, and the Denver City Town Company was organized on November 17, 1858. Larimer shrewdly chose its name in hope of favors from Governor Denver, unaware at the time that he no longer held office.

General James W. Denver remains an almost unknown figure to the city that bears his name. Born in 1817 at Winchester, Virginia, he taught school and practiced law in Ohio, and later edited newspapers in several small Midwestern towns. After service in the Mexican War, he joined the gold rush to California, where he became a State official and a member of the U. S. House of Representatives. He later served as commissioner of Indian affairs and Governor of Kansas Territory.

During the Civil War, as a brigadier general, he commanded troops from Kansas. On his death in 1892, he was buried at Wilmington, Ohio.

By the end of 1858 Denver City had some twenty cabins and Auraria twice that number, including Colorado's first saloon, established by Richens ("Uncle Dick") Wootton, one of the great frontiersmen, who drove in with a wagonload of goods on Christmas Day and won the good will of the settlement by dispensing free drinks from a barrel of "Taos Lightning," a peculiarly potent whisky. A second saloon, later known as the Hotel de Dunk, soon began business, its proprietor being a minstrel named Duncan. Early the next year the log-and-mud Eldorado Hotel, the town's first, was opened by a certain Smoke, and "Count" Murat, its sign a white silk flag floating from a tall pine pole. In May 1859, two stagecoaches of the Leavenworth and Pikes Peak Express, the first on regular schedule, arrived with mail, valuables, and nine passengers after a nineteen-day trip from Kansas. Among the early arrivals was Professor O. J. Goldrick, who appeared upon the scene in plug hat, frock coat, and lemon-colored gloves. Goldrick opened the first school in Colorado, with thirteen pupils from Denver and Auraria, and organized the Denver and Auraria Reading Room Association, with one book. Religious services were first held in a cottonwood grove and in the log cabin of Smith and McGaa, but arrangements were soon made for the use of a room above a gambling hall; usually the players courteously refrained from making too much noise while services were in progress.

Exaggerated reports of gold discoveries inspired a head-long rush into the region early in 1859, which flooded the Cherry Creek settlements with excited men. The majority traveled in covered wagons, but one hardy adventurer came pushing a wheelbarrow loaded with a meager supply of flour, coffee, and sugar, having accepted a boarder en route to help defray expenses. Stores, mills, and hotels sprang up overnight. An intense rivalry existed between Denver and Auraria. Diplomatically, the *Rocky Mountain News* built its office on piles in the middle of Cherry Creek, the boundary between the two camps. Here, on April 23, the first edition of the *News* was published by William N. Byers and Thomas Gibbons, appearing half an hour in advance of the *Cherry Creek Pioneer,* which was immediately sold to its rival.

While officials of the townsite companies were elated at the growth of population, they had cause for worry. No one knew exactly where to look for gold, and when the insignificance of the first strikes became evident, hungry men seethed angrily about town, cursing and threatening to hang those whose glowing tales had lured them westward. The price of staples soared to fantastic heights; flour sold at $20 to $40 a hundred pounds; sugar, coffee, tobacco, and whisky commanded almost impossible prices. Hundreds of gold-seekers abandoned hope and started the long journey back to "America," spreading news of the "Pikes Peak Hoax." The first white child born in the community was named Auraria, and father and daughter were given several town lots for their "enterprise" in helping to populate the community; the mother held so poor an opinion of the gifts, however, that the family soon departed for Oregon.

Word of Gregory's famous strike on the North Fork of Clear Creek, May 6, 1859, brought immense relief to the Cherry Creek settlements, along with certain forebodings to their promoters, for it seemed that the rush to Gregory Gulch might depopulate both Denver and Auraria overnight. But not everyone could find a foothold in the "diggings," and with additional gold-hunters pouring in daily, there remained in Denver and Auraria through the winter of 1859–60 more than 1,000 persons.

In its first extra on June 11, 1859, the *News* published Horace Greeley's letter on the gold fields. On his way to the diggings Greeley had stopped in Denver to deliver a lecture on temperance and had found, so he said, "more brawls, more pistol shots with criminal intent in this log city of 150 dwellings, not three-fourths of them completed, nor two-thirds of them inhabited, nor one-third fit to be, than in any community of equal numbers on earth." Blake Street, the principal thoroughfare, was lined with business and gambling houses, including the Denver House, soon known as the Elephant Corral, where play went on day and night to the accompaniment of clinking glasses and a screechy orchestra.

The first city hospital was opened that year; Baltimore oysters were offered at $16 a gallon; and a stranger from Kansas, equipped with an ax for cutting buffalo chips, bought himself a buckskin bag and started for Pikes Peak to scoop up gold. The first banking firm was established by Turner and Bobbs, with interest rates on loans ranging from 10 to 25 per cent a month, depending upon the collateral security. Clark, Gruber & Company soon established a private mint, later sold to the Federal Government. Although gold coins circulated, gold dust remained the principal medium of exchange. A pinch between thumb and forefinger represented 25¢; larger amounts were weighed on small scales. Freight charges by ox or mule train from the Missouri River ranged from 10¢ to 20¢ a pound; letter postage was 25¢. Although livestock were few, a farmer whose crops had been damaged by roving cattle warned in the *News* that "eny kows that gits into my medders shal have tale cut off by me, Obadiah Rogers."

On April 3, 1860, Denver and Auraria were consolidated under the name of Denver City; at an election in January 1861, 1,291 votes were polled in the settlement, indicating a population of at least 6,000. For some years Denver's fortunes rose and fell with those of the gold camps. As richer surface diggings were exhausted, population dwindled. Travel across the plains was rendered hazardous by raiding parties of Indians who frequently killed and pillaged to the outskirts of the town.

An unexpected flood of usually shallow streams caused a major disaster. The bed of Cherry Creek, normally a mere trickle of water, had been laid out in lots, with buildings erected on piles driven into the sand. On the night of May 19, 1864, heavy rains resulted in a flood that cost twenty lives and great property damage. "Nature shook about us," wrote "Professor" Goldrick in a fine fury in the *News*. "The azure meads of Heaven were darkened as in death and the fair Diana with her starry train, though defended by the majesty of darkness all around her, and by batteries of thick clouds in front, looked down in shuddering silence dimly, as if lost in the labyrinth of wonder and amazement at the volume of the vast abyss into which all of us expected to be overwhelmed." Denver has ever retained a due respect for Cherry Creek and built no more in its channel; the disaster eclipsed the great fire of a year before that had reduced half the business section to ashes.

Preoccupied with its own urgent affairs during the Civil War, the struggling settlement was only indirectly touched by the conflict, although passions of both Northern and Southern supporters ran high. The Confederate flag was raised above a Larimer Street warehouse one April morning in 1861. Unionists angrily demanded its removal, and a compromise was arranged when bloodshed threatened; the flag was to fly until sundown and never again to be raised. Three regiments organized in Denver for the Union Army spent much of their time pursuing Indians and guarding the overland trails, participating in the Sand Creek Massacre (*see Tour 8a*), which caused fierce Indian uprisings that isolated Denver from the East for months. "Cheyenne scalps are getting as thick here now as toads in Egypt," reported the *News* on the troops' return from Sand Creek. "Everybody has got one, and is anxious to get another to send east."

Gradually the high cost of living fell. "Owing to the low price of butter, the fall of Charleston, and other causes," one enterprising merchant advertised, "I have put down the price of coal oil to $5 a gallon." In 1866 Denver's first hook and ladder was hauled across the plains, to be received by a welcoming committee. Late in 1867 the legislature, meeting at Golden, selected Denver as the permanent seat of government. The community was gradually brought into closer communication with the rest of the country. A telegraph line was strung across the plains in 1863, but service remained inadequate for several years, for buffalo herds frequently rubbed down the poles and wires were stripped away by Indians. Disappointed when the Union Pacific Railroad, pushing west from Julesburg, chose easier mountain grades through Wyoming, local promoters financed the construction of the Denver & Pacific Railroad to connect with the transcontinental system at Cheyenne; the first train puffed into Denver on June 24, 1870. The Kansas Pacific Railroad, now part of the Union Pacific System, advanced into the city from the Missouri River two months later. Farmers settled along the railroads and prospered.

"Peltry shops abound," wrote a traveler of the day, "and the sportsman, teamster, and emigrant can be completely rigged out at 50 different stores. . . . At Denver people who come from the East to try the 'camp cure' now so fashionable, get their outfit of wagons, driver, horses, tents, and bedding and start for the mountains. Invalids who cannot bear the rough life in the mountains fill the town's hotels and boarding houses." Many Indians added to the harlequin appearance of Denver streets. Women were few; Isabella Bird saw but five in a day, but "there were men in every rig; hunters and trappers in buckskins; men of the Plains with belts and revolvers, in great blue cloaks, relics of the war; teamsters in leather suits; horsemen in fur coats, caps, and buffalo-hide boots; Broadway dandies in yellow kid gloves; and rich English sporting tourists, supercilious-looking."

In 1873 a band of Ute Indians, poaching on Arapaho hunting grounds to the east, encountered a party of Cheyenne, their traditional enemies. Slaying and scalping a Cheyenne warrior, the Ute hastily beat a retreat to Denver, pitching camp on the outskirts of the city. Enterprising showmen quickly persuaded the Indians to stage a war dance with the scalp, and had their handbills printed before police intervened.

Until 1880 doubt clouded Denver's future. From the time of the earliest gold strikes at Gregory Gulch, Gold Hill, California Gulch, and Buckskin Joe, much of the mineral wealth of the hills had found its way to the community, which had also profited from its trade with ranchers and farmers. But gold mining at best was a sporadic and uncertain venture, and Colorado agriculture was still in its infancy. It remained for the great silver discoveries at Leadville, Aspen, Caribou, Georgetown, and in the San Juan Mountains to give substance to the dream of early promoters who had envisaged a great metropolis at Cherry Creek and the South Platte.

The growth of Denver in the era of the great silver camps was phenomenal. Between 1880 and 1890 population increased from 35,-629 to 106,713. Building progressed so rapidly that piles of structural materials blocked the streets. Large business buildings, foundries, machine shops, and two smelters were built. Manufacturing which had averaged about $5,000,000 annually between 1880 and 1885, more than tripled in 1886. The wealth that poured in from the silver districts founded banks and business enterprises, and Denver became the world's chief producer of mining machinery.

The celebrated Tabor Grand Opera House opened in 1881 with all of Denver society in attendance. A great mining and industrial exposition of Colorado products and resources was held the following year. But water was still sold as a staple commodity as late as 1881, and public hangings attracted many spectators. Lawrence Street became the fashionable shopping district in 1888, in which year the first cable cars began running on Larimer and Sixteenth Streets; at 1649 Lawrence Street stood the famed Silver Dollar Saloon, with silver dollars embedded in the tile floor.

Bonanza kings moved from the mountains to Denver and rivaled the cattle barons in building imposing brick and sandstone mansions. "The distinguishing charm of Denver architecture," wrote a visitor of the period, "is its endless variety. Everyone is ambitious to build a house unlike his neighbor, and is more desirous that it shall have some novel feature than that it shall be surpassingly beautiful." Tabor outdid his contemporaries as usual by purchasing an entire block on Capitol

Hill and erecting an "Italian villa," encompassed by a magnificent lawn embellished with cast-iron dogs and deer.

Gaiety during this sparkling period centered at the Windsor Hotel, where the Colorado senate, awaiting the building of a capitol, occasionally held its sessions. The "Windsor Hotel Crowd" was a term broadly applied to the free-spending throng that dashed about the city in costly carriages and fancy buggies, creating the traffic hazard of their day. Gold, silver, smelter, cattle, and railroad kings, the politically and socially ambitious—all were inviting targets for Eugene Field, who, from his desk at the *Tribune,* recorded their doings with a caustic pen.

Political progress lagged somewhat behind the city's development in other fields. Although Denver was the State capital, its citizens grumbled at finding themselves under a form of State administration imposed by the legislature—a situation popularly ascribed to the desire of rich mine and railroad owners to retain control of the capital city. The governor had appointive power over the Public Works and the Fire and Police Boards. These bureaus, free of local control, assumed great authority, even to the issuance of public improvement bonds on their own responsibility. Constant agitation for "home rule" finally succeeded in 1902 when a constitutional amendment gave cities of 2,000 population or more the right to manage their own affairs.

The prosperity of the 1880's proved sufficient to carry Denver through the dark years of the early 1890's, when a world panic added its gloom to the crash of the silver markets. The great mining camps, with the exception of Cripple Creek, were in distress, and hundreds of families crowded into Denver for relief. By 1895, however, the city had sufficient optimism to celebrate the "end of the depression," and in October of that year staged an elaborate carnival, the Festival of Mountain and Plain, patterned in part on the Mardi Gras at New Orleans and continued annually until 1911. For one week the city gave itself up to unrestrained celebration and merriment, with balls, parades, and street dancing.

The growth of the city since 1900 has been steady. Denver County was created in 1901 from parts of Adams and Arapahoe Counties, and the city and county were consolidated in 1902. Robert W. Speer, the first mayor under the home rule amendment, instituted a broad program of municipal improvements. New streets and boulevards were laid out with an eye to beauty as well as utility; steel and concrete viaducts were constructed across the Platte and the railroad yards; the frequently flooded channel of Cherry Creek was walled and lined with landscaped drives; the park system was greatly improved and extended with the acquisition of land in Jefferson County, the beginning of Denver's mountain parks system, now the second largest in the country. Denver experimented briefly with the commission form of government in 1913, but found it unsatisfactory and returned Speer to office under a new charter granting the mayor unusually broad powers.

In July 1907, the Denver Juvenile Court was established with Benjamin Barr Lindsey as judge. Lindsey treated juvenile delinquency largely as the result of environment. He made great progress, but in 1927 failed of reelection and became a superior court judge in Los Angeles.

Relations between employers and employees in Denver have seldom been attended by violence, but an exception occurred during the depression and general unrest that followed World War I. Clashes in 1920 between striking employees of the tramway company and strikebreakers from other cities resulted in nine deaths and much property damage. Federal troops from Fort Logan were called in to restore order. The tramway employees' union failed to win its demand for higher wages.

Completion of the Moffat Tunnel in 1928 gave Denver a direct short route to the Pacific Coast and opened up undeveloped trade territory; that year natural gas was piped into the city from the Texas fields, 400 miles to the south. In 1939, $3,500,000 was appropriated by the Federal Government for improvement of Lowry Field, established in 1937 as a technical school of the U. S. Army Air Corps and used later by the new U. S. Air Force Academy. In the same year two city markets were established; served by five railroads, they are among the largest west of the Mississippi River. Rapid transportation has ended Denver's comparative isolation. In 1860 it took stagecoaches nineteen days to travel the distance from the Missouri River to the mountains. The steam engine reduced the time considerably. Diesel-powered locomotives now haul streamlined trains between Chicago and Denver, more than 1,000 miles, in little more than fifteen hours. But the airplane, which bridged the miles between Denver and New York in five hours running time, united East and West.

POINTS OF INTEREST

The STATE CAPITOL (*open daily 9–5*) is a granite building of classical design located on Capitol Hill, a ten-acre area on Broadway between E. Colfax and E. 14th Aves. The corner stone was laid July 4, 1890; the building was partially occupied in 1895 but not fully completed until 1907. It cost $2,800,000. It has three stories surmounted by a dome, 272 ft. above the ground and covered with 28-carat gold leaf, of which 200 ounces were applied in 1908 and 50 ounces more in 1950. It is floodlighted at night.

The floor plan is in the form of a Greek cross, 383 ft. long and 315 ft. wide. There are four entrances to the grand staircase in the rotunda, which is made of marble and embellished with sculptured brass. The gold sunburst inside the top of the dome is 150 ft. overhead. Near the top is the Hall of Fame, where the portraits of sixteen pioneers are displayed in stained glass, best viewed from the Inside Observation Gallery. On the main floor of the rotunda are eight huge murals painted by Allen True and embellished with poetry by Thomas Hornsby Ferril; they describe the history of water in Colorado.

The office suite of the Governor is on the first floor. It was remodeled, redecorated and refurnished in 1958. The Governor's office has tawny gold wool carpeting with the seal of the State woven into it. The walls are paneled with natural-finish American walnut. The office has built-in radio, television and motion picture equipment. The offices of the Secretary of State, Treasurer, Auditor, and Attorney General also are located on the first floor. The courtroom and chamber of the State Supreme Court and the Law Library are located on the second floor. The Senate Chamber, accommodating 35 senators, and the House of Representatives, for 65, also are located on the second floor. Plans for numerous changes in the Capitol long have been drawn; there will be a new Supreme Court Building, to shelter also an Appellate Court and the Law Library.

The bronze doors of the elevator have panels symbolizing historic episodes. Much of the wainscoting and pilasters is rare Colorado onyx, each panel carefully matched for color and pattern.

The lawns of the Capitol are ornamented with nearly fifty varieties of trees, including two black walnuts that came from the home of Abraham Lincoln. A bronze statue of a private soldier commemorates Colorado soldiers who died in the Civil War, and whose names are inscribed on tablets. A remarkable group of bronze statuary on the east lawn represents an Indian hunter standing above a buffalo. It is known as The Closing Era and was designed by Preston Powers.

The CAPITOL ANNEX, East 14th Ave. and Sherman St., was erected in 1939. It is seven stories tall and has a facade of white Colorado marble, a base trimmed with gray granite, and interiors finished with travertine. It has the offices of the State Revenue Department, the Industrial Commission, and the Compensation Insurance Fund.

The STATE SERVICES BUILDING, northwest corner of East Colfax Ave. and Sherman St., was built in 1959–1960 at a cost of nearly $4,000,000. It has seven stories and a facade of Vermont marble with gray granite trim. It has the offices of the State Civil Service Commission and a number of State departments.

The COLORADO STATE LIBRARY, in the State Services Bldg., a division of the State Department of Education, is the principal agency administering the Federal Library Services and Construction Act in Colorado, and aiding libraries with workshops, training and advisory services. It has about 100,000 books and thousands of official documents, also films and recordings. It serves State institutions. The LIBRARY OF THE LEGISLATIVE REFERENCE OFFICE in the Capitol is used chiefly by the General Assembly and State agencies. The LIBRARY OF THE STATE SUPREME COURT in the Capitol possesses an extensive collection of legal documents and reports and is used chiefly by the Court and lawyers. Federal matching funds and State grants-in-aid have contributed substantially to the development of libraries in rural areas and towns of 10,000 population and less since the first Library Services Act in 1959.

The STATE OFFICE BUILDING, northeast corner of East Colfax Ave. and Sherman St., is a five-story building completed in 1921. It has a facade of Colorado granite and Colorado and Tennessee marble in the interior. It has the State Department of Education, the Inheritance Tax Department, the Banking Commission, and other agencies.

A new EXECUTIVE MANSION was given to the State in 1960 by the Boettcher Foundation of Denver. It is located at 400 East Eighth Ave. and for about twenty years had been the home of Charles K. Boettcher, notable industrialist and developer of Colorado enterprises. It is a colonial mansion of brick with white stone trim, four stories tall and standing on terraced grounds enclosed by a six-foot iron fence. The gift included luxurious furnishings and rare art objects valued at several hundred thousand dollars, plus $45,000 for three years' maintenance.

The administrative needs of Colorado are served by a number of other buildings not located in the Capitol complex. The STATE DEPARTMENT OF HIGHWAYS completed its new office building in southeast Denver in 1955, at a cost of $2,389,825. This also shelters the Colorado State Patrol. The Highways Department also uses a laboratory, a warehouse, maintenance shops, and other facilities. The STATE DEPARTMENT OF EMPLOYMENT entered its new headquarters at 1210 Sherman St. in 1957. It bought and remodeled a building at Broadway and E. 14th Ave. in 1962. The STATE DEPARTMENT OF PUBLIC HEALTH completed a new office building and laboratory near the University of Colorado Medical Center in East Denver in 1960. The STATE GAME, FISH AND PARKS DEPARTMENT bought an industrial property at 6060 Broadway north of the Denver line in Adams County in 1963. Its former headquarters, 1530 Sherman St., next to the State Office Building, was remodeled for the STATE DIVISION OF ARCHIVES AND RECORDS.

The COLORADO STATE HISTORICAL MUSEUM at E. 14th Ave. and Sherman St. is part of the State Capitol complex. By means of models and materials it provides much data about cliff dwellers, trappers, Plains Indians, settlers, minerals, and reptiles of prehistoric ages. There is a collection of Baby Doe Tabor relics. This is the base of the Colorado State Historical Society and houses the Historical Library. *Open 9–5 daily; weekends, 10–5; free.*

The impressive CIVIC CENTER of Denver, Broadway to Bannock St., W. Colfax Ave. to W. 14th Ave., is a formal expanse of lawns, trees, graveled walks, and esplanades. At the western boundary is the gleaming white crescent of the City and County Building. Plans for the Civic Center were projected in 1904 by Mayor Robert Speer, and work was begun in 1919 in accord with the designs of Frederick Law Olmsted, Jr., of Brookline, Massachusetts; E. H. Bennett, city planner of Chicago, acted as consultant.

The Voorhies Memorial, designed by William E. and Arthur A. Fisher of Denver, a graceful arch of buff-colored sandstone with curved wings supported by Ionic columns, constitutes the north entrance to the Civic Center. Funds for its construction were bequeathed by John H. P. Voorhies, pioneer mining man. Decorating the upper walls are several murals of Western animal life by Allen True, Denver artist. The twin

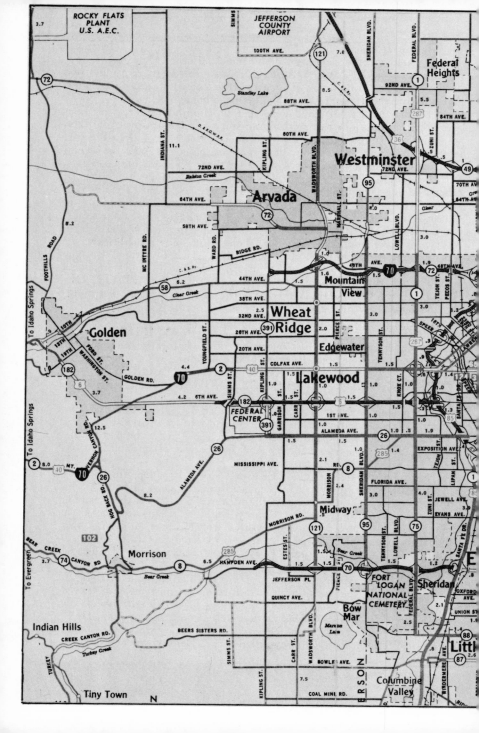

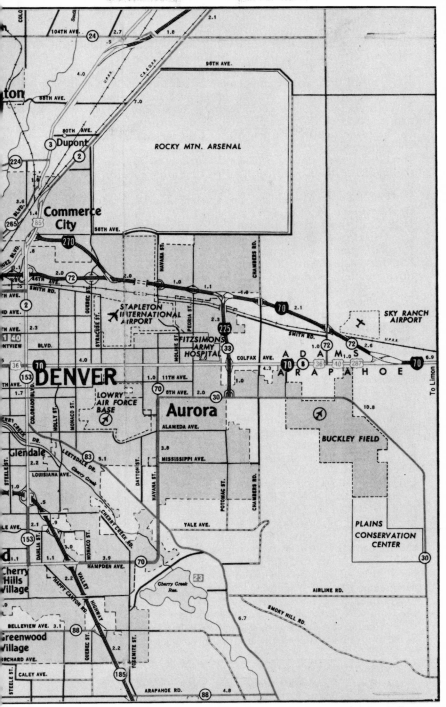

State Dept. of Highways, Division of Highways

statues of children astride sea lions in the shallow fountain pool within the curve of the arch are the work of Robert Garrison.

The Colonnade of Civic Benefactors, S. end of the Center, built in 1919, forms the stage of an open-air Greek theater. The colonnade, designed by Marean and Norton of Denver in the Ionic order of the Erechtheum at Athens, commemorates benefactors of the city whose names appear on the brass plate on the outer eastern wall. At either end of the stage are murals by Allen True depicting early mining and trapping scenes.

The bronze statues, *Bucking Broncho* and *On the War Path,* at the middle of the Center, both by A. Phimister Proctor, were presented to the city by J. K. Mullen and Stephen Knight.

The Pioneer Monument, on a triangular landscaped plot, corner Broadway and W. Colfax Ave., marks the terminus of the old Smoky Hill Trail over which thousands of gold seekers reached the Cherry Creek settlements in 1859–60. Designed by Frederick MacMonnies, the $75,000 fountain was unveiled in 1911. A bronze equestrian figure of Kit Carson surmounts the memorial; around the rim of the fountain are three reclining bronze figures, *The Hunter, The Prospector,* and *The Pioneer Mother.*

In the original design the sculptor had placed a defiant Sioux at the top of the monument, but pioneers rose in wrath, held indignation meetings, and created so much furor that MacMonnies made a special trip from Paris to confer with them. The pioneers were pacified when the figure of the noted scout was substituted. Later, however, criticism was directed at the modeling of the figures. Kit Carson was said to resemble a "rococo cowboy upon a pony of the same extraction."

The DENVER CITY AND COUNTY BUILDING was erected in 1932 from a design by thirty-five leading Denver architects and is a four-story granite building of simple classical lines, with a concave facade of Doric columns and a central portico surmounted by a slender clock tower housing the Speer Memorial Chimes. The Corinthian capitals on the portico columns were carved from 26-ton granite blocks. There are heavy bronze doors, and the lobby columns and interior panelling are of Colorado travertine.

In 1956 the DENVER PUBLIC LIBRARY opened its fine modern headquarters in the Civic Center, which replaced the neo-classical building of 14 tall columns that had served it since 1910. By 1968 it had more than 1,000,000 volumes in its stacks and estimated that 40 per cent of the residents of Denver were registered book borrowers of its system. This system comprised 12 branch and regional libraries, six neighborhood libraries, and the services of four bookmobiles. The library receives more than 100 newspapers and about 2,000 periodicals, besides tons of Government reports. As a State-wide reference center it cooperates with the Colorado State Library, and has enlarged its usefulness by depositing collections at certain locations, supported the Great Books and the Head Start programs, removed the limitation on books available to adults and permitted children to borrow six at one time. More than 60,000 questions are answered annually, demonstrating the reliance placed on the library. The City Council appropriated $2,134,200 for operating expenses in 1967; books cost $221,494.02; the payroll, for 285 staff positions, was $1,681,780.42.

In 1929 Malcolm Glenn Wyer, then director of the library, began the Western History Department, today a most valuable collection of early books, diaries, sketches, lithographs, photographs, negatives, and newspaper files of the Rocky Mountain region. The Department is primarily for reference and research use. The collection of books and sketches signed by Frederic Remington is one of the best; the Adriane diaries of Central City and Black Hawk, 1859–1861, are unique; there are large collections of photographs and negatives by such pioneers as David F. Barry, William H. Jackson, and Horace S. Poley; paintings by western artists, including Bierstadt, Russell, Moran, Catlin, Tallant Mathews, and many others. Bierstadt's painting, "Estes Park," originally executed for the Earl of Dunraven, hangs in the main room of the Department. There is a large section devoted to railroad history and lore, which is frequently consulted by railroad buffs. A writer who prized this collection was Lucius Beebe, who demonstrated his interest by giving the library a substantial legacy.

The Bibliographical Center for Research, Rocky Mountain Region, is located in the Denver Public Library. The Center maintains a union catalogue covering books and journals in fifty American libraries, and has 15,000 vols. of biographical source material.

The DENVER ART MUSEUM, 1343 Acoma Ave., has been bringing a new look to the Civic Center by the construction (1969–1970) of a new building that rises like two connected towers, containing six stories of galleries, but actually is as tall as ten stories. The former Schleier and Oriental Galleries and the Living Arts Center were demolished for the new building; only the South Wing with the Kress Collection of Renaissance Art remained to be united with the new structure. Light gray glass brick has been used freely. The Museum has been designed by James S. Sudler Associates of Denver in collaboration with Gio Ponti of Milan, Italy, and is expected to cost a great deal more than the original estimate of $3,800,000 when fully equipped.

During building operations many of the fine collections had to be placed in storage; however, exhibitions continued in the Interim Gallery, 1201 Acoma, and the Chappell House, 1300 Logan Ave. The Museum has exceptionally representative collections of nineteenth and twentieth century French, Dutch, and American works, including the Barbizon painters, contemporaries such as Picasso, and contemporary Americans. There are large collections of Chinese and Japanese porcelains and bronzes, Colonial china and textiles, and Georgian furniture, and prints; also Indian pottery, and basketry. Rare pieces have been added lately to the pre-Columbian collection. Among recent accessions is a wooden eagle with a wingspread of six feet once atop the Eagle Hotel in Charleston, N. H., well suited to adorn the entrance of the new Colonial Suite. *Hours: 2–5 Sundays, 1–5 Mondays, 9–5 Tuesdays through Saturdays. Closed Dec. 25, Jan. 1, Easter, July 4 and Thanksgiving.*

The UNIVERSITY OF DENVER, oldest institution of learning in Colorado, has its main campus six miles southeast of midtown, around South University Blvd. and East Evans Ave., where are located the College of Arts and Sciences, the College of Business Administration, and the College of Engineering. A fourth unit, the College of Law, 200 W. 14th Ave., occupies a modern structure adjacent to the Civic Center. Chamberlin Observatory is located at 2930 East Warren Ave. Graduate courses are given by the colleges and the Schools of International Studies, Librarianship, and Social Work.

In 1968 the Universtiy enrolled 8,926 students (5,292 men, 3,634 women) and had a faculty of 699—430 full-time. There were 552 law students. The institution was chartered by the Territorial Legislature as the Colorado Seminary of the Methodist Episcopal Church on March 5, 1864. John Evans, the governor, who helped found it, had helped open Northwestern University and had the city of Evanston, Ill., named after him. The Seminary was closed during 1867–1879 and reopened in 1880 as the University of Denver. Its board is still chosen by the Methodist Church but its teaching is nonsectarian. A student's expenses for the nine-month academic year are estimated at $2,545, of which $1,500 is for tuition and $900 for room and board.

The University has profited in recent years by the erection of new buildings and enlarging its facilities. The MARY REED LIBRARY is the central unit of the library system, which has more than 500,000 volumes and many documents, periodicals bound and on microfilm, and special collections, such as the Renaissance Room. Some specialized libraries, such as the Westminster Law Library in the Law Center, are housed in other buildings. The Mary Reed Library has a 100-ft. tower and faces the Harper Humanities Garden, in which is located the Evans Memorial Chapel. Students attend services in the Buchtel Memorial Chapel.

The College of Engineering and the Denver Research Institute occupy twelve buildings in the southern part of the campus. The Institute has a $6,200,000 annual program of contract research for industry and government. Four units are known as the Boettcher Center for Science, Engineering and Research. A new laboratory built on a grant from the National Aeronautics and Space Administration is the Space Sciences Research Building. The College of Business Administration moved into its new four-story building in the northwest section in January, 1968. It has a 200-seat lecture hall and a Computing Center that operates a Burroughs B5500 computer.

Student activities include all form of intercollegiate sports except football. There are four kinds of bands, a symphony orchestra, four choral groups, and numerous chamber music groups. The University Theatre gives five major productions annually. Students publish the *Denver Engineer,* a quarterly; the *Clarion,* a biweekly; the *Kynewisbok,* a yearbook. The *Library Bulletin,* devoted to legal books and periodicals, was begun in 1965. The Westminster Law School was merged with the College of Law in 1957.

Chamberlin Observatory, 2930 E. Warren Ave., at S. Fillmore St., opens its facilities to the public on Tuesday and Thursday, 7–9 p.m., subject to reservations by calling 753–2454. It has two structures, a small one with a 12-ft. dome containing 12-inch and 8-inch reflectors and an 8-inch telescopic sight, and a main building with a 35-ft. dome and a 20-inch Clark refractor. Various astronomical instruments may be inspected. The Denver Astronomical Society of amateur observers holds its meetings here.

The High Altitude Laboratory of the University has two units: the Mt. Evans Laboratory, 14,150 ft., and the Echo Lake unit on the highway to Mt. Evans. The first can accommodate six observers from mid-June through September; the second has two laboratory buildings and a dormitory for fifteen. Pioneering studies of cosmic rays and subatomic particles have been made here.

Tuition for resident and nonresident students is $500 per semester (12 weeks). The university estimates board and room at $300 a semester in residence halls. Apartments outside rent for $130 to $160 per quarter, excluding food. Various forms of student aid are available.

The ILIFF SCHOOL OF THEOLOGY, unaffiliated, is located on the campus at E. Iliff Ave. and So. University Blvd. It was established by the Methodist Episcopal Church to train candidates for the ministry. It was founded by gifts from the family of John Wesley Iliff, pioneer cattleman.

The new COLORADO GENERAL HOSPITAL, 440 beds, is north of the older complex and linked with it via the new Clinical Research Wing, bridging East 9th Ave. In 1966–67 the hospital admitted 13,102 patients and 188,749 visited the outpatient clinics. Linked with the hospital and the School of Medicine is the Colorado Psychiatric Hospital, 79 beds. The Adult Outpatient Psychiatric Division and the Division of Child Psychiatry occupy the Clinic Building, adjoining which is the Children's Psychiatric Day Care Center. The John F. Kennedy Child Development Center was completed in 1968. During 1966–67 the Psychiatric Hospital had 869 patients and 33,589 outpatient visits.

Also part of the Center are the School of Nursing; the Florence R. Sabin Building for Research in Cellular Biology; the Bonfils Tumor Clinic, supported by an annual grant by Miss Helen Bonfils and the U. S. Public Health Service; the Belle Bonfils Memorial Blood Bank, which serves the whole Rocky Mountain area, and the Humphreys Postgraduate Center, in the Denison Library Building, honoring the memory of Mrs. Ruth Boettcher Humphreys and created by her family and the Boettcher Foundation. Affiliated is the Webb-Waring Institute for Medical Research, dealing with diseases of the lungs, and privately financed. The Eleanor Roosevelt Institute for Cancer Research opened 1966 with a grant from the Eleanor Roosevelt Cancer Foundation.

The Charles Denison Memorial Library building was given by Mrs.

Ella Strong Denison in memory of her husband, a physician. In 1969 the library had approximately 82,000 bound volumes and was subscribing to 1,985 medical and scientific journals. The building has an auditorium with 408 seats. The new addition to the library provided space for the James J. Waring room of the history of medicine collection.

The Medical Center was one of the first institutions to develop an artery bank. It has an eye bank and has developed use of the artificial kidney and hypothermia anasthesia. Basic cell biology is one of the many medical subjects of research. The research program of the Center expends more than $7,100,000 annually, and that at Boulder annually expends approximately $10,300,000.

The DENVER CENTER OF THE UNIVERSITY OF COLORADO, 1100 14th St., offers day and evening instructions in undergraduate and graduate courses leading in some areas to baccalaureate and masters degrees, and in others credit toward degrees. The plant includes an instruction building with more than fifty classrooms and laboratories, a library building, and a tower housing faculty and administrative offices. Noncredit courses are offered through the Extension Division. Enrollment in the fall semester, 1968, was 7,007 students, one-fourth of them graduates; 13,000 were enrolled throughout the year. This is one of two urban centers of the University, the other being located in Colorado Springs.

The MEDICAL CENTER of the UNIVERSITY OF COLORADO, 4200 East 9th Ave., has a 32-acre campus where more than 1,200 students and trainees enroll annually. The four-year School of Medicine, opened 1883 in Boulder, was moved here in 1910; it now has fifteen departments, and its refresher courses for practicing physicians are attended annually by 5,000. In 1965 the Center completed a $20,000,000 building program, and in 1966 it applied $10,000,000 to remodelling older facilities. Development continues; a new School of Dentistry will be located here.

LORETTO HEIGHTS COLLEGE, a Roman Catholic college for women, occupies 157 acres on Loretto Heights, south of Amherst Ave. at 3001 South Federal Blvd., in the community of College View, lately annexed by Denver. Founded 1918 it shared the facilities of Loretto Heights Academy (estab. 1891) until 1940. It grants degrees in the humanities, education and nursing, and offers a junior year study program abroad. New construction has included the May Bonfils Stanton Library, the Center for the Performing Arts, seating 1,000; and Walsh Hall, the fourth dormitory. A Parents' Weekend is observed annually in June during the Star Nights musical production. Enrollment is 895.

REGIS COLLEGE, offering a curriculum in the liberal arts and sciences, is administered by the Society of Jesus and occupies 90 acres at West 50th Ave. and Lowell Blvd. It developed from humble beginnings in Las Vegas, N. Mex. Terr., in 1877, and in 1888 moved to Denver as the College of the Sacred Heart. In 1921 it was renamed Regis College, honoring an eighteenth century Jesuit missionary. Main Hall dates from 1887 and Carroll Hall from 1923, but a number of new buildings have been added in recent years: the Chapel in 1949; Regis Fieldhouse'in 1960; the Center in 1957 and 1963; Science Hall, which contains the wellknown seismological unit, in 1966. The Dayton Memorial Library, opened in 1966, has 60,000 volumes and room for 150,000. The college has two regular semesters and a summer session; a student not living at the college pays $735 per semester; one who has board and room there pays $1,360 per semester. The College gives baccalaureate degrees in the arts, classical arts, science (including business administration, accounting and economics); B.S. in chemistry, B.S. in engineering physics, and has pre-engineering and pre-law programs. For ninety years it taught male students exclusively; in the fall 1968, it opened the college to women. It will also accept sixty to ninety students in nurses training at St. Joseph and Mercy Hospitals in Denver for the first year of chemistry and biology. In 1968 the College, which restricts enrollment to below 1,500, had 1,394 students. Regis is a member of the recently organized Rocky Mountain Athletic Conference and competes in all major sports except football.

TEMPLE BUELL COLLEGE, 1800 Pontiac St., is the name bestowed on July 1, 1967, on the former Colorado Woman's College, which had operated as a junior college since 1909. The name was changed to honor Mr. and Mrs. Temple H. Buell of Denver for giving an eventual endowment of $25,000,000, free from restrictions. It is now a 4-year institution for women with an attendance of around 1,000 and limited to 1,500. Founded by Denver Baptists in 1888, the cornerstone for Treat Hall was laid in 1890, but 17 years elapsed before the main building was more than a shell of red sandstone. The first students (13) arrived in 1909.

Impressive is the new Dale and Ida Huston Fine Arts Center, E. Stanley Morse, architect, which includes a theater seating 700 and a music hall seating 300. It has an experimental theater, two art galleries, art and dance studios. Morse also was the architect of the Whatley Chapel, (1962), which has stained glass made in Chartres, France; a meditation chapel, and a baroque organ with 2,116 pipes, 52 ranks and 44 stops, built in Lawrence, Kansas. Adjoining is the Lindsay Memorial Amphitheater, seating 1,200, and the Ollinger Memorial Tower with a carillon of 30 bells. Stanley Morse and Arthur S. Axtens are architects of new residence halls. The Pamela Curtis Porter Library (1947), Victor Hornbein architect, has more than 65,000 volumes and a Teaching Materials Center.

In 1968 the college introduced a Community Relations Program, including a course in minority history. Study abroad is available to third-year students. Project Upward Bound is a coeducational program to benefit high school students of limited means. The Council on Religious Activities promotes interfaith cooperation. Scholarships were worth $290,000 in 1968–1969. Fees are $3,214 for the full-time student in residence; for the off-campus student, $1,649.

The UNITED STATES MINT, W. Colfax Ave., between Cherokee and Delaware Sts., a massive two-story granite building, one of three coinage plants in the United States, is also one of the two chief Federal gold repositories, the other being at Fort Knox, Ky.

Guided tours are available during the summer, 7:45–11, 12:30–3, except for the last week in June and the first in July; rest of year, 9–11, 1–2:30. Closed Saturdays, Sundays and holidays.

In 1863 the Federal Government purchased the private mint of Clark, Gruber & Company, 16th and Market Streets, which had been coining $5, $10, and $20 gold pieces since 1860. The Denver Mint, which began operating in 1869, confined itself at first to melting, refining, assaying, and stamping bullion; no coining was done until 1906. The last gold coins were minted in 1931.

The mint was the scene of a bold and well-executed robbery on December 18, 1922. As a Federal Reserve truck in the charge of 4 guards was being loaded with $200,000 in $5 bank notes, a sedan pulled up alongside and three men leaped out, covered the guards, seized the currency, and tossed it into their car. The bandits opened fire with shotguns loaded with buckshot; guards in the building returned the fire as the car raced off. One bandit was later found dead in the bullet-riddled car parked in a private garage near by.

The historic BROWN PALACE HOTEL, with its modern additions, is a monument of western progress. It was opened August 1, 1892, when a gala dinner was served to the Knights Templar, who had chosen it for their national convention. The principal builder was Henry Brown, a carpenter who had grown wealthy, and who expended $1,600,-000 on it. Maxcy Tabor, son of H. A. W. Tabor, and Bill Bush, who had been associated in construction of the Tabor Grand Opera House and had operated the Windsor and other hotels, spent $400,000 on furnishings. The hotel was built of native red sandstone, and onyx from Mexico was used for panelling. The central rotunda is nine stories tall. The owners suffered a number of financial difficulties and in 1931 the hotel was sold to Charles Boettcher and his son Claude. The Boettcher interests continue to operate the hotel.

In 1959 a new era began for the Brown Palace. The owners built the Brown Palace Tower, a structure of 22 stories, costing $7,000,000, across Tremont from the original building and connected with it. The Grand Ballroom on the second floor of the Brown Palace Tower is panelled on three sides by African mahogany and seats 800 for a meeting and 600 for dining. The widely known Palace Arms and Ship Tavern are unchanged. The former Emerald Room and Coffee House have been converted into the San Marco Room, which has on display two bronze horses modelled after the famous horses on St. Mark's cathedral in Venice. The Prospector Suite and the Brown Palace Club were opened in 1962 and 1963.

The Brown Palace has been a leading center for cattlemen and in turn supports the National Western Stock Show by buying prize steers. Sometimes they are exhibited in the lobby. In 1966 the hotel paid $8 per pound for the grand champion steer of the stock show.

The DENVER HILTON, 1550 Court Place, the city's largest

hotel, was opened in April, 1960. At that time it was the 41st hotel in the chain. It is 22 stories tall and rises north of the Civic Center like a huge monolith, 365 ft. long, 50 ft. wide. It has 884 rooms and a garage for 1,300 cars, and employs more than 800 persons. Its cost was $26,-500,000. Many of the rooms have a western theme in their decorations. It was planned to accommodate conventions and can serve dinner for 2,000 at one sitting.

Other new hotels in Denver are the HYATT HOUSE, 1790 Grant St. with luxurious suites; the HAMPSHIRE HOUSE, 1000 Grant St., opened in 1963 and rising 17 stories, and the DENVER DOWN-TOWNER MOTOR INN, 303 West Colfax Ave., opened in June, 1969, and the fifth largest hotel in Denver. The popular Trader Vic's restaurant is associated with the COSMOPOLITAN HOTEL, 18th St. and Broadway.

The DENVER CONVENTION CENTER, with entrances on 12th and 14th Sts. and located along Champa St., opened its main section to its first guests in April, 1969, while construction was still continuing. This $14,000,000 investment by the city to accommodate national conventions and exhibits represents the most modern facilities for large gatherings, subsidiary conferences, and entertainment. The main floor is 680 ft. long, 240 ft. wide, free of obstructions under a steel webbed roof 46 ft. above the floor. In the white-painted network are clusters of lights that can be lowered to illuminate exhibits. The hall will seat 14,000 and can be divided into two sections of 50,000 sq. ft. each. It is surrounded by a mezzanine floor that has numerous rooms for special purposes reached by escalators. The traffic of 13th St. passes through the basement level, where there are facilities for loading.

The facade of the Convention Center is a notable architectural achievement. Its rust-brown exterior has long narrow slits of windows that extend the full height. The Center is in an urban renewal area.

From the mezzanine floor a bridge leads across Champa St. to the CITY AUDITORIUM, which continues to be the home of the Denver Symphony Orchestra, plays, and sports events. Here the Arena seats 7,800 people and the Theater 2,250. Behind the theater are three floors convertible to three large assembly rooms or twenty smaller rooms.

The Convention Center amplifies the numerous facilities Denver has for spectacles and concerts. The BEARS STADIUM, W. 20th and Decatur Sts., is the home of the Denver Bears of the Pacific Coast Baseball League and the Denver Broncos of the American Football League. The city bought the stadium from Empire Sports, Inc., for $1,800,000 in donations to finance the purchase. By adding 25,000 seats the capacity has been raised to 50,000. The COLISEUM, E. 46th Ave. and Humboldt St., is the hq of the National Western Stock Show and Rodeo in January and also offers ice skating. DENVER UNIVERSITY ARENA, 2241 E. Asbury Ave., has scheduled games of ice hockey. CENTENNIAL TURF CLUB, south of the Denver line on US 85 in Littleton, has racing July–October, except Sunday and Monday.

LARIMER SQUARE, in the 1400 block of Larimer St., is considered a prime example of a "preservation project for profit." Here a run-down section that a century ago was in the center of Denver business life has been restored and refurbished, so that today it has seven restaurants, three galleries and 20 shops fully functioning amid authentic furnishings on their original sites. First buildings here were cabins erected 1858–1859 in what miners called the St. Charles Town Assn., later taken over by Gen. William E. Larimer. Mrs. Dana Crawford, assisted by her husband John W. R. Crawford, led the movement to restore Larimer Square. Langdon E. Morris was the architectural consultant. About $1,600,000 has been spent on restoration. The annual rental base is figured at $4 a sq. ft. The Theatre in the Square gives performances Wednesday through Saturday at 8:30 p.m. and children's bills Saturday and Sunday at 2 p.m.

The FEDERAL COMPLEX, 18th to 21st Sts., California to Stout Sts., is an impressive group of U. S. Government buildings, including the Federal Tower Bldg., the U. S. Court Bldg., the U. S. Customs House, and the U. S. Post Office. Here are the offices of the Internal Revenue Service, the Department of Agriculture, and the Federal Bureau of Investigation. The new Federal Reserve Bank, 17th and Arapahoe Sts. is an impressive example of modern architecture especially when flood-lighted at night.

The DENVER FEDERAL CENTER, Kipling St., between W. 6th Ave. and West Alameda Ave., second largest Federal Center in the country, since June, 1969, is part of the newly incorporated Lakewood. It occupies about one square mile and has more than thirty buildings with the regional offices of the U. S. Bureau of Reclamation, the U. S. Bureau of Mines, the Atomic Energy Commission, the Veterans Administration, the Corps of Engineers, USA, the Civil Aeronautics Agency, the U. S. Fish and Wildlife Service, the U. S. Forest Service, and others of like importance. The Federal Regional Center, an underground structure intended to protect Federal workers during a nuclear attack, was completed at the Federal Center in June, 1969.

The EISENHOWER CHAPEL is located on the second floor of the Denver Club Building, 518 17th St. It is sponsored by the Lions Club of Denver, as "a quiet retreat for meditation or petition" acceptable to individuals of many faiths. It is a tribute to Dwight D. Eisenhower and his expressions of faith in a Supreme Being, including: "Prayer gives you courage to make the decisions you must make in a crisis and then the confidence to leave the result in a higher power." The Lions Club solicited dollar contributions from the public beginning in November, 1953, and in April 3, 1955, dedicated the chapel. A stained glass window shows Hoffman's Christ in Gethsemane. The color of the robe is ruby, the marble of the altar is salmon tinted, carpeting is turquoise, and the wood panelling natural oak. The narthex contains an oil painting of Eisenhower and a statement of his religious philosophy, closing with "Prayer today is a necessity."

A memorial plaque to a distinguished newspaperman has been affixed by the Colorado Press Association to its headquarters in Glenarm Place, opposite the Denver Athletic Club. It commemorates William M. Long, 1915–1964, and reads: "The newspapers of Colorado, their publishers, their editors, their ad men, and their printers, have been truly fortunate; for fourteen years every phase of our industry knew and felt the inspired and vigorous leadership of William M. Long." The plaque was placed February 20, 1965.

Denver has made unusual efforts to provide its residents with many opportunities for recreation and easy access to parks, playgrounds, and scenic drives. Thousands of visitors come annually for its clean air and equable climate and find provision for every form of healthful activity. Of the many areas inside the city limits CITY PARK is best known. It has two lakes; an 18-hole golf course; a miniature railroad, places for tennis, baseball, bowling, horse shoe pitching; rowboats. There are band concerts on summer evenings. The Electric Fountain in the center of the large lake has 2,000 sprays, using 4,400 gallons of water a minute and is illuminated by colors. The Park has the DENVER ZOO and the CHILDREN'S ZOO, with small farm animals.

The DENVER MUSEUM OF NATURAL HISTORY, at the eastern edge of City Park, has extensive exhibits of animals and birds in habitat surroundings. Here also are the Campion collection of flake gold and the H. H. Nininger collection of meteorites; fossil remains of the dinosaur period, and artifacts of prehistoric peoples found in Colorado. The Northwest Wing and the Boettcher Foundation Wing are recent additions at a cost of $2,700,000. More than 700,000 persons annually visit the Museum.

The CHARLES C. GATES PLANETARIUM in the Boettcher Foundation Wing of the Museum is one of the busiest educational agencies in the city, giving programs twice a day and on some days three times. The auditorium seats 236 and can present the sky through projector simulation and live telescope. Daily school programs are given mornings; adult education courses are available through Metropolitan State College.

The Planetarium has demonstrations Monday through Friday, 2:30 p.m. and 4:30 p.m.; weekends and holidays, 2 p.m. and 5:15 p.m.; Monday, Wednesday and Friday evenings, 8:30 p.m. Admission, day, adults 75¢, children 50¢; evening, adults $1, children 75¢.

DENVER BOTANIC GARDENS, 909 York St., are widely esteemed for their extraordinary displays of varieties of flowers. The Botanic Gardens House for administrative offices contains the Helen Fowler Library; on 18 acres adjoining is the Herbaceous Garden. The Boettcher Memorial Conservatory for tropical and subtropical plants is one of the recent additions. There is a Children's Garden that enables young people to practice horticulture. The Gardens are famous for the great variety of flowers exhibited. There are iris in profusion; day lilies, dahlias, petunias, roses, peonies, gladiolas, poppies, and many others. A unit of the Gardens in City Park has a rose garden and the Robert E. More Pinetum (evergreens).

The M. Walter Pesman Alpine Trail is maintained jointly by the Denver Botanic Gardens and the U. S. Forest Service at Mount Goliath,

50 *m.* west between Echo and Summit Lakes, reached by State 5 from Echo Lake. Echo Lake may be reached via State 103 from Bergen Park or Idaho Springs. Open July and August, sometimes in June if weather permits.

The DENVER STOCKYARDS, Lafayette St. near East 46th Ave., are operated by the Denver Union Stock Yard Co. as a strong central market for cattle, sheep, and hogs. The facilities cover 84 acres and include the modern Auction Arena, erected 1966 adjacent to the Livestock Exchange, and the world's largest concrete barn, capable of handling 30,000 sheep. When trucks began to deliver more than 1,500,-000 head of cattle annually a new truck-in division was built with a viaduct carrying cattle from the unloading docks to the commission firms. Marketing facilities have been leased to the Denver Livestock Market, Inc., made up of commission firms operating on the market, which sells all cattle, sheep and hogs at auction. In 1966 Swift & Co., responding to the decentralization of the meat packing industry to rural livestock centers, sold its plants to the Stock Yard company. Six railroads serve the Stockyards, which have completely modern mechanization.

The NATIONAL WESTERN STOCK SHOW, which the Colorado Cattlemen's Assn. has called "the nation's most useful stock event," began under a big tent in 1899 on what is today its 106-acre exhibition area. It is conducted by the Western Stock Show Assn. as a civic enterprise and is self-supporting. In 1909 the Denver Union Stock Yard Co. built the Stockyards Stadium, now used for judging horses and cattle. In the 1940's business leaders and stockmen donated $3,000,000 to the city and county for expansion of facilities, which in addition to a bond issue, made possible the erection of the new COLISEUM at East 46th Ave. and Humboldt, opened 1952 for the horse show and rodeo.

LOWRY AIR FORCE BASE, East Sixth Ave. and Quebec St., was opened in 1938 by the U. S. Army Air Corps for training in aerial photography and bombing. A large assembly of buildings suitable for barracks, schools, hospitals, officers' quarters and hangars was erected and runways were built. When the U. S. Air Force Academy was established in 1954 it started instruction at Lowry Field and used these facilities until completion of the Academy plant north of Colorado Springs in 1958. The Colorado Wing of the Civil Air Patrol, one of 52 state agencies, has its base at Lowry. It is an auxiliary of the USAF. It is composed of volunteers and consists of the headquarters wing, 6 groups, and 40 squadrons and flights. CAP undertakes search and rescue missions and assists in noncombatant and recruiting services for the USAF, besides coordinating aerospace education, workshops, and other duties.

FORT LOGAN MENTAL HEALTH CENTER, in the suburb of Fort Logan west of Federal Blvd. and south of W. Hampden Ave., is a State institution erected on 308 acres obtained from the Federal Government area in 1959. The Center was designed by Alston G. Gutterson. The State annually appropriates nearly $4,000,000 for its maintenance. In 1965 the State opened the CHILDREN'S PSYCHIATRIC

TREATMENT CENTER, a group of five buildings adjoining, built at a cost of $1,075,000.

STAPLETON INTERNATIONAL AIRPORT, 8100 E. 32nd Ave. is the fastest growing airport in the Rocky Mountain States. It is located in the northeast corner of Denver and is reached also via Smith Road and Interstate 70, which passes under the long runway. Since 1963 it has had direct flights to Paris and Rome via Trans World Airlines. From 1960 to 1964 the airport invested $21,000,000 in new facilities and in 1969 began a construction program to cost $43,000,000, including doubling the size of the Terminal Building, providing new parking facilities for a minimum of twenty-four aircraft, including jumbo jets, and a new north-south runway. The growth of the airport is shown in the scheduled flight summary. From 1964 to 1968 total flights rose from 102,262 to 195,124; passengers carried were 2,898,242 in 1964 and 5,980,845 in 1968; similarly air mail rose from 17,968,280 lbs. to 59,-353,423 lbs.; express from 7,088,675 to 9,135,417; freight from 48,234,-266 to 104,523,137. At the present rate of growth Denver will need a new commercial airport in about twelve years and has been viewing the 20,000 acres of Rocky Mountain Arsenal, north of Stapleton, as a possible site. United Airlines conducts a University of the Air at Stapleton Airport.

The DENVER MOUNTAIN PARKS constitute a chain of 27 named parks covering about 13,500 acres in the areas west and southwest of Denver and easily accessible by a superb road system. (*See Tour 15A*) They are maintained by the City and County of Denver and have facilities for all forms of outdoor recreation, including swimming, boating, fishing, golf, mountain rides, and theater performances. The best-known is RED ROCKS PARK, near Morrison, reached by US 285 and State 74, where the Open Air Theatre, on a slope with spectacular rocks forming the stage, is one of Denver's superior summer attractions. WINTER PARK, on US 40, *67m.* out, has facilities for skiing, including three chair-lifts and four T-bars. LOOKOUT MOUNTAIN PARK on the crest of the mountain has the grave of Colonel W. F. Cody (Buffalo Bill) and a museum of memorabilia. (*See Tour 7A*).

CHERRY CREEK RESERVOIR, located just beyond the city limits of Denver on Interstate 225 in Arapahoe County, since 1960 has become a most popular recreation resort for Denver people. The dam was built by the Corps of Engineers, USA, to control Cherry Creek floods, and the reservoir can store 95,000 acre ft. No person may swim, bathe or wade in the reservoir except at the designated swimming beach.

Denver Metropolitan Area

The DENVER METROPOLITAN AREA, comprised, with a few exceptions, of cities, towns, and unincorporated suburbs that contribute to the preeminence of Denver in business, industry, and banking, covers 3,687 square miles in five counties—Adams, Arapahoe, Boulder, Denver, and Jefferson. Golden, the seat of Jefferson County, and Boulder, the seat of Boulder County, are self-contained cities not subordinate to Denver, but are included by the Bureau of the Census in what it designates the Standard Metropolitan Statistical Area (SMSA). The core of this prosperous domain is Denver City and County, an area of 98 sq. m. and a population now estimated at well over half of the Metropolitan Area.

Cities and towns with a population of more than 2,500 in this area are Aurora in Adams and Arapahoe Counties; Brighton, Commerce City, Thornton, Westminster, and Northglenn in Adams County; Englewood, Littleton, and Sheridan in Arapahoe County; Boulder, Broomfield, Lafayette and Longmont in Boulder County, and Lakewood, Arvada, Edgewater, Golden, and Wheat Ridge in Jefferson County. The assessed valuation of this area was about one-half that of the State of Colorado; its revenue was nearly two-thirds of that of the State, the percentage of change from 1960 to 1966 having been more than 55 percent, according to the Colorado Division of Accounts and Control. Bank deposits of Denver City and County were $1,620,000,000 in 1967; of the Denver Metropolitan Area, $2,021,000,000; of the State, $3,023,000,000. Jefferson and Arapahoe Counties are the centers of Colorado's carnation industry. The Arapahoe County Airport, near Arapahoe Road and Interstate 25, open in May, 1968, has about 650 landings and takeoffs daily.

LAKEWOOD (5,355 alt.) was incorporated as Jefferson City on June 24, 1969, by vote of residents of 41 square miles in eastern Jefferson County, living west of Sheridan Blvd., which is the Denver line. The vote for incorporation was 8,478 to 3,371, and the 17 precincts that voted were in Lakewood, Alameda, Green Mountain, Applewood Knolls, and several smaller suburbs of Denver. About 10 percent of the population voted.

Use of the name of Jefferson City had been debated before the incorporation; after it the feeling grew that this would become a source of confusion with the capital of Missouri. On November 4, 1969, the voters were asked to substitute Lakewood, the name of the largest suburb in the complex. The sentiment in favor proved overwhelming, and on November 6 the city council made the name of Lakewood official.

James J. Richey, the first mayor, was reelected on November 4 and installed for a two-year term on January 12, 1970. Mrs. Jean L. Rogers was elected city clerk. The appointed city administrator is Walter Kane. The city leased a former school district administration building with option to purchase, for use as its City Hall.

The population of Lakewood is estimated by local authorities as around 100,000. On June 25, 1970, the U. S. Bureau of the Census gave Lakewood 93,403, making it the fourth largest in Colorado, after Denver, Colorado Springs, and Pueblo. It remains a part of the Denver Metropolitan Area (SMSA) as outlined by the Census Bureau. It is larger than the county seat, Golden.

Although the new city by force of numbers will be able to call itself the fourth largest incorporated community in Colorado, it is not actually comparable with Pueblo or Colorado Springs, which have the industries, hotels, banks, business houses of a complete city. For such elements of urban life Lakewood must continue to rely on Denver, the core city of the area.

The agitation among Denver suburbs to incorporate gained impetus during 1968. Northglenn, newly platted area in Adams County on the Valley Highway north of Denver, was incorporated that year. Planners in Wheat Ridge and Lakewood proposed to incorporate them as one city in 1960 but were defeated in an election. A proposal to incorporate both separately was also voted down. In May, 1969, Wheat Ridge succeeded in obtaining incorporation. It is located west of Sheridan Blvd., north of Edgewater and Lakewood, and has an estimated population of 34,000. Edgewater, lying north of Lakewood, was incorporated as long ago as 1904. It was credited with 5,400 population in 1967.

The center of the new city is bisected by Denver's main east-west artery, Colfax Avenue, along which run US 40 and Interstate 70. The Golden Road leaves Interstate 70 for Golden, which is only 15 miles from Denver. Denver's West 6th Ave. also runs through the Lakewood section, past the Denver Federal Center and thence northwest to Golden. South of the Federal Center runs Alameda Ave., which becomes Alameda Parkway and one of the routes to the Red Rocks Park.

The Denver newspapers looked on the incorporation of Denver's big suburb with ironic detachment. The *Rocky Mountain News* remarked that Denver's neighbors in Jefferson County never had an opportunity to fight City Hall, "and now they have it, a treasured element in any democracy." But now they would have to build a city hall, elect officials, enact a sales tax, "an independent police department, an independent fire department, a jail, a courthouse for municipal legal transactions, a program to provide better streets, sewers, water, parks, recreation, health and welfare, etc. The litany of responsibilities formerly shouldered by Jefferson County is long and costly. Costliness is the name of the game in any kind of government these days . . . We wish you luck. And it is comforting to have you at hand even if only because misery loves company."

In recent decades developers have been exploiting the sugar beet fields to the north and the hilly lands to the northwest, and habitations have been rising along the Valley Highway and as far north as the Eastlake group of reservoirs. But one town, ARVADA, in the Ralston Valley and on State 72 and 121, has a more remote origin; miners built their cabins there in 1859; it was a town by 1880 and incorporated in 1904. Its real growth has come since 1950, when it had 2,358; the current estimate is 37,000. Jefferson County Airport lies six *m.* north on State 121, which in Arvada and Denver is Wadsworth Blvd. The *Arvada Enterprise* is its weekly newspaper.

In Denver's Metropolitan Area to the north are WESTMINSTER, incor., 1911, which had 534 people in 1940 and 18,700 in 1967; THORNTON, incor. 1956, with 14,500, COMMERCE CITY, incor. 1952, with 18,600, and BROOMFIELD, incor. 1961, with 6,600.

On the east Denver's streets continue into AURORA, which has 68,000 people, estimated 1969. Adjoining the Aurora line in Denver is LOWRY AIR FORCE BASE, 800 acres, entrance E. 6th Ave. and Quebec St. The principal east-west highway, State 8, US 36, 40, and 287, moves along Colfax Ave. beside the Capitol. North of the highway in Aurora is FITZSIMONS ARMY HOSPITAL. To the East is BUCKLEY AIR NATIONAL GUARD BASE, leased by the State from the Federal Government and hq of the Colorado Air National Guard.

Like an enclave in the heart of Denver is GLENDALE, 1,650 pop., incorporated as a town in 1952. Directly south of the Denver line are SHERIDAN, incor. 1890, 5,000 pop.; ENGLEWOOD, incor. 1903, 37,400 pop., and CHERRY HILLS VILLAGE, incor. 1945, 3,200 pop. South of Englewood on Santa Fe Drive is LITTLETON, 21,000 pop., seat of Arapahoe County (*see page 369*). At the southwest corner of Denver is Fort Logan, a part of the city, where the FORT LOGAN MENTAL HEALTH CENTER, a State Institution, occupies 308 acres. Adjoining Fort Logan on the west is the incorporated (1958) town of BOW-MAR, 1,200 pop., with a group of lakes, the largest of which, Marston, covers 652 acres.

A study of employment in the Denver Metropolitan Area for one year (1968) disclosed that out of a work force of 499,800 only 14,500, or 2.9 percent were unemployed. Of the 485,100 earning wages or salaries, 109,400 were engaged in wholesale and retail trade, the largest category. Of this number 76,800 worked in stores, food dispensaries, gasoline stations, motor car salons, and all such places in which goods change hands. The Denver area also accounted for a great deal of manufacturing, in which 76,200 were employed, more than one-half in durable goods, of which ordnance and its accessories used 9,000, exceeded only by nonelectrical machinery. The Denver Metropolitan Area also had large numbers engaged in hotel and entertainment services. The city has the largest network of transportation in the State. Airplane transportation averages 6,700 employees; railroads use 4,500; about 8,700 are engaged in truck transportation and warehousing.

Fort Collins

Airports: Fort Collins-Loveland airport (municipal) 4 *m.* east, 7 *m.* south, adjacent to Interstate 25; has runways 100 x 6,500 ft. Metro Airways commuter service to Denver. Fort Collins Airport (private) 2 *m.* east.

Buses: Continental Trailways, Colorado Motor Way.

Highways: State 14 from the east is the direct route into the great national forest area via the Cache la Poudre River route. US 287 and State 1 are north-south routes. Interstate 25, combined with US 87 and State 185, runs 4 *m.* east of Fort Collins and direct to Denver (64 *m.*) and Colorado Springs (130 *m.*).

Railroads: Colorado & Southern, Union Pacific.

Information and Accommodations: Fort Collins Coloradoan, daily except Saturday; *Northern Colorado Star,* weekly. Fort Collins Chamber of Commerce. Also Poudre Canyon Businessman's Assn., Fort Collins. Five radio stations include WWV, service of the National Bureau of Standards, which provides special frequencies and time signals; 6 television channels. Hotels and motels located chiefly in College Ave.; numerous motels, cabins, housekeeping cottages, ranches, in environs, Laporte, and Poudre Canyon route. Poudre Valley Memorial Hospital, 1024 Lemay Ave., has 128 beds.

Recreation: Seven public parks, 5 tennis courts, 3 football fields, public and private swimming pools, 2 9-hole public golf courses, 1 private, basketball courts, baseball fields, boating, bowling. Ski buses to ski areas. Easy access to Roosevelt National Forest, Estes Park, Rocky Mountain National Park, Cache la Poudre Canyon fishing and hunting areas. *See Circle Tours, below.*

Cultural Activities: Programs at Colorado State University; Symphony Orchestra concerts; Fine Arts Festival, Little Theatre Group and Children's Theatre performances. Of the 57 churches 30 are community centers and 31 youth activity centers.

Special Events: CSU football in season, Hughes Stadium, Foothills Campus. Fort Collins Birthday exercises, August. National Western Rodeo, Friday, Saturday & Sunday, first week in May.

FORT COLLINS (4,984 alt., 25,027 pop., 1960; 39,000, 1967, est.), seat of Larimer County, is a prosperous outlet for a large irrigated area, where sugar beets, barley, hay, and vegetables are the chief agricultural products, and industrial interests are multiplying. Retail sales income is derived, in order, from automotive materials, food processing, lumber and building supplies. Ideal Cement Co., 2 *m.* outside the city, makes 57 per cent of the cement produced in Colorado; other industries make speed controls, electrical equipment for internal combustion engines, light airplanes and parts, alabaster products, and prefabricated housing. The Great Western Sugar Co., Woodward Governor Co., and Forney Industries, Inc., are among the principal employers. Dairy products and livestock feeds are profitable. The city also provides supplies for the oil and gas industries of Larimer County.

Long before the founding of the town, this pleasant spot appealed to pioneer travelers as a camping ground. During the great Mormon migration of the 1850's, services were held by members of that faith in the cottonwood groves along the river. The first actual settlement was the small military post moved here in 1864 from Laporte. Named Camp Collins and later Fort Collins for Lieutenant William O. Collins, commanding officer at Fort Laramie, Wyoming, the camp was established for the protection of the few scattered ranchers and farmers in the Cache la Poudre Valley, as well as to guard the Overland Trail, then virtually closed to travel by Indian uprisings.

The military post was abandoned in 1871, but the settlement that had grown up around it retained the name. This village attracted many of the newcomers to north-central Colorado; in 1873 a town company modelled on the successful Union colony at Greeley was organized by General Robert A. Cameron, and Fort Collins was incorporated in 1879. Its growth was stimulated by development of the sugar beet industry in the irrigated sections of the State and the building of a sugar factory here in 1903; property values soared and an increasing number of settlers came into the region. The opening of the Fort Collins-Wellington oil field in 1923 further stimulated growth. Within the next decade the population increased 25 per cent.

The CACHE LA POUDRE River, on which Fort Collins is located, provides not only the chief tourist lure as a prime trout stream, but also the city's principal water supply, via a diversion dam 14 m. west. This is supplemented by water stored by the HORSETOOTH RESERVOIR, 6 m. southwest of Fort Collins. This is a unit of the Colorado-Big Thompson Project, begun by the Bureau of Reclamation in 1937, which collects water on the western slope of the Continental Divide and carries it to the east by way of a 13-mile long tunnel. Horsetooth has a dam of earth 170 ft. tall, impounding a storage area of 1,610 acres and capable of holding 151,700 acre-ft. of water when full.

POINTS OF INTEREST

COLORADO STATE UNIVERSITY, established 1870 as a land grant college and controlled by the State Board of Agriculture, operated for many years as the State College of Agriculture & Mechanic Arts. In the last twenty years it has experienced an increase of students to more than 13,000, and a big expansion in facilities, financed by State and Federal appropriations. Today the University has full scale curricula in eight colleges: Agriculture, Business, Engineering, Forestry & Natural Resources, Home Economics, Veterinary Medicine & Biomedical Sciences, Humanities & Social Sciences, and Natural Sciences.

CSU is located on three sites: the Main Campus of 507 acres in Fort Collins; the Foothills Campus of 1,700 acres two miles west of Fort Collins, largely devoted to engineering research, and Pingree Park,

54 miles northwest in Roosevelt National Forest, a summer camp devoted to forestry, engineering and the biological sciences. A construction program has added 25 major buildings since 1963, and since 1965 $27,000,-000 has been spent on eight additional buildings. Largest of the eight is the Social Science Bldg., 253,960 sq. ft., costing $5,100,000. Its Learning Center, with audio-visual equipment, can handle 5,000 students per hour. The new Physiology Bldg. is part of the planned College of Veterinary Medicine & Biomedical Sciences complex that will cost $17,500,000; the Microbiology Bldg., and the Chemistry Bldg., also are new projects. A recent addition to the Engineering Bldg. is the mathematics wing with classrooms and the CSU Computing Center, which operates a CDC 6400 computer system, installed in 1967. A Computer Science Bldg. is being planned.

The growth of the research facilities at the Foothills Campus exemplifies the tremendous importance of new scientific studies in modern education. Outstanding is the ENGINEERING RESEARCH CENTER, which is drawing an increasing number of graduate students. There are five laboratories: Hydraulic, Fluid Dynamics & Diffusion, Hydrology, Hydraulic-Mechanical, and Atmosphere Simulation. Here also is the Atmospheric Science Bldg., the home of weather modification programs. The Atmospheric Simulation Laboratory has been designed by the National Science Foundation as the nation's test center for cloud-seeding generators. Research devices in fluid dynamics and hydraulics include dam models, water distribution systems, wind tunnels, a space chamber and an electrokinetic laboratory.

The College of Veterinary Medicine & Biomedical Sciences pursues research at the Foothills Campus. Several laboratories of the National Institute of Health make use of its capabilities. The Collaborative Radiological Health Research Laboratory, established in 1964, studies the effects of low-level radiation on a colony of 3,000 beagle dogs, in order to determine its relation to human beings. The practical aspects of radiation control in environmental and public health are part of the University's Radiation Health Training program, which prepares graduate students to fill positions in radiological health agencies.

The Ecological Investigations Laboratory of the U. S. Public Health Service, located here, is headquarters for the communicable disease program in the western United States. Diseases such as bubonic plague, tularemia (rabbit fever), and Colorado tick fever are studied here.

One of the fastest growing units is the College of Home Economics. In two years enrollment increased 33 per cent. The college offers fashion merchandizing, with a work-credit system; fashion tours in Europe, courses in housing and design, child development, family relationships and occupational therapy.

Among the new buildings on the Main Campus are provisions for sheltering faculty and students. There are nine new residence halls, two high-rise dormitories, and three groups of housing for married students.

The WILLIAM E. MORGAN LIBRARY, completed in 1964, houses more than 400,000 volumes and numerous periodicals, journals, newspapers, manuscripts, films, and records. It has reading area for more than 2,000 students, meeting rooms and display areas.

The new HUGHES STADIUM, for football and other contests, is located at the Foothills Campus. It seats 30,000 and cost $2,900,000 to build. The colors of CSU are green and gold.

FORT COLLINS PUBLIC LIBRARY occupies a building of native sandstone, erected 1904 and doubled in size in 1937, in a park on Mathews St., which it shares with the Pioneer Museum. It had more than 80,000 vols. in 1968 and adds approx. 4,000 a year; city and book-mobile circulation is well over 300,000. It has a special collection of Colorado books and a microfilmed newspaper collection dating from 1874.

The PIONEER MUSEUM and ANTOINE JANIS CABIN, 219 Peterson St., have many relics of the old fort and Indian settlements. The cabin of handhewn logs, built 1854–1855, first dwelling on the Poudre, was brought here from its original site west of Laporte. The AUNTY STONE CABIN, 241 Mason St., is a log cabin built 1864 by Judge Lewis Stone as a mess hall for officers at Camp Collins and later conducted as a res-taurant by his wife. It was moved here in 1908.

RECREATION AREAS AND THE CIRCLE TOURS

Fort Collins is known to sportsmen and vacationists as the gateway to the hunting and fishing areas of the Roosevelt National Forest, adja-cent to the canyon of the Cache la Poudre River and other waters. This is "Colorado's Trout Route," where the fisherman can try his skill with rainbow, brown, brook and native cuthroat trout, and in Parvin Lake, a new hybrid—splake. Fishing is available the year around; hunting has a bow-and-arrow season in September and a regular season in October, and there are deer, elk, bear, bobcat, and sometimes mountain lion in the deep woods.

Tours that give access to some of the finest mountain scenery in all the Rockies are available in Fort Collins. Accommodations for vacation-ists are plentiful all through the Poudre Canyon area and include lodges, inns and resorts with meals, supplies, horseback riding, picnics, licenses, and fully equipped cabins for housekeeping. Some inns are open the year around.

Fort Collins has the popular Circle Tours, one-day round trips into the Rocky Mountain country east of the Great Divide. Six tours, cover-ing sites associated with early explorations and camps, are summarized herewith.

RED FEATHER LAKES and DEADMAN LOOKOUT, 116 *m.* Leave Fort Collins on the old stage route north to Owl Canyon, site of highly valued alabaster quarries; continue to The Forks, then west through Livermore up McNey Hill, past Parvin Lake, Colorado Fish and Game Preserve. Twin and Doudy Lakes, open in season for fishing. Next Redfeather Lakes, where 500 private cabins are hidden in the timber surrounding Hiawatha, Shagwa, Ramona, Snake, Letita, and Nokomis. Bellaire Lake, 3 *m.* farther, is stocked with trout. Deadman

Mountain, 14 *m.* beyond Redfeather, is the site of U. S. Forest Service fire watchtower, 10,481 ft. Visitors who climb to the top for views of mountains ranges becomes members of the Squirrel Club. Return to Fort Collins via Pingree Hill, Rustic, and the Poudre, or via Redfeather Lakes, Prairie Divide, Cherokee Park and Laramie Highway.

BUCKHORN VALLEY TOUR, 145 *m.* Leave Fort Collins via Horsetooth Dam, Masonville, follow Buckhorn Creek over Pennock Pass to Pingree Park. Here is located a forestry unit of Colorado State University. Visit Forestry Lodge, then north over the Little South to Bennett Creek and return via Cache la Poudre Canyon.

RIST CANYON Tour, 54 *m.* Take highway northwest through Bellvue and enter Rist Canyon, one-time frontier toll road. Up to top of Stove Prairie Hill, left off main highway to ascend Buckhorn Mountain for panorama of green Poudre Valley interlaced with silver threads of irrigation canals. West to Stove Prairie schoolhouse, north to Poudre Canyon highway (State 14), east to Fort Collins.

GHOST TOWN STAGE ROUTE, 105 *m.* North on US 287 to The Forks, ancient hotel of stage coach days. West through Livermore on old North Park freight trail, used until 1919, when the Poudre highway tunnel displaced it. Ascend McNey Hill to sudden striking view from summit of Great Divide. To Logcabin, then west; at Lady Moon Ranch turn south to Pingree Hill, descend to Rustic, return on State 14.

LARAMIE RIVER and THE RAHWAYS, 180 *m.* Follow the Cache la Poudre River (State 14) past Roaring Creek, Sleeping Elephant campground to Chambers Lake. Head north between Chambers and Lost Lakes, with the vast Rahway Primitive Area on the left. Parallel the Laramie River, flowing north. McIntyre and Rawah Lakes. New and Old Glendevy, rustic resorts. (8,300 alt.). This is the Colorado State Forest. Return via Deadman Park route.

POUDRE CANYON ROUTE, 244 *m.,* especially for fishermen. Start at Ted's Place, 9 *m.* northwest of Fort Collins on US 287, this is Indian country, fought over long ago by Arapahoes and Pawnees. Waterworks Park, 14 *m.,* has fireplaces, swings, trout ponds. Greyrock Mountain Trail, 2 *m.* farther, to a hidden lake in deer hunters' domain. Upper Greyrock was a rustlers' hideout. Poudre Highway passes through a tunnel in solid granite 1 *m.* above Mishawaka, entering Upper Poudre. Fort Collins Mountain Park, 38 *m.* from city, has a shelter house, trails, and facilities. At Big Narrows Dutch George, outlaw, once blocked the road to a hunting area he had preempted. From Rustic, explore Seven Mile Creek and old gold mines of the 1880's. State fish-hatching ponds at Zimmerman Ranch, winter range for deer, big horn mountain sheep. Near Spencer Heights Kit Carson trapped for ten winters. Chambers Lake has skiing until late June. Return via North Park, Walden; State 127 to Laramie, Wyo.; South on US 287 to Virginia Dale, historic haunt of Slade's gang; thence The Forks, to Fort Collins.

Grand Junction

Air Services: Frontier Airlines and United Airlines, at Walker Field, operated by the City of Grand Junction and Mesa County. Two runways, 7,500 ft. and 5,400 ft. About 200 landings and takeoffs daily. Hangar space, charter services, flying instruction provided; about 75 private planes based here.

Highways: Grand Junction is the major junction point of western Colorado. Interstate 70 from Denver (257 *m.*) and the east combines US 6 and US 24 after connecting with State 65. US 50 comes up from the southeast with State 8 and State 789, after a junction with State 141 at Whitewater. A new road, starting at Loma, 30 *m.* west, goes north into the Rangely oil basin. Salt Lake City is 300 *m.*, Kansas City, Mo., 895 *m.* away; almost equidistant are Los Angeles (1,062 *m.*) and San Francisco (1,070 *m.*).

Buses: Continental Trailways.

Railroad: Denver & Rio Grande Western Railroad, main line. Grand Junction depot, 2nd St. and Pitkin Ave.

Information and Accommodations: Grand Junction Chamber of Commerce, 127 N. 4th St., *Daily Sentinel,* evening and Sunday, 634 Main St. Three downtown hotels with from 50 to 100 rooms each; numerous motels, several with 50 to 100 units; total in Grand Junction and Grand Valley, 1,042 rooms and units, 718 trailer court spaces. There are five radio stations and one television channel.

Climate: Precipitation, annual average, 8.29 in.; snowfall, total, 27.9 in.; summer average temperatures, 61°–89°, winter, 20°–38°. Blizzards rare. Sunshine, 71% of year.

Recreation: Eleven public parks, 4 with supervised playground programs; 2 golf courses, 16 tennis courts, 12 baseball fields, 34 basketball courts, 5 football fields, 3 public bowling lanes. Every form of outdoor activity is available in mountains and valleys of Mesa County. Sightseeing trips to Colorado National Monument are available during the summer (*Consult the Chamber of Commerce*). Motor cars may be rented.

Annual Events: National Junior College Baseball tournament, Mesa County Sheriff's Posse Rodeo, VFW Rodeo, Western Slope Horse Show, Sports Car Rally, Rocky Mountain Open Gold tournament, Western Colorado Science Fair, Western Colorado Band tournament, Women's Invitational Softball tournament, Men's District Softball tournament.

GRAND JUNCTION (44,586 alt., 18,694 pop., 1960; 22,735, 1966, est.) seat of Mesa County, is the central marketing, manufacturing and supply city in the Grand Valley of the Colorado, the largest city between Denver (275 *m.* east) and Salt Lake City (300 *m.* west), and 30 *m.* east of the Utah border. Easily accessible via all highways on the western slope, it provides facilities for handling the agricultural and mineral products and the large fruit crop of the area. Retail trade enlists the largest number of employees, 16 percent of Mesa County's activities;

agriculture is next with more than 10 percent. Several thousand extra workers are often used in the Grand Junction area for harvesting the annual peach crop, which reaches 700,000 bu. The dry, sunny climate avoids extreme temperatures, being sheltered by the Rockies to the east. This increases its usefulness as a recreation center and makes tourism a profitable activity. Tourists spend up to $10,000,000 annually in this area. Local promotion outside the state in 1966 brought more visitors from California than from the rest of Colorado.

For many years the Grand Valley was part of the Northern Ute Reservation. In 1880 the Indians surrendered their claims and the next year were removed forcibly to Utah so that the valley might be opened to settlement. Land-hungry settlers poured in so quickly when the opening gun was fired on September 4, 1881, that they caught sight of the rear guard of the retreating Ute. A party of five men from Gunnison, headed by George A. Crawford, ex-governor of Kansas and frontier capitalist and speculator with a reputation for establishing a new town "every decade or so," staked a townsite here. The settlement was first called Ute, then West Denver, and was finally named for its site at the junction of the Gunnison and the Colorado (formerly the Grand) Rivers.

During the 1950 decade Grand Junction became the center of development and administration of the Federal government's uranium exploration and reproduction program. At present the Atomic Energy Commission maintains an administrative agency in Grand Junction.

Uranium ore and natural gas liquids have increased in value in Mesa County in recent years, but there have been decreases in coal, stone, and sand and gravel production, and the loss of clay production. Uranium ore production, up 20,000 tons in 1965, came from 65 operations, but only one operation, Bonanza No. 2 of the Climax Uranium Co., a subsidiary of American Metal Climax, Inc., produced more than 10,000 tons. This mill at Grand Junction, employing up to 200, treated ores for the recovery of uranium and vanadium. In 1966 mineral production in Mesa County had a value of $8,472,144. The major firms in uranium production are Climax, Union Carbide Corp., Beaver Mesa Uranium, Inc., Shipman Mining & Exploration Co., Foster & Sons, and Vanadium Corporation of America.

As the principal processor and shipper of Mesa County, Grand Junction handles much of its agricultural products. In a typical year of the 1960's the county had 58,405 beef cattle and 68,555 sheep and lambs, and a production of 785,981 lbs. of wool. Out of an agricultural income of $13,367,884, livestock sales were $7,131,511, field crops sales $2,810,115, and fruit crop sales $1,779,234. The county produced 250,000 bu. of peaches, 155,035 bu. of apples, and 152,869 bu. of pears. Several thousand workers are recruited in the season to harvest fruit crops. Agriculture, including fruit, employs about 19 to 21 percent of the labor force; all the other categories—mining, manufacturing and trade—employ the rest, with from 3 to 6 per cent unemployed. The Denver Research Institute rated annual family income in Grand Junction in 1960 at $5,371, with an accumulated wealth per capita of $6,335, while the State annual family income was $5,780.

OPERATION FORESIGHT, a cooperative effort by the city and downtown property owners to improve the business district, was instituted in 1962–1963. It called for a total overhaul of downtown streets, sidewalks, gutters, and storm sewer sytem, and provisions for regulating traffic, establishing accessible parking places, and improving appearances. Four blocks on Main Street became the Shopping Park. A gently curving street was built, bordered by trees, shrubs, flower beds, fountains and benches. Side streets were widened and heavy traffic was routed away from the new blocks. Development of contiguous areas has been continued. These projects caused the sponsors of the All-America City Contest to cite Grand Junction as one of 11 cities in the country with a distinguished planning record.

Settlement of the valley was rapid, although the first arrivals looked upon the land as being chiefly valuable for pasturing cattle. For some weeks there was fear of a return of the Ute. Grand Junction was incorporated in December 1881, in which month a store and a saloon were built, and a ditch company was organized to supply water. Early in 1882 the townsite was surveyed and platted on an elaborate scale, with provision for four public parks; a post office was established, and a school was opened.

The first election took place in 1882 when the district was still a part of Gunnison County. It was a school election, with two tickets in the field, one list of candidates being married men, the other single. The bachelors won by an overwhelming majority, due to the influence of the wives of the opposition who held, so it was rumored, that "a married man had no business fooling away his time with school marms." The first teacher was Nannie Blain, of Illinois, whose father was one of the first settlers in the valley and is credited with having planted the first fruit trees, thus laying the foundation of one of the largest enterprises in the State. She was soon a prominent figure in the community, organizing the first Sunday School, conducting the first funeral service before there was a cemetery; the deceased was laid away in a shallow grave in the desert. Sunday School services in early Grand Junction typified the attitude of the pioneer toward religion. Promptly at two o'clock on Sunday afternoons, all places of business closed and the entire population, from unregenerate old soak to the staid business man, repaired to the log schoolhouse to hear "Miss Nannie" read the Scriptures. After the service, shops and saloons were quickly reopened, and the town resumed the even and uneven tenor of its ways.

Building operations progressed rapidly. The Grand Junction House, the first hotel, was built in January 1882, and soon had a number of rivals. The most noteworthy were two hostelries that bore the startling names of The Pig's Ear and The Pig's Eye. By the end of the year the population of the town totaled almost 900; there were several general stores, a drug store, two blacksmith shops, five hotels and restaurants, a meat market, and twelve saloons. The predominance of barrooms was typical of all Western cattle town, and Grand Junction was no less rowdy in its youth than similar settlements. Cowboys from the upper ranges regularly shot up the town on pay days, and respectable citizens bewailed the want of law and order.

Extension of the narrow-gauge Denver & Rio Grande line from Gunnison in 1882 gave the town its first rail outlet and did much to stimulate growth. In 1883 Mesa County was created from part of Gunnison County, and Grand Junction was made the county seat. A company was soon organized to construct a toll road up the Colorado River; after considerable difficulty due to lack of funds, the project was completed and two stage lines began operating to Glenwood Springs.

In 1886 the Teller Institute and Indian School was established here. The citizens of Grand Junction donated 160 acres just east of town, and the Federal Government appropriated $23,000 for buildings. In addition to regular scholastic instruction, practical trades were taught the students, who were the same Ute who had been driven from the valley five years before. Later enrollment included many students from other tribes in Utah and Wyoming; the school was highly successful, continuing until 1911, when Indian education was concentrated at the Ute Reservation (*see Tour 11D and E*).

POINTS OF INTEREST

LINCOLN PARK, 12th St. and Gunnison Ave., the largest of the numerous parks that dot the city, has many of its 130 acres landscaped. Here is the Moyer Natatorium, a swimming pool donated by William J. Moyer.

MESA COLLEGE, founded 1925, has a campus of 40 acres and a complex of modern buildings, most of them erected within the 1960 decade. Besides the humanities it offers courses in agriculture, home economics, nursing, data processing, accounting, automotive mechanics, secretarial and pre-medical subjects. It has upwards of 2,400 students and a faculty of 135, and provides as well a Continuing Education Program for adults. The new Library, recently completed, is available to the public for research. Mesa College has a branch at Rangely, which enrolls up to 350 and has 25 instructors.

MESA COUNTY PUBLIC LIBRARY has two locations, 521 White Ave., and 616 North Avenue. It contains more than 150,000 volumes and receives more than 130 periodicals. It has branches in Fruita, Clifton, and De Beque, and a bookmobile service to other parts of the county. Teletype communication with major libraries in Denver provides a rapid interlibrary loan and reference service. The library has developed a substantial business information section. Other specialized collections in Grand Junction are the medical library at the VA Hospital, the geological and scientific library at AEC, and the County Law Library in the Courthouse.

A TRI RIVER EXTENSION OFFICE of Colorado State University is located in the County Courthouse. The staff provides information and advice on current research in agriculture, home economics, and youth work. Other offices are maintained in Delta and Montrose.

The STATE HOME AND TRAINING SCHOOL occupies 263 acres given to the State by the Federal Government when it closed Teller Institute, and Indian School. The present institution is devoted to rehabilitation treatment of mentally retarded children and physical rehabilitable children, and enrolls between 800–900 annually.

The COLORADO NATIONAL MONUMENT starts 4 m. west of Grand Junction. It is easily reached via US 50 and State 6. Continental Trailways buses reach the entrance to the Monument from Grand Junction, where motor cars also may be rented. Sightseeing trips are available during the summer; inquire at the Chambers of Commerce of Grand Junction and Fruita. This impressive area of rock erosion, disclosing the geological history of uncounted millions of years, covers 28 sq. m. and is administered by the National Park Service.

POINTS OF INTEREST IN ENVIRONS

Colorado National Monument, 4.8 m., Dinosaur Beds, 4 m. (see Tour 9D); Grand Mesa, 30.3 m. (see Tour 5E); Lands End, 45 m. (see Tour 9c).

Greeley

Air Services: Greeley-Weld County Airport, 3 *m.* from center of city, has 5,080 ft. runways. Stapleton International Airport at Denver, 51 *m.* south on US 85 has daily service by 8 airlines.
Buses: Greyhound lines have 6 north, 7 south, daily.
Highways: US 34, east-west; connects with US 87 and Interstate 25, north-south, 14 *m.* west of Greeley. US 85, north-south; State 3, 16, 263.
Railroads: Union Pacific main line, Colorado Southern branch line; six passenger trains daily.

Information and Accommodations: Greeley Chamber of Commerce, 7th Ave. at 9th St.; *Greeley Tribune,* daily, 714 8th St.; *Greeley Journal,* weekly; *Greeley Booster,* weekly; *Mirror,* weekly, Colorado State College. Two hotels, 29 motels, 10 mobile home parks; 54 churches, 2 public libraries, 1 college library; Weld County General Hospital, 351 beds, and Memorial Hospital.

Recreation: Greeley is the gateway to the Rocky Mountain National Park and to numerous areas for hunting, fishing, camping, hiking and skiing. The city has a public recreational program with a director. It has 12 public parks, 2 18-hole golf courses, 1 9-hole course; tennis courts, bowling alleys, swimming pools (1 municipal); 2 ice skating rinks, 1 roller skating rink. The city owns 1 mountain park and 3 mountain lakes. Spectator sports include college contests, basketball, football; also dog racing, horse racing, sailboat races, water skiing.

Annual Events: Go West With Greeley Rodeo, July 2, 3, 4. Weld County Junior Fair, Island Grove Park, August; Weld County Harvest Fair, late August; Fine Arts Festival, Colorado State College, summer session, also weekly plays at Little Theater of the Rockies, CSU summer session.

GREELEY (4,663 alt., 33,300 pop. 1967, est.) seat of Weld County (77,500 pop.), is located in the center of a rich agricultural area, noted for the handling of many head of livestock, processing of sugar beets, shipping of wheat and other grain, and diversified industries producing everything from office desks to fishing rods. The county has large herds of cattle, sheep and hogs, and more than 300,000 head of cattle are marketed every year. A few miles outside of Greeley is a big terminal stockyards complex, costing $300,000, that can accommodate 6,000 head. The county frequently leads the State in the production of wheat, barley, oats, and sugar beets. The Great Western Sugar Co. produces lime at its plant in Greeley, as well as in the environs, including Eaton (1,300 pop.) on US 85, Johnstown (1,000 pop.) on State 257, and Windsor (1,500 pop.) on State 257. The Eastman Kodak Co. in 1969 began building a distribution plant at Windsor, which is projected to employ up to 2,000.

Much of the industry in Greeley is concerned with food processing, meat packing and canning. Elsewhere in Weld County petroleum and coal production make 88 per cent of mineral production and in 1966 reached a value of $8,876,991.

Extensive building in recent years has taken place at COLORADO STATE COLLEGE, which has long specialized in the education of teachers; there also are a new high school, a junior high, a new wing for Weld County General Hospital, and new banking and postal facilities. AIMS JUNIOR COLLEGE, a two-year liberal arts and vocational institution, was opened in 1967, with 950 students.

Greeley is the outgrowth of the Union Colony, a cooperative enterprise conceived by and named for Horace Greeley, noted editor and publisher of the New York *Tribune,* and was founded by his agricultural editor, Nathan C. Meeker. Greeley, who popularized but did not coin the phrase, "Go West, young man!" was so impressed with the agricultural possibilities of the region on a visit in 1859 that he began a spirited campaign to interest "proper persons in establishing a colony in the Colorado Territory." Perhaps no settlement of its size was ever more widely advertised, thanks to the powerful New York *Tribune* and the reputation of Meeker. A group of New Englanders sent a committee, headed by Meeker, to inspect several sites in 1869. Meeker was fascinated by the mountains and had almost decided to establish the colony in South Park (*see Tour 15a*), when he conferred with William N. Byers, editor of the *Rocky Mountain News,* who had first-hand knowledge of the entire country; he persuaded Meeker that South Park was no place for an agricultural community and prevailed upon him to settle along the Cache la Poudre in the South Platte Valley. The area had been settled several years before by Peter Winne, David Barnes, and others; Byers urged Meeker to let them remain on their lands so that he might profit from their agricultural experience. Meeker, however, insisted on settling the site entirely with his own colonists and bought out the original settlers, purchasing 12,000 acres for $60,000; provisional title was taken to an additional 60,000 acres.

The following year 50 families, headed by Meeker, who was determined to be no mere armchair colonist, arrived here on the newly constructed Denver Pacific Railroad from Cheyenne. Members of the organization paid a $5 entrance fee and $150 for their land; no one was permitted to own more than 160 acres. Each colonist was given a town lot, 100 by 150 feet, and his choice of a 5-acre tract near by or an 80-acre farm at a greater distance. Later, those who accepted the 5-acre tracts were given the opportunity to obtain 80 additional acres at $3 an acre, the actual cost of the land to the colony. Building was retarded by the scarcity and high price of lumber, but by mid-year more than 200 houses and small business structures, the majority of adobe, had been constructed.

In the matter of temperance the colony's attitude was unswerving. In his circulars to prospective members and in his speeches, Meeker stated that the idle, immoral, intemperate, or inefficient need not apply; they would not be received, nor would they feel at home. One of the "commandments" was: "Thou shalt not sell liquid damnation within the lines of Union Colony." The first saloon, opened in a sod hut at the edge of town, was brought to the attention of the community during a Sunday service, and the congregation moved in a body to confer with the proprietor. During the argument a fire started in the establishment and destroyed it.

The Greeley Cooperative Stock and Dairy Association was organized in 1870, with 75 head of cattle, which made "a respectable show when stretched out across the prairie." Meeker wrote to the New York *Tribune* that "we mean to cover the unoccupied land in every direction with our cattle." The hard winters of 1871 and 1872, however, drove the cattle southward, and there was not enough hay to feed them. Independent cattlemen, maintaining that "the country was fit only for grazing," ranged their cattle on colony property. To keep livestock out of the fields, colonists erected a 50-mile fence around their lands. With posts at 25¢ each, and wire at 8¢ a pound, the undertaking cost $20,000. Much of the money raised by sale of town lots for civic improvements was spent on this venture.

The fence did not provide complete protection, for the settlers were denied the right to put gates across public roads leading into the colony and were forced to employ watchmen to guard these points.

Meeker established the Greeley *Tribune,* a weekly, in the first year of settlement and gave prominent display to the New York *Tribune's* editorials and articles dealing with the community, together with the many letters received from Horace Greeley. The town's first sizable industry was the tanning of buffalo hides, and the local newspaper reported in 1876 that the plant, the only successful one in the United States, was turning out 12 robes a day, with aggregate sales of $2,000 to $3,000 monthly.

After several warmly contested elections and court battles between 1872 and 1877, Greeley became the county seat and grew rapidly. The second electric light plant in the State was installed here in 1885, and at this time potato raising began on a considerable scale. Large storage warehouses were built; growers organized a Potato Exchange and initiated a marketing program, aided by extensive advertising, which increased the demand for Greeley "spuds." By 1890 more than 2,000 carloads were being shipped annually to eastern and southern markets. A Potato Experimental Station, established in 1915, was later taken over by the Bureau of Plant Industry of the U. S. Department of Agriculture. Sugar beet culture was introduced in 1902 and almost immediately became one of the most important mainstays of the rapidly growing city. German-Russians were imported in large numbers to till the crops; later, Japanese became the largest racial group working the beet fields. They proved unsatisfactory because of their custom of underbidding native labor, and were replaced with Spanish-Americans, who make up a large proportion of the urban and rural population.

POINTS OF INTEREST

COLORADO STATE COLLEGE, which opened in 1890 to supply the need for trained teachers, has carried its present title only since October, 1957. Originally the State Normal School, its name was changed to Colorado State Teachers College in 1911. It was then offering four years of study leading to the bachelor of arts degree. In 1935 it was styled the Colorado State College of Education, to give recognition to its fully developed graduate program. In 1957 the State legislature agreed to shorten the name to Colorado State College. Its graduate school offers work leading to the degrees of master of arts, specialist in education, doctor of education, and doctor of philosophy.

In 1941 this *Guide* reported that the college had 17 buildings and 1,570 students on 65 acres. Today it enrolls more than 7,000 and its 243-acre campus in located in a residential area in the southern part of Greeley. It is in three parts, East, Central, and West. The major buildings are on Central Campus. However, Ross Hall, of Science (1966); Bishop-Lehr, the laboratory school, and McKee Hall of Education, erected 1968 at a cost of $2,900,000, are on West Campus. Three coeducational residence halls on West Campus can house 1,660. Capacity for housing throughout is 3,320. The total physical plant has 61 buildings. The college also owns 80 acres and five buildings adjacent to the city of Estes Park.

The college maintains a laboratory school, which includes an elementary school with kindergarten and six grades, and College High School, with grades 7 through 12. The Special Education School, on the campus, is a cooperative project of a Greeley school district and the college, and enrolls handicapped and disturbed children. A nursery school is maintained by the Dept. of Home Economics. In a number of ways the college provides instructional materials, films and recordings, test programs, off-campus instruction, and correspondence courses. The Insurance Institute give courses in cooperation with the School of Business to prepare students for careers in insurance.

The Library in Carter Hall, bulging with approx. 300,000 vols. and associated research facilities, is being moved to modern quarters in a new Classroom-Library Building on the West Campus, intended eventually solely for the Library. Cost will be $4,700,000, one-third to be paid by the Federal Government. Brelsford-Childress-Paulin are the architects.

The College Center, 19th St. between 10th and 11th Aves., is the focus of student activities. Students may participate in the choirs, bands, orchestra, and the Greeley Philharmonic Orchestra. The Little Theatre of the Rockies presents plays during the school year.

A student's typical first-year expense, without fringe costs, is estimated at $1,795 for a state resident, (tuition and fees, $345; books and supplies, $240; board and room, $860, personal expenses, $350). A student from outside the state pays $795 for tuition and fees.

The MEEKER MEMORIAL MUSEUM, 9th Ave. and 14th St., was the home of Nathan C. Meeker, who, after founding the colony, was appointed Indian Agent at the White River Agency and was slain there in the Ute uprising in 1879 (*see Tour 17*). The front of the building is the original house, a four-room, two-story structure of sod and adobe, with a wooden framework, erected in 1871. It is surmounted with a watch tower inclosed within a wooden railing. The brick addition at the rear and the veranda encircling the south and west sides of the adobe building were constructed later by Meeker. In the museum are Meeker's furniture, saddles, trappings, and papers. Here also is the plow that turned the first sod in the Union Colony.

The GREELEY PUBLIC LIBRARY opened its new quarters in the East Wing of the Civic Center Complex April 1, 1968. It has more than 72,000 vols. and circulates more than 300,000 annually, one-third among young readers. The Children's Room has more than 25,000 vols. The Varvel Memorial Collection contains books about the city and its residents. Another cultural facility is the COUNTY LIBRARY of Weld County, which serves the southwestern part of the city and sends a bookmobile into the rural areas.

The GREELEY MUNICIPAL MUSEUM occupies quarters in the East Wing of the Civic Center Complex, adjacent to the Greeley Public Library. Its exhibits deal with the life and customs of the area.

Leadville

Air Services: Lake County Airport, 1½ *m.* south of Leadville, has a 4,500-ft. runway and hangar facilities.
Bus Lines: Continental Trailways provides two buses a day to and from Denver, and other connections. Bus also between Leadville and Climax.
Highways: Leadville is served by US 24 (with State 4), which is joined by State 91 1 *m.* above Leadville, and State 300. Interstate 70, from Denver west across the State, has a junction with State 91 24 *m.* north of Leadville. Distance to Denver, 115 *m.*; Colorado Springs, 129 *m.*; Aspen, 59 *m.*
Railroads: Denver & Rio Grande Western runs parallel with US 24 north-south. Colorado & Southern provides freight service between Leadville and Climax.

Information and Accommodations: Leadville Chamber of Commerce, Harrison Ave. and 9th St. *Herald Democrat,* issued five evenings a week, and *Carbonate Chronicle,* a weekly. One radio station and 5 television channels by cable from Denver. Vendome Hotel, 701 Harrison Ave. Silver King Inn, north of city line, 40 units. Numerous motels.

Recreation: Leadville has 2 public parks, 1 golf course, 4 tennis courts, 4 baseball diamonds, 4 basketball courts, 3 lakes for boating. Its biggest appeal is as the jumping-off place for countless outdoor activities in Lake County, including fishing, camping, hiking, horseback riding, scenic trips. Easily accessible for fishing are Twin Lakes, Turquoise Lake, Conley Lakes, Clear Creek Reservoir, Arkansas River, Lake Creek, Half Moon Creek, West and East Tennessee Creeks. Streams are stocked four times a season by the hatchery of the U. S. Fish & Wildlife Service at Evergreen Lakes. Cooper Hill, 12 *m.* north of Leadville on US 24, considered the State's best family slope, is open each Saturday and Sunday until May. Vail Village, 37 *m.* north, and Breckenridge, 45 *m.* east, are ski centers. Ice skating is available at the All Purpose Court in Leadville. Travel by jeep over the Mosquito Range and the Collegiate Range is available in the summer. The moderate temperature makes for a cool, invigorating atmosphere: July is 40° to 70°. Yearly snowfall averages 124.7 in.

Touring: A self-guided tour over the entire mining area is possible with the aid of a complete directory, *Travel the Routes of the Silver Kings,* available at the Leadville Chamber of Commerce. The Timberline Tours to ghost towns, mines, lakes and top of the 14,000-ft. Rockies start at 220 W. Second St.

LEADVILLE (10,152 alt., 4,008 pop. 1960; 6,000, 1967, est.) seat of Lake County and often called Cloud City, is located in the upper Arkansas River valley east of the Continental Divide and served principally by north-south highway US 24 and its connections. Within a short drive is the tallest peak in Colorado, Mt. Elbert, 14,431 ft., and the third tallest, Mt. Massive, 14,418 ft. Famous for the fortunes in gold and silver taken out of its surrounding area. Leadville had 40,000 people at the top of its prosperity in 1880; after the panic of 1893 and the repeal of the Federal Silver Purchase Act, it declined to the size of a village. The town's records indicate that anywhere from $600,000,000 to $1 billion worth of minerals was extracted in the county, in the late 19th century, including $60,000,000 in gold and $200,000,000 in silver. All such figures, however, are based on the buying power of a period; today's estimates are best described in the oft-used term, *fabulous*.

These ancient operations still cast a nostalgic glow over Leadville and Lake County, but actually more wealth is being taken out of the mines today than ever before. The mineral is molybdenum, used in hardening steel, which is recovered at Climax, 13 *m*. north of Leadville, by the Climax Molybdenum Division of American Metal Climax, Inc., and with other metals accounts for a valuation of more than $92,-000,000 annually. In 1966 the corporation moved practically all of its approx. 2,700 employees into Leadville, thus adding both to the city's population and retail sales.

Although the legends of the past are kept brightly polished for the entertainment of visitors, the serious business of making Leadville a better place for everyday living engages the officials. New building operations have refurbished older institutions in recent years. There is a new Lake County Courthouse; St. Vincent's hospital has invested $1,000,000 in new construction; the Leadville Medical Center and the Leadville Labor Center, and a new home for the Elks, have brightened the face of the municipality. Colorado Mountain College, a two-year junior institution established at Glenwood Springs, has opened its East Campus at Leadville, and is providing facilities for studying the liberal arts, agriculture, the biological and chemical sciences, the social sciences, and occupational programs all the way from automobile mechanics to recreation supervision and "secretarial science."

The Leadville district, one of the most highly mineralized in the world, has produced gold, silver, lead, zinc, manganese, and molybdenum. Gold came first, early in 1860, when Abe Lee and other Georgians discovered in California Gulch, on the southern limits of the town, one of the State's richest placer diggings. In the summer of that year Oro City was founded, and within two months the gulch had a population of 5,000; two years later, when the gold sands had been exhausted, it was almost deserted. Decay continued until 1875 when "Uncle Billy" Stevens, a prospector from Minnesota, began reworking some of the abandoned claims and took in as a partner A. B. Wood, a trained metallurgist. The latter analyzed the heavy red sands that had long interfered with sluicing, and discovered them to be virtually pure carbonate of lead, with a high silver content. The two men worked quietly in tracing silver-lead lodes and staking out claims, one of which, the Iron Silver, later yielded twenty millions. Scant attention was paid to their activities until Wood sold his interests for $40,000 to Levi Leiter, partner of Marshall Field, the Chicago merchant.

The gulch instantly stirred with new life; old miners prospected north and west to make strikes on Iron and Carbonate Hills. Later, George Fryer opened a rich body of carbonate ore on the adjoining hill that now bears his name. Oro City, which had been moved up California

Gulch, was moved back down again and merged with Slabtown as New Oro City. Here, in January 1878, the miners assembled to incorporate the camp as Leadville, with H. A. W. Tabor as mayor and postmaster; population was estimated at 200 persons.

While not altogether typical of the Carbonate Kings, as the local mining magnates came to be called, Tabor symbolizes Leadville's amazing history. The Vermont-born stonecutter, with his wife and small son, had come in the Pike's Peak gold rush early in 1859, and endured many years of hardships and privation as he drifted from field to field, following each new strike. In California Gulch in 1860 he washed out several thousand dollars' worth of "dust," but his claim was soon depleted. There followed a brief and luckless sojourn at Buckskin Joe, where his wife Augusta kept the family by taking in boarders. By the time of the silver discoveries Tabor was convinced that his luck had run out; he was keeping a small store and acting as postmaster at Oro City.

More to be rid of them than in any hope of profit, he grubstaked two German shoemakers, George Hook and Auguste Rische, who had drifted in from South Park. The men helped themselves to a jug of whisky without Tabor's knowledge, so the story goes, and sampled it appreciatively as they started off prospecting. Climbing a hill within a mile of camp, they set to work digging in the shade of a pine, for to them one spot looked as desirable as another. Almost at once they struck an exceptional silver lode later developed as the Little Pittsburg; according to a report of the United States Geological Survey, they made the strike at the only point where the vein came so near the surface.

Possessed of a third share in the find by reason of his $17 grubstake, Tabor developed "the Midas touch"; his luck, not long since at bottom, was soon the talk of the State and then of the entire country. Duped, Tabor bought a "salted" shaft, sent men to work it to the accompaniment of ribald merriment on the part of those in on the hoax, and promptly hit the great Chrysolite lode, one of the marvels of the district. Having realized $500,000 in dividends from the Little Pittsburg, he sold out within a year for $1,000,000 and invested his profits in even more remunerative enterprises—among others, in the immensely profitable Matchless Mine.

With a fortune estimated at more than $9,000,000, Tabor embarked upon a bizarre public career. He was elected lieutenant-governor of the State, gave generously to the campaigns of the Republican party, presented Leadville with a fire department, organized military companies, and built opera houses and imposing business buildings both here and in Denver. In only one respect was he disappointed. Anxious to become U. S. Senator from Colorado, he had to be satisfied with a thirty-day term, filling the vacancy created by the appointment of Senator Henry M. Teller as Secretary of the Interior in 1883. Divorcing his wife Augusta, whom he had married in Maine in 1857, he married Elizabeth McCourt ("Baby") Doe, a young and beautiful divorcée, to whom he had been attracted in Leadville days. President Arthur attended the lavish wedding party at the Willard Hotel, Washington.

Tabor's fall was as meteoric as his rise. With the collapse of silver prices and the panic of 1893 his over-extended financial empire quickly crumbled. The ruin was complete; virtually penniless, he was postmaster of Denver at his death on April 10, 1899. "Hold on to the Matchless," were his last instructions to Baby Doe, and this she did faithfully, living alone for many years in a rude shack beside the mine shaft, enduring abject poverty until her death in 1935.

In the boom years of the Carbonate Camp, as it was known from the nature of its ores, mines and smelters roared day and night; sawmills droned in the hills; fresh yellow pine lumber was knocked together to create rows of cabins and stretches of sidewalks, no two on the same level. The camp was a wilderness of "tents, wigwams of boughs and bare poles . . . cabins wedged between stumps; cabins built on stumps; cabins half roofed . . . with sailcloth roofs, and no roofs at all. . . . All faces looked restless, eager, fierce." From the mines on almost inaccessible hillsides, hundreds of heavy ore wagons clattered down steep makeshift roads and rumbled through town to the smelters. Whole pine forests were cut down, converted into charcoal, and consumed by smelters and ore-reduction plants, for coal and coke were too expensive for use even when available, which they usually were not.

As one rich strike followed another, an army of newcomers descended upon the roaring camp by stage lines, in freight wagons, and on foot—men and women of all ages, all professions, and, it is said, of all races except Indian and Chinese. The first Chinese who ventured into camp were promptly hanged. During winter months hundreds perished along the icy mountain passes; the route was lined with dead horses and mules, as were the streets in town. Soon the population had risen to 10,000, and still the human flood continued.

Ruthless profiteering by local storekeepers founded many a fortune. Staple groceries sold at four times their price in Denver; a barrel of whisky often netted a $1,500 profit; hay frequently brought $200 a ton. An endless chain of freight teams traveled between Denver, Colorado Springs, and Canon City, laden with bacon and sealskin coats, flour and jewels, champagne and mining machinery. The railheads, 75 miles distant, were a hopeless confusion of freight and men awaiting transportation. Six stage lines served the camp before it was six months old.

Accommodations were wholly inadequate and most expensive. The few hotels turned away hundreds each night, and lodging houses charged $1 for the privilege of sharing a bed with another in makeshift rooms containing a dozen beds. A large tent was pitched on a side street and advertised as the best "hotel" in town. The Mammoth Palace, a vast shed with accommodations for 500, contained double tiers of hard bunks occupied day and night, a guest paying 50¢ for a sleeping turn of eight hours. Thousands fought for permission to curl up on draughty saloon floors, paying high for preferred spots near the stove. Pneumonia claimed scores of victims.

In February 1878, Father Robinson and Parson Uzzell organized their respective churches, Catholic and Methodist. Father Robinson commandeered the first load of brick to reach the town, it is said, and with it Irish miners built his church, topped with a tall steeple; later, the railroad company presented the congregation with the bell that still sounds over the city.

In 1879 was built the first schoolhouse, such as it was, for citizens complained that it was a disgrace to a city of 20,000. At the same time three breweries were running at capacity, with beer at 5¢ a schooner, six for 25¢. But champagne, or what passed for it, remained the drink of splurgers, and immense quantities were consumed.

Every night brass bands assembled along State Street before variety houses and wine theaters to blare in friendly rivalry for an hour or more, afterwards parading the principal streets with banners advertising "cancans, female bathers, daring tumblers, and other dramatic attractions." Charles Sidney Vivian, an English actor, appeared at the Grand Central in 1880, and died here later in the year. Vivian had founded the Jolly Corks in New York in 1867, later reorganized as the Benevolent Protective Order of Elks, and in 1889 his body was removed to Elk's Rest in Mt. Hope Cemetery, Boston.

Almost from the first an orgy of speculation and frenzied finance swept the camp. Mines, prospects, even shallow holes in the ground, were sold and resold many times a day, and always at a profit. Millions were made from grubstakes of a few dollars. Every day brought forth some new and incredible discovery; yokels from the cornfields dug into ground passed over as valueless by experienced prospectors and became wealthy. A prospector died during mid-winter, so it is said, and was placed in a snowbank until friends could hire a man to dig a grave in the frozen ground. After a long delay they visited the cemetery to find that the sexton had struck a rich silver lode while excavating. Within a few days the cemetery was staked out, and the dead man, forgotten, remained in the snowbank until the spring thaw.

By 1880 estimates of Leadville's population ranged from 25,000 to 40,000; the *Chronicle* placed it at 60,000. The constant fire hazard led to the organization of three volunteer fire companies and the Leadville Water Company. As little solder was available, many pipe joints and faucets were "wiped" with silver. Military companies were organized and financed by the Carbonate Kings—the Leadville Guards, the Carbonate Rifles, the Tabor Highland Guards, the Tabor Light Cavalry, the Pitkin Cavalry, among others. Tabor's Highlanders were accoutered in black doublets with blue and red cord and facings, kilts of royal Stuart style, a sporan of white goat's hair, stockings dashed with red and green, and Prince Charlie bonnets; his guards were magnificent in red trousers, blue coats, and brass helmets. Ostensibly formed to resist the Ute, who were never a menace, these gaudily uniformed private armies at once satisfied the Carbonate Kings' craving for splendor and protected their persons and properties.

Harrison Avenue was laid out in 1878 and soon rivaled Chestnut Street as a business thoroughfare. Lots along it sold at $250 a front foot; stores rented at $500 a month. Just above the dance halls, variety theaters, and brothels along State Street and part of Main, was Carbonate Avenue, lined with the dwellings of merchant princes and mining moguls. Tabor, however, continued to live for a time in a small clapboard cottage on Harrison Avenue, later moving it intact to Carbonate Avenue.

When the few police proved powerless against armed ruffians, citizens took the law into their own hands. The formation of Vigilantes, with subsequent hangings and banishment of known thugs, restored some semblance of order. Mart Duggan, notorious bully and killer, was appointed city marshall. Quick with his fists and gun, boasting that he had killed seven men, Duggan hunted down the worst of the ruffians. Occasionally he assaulted the innocent and was often in trouble—once threatening to throw Mayor Tabor into jail—but he retained his position for several years. When he finally resigned and departed, Tabor wired him to return. Duggan was killed in 1888 outside the Texas House by one of three gamblers who had drawn lots to see who should shoot him.

Substantial brick buildings began to appear. Banks were "over-run with deposits," but the post office remained the depository of the miners, who purchased money orders payable to themselves and renewed them on expiration. Money orders averaged $1,000 a day for a long period, more than half the rate in St. Louis, four times that in Kansas City. Two large hotels were built—the Clarendon and the Grand. The latter stood on Chestnut Street and was kept by Thomas F. Walsh, whose profits here later enabled him to discover and operate the noted Camp Bird mine at Ouray (*see Tour 18*).

Tabor built an opera house with elaborate private boxes for himself and "Bill" Bush. Friends in business and politics, they were rivals for the attention of every visiting star. When Gladys Robeson, a popular variety actress of the day, appeared in "red tights that set off her admirable figure," Tabor tossed a handful of silver dollars across the footlights. Bush immediately tossed two handfuls; Tabor, four; their supply of silver exhausted, Tabor and Bush sent to the gambling rooms below for bags of gold pieces. The battle raged, with a whooping audience participating until virtually every coin in the house was on the stage. The actress gathered up some $5,000, the stage hands even more, but the handsome actress declined an introduction to either of the rivals.

Those who founded fortunes here included Meyer Guggenheim, who came from Philadelphia in 1879, and with R. B. Graham bought the A. Y. and Minnie mines, which within a few months were netting a profit of $1,000 a day; a decade later they were valued at $14,000,000. In 1888 Guggenheim and his sons established the Philadelphia Smelter at Pueblo, later sold for $10,000,000. Here in 1880, Samuel Newhouse made the lucky strike that enabled him to hobnob with the Prince of Wales' set in London and to become one of the largest copper operators in the world; it was he who erected the Flatiron building in New York. Alva Adams, three times Governor of the State, father of Alva B. Adams, who became U. S. Senator from Colorado, took a fortune from the Blind Tour. John L. Routt, last Territorial Governor, was owner of rich Carbonate Hill property. Charles Boettcher, pioneer Leadville merchant, later organized the Colorado Portland Cement Company and became one of the State's wealthiest industrialists.

By the end of 1880 the town had 28 miles of streets. Harrison Avenue and Chestnut Street were paved with slag from the smelters, and in summer the dust was laid by a man who ladled water from a barrel and collected what he could from citizens along his route. This derelict was Abe Lee, who, after making the first gold discoveries in California Gulch 20 years before, had squandered two fortunes. Tabor organized a street railway company that failed because the large wooden cars were too heavy for horses to pull up the steep grades. A telephone exchange, established in 1879, was "talking like a charm," and the *Evening Times* reported the arrest of the city's "first insane person," who was charged with spending all of his time in prayer and religious exhortation. In 1880 the tracks of the Denver & Rio Grande Western advanced up the Arkansas to the camp, and those of the Denver & South Park soon entered from the north.

There were 14 smelters and ore reduction plants in the Leadville district in 1881, the first having been established in 1875 at Malta. In the intervening years the district had become the smelting center of the Rocky Mountain region, and the importance of the smelters to the development of the region was second only to that of the mines. The demand for labor in the plants brought in large numbers of Austrians, Croats, Serbs, and Slovenes. Many turned to the mines, attracted by better wages, which led to a second immigration, largely of Mexicans and Spanish-Americans, who replaced other nationalities in the smelting industry. Miners and smelter hands struck in 1880 for higher wages and improved working conditions. Fatalities ran high in the mills and mines, and public sympathy was with the strikers. When Vigilantes and the Carbonate Kings' military companies failed to overawe them, martial law was declared and the strike collapsed, leaving owners in undisputed possession of the field for more than a decade.

Leadville's decline began in 1881. Production of silver reached a peak of $11,473,946 in 1880, although the Morning Star, Chrysolite, Catalpa, Little Pittsburg, Matchless, Iron Silver, and other celebrated mines held production around $10,000,000 for several years. But some of the largest and richest properties, due to reckless exploitation, were nearing exhaustion. When it was revealed that certain mines had been borrowing heavily to pay dividends, stocks dropped from many dollars to a few cents. Charges were made that stock in many companies had been manipulated by insiders. Investors became panic stricken and unloaded their shares, breaking the market. One by one, the banks failed. Tabor and other mining kings abandoned the city for Denver. The sporting gentry left for more lucrative fields. Fires destroyed the Grant Smelter, a few larger hotels, and several department stores, one owned by Dave May, who later established a large chain of such stores in the East and West.

Population dwindled and silver production decreased; but the town itself was as little prepared as Tabor and his associates for the blow that fell in 1893 when the mints in India ceased buying silver for coinage. The Sherman Silver Purchase Act was repealed, and the depression of 1893 sent the price of the white metal tumbling. The fabulous era of silver had ended.

In the winter of 1895 business men organized a Crystal Carnival, building a mammoth ice palace. The castellated structure of Norman design covered five acres; within its ice walls, 8 feet thick and 50 feet high, were a ballroom, a skating rink, a restaurant, peep shows, and curio shops. Frozen into the walls were specimens of ore, produce, and meat; ice and snow statues graced the interior. The palace, visited by thousands, remained open until July 4, 1896, before it melted away.

Leadville experienced a revival late in the 1890's with the discovery of the Little Johnny and other rich gold mines east of the city. The Little Johnny had been worked as early as 1884 by James J. Brown, who had come to Leadville in 1880 in the employ of David H. Moffat. His fame is somewhat eclipsed by that of his wife, who was prominent in New York, Newport, and European society; a heroine of the *Titanic* disaster, she became known as "the unsinkable Mrs. Brown." Later John F. Campion, who had arrived in 1879, purchased the Little Johnny and consolidated it with other properties as the Ibex Mining Company, from which came another great Colorado fortune. Campion later pioneered the sugar beet industry in Colorado, building its first beet sugar factory.

Until the close of World War I, large lead, zinc, and manganese deposits in the vicinity were worked profitably, but declining prices, the exhaustion of rich lodes, and the flooding of shafts subsequently forced the closing of many mines. During the prohibition era numerous isolated and deserted shafts housed whisky stills, and "Leadville moon" was highly regarded and commanded good prices throughout the West. Growth of agriculture, ranching, and tourist business has recently contributed to the city's welfare. During the 1930's population has increased, largely due to the development of molybdenum deposits at Climax and intensive working of old gold, silver, lead, and zinc properties; many abandoned stores and houses have been reconditioned.

POINTS OF INTEREST

Houses built nearly a century ago are preserved today as exhibits of period housekeeping. Two of them, the HEALEY HOUSE and the DEXTER CABIN, Harrison Ave. and East 10th St., are maintained by the State Historical Society of Colorado (*Open June 1–October 15, 9–5*). The Healey House was built in boom days and its furniture was the best of its time. The Dexter Cabin, 1878–1879, is made of logs and contains two rooms, furnished more modestly.

The little TABOR COTTAGE, 115 East 5th St., has been refurnished in period style by its owners, who admit the public (*35¢*). H. A. W. Tabor built it in 1877 in Harrison Avenue, and moved it to its present site when he decided to build his Opera House in Harrison.

A certain melancholy interest attaches to the house because here Tabor lived amicably with his first wife, Augusta, to whom he was married in Vermont in 1857. Augusta is regarded in Leadville as a woman of great character who was gravely injured by her husband's philandering after they had moved to Denver. In 1881 Tabor deserted Augusta to live with Mrs. Elizabeth Doe, "Baby Doe," in the Windsor Hotel in Denver. After the Tabors' divorce Augusta, with a block of Tabor's wealth, frequently visited in Leadville, where her sister occupied her former house. When she died in 1895 she left riches and Tabor was bankrupt.

The HOUSE WITH THE EYE, 127 West 4th St., is a cottage museum exhibiting relics of mining days, including the Tabor grand piano, an electric piano, slot machines, old bottles and glassware, a hearse and "actual nooses from the first lawful and lynch-mob hangings, 1882." The eye is a little window in the attic roof.

At 318 Harrison Ave. a marker commemorates the first store opened in 1881 by David May, whose enterprise led to the establishment of the May Department Stores. May started merchandising in 1877 in a tent.

The TABOR OPERA HOUSE, 308 Harrison Avenue, built by H. A. W. Tabor in 1879, after he became wealthy from silver mining, is today an outstanding historic structure in Leadville. Guided tours, conducted daily from May 30 to October 1, take visitors back to the red plush and gold tinsel decades when the best performers on "the road" appeared there. These included Laurence Barrett, Louis James, Helena Modjeska, Robert Mantell, Lew Dockstader's and Primrose & West's minstrels, and numerous operettas of the past. It was advertised as "the cosiest place for lovers of the legitimate drama to throw off the cares of life and yield to the fascinations of music and imagery." On the ground floor was the Cabinet Saloon, where poker could be played between acts.

The opening night, at which *The Serious Family* and *Who's Who* were presented, was poorly attended because two nights previously the Vigilantes had hanged two men from the rafters of the unfinished courthouse a few steps up the street, and the hushed and uneasy town was in no mood for frivolity. Melodramas, farces, and Shakespearian tragedies held the boards until 1882, when the Emma Abbott English Grand Opera Company arrived. For this gala event "plug hats, heretofore a rarity, suddenly appeared on the heads of male bipeds," so the *Chronicle* reported, and "the ladies came in full bloom; flashy dresses, white opera hats, and colors flying."

Later that year an audience accorded a warm welcome to Oscar Wilde, who stepped upon the stage in a suit of "elegant black velvet, with knee breeches and black stockings, a Byron collar and white neckhandkerchief. . . . On his shirt front glittered a single cluster of diamonds." He spoke at length on "The Practical Application of the Aesthetic Theory to Exterior and Interior House Decoration, with Observations on Dress and Personal Ornament." The miners understood little of what Wilde said in his dull manner, but they liked him, being quite frankly awed by his capacity to drink hard liquor.

After the silver crash of 1893 Tabor lost the Opera House and it became known as the Weston Theatre, managed by Letitia Weston and her husband. In 1905 it was acquired by the local B. P. O. E. lodge and until January 12, 1955, was known as the Elks Opera House. Mrs. Florence A. Hollister, the present owner, has renamed it the Tabor Opera House and restored it to its original appearance.

The site of the CLARENDON HOTEL adjoins the Tabor Opera House to the south. Built in 1879, one of the first large hotels in the city, it was torn down early in the 1930's. Its bar and lobby were the club of the Carbonate Kings, who here gave banquets to President U. S. Grant and his wife, General Sherman, the Duke of Cumberland, Commodore Vanderbilt, and Jay Gould. The food prepared by Monsieur L. Lapierce from Delmonico's, New York, was celebrated. Oscar Wilde stayed here during his engagement, and callers found him reclining on a couch, "some six feet tall, with long hair reaching to his shoulders . . . a languid far-away look in his eyes." Much to their chagrin, he was dressed in tweeds, "without sunflower or lily."

The HOTEL VENDOME, 701 Harrison Ave., a four-story brick structure, its false mansard roof ornamented with cupolas in the manner of the 1880's, was opened in 1885 as the Tabor Grand Hotel and renamed in 1894. The elaborately decorated and furnished bar is said to have had the finest stock in the State. It was tended by "Powder House Billy," quick with his fists, who on one occasion knocked out a guest who refused to pay for his drinks, on the ground that he did not wish to encourage intemperance.

The MATCHLESS MINE (*open daily, May–Sept.*), E. on 7th Ave. to junction with a dirt road, 1.4 *m.*, then left 1.5 *m.*, was Tabor's most prized possession and one of the great bonanzas of the district. On Fryer Hill overlooking the valley, the property was purchased by Tabor in 1881 for $117,000 and netted him $10,000,000, paying $100,000 a month at times. A single shipment of ore from this mine, which Tabor's contemporaries had pronounced worthless, assayed 10,000 ounces of silver a ton. When Oscar Wilde visited the mine, he was met at the bottom of the shaft by a dozen miners, each with a bottle. All of the bottles made the rounds; after the twelfth drink, Wilde was cool and collected, and was "voted a perfect gentleman" by the somewhat tipsy miners. Repairs were made to the surface plant and an electric hoist was installed in 1937, when the mine was reopened.

Just south of the shafthouse in the TABOR CABIN (*open*), a one-room wooden shack with a lean-to, now occupied by the caretaker of the mine. Here "Baby Doc" Tabor lived alone for years, rejecting all offers of assistance, stubborn in the belief that some day the deep veins of the Matchless would again produce a silver fortune. She was found dead here on March 7, 1935, having died a day or two before. One end of the cabin was piled high with mementoes of the Tabors' lives, bundles of newspapers, and a miscellany of unopened presents sent by unknown friends who admired a faith that could not be shaken.

Adjoining the Matchless mine on the south stands the last of the long-abandoned buildings of the ROBERT E. LEE MINE, Leadville's greatest bonanza. Long an undeveloped claim on Fryer Hill, it was bought in 1879 by Jim Baxter, who sank a 100-foot shaft, found no ore, and sold it for $30,000. The following morning the new owners put in a single shot of dynamite and exposed a vein of almost pure silver. More than $500,000 was taken out within three months; in one 24-hour period $118,500 was mined; an operator, it is said, offered $10,000 for permission to work an hour on an area four feet square, and was scornfully refused.

What is described as "the largest underground mining operation in the world" is located at Climax, 13 *m.* north of Leadville on State 91. This is the plant of the Climax Molybdenum Division of American Metal Climax, Inc., which in 1967 mined 15,400,000 tons, a rate of 42,900 tons a day. Its value was 25 per cent of the total mineral value of Colorado, exceeded only by petroleum. The mine is located in Bartlett Mountain on the Continental Divide, a height of 13,335 ft. A new plant that recovers molybdenum from oxide ores will have a capacity of 3,000,000 lbs. a year when in full operation. Climax also recovers monazite, a combination of rare earth phosphates, wolframite and tungsten, from mill tailings. The first mining at Bartlett took place in 1903 when a Nebraska banker dug a tunnel into the mountain in order to intercept a gold-bearing vein from the opposite side. He failed to find it. In the 1930's a 500-ft. shaft was sunk to the Phillipson level; today miners are drilling 600 ft. below that. In 1967 the company began operating its Urad mine in Clear Creek County and testing its newly discovered Henderson Deposit nearby, which has reserves of more than 236,000,000 tons.

Pueblo

Air Services: Frontier Airlines, Trans-Central. Pueblo Memorial Airport, 6 *m.* east on State 96, US 50.

Bus Lines: Continental Trailways, Denver-Colorado Springs-Pueblo Trailways, Greyhound Lines.

Highways: Interstate 25, north-south, takes the route of US 85 and US 87; US 50, east-west, has State 6; other State routes are 18, 76, 96, 227, 209.

Railroads: Santa Fe, Colorado & Southern (Burlington), Denver & Rio Grande Western, Missouri Pacific.

Information: Pueblo Chamber of Commerce; Pueblo Council of Churches, 314 Jackson St., for *Church Directory;* Pueblo *Chieftain* (morning), Pueblo *Star-Journal* (evening), Star-Journal *& Chieftain* (Sunday), 825 W. 6th St. There are 7 radio stations, 3 local and 5 Denver television channels.

Climate: U. S. Weather Bureau annual averages: mean, 51.9°; precipitation, 11.50 in.; snowfall, 29.1 in.; sunshine 74%.

Recreation and Sports: All forms of outdoor activity and recreation are available. There are 12 public parks. City Park has a 9-hole and an 18-hole course and two miniature courses. It also has a swimming pool, a zoo, groups of elk, deer and buffalo; a children's farm, a pool for fishing by youngsters of 11 and under; horticultural exhibits, band concerts, riding.

Mineral Palace Park and Minnequa Park have swimming pools; there are pools with trout for children's fishing. All parks have tennis courts; roller skating is available; horses may be hired; there are numerous bowling alleys. Indoor swimming at Y. M. C. A. and Y. W. C. A. Private swimming at Pueblo Country Club and Minnequa Club. Shooting available to visitors at Municipal Shooters, City Park, 7-10 p.m.; Trap & Skeet Club, north edge of City Park, Sundays, 8:30 a.m. to 1:30 p.m. Square dancing ($1) at City Park, Red Barn, Baxter School, during weekdays, consult newspapers.

Horse racing takes place at Pikes Peak Meadows, 21 *m.* north of Pueblo on Interstate 25 in the late spring; greyhound racing at Pueblo Greyhound Park, 3215 Lake Ave. every night. Stock car racing at Beacon Hill, n. of Pueblo on Highway 85-87 every Sunday at 7 p.m., June–October. Rodeos are held at the State Fair in August and in Beulah and Rye.

In winter there are numerous ski slopes within easy driving range, as well ice skating at Lake Isabel and other lakes.

Tours: CF&I Steel Corp. plant, Indiana Ave. gate, Monday through Friday, 9:45 a.m. Pueblo Army Depot, for appointment call 947–3341. Star-Journal & Chieftain, 825 W. 6th St. Walter Brewing Co., Tuesday, Wednesday, Thursday, 1:30 p.m. Colorado State Hospital, 1600 W. 24th St., 10 a.m. to 2:30 p.m., by appointment, 543–1170. Rainbo Bakery, 330 W. 4th St., weekdays. Southern Colorado State College, call 545–4420 for time of tour.

Special Events: Fine Arts Festival, Southern Colorado State College, April. Colorado State Fair, August–September. Broadway Theater Guild sponsors four traveling companies a year at Pueblo City Auditorium. Little Theatre of Southern Colorado State College gives plays (call 545–4220 for listing). Impossible

Players Playhouse, 208½ N. Main St., 2 shows a year. In July and August the Beulah Melodrama is performed at the Valley Ho Bldg. in Beulah. All State Games, basketball and football, are held in the Public School Stadium.

Art exhibits at Arkansas Valley Bank Art Show, 211 W. 8th St. Seventh Red Door Art Gallery, 1401 Elizabeth Ave. El Pueblo Museum Art Gallery, 905 S. Prairie Ave. McClelland Public Library Art Gallery, 100 E. Abriendo Ave. Pueblo Art Guild Gallery, Mineral Palace Park. In mid-July the annual Beulah Art Show is held in the streets and byways of Beulah, Colo., 20 *m.* southeast on State 76.

PUEBLO (Sp. town) (4,695 alt., 91,181 pop. 1960; 103,000 1967, est.) is a steel manufacturing center on the eastern slope of the Rockies and the second largest city in Colorado. It is located on the Arkansas River below its confluence with Fountain Creek. A great network of highways makes Pueblo easily accessible; it is on the main north-south and east-west roads, Interstate 25 connecting it with Trinidad, Colorado Springs, Denver, and Fort Collins.

Highways and railroad connections have attracted a variety of light and heavy industry, employing about one-fourth of the County's available labor supply. Vocational training is part of the public high school programs, and youths, adults and veterans have access to the well-equipped shops at Southern Colorado State College.

The principal employers in Pueblo are the CF & I Steel Corp., the Pueblo Army Depot, the Santa Fe Ry., the Denver & Rio Grande Western Ry., Triplex Division of the Perfect Circle Corp., the Rock Wool Division of the American Gypsum Co., the American Stores Packing Co., the Mountain States Telephone Co., and the Star-Journal Publishing Corp.

The CF & I Steel Corp. has one of the most diversified steel mills in the country on the southwestern edge of Pueblo, where it employes up to 8,000. Established in 1881 and acquired by Rockefeller interests in 1892, it continues to expand on its 639 acres. In 1966 the corporate title of the CF & I Corp. was changed to CF & I Steel Corp. because it manufactures 1,200 different steel products. A new wide flange beam mill, to serve construction, began operation in 1963. The Morgan Rod Mill was built at a cost of $5,000,000. A seamless tube mill, supplying tubes for the oil industry, cost $27,000,000, and a new oxygen steelmaking process costing $16,000,000 was added in 1960. The 20-inch mill was modernized by 1968. The payroll of the corporation in Colorado exceeds $3,-600,000 per month. The corporation has voted to spend nearly $115,-000,000 in improvements by 1972. A new bar mill, to cost $41,000,000, with a capacity of 450,000 tons annually, was scheduled for 1971. It owns the Colorado & Wyoming Railway, which serves the Pueblo plant, the Allen mine, and the Sunrise iron ore mine. On July 15, 1969, the Crane Company acquired 82 percent of the stock and control of the corporation.

The Bureau of Reclamation of the U. S. Dept. of the Interior has its headquarters at 219 W. 5th St., Pueblo. It is in charge of the huge FRYING PAN-ARKANSAS PROJECT, which will divert water from the western slope of the Continental Divide and control water and hydroelectric power distribution on the eastern slope all the way from Leadville to Pueblo. Work on the southernmost unit, the PUEBLO DAM AND RESERVOIR, 6 *m.* upstream from the city on the Arkansas River, was begun in 1967 when 16 miles of Denver & Rio Grande Western railroad track were shifted to a new location. The Reservoir, to be completed by 1972, will become the principal water supply of Pueblo, which now gets its water from the Arkansas River and standby wells.

Pueblo Dam will be an earthfill dam 185 ft. high, 10,600 ft. long, and the Reservoir will be able to store more than 300,000 acre-ft. of water at full capacity. Pueblo is one of the cities that will draw on 20,-500 acre-ft. of water annually. Discharges from the Pueblo Reservoir will be made through the Pueblo Power Plant, the final one of seven that will use the water as it descends the east slope.

In 1963 Pueblo voted a $4,000,000 bond issue to supplement a $3,000,000 appropriation for a high-volume water distribution pump and reservoir system for its suburban areas. Pueblo treats its water for sedimentation and applies chlorination.

The site of Pueblo is supposed to have been visited in 1706 when Juan de Uribarri traversed this area while pursuing runaway Indian slaves from Santa Fe. In 1806 Lieut. Zebulon Pike camped here five days and built a 5-ft. breastwork of logs open at the river's edge. Jacob Fowler, a trapper, built a three-room log house here in 1822.

The settlement and naming of Pueblo are credited to James P. (Jim) Beckwourth, a mulatto trader. Beckwourth and his party reached the Arkansas here in October 1842, and erected a trading post. They were soon joined by 15 to 20 independent trappers, with their families. "We all united our labors, and constructed an adobe fort 60 yards square," wrote Beckwourth in his autobiography. "By the following spring we had grown into quite a little settlement, and we gave it the name of Pueblo."

To the Bostonian eye of Francis Parkman, who visited the Pueblo four years later, it was a wretched fort of primitive construction, "being nothing more than a large square enclosure, surrounded by a wall of mud, miserably cracked and dilapidated," inhabited by a few squaws and Spanish women, and a few Mexicans, "as mean and miserable as the place itself." Ushered into the state apartment of the Pueblo, he found it "a small mud room, very neatly finished, considering the material, and garnished with a crucifix, a looking-glass, a picture of the Virgin, and a rusty horse-pistol . . . There was another room beyond, less sumptuously decorated, and here three or four Spanish girls, one of them very pretty, were baking cakes at a mud fireplace.

Here, too, Parkman found the canvas-topped wagons of a large party of Mormons sent in advance of the main body of emigrants. They unyoked their oxen among the cottonwoods along the river on August 7, 1846, after an 800-mile journey from the Missouri River, and began building log cabins.

The settlement, the largest in the region until gold-rush days, served as a rallying point for the Mormon Battalion during the Mexican War; in 1847 the families moved on to join the main body in Utah. Nothing remains of Mormon Pueblo; even the graves of those who died here were soon obliterated by the flood waters of the Arkansas.

After his remarkable feat of driving 9,000 sheep from New Mexico to California, "Uncle Dick" Wootton, Mountain Man, trader, freighter, and herder (see Tour 12c), came in 1853 to trade with the many emigrants passing through Pueblo. He swapped fresh oxen for footsore and broken-down animals, usually obtaining three or four for one. He sent the lame cattle to his ranch, and after they had been pastured a few weeks, they were traded for other disabled cattle. "In this way I increased my herd very rapidly," wrote Wootton.

The Ute in the vicinity were acting suspiciously just before Christmas Day, 1854, and Wootton cautioned the inhabitants not to allow the Indians to come into the fort, but Wootton's advice was disregarded. "Taos lightning" flowed freely that day; all of the 17 Mexicans in the fort got gloriously drunk and invited the "friendly" Indians to enter. The latter turned upon their hosts and killed all but a young Mexican girl, two children, and one man, Romaldo, who lived long enough with a bullet through his tongue to tell the tale in Indian sign language. The massacre marked the end of Pueblo as a rendezvous for the Mountain Men. Passing by in 1855, Lieutenant E. G. Beckwith reported that a Spaniard named Massalino and his Pawnee wife were the only occupants of the Pueblo, which was avoided by the Mountain Men because it was believed to be haunted by headless Mexican women.

The first definite proposal for a new state originated with the citizens of Fountain City, who on April 7, 1859, "without distinction of party, unanimously declared in favor of a new state." Seventy-five registered citizens exercised their franchise that fall to select a governor and legislature for the provisional and extra-legal government of "Jefferson Territory." Hickory Rogers, sent from Denver to canvass the vote, stopped on his way back to Denver and wrote 1,150 additional ballots.

The rival town of Pueblo City was laid out by Denver promoters in 1860; one of its earliest establishments was Jack Allen's "Taos lightning factory." The new town quickly absorbed the residents of Fountain City, which was soon occupied by Spanish-American farmers.

The first issue of the Pueblo *Weekly Chieftain* appeared on June 1, 1868, carrying a notice of the death of Kit Carson. Some of the early issues were printed on brown wrapping paper when Indian uprisings on the plains cut communication with the East. Four years later the newspaper became a daily.

By 1870, when it was incorporated as a town with a population of 700, Pueblo was a quiet settlement of adobe houses. When General William J. Palmer's narrow-gauge Denver & Rio Grande Railroad was extended to Pueblo in 1872, the little engine *Ouray* puffed in from Denver at 20 miles an hour and was greeted with a joyous celebration, although few realized what a marked change it would make in the town. The railroad and the supply of coal at Trinidad to the south made Pueblo a workshop for the mines in the mountains. Pueblo was incorporated as a city in 1873; building and population rapidly increased; the Atchison, Topeka & Santa Fe, known locally as the "Banana Line" because of its yellow cars, reached Pueblo in 1876, and was extended to Denver a year later. The Colorado Coal & Iron Company, subsequently the Colorado Fuel & Iron Corporation, blew in its Minnequa blast furnace in 1881. The Mather and Geist smelter was built in 1882, the Eilers smelter the next year, and the Guggenheim smelter in 1888. Coal from Trinidad was used to smelt ores from Leadville, for Pueblo occupied a strategic position on the rail lines. The steel company, operating its own coal mines, became the largest coal and steel concern in the West. Pueblo's population rose from 3,217 in 1870 to 24,588 in 1880—an eight-fold increase.

The 1890's were a difficult decade for Pueblo, as for the rest of the State; the panic and unrest were reflected in the railroad strike of 1894, which tied up traffic at Pueblo and its coal supply base, Trinidad. The Cripple Creek gold strike in 1893, however, stimulated the city's growth, and as farmers continued to settle in the Arkansas valley, Pueblo realized that it also commanded a rich agricultural market. To meet the demands of a constantly enlarging consumer area, numerous small and medium-size factories were established here.

On July 3, 1921, the Arkansas River, swollen by cloudbursts, overran its banks and inundated a large part of the city. The next morning houses and business buildings were floating in the swirling waters, which covered the lower business section to a depth of 12 feet. More than 600 houses were swept away; 350 business houses were badly damaged and had to be condemned; property loss was estimated at $16,000,000, while loss of stock and equipment, accounts and business, brought the total to $30,000,000. Perhaps 100 people—the exact number has never been ascertained because many of the families living along the river bottom were migrants—lost their lives. To guard against a repetition of the disaster, the river was diverted in 1924 to a new channel and imprisoned behind reinforced concrete levees.

POINTS OF INTEREST

EL PUEBLO MUSEUM, 905 Prairie Ave., is one of the newest of museums that aim to demonstrate the essentials of social and industrial history by reproductions and tangible materials. In 1959, a century after the first goldseekers rushed up the Arkansas River, the State Historical Society of Colorado sponsored the museum, and the city donated for its quarters a building that once housed the municipal airport. The most effective historical display is a full-sized reproduction of the original fortification built by traders in 1842 close to the river, in an area near the present railroad station and City Hall. James Grafton Rogers, chairman of the board of the State Historical Society, writes that the so-called fort "was a little walled quadrangle built of mud bricks (adobe), mud-plastered wicker work (jacal) and cottonwood logs (vigas), 60 or 80 ft. square, and 8 or 10 ft. high. It had a heavy wooden gate and two towers at diagonal corners for riflemen. Its purpose was defense against marauding Indians. Inside the walls were adobe huts, a store, a small corral for horses."

The CF & I Steel Corp. has donated exhibits showing its development. There are numerous artifacts and examples of Indian living. The museum is open Tuesday through Friday, 9–5, Sunday and holidays, 10–5, closed Monday. The Museum Art Gallery has similar hours (free).

SOUTHERN COLORADO STATE COLLEGE, began as Pueblo Junior College in 1933 and was made a senior college in 1961. Its first 4-year term began in 1964 and by 1967 it had 5,000 fulltime students. In addition to the regular academic programs leading to degrees of B.A., B.S., Assoc. in Arts, and Assoc. in Applied Science, the college gives special technical and academic courses for adults, enrolling as many as 700 students in evening classes at Colorado Springs. Its institute of Regional Service concentrates on regional and community problems. The college is moving to a new campus of 850 acres north of Pueblo, where new buildings are under way. The Library in 1966 received a joint award for design by the American Institution of Architects and the U. S. Office of Education.

The McCLELLAND PUBLIC LIBRARY, 100 E. Abriendo Ave., opened its new main building June 1, 1965. It had been erected on the site of the library built 1903–1904 with the aid of $60,000 from Andrew Carnegie, when there were 1,072 volumes; today the Library circulates around 400,000. James M. Hunter and Associates were architects of the new building. It is open daily except Sundays and holidays, 9–9. Its garden level holds the Children's Library, the Periodical Room and the Bookmobile area. The Main Level has the circulation section and an Art Gallery; the second has genealogy and a collection of Colorado and the West, chiefly the legacy of Governor Adams, and U. S. Government Reports. There are a branch library at 1551 Bonforte Blvd. and four school stations.

CITY PARK lies south of the Arkansas River and north of Thatcher Ave. (State Highway 96) and can be entered at Goodnight and Calla Aves. It is the largest of 12 parks and contains in its 100 acres a swimming pool, a zoo with elk, deer and buffalo; a children's farm, riding trails, horticultural exhibits, and an amusement area. Band concerts, trap and skeet shooting, are provided and there are regular square dances. MINERAL PALACE PARK, 13th and Main Sts., has an art gallery and a museum of minerals. MINNEQUA PARK is located at Lake Minnequa. Both City and Minnequa Parks have pools where children of 11 and under may fish; the pools are stocked three times a year.

COLORADO STATE HOSPITAL, occupying 500 acres starting at 13th and Frisco Sts., has been treating the mentally ill since 1879. The 6,000 patients of former years have been reduced to around 3,600 by

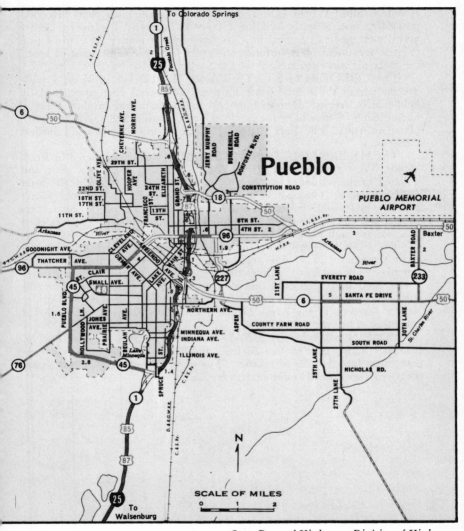

State Dept. of Highways, Division of Highways

transfers. Since World War II the State has spent more than $16,000,-000 here, most recently building a 60-bed Childrens Treatment Center and a new medical-surgical unit. It has begun a modern system of psychiatric treatment in 12 autonomous units. The per capita cost of treating a patient was estimated in 1963 at $3,323.

The COLORADO STATE FAIR GROUNDS in West Pueblo are the site of the annual State Fair and Industrial Exposition, usually held late in August. Besides livestock and agricultural exhibits there is horse racing. A new barn for cattle exhibits, costing $388,800, was completed in 1964. The Fair is publicized as having "the world's largest rabbit show."

The METROPOLITAN MUSEUM of Pueblo is located in Rosemount, West 15th St. and Grand Ave., a mansion erected in 1891 and donated to the Museum Association on November 1, 1968, by the heirs of Raymond C. Thatcher. The donation also included $20,000. Many of the exhibits were collected by Andrew J. McClelland during travels abroad and chosen for their educational usefulness. The museum is open Tuesday through Saturday, 9–5; Sunday, 2–5.

The PUEBLO ARMY DEPOT occupies part of a U. S. Government terrain of 42 sq. mi. starting 15 m. east of Pueblo. Originally organized for ordnance, it now handles military supplies of many categories, including missiles. It has about 3,500 employees and its expenditure of about $25,000,000 annually is a source of income for Pueblo. At the entrance to the Army Depot is HI PODNER PARK, which has a collection of historic ordnance.

The PUEBLO MEMORIAL AIRPORT, 6 m. east of Pueblo, has daily flights by Frontier Airlines and Trans-Central, and full-scale equipment for all needs of aviation. The major runway is 8,800 ft. long. Three private agencies offer charter service.

Trinidad

Air Services: Trans-Central Airlines makes four flights daily between Denver and Albuquerque with stops at Las Animas County Municipal Airport, 12 *m.* east of Trinidad. Has 5,500 ft. runway.

Buses: Continental Trailways, Greyhound Lines.

Highways: Interstate 25, US 85, 87, 160 and State 1 from Denver, Pueblo, Colorado Springs, continue south into New Mexico. US 350 and State 12 cross the prairie to La Junta, then south to Trinidad. State 12 runs northwest after Trinidad, joins US into the Rockies.

Railroads: Santa Fe main line, Colorado & Southern (Burlington line), Colorado & Wyoming short line in coal mining area.

Information: Trinidad Chronicle-News, daily; Chamber of Commerce, 212 Nevada Ave.

Climate: Annual mean temperature, 51.4°; precipitation average, 14.32 in.

Recreation: Kit Carson Park, on the old Santa Fe Trail, and Central Park, are equipped for ball games, picnics, barbeques; Monument Lake, 35 *m.* west on State 12 is a municipally-owned area of 1,200 acres for fishing, boating, camping, etc. Golf at Trinidad City Gold Course and Country Club.

Special Events: Roundup Time, rodeo and Old West parade, Labor Day week.

TRINIDAD (Sp. Trinity) (6,025 alt., 10,800 pop.), seat of Las Animas County, owes its birth to its position on the Mountain Branch of the Santa Fe Trail at the foot of Raton Pass, and its growth to several decades of coal-mining prosperity. Built on a foothill chain of the Culebra Range, its deviously angled streets give the city a curiously foreign aspect, heightened by the numerous sod-roofed, square adobe dwellings that still remain in the outlying sections. Along the older streets have passed Indians, Mexican farmers and sheepherders, hard-bitten trappers, freighters, and brawling railroad construction huskies. Many of the two-and-three-story stone and brick buildings along Main and Commercial Streets, principal thoroughfares of the business district, have served for more than half a century. The Purgatoire River, spanned by bridges, separates the residential districts from the business section.

Before the whites came, the site was an Indian ceremonial ground. Juan de Oñate, on a gold-hunting expedition north from Taos in 1598, led his party into the valley. Three years later he again passed by on another expedition that penetrated as far north as the South Platte River. Oñate was followed by other Spanish explorers, priests, and fighting men during the seventeenth and eighteenth centuries—Archuleta, Uribarri, militant Governor Anza when returning from pursuit of Comanche raiders, and the ill-starred party whose massacre on the banks of the river led to its being named the Purgatoire, the French translation and contraction of the Spanish El Rio de Las Animas Perdidas en Purgatorio, or the River of the Souls Lost in Purgatory. Still later, the spot was a camping ground for trappers, traders, and hunters on the route from the east to Santa Fe and Taos.

In 1846 Colonel Stephen W. Kearney passed this way on his march from Kansas to the bloodless conquest of New Mexico. The Colorado troops in Kearney's Army of the West joined him near Bent's Fort 100 miles to the northeast, and the entire force proceeded down the old trail toward the pass, camping here overnight. Two years later the forces of General Sterling Price bivouacked here on their march to reconquer Santa Fe and Taos after the rebellion of 1847, in which the Mexican and Indian population of New Mexico attempted to overthrow their new rulers from the United States, killing Governor Charles Bent (*see Tour 9A*) and many others.

Until 1859, when Gabriel Gutierrez and his nephew came from New Mexico to find a range for their sheep, there was little attempt at permanent settlement here. The two men built a cabin on the south bank of the river near where the library now stands. Other settlers came from New Mexico and took up farms along the river; men from the East drifted in—settlers, traders, and desperadoes of all descriptions —and Trinidad became known as a "tough place."

At a time when relations between the United States and Mexico were still strained by memories of the war, there was constant friction between the men from the "States" and the more-established settlers of Spanish and Mexican descent. Clashes between the two groups were frequent, culminating in the so-called "Battle of Trinidad" on Christmas Day, 1867, when a wrestling match developed into a riot with almost a thousand people engaged. During the free-for-all, a wrestler of the Spanish-speaking group was killed, and his slayer, a stage driver, was arrested. Friends of the stage driver rallied in his behalf, broke into the jail, and freed him. The prisoner and his liberators fled to an empty adobe building where they were besieged by the sheriff and a sizable posse. The siege lasted four days, during which several persons were killed. A war party of Ute appeared and offered to help the posse overcome the English-speaking whites. The offer was declined by the sheriff, who threatened to arrange a truce with the besieged and combine the whole force against the Indians if they did not withdraw. The Ute thereupon departed. On the fourth day cavalry from Fort Lyon and Fort Reynolds appeared and placed the city under martial law. The soldiers were withdrawn several weeks later when the opposing factions, resenting the strict discipline of the military, again threatened to unite against the troops. For many years the hostility engendered by the affair continued, although it never again reached such a violent height.

Situated near Ute hunting grounds, Trinidad was often subjected to Indian alarms. The town was never attacked, but Ute war parties on their way to and from raids on their plains enemies frequently camped on the surrounding hills; during these unwelcome visits, citizens armed themselves and posted guards against possible surprise.

Las Animas County was created in 1866, and Trinidad was chosen as its seat; ten years later the town, with a population of 2,000, was incorporated and named for Trinidad Baca, daughter of a pioneer. It is the largest county in Colorado, with 4,798 sq. mi. Much of its area east of the mountains is devoted to grazing, but income from livestock and farm products was curtailed for several years of the 1960's by lack of precipitation. Efforts to extend irrigated areas have been made by building Fishers Peak and Carbon Arrroyo dams, and plans have been completed for the Trinidad Reservoir on the Purgatoire River, to hold 114,500 acre-ft. of water and add to irrigation of 19,000 acres below Trinidad.

During World War I more than 5,000,000 tons of coal were mined annually. The county still has a high coal production, much of it from the Allen mine of the CF&I Steel Corp., which converts it to coke at Pueblo for use in steel making. Clay for firebrick is mined by A. P. Green Refractories Co., Harbison-Walker Refractories Co., and Scott Mining Co. In 1966 the value of minerals produced was $5,571,654.

POINTS OF INTEREST

KIT CARSON PARK, San Pedro St., between Kansas and Topeka Sts., is a landscaped area on a low hill. Crowning the rise is a bronze equestrian statue of the famous plainsman and scout. Carson (*see Tour 9a*) spent much of his life along the Santa Fe Trail as hunter, scout, and guide, and was a frequent visitor in Trinidad at that time and later when he was Indian Agent.

The KIT CARSON MUSEUM (*open daily*), 620 Main St., an adobe structure dating from early settlement, houses a large collection of pioneer relics and Indian artifacts, and an elaborate hunting coat presented to Kit Carson by a Cheyenne chief.

The FORT WOOTTON MEMORIAL (*open 8–12 a.m., 1–5 p.m. weekdays*), SE. corner of First and Chestnut Sts., was constructed by the Work Projects Administration in cooperation with Las Animas County and Veterans' organizations. The design of the large gray stone structure was inspired by Bent's Fort (*see Tour 9A*). It honors Richens L. (Uncle Dick) Wootton, trapper and scout (*see Tour 12c*), who constructed a toll gate below Raton Pass; Wootton was a well-known figure in early Trinidad.

The SANTA FE TRAIL MARKER, on the Columbian Hotel, NW. corner Main and Commercial Sts., indicates the course of the trail across the city. This bronze plaque, erected by the local D. A. R., commemorates the days when cavalcades of horsemen and creaking *carretas* passed along this street on their way to and from the chief city of the Southwest. This northern or Mountain Branch of the Santa Fe Trail played an important part in the development of Colorado. It constituted the link between the New Mexican metropolis, the Missouri Valley markets, and the trading posts along the Arkansas.

TRINIDAD STATE JUNIOR COLLEGE, founded 1925, is a two-year institution supported by Las Animas County. It gives degrees of associate in the arts and applied science. It occupies the former quarters of Tillotson Academy, and in recent years has been erecting a new Library, a vocational training building, a girls' domitory, and a students' union, and will add a new science unit. Among its special courses are electronics, gunsmithing, and law enforcement. It enrolls up to 1,200 students with a faculty of 58.

COLORADO STATE HOME FOR THE AGED, founded 1953 by the State, provides shelter, rehabilitation, and nursing services for about 160 aged. Residents must be 60 years old or older, have resided in the State five out of the past nine years and be free of tuberculosis or senile psychosis.

ROUND-UP PARK, on US 85 at the northern edge of the city, is the scene of the annual Kit Carson Round-up, Trinidad's chief festival. A grandstand with a seating capacity of 1,500 overlooks the race track and the rodeo ring, converted into a softball diamond during the season; there is also a swimming pool. The park is enclosed within a low adobe wall of the Spanish type.

The BLOOM MANSION, erected 1882 by Frank G. Bloom, merchant, banker, and cattleman, was presented to the State by the Trinidad Historical Assn., and the Friends of Historical Trinidad in 1961. Its architecture is rococo Victorian, an example of the opulence of the period.

The OLD BACA HOUSE and PIONEER MUSEUM are two structures of major historic value. The group was acquired by the State Historical Society and dedicated in September, 1960. Baca House, built 1869, was the home of Don Felipe Baca, rancher, for about fifty years. The Santa Fe Trail ran past the house. A 10-room adobe across the courtyard, probably for servants, is now the Pioneer Museum (*open 9–5, May 15–Oct. 15*).

MONUMENT LAKE, a 1,200-acre recreation area owned by the city, is located near State 12 and State 111 in the Stonewall Valley 35 *m.* west. This is near the southern limit of a segment of San Isabel National Forest, part of which is in Huerfano County.

PART III

Up and Down and All Around

CCCCCCCCCCCCCCCCCCCCCCCCCCCCCCC

Tour 1

(McCook, Nebr.) — Holyoke — Sterling — Fort Morgan — Denver — Georgetown — Loveland Pass — Glenwood Springs — Grand Junction — (Thompsons, Utah) ; US 6.
Nebraska Line to Utah Line, 493.5 *m.*

State 176 enters Phillips County from the border town of Venango, Nebr. At 8 *m.* AMHERST, a small farm town. At 18 *m.* it connects with US 6 and State 14, east-west highways, and US 385 and State 51, north-south highways in Holyoke.
Chicago, Burlington & Quincy R.R. parallels route between Nebraska Line and Sterling; Union Pacific R.R. between Sterling and Fort Morgan; Chicago, Burlington & Quincy R.R. between Brush and Denver.
Good accommodations.

The route crosses semiarid plains devoted to ranching and dry farming, then traverses the productive valley of the South Platte River to Denver and into the foothills and mountains beyond. Ascending through a region of great beauty, US 6 crosses the Continental Divide, continues over Vail Pass, and descends the Eagle River and the Colorado into Utah.

Section a.   NEBRASKA LINE to DENVER; 185 m. US 6

US 6 crosses the Nebraska Line, 0 *m.,* 93 *miles* west of McCook, Nebr.

HOLYOKE, 13 *m.* (3,745 alt., 1,555 pop.), named for the city in Massachusetts, is the seat of Phillips County. Grain elevators and livestock and dairy products exchanges are an index to the character of business and home life of villages in this area.

Farmer's Night is an annual featured event. The County Fair is held here. Holyoke has new hospital, church, and recreation facilities. The *Enterprise* is its weekly newspaper.

West of Holyoke the highway crosses a grain-growing section to PAOLI, 23 *m.* (3,873 alt.), a trading and supply center. Level broad prairies, interspersed with grain fields, border both sides of the route. This area, unprotected by hills or trees, with an average annual rainfall of 15 inches, embraces three-fourths of the 22 million acres of the potential dry-farming acreage in Colorado. To be a successful dry farmer, one must understand the principles of water movement in the soil and its conservation in order to take advantage of rains when they fall. Plowing must be deep; for fall crops it is performed in spring and early summer. Winter wheat is planted in September in ground plowed, disked, and harrowed in June and July. As high winds prevail their force is lessened by leaving the ground rough and by planting crops in strips, alternating corn and sorghums with grains (*see Farming*).

HAXTUN, 31 *m.* (4,000 alt., 1,027 pop.), is a shipping point for farmers. The flat brown country through which the highway continues is the habitat of the coyote, smaller than the wolf but more cunning, which thrives near the habitations of man. The coyote hunts rabbits and other small animals, but it is a night marauder, preying upon chickens, even young lambs and calves. Its yelp has an uncanny sound, and one coyote may sound like a dozen. Coyote hunting has long been a popular sport. Formerly the riders moved across the plains with a two-wheel cart bearing a cage in which were hounds. When a coyote was "jumped," the cavalcade halted, dogs were released, and hunters followed. If the chase lasted more than a mile the animal usually escaped. Now the automobile has supplanted the horse, and a trailer carries the hounds. On level open ground, the coyote is often pursued by car until it is near exhaustion, when the dogs are released.

The road traverses the valley of the South Platte, where the prairies merge with low rolling hills. The highway enters a country of rich farms, irrigated from the South Platte. Beyond the river bottom the broken swells are covered with buffalo grass and gray-green sweeps of sagebrush.

The lower valley of the South Platte is one of the most productive sugar-beet districts in the country. Farmers contract with the sugar companies for sale of their produce before the beets are planted. Sugar-beet farming used to require a great amount of "stoop labor," and until mechanization in recent decades this was done by migrants. German-Russians, Spanish-Americans, and Mexicans succeeded one another. During the 1930's the Great Western Sugar Company aided the development of machines and in 1935 had the first Silver-Roberts plyers built. A ton-a-minute field loader for harvested beets came in 1938. A Colorado farmer built a harvester that pulled and harvested beets better than others and when the John Deere Co. put it on the market in 1942 it became widely used. Other models have been made since by International Harvester, and by 1954 95 per cent of all Great Western beets were handled by machines.

The sugar beet is used for many useful purposes in agriculture. Beet tops are livestock feed, and also may be plowed back to enrich the soil. The beet crop of one acre can yield 5,000 pounds of sugar. Beet pulp and molasses are used in beet fattening. Dried pulp in pelletized form is especially easily handled for feeding cattle and sheep. The uses of sugar in many other products is well established. The chemical ingredients for beet sugar and cane sugar are the same.

Sunshine and water are needed to produce beets. Colorado had plenty of sunshine but not enough water until irrigation made possible the improvement of fields. When the beets are harvested in late September or early October farmers use tractors to pull machines with six to twelve-row units, which top and uproot the beets and pile them into trucks.

Formerly all the work of uprooting and topping beets was done by manual labor.

At some receiving stations the trucks, after being weighed, ascend a ramp where they are picked up bodily and dumped. A random sample of each load is taken, and calculations are made to determine the tare—the approximate amount of earth and foliage remaining. At other stations, where it is necessary to build huge storage piles, machines unload trucks on the ground.

Although the sugar beet was known to the ancient Mediterranean peoples, it is said that Napoleon gave it to the modern world in 1811. After bestowing the Cross of Honor on Benjamin Dellessert, who had set up a factory at Passy and produced a small amount of crystallized sugar, the Emperor notified his Minister of the Interior: "All steps shall be taken to encourage this culture and to establish schools for teaching the manufacture of beet sugar—advise cultivators that the growing of sugar beet roots improves the soil and the residue of the fabrication furnishes excellent food for cattle."

A complete sugar manufacturing outfit, purchased in France by the Mormons in 1852, was brought to Fort Leavenworth by boat from New Orleans, loaded into covered wagons drawn by 52 ox-teams, and carried across the plains to Provo, Utah. The experiment was a failure; the factory produced a syrup so acid that "it would take your tongue off."

Peter Magnes, a farmer living near Littleton, wrote in the *Rocky Mountain News* in 1876: "If we had beet sugar factories in Colorado . . . so that the farmers could raise beets . . . and get them manufactured the same as we now get grain manufactured into flour and meal, I imagine Colorado farmers would produce more gold than all the miners of the mountains"—a true and far-seeing prophecy.

Sugar towns come to life in October and November, when growers receive their largest checks from factories. Beet pay day is a gala event. Streets are jammed; stores, decorated for the occasion, advertise bargain sales; sidewalk stands dispense soft drinks and souvenirs; carnivals set up their tents and barkers exhort the crowds.

SHERWIN RANCH, 61 *m.*, pastures a herd of buffalo; sometimes the shaggy beasts are visible from the highway.

OVERLAND PARK, 62 *m.*, contains the LOGAN COUNTY MUSEUM.

STERLING, 63 *m.* (3,935 alt., 11,600 pop. 1968, est.) seat of Logan County (pop. approx. 22,000) on the South Platte, is served by the Union Pacific and Burlington Rys., US 6, 138, State 2, 14, and Interstate 80S (across the River); Continental Trailways, and maintains a municipal airport. Sterling profits by the farm and livestock production and the petroleum and natural gas output in 76 fields of Logan County. Pioneers started here with sod houses and named the place for Sterling, Illinois, home town of David Leavitt, Union Pacific Surveyor.

The new MUNICIPAL AUDITORIUM, seating 1,700, and the OVERLAND TRAIL MUSEUM, are attractions. NORTH STERLING RESERVOIR is a recreation area. NORTHEASTERN JUNIOR COLLEGE, founded 1941, has more than 1,700 students and a faculty of 92. It offers the humanities and technical courses, including surveying, electronics, civil technology, nursing. Its summer semester continues regular work.

Industries are expanding. The GREAT WESTERN SUGAR COMPANY is the largest employer; Logan County raises up to 265,000 tons of sugar beets annually. The STERLING COLORADO BEEF COMPANY, a new aquisition, can process 700 hd. a day. The *Sterling Journal-Advocate* is the daily newspaper.

Processing Sugar Beets: Beets enter the factory over a flume of warm water which is agitated by rotating paddles. They fall upon hopper scales, are weighed, and then drop into a slicer that cuts them into long thin strips, called "cossettes," but known as "chips" to the workers. These are carried along high-speed belts into a battery of cylindrical tanks where hot circulating water extracts the juices. What remains is diverted either to the wet-pulp silo and stored, or is passed through heated drums where the pulp is dried. Part of the dried pulp is pressed into blocks known as "bull biscuits." The men handling the pulp, which has an unpleasant odor, as well as the trucks transporting it, are called "high smellers."

The juice is put through several chemical processes, repeatedly filtered, and run into evaporators, to emerge as "evaporator thick juice." Treated with sulphur gas and carefully filtered, the clear sparkling liquor, known as "blowup thick juice," passes into vacuum pans and is boiled until the sugar begins to crystallize. High speed centrifugal machines separate sugar crystals from the syrup. The wet sugar passes into granulators, where it is dried and screened; the dry sugar is sent to the warehouse for packing in barrels, sacks, and small packages. Workers engaged in the latter process say they are "making pups."

The two kinds of syrup produced, "high green" and "high wash," are again filtered and returned to the vacuum tanks to be boiled and stirred for the recovery of some of the remaining sugar. After a third boiling the high green or mother liquor, called molasses, is sent to factories where the Steffen process is used to extract yet more sugar.

The sugar content of beets ranges from 14 to 18 per cent. Beet pulp, both wet and dried, as well as molasses and green beet tops, are valuable stock feed. The weight of beet tops ranges from one-half to two-thirds of the weight of the beets, and the tops from an acre of beets have a feeding value equivalent to a ton of hay. An acre of beets, it is estimated, produces enough by-products to fatten 10 lambs or put 150 pounds of meat on a steer.

Sterling is at the junction with US 138 and State 14. Right from Main Street in Sterling on a graveled road to PIONEER PARK. West of Sterling the highway follows the winding course of the South Platte to ATWOOD, 69.5 *m.* (3,993 alt.), an unincorporated village in the dry farm area.

Left from Atwood on State 63 to the junction with a dirt road, 8 *m.;* L. here to the SUMMIT SPRINGS BATTLEGROUND, 13 *m.,* scene of the last important Indian battle fought in northeastern Colorado. On July 11, 1869, a large band of Cheyenne, under Tall Bull, were defeated by 285 white scouts and troopers with their Pawnee allies. Tall Bull and 52 of his warriors were slain. Two women, who had been taken prisoner by the Indians, were the only white casualties. Traveling Bear, a Pawnee scout who killed and scalped four Cheyennes single-handed, was awarded a Congressional medal. A granite monument marks the site of the battleground.

MERINO, 75.5 *m.* (4,042 alt., 1,655 pop.), originally called Buffalo, was renamed in 1881 when Merino sheep were brought here.

East of US 6 and west of Interstate 80S in Washington County is PREWITT RESERVOIR, 2,431 acres, 32,900 acre-ft.

Where the highway crosses to the southern bank of the Platte, 78.2 *m.,* is the SITE OF FORT WICKED (R), once a ranch and station on the Overland Trail. On January 14, 1865, Indians attacked every ranch between Fort Sedgwick, near Julesburg, and Fort Morgan, a distance of almost 100 miles. Many ranches were burned, and their occupants massacred or put to flight. H. Godfrey, station master of the Overland here, had prepared for such an emergency and while his wife and daughter supplied him with powder and bullets, Godfrey continued firing at the raiders. The Indians soon rode off, carrying dead and wounded, and thereafter referred to Godfrey as "Old Wicked."

At 97.5 *m.* is the eastern junction with US 34 (*see Tour 3*) ; US 6 and US 34 are united for 24.5 miles.

BRUSH, 98.5 *m.* (4,231 alt., 4,750 pop. est.), is a sales center for livestock, with large feeding pens. It processes milk, sugar beets, cheddar cheese. Named for Jared L. Brush, pioneer cowman, it has an amateur rodeo July 3 and 4, and the Morgan County Junior Fair in August. The Brush *News-Tribune* is its weekly newspaper. It is a junction for US 34, State 14, with Interstate 80S, US 6, State 2 and State 71.

FORT MORGAN, 108.1 *m.* (4,240 alt., 8,000 pop.), seat of Morgan County, is the trade capital of an area that produces four per cent of the beet sugar refined in the United States; thousands of sheep are fattened here on beet pulp. Grain, beans, and dairy products provide other income. A municipal light plant provides residents with free current for porch lamps. It is known as the City of Light.

During the gold rush the town was a station and a military post, on the Overland Trail, known first as Camp Tyler, then as Camp Wardell. In 1866 it was named Fort Morgan in honor of the first commander, Colonel C. A. Morgan. The SITE OF FORT MORGAN is marked by a monument on Riverview Avenue. Indian relics at the V.F.W. Museum include Yuma and Folsom artifacts.

The Great Western Beet Sugar Co. has a large refinery here. Oil, natural gas, and natural gas liquids of the county help Fort Morgan's business. The *Fort Morgan Times* is its daily newspaper.

Bijou Lake and Jackson Lake, northwest of Fort Morgan are reservoirs with recreation facilities.

At 122 *m.* is the western junction with US 34 (*see Tour 3*).

Southwest of WIGGINS, 123 *m.* (4,443 alt.), a supply center, a range of low hills (L) rises above the shallow undulations of the prairies; the hills are composed of vast beds of small sea shells, which are ground up to produce a mineral food for livestock.

The road threads its way across brown plains relieved occasionally by low gray hills and clumps of bright-green cottonwoods fringing water courses. At home in the cottonwoods are the kingbirds, the white-rumped shrikes, and the melodious western mockingbirds. Most conspicuous is the ever-chattering, long-tailed magpie, master architect of the bird kingdom. Its huge domed nest, weather-proofed with mud and occupied but one season, often becomes the home of the grotesque long-eared owl.

COMMERCE CITY (5,150 alt., 18,600 pop., 1967) north of Denver's 50th Ave., and west of the ROCKY MOUNTAIN ARSENAL, had 1,200 people when it was incorporated in 1952. By annexations it has grown to 3,840 acres. Besides US 6 it is served by State 2, State 285 (Brighton Blvd.) and State 85; the last connects with Interstate 70 by a short Interstate 270. Most of the citizens work in Denver. The Mile High Kennel Club seats 15,000 and averages 10,000 people a night during its sixty-day season of greyhound racing. Numerous carnation greenhouses are located here.

In DENVER, 185 *m.* (5,280 alt., 493,837 pop.) (*see Denver*), are junctions with US 6, US 36, US 40, US 85, US 87, US 285, US 287, Interstate 25 and Interstate 75.

Section b. DENVER to UTAH, 308.5 m. US 6; Interstate 70

This section of the tour traverses a mountainous area colored with the robust history of early mining camps. The highway three times crosses the Continental Divide, the geologic backbone of North America.

West of Denver, 0 *m.,* US 6 and US 40 (*see Tour 7*) are united for 43.6 *miles* (*see Tour 7b*). At 43.5 *m.* US 6 branches (L) south from US 40, following the South Fork of Clear Creek. Interstate 70 and US 6 remain together. Marking the hillsides are numerous mine dumps.

GEORGETOWN, 47 *m.* (8,549 alt., 500 pop.), walled in by high barren mountains where the valley narrows at the foot of the Continental Divide, is the seat of Clear Creek County, which produces gold, silver, copper, lead, and zinc in small quantities today and has the Urad mine of Climax Molybdenum Co. The town came into existence with the discovery of gold here in 1859, and prospered until placer claims gave out. There was a boom in the 1870's, when lode mining was developed. Prior to the great Leadville strike in 1878 it was the most important silver camp in the State.

LOVELAND BASIN and LOVELAND VALLEY are two major ski areas on US 6 (Interstate 70) near Georgetown, 54 m. from Denver. They open October 15 with artificial snow on a 4,100 ft. run served by 2 chair lifts. Regular season November 1 to mid-May. Have 4 double chair lifts, 1 T-bar, 1 rope tow, 1 Pomalift, total capacity 7,000 skiers per hour; 22 runs, vertical drop, max. 1,430 ft. Ski patrol, ambulance, ski school. Shops, inns, restaurants in Georgetown and Idaho Springs. P. O. Box 455 Georgetown, or phone 303–569–2288; direct Denver line, 255–7103.

With the decline of silver mining in the 1890's Georgetown entered a second decline. A few prospectors, some gold miners, and many tourists kept the town alive. Curio hunters ransacked uninhabited houses in search of relics of by-gone days. One man rented a stable for a summer studio and found files of several of the State's earliest newspapers—priceless for the historian—thrown into an attic as rubbish. In 1933 higher prices for gold and silver caused many mines to reopen. Houses and picket fences are now brightly painted, set off by blue-grass lawns. Livery stables have been transformed into garages and filling stations. The old FIRE STATION, a tall wooden tower in the center of the village, for many years housed a hose reel, a two-wheeled vehicle pulled by volunteer firemen.

The HOTEL DE PARIS, one of the most celebrated hotels west of the Mississippi during the 1880 and 1890 years, retains bits of its former glory. Its rococo elegance of furnishing and decoration, its exotic cuisine, and its curious owner were talked of throughout the mountain region, where opulence was common but discriminating taste was not. Louis du Puy, its builder and presiding genius, was born Adolphus Francis Gerard at Alençon, France, in 1844. He has been described as "an innkeeper who hated his guests, a philosopher, and poet who left no written record of his thought, a despiser of women who gave all he had to one, an aristocrat, a proletarian, a pagan, an arcadian, an atheist, a lover of beauty, and, inadvertently, the stepfather of domestic science of America."

The last title is his because of the influence his knowledge of food and wine had upon Dr. James E. Russell, high priest of domestic science in America, dean of Teachers' College, Columbia University, who first gave domestic science academic status. The idea was born during a visit to the Hotel de Paris in 1896, when Russell was fascinated, as he confessed, by Du Puy's philosophies concerning food and man. "French Louis' " tastes were epicurean to the extreme; a French guest once remarked, "I would have slave girls and music at dessert; with my wines I would have the ceiling to open and orange blossoms and roses to fall upon the table." His host answered, "I make one to smell the roses and imagine the slave girls by my wine!"

He was altogether a strange type of find in a frontier town, and there was a fantastic life behind him. Born to wealth and position, he squandered his inheritance and then tried journalism in Paris, London, and New York with indifferent success. He served in the French and the American armies, deserted from both, drifted through a succession of odd occupations, and, inevitably, wound up in the mining camps, taking the name Du Puy. He came to Georgetown in 1869 and was seriously injured in a mine explosion four years later.

A collection was taken up to establish him in business, and the Hotel de Paris was the result. In 1875 Du Puy bought the Delmonico

Bakery building on Alpine Street, excavated cellars, and added another story to provide space for eight bedrooms, each 12 by 20 feet, divided by a large central hall. He did almost all the work himself. Although the building was ready to be opened at Christmas, work continued for another year before Du Puy was satisfied. The two-story hotel is built of huge block bricks, with lintels and facades of brown stone, crowned with a *cheval-de-frise* of gilded spikes. A wide wooden veranda, garnished with scroll work, occupies one whole side of the building. There formerly was gilt on the lion guarding the gate, on the metal stag decorating one wall, on the heroic statue of Justice on the peak of the roof; there was more gilt on the legends "Hotel de Paris" and "Louis du Puy" emblazoned over the doors. The inner decorations were lavishly Parisian—mirrors, sculpture, paintings, hangings, and more gilt; many of these trappings remain.

The establishment of the hotel was due to the kindness of the citizens of Georgetown, but its success was due wholly to Louis du Puy's own efforts, and fully aware of this he established himself as a feudal lord, refusing to pay taxes, even threatening to shoot the collectors and burn the hotel with himself inside. He was equally high-handed in his selection and treatment of guests. Visitors who did not please him were not permitted to register, and others were ordered out instantly on incurring his displeasure. This was not such bad business, for everyone was eager to be accorded the privilege, something in the nature of an accolade, of being accepted at the Hotel de Paris. Women were never welcome; at best, they were accepted grudgingly if accompanied by one of Du Puy's favored gentlemen. Their marital status, however, was a matter of complete indifference. His attitude toward guests he explained to Dr. Russell, "If you are a college man, surely you know that no gentleman invites himself to be the guest of a stranger. This house is my own, and if I want guests I invite them."

Du Puy was fond of children, and there was one woman to whom he was kind. She was Sophie Galet, "Aunt Sophie," the widow of an old French cabinet maker, and at her husband's death Du Puy took her in. Her position in his establishment was ambiguous; Du Puy said that he asked her to do nothing, but she seemed to do everything. She became chatelaine, housekeeper, and maid of all work. She may even have done the cooking, but this is doubtful—Louis du Puy was jealous of this province. On his death in 1900 it was found that he had willed the hotel to her. She survived him but four months. The hotel is owned by the Colonial Dames of America in Colorado.

The CABIN CREEK HYDROELECTRIC STATION at Georgetown is the largest in Colorado. During peak demand for electricity by Denver water is released from the upper reservoir to generate electricity, pumped back up from the lower reservoir at night when demand is less. The Public Service Co. of Colorado has been spending approx. $31,000,000 for improving the facility, which can produce 324,000 kw of electricity for Denver's use.

West of Georgetown the highway begins a long ascent, passing (L) the SITE OF THE GEORGETOWN LOOP, 47.8 *m.*, where the narrow-gauge tracks of the Colorado & Southern Railway formerly looped over themselves for easier grade. The road was abandoned in 1939, the tracks were removed, and the high trestles torn down. At one time excursion trains carrying hundreds of awed passengers daily passed over the loop.

Mountain walls slope steeply on either side of SILVER PLUME, 49 *m.* (9,175 alt.), another formerly prosperous mining town, described by early Colorado historians as a "pretty village." It shared in the early silver prosperity of the region, but most of the mines ceased operations after 1900. A high-quality granite, quarried near by, is used for most of the State historical markers.

The highway follows the South Fork of Clear Creek, a thin sparkling stream running between willow and aspen thickets, its bed broken by numerous pools and eddies where trout abound. The canyon is overshadowed (L) by the massive forms of GRAYS PEAK (14,274 alt.), ninth highest summit in the State, and TORREYS PEAK (14,264 alt.), tenth highest. The peaks were named for the eminent American botanists, Asa Gray and John Torrey.

The boundary between Pike and Arapaho National Forests is crossed, 52.1 *m.*, and the highway ascends steadily through forests of dark green Engelmann spruce, the trees almost identical in size, shape, and color. Away from the highways this is a primitive area, the habitat of deer, elk, and some bear.

At 54.7 *m.* is (R) the entrance to BETHEL, an improved camp ground of the Forest Service (*fireplaces; sanitary facilities*).

LOVELAND PASS (11,992 alt.) 62 *m.*, has been the second highest motor traverse in the State. It was named for W. A. H. Loveland, railroad builder. Often impassible in winter, it was not used as a motor highway until 1931. In 1966 work was begun to pierce the mountain with two tunnels (Straight Creek) 8,400 ft. long, to carry combined US 6 and Interstate 70 under the Pass, replace the 992 ft. climb and reduce the distance from Loveland Ski Area to Dillon by 10 *m.*

DILLON, 76 *m.*, (8,600 alt.) is a new town overlooking Lake Dillon, a reservoir covering 3,300 acres and holding 261,700 acre-ft. of water. Dillon Dam, 231 ft. tall, on the Blue River, was completed in 1963. It obliterated the old mining town of Dillon, some of whose residents moved to Breckenridge and Silverthorne. The new town has an annual lake regatta. The west portal of the new Harold D. Roberts Tunnel is located near Dillon. It was built to carry water from the Blue River to the North Fork of the South Platte at Grant to aid the Denver water supply. Arapahoe Basin, 11 *m.* east of Dillon, is part of the great winter ski area.

At 77.1 *m.* is the junction with State 9 (*see Tour 16*).

FRISCO, 79.6 *m.* (9,097 alt.), a lively mining camp during the 1870's, was practically deserted until the rise of gold and silver prices in 1932. Then weather-beaten shacks were re-roofed and painted, and boarded windows were refitted with glass.

At 85.6 *m.* is the junction with a paved road, the former US 6.

Left (straight ahead) on this road to KOKOMO, 8 *m.* (10,618 alt.), the highest incorporated town in Colorado, formerly a gold camp. Today it is a huddle of cabins, except for a cafe built on the hillside, down which pours a lively mountain stream.

The highway crosses the Mosquito Range to the eastern slope of the Continental Divide over FREMONT PASS (11,320 alt.), 12.3 *m.,* named for Lieutenant John C. Frémont, explorer and pathfinder. The pass marks the boundary between the Arapaho and Cochetopa National Forests.

At the top of the pass is CLIMAX (11,320 alt.), the highest post office in the United States and Colorado's most prosperous mining town. Here Climax Molybdenum Division of American Metal Climax, Inc., produces molybdenum, a rare metal used in making radio tubes, chemicals, and dyes, and in hardening special steels for automobiles and aircraft. The plant has been built at the foot of BARTLETT MOUNTAIN, a mountain of molybdenum, with known ore reserves of 100,000,000 tons and a large unexplored area. Climax presents a busy and efficient scene with its great white silt dumps, and its miles of trestles on which ore cars run between mine cuts and sprawling gray flotation mills where the ore is processed. Mining is done by the caving system, a modification of Alaskan mining practices, which has eaten away a large gash in the face of the mountain. Ore bodies are undercut horizontally and broken down with dynamite. Its approx. 2,700 employees live in Leadville.

Molybdenum was first discovered by gold seekers; they ignored it, thinking it lead. Later it was believed to be galena; but in 1900 it was properly identified by the Colorado School of Mines. There was little market for the metal until 1914, when its value as an alloy for toughening steel was recognized; the outbreak of the World War sent it skyrocketing in price. After the war the market slumped, and for several years mining operations virtually ceased. The company began an intensive and successful campaign to interest steel manufacturers and others in use of the metal, and almost overnight the production of molybdenum became one of the State's important industries.

In 1966 Lake County had the highest value of mineral production in the State, due to an increased molybdenum output at the Climax mine. It was also the source of pyrites, rare earth minerals in monazite concentrate and tin and tungsten concentrates. Concentrated "moly," as it is known to miners, is shipped in paper-lined jute sacks for domestic use, and in oak barrels for foreign consumption.

South of Climax the road descends through forested slopes into the upper Arkansas Valley, crossing a boundary of the Pike National Forest, 15.3 *m.* The surrounding mountains do not appear exceptionally high, although they rise to greater elevations than elsewhere in Colorado. Ahead are Mount Elbert and Mount Massive, the State's two highest peaks.

In LEADVILLE, 25.4 *m.* are junctions with US 24 and State 300.

US 6 crosses the Continental Divide, follows the Vail Pass highway, and descends the western slope of Vail Peak, 11,200 ft. to make a junction with US 24 at Dowd, 110.4 *m.* Before reaching Dowd US 6 passes through a new ski area. From the summit of Vail Mountain to the Village of VAIL at 8,200 ft., trails drop 3,050 ft. over three miles. Here 63 four-passenger gondolas move from the terminal to Mid-Vail, where food is available. A 4,500 ft. double chairlift moves to the summit, 1,000 ft. above. Vail has Alpine and Scandinavian type houses and inns.

Between this point and GRAND JUNCTION 274.5 *m.* US 6 and US 24 are one route (*see Tour 5C*).

West of Grand Junction, US 6 and US 50 are one route, crossing the Utah Line 308.5 *m.* 45 miles east of Thompsons, Utah.

Tour 1A

(North Platte, Nebr.)—Julesburg—Sterling; US 138.
Nebraska Line to Sterling, 62 *m.*

Two-lane, paved road throughout. Union Pacific R.R. parallels entire route.

This route, following the former South Platte River Trail, has been closely associated with the development of Colorado. Along the banks of the shallow many-islanded stream passed the Spanish explorer, Pedro de Villasur, in 1720; a century later came trappers for beaver skins, and fur traders who built well-fortified posts and bartered with Indians for buffalo hides; next, the Fifty-niners, lured by tales of fabulous gold strikes; then, an ever-increasing tide of settlers, pushing into a virgin country; and now, the tourists.

Low rolling hills, once covered with short curling buffalo grass, the range first of bison and then of vast herds of cattle, are now dotted with dry farms growing wheat and corn, and with fields irrigated for sugar beet culture. Farmers have plowed up the grass and fenced the open ranges. The rutted trail has become a broad paved highway.

US 138 crosses the NEBRASKA LINE, 0 *m.*, at the extreme northeastern corner of Colorado, 61 miles west of North Platte, Nebr.

JULESBURG, 2 *m.* (3,477 alt., 1,880 pop.), lying among the broken hills in a curve of the South Platte River, is the only remaining town of four of the same name, each in its time an important stopover on the main trail to Denver. The present town, founded in 1881 when the Union Pacific Cutoff to Denver was projected, and still a division point on the main line, is the trading center for a large agricultural region.

Left from Julesburg on State 51 to the junction with a graveled road, 1.6 *m.;* R. here 3.6 *m.* to the ITALIAN'S CAVE, an enlargement of a natural fissure. Although legend has it that this was once the hide-out of Jules Beni, founder of Old Julesburg and subsequently an outlaw, the cave as seen today was the creation of Uberto Gabello, a miner from Cripple Creek, who enlarged the opening to obtain material for the construction of his house. Later he further enlarged the tunnel structure and derived a considerable revenue from visitors to this partly man-made cavern.

The SITE OF THE SECOND TOWN OF JULESBURG (R) is at 6 *m.* This town sprang up following the destruction of the first Julesburg, and was abandoned in 1867 when the third Julesburg was established.

On the SITE OF OLD JULESBURG, 9 *m.*, stood the first of the towns of that name, a station on the Overland Stage and the Pony Express routes, and a rendezvous for traders, Indian fighters, buffalo hunters, adventurers, bandits, and desperadoes, who rode into town to divide their loot and squander it riotously. Jules

Beni, the sullen bear-like French-Canadian station master, was the reputed leader of a band of outlaws in league with the Indians. Hostility of the Indians broke out into open warfare after 1862. Wagon trains were attacked and burned, and travelers were murdered. While the outrages were blamed on the numerous Indians in the region, the presence of white men in some of the war parties was attested by more than one survivor. As coaches carrying the largest specie shipments were singled out for attack, Jules Beni was believed to have instigated these raids. Although proof was lacking, the stage company finally dismissed Beni and appointed Joseph (Jack) Slade as station master. Slade, one of the toughest men on an extremely tough frontier, immediately found himself a target for the hostility of Jules Beni, who brooded over his displacement as station manager. The feud reached a climax when Beni filled Slade with enough buckshot to kill an ordinary man. Slade lived, however, to boast that he would cut off Jules' ears and wear them as watch charms. He captured Beni near Fort Laramie, Wyo., and killed him, so legend has it, after prolonged torture; there were many who asserted that they had seen the tokens of Slade's vengeance dangling from his watch chain. Slade in turn was later accused of robbing wagon trains along the Overland Trail, but all the evidence seems to be against it. Relieved of his post because of his violence when drunk, Slade was soon hanged by Vigilantes in Virginia City, Mont.—for disturbing the peace.

There are many who believe that the robbers buried much of their loot near Julesburg—the Italian's Cave being one of the favorite spots for treasure seekers—but none has ever been found. This Julesburg was completely destroyed during an Indian raid in 1865.

A granite marker, 9.6 m., indicates the SITE OF FORT SEDGWICK (R), a military post established to protect travelers and named for General John Sedgwick of the Union Army. The post, built in 1864, was garrisoned until 1871, when the Indians of this area were subjugated. Only traces of the old buildings remain; the wooden stockade has disappeared.

At 10 m. is the junction with a dirt road. Right 1.6 m. on this road, crossing the South Platte River, to OVID.

At 5 m. on US 138 is the junction with a dirt road. Right on this road to a siding known as WEIR, 0.25 m., the site of the third town of JULESBURG, once called "the wickedest little city east of the Rockies." Like Old Julesburg, it was headquarters for the riffraff of the West. Railroad huskies mingled with painted ladies, gamblers, soldiers, and frontiersmen in the dusty plains city, with its narrow, crowded streets, dance halls, barrooms, and gambling dens. This Julesburg came into being as a construction camp when the Union Pacific was building its tracks westward across Nebraska, Colorado, and Wyoming, to meet the Central Pacific and tie East to West. "Blacksnake" Lachut came in 1867 and was employed as a teamster. His command of profanity was surpassed only by his proficiency with the whip, and Julesburg soon came to know and fear that whip. A drunken laborer jostled Lachut; like a snake, the latter's long whip uncoiled and knotted itself around the neck of the husky. After dragging his victim through the streets, the teamster loosened the thong and then cut the man to pieces with the lash. For amusement "Blacksnake" snapped cigars from the mouths of bystanders and broke the necks of bottles a room's width away; he delighted in flicking off the ornate buckle that supported the single strap of a dancing girl's costume. This sadistic bully left Julesburg in 1870 and disappeared into Mexico.

A more somber figure was Gypsy, who foretold the death of many, all of whom died violently within a few hours. One evening she embraced a young man, her favorite at the time, and sobbed that she did not want him to die. He laughed. She refused to be comforted on what she said would be their last evening together. The boy was fatally shot that night. Gypsy became dreaded in the town; men and women evaded her eye lest it bring death. Finally, so the story goes, she walked into a saloon one night and announced that she would not see another sunrise; when morning came, she was found dead in bed, whether from violence or natural causes is not recorded.

OVID, 9.5 *m.* (3,500 alt.), is a flourishing trading center and a sugar refining town.

SEDGWICK, 17.5 *m.* (3,500 alt.), is a shipping point in the heart of rich sugar-beet country.

CROOK, 33.4 *m.* (3,700 alt.), in the beet area, has a consolidated high school serving a large district. The surrounding country was the scene of great cattle round-ups in the 1880's. PROCTOR, 42 *m.* (3,770 alt.) is another Logan County farm town shipping sugar beets.

ILIFF, 49 *m.* (3,998 alt.), was the site of the principal ranch house of John W. Iliff, chief of the cattlemen who became wealthy through grazing herds on buffalo grass. At one time Iliff owned 35,000 head of cattle and controlled most of the South Platte Valley. He opposed the coming of homesteaders, foreseeing the destruction of the open range. By having his numerous retainers take up homesteads throughout the region, Iliff maintained his seigniory for many years. Eventually his great ranch was broken up. The Iliff School of Theology (*see Denver*) was founded by his widow.

At 52.4 *m.* is the junction with State 113.

Right on this graveled road is PEETZ, 16.5 *m.* (4,300 alt.), serving a dry-farming region.

Left from Peetz 26 *m.* on a dirt road to CHIMNEY CANYONS. In early days these rugged canyons were covered with red cedar trees, many of them 75 feet high. As they provided the only source of firewood, lumber, and fence posts for settlers as far distant as Julesburg and Sterling, the larger trees were cut down. The canyons are popular picnic and camp grounds.

In STERLING, 62 *m.* (3,947 alt.,11,600 pop.) is the junction with US 6 (*see Tour 1a*).

〔⟨〕

Tour 2

Sterling — Fort Collins — Cameron Pass — Walden — Muddy Pass (Junction with US 40) ; 241.4 *m.,* State 14.

Paved highways. Cameron Pass closed Sept. 15-May 15.

This route, traversing miles of prairie land, crosses North Park, a great saucer-shaped valley noted for its hunting and fishing, to terminate on the crest of the Continental Divide. The road between Sterling and Ault is little used, but the section west of the junction with US 85 is heavily traveled during summer.

In STERLING, 0 *m.* (3,947 alt., 11,600 pop.) State 14 branches west (R) from US 6 (*see Tour 1a*).

The highway crosses a narrow belt of country irrigated by waters of the South Platte River, and enters an area of brown hills, covered with sagebrush, relieved by low sand bluffs and occasional outcroppings of rock. Farmers struggled to cultivate this arid inhospitable land, but unpainted and sun-warped buildings, now deserted, indicate that many have given up the struggle.

Settlement brought about destruction of this region's natural resources. Less than a century ago the rolling hills were the empire of the Pawnee, who lived in skin tepees and hunted buffalo. Their villages, clustered along the banks of PAWNEE CREEK, 12.8 *m.,* were soon disturbed by the coming of the white man. Earliest of these were French-Canadian traders who bartered with the natives for peltry and buffalo hides. Professional hunters made short work of the buffalo herds; and as the Pawnee and other Indians vanished with their food supply, the country began to fill up with Texas longhorn cattle.

For several decades northeastern Colorado remained a vast unfenced range, the scene of large cattle operations, from which a few gained fortunes. The cattle barons were not long to themselves, for homesteaders crowded into the country and gradually fenced in the great ranches. What is known now was not known then—that this submarginal land was unfit for cultivation. Steel plows broke the grassy protecting mat and exposed the soil to the unceasing high spring winds. As years passed, the erosion of the topsoil increased; each wind brought its dust storm; and fields became shifting sand dunes. Irrigation was impossible; either the fields were too high above the rivers, or available water had been appropriated by earlier settlers.

STONEHAM, 25.6 *m.* (4,583 alt.), is a trading hamlet in this dry-farm area. A few weather-beaten stores line the main street. Here is a junction with State 71.

West of Stoneham is the PAWNEE NATIONAL GRASSLAND. Great gullies break the hills—more evidence of destruction induced by attempts to plant crops.

RAYMER, 35.1 *m.* (4,779 alt., 1,464 pop.), the largest village between Sterling and Ault, has experienced two successive waves of immigration. First settled in the early 1890's, the town suffered from a series of crop failures. The need of a local trading center for surrounding farms gave it another start. The second town was called New Raymer but today Raymer is the P.O., and has a junction with State 52.

The area west of BUCKINGHAM, 42.5 *m.* (4,945 alt.), was once a part of the Seven Cross Ranch, one of the largest cattle holdings of northeastern Colorado, known for its annual round-ups, drives to market, and pay-day sprees.

At 45.2 *m.* is the junction with State 155.

Right on this graveled road is KEOTA, 5.5 *m.* (5,000 alt.), the shipping point for grain and livestock on the Holyoke branch of the Chicago, Burlington & Quincy Railroad.

Northeast of Keota, 14 miles across the prairie, rise the PAWNEE BUTTES, limestone cliffs fretted by wind and rain, which from a distance resemble an eerie ship sailing on the hazy blue expanse. Their chief interest is the remains of animal life found in their strata. Some catastrophe of the Pliocene and Miocene ages caught innumerable plains animals here. An ancient sea laid over their remains a covering of mud and sand which in the course of centuries turned to limestone. Pawnee Buttes are known to scientists throughout the world. As early as 1875 Professors Cope and Marsh of Yale University were engaged in studying the fossilized remains of a prehistoric horse and camel found here.

At 60.3 *m.* is the junction with a dirt road.

Right on this road to SEVEN CROSS HILL, 2 *m.*, rising high above the surrounding country, which served as a lookout for riders of the Seven Cross Ranch, who kept watch for stray horses and cattle, chance travelers, cattle rustlers, and occasional Indian raiders. An intricate system of mirrors, based on this focal point, relayed messages from ranch headquarters to range riders.

BRIGGSDALE, 62.1 *m.* (4,950 alt.), is the terminus of a spur line of the Union Pacific that serves the dry farming region. It has the usual grain-buying exchange, stock-shipping pens, and general merchandise stores. Dust storms and blistering sunlight have joined with other elements to create the weather-beaten appearance of the frame buildings.

West of Briggsdale the highway crosses CROW CREEK, 62.5 *m.*, a tiny stream named to commemorate an ancient Indian battle in which the Pawnee decisively defeated their enemies, the Crow.

PURCELL, 76.6 *m.* (5,024 alt.), at the terminus of another spur line of the Union Pacific, has a grain elevator, milk station, and general store. Large shipments of grain and cattle from the surrounding farming region are made here.

The landscape west of Purcell changes abruptly; hills dwindle, and tawny brown buffalo grass is relieved by touches of green as the highway approaches an irrigated area.

AULT, 87.6 *m.* (4,940 alt. 810 pop.) (*see Tour 12a*), is at the junction with US 85 and State 3.

The route traverses a section irrigated from the Cache la Poudre River, where fields remain a rich green throughout most of the summer. Huge cottonwoods and willows, planted a half century ago as windbreaks, shade the highway and side lanes. Black soil produces heavy crops of sugar beets, grains, vegetables, and hay. Cattle feeding is an important activity; livestock, pastured on the foothills and mountain ranges throughout the summer, is brought into the valley during winter to be fattened for market. Dairying is profitable.

In FORT COLLINS, 106.4 *m.* (5,100 alt., 39,000 pop.) (*see Fort Collins*), are junctions with US 87 (*see Tour 13*) and with US 287, which unites with State 14 as far as TED'S PLACE, 115.7 *m.* and with Interstate 25.

The route enters the canyon of the Cache la Poudre River, a popular vacation area. For almost its entire length the river (*good fishing*) is lined with summer cabins and resorts. Low foothills are covered with a sparse growth of juniper and scrub cedar; the soil is dun-colored, but here and there are dark outcroppings of underlying granite. A long ridge of red Morrison sandstone thrusts up through the foothills.

At 119 *m.* the highway crosses the eastern boundary of ROOSE-VELT NATIONAL FOREST, most accessible of Colorado's national forests, extending west to the Medicine Bows, north to Wyoming, and south to Clear Creek (*see Tour 7*). Its area of 771,385 acres was originally part of the Medicine Bow Forest Reserve. The name was officially changed in 1932 in honor of Theodore Roosevelt, ardent champion of conservation. In the dense forest are 17 varieties of conifer and broadleaf, and numerous picnic and camp grounds. At the more attractive of these the Forest Service has provided fireplaces, sanitary facilities, and other conveniences.

West of the boundary the highway penetrates heavily wooded hill country. Between wine-colored cliffs the waters of the Poudre lash the boulders in its course. Although neither sheer-walled nor rugged at this point, the canyon is attractive for its pastel shadings.

At 124 *m.* is the junction with a trail.

Right on this trail to ROBBERS ROOST, 5 *m.*, a high tor. According to local tradition, this area was a hide-out for stage robbers when the Overland Express used the route between La Porte (*see Tour 13A*) and Fort Laramie, Wyoming. Approached only by this rocky trail, the Roost served as an almost impregnable fortress and the outlaws were driven out only by a threat to use artillery, according to old-timers.

The highway winds tortuously through the LITTLE NARROWS, its high steep walls varying from deep maroon, when in shadow, to brilliant scarlet in the sunlight. Where the Little Narrows open into a wide valley the road follows the grade of an abandoned railway, the projectors of which visualized a transcontinental route to the Pacific.

The highway parallels the Poudre through BIG NARROWS, a long defile winding in and out between granite walls. Like the Little Narrows, the cliffs are of red granite, and tower in great battlements and castles. Lichens and scrawny pines have secured footholds in recesses of the rock and relieve the grimness of the cliffs.

The FORT COLLINS MOUNTAIN PARK (*picnic grounds*), 138.4 *m.*, comprises several hundred acres of municipally owned land in a broad wooded valley. The Nature Trail, constructed by the Rocky Mountain Climbers Club, is so laid as to pass by at least one specimen of every variety of tree in the forest. Wild flowers and shrubs native to the mountains are planted along the trail, each variety labeled and its distinctive feature indicated.

EGGERS, 140.5 *m.*, is a summer post office and resort (*accommodations*) in Poudre Canyon. West of Eggers the road skirts INDIAN MEADOWS, a long narrow grassland bordering the river, once the heart of rich Indian fishing and hunting territory and the site of numerous battles. Arrowheads, stone axes, ornaments, and other relics are occasionally found here.

Through this area the highway winds to RUSTIC, 146.2 *m.*, a filling station, and on to GLEN ECHO, 148 *m.,* a resort at the foot of PINGREE HILL, its steep sides scarred with abandoned mine shafts and prospect holes. The Cache la Poudre River here marks the northern boundary of the COLORADO STATE GAME REFUGE, an area extending more than 50 miles north and south, and approximately 15 miles east and west. In autumn, deer driven from the mountains by snow graze in the foothills and are frequently seen along the road.

OLD MAN'S FACE, 149.8 *m.,* a rock silhouette, is one of many fantastic conformations wrought by nature.

HOME, 152.6 *m.,* is a three-story, red-brick hotel, built by John Zimmerman in 1882 as headquarters of his mountain ranch. The route passes several small resorts and skirts CHAMBERS LAKE (9,000 alt.), named for Robert Chambers, an early trapper who was slain by Indians. The lake, artificially enlarged, is used as an irrigation reservoir. CAMERON PEAK (12,124 alt.) shuts out the sky (R), and left rise the peaks of the Mummy Range, lying within Rocky Mountain National Park. Alpine and subalpine growths cover the higher slopes; five varieties of bog orchids are found near the lake shore.

On the last lap of its long climb over the Continental Divide the highway skirts the base of CLARK PEAK (12,965 alt.), southernmost eminence of the Medicine Bow Range. Practically the entire eastern slope of the range is included in the CAMERON PASS PRIMITIVE AREA, set aside by the Forest Service to be preserved in its natural condition. No roads or improved trails are to be constructed here, and erection of buildings is prohibited. The area offers excellent opportunities for "high country" trips with guides and pack horses. These excursions are usually undertaken by experienced campers, but a tenderfoot, with the aid of a guide and adequate equipment, can have an enjoyable outing.

CAMERON PASS, 175.7 *m.* (10,285 alt.) named for its discoverer, General Robert Cameron, pioneer railroad builder, is a narrow forested defile between Clark Peak and MOUNT RICHTHOFEN (12,953 alt.), through which the road winds for 9 miles. A granite and bronze marker indicates the highest point on the pass. In winter it is sometimes necessary to use dynamite to clear the snow-and-ice-packed highway.

West of the pass the highway is bordered with dense stands of lodgepole pines as it descends by fairly easy grades into NORTH PARK, a level grassland. On the edge of the COLORADO STATE FOREST is NORTH MICHIGAN LAKE, stocked for fishing. GOULD, first town in Jackson County, has busy lumber mills.

WALDEN, 206.5 *m.* (8,300 alt., 850 pop.), a ranching supply center and seat of Jackson County, is the only town of consequence in North Park. Walden has a municipal airport with a 6,000-ft. runway. Its mills are busy cutting lumber from Routt National Forest. It contracts for natural gas produced in Jackson County.

Walden is at the junction with State 125. State 14 turns southwest toward Steamboat Springs.

At 220.4 *m.,* is the junction with an unimproved road.

Right on this road is COALMONT, 3.6 *m.*, (8,500 alt.), a collection of rambling frame and corrugated iron buildings, terminus of the Laramie, North Park & Western R.R. Here coal is mined by strip mining.

South of the junction the route crosses the rough foothills of the Rabbit Ears Mountain, named for the two colossal granite upthrusts that from a distance resemble rabbit ears.

MUDDY PASS, 241.4 *m.* (8,772 alt.) on the Continental Divide, is at the junction with US 40 (*see Tour 7b*).

❰❂❰ ❖

Tour 3

(McCook, Nebr.) — Wray — Brush — Greeley — Estes Park Village—Rocky Mountain National Park—Junction US 40 (Granby); US 34.

Nebraska Line to Junction US 40, 265.3 *m.*

Paved road entire distance. The Burlington parallels route between Nebraska Line and Wiggins.

US 34 traverses the heart of the plains country, once grazing land for buffalo herds, and the habitat of hostile Indians. Now the area is devoted to dry-land farming and cattle raising. The highway crosses an irrigated section before penetrating the foothills to the mountain gateway of Estes Park.

US 34 crosses the Nebraska Line, 0 *m.*, 93 miles west of McCook, Nebr.

WRAY, 10 *m.* (2,516 alt., 2,100 pop.), seat of Yuma County, unlike many eastern Colorado towns, lies in moist river land and is a mass of verdure throughout spring and summer. On the southeastern edge of town, reached by a winding drive from Main Street, is FLIRTATION POINT, a limestone formation away from the cliffs (L) that hem in the valley. In the eastern wall was reputedly an Indian temple of demon worship.

The Reverend Moses Anderson, the first minister, who held services hereabout in 1880, was assisted in his work by several cowhands, who, so the story goes, decided that it was too much to expect a man of God to save souls on his meager income. Bolstered by good thoughts and many drinks after a meeting in a saloon, they canvassed the town, and hesitant citizens were "persuaded" to contribute. Late that night the tipsy delegation presented the clergyman with a purse containing $200.

Left from Wray on State 51 to the junction with State 53, 5.6 *m.;* L. here to BLACK WOLF CREEK, 16.1 *m.,* a small stream flowing through a dense growth of cottonwoods and flowering wild currants, named for the black prairie wolves prevalent in early days. Hills and breaks along the stream were their favorite breeding grounds. According to Indian legend, a malignant prairie spirit in the form of a gigantic black wolf dwelt above the creek.

At 17.4 *m.* is the BEECHER ISLAND BATTLEGROUND, scene of a combat between U. S. Troops and Indians that continued for more than a week and broke the power of the Indians in the Plains States.

In 1868, Colonel George A. Forsythe and Lieutenant Fred Beecher, with 50 soldiers and scouts, moved up the Arickaree Valley on the trail of a hostile band of Cheyenne. Unaware of a general gathering of "hostiles" in that region, they made camp beside the river. When morning came the bluffs around were swarming with Indians; realizing that they were cut off from help, the men withdrew to a low flat island in midstream, where they dug in. The Indians numbered more than a thousand Northern and Southern Cheyenne and their allies, the Arapaho and the Ogallala Sioux. Their commander was Roman Nose, a great Cheyenne war chief. Soon after dawn he ordered a charge down the slope and across the river. The attack was halted by the soldiers, and Roman Nose was among those killed. Other charges made during that day of short-range fighting were repelled by the besieged, and the Indians took to the tall grass along the river and showered their enemies with bullets and arrows.

Day after day Forsythe and his men held their position. As horses were killed, their bodies served as breastworks after edible portions had been cut away. Horse meat supplemented by a few wild plums comprised the food supply during the eight-day siege. Water came from holes dug in the sand. Lieutenant Beecher and several men killed; nearly all of the survivors suffered one or more wounds. Four scouts, who slipped through the Indian lines, carried word to Fort Wallace, Kans. A strong force hurried to Forsythe's aid and arrived at the moment when defenders of the island, despairing of rescue, were about to charge and die in open conflict. The course of the river has changed and obliterated the island; monuments erected by Colorado and Kansas were swept away by flood in 1934.

In the brick BEECHER ISLAND MEMORIAL AUDITORIUM, seating 1,400, erected on a near-by hill by the Beecher Island Memorial Association, reunions and a pageant commemorating the battle are held annually during the third week of September.

To the north rises the low cone-shaped mound of SQUAW HILL, from the crest of which the women and children of the Cheyenne watched the battle. Here, according to legend, Roman Nose defied the gods of his people and sealed his own doom. A prophetess of his tribe had predicted that he would become one of the greatest of Cheyenne leaders, but had warned that if he ever ate food touched by metal he would become vulnerable to the weapons of his enemies. A few days before the Forsythe attack, while feasting at the Ogallala camp, he ate bread that had been cut with an iron knife. Before the long ceremony of purification was completed, the advance of Forsythe's scouts was discovered. Roman Nose directed the onslaught from a bluff; not heeding protests of the medicine men, he participated in the battle and was killed.

North and west of Beecher Island lies an oil field.

West of Wray is a monotonous stretch known as "drylands flats," where small farms dot rolling arid hills, gray with sage and needle-pointed soapweed. Occasionally a cottontail is glimpsed, and jackrabbits are so numerous in this and other parts of the eastern plains region as to menace field crops and gardens. Drives are periodically held to exterminate the "jacks." Beaters, often numbering hundreds, encircle an area and close in, shouting and beating on tin pans. The frightened rabbits flee toward the center where a pen of close-meshed wire has been built. Frequently thousands of rabbits are thus forced into a trap; hunters enter armed with clubs, and whosesale slaughter begins. Such drives attract large crowds from near-by towns, who cheer lustily when, during the melee, a hunter happens to be knocked flat by a wildly swung club. Welfare organizations once distributed the carcasses of the rabbits, a practice discontinued when many of the animals were found to be infected with tuleremia.

YUMA, 36.5 *m.* (4,132 alt., 2,084 pop.), named for an Indian tribe, is in the heart of a dry-farming district, where oats, winter rye, macaroni wheat, and spelt, a German wheat, are the principal crops.

The FEDERAL GOVERNMENT AGRICULTURAL EXPERIMENT STATION (*open 9–5 daily*), 62 *m.,* covers 160 acres laid out in orchards and fields planted to more than 1,600 varieties of wheat, corn, oats, and other crops, which are rotated in 20-year cycles. Experiments here are of vital importance to the region, since they point the way to new methods in soil conservation.

AKRON, 63.5 *m.* (4,662 alt., 1,800 pop.), seat of Washington County, was the only town site on the new Burlington Railroad at the time of its founding in 1882, and herds of antelope grazed on the surrounding plains. The town is still a division point on the railroad, and its shops provide employment for many.

At 85.5 *m.* is the junction with US 6, 1 mile east of BRUSH, 86.5 *m.* (4,280 alt., 4,750 pop.) (*see Tour 1a*). US 6 and US 34 are united for 24.5 miles (*see Tour 1a*).

At 110 *m.* is the western junction with US 6, 1.5 miles north of Wiggins (*see Tour 1a*).

DEARFIELD, 122 *m.* (4,225 alt.), was founded for his race by C. T. Jackson, a Negro, who came to Colorado in 1887 and seven years later began farming near Boulder. Inspired by Booker T. Washington's *Up From Slavery,* and advised by Governor John F. Shafroth in whose office Jackson was a messenger, the Dearfield tract was selected in 1910 and settled the next year when seven families built houses here. Without adequate capital and unfamiliar with scientific methods of dry farming the colonists suffered discouraging set-backs. In time they learned the principles of soil-moisture conservation and grew increasingly independent. The name of the community was suggested by one of the settlers, who said that the labor expended upon the development of their fields would make them very dear.

Traversing undulating semi-arid hills that fringe the Platte Valley, US 34 swings again into rich irrigated country, the center being KERSEY, 140.5 *m.* (4,614 alt., 443 pop.), with elevators and feed mills.

On the O. A. Gordon farm, 146.5 *m.,* a monument marks the SITE OF FORT LATHAN, established as a station on the old Overland Stage Line in 1862. At 143 *m.* is a junction with a dirt road. Right on this road to SCOUT ISLAND 2.5 *m.,* in a heavy grove of cottonwoods at the confluence of the South Platte and Cache la Poudre Rivers.

The route continues along the Platte Valley through a rich section

Sports and Recreation

ACTION AT ONE OF COLORADO'S FORTY ANNUAL RODEOS

ROPING A CALF AT A RODEO

Colin Lofting Photo, Rodeo Cowboy Assn.

POLO AT COLORADO SPRINGS

Continental Oil Company

LIFT CARRIES SKIERS TO TOP OF SLOPES

RIDING PLATTERS AT HIDDEN VALLEY

YACHTING ON GRAND LAKE

Colorado Visitors Bureau

GOLF MATCH, COLORADO SPRINGS

Bob McIntyre Photo, Broadmoor Hotel

MOTOR LAUNCHES IN LAKE GRANBY

CAMPING, ROCKY MOUNTAIN NATIONAL PARK

National Park Service

HOW HIGH IS UP? GUIDE AND TOURISTS

FISHING IN ONE OF THE SWIFT TROUT STREAMS

Colorado Dept. of Public Relations

FISHING IN BOX LAKE, ROCKY MOUNTAIN NATIONAL PARK

ONE MAN'S RECREATION, EAGLE CLIFF

known in the Rocky Mountain region as the cradle of irrigation farming. Water is a precious commodity in Colorado, for much of the land is of little value unless irrigated. When buying a farm in irrigation districts, a "water right" is either included in the price or must be purchased separately. This right, defined by State statute, entitles the holder to use a specific amount of water at stated periods during the growing season. Private concerns build reservoirs in which to store water taken from the streams, construct and maintain canals to convey it to hundreds of farms, and employ "ditch riders" to superintend its distribution. The canals are tapped by ditches through which water flows to the fields where it is distributed by means of furrows or laterals. Small grains, alfalfa, and clover are irrigated by flooding. Irrigation began in Colorado on a small scale almost as early as gold mining. There are records of primitive irrigation projects established by Spanish colonists in 1598.

GREELEY, 149.5 m. (4,663 alt., 33,300 pop.) is at the junction with US 85 (see Tour 12a).

West of Greeley the country is comparatively level, although the highway crosses several low hills, from the crests of which is visible the imposing blue wall of the Front Range of the Rocky Mountains as it fades away into the badlands of Wyoming. Most impressive of the mountain peaks that splinter the western sky-line is the jagged spire of LONGS PEAK (14,255 alt.).

From the summit of a hill, 160 m., the Big Thompson and Cache la Poudre River Valleys come into view, both green and fertile agricultural regions, which produce quantities of sugar beets and grains. On clear days looms (R) the blunt bulk of HORSE TOOTH MOUNTAIN (7,252 alt.).

The highway descends into the lower Big Thompson Valley and traverses level farming country to KELIM, 163.5 m. (4,960 alt.), an agricultural community founded in the early 1900's by German immigrants who had knowledge of sugar beet culture and aided in the developing of the new industry.

An EXPERIMENTAL FARM (open 9–5 daily), 168 m., is maintained by the State College of Agriculture and Mechanic Arts. Office and laboratories are housed in a white frame building surrounded by well-tended lawns. Here is the eastern edge of the prosperous fruit-growing region around Loveland. Apples and cherries are the principal crops. In spring the valley is a sea of pink and white blossoms.

LOVELAND, 171.3 m. (4,982 alt., 15,000 est. 1968) calls itself Sweetheart Town and uses a heart-shaped cachet because annually thousands send their valentines through the local postoffice. It is at a junction of US 287 with State 1, 6 m. west of Interstate 25 and US 87. It is on the direct route to Estes Park and Rocky Mountain National Park. The Great Western Sugar Beet refinery employs 400 seasonally, and the Hewlett-Packard electronics plant employs 1,500.

Loveland, named for W. A. H. Loveland, one of the State's early railroad builders, was founded in 1877 with the construction of the Colorado Central R. R. The first station was a tent in a wheat field.

The harvesting of a bumper crop delayed platting the town site. Later, when selling of lots began, many houses were removed from St. Louis, a near-by settlement. Disappointed prospectors, returning from the gold fields, took up land here and raised vegetables and other produce that brought fabulous prices in Denver. Butter sold at $2 a pound; eggs, $1.50 a dozen. Hay cut from bottom lands and hauled to Central City and Blackhawk by ox-teams brought $100 to $150 a ton. The *Reporter-Herald* is its daily newspaper, and the *Larimer County Times-News* a weekly. It promotes the County Fair and Rodeo, a horse show, a soapbox derby, greyhound races and the Open Water Ski Tourney. Loveland shares in the new Fort-Collins—Loveland Airport on Interstate 25, which has runways 6,500 ft. long.

In JOHNSON'S PARK (Lakewood) (L), 172.1 *m.,* a marker indicates the SITE OF FORT NAMAQUA, the first settlement in the vicinity. Here, early in 1858, Mariano Modeno, accompanied by his family and a body of retainers, built a fortified ranch house which later became a station on the Overland Stage Line. Modeno also built the first bridge across the Big Thompson at this point. Artificial LOVELAND LAKE, opposite the park, provides boating and fishing.

The rolling terrain south of the lake marks the beginning of the Rocky Mountains. Above the acres of cherry orchards in the valley rise brick-red formations, erosive debris of Triassic sandstone, curiously wrought and twisted by wind and water.

West of WILD'S JUNCTION, 175.5 *m.,* with important gypsum deposits, the route passes through an opening in the DEVIL'S BACK-BONE, a great hogback. Here have been found fossils of giant sea turtles, for the hogback was an island when most of Colorado was the bed of an ancient sea. At 178.5 *m.* is a junction with a dirt road.

Right on this road to SYLVANDALE, 5 *m.,* summer headquarters of Cotner College, Lincoln, Nebr. The grounds include 190 acres, with a dormitory, classroom, and assembly building, all neat white frame structures. Accommodations are provided for 150 students.

The highway crosses the eastern boundary of Roosevelt National Forest, 180.7 *m.;* at intervals, where softer rock is exposed, the river has cut out small grassy and forested glades. In one of these (R), 183.9 *m.,* is LOVELAND MOUNTAIN PARK. The 400-acre tract, framed by the sloping walls of a natural bowl, has sports and picnic facilities, including fireplaces set at well-selected points along the winding trails.

At 187.7 *m.* is the resort village of DRAKE.

Right from Drake on a dirt road, an alternate route to Estes Park Village, is GLEN HAVEN, 7.5 *m.,* one of the oldest cabin colonies in the region. The road, the original entrance to the park, follows the North fork of the Big Thompson, winding among rock-crowned hills of increasing height, clothed with deep forests of aspen that flame scarlet and yellow in the fall. At the top of rugged DEVIL'S GULCH, 12 *m.,* is the hunting lodge built by Lord Dunraven, Irish nobleman, who became fascinated by the beauty of the canyon. The route continues beyond the gulch to Estes Park Village, 14.5 *m.*

US 34 cuts deeper into the mountains, and makes an abrupt entrance into the highlands of ESTES PARK. LAKE ESTES, 1½ *m.* east of the village, is a reservoir on the Big Thompson River, impounded by Olympus Dam.

US 34 crosses the western boundary of Roosevelt National Forest, 197.1 *m.,* into ESTES PARK VILLAGE, 199.8 *m.* (7,500 alt., 1,518 pop.), at the junction with State 7.

Between Estes Park Village and the western boundary of Rocky Mountain National Park, 248.7 *m.,* US 34 is known as the Trail Ridge Road (*see Rocky Mountain National Park Tour 1*).

At 249.2 *m.* is the junction with an improved road.

Left on this road is GRAND LAKE VILLAGE, 1 *m.* (8,380 alt., 350 pop.), a summer resort on the lake shore. The cabins and many other buildings of peeled logs harmonize with the natural surroundings. GRAND LAKE, one of the largest in the State, was created ages ago when the valley of the Colorado was dammed by a glacial moraine. The Ute abhorred the vicinity, because according to legend, a large village of the tribe encamped on the lake shore was attacked by Cheyenne and Arapaho. Most of the Ute warriors were killed, while women and children, who had been placed on a large raft for safety, were left at the mercy of a rising storm. The raft was driven to the center of the lake where it capsized, and all were drowned. Mists rising from the waters were believed by the Ute to be the spirits of the unfortunates. Extremely deep—in places the bottom has never been sounded—the lake remains a constant blue. Most of the pine-fringed shore is privately owned. The Grand Lake Yacht Club holds annual yacht races here in August; boating and fishing are popular, and there is some swimming notwithstanding the coldness of the water.

South of the junction, US 34 descends the wide valley of the Colorado, a stretch of rolling grassy hills dotted with pine and aspen.

STILLWATER, 254.3 *m.,* has a Ranger Station and campground.

The GRAND LAKE ENTRANCE to the Rocky Mountain National Park is on US 34 near the head of Grand Lake. To the south and outside the Park is the SHADOW MOUNTAIN NATIONAL RECREATION AREA, 18,240 acres, which has two important units of the Colorado-Big Thompson irrigation project, developed since 1952 by the U. S. Bureau of Reclamation: SHADOW MOUNTAIN LAKE, which covers 18,400 acre-ft., and LAKE GRANBY, 539,800 acre-ft. The Granby Dam is 298 ft. high; the Shadow Mountain Dam only 63 ft. high, but 3,077 ft. long. Water is lifted from Lake Granby 85 to 186 ft. into Shadow Mountain Lake and thence to Grand Lake. Water from Grand Lake is moved via the ALVA B. ADAMS TUNNEL, 13.1 *m.* through the Continental Divide at 550 cu. ft. per second to a point 4.5 *m.* southwest of Estes Park.

(❖

Tour 4

Junction US 287—Boulder—Lyons—Estes Park Village; 63.2 *m.,* State 7.

This route, used chiefly as a short cut from central Colorado to Estes Park Village, traverses rich farming lands in Boulder Valley to reach the foothill country where ranching is the principal occupation. Ascending through colorful South St. Vrain Canyon, the highway terminates at the entrance to Rocky Mountain National Park.

State 7 branches west from US 287 (*see Tour 13*), 0 *m.,* 25 miles north of Denver (*see Denver*).

The highway pursues a straight course across low rolling hills dotted with farms, the majority under irrigation. The principal crops are alfalfa and small grains.

BOULDER, 9.5 *m.* (5,350 alt., 56,000 pop.) (*see Boulder*), is at the junction with State 119 (*see Tour 6*).

North of Boulder the highway follows a rapidly rising grade. Much of the country is included in the Colorado Game Preserve, and glimpses of wild life are frequent. Chipmunks, gophers, and black squirrels scamper along the roadside; occasionally a porcupine wanders among the pines. Although this large rodent frequents the mountain country, it is somewhat of a gypsy and is often found on the plains. Many have been encountered on Denver streets. Deer, singly or in groups, approach the highway to stare at motorists as they stop to photograph them.

The route crosses LEFT HAND CREEK, 18.3 *m.,* named for the Arapaho chief, Niwot (Ind. left hand), killed at Sand Creek (*see Tour 8a*). The valley here was settled shortly after the gold rush of 1859 by men who had become discouraged in their search for "color." As the country had no established courts, settlers worked out their own code for establishing titles to lands.

ALTONA, 18.5 *m.* (5,360 alt.) was planned in the early 1860's as a mountain metropolis. Toll roads were to radiate from here to the more important mining camps. But the plan collapsed when a toll road was constructed from Boulder to the camps, and the railroads avoided the settlement.

Left from Altona on a graded road through rugged LEFT HAND GAP, across the boundary of ROOSEVELT NATIONAL FOREST (*see Tour 2*), 3.3 *m.,* to JAMESTONE, 8 *m.* (6,920 alt.), the supply base for mines along Jim Creek. The route continues through a country of impressive beauty to the junction with State 160 (*see Tour 6*), 14.5 *m.*

The ascending route is lined with massive slabs of vividly colored stone. The dark red sandstone, prominent in many mountain formations of the West and known as the Lyons formation, was first studied by geologists in this area.

At 25.1 *m.* is the junction with State 66.

Right on this improved road is an alternative and shorter route to Estes Park Village, 20 *m.* (*see Tour 3 and Rocky Mountain National Park*).

LYONS, 26.5 *m.* (5,375 alt., 800 pop.), a mining center, lumber camp, and cow town, was named for Mrs. Carrie Lyons, pioneer editor of the Lyons *News.*

West of Lyons the highway along the canyon of the South St. Vrain is bordered with small farms and ranches. The country becomes more rugged and sparsely settled as the route crosses the eastern boundary of ROOSEVELT NATIONAL FOREST, 29.5 *m.,* embracing Rocky Mountain National Park on three sides and forming part of the great Colorado State Game Refuge (*see Tour 2*).

The road reaches South St. Vrain Canyon and enters THE NARROWS, 30.1 *m.,* winding three miles between jagged cliffs. Where The Narrows open suddenly, rock-torn slopes, dark with evergreens, fall back on both sides of the route. The bed of the stream is strewn with rock fragments of grotesque shape. Around the base of ELEPHANT ROCK, 34.3 *m.,* a mammoth boulder, the stream is a brawling white torrent. Indians believed that in these rapids lurked the Underwater People, demons who dragged the unwary to their death.

Here, and along other noisy mountain streams, the American dipper, also known as the water ouzel, dives recklessly into the torrent for its dinner. Although its feet are not webbed, the dipper is as much at home in the water as a gull, using its strong wings for swimming. Their nests, resembling dutch ovens, are built in damp rock crevices.

The bronze MORE MEMORIAL PLAQUE, set in a slab of rock (L), 37.1 *m.,* bears the legend: "Daddy More (1846–1930). A friend to man." This simple tribute was paid to an old prospector who bestowed place-names upon many points in the region. He loved to trace resemblances between rock formations and actual living creatures, and was adept at weaving tall tales about these curiosities. Many bus drivers used to stop at his cabin so that passengers might be amused and thrilled.

RIVERSIDE, 39.3 *m.* (7,364 alt.), and RAYMOND, 41.5 *m.* (7,711 alt.), are resort villages.

At Raymond is the junction with State 160 (*see Tour 6*).

Northwest of Raymond the road ascends from the basin of the South St. Vrain to the crest of the ridge separating this stream from the headwaters of the North St. Vrain. Ahead is Longs Peak, with the Arapaho Peaks (L) to the west.

ALLEN'S FIREPLACE, 46.6 *m.,* an old landmark (R), is part of the chimney of a cabin built in 1864 by Alonzo Allen, an early settler and prospector. The highway follows a weaving course along piney slopes through the heart of a resort district bordering the eastern side of Rocky Mountain National Park. CHIEF'S HEAD MOUNTAIN, 51.5 *m.*, its serrated crest suggesting the profile of an Indian warrior, is outlined against the sky.

COPELAND LAKE, 48.8 *m.* (9,200 alt.), is a resort on North St. Vrain Creek at the eastern edge of the Wild Basin area, one of the most rugged sections of Rocky Mountain National Park.

Left from Copeland Lake on a dirt road to a PUBLIC CAMPGROUND, 2.2*m.*, within the boundaries of the park; here marked foot trails lead west to OUZEL LAKE, 4.5 *m.*, and BLUE BIRD LAKE, 6 *m.*, both at the foot of OUZEL PEAK (12,600 alt.), and to THUNDER LAKE, 6.5 *m.* at the foot of TANIMA PEAK (12,417 alt.).

LODGE ST. MALO (L), 52 *m.*, is a summer camp for youths of the Roman Catholic parishes of Denver. The fieldstone CHAPEL is built on an outcrop of rock overlooking the road.

At 52.9 *m.* is the junction with a dirt road.

Left on this road to the LONGS PEAK CAMPGROUND, 0.9 *m.*, official starting point for the climb to the summit of Longs Peak. At 53.8 *m.* is the junction with a foot trail. Right on this trail across an open meadow and over a series of switchbacks to the summit of TWIN SISTERS MOUNTAIN, 3.8 *m.;* the trail ends at the RANGER STATION of the Twin Sisters Fire Lookout in the saddle between the peaks.

At 62.6 *m.* is the junction with US 34 (*see Tour 3*), which unites with State 7 to ESTES PARK VILLAGE, 63.2 *m.* (7,500 alt.,1,518 pop.), the principal entrance to Rocky Mountain National Park.

The east portal of the ALVA B. ADAMS TUNNEL is located 4.5 *m.* southwest of Estes Park. It carries water from Grand Lake through the Continental Divide, 13.1 *m.* at 550 cu. ft. per second. The water then moves 4.3 *m.* to the Big Thompson River. It serves St. Marys power plant, 2½ *m.* southwest of Estes Park; Estes power plant, on LAKE ESTES, formed on the Big Thompson River by Olympus Dam; Pole Hill power plant, 10 *m.* east of Estes Park, and two other power plants near Loveland. After leaving Pole Hill the water is stored in Flatiron Reservoir and by pumping into CARTER LAKE in Larimer County. The Carter dam is 285 ft. high, highest in the State; the lake, 1,140 acres, has a capacity of 112,000 acre-ft.

Tour 5

(Goodland, Kans.)—Burlington—Limon—Colorado Springs—Buena Vista—Leadville—Tennessee Pass—Mount of the Holy Cross—Glenwood Springs—Rifle—Grand Junction; US 24. Interstate 70 enters Colorado with US 24; 1 *m.* west of Limon it turns northeast to Denver. Kansas Line to Grand Junction, 484.8 *m.*

The Chicago, Rock Island & Pacific Ry. parallels the route between Burlington and Colorado Springs.

Interstate 70 follows US 24 much of the route, but runs south of it at Burlington, Bethune, Stratton, to a point 3 *m.* west of Seibert.

Crossing the seemingly limitless High Plains, barren and semiarid land devoted to cattle raising and dry farming, US 24 ascends to the base of the mountains at Colorado Springs. West of this sophisticated center, with its surrounding vacation area, the highway skirts Pikes Peak and traverses a rugged region of great natural beauty. Tales of Indian battles, gold strikes, and subsequent "rushes" lend glamour to the hills and old towns along the way. The tour winds through four of the State's national forests before entering the fertile Grand Valley nestled in the semimountainous plateau country of the western part of the State.

Section a. KANSAS LINE to COLORADO SPRINGS; 163 *m.*
US 24

US 24 crosses the KANSAS LINE, 0 *m.,* 19 miles west of Goodland, Kans. In the 1870's and 1880's the plains along the boundary were overrun by herds of cattle; now agriculture is practically the sole occupation.

US 385, combined with State 51, is the easternmost north-south highway in Colorado. Its chief town in Kit Carson County is Burlington. Just north of the county line in Yuma County it runs by Bonnie Reservoir, which covers 8,470 acres and holds 362,000 acre-ft. of water.

BURLINGTON, 12 *m.* (4,166 alt., 2,800 pop.), is the seat of Kit Carson County and was laid out in 1889 when the county was formed from Elbert County. The Rock Island Railroad and Greyhound Bus lines serve the town, which has an airport for light craft. The county was second in value of wheat produced, fifth in crops generally, and raises cattle. The *Burlington Record* is its newspaper.

BETHUNE, 20.5 *m.* (4,294 alt.), a dry-farming settlement, was founded during World War I when high grain prices brought an influx of farmers. Farmers in this section of eastern Colorado are mostly of English, Scottish, Dutch, and German stock, with some Irish. Slavs and Latins are few. Dry farms range from 80 acres to 640 and more. Wheat and corn are the principal crops; oats, rye, barley, beans, and forage crops are also grown.

Not so very long ago, fall wheat threshing took on the color of a festival. Farmers and their wives traded help when a thresher moved through the countryside harvesting grain at a few cents a bushel or at a flat price for a field. The men worked hard in the fields, and ate prodigious meals of meat, vegetables, and pie provided by hard-working housewives. But threshing machines are fast being replaced by combines that thresh the grain as it is cut; outmoded threshers stand rusting among high weeds on many farms.

Corn harvesting is sometimes still performed by manual labor. After the first freeze, through November and December, sometimes as late as February, wagons move slowly through the fields, and their high bangboards resound to thumps of ears of corn as deft huskers move between rows of brittle yellow stalks. To husk 70 bushels of corn a day is good work; to husk 100 bushels gives one high standing among one's fellow. Work begins before sunup and continues until after sundown, or, as the phrase is, "from can see to can't see."

When the corn has been harvested, plains farmers look forward to a winter of rest. They play pitch, attend dances, and cheer at the basketball games in which their children participate. When warmth again floods the prairies, crop planting begins.

The country west of STRATTON, 29.5 m. (4,404 alt., 750 pop.), a dusty prairie town, was settled during the late 1890's when thousands homesteaded on what had been grazing land. Irrigation is impossible, but careful dry farming has permitted cultivation of an area once known as the Great American Desert.

When this region was young, many frauds were perpetrated by men who "homesteaded" under false pretenses, solely for the purpose of selling their claims. Some would place four sticks around a hollow square and file notice with the land office that foundations for houses had been laid. "Improvements" often consisted solely of such a foundation of logs, but the owner would appear at the land office with a witness and swear that he had erected a habitable dwelling.

Other farm towns along this route are Vona (130 pop.), Seibert (250 pop.), Flagler (725 pop.), Arriba, in Lincoln County (300 pop.), and Genoa (165 pop.).

LIMON, 88 m. (5,366 alt., 2,000 pop.) largest city in Lincoln County, is at the junction with State 71, State 8, and US 40 and US 287. Interstate 70 here leaves US 24 and parallels US 40 to Denver. It is a junction of the Union Pacific and the Rock Island and was named for a railroad foreman. The *Limon Leader* is its weekly newspaper.

The highway traverses miles of prairie carpeted with white and yellow daisies, golden pea, and butterweed during spring; later, with loco weed, prickly poppy, and sunflowers. Large areas are covered with

Russian thistles, more commonly known as "tumbleweeds," native to Russia and transported to this country by seeds mixed with imported grains. With the sandbur, it is the chief vegetable pest of the arid West.

The thistles grow in thick mats, sending down many roots and entangling their branches until a whole field seems to be covered by a single plant. Bushes are roughly globular in shape, some attaining great size, and the upcurving stems are studded with tiny thorns. They are green with streaks of lurid purple during spring and early summer, but turn brown as the season progresses. When completely dry, they break away from their roots, to be caught up by the wind and tumbled along over hills and plains, leaping and twirling in a grotesque parody of a spring song. Scattering seeds as they go, they eventually come to rest, heaped in fence corners, ditches, or sand blows. Their high inflammability when dry has resulted in miles of weed-covered prairie going up in sheets of flame.

At 88 *m.* is the eastern junction with US 40, which unites with US 24 for 3.5 miles (*see Tour 7*). To the southwest, the blue Rockies are visible in clear weather. Pikes Peak, ahead and slightly to the south, stands as a guardian sentinel detached from the massive barrier that fades away in the haze to the north.

Passing MATHESON, 108.8 *m.* (5,591 alt.), the highway crosses the last of the plains country, and the prairies give way to broken rocky knolls spotted with scrub pine.

SIMLA, 115 *m.* (6,029 alt., 500 pop.), and RAMAH, 119 *m.* (6,094 alt.), settled in the late 1880's when the Rock Island Ry. was extended through this territory, are said to have been named by the wife of a railroad official who happened to be reading a book on India.

At the head of Big Sandy Creek, CALHAN, 128 *m.* (6,508 alt., 417 pop.), was founded in 1888 by a contractor who built this section of the Rock Island and perpetuated his name. The route continues across miles of level barren country cut by numerous arroyos, dry for the greater part of the year. In the early 1880's this district grazed many cattle, and PEYTON, 138 *m.* (6,789 alt.), was named for the owner of a large ranch.

COLORADO SPRINGS, 163 *m.* (6,012 alt., 118,000 pop., est.), is at the junction with US 85 and Interstate 25.

Right from Colorado Avenue (US 24) on Ridge Road, passing the granite Ute Trail Monument, 2.6 *m.*, marking the spot where an Indian trail crossed the ridge toward Ute Pass, to the Entrance of the Garden of the Gods (*municipal park; free*), 5.2 *m.* Framed in a natural gateway between Gray Rock (L) and Red Rock is an excellent view of Pikes Peak.

The Garden of the Gods, a hilly area studded with a variety of grotesque rock masses of red Morrison sandstone, with a few upthrusts of gypsum, has several pinnacled and grottoed ridges of impressive size. The highest (300 alt.) is broken by numerous lofty crannies in which doves and swallows nest. The sandstone formation here is a part of the outcrop that extends from the highlands of Wyoming southward across Colorado for more than 300 miles.

The name of the park originated in a remark made in 1859 by R. E. Cable, a Kansas City lawyer, who visited the site of the company with a Mr. Beach.

"This would be a fine place for a beer garden!" exclaimed the latter. "Beer garden?" replied Cable, "why, this is a fit place for the gods to assemble—a garden of the gods!" Helen Hunt Jackson, American novelist, described it as a wonderland of "red rocks of every conceivable and inconceivable size and shape . . . queer, grotesque little monstrosities looking like seals, fishes, cats, and masks . . . colossal monstrosities looking like elephants, like gargoyles, like giants . . . all motionless and silent, with a strange look of having been stopped and held back in the very climax of some supernatural catastrophe." But Julian Street, in his *Abroad At Home,* called it "a pale pink joke."

The road runs along the foot of Red Rock, which almost overhangs the highway; at one point its top has been eroded to form figures of the KISSING CAMELS. Red Rock can be climbed by a series of hand-hewn steps, but inexperienced climbers are advised not to attempt it.

HIDDEN INN (R), 5.3 *m.,* at the foot of Red Rock, contains a collection of Indian jewelry, blankets, and novelties. From the balconies is a good view of the slender towering CATHEDRAL SPIRES, south across the Garden. South from the inn at the base of Gray Rock (L) is a NATURAL AMPHITHEATER, in which Easter sunrise services have been held under the joint sponsorship of Colorado Springs churches.

Formations along the road are, in order, the THREE GRACES, INDIAN HEAD, BEAR AND SEAL, BUFFALO, HARRY LAUDER ROCK, SIAMESE TWINS, SLEEPING GIANT, PUNCH AND JUDY, WASHERWOMAN, BEEHIVE, and TURTLE. To distinguish most of them requires a guide.

The road passes between BALANCED ROCK (R) and STEAMBOAT ROCK (*parking space*), 7.8 *m.;* from the summit of the latter is an excellent view of the Garden, with the Kissing Camels plainly visible. West of Balanced Rock is a small area known as MUSHROOM PARK for the hundreds of rock formations resembling that fungus.

At the western entrance to the garden, 8.1 *m.,* is the junction with Manitou Boulevard; R. on this road to RED CRAGS MANOR, 8.3 *m.,* a frame and red sandstone structure built on a high crag by Henry Van Brunt, an architect who designed some of the buildings at the Chicago World's Fair of 1893. Unoccupied for many years except by caretakers, it was once said to be haunted. An engineer solved the mystery when he discovered that the rock stratum on which the manor rested extended under a street car track, and passing cars caused the building to vibrate.

At 9 *m.* is the junction with US 24 in MANITOU SPRINGS (*see below*).

Section b.   COLORADO SPRINGS to LEADVILLE; 137.0 m. US 24

The highway enters the mountains through Ute Pass, skirting the northern base of Pikes Peak, and crosses the wide expanse of South Park as it approaches the Continental Divide. Along this route thousands of miners thronged to the gold fields of Cripple Creek and Leadville.

West of COLORADO SPRINGS, 0 *m.,* US 24 follows FOUNTAIN CREEK, a stream known to pioneer fur traders as Fontaine qui Bouille (Fr. fountain that boils), now lined with tourist camps and cottages.

MANITOU SPRINGS (Ind. Great Spirit), 6 *m.* (6,336 alt., 5,000 pop. 1968 est.), a resort lying in the foothills that swell upward toward Pikes Peak, was founded in 1872 by Dr. William A. Bell and General William Palmer, railroad builder (*see Colorado Springs*). The proposed name of Villa la Font was changed to Manitou when a resort hotel was opened, then to Manitou Springs in 1912 when the town enjoyed its greatest popularity. Restaurants, curio shops, and the usual variety of resort amusements line the main thoroughfare. The town hibernates from October to June when the majority of hotels and shops are closed.

The great springs here were long known to the Indians, who marked off the area surrounding them as a sanctuary; the neutral ground is said never to have been violated. French traders visited the region during the late 1730's; Frémont stopped here in 1843 and made an analysis of the waters, which for a time were known as Fremont Soda Springs. The three main springs today are Ute Chief Springs, Manitou Health Spa, and Wheeler Springs (*all free*). Hot mineral baths, massage and physio-therapy are available. Four museums in Manitou Springs are Cameron's Doll & Carriage Museum, the Antique Auto Museum, the Cliff Dwellings Museum, and Manitou's Indian Museum.

An inclined railway runs between the town and the top of Mount Manitou (9,455 alt.). The Manitou & Pikes Peak Cog Ry. runs to Summit House at top, 14,110 ft., twice daily (adults, $7; children under 12, $3.50).

Right from Canon Avenue on an oiled and graveled road (*one way only*) into WILLIAMS CANYON, a rugged gash cut through layers of white Sawatch sandstone and dove-gray Manitou limestone; at THE NARROWS, 1 *m.*, the cliff walls almost overhang the highway.

The CAVE OF THE WINDS (*40 min. guided tours*), 2 *m.*, has been hollowed out of the western limestone wall of Williams Canyon by underground waters. Numerous stalactites and stalagmites are in all seventeen compartments of the cave. One chamber is known as OLD MAIDS KITCHEN, and legend has it that if a girl leaves a hairpin here she will be married within a year; thousands of hairpins are heaped against the walls. Left from the Cave of the Winds the road continues along SERPENTINE DRIVE to the junction with US 24, 4.4 *m.*, at the western edge of Manitou Springs.

West of Manitou Springs, US 24 ascends by easy grades, crossing the eastern boundary of PIKE NATIONAL FOREST, 7.5 *m.*, one of the largest forest preserves in Colorado. Of its 1,417,903 acres, 1,093,657 are owned by the Federal government, the remainder by the State, municipalities, and private individuals. This section of the forest is included within the Pikes Peak State Game Refuge, in which hunting is forbidden. The first unit was established by President Harrison in 1892, and in 1929 mountain areas north and west of South Park were added. Englemann spruce trees are most numerous; other species are Western yellow pine, Douglas fir, and lodgepole pine. Foot and bridle trails thread the forest, and many streams offer good trout fishing.

A hundred yards west of the boundary is RAINBOW FALLS, spanned by a concrete bridge and surrounded by a dense stand of pine. Blue and white columbines, the State flower, grow profusely in the vicinity.

The highway enters UTE PASS, 8.5 *m.*, walled in by dark granite cliffs. Except at midday, the canyon is dark and forbidding. Even before the advent of white men, this was one of the important mountain passes of the region. The Ute, who held the mountain country successfully against the Plains Indians, fell back only when the gold rush began in 1859. Until 1920, Ute outposts, small forts with walls five feet high, stood in the neighborhood of the past.

In the winter of 1860, H. A. W. Tabor (*see Leadville*), hearing rumors of gold strikes, sold his cow to buy supplies, and with his wife and several boarders, left Denver in a battered old wagon drawn by oxen. They reached Fontaine qui Bouille, prospected there for a time, but finding little "color," hired out as laborers on a toll road being built up Ute Pass. News of fresh strikes beyond sent them up the pass. The grade was so steep, and travel so slow, that they often saw the "smoke sent up by the dying fire of the camp of the night before."

Travel along this rutty wagon trail was often perilous; during the late 1860's the route was infested with outlaws who preyed on travelers going to and from the mining camps. Through it prowled the "Bloody Espinosas," two brothers who declared that they had been inspired by the Virgin Mary during a dream to kill all Gringos. Twelve of their 32 victims were murdered in and near Ute Pass. This reign of terror ended when Tom Tobin, frontier scout, walked into Fort Garland (*see Tour 11b*), carrying the head of the last of the brothers; the other had been killed by a posse of miners.

Ute Pass has been the scene of many mysterious deaths. In 1866 a neighbor visited the cabin of a Mrs. Kearney, to find the table set for three persons, the food untouched, and no trace of the occupants. A search revealed the woman's decapitated body hidden in a barrel and her grandson's body in a grain sack. Neither the murderer nor his motive was ever discovered. In 1873 a four-horse stage carrying five passengers and $40,000 in gold is said to have entered the pass and to have disappeared without a trace. Four years later J. T. Schlessinger, secretary to General William Palmer, rode into the pass and did not return. Several days later his body was found with a bullet through the heart. The ground near by had been marked off as for a duel, and on the body lay a woman's glove and silk handkerchief; his slayer remains unknown.

The highway continues through the narrowest part of the pass, winding along Fountain Creek, here a brawling stream. A series of dams prevents flood waters from damaging Manitou Springs and Colorado Springs.

CASCADE, 11.5 m. (7,773 alt.), a resort with cabin and cottage accommodations, was founded by Kansas promoters in 1886. Thomas Cusack, head of a billboard advertising company, purchased the town in 1930, and the yellow stucco Community House was built by his estate as a memorial to him. General William T. Sherman, Elihu Root, and John Hay spent many summers in this vicinity; Hay wrote part of his *Life of Abraham Lincoln* here.

Cascade is the locale of an interesting lawsuit in irrigation history.

When farmers on the plains attempted to divert water from the river above the town, the promoters of Cascade resisted, claiming that they had first utilized the water, for the spray from the waterfalls had irrigated trees in the canyons, an important factor in the development of the resort. The Colorado Supreme Court held that the resort's use of the water was prior in time, but as the method used—that of allowing the cascades to spray a fine mist over the trees—was wasteful, the farmers could appropriate the excess water.

Cascade is at the junction with a graveled road (*see Tour 5A*), which leads to the summit of Pikes Peak.

The route crosses a wide park-like valley, its grassy floor ending abruptly in red forested hills. Many Colorado Springs families have summer cottages here.

At 13.5 *m.* is the junction with a graveled road. Left on this road is GREEN MOUNTAIN FALLS 1 *m.* (7,694 alt.), named for a series of cascades about 200 feet in length.

WOODLAND PARK, 20.5 *m.* (8,500 alt., 1,600 pop.), is a shipping point for railroad ties and mine props. The log and frame houses of the village are set in a wooded valley overlooked by Pikes Peak on the south, the Front Range on the east, and an irregular ridge of hogbacks on the north.

Swinging south, the highway traverses foothill pasture country to DIVIDE, 27 *m.* (9,183 alt.), in the early 1890's the terminal of a toll road into the Cripple Creek district. The town ships lettuce, potatoes, and hay grown on the surrounding slopes.

Divide is at the junction with State 67 (*see Tour 5B*).

The highway follows the abandoned grade of the Colorado Midland, until 1918 the shortest rail route through the mountains. Keeping the track open during winter proved expensive, and when mining of ore dwindled, the tracks were torn up.

FLORISSANT, 35 *m.* (8,178 alt.), once a busy division point on the Midland, now depends upon local and tourist trade for its existence. Several dude ranches are in the vicinity.

Left from Florissant on State 143 to the PETRIFIED FOREST (*adm. fee*), 2.5 *m.* Delvers into the past relate that giant Sequoias, similar to the huge trees in California, once grew here. During the Tertiary era an upheaval caused silica-laden water to overspread the living forest, and wood cells were changed in time to red sandstone. Another disturbance came, the lake drained away, and the forest appeared as trees of stone. Men looking for gold first found this petrified forest. Then came curio hunters, and so many souvenirs were broken off and carried away that now little more than stumps remain. One measures 74 feet in circumference; another, 61 feet. This region won additional scientific attention when insect fossils of many species were discovered Dr. T. D. A. Cockerell assembled a valuable collection of Florissant fossils, now on display in the University of Colorado Museum (*see Boulder*). An early trapper who visited this forest graphically described it to his companions upon returning to Taos, New Mexico, "Pa'dners, I seed a *pewtrified* forest of *pewtrified* trees, with their *pewtrified* limbs chock-full of *pewtrified* birds a-singing of *pewtrified* songs."

The route crosses a boundary of the Pike National Forest, 37.3 *m.*, and continues along the abandoned railroad grade to LAKE GEORGE, 42.3 *m.* (7,963 alt.), center of an extensive potato-growing area. Brands of various ranches in this region are burned into the door jam of the CATTLEMEN'S TRADING POST.

At Lake George is the junction with State 77. Left from Lake George on a rough dirt road (*difficult*) to ELEVEN MILE RESERVOIR, 11 *m.* (*picnic grounds; trout fishing above dam*), an azure lake lying between precipitous canyon walls. The lake (8,564 alt.), a part of the Denver water supply system, was created by damming the South Fork of the South Platte River and holds a maximum of 26,393,000,000 gallons.

West of Lake George the highway ascends WILKERSON PASS, 53.3 *m.* (9,524 alt.), crosses the western boundary of Pike National Forest, 54.8 *m.*, and descends into SOUTH PARK, a flat grassy basin some 40 miles from north to south, with an average width of 30 miles, the favorite hunting ground of the Ute. Early frequented by the Mountain Men, it was a scene of great excitement during the gold rush days (*see Tour 15a*).

HARTSEL, 68.4 *m.* (8,875 alt.), is a resort near a number of hot springs.

At 69.4 *m.* is the junction with State 9. At 77.3 *m.* is the junction with a graveled road.

Right on this road to ANTERO RESERVOIR, 2.5 *m.*, another of the chain of reservoirs of the Denver water supply system. The lake, formed by damming the South Fork of the South Platte, has a capacity of 10,843,000,000 gallons. The soil around the lake is streaked with white patches of alkali, evidently seepage from underground waters.

On the McQuaid Ranch, 4.8 *m.*, are the boilers and high smokestacks of an old SALT MILL (*open*), which supplied gold camps during 1861.

The road rejoins US 24, 7.2 *m.*

At 81.2 *m.* is the junction with US 285 (*see Tour 15a*), which unites with US 24 for 15.5 miles.

West of the junction is an impressive view of the Mosquito Range. From south to north the jagged peaks of the range are MOUNT SHERMAN (14,037 alt.), MOUNT DEMOCRAT (14,142 alt.), MOUNT BROSS (14,170 alt.), MOUNT LINCOLN (14,284 alt.), and QUANDARY PEAK (14,256 alt.).

TROUT CREEK PASS (9,346 alt.), 85.2 *m.*, the dividing point between the drainage basins of the Arkansas and South Platte Rivers, was once used by both the Colorado Midland and the Denver, South Park & Pacific Railroads. The eastern boundary of SAN ISABEL NATIONAL FOREST (*see Tour 9b*) is crossed at the pass, west of which lies the BUFFALO PEAKS STATE GAME PRESERVE embracing 192,640 acres. The highway continues through a deep canyon and traverses a region of barren hills. At intervals are miners' log cabins. Now abandoned, their roofs have fallen in, and their doors creak in the wind. Concrete and stone abutments are all that remain of NEWETT, 86 *m.*, once a railroad town.

West of Newett the route enters the Arkansas River Valley, a level winding basin producing large crops of hay and vegetables. On the west are the majestic peaks of the COLLEGIATE RANGE, one of the highest in the State. The chief peaks were measured in 1869 by Prof. J. D. Whitney and his party, who named MOUNT HARVARD (14,420 alt.) in honor "of the university to which most of the members belonged as teachers or students." MOUNT YALE (14,194 alt.) was named for the university from which Whitney was graduated. MOUNT PRINCETON (14,197 alt.) was named a few years later by Henry Gannett, also a member of Whitney's party. The highway crosses a boundary of Cochetopa National Forest, 92.1 *m.*, to the western junction with US 285, 96.7 *m.* (*see Tour 15a*).

US 24 turns sharply north up the Arkansas Valley, here devoted to mountain lettuce cultivation. Little was grown until 1918 when G. D. Isabel of Buena Vista (*see below*) planted an experimental 10 acres that netted him $7,000. By 1926 more than 13,000 acres were under cultivation, averaging 100 crates an acre. The best mountain lettuce is grown between altitudes of 7,000 to 9,000 feet on sandy soil rich in leaf mold, preferably land from which aspens have been removed. Seed is planted in June; after thinning, plants stand about a foot apart. Irrigation during the growing season is essential. During late August and September the lettuce is harvested and shipped in refrigerator cars to eastern markets. Preferred varieties are Western and Mountain Iceberg. The Colorado crop is marketed when production in eastern states is at a minimum.

The COLORADO STATE REFORMATORY, 97.6 *m.*, which has been adding new buildings in recent years, was established in 1891 for offenders between 16 and 26 years of age. The 560 inmates grow much of the foodstuffs they use, and make their own clothing and shoes in the institution's shops.

A STATE FISH HATCHERY (*open 9–5 daily*), with spawning beds and nursery ponds, occupies a portion of the reformatory grounds. This is one of 16 State-owned-and-operated hatcheries with a combined annual capacity of 75,000,000 trout. Brood fish are "stripped" by hands; the eggs are fertilized by "milt" from the males stirred in water, and are then left in trays from 30 to 60 minutes until the adhering stage is passed. A two-year-old fish produces 500 to 700 eggs; those six years old, some 1,500. Eggs for near-by hatcheries are transferred immediately; others are held at the point of collection until reaching the "eyed" stage, a period of three days when eyes of the developing embryo are discernible. Trays covered with wire cloth are submerged in troughs of running water until the eggs are hatched, requiring from 25 to 50 days, depending upon the temperature of the water. The fish are then placed in open ponds, or nurseries, and are fed six times a day, usually ground beef heart and liver. When four to seven inches long, they are termed "fingerlings" and are transplanted to streams and lakes throughout the State. If the journey takes less than 10 hours, finger-lings are transported in ordinary 10-gallon milk cans; for longer trips, motor tank trucks are used; in these specially built tanks compressed oxygen flows through ice-cooled compartments to aerate the water. The State maintains three large reservoirs for egg-spawn purposes, replacing the natural lakes used in former years. In addition to State and Federal hatcheries, numerous private hatcheries supply local markets.

BUENA VISTA (Sp. good view), 99.2 m. (7,800 alt., 2,500 pop.), at the confluence of Cottonwood Creek and the Arkansas River, six miles northeast of the base of Mount Princeton, is a shipping point for products of mines and farms. The town, founded in 1879 by silver prospectors, became the seat of Chaffee County later that year when a group of citizens chartered a locomotive and flat car and one night removed the county records from Granite (*see below*), where they had been stored in a hall above a brewery. Salida is now the county seat. Buena Vista was once the center of mining operations, but today Chaffee county produces sand, gravel, stone and peat. The town was the terminus of the railroad before its extension to Leadville and was headquarters for gamblers, bunco men, and desperadoes, who were driven out by the "respectables" in 1880. MUNICIPAL PARK contains a community house and library. Lettuce Day, combined with a rodeo, is celebrated annually in September.

North of Buena Vista the valley is walled in by rough hills. The eastern wall is of pink granite; the western is a glacial terrace of con-glomerate rock and unconsolidated gravel, covered by a dense growth of sagebrush.

The highway passes RIVERSIDE, 106.7 m. (8,374 alt.), where the valley narrows. Directly east is MARMOT MOUNTAIN (11,-841 alt.), containing a solitary outcrop of limestone and quartzite in a region otherwise composed of granite. Glacial debris is deposited in long ridges across the valley.

The highway crosses a boundary of San Isabel National Forest, 109.2 m., and then skirts CLEAR CREEK RESERVOIR (*fishing, boating, and near-by camping facilities*), 114.2 m., which supplies water to the valley farms.

GRANITE, 116.5 m. (8,943 alt.), a collection of weathered frame houses at the bottom of a ravine, was the scene in 1859 of the first gold discoveries in this section. The diggings along Cache Creek and at Kelley's Bay were later abandoned in favor of richer deposits up the Arkansas at California Gulch. Dredges have successfully reworked the creek sands.

At 121.5 m. is the junction (L) with State 82 (*see Tour 5C*).

North of this junction appear (L) the twin peaks of MOUNT ELBERT (14,431 alt.) and MOUNT MASSIVE (14,418 alt.). The first-named has been officially measured by the U. S. Geological Survey as the highest peak in Colorado, but Mount Massive appears to be the higher of the two; residents here continue a long-standing feud over their relative altitudes. Elbert is a sharply pointed peak, while

Massive, standing a little to the north and west, is a double-peaked mountain marked by a great semicircular gash. Livestock is grazed on the mountain sides during the summer and wintered in the valley, protected by the surrounding mountains against severe cold. In late summer and fall the fields along the river are dotted with brown hay stacks.

At the head of the valley is MALTA, 133 m. (9,570 alt.), a railroad junction point for Leadville. During the 1880's this was the prosperous and populous center of an extensive charcoal-burning industry that supplied the fuel needs of the smelters of the Leadville district. A FEDERAL GOVERNMENT FISH HATCHERY (*open 9–5 daily*), is used exclusively for the propagation of trout, shipping fingerlings and eggs, transporting them in special vehicles.

The road swings sharply east and traverses the lower end of CALIFORNIA GULCH, the ravine that first made this region famous as a mining center. Prospectors, disgusted with their luck in Clear Creek Canyon (*see Tour 7b*), stopped here early in 1860 to dig through four feet of snow and pan some of the frozen sand. Few traces of color were found, and the men prepared to move on, when suddenly Abe Lee shouted, "I've got Californy right in my pan!" The rich strike brought a rush to the new diggings. The straggling settlement in the gulch was known first as Boughtown, later as Oro City (Sp. gold). At the end of 1860 the camp sheltered 5,000 persons and in 1861 was the most populous in the region.

The usual miscellany of miners, speculators, gamblers, and prostitutes descended upon the camp; saloons, gambling houses, and brothels lined the streets. "Money was of no account here," wrote Augusta Tabor (*see Leadville*) of that time. "Ordinary workmen were paid $6 in gold and spent it before morning." The placers were so rich that some mine owners reported taking out "a panful of almost pure gold a day." Before the claims were exhausted, California Gulch produced more than $5,000,000 in gold. By 1870 the gulch was almost abandoned; today the few houses along the road are occupied by workers at the smelter.

Gold has been displaced by molybdenum, which today accounts for 96 per cent of the total value of mineral production in Lake County. In 1966 the county had the highest value of mineral production in the State, as well as the largest increase over that of 1965, a rise of $11,-900,000. This was due primarily to the molybdenum output increase of 6,000,000 lbs., worth $10,200,000, at the Climax mine, which also was a sources of pyrites, rare-earth minerals in monazite concentrate, and tine and tungsten concentrates, all by-products of molybdenum ore. Only 8 troy ounces of gold and 2 troy ounces of silver were recovered in 1966 in Lake County, but new efforts were made on a lead-zinc-silver property near Leadville.

In LEADVILLE, 137 m. (10,152 alt., 6,000 pop. est.) is the junction with State 104 (*see Tour 5D*).

Section c.   LEADVILLE *to* GRAND JUNCTION; 184.8 m.

US 24

This section of the route ascends the Arkansas Valley by easy grades through a region of glacial moraines to the crest of the Continental Divide, traverses three of the State's national forests, descends the Eagle River to its junction with the Colorado, and enters the rich horticultural area of the Grand Valley.

North of LEADVILLE, 0 *m.,* the highway climbs through rolling wooded country to TENNESSEE PASS, 9.9 *m.* (10,427 alt.), a high saddle between pine-covered hills. Although the pass was long used by Indians, the first recorded crossing by white men was made by Lieutenant John C. Frémont and his party on their way to California in 1845.

The road descends into the valley of the EAGLE RIVER, tributary to the Colorado, passing abandoned kilns, 12.5 *m.,* once used to burn charcoal for the Leadville smelter. Following the Eagle River, the highway descends by hairpin curves to the floor of Eagle Park, in prehistoric times the bed of a lake. Along the valley wall (L) is an outcrop of glassy white quartzite laid down as sand on the lakeshore and formed by deposits of silica in the pores of the early sandstone.

PANDO (*cabins; good fishing*), 19 *m.* (9,200 alt.), has a sawmill operated by water power set back in a grove of pines.

MOUNT OF THE HOLY CROSS (13,978 alt.) is visible directly ahead, 21 *m.,* the only view from US 24 of the northern or cross-face of the noted peak. The outlines of the cross are seen most distinctly in late spring and early summer. The peak, scarcely known before 1869, was not named until several years later. Longfellow's poem and the widely published sketches of Thomas Moran made the unique formation known to the world. The upright of the cross is 1,500 feet in length, and the arms extend 750 feet on each side. In spring the ravines forming the cross are filled with snow drifts 50 to 80 feet deep. Other drifts form an image of the SUPPLICATING VIRGIN, at the foot of which is a body of water known as the BOWL OF TEARS.

The route passes the HOMESTAKE CAMPGROUND, 23.5 *m.,* maintained by the Forest Service, to the junction with a dirt road, 24.1 *m.,* with a marker pointing to Mount of the Holy Cross.

Left on this unimproved road to GOLD PARK, 10 *m.,* a ghost town, one of the nearest automobile approaches to Mount of the Holy Cross.

Right 9.8 *m.* on a trail from Gold Park to Camp Tigiwon (*see below*), at the foot of Mount of the Holy Cross.

North of the junction, US 24 traverses a narrow canyon to REDCLIFF, 25 *m.* (8,750 alt., 600 pop.), a mining settlement. Many of the weathered houses, set on the steep slopes, are reached by long stairways from the highway. The important deposits in the vicinity are silver, lead, and zinc. The surrounding area offers excellent hunting and fishing (*guides; equipment*).

Climbing 400 feet in less than three miles, the highway ascends BATTLE MOUNTAIN (10,956 alt.), named for an encounter between the Ute and Arapaho in 1849. The granite and quartzite cliffs, capped with a layer of Leadville limestone rich in zinc, are honeycombed with tunnels driven in search of gold. Perched precariously on the slopes of the mountain is GILMAN, 28 m. (9,000 alt.). Drifts of the EAGLE MINE, producing gold, silver, lead, zinc, and copper, crisscross the interior of the mountain; the shafthouse and mill are partially underground. Ore and supplies are carried by aerial trams from the railroad station at the foot of the mountain; passengers reach the town by a series of stairs.

At 31 m. is the junction with a dirt road, marked with a sign indicating the Mount of the Holy Cross. Left on this road to CAMP TIGIWON, 3 m., a community house established by the Forest Service. An annual pilgrimage is made in July by the Mount of the Holy Cross Association.

Right 9 m. on a trail from Camp Tigiwon to NOTCH MOUNTAIN (*shelter house*), from which the arms of the cross are a half-mile distant.

The highway issues from the White River National Forest beyond MINTURN, 34 m. (7,825 alt., 800 pop.), a railroad lumbering town. The road winds through a narrow canyon between two segments of the Forest. DOWD, 36 m., is the junction for US 6 and Interstate 70 from the east, joining US 24 to Utah. The D. & R. G. W. parallels the highway. AVON, 40 m. (7,455 alt., 200 pop.) lies at the foot of RED PEAK (12,382 alt.). EDWARDS, 44 m., is a farm town.

Before construction of the Moffat Railroad through northwestern Colorado, WOLCOTT, 51.3 m. (6,975 alt., 115 pop.), was an important supply point for ranches to the north. Here State 131 joins US 24 from the north.

In Wolcott is the junction with State 11 (*see Tour 7B*).

The road continues through a narrow canyon in which the vividly colored Triassic sandstone walls resemble masses of red-hot iron. Willows, cottonwoods, and spruce border the river. The route descends a broad valley dotted with farms to EAGLE, 61.5 m. (6,602 alt.), seat of Eagle County and center of an agricultural district. In 1966 the County produced minerals worth $10,200,000.

West of Eagle the highway leaves the mountains and traverses the high plateau country of western Colorado, described as "the badly weathered western roof of the Continental Divide." Vegetation becomes sparse, evidence of a diminishing amount of rainfall. South of GYPSUM, 69 m. (6,325 alt.), a potato-growing community, rise the high limestone cliffs for which the community was named.

Right from Gypsum on a dirt road to the SWEETWATER LAKE COUNTRY (*camp grounds and accommodations at Sweetwater and Gypsum Lakes*), 8 m., noted for its excellent hunting and fishing.

A stratum of black rock (R), 74.2 *m.,* is one of the best examples of lava flow in the State.

DOTSERO, 75.5 *m.* (6,155 alt.), is the junction point of the Royal Gorge and Moffat Tunnel routes of the Denver & Rio Grande Western Railroad. The Dotsero Cutoff, completed in 1935, links the D. & R. G. W. with the Denver & Salt Lake (Moffat) Railway at Orestod (*see Tour 7B*), the latter name being Dotsero spelled in reverse.

From the broad valley formed by the junction of the Eagle and Colorado River, White River Plateau is visible (R), a high level country visited by Theodore Roosevelt on one of his many western hunting trips. The Colorado River, once known as the Grand above its junction with the Green River in Utah, rises in Middle Park and flows alternately across flat treeless areas and through numerous canyons. In Gore Canyon (*see Tour 7B*) it becomes a roaring torrent, falling 360 feet in 5 miles, the greatest drop in the upper river below its headwaters.

The highway swings southwest between slate-colored cliffs as it follows the valley of the Colorado to the mouth of Glenwood Canyon, trenched through sedimentary rock and underlying granite for 15 miles, one of the outstanding scenic attractions of Colorado. Sheer walls here and there rise 1,000 feet above the foaming river as it cascades down a series of rapids. Throughout the canyon are alternate bands of limestone, granite, and red sandstone. High on the serrated walls pine trees cling precariously. Frequenting the sheer precipices are the canyon wren, mouse-like in color but eloquent in song, and colonies of white-throated swifts, birds possessed of such tremendous powers of flight that they have developed wing feathers stiff as steel needles.

The route enters the western segment of WHITE RIVER NA-TIONAL FOREST, 81.2 *m.,* the first national reserve created in Colorado (1891) and the second in the United States. It embraces 1, 960,931 acres, 114,000 privately owned. In 1945 Holy Cross National Forest was joined to White River. Within the forest is the White River Plateau, or Flat Tops, embracing 400 sq. mi., much of it bordered by rimrock.

At 83.5 *m.* a trail leads to Hanging Lake, where the Bridal Veil Falls pour from the cliff into a basin 500 ft. wide. There are 1,500 trails in this forest, many campgrounds, good fishing. *Write Forest Supervisor, Glenwood Springs.*

About 27,000 cattle and 100,000 sheep graze on the summer range. The spruce bark beetle, which killed many trees, has been eradicated.

A concrete dam, 84.5 *m.,* diverts water through a 2.7 *m.* tunnel to the Shoshone hydroelectric plant of the Public Service Co. of Denver, which supplies light and power.

GLENWOOD SPRINGS, 93.5 *m.* (5,736 alt., 5,200 pop.) seat of Garfield County, at the western end of Glenwood Canyon, and the confluence of the Colorado and the Roaring Fork Rivers. The Flat Tops rise nearly 10,000 ft. north of town and MOUNT SOPRIS, 12,823 ft.

looms over the valley of the Roaring Ford to the south. The place has been famous since Indian times for its hot springs, which supply a 600-ft long pool. Isaac Cooper, president of the Defiance Town & Land Co., laid out a town site of 400 acres, first calling it Glenwood, after an Iowa town, then added the Springs. An English, syndicate, interested in the region as a health resort, built the open-air swimming pool and bath-house in 1891. Previously, the bath tubs of early settlers had been holes scooped in the ground and shielded by pine boughs, and idea borrowed from the Indians who brought their sick here for treatment. The Ute continued to visit the springs long after they had been removed to their reservation.

Famous for years for sulphur baths with curative powers, the city has doubled its attractions as a winter ski resort. SUNLIGHT SKI, opened 1966–67, is 10 m. south on State 82 and can accommodate 2,500 per hr. It has 18 runs, 2 chairlifts, 1 pomalift (*day, $5.75, half-day, $4.25, children, $2.*) The Colorado Hotel, built 1893, is now called Glenwood's Village Inn. The Frontier Historical Society operates a regional museum on West 8th St. Two springs with a daily maximum of 9,000,000 gals. furnish the city's water, which is chlorinated. Straw-berry Day in June is attractive to visitors because fresh berries are served to all comers on tables set along one of the streets. The city is a distribu-tion center for livestock and farm products.

Colorado Mountain College was founded by popular vote in 1965 and opened in September, 1967, as a junior college. It has campuses at Glenwood Springs and Leadville.

West of Glenwood Springs US 24 skirts Red Mountain, noted for its coloring and strange formations, and traverses an irrigated valley to NEWSCASTLE, 108 m., a former coal camp, which was abandoned when fire in the underground works of a mine could not be extinguished.

West of SILT, 112.5 m. (4,452 alt., 500 pop.) a cattle and potato shipping point, is the beginning of a semi-arid region, the true mesa country of western Colorado. Vegetables and alfalfa are grown by irriga-tion, but a large area is wasteland.

RIFLE, 120 m. (5,345 alt., 3,000 pop.) at a junction with State 13, in a cattle raising area, in recent years has attracted industry for minerals. In 1966 Garfield County produced minerals valued at more than $3,000,000, chiefly vanadium, uranium, and coal. In 1924 the U. S. Vanadium Co. mined vanadium 12 m. north of Rifle and processed it in a mill east of town. It became a subsidiary of Union Carbide. The mill was closed in 1932 and reopened in the 1940's. Later Union Carbide dismantled the mill and built a new one west of Rifle. The uranium procurement program of U. S. Atomic Energy Commission keeps the mill running.

The U. S. Bureau of Mines operated an experimental shale oil plant in Rifle 1954–56. In 1964 it leased the plant to the Colorado School of Mines Research Foundation, which had the initial support of $5,000,000 from Socony Mobil Oil Co., and Humble Oil & Refining Co.

The road parallels the Colorado River and skirts the foot of Battlement Mesa (10,000 alt.). On the north the precipitous Book Cliffs, topped with evergreens, resemble a row of gigantic volumes.

GRAND VALLEY, 135.5 m. (5,104 alt.) is a small farm town in the Parachute Creek Oil Mining District, part of the Naval Oil Shale Reserve that extends west to Uinta Basin and contains many millions of barrels of potential oil.

Colony Development Co. has been formed by Standard Oil Co., Cleveland-Cliff Iron Co., and The Oil Shale Corp. to operate a prototype oil shale plant north of Grand Valley. If all hurdles are overcome The Oil Shale Corp. will build an oil production plant that can achieve 58,000 bbl. a day in two years. A retort process is expected to take oil out of shale at a cost much lower than operation of oil wells.

PROJECT RULISON. On September 10, 1969, the U. S. Atomic Energy Commission, in cooperation with CER Geonuclear Corp. and Austral Oil Co., detonated a 40 kiloton nuclear device 8,442 ft. below ground 6 m. south of Grand Valley. The object was to release a reservoir of natural gas stored in the rock. The hole for the device was 15 in. in diameter, and the nuclear device was a cylinder 10 in. in diameter and 15 ft. long. Roads were closed within 15 m. to avoid possible rock falls and residents within 5 m. were evacuated, but many near the area refused to move. There was no visible damage. The internal well was not to be opened for six months, to counter radioactivity.

DE BECQUE, 149.5 m. (4,956 alt.) is a trading village in Roan Creek Valley.

North on State 13, 3 m. and northeast on State 325 to RIFLE GAP DAM and RESERVOIR, completed 1967. North on Rifle Creek to the large TROUT HATCHERY of the State Game, Fish & Parks Dept. Along Rifle Creek is the BIG BOX CANYON and the municipal recreation area of Rifle Mountain Park, 440 acres.

Left from De Becque on a dirt road 6 m., to Devil's Playground, where dinosaur fossils have been found, notably a brancheosaurus, 30 ft. tall, 140 ft. long, weighing 100 tons (est.) in life, now in Field Museum of Natural History, Chicago.

The main highway traverses Colorado Canyon to GRAND VALLEY DAM, 163 m., which diverts water for irrigation into High Line Canal through a 6 m. tunnel built through solid rock.

At 165.5 m. is a junction with State 65. At 170.5 m. is a dirt road. Right on this road to CAMEO, a coal town. The road descends into Grand Valley, 50 m. long and 20 m. wide, an irrigated area known for its peach orchards which extend to the surrounding mesas. Approximately two thirds of the State's peach crop is raised here. In mid-August thousands of workers, often with their families, converge here from Kansas, Missouri, Oklahoma, Texas, and other States. Rooming houses are filled; many workers pitch their tents on the outskirts of small towns; some occupy trailers. These workers, often referred to as "fruit tramps," are paid both by the day and on a piece-work basis. Peach "fuzz" is the bane of pickers; many of them dust their necks and shoulders with starch or powder to counteract the irritation, and take several shower baths daily to relieve the intense itching produced by the fuzz.

There are two types of packing: the "field pack," in which each grower does his own grading and packing; and the "shed pack," performed in a centrally located plant. During the peak of the season hundreds of cars and trucks are daily packed and dispatched from the valley. Most popular of the peaches are the Elberta, averaging 60 to a crate, and the Hale, a larger variety, which runs as low as 20 to a crate.

In the midst of this orchard area is PALISADE, 172.2 m. (4,727 alt., 1,000 pop.), an important fruit-shipping center, named for the high serrated cliff of white shale extending for miles along the northern rim of the valley. During the picking season carnival companies follow the workers to set up street and tent shows in the small valley towns.

West of CLIFTON, 178 m. (4,800 alt.), the highway follows the Book Cliff Mountains, a continuation of the palisades extending westward 190 miles, far into Utah; they form the southern rim of the trough known as the Uinta Basin.

GRAND JUNCTION, 184.8 m. (4,602 alt., 22,735 pop.), is at the junction with US 50 and Interstate 70 (see Tour 9c).

I❖◄ I❖◄ I❖◄ I❖◄ I❖◄ I❖◄ I❖◄ I❖◄ I❖◄ I❖◄ I❖◄ I❖◄ I❖◄ I❖◄ I❖◄ I❖◄ I❖◄ I❖◄ I❖◄ I❖◄ I❖◄ I❖◄ I❖◄ I❖◄ I❖◄ I❖◄ I❖◄

Tour 5A

Junction US 24—Summit of Pikes Peak; 18 m., Pikes Peak Highway.

Graveled road; usually open by May or June, depending on snowfall.

The Pikes Peak Highway, built as a toll road in 1915 and a free highway since 1937, is the second highest automobile road in the State; that up Mount Evans is the higher. Pikes Peak Auto Hill Climb for the Race to the Clouds is held about June 30. Participants drive standard racing models. The races draw great crowds that line the upper reaches.

Pikes Peak, although surpassed in height by 27 in Colorado, is the most noted of the State's mountains, principally because it is isolated from the higher ranges and affords a magnificent view of the mountain and plain country. The peak was early made accessible by the Manitou & Pikes Peak Railway, better known as the Cog Road; the first train of tilted cars reached the summit on June 30, 1891.

The Ute legend of creation centers on this mountain. The Ute believed that the Great Spirit formed it by pouring ice and snow through a hole He had made in the sky by turning a large stone around and around. He then stepped from the clouds to the mountain top, descended part way, and made trees and plants by putting His fingers in the ground. As the snow melted, He formed rivers by drawing channels with the small end of His staff, made birds by blowing upon leaves, and created animals out of His staff. The grizzly bear came from the large end of the staff and was master of all animals. Later, the daughter of the Great Spirit, venturing far from home, fell into the power of the Grizzly, who forced her to marry him. The Indians, fruit of this union, were taken under the protection of the Great Spirit, but the bears were punished by being compelled to walk on all fours.

Another legend on the origin of Pikes Peak, well known to the Plains Indians, parallels stories of the Flood. What is now Colorado, according to the legend, was given by the Great Spirit Manitou to the Indians as a paradise. Soon tiring of its perfection, they decided to leave the earth and journey to the Happy Hunting Ground. They gathered great sacks of earth, rock, and maize, so that they might have with them some of what seemed good to them on earth. When they were about to pass through the Portal of the Sun into the presence of the Manitou, their wizards commanded the seas and rivers to loosen their waters and destroy the earth. Suddenly the voice of Manitou thundered above them, commanding them to put down their burdens. The frightened Indians dropped their sacks into one vast heap, which rose high above the flood water—Pikes Peak.

The first extended mention of the peak occurs in the memoirs of Lieutenant Zebulon M. Pike, who saw it in 1806, probably first from what is now Las Animas (*see Tour 9a*). Pike estimated its height at more than 18,000 feet and described it in his journal as "so remarkable as to be known to all savage nations for hundreds of miles around, to be spoken of with admiration by the Spaniards of New Mexico, and to be the bounds of their travels northwest." He and his followers endeavored to scale the height, but lack of provisions and intense cold prevented.

Although Pike predicted that the "Great Peak," as he called it, would never be scaled, the first recorded ascent was made in 1820 by Dr. Edwin James, botanist and historian of Major Stephen F. Long's expedition. Long named it James Peak, while maps published in 1814 and 1818 used the name "Highest Peak." Trappers and hunters continued to call it Pikes Peak, and it was so recorded on a map made in 1835 by Colonel Henry Dodge.

During the gold rush of 1859, Pikes Peak was the landmark that guided an army of prospectors westward. Thousands of Conestoga wagons crossed the plains, their canvas covers bearing the crudely lettered inscription, "Pikes Peak or Bust!" Many soon turned back with "Busted, by God" daubed below. For many years the entire mountain region was commonly known as the Pikes Peak Country. Fabulous tales were circulated about the richness of the area. "We learn from a man just returned from Pikes Peak," wrote an Iowa newspaper in 1860, "that gold there lies in bands or strata down the slope. The custom of the best miners is to construct heavy wooden sleds with iron ribs similar to a stone boat. These are taken to the top of the peak, several men get into each one and guide it down over the strata. The gold curls up on the boat, like shavings, and is gathered in."

Take Midland Expressway or Colorado Ave. in Colorado Springs, follow US 24 through Manitou Springs, 6 *m.*, and Ute Pass to CASCADE, 11 *m.* (7,773 alt.) Follow Pikes Peak Auto Highway signs to NORTH POLE, with Santa Claus' toymakers and animals.

The road passes the old TOLL STATION, 1 *m.*, the beginning of a steep climb along the western slope of the densely forested mountain to PENGUIN ROCK, 1.1 *m.*, a curiously formed outcrop resembling a penguin on a cake of ice. Traversing a growth of young spruce and aspen, part of a Forest Service project, the route in its ascent makes numerous hairpin turns and switchbacks. From many points are views of summer cabins below in Fountain Creek. The mountains to the west resemble an expanse of crumpled paper.

The Pikes Peak Cog Railway moves to the summit by a route on another side of the mountain, by way of Cameron's Cone, 10,705 ft. alt.

Wild flowers border the route during summer. Blueberry shrubs carpet much of the shaded forest floor, and in moist open spaces are patches of bluebells, purple monkshood, and yellow butterweed, often waist-high. Near timberline, fragrant and brilliantly colored alpine flowers grow in clusters among the rocks; here are forget-me-nots, mountain pinks, and the fragile alpine gentian, its funneled waxy blossoms streaked with blue and stippled with purple.

From Glen Cove the highway rises sharply to reach timberline (11,400 alt.), 12.3 *m.* Gnarled pines are numerous, their bark stripped away by constant winds. Portions of the slopes remain snow-covered throughout the year. At the edge of the snow fields, and often in them, grow white marsh marigolds, dogtooth violets, and the alpine primrose. Here is the home of the American pipit, the rosy finch, and the white-tailed ptarmigan, or snow quail.

Pikes Peak now rises abruptly, and the highway ascends by a series of switchbacks along the edge of a high bluff, each turn offering a panorama of mountains and plains. The BOTTOMLESS PIT (L), 14.8 *m.*, is a vast chasm approximately 1,000 feet deep. From a parking space the giant pines in the pit appear no larger than matchsticks.

The BOULDER FIELD, 15.5 *m.*, consists of great red granite boulders strewn over the summit of the mountain; from a hairpin turn, 16.5 *m.*, is (L) an impressive view of the Cripple Creek district (*see Tour 5B*).

SUMMIT HOUSE, 18 *m.* (14,110 alt.), erected in 1882 as an observation station for the U. S. Signal Corps, is surmounted with a 25-foot tower. The plains appear as a sea of blue haze; Colorado Springs is a green spot in the foreground. This scene inspired Katherine Lee Bates's poem, "America the Beautiful" (1911). The Summit House is the upper terminal of the Pikes Peak Cog Road (*see Tour 5b*).

On the summit is held the annual New Year's Eve fireworks display of the AdAmAn Club. As its name implies, this organization adds one member annually, initiating him with the strenuous cold climb to the summit. The organization was formed in 1922 with a membership of five.

Cheyenne Mountain, a rough black hill marked with tiny outcrops along its ridge, is visible below to the southeast (*see Colorado Springs*). The Indians regarded this mountain as the carcass of the Thirst Dragon summoned by the Manitou to drink up the great flood. The dragon drank so much that, in attempting to climb to heaven, he fell and burst.

In 1880 the U. S. Signal Corps on the summit was in charge of Sergeant John T. O'Keefe, a youth who, when in his cups, sent amazing reports to headquarters. He pictured an eruption of Pikes Peak as occurring on the night of October 29 when "a bright flash clove the darkness and after some laborious climbing we arrived some 200 yards from the crater. The heat . . . was very oppressive, and the ground about us covered with pulverized ashes and lava. I was lost in astonishment. The snow for nearly half a mile around the crater had disappeared. This was all the more remarkable as on the previous day the snow had been several feet deep."

The second eruption occurred on the night of November 7, so O'Keefe reported, and the majesty of the scene was the grandest he had ever seen, not excepting the eruption of Vesuvius in 1852, seen by him when a lad in Italy. "It began with a tremendous burst which shook Pikes Peak to its very foundations, hurling into the air dense clouds of ashes and lava. The explosions succeeded each other with rapidity and increased in violence for about an hour when the volcano seemed to enter a profound sleep . . . no doubt Colorado Springs will meet the same fate as Pompeii and Herculaneum." O'Keefe added other tall tales to the legends of the area before someone in authority stopped their circulation.

Tour 5B

Divide (Junction US 24)—Cripple Creek—Victor—Florence (Junction US 50) ; 50.7 *m.,* State 67.

Paved and graveled road open all year, but subject to heavy snows.
Limited accommodations.

State 67 crosses one of the world's most famous gold fields—the Cripple Creek district. This region, long pronounced worthless by mining experts, has produced $380,770,422 of yellow metal since 1891. The history of the field is a saga of·tenderfoot luck and the confounding of experts, for this $300,000,000 cow pasture" was proved by amateurs who did their prospecting with pitchforks.

In 1858 a Captain Norton, heading a party of explorers, picked up rock here that revealed the presence of gold, but no attempt was made to find the vein. During the Pikes Peak Rush of 1859, when every square mile of the territory was critically examined, prospectors found some "color" in the field but did not consider their finds worth investigating. Hayden H. Wood, of the U. S. Geological Survey, and A. H. Kidney, a mining engineer, discovered gold near the eastern slope of Mount Pisgah (*see below*) in 1874, but their reports were not taken seriously.

Mount Pisgah gave the field a bad name 10 years later. In April 1884 rumors of rich discoveries on this dark solitary cone west of the present town of Cripple Creek brought prospectors from Leadville and other camps nearby. Thousands explored the hill but found gold only in the prospect hole of those who had reported the discovery. "Salting" —the practice of planting gold on a claim in order to sell it—was suspected, and this seemed to be confirmed when one of the owners was caught with a bottle of chloride of gold in his possession. Threats of lynching followed, but as no one had been injured, the affair terminated with a picnic and general drunk, and the experts' adverse reports on the district were even more generally credited.

Gold was again reported in this area a year later by Theodore H. Lowe, another member of the Geological Survey, and an uncle of Robert Womack, the young cowhand destined to open one of the world's fabulous treasure vaults. While riding the range for Horace Bennet and Julius Myers, of Denver, young Womack dug so many holes that his employers reprimanded him because of danger to the cattle. In 1891 two Colorado Springs prospectors, L. M. De La Vergne and F. B. Frisbee, traversing Poverty Gulch (*see below*), found Womack working at the bottom of a 48-foot shaft, in which he had uncovered a promising vien.

Womack named this claim the El Paso and took specimens of ore to Colorado Springs.

Ore from the El Paso, the first in the district, assayed almost $250 a ton, and the cowboy went on a roaring drunk, sold his claim for $500, and galloped through the streets of Colorado City, now West Colorado Springs, celebrating his luck. Subsequently, the El Paso was developed by the Gold King Mining Company and produced $5,000,000. Womack died impoverished in Colorado Springs, a ward of loyal friends.

Reports of Womack's discovery did not precipitate an immediate rush. Experienced miners refused to believe that any large body of ore would be found, and the Mount Pisgah hoax was still fresh in mind. In May 1891, however, Frisbee and De La Vergne interested Winfield Scott Stratton, a Colorado Springs carpenter and prospector, in the district. Stratton found traces of gold on Battle Mountain (*see below*), and on July 4th staked out the Washington and Independence mines; nine years later he sold out to an English syndicate for $11,000,000. Stratton had not pushed development of his claims, preferring to let the gold remain in the ground until needed. "The banks," he said, "will go bust."

Late in 1891 Bennett and Myers, advised by their ranch foreman that prospectors were beginning to overrun the country, platted an 80-acre townsite. The newcomers were generally regarded as a nuisance. Almost $200,000 was taken from the district that year, but skepticism remained so strong that it was difficult to obtain capital for development. Prospectors continued to swarm in, however, and new discoveries were made. In 1892 several thousand men were mining in the field, and gold production reached $600,000. Two years later the population had increased to 18,000, and by 1896 gold production had jumped to $8,750,-000. During 1901, the peak year, as long ore trains rolled out day and night toward Colorado Springs, $24,986,990 in gold was taken from the field, which was surpassed only by the Witwatersrand in the Transvaal, South Africa. At this time the district had an estimated population of 50,000.

The region is named for the little stream that meanders southward from the plateau, but the origin of the name is uncertain. One story has it that the stream was named because so many cattle were lamed in the bogs along its course.

The topography of the country delayed mining discoveries here, for the Cripple Creek district has few outcrops and heavy volcanic debris on the rounded hillsides makes digging difficult. The gold-producing area, about six miles square, lies on a plateau ranging in altitude from 9,500 to 11,000 feet, through which great masses of volcanic rock were spewed up at intervals in ancient times. Gold is found in this eruptive material, usually in the form of free gold or telluride of gold.

A gold-mining district seldom enjoys an extended prosperity, but Cripple Creek has again confounded experts. Gold was mined in great quantities for almost two decades before the veins began to be depleted. After 1914 there was a long period of stagnation, but in the early 1930's the district took on new life, and in 1938 the population trebled when gold production rose to $5,109,055.

At the height of its glory the gold field had eleven camps—Cripple Creek, Victor, Goldfield, Independence, Ananconda, Gillett, Elkton, Altman, Lawrence, Arequa, and Mound City—all connected by a network of electric tramways. Two electric lines connected Cripple Creek and Victor, the major settlements; two railroads were built into the district during 1894–95—the Florence & Cripple Creek R. R., or "Short Line," and the Midland Terminal. Business was so profitable that the Florence & Cripple Creek is said to have paid for itself within a year. Its roadbed is now traversed by the Corley Gold Camp Highway, owned by the National Forest Service. The millions in gold taken from approximately 5,000 shafts in and around Cripple Creek went far toward stabilizing economic conditions in the State in 1893.

Turbulence and bitterness marked the early labor history of the Cripple Creek area. Trouble first occurred in 1893, when some mines attempted to reduce the prevailing $3 wage scale for an eight-hour day. The Western Federation of Miners, with a membership of 800, went on strike from February 1 to June 10, during which time several men were killed and one mine was dynamited. After the National Guard had been ordered into the district, differences were arbitrated and the prevailing wage rate remained in force.

More serious trouble developed when employees of the Standard Mill at Colorado City (*see Colorado Springs*) struck in February 1903, in protest against the discharge of union men; a sympathetic strike was called by the Western Federation of Miners at Cripple Creek against "unfair" mines, or those that continued to ship ore to the struck mill at Colorado City. This dispute was settled on March 31, but Colorado City mill employees again went on strike on July 3 for a wage increase and reinstatement of union men who had walked out in the previous strike. Union miners in Cripple Creek laid down their tools in August, and by the next day 3,552 men were idle. Two months later 1,000 union men were employed in the "fair" mines, and 1,700 non-union men and strike breakers were at work in the others.

With neither side inclined to yield, friction soon developed. In September 1,000 militiamen established stations on every commanding hill. Union leaders were arrested; when a hearing was held for their release on writs of habeas corpus, the Cripple Creek courthouse was guarded by sharpshooters and a gatling gun. Accusation of terrorism and intimidation were made by both sides, and acts of violence multiplied. On November 21, when the superintendent and the shift boss of the Vindicator Mine were killed by an explosion in a shaft, W.F.M. members were again arrested, but none was convicted. Union miners, on their part, charged that these disturbances were a part of a plot to discredit their organization.

December found the entire district under martial law; while efforts were being made in Denver to arbitrate the strike, word came of a tragedy at the Independence Mine, where a cable hoist to the shaft-house parted and plunged 15 men to death.

Quiet reigned early in 1904, and troops were withdrawn. But the lull was deceptive. In June a mysterious explosion wrecked the rail-road station at Independence (*see below*), killing many non-union miners. Mines were closed and business temporarily suspended; a com-mittee of mine owners forced the Teller County sheriff to resign; furious rioting broke out in Victor, where two men were killed and many wounded; W.F.M. stores and offices of newspapers favorable to the union were ransacked and pillaged; troops were again brought in. A blacklist against union members was established by mine owners, and scores of union men were escorted out of the district, some as far as the Kansas and New Mexico Lines. Hundreds of others left of their own accord. The strike collapsed, and with it the W.F.M. as an effective organization in the Cripple Creek field.

In DIVIDE, 0 *m.* (9,183 alt.) (*see Tour 5b*), State 67 branches south from US 24 (*see Tour 5b*) and winds through hilly country with frequent views (L) of Pikes Peak and other summits of the Rampart Range, and (R) of the rough and jagged outline of the Sangre de Cristo Mountains. South of MIDLAND, 5.5 *m.* (8,270 alt.) with private fish hatchery, the route follows the crest of a small ridge, skirting the western edge of Pike National Forest and the Pikes Peak Game Refuge (*see Tour 5*). RHYOLITE MOUNTAIN (10,771 alt.), rising sharply (R) from a comparatively level terrain to an almost perfectly rounded summit, contains the northernmost gold deposits of the Cripple Creek district; a strike yielding $100,000 was made here in 1891.

At 13 *m.* is the junction with a dirt road.

Left on this road to GILLETT, 1.1 *m.* (9,938 alt.), now a handful of aban-doned houses, once a busy town of several hundred with a large reduction mill and a race track. One of the few bull fights in the Spanish manner ever held in the United States was staged here by "Arizona" Charlie Wolf on August 24, 1895. Toreadors and bulls were imported from Mexico, a wooden arena was built, and excursion trains were run from Colorado Springs and Denver. One bull was killed before authorities interfered.

CRIPPLE CREEK, 16.2 *m.* (9,375 alt., 545 pop. 1967), sur-rounded by hills dotted with gray mine dumps and overshadowed by the sharp regular cone of MOUNT PISGAH (10,400 alt.), looks old and worn beyond its years. Although new structures have come into the business district, not a building was erected from 1914 to 1934, at which time a five-room house was built. The news flashed along press wires, for almost everything that has happened in Cripple Creek since its found-ing has been news. Many miners had modernized old shacks; and it is not uncommon for a house, unpainted for 25 years, to be equipped with an electric range, refrigerator, radio, and the newest furnishings.

The seat of Teller County since its creation in 1899 and its largest town, Cripple Creek once had a population of 20,000. The two decades following its incorporation in 1892 constituted a heady mixture of mod-

ern progress and the wildest of the Wild West. It was born when gold
ore began to pour down from the hills and gold coins filled every pocket.
Here were the ubiquitous saloons, dance halls, and bawdy houses, side
by side with outfitters' tents selling everything from diamonds and silks
to picks, shovels, bacon, flour, and tobacco.

Gambling increased as wealth piled up; high-graders operated singly
and in gangs; beautiful or lucky "professional" women married million-
aires. Everybody speculated heavily in mining shares; brokerage offices
vied with saloons for choice sites along the principal streets, and their
scouts combed the hills daily for news of fresh strikes. Early accommodations were limited; lines formed outside hotels and restaurants at
meal hours; finding a house to buy or a room to rent was as difficult
as finding an unstaked claim. Miners returning from work at night
sometimes found their cabins appropriated or removed to another site.
Yet it was Cripple Creek's romantic boast during this fevered period
that houses were seldom locked and a woman could walk any street day
and night unmolested—provided she kept her eyes straight ahead and
kept moving.

As befell the majority of flimsy early mining camps, Cripple Creek
had its fire. In 1906 an overturned stove in a Myers Avenue hotel
lighted a conflagration that destroyed much of the town. A second fire
two days later leveled what remained. The town was soon rebuilt with
stone and brick structures. At the beginning of the century the camp
had 41 assay Offices, 91 lawyers, 46 brokerage houses, 88 doctors and
dentists, 14 newspapers, 70 saloons, and one coroner.

Two brothers, A. E. and Leslie Carlton, who began a freighting and
transfer business, bought the First National Bank; with Spencer Penrose
of Colorado Springs, whose fortune also came from these fields, they invested heavily in mining enterprises. In time the Carlton interests controlled most of the production of the gold field.

Many names now celebrated in one way or another have been associated with Cripple Creek. Here Texas Guinan launched her career as an
entertainer, and Lowell Thomas carved his initials on a schoolroom
desk. Governor Ralph L. Carr of Colorado (1940) also attended school
here and worked for a time on a newspaper. Jack Johnson, first Negro
world heavyweight champion, was once a bouncer in a local saloon; William Harrison (Jack) Dempsey worked as a mucker in the mines and
fought a long and bloody battle here for a $50 purse.

Few landmarks of the old camp remain. During its dormant period
hundreds of buildings were torn down for their lumber, and scores of
houses were removed to Manitou Springs and Colorado Springs. Some
ramshackle buildings still stand along Myers Avenue, the early red-light
district. When Julian Street, magazine writer, visited the town in 1914,
he interviewed Madam Leo, known as "Leo the Lion," an inmate of the
district, who told him she would give him a story "hot enough to burn
the paper on which it is written." Street's article, which concerned itself
much more with Myers Avenue than with the mines and the more respectable parts of the community, incensed the town fathers, who declared

that the writer had been too frightened to venture more than a block from the depot and retaliated by wittily calling the notorious thoroughfare Julian Street.

The CRIPPLE CREEK DISTRICT MUSEUM occupies the former Midland depot and exhibits relics of mining days. Adjoining it is the Art Gallery, showing work by regional artists. The Imperial Hotel, erected 1896, retains its original decor. In summer visitors attend its Melodrama in the Gold Bar Room. The *Cripple Creek Gold Rush* is the weekly newspaper of Teller County, Chief products today are peat, sand, gravel, and stone.

Left from Bennett Avenue in Cripple Creek on a dirt road winding up Poverty Gulch to the GOLD KING MINE, 0.4 *m.*, where in 1891 Bob Womack made his gold strike.

South of Cripple Creek State 67 winds tortuously between rounded hills marked by mine dumps and decaying shaft houses. At 18.7 *m.* is the junction with a dirt road.

Left on this road to ELKTON, 0.3 *m.*, a few houses grouped about the corrugated gray iron superstructure of the ELKTON MINE discovered in 1895 by John W. Bernard, who, walking from Colorado Springs, spent his first night sleeping on the ground. Ignorant of prospecting, he staked out a claim around the first likely looking rock pile, naming the mine, which has yielded $13,000,000, for a pair of elk horns lying nearby.

East of Elkton the narrow rough dirt road ascends Eclipse Gulch to the CRESSON MINE. Originally it produced low-grade ore, but in 1915 a new 1,700-foot shaft opened a "vug," a pear-shaped hollow in a lode, known to geologists as a geode. The walls and ceilings were lined with tellurium with an extraordinarily high gold content, and the floor was carpeted with gold ore that was scooped up with a shovel. So rich was the discovery that a vault door was placed at the opening of the chamber. Shipped to Colorado Springs with armed guards riding the box cars, the ore yielded from $5,000 to $10,000 a ton; the richest of it assayed at more than $100,000 a ton, or $50 a pound.

VICTOR, 19.7 *m.* (9,900 alt., 350 pop.), is a twin of Cripple Creek, but rivalry has always marked their relationship. Some thoroughfares in Victor are literally paved with gold, for in early days only high-grade ore was shipped; low-grade was used to surface the streets. In 1936 the town realized $5,000 from ore mined in the street in front of the post office. The Gold Coin, one of the richest surface mines in the district, was discovered while excavating for a hotel basement. The County Store Museum recalls the past; the 20th century home of Lowell Thomas, one-time reporter in Cripple Creek, is preserved.

1. Left from Victor 0.7 *m.* on a steep dirt road to the PORTLAND MINE, largest and richest of the mines operating in the district. Buildings and great dumps cover 180 acres on BATTLE MOUNTAIN. More than $65,000,000 in gold has been taken from the 3,000-foot shaft, deepest in the Cripple Creek district. In 1892, two young Irishmen, James Doyle, a carpenter, and James Burns, a plumber, found about one-sixth of an acre of unclaimed land on Battle Mountain, staked out a claim, and began digging. Funds exhausted, they took in a third partner,

John Harnan. Soon they struck ore so rich it "made their eyes bug out." Fearing that their claim might be jumped or claimed by neighboring mines, they worked in secret, taking out ore only at night, until they had accumulated $90,000; with this they successfully defended their holdings.

Below the Portland properties on Battle Mountain is the INDEPENDENCE MINE, staked by Winfield Scott Stratton on July 4, 1891, which has produced $30,000,000. The $1,000,000, commission paid Verner Z. Reed of Denver for negotiating the sale of the Independence and Washington mines to the Venture Corporation of London, England, founded another of Colorado's great fortunes.

2. Left from Victor 0.8 *m.* on another dirt road that skirts the south foot of Battle Mountain to an old brick schoolhouse and a dozen ramshackle frame dwellings, all that remain of GOLDFIELD, established in 1895 by the owners of the Portland Mine. Lying between Battle Mountain (L) and Big Bull Mountain, the community once had a population of 3,000, and with four schools was known as a "family town." Three fourths of the ore mined in the Cripple Creek district was shipped from the stations formerly maintained by three railroads here.

On the southeastern slope of BULL HILL (L), 2.5 *m.* is the SITE OF INDEPENDENCE, another mining settlement and scene of a terrific explosion during labor troubles in 1904. Authorities believed that someone at a distance pulled a wire that fired a shot into more than 200 pounds of dynamite placed under a railroad station, killing thirteen miners waiting for a train.

All that remains of ALTMAN (10,610 alt.), 2.8 *m.*, are a few crumbling shacks. Prior to 1900 it had a population of 2,000, mostly miners. As the majority of elected officials were members of the W.F.M., the town became one of the headquarters of the strike of 1893 and 1903–04. So numerous were the shooting scrapes that an undertaker offered party rates if all killings were scheduled on Saturdays. Altman lies on the eastern flank of Bull Hill (10,814 alt.), a commanding eminence fortified by striking miners in 1893; an attack by a large force of deputy sheriffs was thwarted by the intervention of the National Guard.

South of Victor the route winds through Phantom Canyon to FLORENCE, 50.7 *m.* (5,187 alt., 3,000 pop.) (*see Tour 9b*), at the junction with US 50 (*see Tour 9b*).

Tour 5C

Junction US 24—Twin Lakes—Independence Pass—Aspen—Glenwood Springs; 82.5 *m.*, State 82.

Paved road; narrow, with many sharp turns, between Twin Lakes and Independence Pass; pass is usually closed by snow from November to late May.
Branch line of Denver & Rio Grande Western R.R. parallels route between Aspen and Glenwood Springs.

Crossing the Continental Divide near its highest point, the highway pierces the heart of the Pitkin County mining district. Not so heavily traveled as other east-west highways, the route is unexcelled for its views of lofty mountains, tumbling snow-fed streams, and forests of pine and aspen. The streams are among the best in the State for fishing; in season there is good hunting.

State 82 branches west from US 24, 0 *m.* (*see Tour 5b*), 15 miles south of Leadville (*see Leadville*), skirting the northern shores of the TWIN LAKES RESERVOIR. The gray bulk (R) of MOUNT ELBERT (14,431 alt.) and, behind it, MOUNT MASSIVE (14,419 alt.), shoulder the sky; TWIN PEAK (11,000 alt.) seems dwarfed. Twin Lakes Reservoir and Sugar Loaf Reservoir, which now hold 70,675 acre-ft., are to be enlarged to hold 377,000 acre-ft. The eastern slope will have water enough for seven power plants with 123,900 kw capacity. This is part of the Frying Pan-Arkansas Project.

The road crosses the eastern boundary of SAN ISABEL NA-TIONAL FOREST, 2.6 *m.*, a reserve embracing 1,103,837 acres of Federal lands. The original reserve was enlarged when old Leadville Forest and part of the upper Arkansas River watershed were added. The San Isobel National Forest now embraces the headwaters of the Arkansas River, the mountain region north and west of the San Luis Valley, and the Tomichi Creek drainage basin to the west over the Continental Divide.

TWIN LAKES, 4.7 *m.* (9,015 alt.), a popular resort (*campgrounds; horses and burros available*), was settled after the Leadville silver rush of 1878–79 (*see Leadville*), when prospectors found in the vicinity the first traces and outcrops of the Gordon, Tiger, Little Joe, and other rich lodes. Attracted by the Leadville rush, newcomers discovered at Twin Lakes a summer vacation ground. Against the flanks of Mount Elbert are groves of quaking aspen. Here fields of wild roses, lupines, and bluebells vie with huge granite boulders for attention. Streaking upward through the lighter green of the aspens are the darker evergreens. Lakes and streams offer splendid fishing, especially for Mackinaw trout, in the fall, and good duck hunting in season. Numerous trails lead back into the Sawatch Range where the climber, amateur or professional, can test his skill in a wilderness of crags.

West of Twin Lakes the highway swings into the narrow, heavily-forested canyon of Lake Creek, in the shadow of massive LA PLATA PEAK (14,342 alt.), which dominates the sky line for miles.

TWIN LAKES FALLS, 7 *m.*, is a turbulent plunging mass of water and upthrown spray. West of Twin Lakes the creek falls 3,000 feet within twelve miles, a great potential source of water power.

EVERETT, 9 *m.*, is a deserted station on an old stagecoach route across the Divide to the mining towns of the Western Slope. Along this road passed pack trains carrying silver ore from Aspen to the Leadville smelter; these trains often consisted of strings of burros more than a quarter-mile long.

At 13 *m.* is the junction with a dirt road.

Left on this road along the South Fork of Lake Creek (*fair fishing*), which was once traveled by stage coaches and freight wagons crossing Lake Creek Pass

(12,226 alt.); the route today is a rutted pack trail mainly used by forest rangers.

The EAST PORTAL OF THE TWIN LAKES DIVERSION TUNNEL (L), 15.5 *m.*, an irrigation project designed to bring waters from the Western Slope to the plains, pierces the Continental Divide just south of Independence Pass. The bore, nine feet in diameter, was drilled four miles through almost solid rock; completed on May 1, 1935, it cost $1,200,000. Funds for the project were obtained through the Reconstruction Finance Corporation by the Twin Lakes Reservoir and Canal Co. Water sufficient to irrigate 50,000 acres, brought from the Roaring Fork, is stored in Twin Lakes Reservoir pending release into the Arkansas River to be used by farmers living 220 miles from the source of supply. The tunnel was driven from both ends, and so accurate were engineers' calculations that the two bores were off only one inch in grade and seven in alignment.

West of the tunnel the valley of Lake Creek widens into grassy meadows. After a wide sweep to the north, the highway rises in a series of loops and curves toward the crest of the Continental Divide. Thinning pines, gnarled and stubby from their fight for existence, give way at timberline to bare boulders, hardy grasses, and the alpine vegetation of a world above the clouds. The road along the sheer face of the mountain, while steep, is one of the safest traversing a pass in Colorado.

A stone monument (R) and several small lakes, 22 *m.*, mark the SUMMIT OF INDEPENDENCE PASS (12,095 alt.), the highest and probably the most impressive automobile pass in the State. An arctic meadowland overshadowed only by the topmost notches of the Sawatch Range, it rises far above the peaks that towered high when viewed from Lake Creek Valley. No matter what the temperatures farther down the slope, it is apt to be chilly here even in summer. The pass is closed in winter.

West of Independence Pass, State 82 descends into the valley of the ROARING FORK RIVER by easy grades. As timberline is reached, the heavier forest growth of the Western Slope is marked. Fishermen esteem this remote district as the best in the State, and throughout the season the Roaring Fork and its tributaries attract many anglers.

INDEPENDENCE, 26.2 *m.*, a scattering of weather-beaten, roof-less log shacks clinging to the mountain side, was once a flourishing settlement. In summer a handful of die-hard prospectors, still tramping the surrounding hills in quest of "color," make this ghost town their headquarters. West of the LOST MAN RANGER STATION (L), 27.2 *m.*, in White River National Forest, dominated by Mountain of the Holy Cross, 14,005 ft., the highway descends rapidly as it follows the cascading Roaring Fork to the valley below.

At 31.5 *m.* is the junction with a dirt road.

Left on this road across the Roaring Fork to the GROTTOES, 0.4 *m.*, a series of fantastic excavations carved by downrushing waters in the solid rock of what was once part of the river bed. Since grinding out the rock, the river has swerved and cut a new channel about 50 feet nearer the highway. Best reached by climbing down the opening in the old river bed, the several grottos, many of them of large size, indicate the tremendous erosive force exerted by a mountain stream.

The rough road, following Lincoln Creek some 11 miles into a rarely visited mountain country, is used by occasional hunting and fishing parties.

ASPEN, 40.9 *m.* (7,908 alt., 1,700 pop. 1967, est.), seat of Pitkin County, is Colorado's prime example of Emerson's mouse-trap aphorism, for the world has sought out this relatively isolated town in the topmost part of the Continental Divide for three different reasons in two generations. About eighty years ago it was a famous silver camp, taking metals worth up to $6,000,000 a year from the mines called Molly Gibson, Durant, Midnight, Newman, Aspen, Montezuma and Smuggler. Today, from Thanksgiving Day to April, it is a high-ranking winter sports area, and in the summer it draws scholars and students from far places for a cultural feast. It is the last function that has made its name internationally known and during those months adds substantially to its population.

Aspen is reached by motor car from Denver, 173 *m.,* on Interstate 70, US 6, turning south at Dillon to the junction with State 91 to Leadville, then south from Leadville on US 24 to the junction with State 82, then northwest to Aspen, 44 *m.* Aspen Airways, 8 flights a day nonstop from Denver, also Grand Junction and Rifle. Frontier and United Airlines service from Grand Junction, 130 *m.* to Aspen. Denver & Rio Grande Western to Glenwood Springs, 40 *m.* from Aspen; bus connections to Aspen. Continental Trailways, express daily from Stapleton Airport, Denver, to Aspen, 5 hrs.

The cultural movement in Aspen dates from 1949 when Walter P. Paepcke founded his Institute for Humanistic Studies. Here many scholars lecture or conduct seminars in the arts, government, labor, science and theology. The Aspen Music School is open through July and August. The American Theatre Institute, founded 1966, has classes and repertory preformances in the summer. The Writers' Workshop meets in the summer and the Writers' Theater gives plays. The Music Associates give concerts three times a week in the Auditorium in Aspen Meadows, where the Aspen Health Center is also located.

Skiing is now a major industry in the environs of Aspen; accommodations in hotels, motels, lodges, inns are excellent and the attendance is larger every season. The Colorado Ski Information Center, a division of the Colorado Visitors Bureau, annually publishes a comprehensive booklet on skiing, giving routes, accommodations, rates, ski slopes, facilities, and answering all questions. Write the Center at 225 West Colfax Avenue, Denver, and phone for snow conditions "24 hours a day, 7 days a week," at Area Code 303—222-0671. The ski centers near Aspen are:

ASPEN MOUNTAIN (p. o. box 1248, Aspen, 81611) Thanksgiving to April 6; 7 chairlifts carry 5,775 skiers per hour to 45 runs up to 2 m. long. Max. vertical drop, 3,000 ft. Ice skating in rink, ski-joring, dog sledding. Summit elevation, 11,212 ft. One day $7; children under 12, $2. Ski school.

ASPEN HIGHLANDS (p. o. box T, Aspen) Descent 3,800 ft., longest in Colorado. 8 chairlifts carry 5,700 per hour; 30 runs up to 5 *m.* long. Restaurants at top and base. Rates as above.

BUTTERMILK-TIEHACK (p. o. box 1248 Aspen) Dec. 20 to Mar. 31. Shuttle service from Aspen. 22 runs total 35 *m.* Max. drop 2,000 ft. 3 double chairlifts, 2 t-bars, capacity 4,000 per hour. Summit, 9,840 ft. Rates as above.

SNOWMASS AT ASPEN (p. o. box 5566, Aspen). Nov. 28 to Apr. 6. 5 double chairlifts carry 5,200 per hour over 50 *m.* of runs up to 3 *m.* long. Max. vertical drop, 3,500 ft. Summit, 11,864 ft. Guided tours into Moraine Valley and East Alpine. Rates as above.

All ski centers have ambulances at areas and doctors and hospital facilities in Aspen, which also provide baby-sitting and day nursery. Ski schools ask about $8 a day, $6 a half day, and make arrangements for groups.

West of Aspen, State 82 uses the roadbed of the abandoned Midland Ry.; descending into the pleasant valley of the Roaring Fork, once a Ute hunting ground, it winds between level meadows in which wild hay and alfalfa provide winter forage for large cattle herds.

At 42.4 *m.* is the junction with a graveled road. Left on this road along Maroon Creek to MAROON LAKE, 9.2 *m.,* known for its mountain setting and excellent trout fishing. SNOWMASS MOUN-TAIN (14,077 alt.), MAROON PEAK (14,126 alt.), and HAGER-MAN PEAK (12,600 alt.) form a majestic western skyline.

SNOWMASS, 55.5 *m.,* is one of the newest ski runs in the Aspen area. Also noted for fishing in the Roaring Fork River and Aspen Creek. Lodges, apartments, guided tours, tennis, swimming, sauna.

BASALT, 59.4 *m.* (6,624 alt., 300 pop.) on the Frying Pan and Roaring Fork Rivers, noted for fishing, has year-round accommodations for sportsmen. Junction with State 104. Ruedi Dam and Reservoir are 15 *m.* east.

At 71.9 *m.* is the junction with State 133.

Left on this road is CARBONDALE, 1.8 *m.* (6,181 alt., 750 pop.), near the junction of the Roaring Fork and Crystal Rivers, in a highly developed irrigated district., Large crops of Irish potatoes, oats, and alfalfa are grown in the rich red soil.

South of Carbondale the route parallels Crystal River and the San Juan R.R., much of its roadbed ballast being white Colorado marble from the great quarries at Marble (*see below*), and traverses the broad Crystal River Valley. Here are commodious farm houses surrounded by fields of hay and oats. Rising to the south is MOUNT SOPRIS (12,823 alt.). Where the valley narrows, the landscape becomes rugged, and at intervals among the pine-clad bluffs the gaunt superstructures of coal mines appear. Underlying much of this country is a vast coal reserve; mining today is limited to local demand.

REDSTONE, 18.3 *m.* (7,202 alt.), was founded at the beginning of the century by J. C. Osgood, official of the Colorado Fuel & Iron Corporation who built a model industrial village on the aspen- and pine-covered slopes. With the decline of mining here, the workers moved away, and the cottages, no two painted alike, were sold as summer residences. The original inn, a sandstone structure of Dutch design has a high square clock tower.

Left from the inn an electrically lighted road follows the eastern bank of Crystal River to the former Osgood estate laid out in 1903 as a private hunting and fishing preserve. Redstone Lodge, 40 rooms, includes in its accommodations suites in the Country Club Manor House.

South of Redstone the highway enters rougher country. CAPITOL PEAK (14,100 alt.) stands sentinel-like (L) to the northeast; farther south (L) is PYRAMID PEAK (14,000 alt.). South of the LILY LAKE RANGER STATION (L), 25 m., are several steep grades.

MARBLE, 29.8 m. (7,800 alt.), site of the quarries and mill of the Vermont Marble Co., opened in 1905. Its one-time population of 2,000 dwindled with the decline of marble prices in 1917. The stone, known commercially as Colorado Yule marble, is both pure white and veined in pale brown. The former, also known as statuary marble, has been compared with the Carrara marble of Italy. Among notable structures using this marble are the Lincoln Memorial at Washington, D. C., the Tomb of the Unknown Soldier in Arlington Memorial Cemetery, and the municipal buildings in New York City and San Francisco. More than a year was required to quarry the 100-ton block of marble, reduced to 65 tons when sawed, for the Tomb of the Unknown Soldier.

Good fishing streams in this region are the Yule, Silver, and Lost Trail Creeks. Snowmass Mountain (14,077 alt.) is prominent (L) on the eastern skyline, and to the west rises Chair Mountain (12,800 alt.), its scooped-out face resembling a gigantic arm chair.

Trips by jeep to the Quarries, 4 m. south. Housekeeping cottages are available at Beaver Lake Lodge.

North of the junction with State 133, State 82 winds through farming and ranching country to CATTLE CREEK, 74.9 m. (6,000 alt.), a shipping point.

In GLENWOOD SPRINGS, 82.5 m. (5,747 alt., 5,100 pop.) (see Tour 5c), is the junction with US 24 (see Tour 5c).

Tour 5D

Leadville—Carleton Tunnel—Nast—Meredith—Basalt; 52.7 m., State 104.

Graded road; open all year.
Accommodations limited.

This route follows the abandoned roadbed of the Colorado Midland Ry., crossing under the Continental Divide through the Carleton Tunnel, to traverse the valley of the Frying Pan River, one of the best hunting and fishing areas of the State. For many miles the road lies within the San Isobel and White River National Forests; at no point does the grade exceed four per cent.

In LEADVILLE, 0 *m.* (*see Leadville*), State 104 branches west from US 24 by way of West 6th Street. For several miles the scene is one of pleasantly wooded slopes, with the massive peaks of the Sawatch Range, the highest in Colorado, dominating the horizon. At 5 *m.* is the junction with a graded dirt road.

Left on this road to the NATURAL SODA SPRINGS (*picnic grounds*), 1.3 *m.*, its water pleasant and faintly astringent to the taste. Here the road winds through large groves of pines, presenting occasional glimpses of the crests of Mount Massive and Mount Elbert. A FEDERAL GOVERNMENT FISH HATCHERY (*open 9–5 daily*), 1.8 *m.*, propagates trout for restocking streams in the neighboring national forests.

At 2.1 *m.* is the junction with a side road.

Right here 0.5 *m.* to EVERGREEN LAKES, two small bodies of water gleaming against the Sawatch Mountains as backdrop.

The Soda Springs road winds down from the forest through rich haylands of the Arkansas Valley to MALTA, 3.5 *m.* (*see Tour 5b*).

State 104 proceeds through hill country to TURQUOISE LAKE, 6.5 *m.,* colored like the jewel for which it is named. The highway roughly parallels the northern shore line for 2 miles, the water gleaming at intervals through the fringe of trees, and crosses the eastern boundary of San Isobel National Forest, 7.6 *m.*

At 8.9 *m.* is the junction with a foot trail. Right on this difficult trail to TIMBERLINE LAKE, 4.2 *m.*

The highway reaches the EAST PORTAL OF THE CARLETON TUNNEL, 12.9 *m.* (11,528 alt.), through which it formerly crossed to the western slope, thus cutting miles off the tour. This 9,394-foot bore, driven through almost solid granite at a cost of $1,250,000, was begun in 1890 as a private enterprise, the promotors hoping to lease or sell it to the Colorado Midland Railway. Ultimately they were forced to sell it at a fraction of the cost, for the railroad, never profitable, was junked during World War I. In 1922 the owners quit-claimed to the State Highway Department all the right-of-way except that through the tunnel. The tunnel has since been closed.

The WEST PORTAL of the tunnel, 14.2 *m.* (11,500 alt.), was protected by a 600-foot snow shed, which insured an open tunnel during winter. In its descent from the tunnel the road passed the ruins of many conical brick charcoal ovens, suggesting a primitive village.

From HELLGATE, 17.9 *m.,* a soaring promontory where the rock-crusted slope drops sheer from the edge of the road, is a view seldom seen even on the high mountain highways. Far below, the clustered buildings of Nast, about four miles as the crow flies, appear as tiny dots among the trees; in the background is the rough, wooded, and almost unvisited basin at the headwaters of the Frying Pan River, walled in on the east by the tremendous shoulders of Mount Massive and Mount Elbert.

State 104 follows an easy winding grade along the Frying Pan River to NAST, 27.8 *m.* (9,060 alt.), summer resort and supply town. West of Nast the road passes several hamlets, former stations on the old Midland Railway; residents are now mainly dependent upon tourist and sportsmen trade. Throughout the attractive green-and-red valley of the Frying Pan are many campgrounds established by the Forest Service. Private resorts offer more elaborate services.

RUEDI DAM AND RESERVOIR, 37 *m.* is part of the project of the Bureau of Reclamation to divert 69,200 acre-ft. of water from the Frying Pan and Roaring Fork rivers of the west slope to the Arkansas River on the east slope. Ruedi, begun 1964, will hold 101,000 acre-ft. About 70 miles of canals and tunnels above 10,000 ft. altitude collect mountain runoff of Frying Pan and Roaring Fork rivers. Seven power plants were to make use of the water, providing 123,900 kw. Colorado Springs, Pueblo, Rocky Ford, Manzanola, La Junta, Las Animas and Eads will have access to the water, which also will irrigate 280,600 acres of land.

The prevailing red tones in the valley come from the vermilion cliffs that occasionally break through the slopes along the river. On the northern bank (R), 48.5 *m.,* are the SEVEN CASTLES, great masses of carmine rock, weathered into towering shapes resembling medieval strongholds.

BASALT, 52.7 *m.* (6,600 alt., 300 pop.) (*see Tour 5C*), is at the junction with State 82 (*See Tour 5C*).

K◆·K◆·K◆·K◆·K◆·K◆·K◆·K◆·K◆·K◆·K◆·K◆·K◆·K◆·K◆·K◆·K◆·K◆·K◆·K◆·K◆·K◆·K◆·K◆·K◆·K◆·K◆

Tour 5E

Grand Junction—Grand Mesa—Skyway—Cedaredge—Delta; 63.6 *m.,* State 65.

This route leads across the top of Grand Mesa, largest tableland in the Rocky Mountain region, and through the heart of a popular vacation area. Grand Mesa, with its superb scenery and facilities for outdoor sports, is a favorite playground.

Starting from Grand Junction, US 6, US 24, and Interstate 70, proceed northeast to where US 65 at right turns east. A granite monument, dedicated to pioneers who made the trail now followed by US 24, marks the junction.

The highway crosses PLATEAU CREEK and enters PLATEAU CANYON, a narrow, winding gorge lined with odd rock formations, among them (L) the DEVIL'S WINGS, 3 *m.* Dislodged from high walls, huge masses of rock are scattered along the edges of the road as it ascends steeply to debouch into a shallow valley.

A great ledge (L), 10.5 *m.*, bears sprawling INDIAN PICTOGRAPHS, carved more than a century ago by the Ute on their seasonal visits to Mesa Springs. Although the writings refer to a near-by burial ground, according to legend, it is believed that the symbols are merely records of tribal passage.

The highway again crosses Plateau Creek; southwest of the bridge, where the road forks, stands (L) the SURRENDER CEDAR TREE, under which the women and children taken prisoners by the Ute at the Meeker Massacre (*see Tour 17*) were delivered to General Charles Adams and other officials who met Ouray and other chieftains here late in 1879 to effect return of the captives and negotiate a treaty.

Left from this fork is the small supply town of PLATEAU CITY, 10 *m.* (6,000 alt.), and COLLBRAN, 11.4 *m.* (6,000 alt.), a cattle town.
Left from Collbran on an unnumbered side road to partly excavated PUEBLO INDIAN RUINS, 2 *m.;* this buried city promises to be of archeological significance, as it lies more than 200 miles from any previously discovered Pueblo structures.

From the fork, the right branch of State 65 skirts ranches and small farms to MESA, 10.6 *m.* (6,500 alt.), a cattle town below the north rim of Grand Mesa. Through a region devoted largely to hay ranches, the highway winds up a mountain boulevard bordered by thick growths of quaking aspen, crossing the boundary of GRAND MESA NATIONAL FOREST, 18.5 *m.,* which contains 360,964 acres forested with conifers and broadleaf trees. The mesa has more than 200 lakes, 63 of them stocked with mountain trout. Wildlife includes bear, deer, elk, rabbits, squirrels, and other smaller animals. Desert plants grow along the base of the mesa, and cedar, piñon, oak, yellow pine, Douglas fir, aspen, Alpine fir, and Engelmann spruce on the higher slopes. Vast sections of the forest are used for grazing.

In the southwestern corner of the forest, GRAND MESA, approximately 53 square miles in area, rises to an altitude of 10,500 feet. It was formed by a lava flow 100 to 400 feet thick, which covered softer sedimentary formations and prevented erosion. Where softer formations are not protected, they have been worn away until the mesa stands high above the surrounding land in splendid isolation, displaying on its serrated slopes various strata of the tableland; darker oil shale and seams of coal form distinct layers, each supporting a slightly different type of vegetation.

The entire region was a hunting ground of the Ute, who called the mesa Thigunawat, or home of departed spirits. The mystic beauty of this curiously detached upland seemed to them a perfect setting for the wandering souls of departed warriors. The mesa, so the Ute believed, was the home of three pairs of great eagles, known as Bahaa-Nieche, or thunder birds, which nested along the north rim of the plateau; the white rock slides on the slope at that point were supposedly formed of bones and debris from their nests. These birds not only carried off deer and antelope, but captured Indian children.

One day a great Bahaa-Nieche siezed the son of Sehiwaq, a chieftain, and carried him off to its aery. The father, bent on revenge, wrapped himself in the bark of the Basthina, or red cedar tree, and thus disguised, started up the side of the mesa. To the Ute the cedar was sacred for its never-dying green, its aromatic fragrance when burned as incense at religious ceremonies, and for its durability and fine texture, which made it particularly suitable for lance shafts and tepee poles. The Ute believed that the cedar had originally been a pole, at the top of which their ancestors had fastened the scalps of their enemies, and that the heart of the tree had been stained red by the blood that trickled through its fibers.

It took Sehiwaq all day to scale the mesa. Whenever a thunder bird soared over him, he stood still and pretended to be a tree. Finally, he reached the nests, pulled out the young birds, and sent them tumbling down the slope. A large serpent, Batiqtuba, lived near the foot of the slide, and as the eaglets rolled near him, he captured and devoured them. When the Bahaa-Nieche returned to their nests and saw what had happened, they suspected the serpent, carried him many miles into the air, and tore him to pieces. As the pieces fell to earth, they made deep pits in the ground. So great was the rage of the thunder birds that fire streamed from their eyes and thunder shook the mountain; torrents of rain fell and filled the pits, forming the many lakes on the mesa.

SKYWAY, 23.6 *m.* (9,800 alt.), named for its altitude, is a resort in the center of the MESA LAKES GROUP, composed of Mesa, Sunset, Lost, and South Lakes. Just under the north rim of Grand Mesa, this group lies in a great basin hollowed from slide rock and rimmed with heavy stands of fir and spruce. The highway winds among them, circling MESA LAKE, 24 *m.*, the loveliest of the four. Numerous smaller lakes stud the forest country below the rim, glittering among the trees like crystal plaques.

At 25.5 *m.* is the junction with a side trail.

Left on this trail to the BULL CREEK LAKES GROUP, 4 *m.*, five large and several smaller lakes, and the COTTONWOOD GROUP, 7 *m.*, five large lakes and a cluster of ponds. Most of the smaller lakes are blanketed with lilies. Bull Creek and Cottonwood Lakes, stocked with rainbow, brook, greenback, and yellow-fin trout, provide some of the best fishing in Colorado.

The highway follows the north rim, piercing slides of shattered rock lying between towering basalt cliffs, to the TOP OF GRAND MESA, 26 *m.* Here a vast meadow, gay with wild flowers in summer, stretches for miles. Much of the tableland is so level that it can be crossed by cars in any direction. Among the patches of sage and greasewood are sage hens and the diminutive gray sparrow. Often a spindle-legged road-runner, extraordinarily fleet of foot, appears on the road to pace a car. The bird lives principally on insects and lizards, but apparently for sheer sport and relaxation this feathered warrior hunts out and kills snakes. In the dense spruce forests surrounding the meadows are deer and small game; wild turkey once were plentiful but are almost extinct.

At 27.5 *m.* is the junction with a side road.

Right on this road to LANDS END, 11 *m.*, a stark promontory on the rim of the mesa. Below is a wide panorama, embracing the fantastic Book Cliff mountain country norch of Grand Junction, the Grand Valley, and the distant blue mountains of eastern Utah. Here a glass-walled rest house on the edge of the promontory overlooks a large winter sports area with ski courses and toboggan runs. Below Lands End the route descends by many curves and switchbacks to WHITEWATER, 24 *m.* (*see Tour 9c*).

The highway winds through a pine and spruce forest, passing (R) the ODD FELLOWS CLUB HOUSE, 30 *m.*, a large two-story log building and three smaller cabins on 10 acres of land. The club house contains the Lodge Hall and sleeping rooms for members; visiting members are housed in the smaller cabins.

State 65 skirts ISLAND LAKE and WARD LAKE, 32.1 *m.*, which form the northern end of a chain known as ALEXANDER LAKES. Descending the southern slope of the mesa in a series of hairpin turns, the road crosses the southern boundary of Grand Mesa National Forest, 39 *m.*, and traverses an area of apple and peach orchards. In the heart of the fruit belt is CEDAREDGE, 47.8 *m.* (6,100 alt., 549 pop.); here is a STATE FISH HATCHERY. At 53 *m.* is ORCHARD CITY (5,800 alt., 1,021 pop.).

At 59.5 *m.* is the junction with State 92 (*See Tour 9c*).

DELTA, 63.6 *m.* (4,961 alt., 4,100 pop.), is at the junction with US 50 (*see Tour 9c*).

Tour 6

Idaho Springs—Central City—Blackhawk—Nederland—Boulder; 43 *m.;* State 279 and State 119.

This route traverses a section in which the first important gold strikes of the State were made; later, silver and tungsten were mined. Few mines remain in operation in this district where canyons, gulches, and mushroom camps once swarmed with miners, prospectors, and those who followed to share in the squandering of new-found gold. Here, within a few short years, laborers became millionaries, and broadcloth supplanted overalls; steel rails pushed swiftly into remote gulches;

flimsy wooden buildings made way for stone and brick structures. North of Nederland are large glaciers in cirques and crevices. The whole area is dotted with summer houses and campgrounds.

In IDAHO SPRINGS, 0 *m.* (7,500 alt., 1,500 pop.) (*see Tour 7b*), State 279 branches north from US 40 (*see Tour 7b*). Looping and twisting its way up Virginia Canyon along a new road that has replaced the steep and dangerous early stage route along the bottom of the ravine, State 279 swings northward to RUSSELL GULCH, 5.9 *m.* (9,500 alt., 93 pop.). The town and the gulch were named for Green Russell, a Georgian, whose party of several hundred members panned more than $20,000 of gold here in 1859. In September of that year 900 men were panning sands here and taking out an average of $35,000 a week. In 1862 Russell went South to join the Confederate Army, but was arrested in Santa Fe, N. M. Soon released, he returned to Colorado and remained until 1875, when he went to join the Cherokee in Indian Territory, now Oklahoma, for his wife was a Cherokee from Georgia.

Passing numerous mine shafts and ore dumps, State 279 ascends a high ridge known as QUARTZ HILL and descends to CENTRAL CITY, 8.1 *m.* (8,560 alt.), seat of Gilpin County, once known as "the richest square mile on earth." The first impression is that the worst possible site was chosen for a settlement. Gregory Gulch, along which the town wanders, ascends steeply from the North Fork of Clear Creek, and houses cling precariously to the steep slopes of the gulch. Although some mining is carried on, Central City bears the marks of neglect and decay. Near the junction of the three principal streets are grouped the larger business structures of weathered frame and stone. Many have been abandoned but still flaunt old signs painted in the golden era when saloons and dance houses were crowded day and night. The surrounding hills, long since stripped of timber, are scarred with mine shafts and ore dumps. Near the center of town is a great yellow mound of mill tailings from the Glory Hole (*see below*) on Quartz Hill.

Within a few weeks of Gregory's rich strike here in 1859, this and neighboring gulches swarmed with thousands of gold seekers. The rush almost emptied the Cherry Creek settlements of Auraria and Denver City, which were seething with discontent as gold-hunters cursed the "Pikes Peak Hoax" that had brought them across the plains. Upon the scene appeared Horace Greeley, editor of the New York *Tribune,* who was determined to investigate for himself the mineral resources of the country. Miners welcomed him by "salting" a placer mine, shooting gold dust into it with a shotgun. Invited to take a pan and wash out gold, he did so and was amazed, as the miners had expected him to be. His glowing account of the richness of the Gregory diggings was published throughout the country and the rush increased.

Many camps sprang up along the gulch: Blackhawk, Gregory Point, Mountain City, Central City, Missouri City, and Nevadaville. Rivalry among them was intense; when a section of Nevadaville decided to break away and become a town, the Nevadaville authorities arrested the newly elected officials for "secession." Central City, named for its situation midway up the gulch, gradually outstripped other camps, absorbing several of them. Although one of the richest, it was also one of the quietest of the gold camps. At first a motley collection of log cabins and shacks, it was substantially rebuilt after a fire in 1874.

The young Colorado Territory might not have survived its first few years had it not been for the outpouring of wealth from the golden "Kingdom of Gilpin." Other fields were soon depleted, and only the mines of Gilpin County—one of the original seventeen counties of the Territory—maintained a fairly stable population on the mountain frontier. Here was the cradle of much of Colorado's mining law; miners' courts were organized within a few weeks of the first strike. On the model of California camps the diggings were organized as a mining district with a president, sheriff, and recorder of claims. No miner, except the original discoverer, could hold by right of discovery more than one creek, one gulch, and one mountain claim. Once staked, a claim had to be worked within 10 days to establish title. A lode claim was limited to 100 feet in length and 50 feet in width; a gulch claim, 100 feet in length, and extending from bank to bank; placer diggings, to an area 100 feet square. Gold seekers were more concerned with justice than legal procedure, as evidenced by an early rule that no man might employ a lawyer unless his adversary happened to be one.

Central City's history has been one of varying fortune. The first miners sought chiefly for rich placer beds and "blossom rock," a gold-bearing decomposed quartz so soft that it could be dug from hillsides with pick and shovel. As these quartz veins pinched out and placer deposits were exhausted, production of the mines dropped until by 1864 only a few were being worked. When methods were perfected in the late 1860's for treatment of refractory ores, the district enjoyed another boom. Mills and smelters were built in Blackhawk; the Colorado Central Railway was extended from Golden to Blackhawk in 1872, and later to Central City.

Again, as more valuable ore veins were exhausted, the mines became less profitable, and a new decline set in. Finally, mines and mills fell silent and many miners departed. Shaft houses collapsed and tunnels became choked with debris; even the herds of burros, once part of the scene, disappeared—probably, as one miner put it, because "everybody claimed them in summer and nobody owned them in winter." Nevadaville became a ghost town, and Central City and Blackhawk languished. The district, from which more than $67,000,000 has been produced since Gregory's strike, now mines from $10,000 to $100,000 of metals annually.

From Gregory Gulch came many men later prominent in the political and financial worlds. Among them were Henry M. Teller and Jerome B. Chaffee, first United States Senators from Colorado. Teller, who served in the Congress for 29 years, was also Secretary of the Interior in President Chester B. Arthur's cabinet. Others were Henry R. Wolcott, smelter manager, later State senator and long a Republican leader in Colorado; George Pullman, who perfected the sleeping car; and W. A. Clark, who worked the Bobtail Mine (*see below*), later going to Montana where he became a copper king and U. S. Senator.

The tradition that Cornish miners brought yellow roses to Central City in 1866 is commemorated annually in July with a ball at the Teller House.

Central City is perhaps the best known of all old Colorado mining towns because of the play festival (*see The Arts*) held each July at the OPERA HOUSE, Eureka St., W. of Main St., erected after the fire of 1874 had destroyed the town's ramshackle playhouses. Four years later the stone building with its four-feet walls was completed. The theater proper is admirably proportioned and decorated simply in Empire style. On its stage appeared Edwin Booth, Lotta Crabtree, Christine Nilsson, Janauschek, Modjeska, and other celebrated players and singers of the day. Although Central City early displayed a love for the theater, the opera house was not a financial success, and at one time it was proposed to convert it into a courthouse. The structure at length passed into the hands of Peter McFarlane, one of the original contractors, whose heirs presented it to the University of Denver in 1931. Through the sale of memorial chairs the building was renovated, and the dimmed frescoes, painted by Mossman, a San Francisco artist, were restored by Allen True of Denver. Under the sponsorship of the Central City Opera House Association, the first play festival was held in 1932, with Lillian Gish in *Camille*. In subsequent seasons operas have been produced with stars from the Metropolitan, New York, in leading roles; in 1968, for instance, the bill was *Rigoletto, The Pearl Fishers,* and *The Crucible* of Robert Ward. Ward's *The Lady from Colorado* was given the same year as Puccini's *Madama Butterfly*. In June, 1969, the opening was a social triumph and performances were given of *Tosca* and *Die Fledermaus* on alternate evenings. Many attend the theater in old-time costumes; night clubs, bars, and a livery stable converted into a dance house of the 1860's are crowded nightly.

The TELLER HOUSE, Eureka St. between the opera house and Main St., a plain brick structure, was the last word in frontier hostelries when completed in 1872. At the time of President Grant's visit in 1873, he walked from the stagecoach to the hotel on a path of silver bricks. Such evidence of respect on the part of their elders did not deter small boys from mounting to the roof of a stable opposite and throwing snowballs at Grant's plug hat. The hotel is conducted in conjunction with the Opera House. Original murals in the bar were uncovered in 1932 after twelve layers of wallpaper had been removed.

Left from Central City on a dirt road is NEVADAVILLE, 2.9 *m.,* which once had a population of 800, now a true ghost town. A few people live here, but the doors of most of the weathered and dilapidated buildings creak idly in the wind, and the city hall and fire station stand empty.

Left 0.1 *m.* from Nevadaville to the junction with a dirt road; L. here 0.6 *m.* along the step face of Quartz Hill to the GLORY HOLE, one of the most impressive sights in the Central City district. This great mining pit is a huge rift almost 1,000 feet long and 300 feet deep in places. Shafts of old mines here were filled with dynamite and exploded, which literally blew out the heart of the mountain.

At the boundary between Central City and Blackhawk a granite monument marks the SITE OF THE FIRST GOLD LODE DISCOVERY IN COLORADO, made by John H. Gregory on May 6, 1859. After mining $900 from the outcrop, he sold his claim for $21,000; it proved to be one of the richest in the history of the State.

Almost a unit with Central City, distinguishable only by the highway signs that mark the boundary, is BLACKHAWK, 9.5 *m.* (8,032 alt.), one of the first settlements in Gilpin County; it extends a mile along North Clear Creek and around the sharp promontory of CASEY'S POINT, named for Pat Casey, who came into the region as a roustabout and discovered a rich lode that made him wealthy. He bought the finest clothing in town and drove about in an expensive carriage drawn by a span of spirited black horses. Although unable to read or write, he carried a memorandum book on which to jot down his business transactions. "I use up tin pincils a day," he often boasted, "and thin don't get half through me business."

The first smelter in Colorado, constructed here in 1868 by Prof. Nathaniel P. Hill, later a U. S. Senator, was removed to Argo, near Denver, ten years later. Here, too, the Hendrie brothers established the first mining machinery foundry in the Rocky Mountains. Among the celebrated lodes here was the Bobtail, so named because the first ore was hauled to the sluices by a bob-tailed ox harnessed to a forked limb over which rawhide had been stretched.

The highway ascends a shallow canyon dotted with ruins of abandoned mines. Here and there new mills are operating, reducing ores from the still valuable deposits of Gilpin County. Within the solid walls of many of the abandoned mills stands the original machinery, left to rust when the roofs collapsed.

In Blackhawk is the junction with State 119, which the route now follows. At 14.7 *m.* is the junction with State 58.

ROLLINSVILLE, 22.2 *m.* (8,200 alt.), was a shipping point on the Denver & Salt Lake (Moffat) Railway. Much gold has been found here along South Boulder Creek.

At 24.2 *m.* is the junction with State 72.

Right on this winding graded road into COAL CREEK CANYON; below the highway, the tracks of the Denver & Rio Grande Western Ry. pass in and out of tunnels and over high trestles as they ascend the steep grade toward the Moffat Tunnel (*see Tour 7b*).

Only one town, PINE CLIFF, 4.5 *m.* (7,500 alt.), is passed, but numerous summer cabins and ranches are seen along the road, which extends to Denver, 33 *m.*

The highway gradually descends through an area spotted with deserted mills and shaft houses to the junction with a graded road, 26.2 *m.* Left on this road is ELDORA, 3 *m.* (8,700 alt.), an old-time gold camp and shipping point for the Caribou mines, which has been rejuvenated as a ski center, with 3 T-bar lifts, and starting point for Arapahoe peaks and glacier.

The road sweeps northward through densely forested country, a region drained by numerous trout streams and dotted with campgrounds. At intervals, from the crests of the higher hills, is glimpsed the entire Front Range of the Rockies, from Mount Evans on the south to Longs Peak on the north.

NEDERLAND, 26.7 *m.* (8,200 alt., 458 pop.), a mining and resort village on the western shore of the lake formed by Barker Dam (*see below*), was formerly an important shipping and milling center for ores from mines farther west. "A dismal little mining town," wrote Helen Hunt Jackson in 1877, "only a handful of small houses and smelting mills. Boulder Creek comes dashing through it, foaming white to the very edge of town." It was named by the Dutch syndicate that owned the mines at Caribou (*see below*). While the town grew up as a gold and silver milling center, it was the center of the tungsten industry in the district from 1914 to 1918. The presence of tungsten in local ores was early known, but not until the first part of the twentieth century did its value as a steel hardener become known. At present a tungsten mill and several mines in the vicinity are operating. The beautiful scenery of the area formed a backdrop for the film "Stagecoach" produced here in 1965.

1. Left from Nederland on State 160, a well-maintained graveled highway, a route of great beauty connecting with roads to Estes Park and Rocky Mountain National Park (*see Rocky Mountain National Park*). The road traverses a high country of forests and meadows, paralleling (L) the Continental Divide. Bright wild flowers grow in profusion in the three-ringed glades, and the many tiny streams are fringed with willows and shrubs.

LAKEWOOD, 7.3 *m.,* now but a point on the map, was once the site of the largest tungsten mill in the United States; only its concrete foundations remain.

Left from Lakewood 4 *m.* to the improved RAINBOW LAKES CAMPGROUND.

From the campground a foot trail winds 7.8 *m.* upward to the ARAPAHO GLACIER, resting high on the face of Arapaho Peak, easily visible from the plain. The ice flow is several hundred feet long, but its depth has never been determined. The glacier moves about 37 feet a year, which causes great fissures in the ice (*trail fairly well-marked, but should not be attempted without a guide*). Numerous climbers come here, particularly groups organized at the University of Colorado. Participation in one of these groups is advised, as lone hikers are sometimes lost on the heights where nights are very cold throughout the year.

On State 160 is WARD, 12 *m.* (9,250 alt.), another former mining town with streets that wind up and down steep slopes between clusters of old buildings, the majority deserted. One of its mines produced more than 2,000,000 ounces of silver during its three-year existence. The fireplace of the WARD HOTEL is constructed of gold ore. It has been suggested that the hill on which the town stands should be leveled for the mineral it contains.

At 12.2 *m.* is the junction with a graded road.

Left here 3.8 *m.* to the BRAINARD LAKE CAMPGROUND, at the eastern end of BRAINARD LAKE, a small but beautiful body of water near the foot of the Continental Divide.

From this campground a well-marked foot trail leads past LONG LAKE, 1 *m.,* and LAKE ISABELLE, 3 *m.,* both fed by glaciers, to ISABELLE GLA-

CIER, 7.3 *m.* This glacier, one of the most spectacular in the State, is set in a great cup formed by three jagged shafts of Kiowa, Navaho, and Apache peaks, all of them rugged and stark, gouged and scored by ice sheets. From Brainard Lake Campground the climb to the glacier and return can be made within a day.

State 160 enters PEACEFUL VALLEY, 19.1 *m.,* a summer resort in South St. Vrain Canyon (*cabins and hotel*).

Left here on a trail (*trip requires two days; do not attempt without guides and proper camping equipment*) to ST. VRAIN GLACIER, 10 *m.,* near the head of South St. Vrain Creek; in the immediate vicinity are ROBERTS GLACIER and MILDRED GLACIER.

State 160 terminates at RAYMONDS 22 *m.,* at the junction with State 7 (*see Tour 4*).

2. Left from Nederland on a dirt road along North Beaver Creek is CARIBOU, 5.5 *m.* (10,000 alt.), a silver camp established in 1869. The next year a half interest in the first strike sold for $50,000; it yielded $70,000 that year, and three years later it was sold to a Dutch syndicate for $3,000,000. The year of peak production was 1875 when $200,000 worth of ore was mined.

The highway follows the irregular line of the lake shore to BARKER DAM, 28.6 *m.,* a 185-foot concrete structure which stores water for use in the Boulder Canyon Hydroelectric Plant.

TUNGSTEN, 29 *m.* (7,800 alt.), supported several ore mills during the First World War when tungsten was in great demand. Traffic on the highway became so heavy that guards were maintained at all curves in the canyon. As the price of tungsten declined, the mills were closed, but today Colorado's production is second only to California.

East of Tungsten the route traverses a broad grassy park, inclosed on all sides by densely forested hills, to CASTLE ROCK, 30.6 *m.,* a huge serrated mass of black rock rising 300 feet above the canyon floor. Difficult of ascent, its summit is a popular goal for climbers. The walls of the canyon close in to form THE NARROWS, through which plunges Middle Boulder Creek.

At 34.3 *m.* is the junction with an improved foot trail. Left here to BOULDER FALLS, 75 *yds.,* the chief attraction of a five-acre park. Here the waters of North Boulder Creek spill 75 feet over the canyon wall to join those of Middle Boulder Creek.

State 119 follows the widening canyon between hills, a mass of green throughout the year, and crosses the eastern boundary of Roosevelt National Forest, 37.5 *m.* At 37.6 *m.* is the junction with a dirt road. Left on this road to SUGARLOAF, 4 *m.* (8,000 alt.), another old mining town. Here in Switzerland Park, a high fertile valley, mountain peas and potatoes are grown.

At 37.9 *m.* is the junction with another dirt road. Right on this road to MAGNOLIA, 2.5 *m.* (7,500 alt.), a busy town after the discovery of gold in 1875, now a resort.

The highway descends Boulder Canyon, passing the BOULDER HYDROELECTRIC PLANT (R), 39 *m.,* a unit of the Public Service Company of Colorado, which supplies a large part of the electric power used in northern Colorado.

At 39.3 *m.* is the junction with the Flagstaff Mountain Road. Right on this highway through the Boulder Mountain Parks system to the summit of FLAGSTAFF MOUNTAIN (7,047 alt.), 3.5 *m*. The road winds down to BOULDER, 7 *m*.

State 119 descends the canyon, passing numerous summer houses and cabins, to the junction with Four Mile Canyon Road, 40.1 *m*.

Left on this improved road to the heart of the once-rich Boulder County mining district. The highway follows the winding course of Four Mile Canyon; along the willow-fringed banks of Four Mile Creek flowers are in blossom most of the summer. In April and May appear numberless purple anemones (in *picking flowers, watch for wood ticks, carriers of Rocky Mountain spotted fever*). Later in the season, asters, daisies, wild roses, Indian paintbrush, and bluebells appear.

CRISMAN, 3.5 *m*. (5,300 alt.), dates from the discovery of gold here in 1875; today, unoccupied houses and store buildings are falling to decay.

The Four Mile Canyon Road gradually ascends; grades are steep, curves sharp, and the road is narrow (*drive carefully*).

At 5.3 *m*. is the junction with a dirt road.

Right here 1.7 *m*. to SUNSHINE (7,200 alt.), founded in 1874 when gold and silver mines here were among the most productive in the district. An early prospector mined $17,500 of gold from a cut 10 feet deep and 20 feet long. Fearing his luck would not last, he sold his mine for another $17,500; the new owners took out $196,000 worth of ore in twenty months. At one time the camp had a population of 1,200. Although the rich lodes have apparently been exhausted, including the celebrated Inter-Ocean, the mines are still intermittently operated.

On the Four Mile Canyon Road is SALINA, 5.8 *m*. (6,500 alt.), an old mining camp founded by a group from Salina, Kans.; it lies at the confluence of Four Mile and Gold Run Creeks; along the latter the first gold discoveries in the Boulder district were made in 1858.

GOLD HILL, 8.8 *m*. (8,500 alt.), the first mining camp in the county, came into existence when gold was found here on January 15, 1859. Soon the Horsfal Lode, a great body of rich ore, was discovered and worked for many years. Gold Hill is now a popular summer resort. Still standing is the MINERS' HOTEL (*visitors admitted*), a 25-room log building erected in 1872, now the property of the Chicago Holiday Association, a social organization. Many of the original furnishings and decorations have been preserved; the weather boarding that once sheathed the building has been removed to expose the log walls. The hotel was renowned for its fine food, of which Eugene Field wrote:

4   'Nd I feel a sort of yearnin' 'nd a chokin' in my throat
       When I think of Red Hoss Mountain 'nd of Casey's tabble dote.

The Gold Hill Mining District was created March 7, 1859, and adopted many regulations that established basic principles for present mining law. A leather-bound volume, containing the original handwritten regulations, is in the county office at Boulder.

The highway leaves Boulder Canyon, 46.9 *m.*, sweeping into more level country. Prominent are the FLATIRONS, a series of great rock slabs rising steeply up the face of the foothills. Climbing the Flatirons is dangerous; several persons have been killed by falls down the steep smooth face of these rocks.

BOULDER (5,430 alt., 56,000 pop.), 43 *m.*, is at the junction with State 7 (*see Tour 4*).

Tour 7

(Sharon Springs, Kans.)—Cheyenne Wells—Limon—Denver—Idaho Springs—St. Marys Glacier—Berthoud Pass—Hot Sulphur Springs— Steamboat Springs—Craig—(Vernal, Utah); US 40.
Kansas Line to Utah Line, 497.5 *m.*

Gravel-surfaced road between Kremmling and Muddy Pass; elsewhere oil-processed. Road between Kremmling and Steamboat Springs sometimes closed by winter storms; alternate route by way of Gore Pass, on State 84 between Kremmling and Toponas, and on State 131 between Toponas and Steamboat Springs. Route paralleled between Kansas Line and Denver by Union Pacific R.R.; between Denver and Empire by.Colorado & Southern Ry.
Good accommodations.

US 40, one of the great transcontinental highways, traverses the dry eastern plains, ascends to the well-watered uplands along the foothills, and penetrates the mountains to reach the vast northwestern plateaus, crossing the Continental Divide three times en route.

Section a.   *KANSAS LINE to DENVER; 193 m. US 40*

This section of the tour follows the dry and dangerous trail trudged in the late 1850's and early 1860's by gold-hunters bound for the rich placer mines in the Rockies. This route, known as the Smoky Hill Trail, named for the Smoky Hills, a low clay ridge separating the drainage basins of the Smoky Hill and Republican Rivers, was a middle passage between the Overland Trail along the Platte to the north and the Santa Fe Trail along the Arkansas to the south. Branching from the Santa Fe Trail west of Council Grove, Kans., it was a shorter route, but lack of water and game made travel along it hazardous and earned it the grim nickname of "Starvation Trail." During the Pikes Peak Gold Rush of '59, thousands hurried along it—on foot, often pushing heavily loaded handbarrows, on horseback, singly or in parties, and in wagons and wheeled vehicles of every kind. Scores died of hunger, thirst, and exhaustion, or were killed by outlaws or Indians, who were roused to fury by the invasion of their buffalo lands. Tales of starvation, murder, and even cannibalism were told of the trail, but the tide to the gold fields mounted ever higher.

Later, one of the many stage lines between Denver and the Missouri River towns chose the Smoky Hill route, established stations 10 to 25 miles apart, and employed 100 Concord wagons and 1,000 mules on its run, which took from 10 to 12 days. The fare was $75 to $100; for shorter distances the charge was 25¢ a mile. The Concord wagon, named for the city of its manufacture, had canvas top and sides, and was less top-heavy than the usual stagecoach built entirely of wood. Filled with passengers and balanced by a proper distribution of baggage in the "boot," its motion was easy and elastic, although cramped accommodations and rough roads made travel decidedly uncomfortable at best.

Soon after steam supplanted horse power, a few ranches built sod dugouts on the plains here, and range cattle were driven north along the Texas trails to be shipped to market. Riders fought Indians and rustlers, lived a hard life, and often died with their boots on. The round-up of beef cattle took place in the fall, when large outfits bunched their herds at the railhead, crowding in as close as the supply of grass and water permitted. Soon a general store and saloon was built for thirsty cow-hands, and another town was born. Almost every town in this section began as a railroad cow camp. From many of these towns 30 cars of cattle left every hour for eastern markets for days at a time. Sometimes shipping schedules got tangled and an outfit lost its turn. This invariably led to fighting—fist affairs between two men, or six-gun battles with scores of riders on each side.

US 40 crosses the KANSAS LINE, 0 *m.,* 16.5 miles west of Sharon Springs, Kans.

West of ARAPAHOE, 7.3 *m.* (4,012 alt.), rolling prairies swell slightly upward toward the yet invisible mountains. Rainfall is heavier here than in districts farther west; the soil is rich and grows relatively profitable crops of corn, cane, millet, maize, and small grains. Across the valley of the Smoky Hill River appears (R) the low ridge of the SMOKY HILLS, ten miles distant.

CHEYENNE WELLS, 17 *m.* (4,282 alt., 1,020 pop.), a farming town and seat of Cheyenne County, dates from the 1860's when it was a station on the Butterfield Overland Dispatch. When Bayard Taylor, novelist and poet, passed through in 1866 as correspondent of the New York *Tribune,* he found "a large, handsome frame stable for mules, but no dwelling. The people lived in a natural cave extending for some thirty feet under the bluff." The community later became a typical cow town.

Before the fall round-up it was customary for one of the large ranches to "throw" a dance. Cattlemen and their households arrived by chuck wagon, buckboard, and on horseback, with bedrolls and personal articles for a two-day stay. The women brought coffee and home-cooked delicacies; the ranchman furnished meats, vegetables, and other staples, including several cases of whisky in pint bottles. Each man took his bottle, cached it in some safe place, and resorted to it whenever he was thirsty—which was often. When the pint was emptied, he called for another. No man touched another's bottle. After a big dinner at sundown, festivities began in the ranchhouse living room, which was usually large enough to accommodate two dance sets of four couples each, with space for all fancy side steps and "pigeon wings."

The orchestra usually consisted of a guitar, banjo, harmonica, and a violin or two.

With boot heels hooked over rungs of chairs tilted back against the wall, with a sand box spittoon within easy range, the musicians swung into such popular ditties as "Sandy Land," "Turkey in the Straw," "Money Musk," and "Good Old Turnip Greens." The "caller" stamped his feet, screeched a wild "ye-ow" to loosen up his vocal chords, and the dance was on. The cadenced thud of heeled boots, the clapping of hands, and the periodic yelps of the dancers continued until morning.

After breakfast the guests slept until noon, when horseshoe pitching, horse and foot races, pistol and roping contests were held. Around the campfire that evening, men and women joined in singing "The Lily of the West," "Clementina," "Sucking Cider through a Straw," and

> Old Aunt Sukey, a fine old squaw,
> Finest ever stepped along the Arkan-saw . . .   8

Right from Cheyenne Wells on State 51 to the junction with a dirt road, 9.5 *m.;* L. here to a field, *2m.;* R. here 0.3 to the WATER WELLS for which Cheyenne Wells was named. These wells, at present dry, were of great importance in covered-wagon days as they constituted the only reliable water supply for miles in any direction.

West of Cheyenne Wells the road traverses rolling prairie, broken at intervals by small hills, to FIRSTVIEW, 28 *m.* (4,580 alt.), from which, on clear days, the far-off mountains are first seen.

KIT CARSON, 42 *m.* (4,285 alt., 390 pop.), named for the western scout (*see Tour 9a*), began its existence as a trading station and military post in 1860. During the construction of the Kansas Pacific Railroad the settlement was "the end of track" for a time, a busy outfitting point for traders whose wagon trains plodded on toward mountain points. Skirmishes with Indians were frequent; burned to the ground, the town was rebuilt here, a few miles north of the original site.

WILDHORSE, 53.2 *m.* (4,435 alt.), derived its name from a near-by creek, once a watering place for large bands of wild horses. These animals, presumably sprung from horses brought to America by Spanish explorers, were numerous in the region during the early years of the last century. Lieutenant Pike reported sighting a great herd of them in 1806; when they saw Pike's party, they came charging up quite close, "making the earth tremble under them like a charge of cavalry." The Spanish gave them the name of *broncho,* meaning rude or rough, and in time such names as bronc, mustang, and cayuse were conferred upon the cow pony. The capture and breaking of wild horses was often a side line of the cattle business, although the animals were usually inferior to cow ponies brought from Texas.

The highway continues across miles of brown prairie land relieved by clumps of yucca, thistles, and cacti. In summer mirages are sometimes seen—sparkling lakes, green fields, and dwellings appear, recede, and finally fade away in shimmering heat waves.

HUGO, 86.2 *m.* (4,970 alt., 890 pop.), seat of Lincoln County and supply town for grain farms, was established as a trading post in 1880. The *Eastern Colorado Plainsman* is its weekly newspaper.

Northwest of Hugo the road ascends the low divide between the basins of the Arkansas and South Platte Rivers. Rainfall in this northern edge of the "dust bowl" is scant, and many fields have been eroded by high winds. A conservation program has introduced contour plowing throughout the area; deep furrows are ploughed to break the force of the wind, and to catch and retain moisture.

At 100.9 *m.* is the junction with US 24 (*see Tour 5a*), which unites with US 40 for 3 miles (*see Tour 5a*).

LIMON, 102.9 *m.* (5,336 alt., 2,000 pop.), a trading center and shipping point for an extensive agricultural district, was founded in 1888 as a railroad camp. The *Limon Leader* is published here.

Northwest of Limon, US 40 crosses a sparsely settled dry farming district to DEER TRAIL, 135.2 *m.* (5,183 alt., 425 pop.), once center of a large sheep and cattle-grazing area; agriculture is the principal occupation today.

BYERS, 147.8 *m.* (5,202 alt.), was founded in 1868 as a shipping point for livestock by Oliver P. Wiggins, frontiersman and scout. Laid out as a townsite in 1888, it was named for William N. Byers of Denver, pioneer editor of the *Rocky Mountain News.* To stimulate sale of lots, excursion trains were run from Denver and a great barbecue was staged, "the longest free ride and biggest free lunch in the history of the State," as the Denver *Republican* stated.

Passing STRASBURG, 152.8 *m.* (5,576 alt.), established as a railroad siding in 1875, the route traverses sun-baked plains, crossing several dry creek beds, to the junction with a graveled road, 184.6 *m.*

Right on this road to FITZSIMONS GENERAL HOSPITAL (*open 3–5, 6–8 daily*), 0.5 *m.*, largest U. S. Army hospital in the United States, admitting beneficiaries of the Veterans' Administration and military personnel.

AURORA, 186 *m.* (5,342 alt., 68,000 pop. 1968 est.), fifth largest city in Colorado, is located east of the Denver city limits in both Adams and Arapahoe Counties and reached by US 36, 40 and 287. It is sometimes called the Gateway to the Rockies. It was settled in 1890, incorporated 1903 as Fletcher, and changed its name to Aurora in 1907. It shares in the industrial and residential growth of the Denver area and profits from its nearness to Lowry Air Force Base, Fitzsimons General Hospital, USA, Rocky Mountain Arsenal, and Buckley Field. The largest manufacturers of fishing equipment in the United States are located here. Aurora has joined Colorado Springs in the Homestake Water Project to guarantee an adequate supply for future needs. Stapleton Airport of Denver is north of Aurora's city limits.

Section b. DENVER *to* CRAIG; *212 m.* US 40

West of DENVER, 0 *m.,* US 40 and US 6 are united for 40.1 miles; the route proceeds through a suburban district toward rolling foot-hills that obscure the higher peaks beyond.

The J.C.R.S. SANITORIUM, 4.5 *m.,* a non-sectarian charitable insti-tution maintained by the Jewish Consumptives' Relief Society, receives tubercular patients from all parts of the United States. A dairy and farm supply much of the institution's food. Its post office station, called Spivak, honors the institution's first superintendent.

The highway turns southward between two hogbacks and swings west into Mount Vernon Canyon to ascend by easy grades to a ridgetop, of which Lookout Mountain is the northeastern extremity. At the sum-mit, 18.7 *m.,* is the western junction with the Lookout Mountain road (*see Tour 7A*).

GENESSEE MOUNTAIN PARK, 19.7 *m.,* contains 2,403 acres, being the largest of the mountain parks owned by the city of Denver.

At the park entrance is the junction with a graveled road.

Left on this road to GENESSEE MOUNTAIN (8,274 alt.), 2.7 *m.* From a parking space near the summit, stone steps lead to the highest point, where a monument has been erected. The road descends in a wide semicircle through heavily forested country. At intervals, where the timber thins, are good views of the plains. This section of the foothills is noted for its abundance of wild flowers, which carpet the ground throughout the summer. Passing (L) the GENESSEE MOUNTAIN SKI COURSE (*open*), 3.7 *m.,* the road winds through the DENVER MOUNTAIN PARK GAME PRESERVE; deer, elk, and buffalo are frequently seen grazing behind high wire fences. A herd of sixty buffalo usually are kept here.

At 5.7 *m.* the road rejoins US 40.

Proceeding northwestward, US 40 crosses rolling mountain country to the top of FLOYD HILL (10,000 alt.), 27 *m.,* and descends into the canyon of Clear Creek, which today belies its name; its waters are roiled and discolored with mine tailings. The stream has been the source of almost endless litigation between miners, who need it for their opera-tions, and farmers on the plains, who want it for irrigation.

The ARGO TUNNEL, 32 *m.,* seen against a steep slope (R), one of the most ambitious mining enterprises ever undertaken in Colorado, was formerly named the Newhouse. From Clear Creek the tunnel runs under the mountains for some four miles, opening at Central City (*see Tour 6*). It intersects several important lodes in the Clear Creek and Gilpin County districts, and drains a number of mines. Quantities of ore are hauled through it for shipment.

A boulder, 32.1 *m.,* marks the SITE OF THE FIRST MAJOR GOLD STRIKE in Colorado. George Jackson, Indian trader, miner, and cousin of Kit Carson, working his way alone down Chicago Creek, a small tributary of the South Fork of Clear Creek, reached the junction of the streams here early in January 1859. He built a fire upon a sand bar and kept it burning throughout the night to thaw out frozen sand and gravel. In the morning he "removed the embers and panned out eight treaty cups of dirt, and found nothing but fine colors; with one cup I got a nugget of gold." Jackson continued to dig until his knife blade was worn out; having obtained about a half ounce of "dust," he filled up the hole again, marked a near-by fir tree, and cut off the top of a small lodgepole pine on a line between the fir and the hole. Making his way back to Denver, he said nothing of his discovery. In the spring he returned and panned out several thousand dollars in gold. The news brought a wild stampede into Clear Creek Canyon. Jackson organized the Chicago Mining Company, which began the first profitable large-scale mining in the Pikes Peak country.

During the peak of the gold rush the canyon was a confusion of tents, cabins, wagons, and livestock; men worked feverishly stripping sand bars, building dams and sluices, and shoveling "pay dirt." Some used the regulation shallow pan; others mounted pans on rockers to form a cradle; still others used a log hollowed into trough—known as a "Long Tom" —rolled from side to side with a stick handle. Larger operators employed long wooden troughs or sluice boxes, with riffle boards across the bottom. Behind the cross-bars were pools of quick-silver to catch and hold the heavy gold as sand and gravel were shoveled into the sluices and washed down by a steady stream of water. When the placers were worked out, quartz formations were mined on both sides of the canyon. The primitive hand windlasses employed to hoist the rock up the shafts were later replaced with a "whip," a gallows with a pulley arrangement, by which a mule, driven straight out and back again, hoisted and lowered an ore bucket. This soon gave way to the "whim," a large wooden drum pulled around by a mule or horse. This in turn gave way to the steam engine, protected by a shaft house.

IDAHO SPRINGS, 32.8 m. (7,500 alt.,1,500 pop.), a mining and resort town near the scene of Jackson's gold discovery is strung along the narrow canyon. Before 1860 it was known as Sacramento City, Jackson Diggings, Idahoe, and finally Idaho Springs. The name is said to be derived from Ee-da-how, an Indian word signifying that the sun is coming down the mountains. A correspondent of the *Rocky Mountain News* in 1860 had a more ingenious explanation, declaring that "the aboriginal legend hath it that where now stands the proud city, the first gold discovery of the country was made long ago, by a dusky maid of the forest, named Ida, with her hoe." The placers hereabouts were soon worked out, but lode mining near by kept the settlement alive; later, through the exploitation of its hot springs, the town prospered as a spa.

The widely known RADIUM HOT SPRINGS, long visited by Indians, attracted health-seekers as early as 1868, when "a mammoth frame building with hot and cold shower baths, parlors and dressing rooms elaborately furnished," was erected.

Nine large ski areas are within easy driving distance of Idaho Springs. There are two good routes to the top of Mt. Evans, 14,260 ft., one via US 103 through Chicago Creek Canyon to Echo Lake, the other via Bergen Park and Squaw Pass to Echo Lake; then from the lake on State

5 to the top. The Ranger Station of Arapahoe National Forest and the Jackson Monument, where gold was discovered in 1859, are on US 103.

In Idaho Springs is the junction with State 119 and with State 103.

Right from Idaho Springs on a dirt road to the EDGAR MINE (*open by permission*), 13 *m.*, maintained by the Colorado School of Mines (*see Tour 7A*) for practical undergraduate work in mining, including mine surveying, mining geology, stoping, drifting, drilling, blasting, use of explosives, and general mining engineering. Graduate students also use the mine for research work.

At 34 *m.* is the junction with an unimproved road.

Right on this road to the KAMINKY MINE, 9.6 *m.;* L. here on a foot trail, skirting the southern shore of SILVER LAKE, 0.3 *m.,* to ST. MARYS LAKE, 0.8 *m.,* a small sheet of startlingly blue water framed against the white backdrop of the glacier to the north.

Left from the lake on a foot trail to ST. MARYS GLACIER, 1.3 *m.,* its hard-packed snows covering an area a half-mile long and one-tenth mile wide, lying in a great cirque on the southern shoulder of KINGSTON PEAK (12,136 alt.). The glacier feeds St. Marys Lake by a small unnamed stream which, at its point of emergence, has hollowed out weirdly beautiful ICE CAVERNS in the heart of the glacial drift. St. Marys is the most accessible of all Colorado glaciers. Skiing is enjoyed here throughout the year, and an annual meet is held on July 4th. From the shoulder of the mountain, 2.3 *m.,* is an impressive view of JAMES PEAK (13,259 alt.) to the west.

The route continues along Clear Creek Canyon, which was black with prospectors during the early 1860's, to DUMONT, 37.4 *m.* (7,955 alt.), founded as Mill City in 1860, when many ore-crushing mills were built here.

At 40.1 *m.* is (L) the junction with US 6 (*see Tour 1b*).

EMPIRE, 41.4 *m.* (8,603 alt.), at the confluence of Lyons and Bards Creeks, is the last of the mining towns between Idaho Springs and the Continental Divide. The highway crosses the eastern boundary of ARAPAHO NATIONAL FOREST, 42.4 *m.;* created in 1908, it contains 987,630 acres owned by the Federal Government. Headquarters are in Golden.

BERTHOUD PASS, (11,315 alt.), named for an engineer who surveyed it in 1861, has a ski area that is open weekends and holidays, with T-bar, double chair lifts, 2,200 ft. long, 685 ft. rise. Ski school.

The MOFFAT TUNNEL (9,094 alt.) used by the Denver & Rio Grande Western Ry., was completed July 7, 1927, at a cost of $18,000,-000, and named for David H. Moffat, Denver banker. The tunnel is 24 ft. wide, 18 ft. tall, 6.4 *m.* long. Beside it is the MOFFAT PIONEER TUNNEL, 8 by 8 ft., which carries water from the west slope to the Ralston Reservoir in Jefferson County, north of Golden.

WINTER PARK is a complete ski resort, mid-December to mid-April, attracting thousands every season. Its 4 chair lifts and 4 T-bars carry 7,700 uphill every hour. Of 32 runs the longest is 1½ *m.* with a vertical descent of 1,700 ft. There are 7 jumping hills, an instruction area, a ski school, a skating rink. National ski patrol, with medical personnel. Snoasis warming house at midway. Numerous chalets, motor lodges, restaurants in the area. Reached by D. & R. G. W. Ry., Continental Trailways, and charter planes to Granby Airport. Address Winter Park Information, P. O. Box 45 or phone 303-726-5331.

SKI IDLEWILD, 2 m. west of Winter Park, and HIDEAWAY PARK are also attractive resorts in the ski area. Ski Idlewild is exclusively for beginners, with a double chair lift, and T-bar, 5 slopes and 5 trails up to 400 ft. wide. Ski school, day nursery and private babysitting, family accommodations.

FRASER, 71 m. (8,550 alt.) gets into the weather news bulletins for its low temperatures. TABERNASH, 75 m. (8,337 alt.), founded in 1905 as a railroad camp, was named for a Ute chief slain hereabouts in 1879.

West of Tabernash the highway traverses MIDDLE PARK, one of a series of high valleys stretching down the center of Colorado and walled in on all sides by high mountains. Ranching, farming, and logging are its chief enterprises. Numerous clear streams, fringed with cottonwoods, trace a weaving course across a grassy level plain. Due to the scanty knowledge of Rocky Mountain geography during the first part of the nineteenth century, this great basin, approximately 70 miles long and 30 miles wide, visited and named by General John Frémont in 1843, was never formally acquired by the United States, except that it was included in a tract formally surrendered by the Ute. The Louisiana Purchase extended only to the eastern side of the park, while the territory ceded by Spain extended only to the Park and Gore Ranges on the west. By the time this was discovered, the United States had established dominion over the area by repeated acts of sovereignty, but on August 9, 1936, at a ceremony at Breckenridge (see Tour 16), the American flag was raised by Governor Edwin C. Johnson (1933–1937), who formally claimed this "no man's land" as a part of Colorado.

GRANBY, 85.9 m. (7,935 alt., 600 pop.), in the heart of a vegetable-growing district, is noted for its mountain lettuce. Granby is in the Winter Park ski area and has motor inns and lodges for visitors. Dude ranches invite summer tourists.

At 87.4 m. is the junction with US 34.

At 89.5 m. is the junction with State 125 (see Tour 14).

HOT SULPHUR SPRINGS, 97.1 m. (7,655 alt., 250 pop.), seat of Grand County, is a resort at the mouth of Byers Canyon. According to a Ute legend, the springs acquired medicinal properties in answer to the prayers of an old chief who had been left by his tribe to die. The chief built magic fires within the springs, and after drinking the waters and bathing in them he was restored to health and rejoined his people. A ski meet, to which snow trains come from Denver, is held here annually in February.

The route traverses BYERS CANYON, hemmed in by orange sandstone cliffs, to KREMMLING, 114.5 m. (7,364 alt., 850 pop.), market center of the western part of Middle Park and the rich valleys of the Troublesome and Muddy Creeks, an area producing hay and vegetables. Even after the advent of the railroad in 1905, letters for the settlement were often addressed, "118 miles west of Denver."

Kremmling is at the junction with State 9.

At 121.5 *m.* is the junction with State 84.

Left on this graded road, an alternate route to Steamboat Springs when US 40 is closed by snow, to the eastern boundary of Routt National Forest (*see below*), 6.6 *m.* The highway, climbing GORE PASS (9,000 alt.), 10 *m.,* named for Sir George Gore (*see Tour 7B*), descends into the Yampa Valley, which is largely dependent upon agriculture, ranching, and coal mining.

In TOPONAS, 26 *m.* (8,246 alt.), a lumber- and lettuce-shipping point on the Moffat Road, is the junction with State 131, which the route follows north, passing FINGER ROCK, 33.8 *m.,* a rugged gray shaft, volcanic in origin, which stands apart from the surrounding hills—a solitary spire rising 300 feet above the valley floor.

YAMPA, 36.1 *m.* (7,884 alt.), the center of a section of the valley known as Egeria Park, is surrounded by rich bottom lands extensively irrigated. At 39.6 *m.* is a natural gateway between red granite cliffs stained with lichens and dotted with trees growing in crevices high up on the walls.

OAK CREEK, 46 *m.* (7,401 alt.), in good farming and dairying country, is largely supported by coal mining. North of the town, and virtually a part of it, are three coal camps: OAK HILLS, 46.5 *m.;* ROUTT, 47.8 *m.;* and HAYBRO, 49.1 *m.* The mines near Oak Creek produce high-grade bituminous and normally employ about 1,200 men.

At 62.7 *m.* is the western junction with US 40.

US 40 passes through sage-covered hills to the foot of Rabbit Ears Range and crosses the Continental Divide at MUDDY PASS (8,772 alt.), 142.4 *m.,* which is at the junction with State 14 (*see Tour 2*). For a few miles the route traverses the eastern slope in a high corner of North Park. The pass marks the eastern boundary of ROUTT NATIONAL FOREST, which occupies both slopes of the Continental Divide and contains 1,144,813 acres; approximately 50 per cent of the timber is lodgepole pine. The road recrosses to the western slope of the Divide by way of RABBIT EARS PASS, 146.9 *m.* (9,680 alt.), named for the peculiar formation at the top of RABBIT EARS PEAK (10,-719 alt.), and descends into Yampa Valley, crossing the western boundary of Routt National Forest, 159.2 *m.*

At 165.5 *m.* is the junction with State 131 (*see above*).

STEAMBOAT SPRINGS, 169.9 *m.* (6,695 alt. 2,200 pop.), seat of Routt County, founded by James H. Crawford who homesteaded the site in 1875, is the center of a popular year-round recreation area. Within and adjacent to the town are 150 medicinal springs with the combined flow of 2,000 gallons a minute, their temperature varying from 58 to 152 degrees. The majority are public, but some have been privately developed with bathhouses and swimming pools. The spring for which the town was named, a fountain which emitted a chugging sound suggestive of a river boat, was destroyed during the construction of the Moffat Road.

Steamboat Springs is one of the most popular ski resorts in Colorado. Many world records for ski jumping have been set on the Graham Jump, 90-meters. Mt. Werner, formerly Storm Mountain, 3 *m.* east, has excellent facilities. The annual Winter Carnival (February) has been well-known for its competing events for more than fifty years. Mt. Werner ski school gives professional instruction.

The PERRY MANSFIELD THEATRE FESTIVAL is held in July and August at the Julie Harris Theatre of Perry Mansfield Camp for Girls in Strawberry Park. The TREAD OF THE PIONEERS MUSEUM exhibits Colorado memorabilia (*Memorial Day to Labor Day, 1–9 p.m.*). YAMPA VALLEY COLLEGE is a private four-year liberal arts college.

The country around Steamboat Springs contains many lakes and trout streams, camping grounds, and points of interest reached by foot and bridle trails. Grouse, ducks, and sage hens are plentiful; in the higher wilder sections big game is hunted in season. West of Steamboat Springs, US 40 follows the valley of the Yampa River across level bottom lands, to a junction with State 129, 171.9 *m.*

Right on this road through forested hill country, lying between the Elkhead Range (L) and the massive barrier of the Continental Divide (R), to the HAHNS PEAK COUNTRY, one of the best hunting and fishing areas in the State. Deer, elk, and sage hens are numerous; streams and lakes are well stocked with mountain and rainbow trout.

CLARK, 17.5 *m.* (7,872 alt.), is dependent upon a single mine producing gold silver, and copper.

In HAHNS PEAK, 24.5 *m.* (8,200 alt.), at the foot of the mountain of the same name (10,824 alt.), placer gold was discovered by a wandering prospector in 1864. Two years later Joseph Hahn with a party of 40 men arrived from the central Colorado fields to prospect. Hahn perished in a storm while attempting to cross the Gore Range that winter, and several years passed before mining was resumed. By 1879 Hahns Peak was the chief town of the region and the seat of Routt County. In those days lawyers traveled from Steamboat Springs and other towns on snowshoes when court was in winter session here. In 1912 diminishing returns from the mines led to a decline, and the county seat was removed to Steamboat Springs. Some mining is still carried on, but the town is chiefly supported by hunters and fishermen.

The road crosses a boundary of Routt National Forest, 26.2 *m.*, to COLUMBINE, 29 *m.* (8,892 alt.), a former mining camp, and continues through the forest to its northwest boundary, 36.4 *m.*

At 50 *m.* State 129 crosses the Wyoming Line, 79 miles s.e. of Creston, Wyo.

The highway parallels the Yampa River to the confluence of TOW CREEK, 183.8 *m.* Oil wells, producing about 86,000 barrels annually, have been drilled in the wide valley.

West of BEAR RIVER, 186.4 *m.* (6,413 alt.), a coal-mining town, the road traverses barren country to MOUNT HARRIS, 188.1 *m.* (6,327 alt., 265 pop.), largest of the Yampa Valley coal towns, with the buildings of one coal company painted gray and those of its rival a vivid yellow.

HAYDEN, 194.9 *m.* (6,350 alt., 900 pop.), a shipping point for sheep grazed in Routt National Forest, was established as a trading post in 1874 and became the seat of Routt County in 1878. When the town was threatened with an Indian raid the next year, the records were removed to Hahns Peak.

Much of the country around Hayden was homesteaded in the early 1900's; newcomers worked from sunup to dark, grubbing the soil and fighting gophers, groundhogs, rabbits, and porcupines. When the harvest was in, a pioneer celebration was held in one of the larger towns, which was decorated for the occasion. A novelty race in the afternoon attracted the most attention; men raced their horses to the end of the track, jumped off, and opened the bundles they carried, which contained discarded odds and ends of feminine clothing; each man donned whatever garment fell to his lot—corset, nightgown, underskirt, or bloomers—and raced back to the starting point.

Section c. CRAIG to UTAH LINE, 92.5 m. US 40

CRAIG, 212 m. (6,185 alt., 3,984 pop. 1960, 5,000 est., 1968) at a junction with State 789 and 13, is the seat of Moffat County and a major shipping point served by the Denver & Rio Grande Western, Continental Trailways and Wilderness Transit Co. It became a home-rule city in 1966. It profits from cattle and sheep raising in the county and annually ships 3,500,000 lbs. of wool. It planes lumber and processes gilsonite, an asphaltic product used in insulating. In contiguous areas are large deposits of bituminous coal, oil, natural gas, uranium and shale; the first oil well was found 15 m. S. of Craig in 1924. The Juniper water project is to be developed on the Yampa River 20 m. west. There is a Craig-Moffat airport for light planes, which also supplies aerial spraying and charter service. The CRAIG-MOFFAT LIBRARY, a joint city and county enterprise, enlarged its quarters in 1966. Craig is a focal point for big game hunting (deer, elk, bear, also grouse, partridge, wild turkey), fishing, hiking and skiing; it puts on a weekly rodeo and the annual Ride 'n Tie Rodeo in the fall. Its daily newspaper is the *Northwest Colorado Press;* there are two weeklies, the *Empire Courier* and the *Yampa Valley Flashes.* The temperature is moderately warm, with a mean annual mark of 59° and mean annual precipitation 13.42 in. An exceptional extreme was −45° in January, 1963.

Agriculture and livestock were long leaders in income in Moffat County, but today mineral production (oil, natural gas, coal) exceed the former by more than $1,000,000 in value annually. The second-largest county, it had an estimated 8,100 people in 1965, a little more than 1.5 persons per sq. mi.

LAY, 19 m., at Big Gulch and Lay Creek, a Federal camp in 1880, is a small supply point. At 23.7 m. a road leads to Juniper Springs at the base of Juniper Mountain. MAYBELL, 31 m., is at the confluence of Deception and Spring Creeks. A few miles west State 318 joins US 40 *(see Tour 7C).* At 52 m. is ELK SPRINGS; at 70 m. BLUE MOUNTAIN. These small settlements supply their areas.

At 85 m., two miles east of the town of DINOSAUR, the National Park Service has its hq for DINOSAUR NATIONAL MONUMENT. Here visitors get permits for fishing and camping; no hunting.

There is a fossil exhibit and an audio-visual program describing the wilderness beyond. A road leads north over Blue Mountain Plateau into the park.

Dinosaur National Monument is a huge wilderness in northwest Colorado that is increasingly visited for recreation and archaeological study. It was set aside October 4, 1915, and has since been enlarged to approx. 326 sq. mi., with 146,833 acres in Colorado and 47,988 in Utah. Its greatest attractions are the rock formations holding the fossil remains of dinosaurs and other prehistoric creatures, but impressive also are the tumbling waters in dark canyons, and the opportunities for camping in an unbroken wilderness. While the canyon of Green River and the cascades of Lodore are in Colorado, the Quarry, where dinosaur bones are removed in full sight of visitors, is in Utah, and may be reached by continuing across the Utah line on US 40. A road that moves to the park from Elk Springs parallels the Yampa River to its confluence with Green River. This is the area of Echo Park, 5,080 ft. elevation; Harpers Corner, 7,528 ft. and the famous Steamboat Rock, 6,066 ft. (*see Tour 7C*).

Fishing for catfish, squawfish, rainbow and brown trout is popular, but both Colorado and Utah require licenses. Hunting is not allowed, and deer, bobcats, coyotes, and lesser animals thrive. Boating is great sport but requires a permit from the Park Superintendent, or a guide. Nature trails are available for hikers, and naturalists give illustrated talks at camps during the summer. Red Rock, Plug Hat, and Harpers Corner are recommended for nature trails. Roads into the canyon country off US 40 are blocked by snow from October 15 to May 15.

State 64, from Meeker and Rangely, joins US 40 at Dinosaur. Vernal, Utah, is 31 *m.* west on State 64. Visitors wishing to proceed direct to the Quarry Visitor Center follow US 40 to Jensen, Utah, and turn north on Utah 149. This part of the Monument is open all year.

Tour 7A

To Golden and Lookout Mountain—Junction US 40; 11.5 *m.*, State 58.

The Golden Road branches west from US 40, 0 *m.* 10.1 miles west of Denver.

West of the junction the route passes through CAMP GEORGE WEST, where the Colorado National Guard holds annual June encampments. The AMPHITHEATER, built against the hillside seats 2,500. The Camp has 102 structures and occupies 675 acres.

Denver, the Capital City

Colorado Visitors Bureau

DENVER CITY AND COUNTY BUILDING, CIVIC CENTER

THE HEART OF DENVER. STATE CAPITOL IN FOREGROUND,

FLANKED BY STATE OFFICE BUILDINGS, FACING THE CIVIC CENTER

BRONCO BUSTER, BY GEORGE RIDINGS, SR., AT CIVIC
CENTER BELOW THE CAPITOL

THE DENVER HILTON

HYATT HOUSE HOTEL

BROOKS TOWER AND FEDERAL RESERVE BANK

IN LARIMER SQUARE, OLD DENVER RESTORED

University of Denver

BOETTCHER CENTER FOR SCIENCE, ENGINEERING AND RESEARCH

LAW CENTER ADJOINING CITY AND COUNTY BUILDING

THE FIRST DENVER MINT

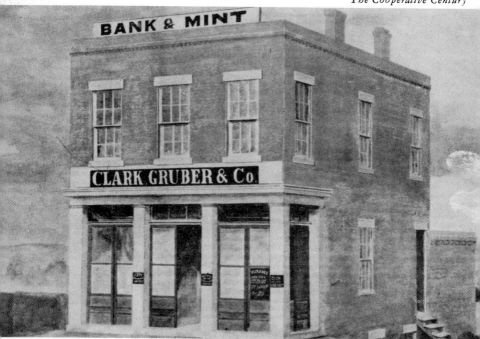

The highway skirts the southern edge of (R) SOUTH TABLE MOUNTAIN (6,215 alt.), 0.7 *m.*, a mesa rising 400 feet. Stone quarried on it was used in building Camp George West, and for rip-rapping the channel of the South Platte River in Denver. Beyond, to the north, is the twin mass of NORTH TABLE MOUNTAIN (6,500 alt.). These small basaltic plateaus, divided by the valley of Clear Creek, were created by volcanic eruptions.

LOOKOUT MOUNTAIN SCHOOL FOR BOYS, 2.1 *m.*, founded 1881, a State institution, receives boys aged 10 to 18 from the juvenile and county courts. More than 350 are usually enrolled. Not all boys are law-breakers, and psychiatric help is emphasized. The school operates a farm; its products are used by this school and the Mount View School for Girls near Morrison.

GOLDEN, 2.5 *m.* (5,675 alt., 8,656 pop. 1967, est.) seat of Jefferson County, is 15 *m.* from the center of Denver and statistically a part of the Denver Metropolitan Area, which counts 205,000 pop. in the county. Since 1957 it has added 2,000 acres. It is served by US 6 and 40 and State 58 and 93.

Founded in 1859 by the Boston Company and named for Tom Golden, an early miner, the town soon supplanted Arapahoe Bar, a placer camp farther east on Clear Creek. Because of its proximity to the mountain mining camps, it rivaled Denver for several years as the chief settlement of the Territory. The legislature of the Provisional Territory of Jefferson met here in the winter of 1860, and in 1862 the town was named the capital of Colorado Territory, remaining so until 1867 when Denver was made the permanent seat of government. Golden's distinction was more or less an empty one, for officials insisted upon transacting their business in Denver. Governor Alexander Cummings, however, loaded his executive records into a wagon and brought them to Golden in 1866, but remained only a month. The Fifth and Sixth Legislatures of the Territory held their meetings in what is now the Mercantile Grocery, Washington Ave. and 12th St.

The gold-capped cupola of GUGGENHEIM HALL, at 15th and Illinois Sts., has been a famous landmark since 1905. It is the administration building of the COLORADO SCHOOL OF MINES and is flanked by numerous modern buildings of recent construction. Mines, as it is familiarly called, is considered the country's foremost university of earth sciences, with many leading mining engineers among its alumni. It has approx. 1,500 students and a faculty of 156.

In 1869 Bishop George M. Randall of the Episcopal Church of Colorado started Jarvis Hall with help from the Territorial Legislature in order to provide technical training in mining. It was located on the present grounds of the LOOKOUT MOUNTAIN SCHOOL FOR BOYS. In 1874 it became the State School, supported by taxation and managed by a board of five trustees appointed by the Governor. Its extensive laboratory and field facilities cover all categories of geological, geophysical, metallurgical, mining, petroleum and chemical, and petroleum-refining engineering. The School operates its own experimental mine at Idaho Springs.

ALDERSON HALL, opened 1953, contains the Chemical and Petroleum-Refining and the Petroleum Engineering Laboratories. The Petroleum Engineering Field Camp is located near Rangely. BERTHOUD HALL, 1940, in Italian Renaissance style, houses the departments of geology and geophysics, and the GEOLOGY MUSEUM. The Well-Sample Library, in Berthoud Hall, contains samples from approx. 2,000 wells in the western states, one-fourth in Colorado.

In 1961 the Colorado School of Mines Foundation, Inc., built the CECIL H. GREEN GEOPHYSICAL LABORATORY at Bergen Park. It has a number of seismographs and other sensitive instruments, some located in Denver. COOLBAUGH HALL contains chemical and research laboratories. CHAUVENET HALL houses mining and basic engineering. NATHANIEL P. HILL HALL, metallurgy, was opened in 1958. PAUL MEYER HALL accommodates the physics department.

A new COLLEGE UNION, with a cafeteria seating 500, was completed in 1964, and a new tri-level GYMNASIUM in 1959. It is connected with STEINHAUER FIELD House. BROOKS FIELD, west of 12th St., seats 5,500. Two new dormitories were built in 1967, making four on the campus. Married students are accommodated in the new 75-unit Prospector Village.

The ARTHUR LAKES LIBRARY, built 1954, has more than 126,000 volumes of highly specialized works, approx. 49,000 geological and topographical maps, and receives world-wide technical publications. The Research Foundation, founded 1949, does research for industrial and government sponsors. In 1964 it obtained a lease from the U. S. Government on the Anvil Points Old Shale Research Center near Rifle. In 1966 it bought research property of the Kerr-McGee Industries, east of Golden.

Information may be obtained at the College Union, 16th and Maple Sts. Geology Museum is open 9–3:30 weekdays, 1:30–4 Sundays.

The COLORADO RAILROAD MUSEUM, 17155 West 44th Ave., at the foot of Table Mountain, furnishes substantial evidence of the State's railroading in the pioneer days of the 1880's. The building is a replica of a masonry depot of the early days and contains a ticket office, telegrapher's instruments and other objects associated with railroading. On the grounds are locomotives and rolling stock of the narrow gauge and standard gauge lines, including the State's oldest extent locomotive, a Denver & Rio Grande Western veteran of 1881, and one of the latest steamers of the Burlington. There also are trolley cars, cabooses, wooden coaches, switches, and a wooden water tower.

The MUNICIPAL BUILDING, 911 10th St., erected 1961, contains the City Hall, police and fire headquarters, the Golden Branch and main offices of the JEFFERSON COUNTY LIBRARY, and the GOLDEN MUSEUM, sponsored by the D. A. R.

The ADOLPH COORS CO. brewery, and the Coors Porcelain Co. constitute the largest industries in Golden, employing more than 2,000. The brewery was established in 1873 and is famous throughout the west (*tours daily except Sunday, 9–4*).

Right from Golden on graveled State 58, an old route to the mines of Gilpin County (*see Tour 6*), into GOLDEN GATE CANYON, 1.5 *m.* In May 1859, Albert D. Richardson, author of *Beyond the Mississippi,* traveled this route with Horace Greely and wrote, "We found Clear Creek greatly swollen, so we left our coach, saddled the mules and rode them through the stream amid a crowd of immigrants who sent up three hearty cheers for Horace Greeley. The road was swarming with travelers; in the distance they were clambering right up a hill as abrupt as the roof of a cabin. . . . This road, only five weeks old, was beaten like a turnpike; and far above toiled men, mules, and cattle. Wagons carrying less than half a ton were drawn by 20 oxen, while those descending dragged huge trees in full leaf and branch behind them, as brakes." Upon his return three weeks later Richardson was amazed to find the hill road abandoned and a newly cut thoroughfare threading the canyon.

The road leaves the canyon and ascends GUY HILL, 8 *m.*, its western slope so steep that stage coaches were once raised and lowered by means of ropes and pulleys attached to a huge tree. West of the hill the route follows Guy Gulch to the junction with a dirt road, 17.2 *m.*, known as the Dory Hill Short Cut.

Left on this road 8.5 *m.*, to BLACKHAWK (*see Tour 6*).

At 17.6 *m.* on State 58 is the junction with a dirt road.

Left here 4 *m.* to DORY HILL CEMETERY, with graves of many early settlers of Blackhawk and Central City.

At 18.1 *m.* is the junction with State 119 (*see Tour 6*), 6.2 miles north of Blackhawk.

South of Golden, 4 *m.,* State 58 passes through ornamental FINLAY L. MacFARLAND MEMORIAL GATEWAY, supported by salmon-colored sandstone towers. MacFarland was a leader in the development of the Denver Mountain Park System (*see Tour 15A*). The road begins the ascent of LOOKOUT MOUNTAIN along a series of hairpin curves; the grade is fairly easy and the roadway wide. Golden and Clear Creek Canyon, with its thread of water, drop away far below; Denver and miles of hazy blue-and-silver plains appear to the east; at night this great expanse sparkles with electric lights.

At the crest of Lookout Mountain, 9.3 *m.,* is the junction with a short circular drive. Right on this drive to the GRAVE OF BUFFALO BILL (William F. Cody), 0.2 *m.,* on the highest point of the mountain (7,375 alt.). The body rests under a concrete slab inclosed within an iron railing. Visitors toss coins into the inclosure for luck, the money being used for maintenance of PAHASKA TEPEE, a rustic lodge built on the drive just below the grave. The lodge houses a collection of relics, including ornaments, early photographs, and clothing worn by scouts and Indians.

William Frederick Cody, hunter, Indian fighter, showman, and hero of dozens of dime novels, was born in Scott County, Iowa, on Feb. 26, 1846. Orphaned at an early age, he turned to the adventurous life of the plains. According to his niece, Helen Cody Wetmore, who with Zane Grey wrote *The Last of the Great Scouts,* Cody was a Pony Express rider through the Indian country in 1859–60 when only 13 years old. Later, he became a scout for the Army, serving in the Indian campaigns of 1867. He attracted the attention of General Phil Sheridan, who made him chief of scouts. Cody's Indian name, Pahaska, or Long Hair, was given him at this time by Pawnee scouts in the Army. The nickname Buffalo Bill, by which he was known to millions throughout the world, came from his prowess as a hunter; he is credited with having killed as many as seventy bison a day when under contract to supply meat to railroad construction gangs. Probably the most publicized of Cody's exploits was his duel with the Cheyenne Chief, Yellow Hand, during the Sioux War of 1876. The most popular of several versions of this affair has Cody slaying the chief in a hand-to-hand encounter between opposing ranks of Indians and soldiers. Tall, striking in appearance, Cody was the beau ideal of a frontiersman. In the early 1880's he capitalized on his appearance and reputation by organizing a Wild West Show, hiring cowboys, Indians, and trick riders, with whom he toured the world for 20 years. Profits from this venture he invested in lands in Nebraska and Wyoming. Subsequently he served in the Nebraska Legislature and as judge advocate general of Wyoming. At the time of his death in Denver, Jan. 10, 1917, financial reverses had wiped out his fortune.

At 11.5 *m.* is the junction with US 40 (*see Tour 7b*), 18.7 miles west of Denver.

Tour 7B

Kremmling (Junction US 40)—State Bridge—Wolcott (Junction US 24) ; 41.3 *m.*, State 11 and State 131.

A link between two arterial highways, US 40 and US 24, this route is little used by Coloradoans. The highway is narrow, with many steep grades, and is often closed by winter snows.

In KREMMLING, 0 *m.* (7,364 alt., 850 pop.) (*see Tour 7b*), State 11 branches southwest from US 40 (*see Tour 7b*) and crosses the Colorado River.

The highway crosses the BLUE RIVER, 3.2 *m.,* near its junction with the Colorado, and ascends by many curves and sharp turns into rough and rugged mountain terrain, sharply contrasted with the green and pleasant lowlands of Middle Park seen in broad and sweeping panorama to the north. Higher in the mountains, hay and small grains are raised in many small valleys. The up-and-down road winds into a narrow valley and again ascends, swinging out on a narrow shelf of rock, twisting around the face of cliffs, affording a constantly changing view. At intervals, high ridges wall in the route; masses of somber spruce and jade aspen, brilliantly colored ledges, and tumbled metallic-hued boulder slides form a pattern vivid as a Persian mosaic. Far below, the glittering serpentine Colorado River traces its course through tiny parks and meadows, which resemble patches of bright green moss. The Denver & Rio Grande Western R. R. follows the course of the river between Kremmling and State Bridge (*see below*) by way of the Dotsero Cutoff (*see Tour 7b*). To the north are the high flat-topped mountains of the "bad lands"; to the south and southeast the Gore Mountains lift their dark and jagged outline against the sky.

South of this shelf rock another abrupt descent necessitates careful driving. The highway skirts a forest of twisted scrub cedar and proceeds into Sheep Horn Valley. Following the contour of the mountains at river level, a comparatively straight course, the road ascends a steep and dangerous grade, too narrow in places for cars to pass, and descends gradually through an amazingly colorful region to STATE BRIDGE, 28.1 *m.* (6,728 alt.) at the northern foot of Rainbow Mountain, named for its many-hued rock formations. Here State 11 joins State 131, which comes in from the north.

Ranching is the chief occupation of this region. As late as 1915 it was the scene of an almost continuous struggle between cattlemen, who first settled here, and sheepmen who later drove in their flocks. The ill feeling finally subsided, and stockmen now live at peace.

The GORE MOUNTAINS (L) were named for the Irish baronet, Sir George Gore, who visited Colorado in 1855. His hunting party, one of the largest ever to roam the early West, included 40 retainers, 14 dogs, 112 horses, 6 wagons, 21 carts, and 12 yoke of oxen. Gore hunted through North, Middle, and South Parks before turning northward into Wyoming and Montana; the party is reported to have killed some 3,000 buffalo, 40 grizzly bear, and unnumbered antelope and deer. The slaughter was so great and so wanton that the Indians, fearing for their food supply, thought seriously of slaughtering this Celtic Nimrod and his play-boy followers. Many stories are told of Gore's irascible temper. On one occasion he attempted to ship out some hides, but the American Fur Co., which controlled transportation to the Missouri River, demanded what he thought was an exorbitant carrying charge. In a rage Gore burned all the hides, and then his wagons, dumping the remaining iron work into a river.

Some pioneers of the West maintained that gold was first discovered in Colorado by a member of that party. When Gore saw the gold, he exclaimed, "This is gold, but I did not come here to seek gold! I don't need it. This is a pleasure hunt." Fearing the gold might cause his men to desert, he broke camp immediately. The man who had found the gold was unable to locate the spot again.

South of State Bridge the road ascends from the Colorado River Valley over a steep grade gouged out of solid shelf rock. WHISKY SPRINGS (L), an old landmark, was named for the many bottles left at the water hole by trappers, hunters, and stagecoach passengers. It is a matter of record that many travelers insisted that they needed several bottles of stimulant before proceeding farther along this hazardous road.

The highway reaches the top of a low divide, 35 *m.,* and descends into the valley of the Eagle River through arid hills covered with sage-brush. There are few trees here, and the prospect is monotonous and uninteresting compared with the rough wild beauty of the northern section of the drive.

At 39 *m.* is the junction with an unimproved road.

Left on this road to TRACY'S HIDEOUT, 3.5 *m.,* an old ranch house reputed to have once sheltered a notorious gunman who finally met his death in a gun fight in Wyoming. An almost-perfectly preserved fossil of the head of a prehistoric three-toed horse, found near the ranch house in 1934, is in the Museum of Natural History at Denver (*see Denver*).

WOLCOTT, 41.3 *m.* (6,965 alt.), is at the junction with US 24 (*see Tour 5c*).

❧❧❧❧❧❧❧❧❧❧❧❧❧❧❧❧❧❧❧❧❧❧❧❧❧❧❧❧❧❧

Tour 7C

Junction US 40—Sunbeam—Greystone—Lodore Canyon Camp; 58.7 *m.,* State 318.

This tour traverses a far northwestern corner of Colorado to Yampa Canyon of the Yampa River and Lodore Canyon of the Green, two of America's great river gorges. Although remote from good highways and little known except to explorers, parts of both canyons are accessible by motor and pack train, provided the visitor is accustomed to roughing it and is properly equipped. The canyons are within the Dinosaur National Monument, the extent of which is described under *Tour 7c.*

State 318 branches northwest from US 40, 0 *m.,* 74.5 miles west of Craig.

Northwest of SUNBEAM, 7.3 *m.* (6,000 alt.), the route traverses rolling mountain country covered with sage and rent by deep dry gullies, crossing LITTLE SNAKE RIVER, 21.3 *m.,* a tributary of the Yampa. Near the Wyoming Line, headwaters of this stream, Jim Baker, early western scout, once had his cabin.

At 39.9 *m.* is the junction with a dirt road.

Left on this road (*high centers*) to FIVE SPRINGS RANCH, 13 *m.* The houses and barns of peeled cedar logs are sheltered in a hollow near the crest of DOUGLAS MOUNTAIN, also known as the Escalante Hills, a sandstone ridge marking the eastern extension of the Uinta Mountains of Utah.

Left from Five Springs Ranch by an unmarked horse trail to WARM SPRINGS DRAW, 7 *m.* (*do not attempt without guides*). Here in YAMPA

CANYON, part of the Douglas State Game Refuge, deer and elk are numerous and tame; bear and mountain lion are occasionally seen. Unlike gloomy Lodore Canyon (*see below*), Yampa Canyon is gay and sunny throughout most of its length, the light bringing out its vivid coloring. The canyon is U-shaped, with imposing walls 1,000 to 1,600 feet high, almost vertical, and with few ledges and practically no vegetation. To the south a series of broad benches rise to the Yampa Plateau; to the north is Douglas Mountain. Bones, corn grinders, awls, and other artifacts, found in the canyon lead archeologists to believe the country was once inhabited by a Pueblo people.

Right from Warm Springs Draw down the canyon to PAT'S HOLE, 14 *m.*, at the confluence of the Yampa and Green Rivers; here the canyon suddenly broadens into a rectangular mile-square area, surrounded by high unbroken walls except where the rivers and Pool Creek enter. At the exit of the Green River at the western side of the Hole rises the great sandstone mass known as STEAMBOAT ROCK, the sheer face of which has never been scaled. The sides of Steamboat Rock and the walls encircling Pat's Hole provide excellent sounding boards; in certain places four distinct echoes can be heard. First named Echo Park by Major John Wesley Powell (*see below*), who descended the Green River in 1869, its present name honors Pat Lynch, who lived here hermit-like for years before others settled in the vicinity. Lynch had a pet mountain lion named Jenny Lind. Though no one ever saw the animal, Pat frequently demonstrated her presence to visitors by shouting "Jenny" at a rock and being answered with a roar. After the reverberations had ceased, Pat always remarked, "Jenny Lind never sang a sweeter note." The floor of Pat's Hole is covered with cedar, grass, and sagebrush, tall as a man on horseback. The grass here often remains green until January.

Right from Pat's Hole up Lodore Canyon (*see below*) to the lower end of HELL'S HALF MILE, 5 *m.*, a stretch of rapids where the Green River churns its way among huge boulders. Horses must be used, for the river is forded ten times, and the rapids are too swift and treacherous for a man on foot. Those wishing to see more of Hell's Half Mile must proceed on foot along the narrow ledges high on the canyon walls (*difficult and not recommended; upper Lodore Canyon is not accessible from the eastern or Douglas Mountain rim*).

GREYSTONE, 40.9 *m.* (6,500 alt.), consists of a general store and post office, with gasoline, food supplies, and limited overnight accommodations.

Northwest of Greystone the narrow rough dirt road, impassable in wet weather, winds through hilly country, crossing the eastern boundary of DINOSAUR NATIONAL MONUMENT, 57.6 *m.*, originally created in northeastern Utah in 1915 but enlarged by presidential proclamation ·in 1938 to include 47,988 acres in Utah and 146,833 in Colorado. The rich fossil beds throughout the monument are of the greatest scientific interest. *See Tour 7 for description.*

LODORE CANYON CAMP, 58.7 *m.* is situated near a spring on the eastern side of the Green River at the mouth of Lodore Canyon. The canyon begins at the eastern end of BROWN'S PARK, also know as Brown's Hole, an almost level valley 30 miles long and 5 miles wide, lying in both Colorado and Utah. Known to white men for a century, the park became a rendezvous for the Mountain Men about 1830, when Baptiste Brown, a French-Canadian fur trader, settled here. A one-story trading post of mud and cottonwood logs, named Fort Davy Crockett, was built in 1837 by Philip Thompson and William Craig on the north bank of the Green River above the mouth of the canyon. This post never prospered, and was known among the trappers as Fort Misery. When Dr. F. A. Wislizenus of Germany, author of *A Journey to the Rocky Mountains in 1839,* visited the post, he found its hungry inhabitants contentedly eating a lean dog they had purchased the day before. Wislizenus found the dog meat was not so bad. Fort Davy Crockett was abandoned about 1840, and the Mountain Men and their Indian squaws departed.

A frontier atmosphere still pervades the park. Many ranches are scattered along its length, but it is too barren and remote from markets to attract settlers. For this reason it was once a favorite haunt of outlaws, the best known of whom was Butch Cassidy (George LeRoy Parker), leader of the Wild Bunch. A stocky good-natured man with a hearty smile, Cassidy grew up much as any young Utah cowboy of the 1880's; by the time he crossed into Wyoming in 1889, he had done some cattle rustling; knew the secret places of the Uncompahgre and of Brown's Park, and the trails along the "high lines" that commanded a view of the country across which "the law" must ride.

Cassidy was arrested in Wyoming for stealing horses in the spring of 1894, but received a pardon two years later upon his promise "not to worry Wyoming." He was too honest to promise to reform entirely, but he kept his word in this matter. Thereafter the tousled-haired cowboy, whom few men could help but like went from bad to worse. He became an outlaw, together with Logan, Harney, Lovie, Longabough, Curry, and Camella Hanks, and was their acknowledged leader. Among other crimes, he is said to have participated in the robbery of a bank at Montpelier, Idaho, where several thousands of dollars were taken; a payroll robbery in broad daylight at Castlegate, Utah; the robbery of a train at Wagner, Mont., where the loot amounted to more than $100,000 in unsigned currency; and the robbery of a bank at Winnemucca, Nev., of more than $20,000.

Soon after the beginning of the century the Wild Bunch was broken up, and Cassidy was forced to flee the country, along with Longabough. According to reports, the two men died in 1904, near the Argentine-Chile border when surrounded by Chilean soldiers who suspected them of cattle rustling. Longabough was killed; Cassidy fought alone through the night and finally put a bullet through his head. The soldiers shot in this encounter are said to have been the only men he ever killed.

Left from the camp is a three-mile boat trip through the upper part of LODORE CANYON. The voyage stops short of Disaster Falls, which, with Triplet Falls and Hell's Half Mile (*see above*), are the most dangerous rapids. The 17-mile gorge begins a short distance below the mouth of Vermillion Creek and terminates at the confluence of the Green and Yampa Rivers. Within this distance the river drops an average of 15 feet a mile. The northern approach to the canyon, where the Green River eats its way into and through a spur of the Uinta Mountains, is spectacular in the extreme. Visible for miles, the great red sandstone cliffs at the canyon entrance rise a sheer 2,000 feet and were named the Gate of Lodore by Major John Wesley Powell, who on his many geological surveys in the West twice "shot" the gorge, in 1869 and 1871. He took the name from Southey's poem "How the Waters

Come Down at Lodore," which he was fond of reciting as he journeyed down the river. Disaster Falls, as most physical features of the canyon, was named by him when one of his boats, the *No-Name,* was wrecked there on his first voyage.

The canyon cuts directly through the Uinta Range, one of the few ranges in the United States that run in an east-west direction. Pointing out that the normal course of the river would be around the mountains, Powell explained that "the river had the right of way. In other words, it was running ere the mountains were formed; not before the rock of which the mountains are composed were deposited, but before the formations were folded, so as to make a mountain range." Powell believed that the fold or ridge rose slowly, permitting the river to keep its original channel and cut it in two.

Within the gate Lodore Canyon is wild and impressive with its dark red cedar-studded cliffs rising far overhead. Of this first section General William Henry Ashley wrote in 1825: "As we passed along between these massive walls, which in a great degree excluded from us the rays of heaven and presented a surface as impassible as their body was impregnable, I was forcibly struck with the gloom which spread over the countenances of my men; they seemed to anticipate a dreadful termination of our voyage." Ashley, a former lieutenant-governor of Missouri, became known as General Ashley on his second fur trading expedition west from St. Louis in 1823, when he joined soldiers in quelling a war party of Indians. While on his third expedition in 1824–25, he painted his name on a huge rock on the eastern wall of the canyon here near a 10-foot cascade, now known as Ashley Falls; the lettering was discernible as late as 1911.

The next authenticated shooting of the rapids was by William L. Manley, who, with six companions, grew tired of the dusty Overland Trail to California during the gold rush of '49 and set out down the river in an old flat-bottomed boat. Their venture came to grief at Ashley Falls, but the men hewed two canoes from logs and reached the Uinta Basin in safety. Here they were persuaded by friendly Indians to give up the perilous river trip and resume their overland march.

Perhaps the most notable shooting of the rapids was the single-handed exploit of Haldane (Buzz) Holmstrom in October 1937, when he safely navigated a home-made boat down the Green and Colorado Rivers from Green River, Wyo., to Lake Mead, at Hoover Dam, in the far corner of Nevada and Arizona.

❧❧❧❧❧❧❧❧❧❧❧❧❧❧❧❧❧❧❧❧❧❧❧❧❧❧❧❧❧❧❧

Tour 8

(Tribune, Kans.)—Eads—Ordway—Pueblo—Westcliffe; State 96. Kansas Line to Westcliffe, 214.2 *m.*

In its approach to industrial Pueblo, Colorado's second largest city, State 96 crosses a plains region. West of Pueblo the highway traverses an irrigated belt along the Arkansas River, ascends the foothills, and threads its way through a series of canyons into the Wet Mountain Valley country.

Section a.   *KANSAS LINE to PUEBLO; 157.2 m. State 96*

The semiarid plains of southeastern Colorado once were the grazing lands of the buffalo and the hunting grounds of Cheyenne, Arapaho, Kiowa, and Comanche Indians. Droves of longhorn cattle, driven north from Texas, supplanted the buffalo, and between the 1860's and 1890's the open range was held by a few large ranch owners. Construction of the Missouri Pacific R. R. opened the country to homesteaders, and a number of small towns, named in alphabetical order, sprang up along the tracks.

State 96 crosses the Kansas Line, 0 *m.*, 18 miles west of Tribune, Kans.

TOWNER, 2 *m.* (3,923 alt.), is a village in the dry farming area. South of Towner, in March 1931, a rural school bus was caught in a spring blizzard. The driver left his 22 charges in the bus and set out afoot to bring aid. He perished in a field a few miles away. Five of the children died from exposure. Others would probably have met a similar fate had it not been for Bryan Unteidt, one of the pupils, who compelled the others to exercise and play games and thus keep warm. In recognition of his heroism Bryan was invited to the White House by President Hoover and publicly honored.

SHERIDAN LAKE, 13.8 *m.* (4,080 alt.), a farm community, has a junction with US 385 and State 51, north-south. Near BRANDON, 20 *m.*, is CHIVINGTON RESERVOIR.

Beyond SAND CREEK, 26.2 *m.*, a small stream that in 1864 was the southern boundary of the territory then held by the Plains Indians, is CHIVINGTON, 27.9 *m.* (3,890 alt.), named for Colonel John Chivington who commanded at the Sand Creek Massacre.

Right from Chivington on a dirt road to the SITE OF THE SAND CREEK MASSACRE, 10 *m.*, perhaps the most disputed incident in Colorado's early history. The scene of the conflict in which an Indian village was virtually wiped out in a surprise attack by white soldiery, is unmarked.

When many Federal troops were withdrawn from Colorado Territory at the beginning of the Civil War, the Plains Indian tribes began to attack settlers and wagon trains. Sporadic forays continued despite the signing of a treaty with the Cheyenne and Arapaho at Fort Lyon, whereby the two tribes agreed to give up all lands east of the mountains between the Arkansas and the Platte in return for $450,000, to be paid in five yearly installments. The Federal Government's failure to fulfill the treaty obligations resulted in starvation among the Indians and precipitated trouble.

Conditions grew steadily worse—the Santa Fe Trail being closed at times to travel—until the summer of 1864, when Territorial Governor John Evans called a grand council of Indian chiefs to settle the difficulties. Black Kettle, chief of the Cheyenne, insisted that the raiding was being done by the Sioux and Comanche, together with a few irresponsible members of his own tribe, and asserted that there was no offensive alliance between his people and the Arapaho with the "hostiles." While admitting that most of the raiding was done by the Sioux, the white leaders blamed the two tribes that had signed the peace treaty. A deadlock resulted, and Governor Evans turned matters over to the military.

Colonel John Chivington, formerly a presiding elder of the Rocky Mountain

District of the Kansas-Nebraska Methodist Conference, had shown talent as a soldier and his promotion had been rapid. Declaring that his policy always was to fight his enemies "until they are beaten and lay down their arms," he ordered all Plains tribes to report at the nearest garrison post and surrender. Governor Evans authorized the mobilization of an emergency Third Regiment, then departed for Washington to remain until the following spring.

According to Major Wynkoop, commandant at Fort Lyon, Black Kettle and his Cheyenne soon appeared to the post to surrender under Chivington's terms. Major S. G. Collery, Indian agent at the fort, and John Smith, an interpreter, supported Wynkoop in this statement. Yet Major Scott J. Anthony, a friend of Chivington, who relieved Wynkoop as post commander in the fall of 1864, swore that the Indians encamped near the fort on his arrival were not Cheyenne but Arapho. Actually, they were of both tribes, although the majority were Cheyenne. In light of the controversy that subsequently raged, much depends upon whether Chivington knew that the Indian encampment at Sand Creek was that of Black Kettle's band, or whether he believed it to be a hostile camp. Black Kettle's good faith has also been questioned by some historians who assert that he was continuously in contact with the hostiles and had merely adopted the not uncommon Indian strategy of surrendering during the cold season while preparing to take the war trail in the spring after his people had rested and gathered supplies. In any event, Major Anthony ordered the band away from the fort, saying that he could no longer feed them. He admitted that when a delegation of Cheyenne later expressed a desire to make peace he informed them that he had no authority to establish treaties and could not permit them to visit the fort.

Meanwhile the 100-day recruits of the Third Regiment in Denver became tired of camp life. They wanted action and got it when Chivington suddenly and secretly marched them south in a blizzard. On the way they were joined by Captain Wilson and 125 men of the First Colorado Cavalry. On Nov. 28, 1864, they reached Fort Lyon. Chivington threw a cordon around the post so that word of their arrival would not leak out. Anthony told Chivington that in a village on Sand Creek were a number of lodges of hostile Arapho.

His force augmented by 125 more First Colorado Cavalrymen and a howitzer battery, bringing the total number of soldiers to 750, Chivington marched north that same evening, and at dawn his troops closed in upon the sleeping village and opened fire. Chivington had given orders that no prisoners were to be taken, and his orders were obeyed. Smith, the interpreter, who was in the camp at the time, later testified that of the 650 Indians in the encampment, 450 were women and children. The exact number of Indians killed has never been determined, estimates ranging from 150 to 500, but their losses were unquestionably heavy. The majority of the victims were old men, women, and children, who were shot down indiscriminately. Black Kettle escaped, but his brother chief, White Antelope, was killed. Left Hand, a head chief of the Arapaho, was slain in front of his tent as he stood with folded arms defying his foes. By midafternoon the troopers had broken all resistance and that night burned the village.

The Sand Creek Massacre aroused such a country-wide storm that a Senatorial investigation resulted in January 1865. Chivington was cited for court martial but was never brought to trial. Testimony before the committee brought out that the bodies of slain Indians, women and men alike, had been horribly mutilated by the soldiers. Lieutenant Cramer of the First Colorado Cavalry stated, "The slaughter was continuous; no Indian, old or young, male or female, was spared." Some soldiers declared that fresh white scalps were found hanging in the Indian lodges, indicating that the braves had been on the warpath, but if this were true, the scalps were burned with the village.

Chivington stated in his official report: "My reason for making the attack on the Indian camp was that I believed the Indians in the camp were hostile to the whites. I believed that they were of the same tribes as those who had murdered many persons and destroyed much valuable property on the Platte and Arkansas Rivers. . . . I had reason to believe that Black Kettle and the Indians with him were not in good faith at peace with the whites. . . . I do not know that any Indians were wounded that were not killed. It may perhaps be unnecessary to state that I captured no prisoners." Chivington added that in his opinion most of the women and children in the camp escaped.

The highway traverses prairie lands to EADS, 42 *m.* (4,262 alt., 1,050 pop.), seat of Kiowa County, named for James B. Eads, engineer, has a junction with US 287 and State 59. The town is the center of a dry farming area growing wheat, barley, and cane for forage; the Missouri Pacific Railroad maintains a stockyards here. The annual Kiowa County Seed and Poultry Fair is held in Eads during the fall.

West of Eads the route crosses a succession of desolate brown hills relieved by clumps of yucca and matted stretches of prickly pear and ball cacti. In spring the silky yellow blossoms of the prickly pear blend with the deep pink flowers embedded among the spikes of the ball cactus. The yucca, better known as Spanish bayonet or soapweed, bristles with dagger-like leaves and bears tall spikes of ivory white blossoms, often referred to as Madonna candles. From the fiber of this plant Indians made a stout rope; the roots, which produce a lather in water, were used for soap; early Spanish colonists planted the yucca around their fortifications as protection against invaders, hence its name.

TODD POINT (R), 90.5 *m.,* a large butte looming above the flat prairie, served as landmark and signal point in early cattle days.

SUGAR CITY, 99.1 *m.* (4,325 alt.), is the center of a prosperous stock raising and general farming district. The National Sugar Manufacturing Co. processes thousands of acres of sugar beets annually.

At 99.5 *m.* is the junction with a dirt road. Right on this road to LAKE HENRY, 2.5 *m.* At 100.8 *m.* is the junction with another dirt road. Left on this road to LAKE MEREDITH, 1.3 *m.*

ORDWAY, 104.5 *m.* (4,312 alt., 1,300 pop. est), is the seat of Crowley County, which is largely agricultural. Melons are an important crop. Prepared food for animals is processed in Ordway. The county's weekly newspaper, *New Era,* is published here.

CROWLEY, 111.5 *m.* (4,275 alt.), was named in 1880 for the owner of a large ranch on which wild horses were caught, broken, and shipped to England for use in the army. Western Canning Co. has a plant at Crowley. Big events are the Fourth of July Rodeo and County Day, Aug. 1, when there is livestock competition and a free barbecued dinner.

West of OLNEY SPRINGS, 116.5 *m.* (4,400 alt.), the western end of the irrigated belt, State 96 parallels US 50 (*see Tour 9a*) into Pueblo, the two roads following opposite banks of the Arkansas River.

NORTH AVONDALE, 142.6 *m.* (4,500 alt.), is populated chiefly by Italians and Slavs who supplement farm earnings by working in the Pueblo steel mills.

PUEBLO, 157.2 *m.* (4,700 alt., 103,000 pop. 1968, est.), is at the junction with US 50 (*see Tour 9*) and US 85 (*see Tour 12*).

Section b. PUEBLO to WESTCLIFFE; 57 m. State 96

Along this section of the route are reminders of the old Texas cattle trails, the Mormons' trek to their promised land, and the explorations of Lieutenant Pike and Kit Carson. From barren prairies the highway penetrates forest growth that cloaks the mountains. Here and there are crumbling ghost towns that knew a glamorous past. Many generations of Spanish and German farmers have wrested a living from the fertile lands of the Wet Mountains.

West of PUEBLO, 0 *m.*, the highway passes the old GOODNIGHT RANCH (R), 2 *m.*, once owned by Colonel Charles Goodnight, noted in western annals as a cattle king and the founder of the Goodnight Trail, over which thousands of longhorns were driven from Texas to Colorado. Fields of alfalfa, oats, and other crops border the Arkansas.

The highway crosses the BESSEMER DITCH, which conveys water from the Arkansas River to the steel mills at Pueblo, and traverses rough prairie land; weathered frame and adobe farmhouses appear at intervals. Small herds of cattle graze upon the plain; the presence of artesian wells is indicated by the green fields of corn and hay as the route approaches the WET MOUNTAINS, once the hunting ground of the Ute. Crossed by Lieutenant Zebulon Pike and his company in 1806, the mountains were named by a party of Mormon immigrants (*see Pueblo*), who rejoiced to see these green and wooded slopes, with heavy rain clouds hovering above them, after their long march across the dry prairie. Curiously, both the Spanish and the Indians had so named the range in their respective tongues. The gently rolling eroded summits and the lower heights of the Greenhorn Range of the Wet Mountains, one of the oldest geologically in the State, rather more resemble the mountains of the East than of Colorado.

WETMORE, 28 *m.* (6,000 alt.), site of a stagecoach station in pioneer days, was named for pioneer rancher Billy Wetmore. Old frame buildings jostle log cabins of summer residents in this once much larger town, framed by a forest of conifers. Stock raising and farming are chief occupations of the region.

Right from Wetmore on State 67, a graded dirt road to MINERAL CREEK, 5 *m.*, which with its tributaries, Adobe and Newlin Creeks, furnish the water supply for the town of Florence (*see Tour 9b*). The OIL WELLS, 7 *m.*, are in a field developed in 1876, one of the earliest in the United States; a few of the original wells are still producing. At 9 *m.* are a number of coal mines and an old oil field, dating back to the early 1860's.

FLORENCE, 12 *m.* (5,187 alt., 3,000 pop.), is at the junction with US 50 (*see Tour 9b*).

The route follows Hardscrabble Creek, along which a band of Ute fled in 1855 after the Christmas Day Massacre at Pueblo. The Indians were pursued and later declared, so it is said, that they had a "hardscrabble" to escape. Scrub oak and willow hug the banks of the creek; fields on the steep slopes grow potatoes, lettuce, and celery.

The highway crosses the eastern boundary of SAN ISABEL NATIONAL FOREST, 30.1 *m.,* a preserve containing 1,103,837 acres of Federal land and also private, State, and municipal land.

On KIT CARSON ROCK (L), 30.3 *m.,* the famous scout carved his name and the initials of his wife, J. J. (Josefa Jaramillo). The rock is cemented and protected with iron rods. When first set up, it was stolen; the thief was threatened with lynching and the stone reappeared as mysteriously as it had vanished. This section of the road, known as the KIT CARSON TRAIL, was often used by the frontiersman in his expeditions into the mountains.

The road ascends through a narrow canyon, its steep slopes covered with white pine, fir, ponderosa pine, and blue spruce. The latter, also known as silver or Colorado spruce, the unofficial State tree, is in demand for landscape planting. Only occasional specimens show the desirable silvery bloom on the needles. Lance-leaf cottonwoods fringe the narrow creek, which cascades down in miniature falls as the ascent becomes steeper; goldenrod, larkspur, Indian paint brush, and mountain daisies bloom profusely in the meadowland. Scattered through this area are picnic grounds with benches and fireplaces. The route crosses the western boundary of San Isabel National Forest, 36.5 *m.,* to the junction with State 76 (*see Tour 8A*), 37 *m.*

CARTER FLATS (9,000 alt.), 41 *m.,* offers an impressive view of the Sangre de Cristo Range to the west.

At 42 *m.* is the junction with State 143.

Right on this narrow rough road, which follows Oak Creek through interesting farming and mining country, to ISLE, 4 *m.,* an old mining camp. At the western border of San Isabel National Forest, 12 *m.,* juniper and piñon give way to pine, spruce, and fir.

BASIN RANCH, 16 *m.,* in a mountain hollow, is a rendezvous for hunters of predatory animals; from this point is an excellent view of the Arkansas Valley and the fruit orchards in the vicinity of Florence.

The route crosses the eastern boundary of San Isabel National Forest, 17 *m.,* and descends abruptly to ROCKVALE, 19 *m.* (5,260 alt., 710 pop.), a coal-mining hamlet.

At 21 *m.* is the junction with US 50 (*see Tour 9b*), 2 miles west of Florence (*see Tour 9b*).

The highway passes through rough, barren country to the BASSICK MINE (R), 46 *m.,* once one of the richest gold and silver mines in the State, now an abandoned tunnel, marked by a deserted shack bearing the name of Mount Tyndall. The mine was discovered in 1887 by John M. True, who opened the first shaft but abandoned it as worthless. Later, E. C. Bassick sank a deeper shaft and received more than $12,000 from the first shipment of ore; the mine continued to pay large dividends; $750,000 of ore was taken out under Bassick's management; in 1889 it was sold to a New York company for $330,000. The richness of the mine encouraged development of the region and resulted in the founding of Silver Cliff, Rosita, and Querida (*see below*).

QUERIDA (Sp. sweetheart), 47 *m.,* now a ghost town, was

founded in 1887 by David Livingstone, nephew of the noted African explorer. At one time it had a population of 500, largely employed in a concentration mill and the offices of the Bassick Mining Company.

Left from Querida on a dirt road is ROSITA, 2 m., so named for the profusion of wild roses in the vicinity. Once the seat of Custer County, it is now another ghost town; the settlement was founded about 1872 and by 1875 had a population of 1,500.

State 96 traverses the weed-grown prairie of WET MOUNTAIN VALLEY. "The altitude, the climate, and the surroundings of this valley," remarked a writer in the 1870's, "are calculated to produce the highest types of human energy and intellect, and also the finest beef and butter in the known world."

SILVER CLIFF, 55 m. (8,000 alt.), once a boom silver camp, was named for the great argentiferous cliff that faces the town. The discovery of horn-silver, so termed because it is found in tinfoil-like layers between rock strata, brought the settlement into existence in 1879. Two years later, claiming a population of more than 5,000, it was the third largest city in the State and aspired to become the capital. Until a waterworks was constructed, water was hauled from a spring several miles away and delivered to consumers at 40¢ a barrel. It had a police department of five men, "handsomely uniformed"; an "efficient chain gang" conditioned the streets.

During its heyday Silver Cliff had two daily and three weekly newspapers. In the summer of 1880 the *Daily Prospect* complained that a blast from a near-by mine "threw a rock that fell with considerable force in front of the Little Chief Saloon, barely missing Harry Dougan. This sort of thing is becoming an everyday occurrence and will end with somebody being brained." The same issue carried the news that Louis Phillips, agent of the Colorado State Lottery, "will give you a chance to make your fortune for $2," and that "the Canon stage came in yesterday loaded to capacity, among its passengers being several bodies."

Silver Cliff and Rosita contended fiercely to become the seat of Custer County. Westcliffe (*see below*), then a station on the Denver & Rio Grande Railroad, supported Silver Cliff's claim. Silver Cliff won and, in appreciation of Westcliffe's support, built the county courthouse between the two towns. After the demonetization of silver in the 1890's Silver Cliff rapidly declined; today it is a town of empty buildings. The first station, housing old fire-fighting equipment, stands as it was in the last century. A church, its belfry crumbling, its pews dusty and long unoccupied, has an antiquated street lamp at its door. The OLD CUSTER COUNTY COURTHOUSE (L), 55.5 m., is abandoned.

WESTCLIFFE, 57 m. (7,800 alt.), is at the junction with State 69 (*see Tour 11B*).

K❖K❖K❖K❖K❖K❖K❖K❖K❖K❖K❖K❖K❖K❖K❖K❖K❖K❖K❖K❖K❖K❖K❖K❖K❖K❖K❖K❖

Tour 8A

Pueblo—Goodpasture—Junction State 96; 46.8 *m.*, State 76.

This route, an alternative to State 96, crosses prairie lands and enters a wooded mountain region, much of it in the eastern part of San Isabel National Forest, in which are the summer houses of many Pueblo residents.

In PUEBLO, 0 *m.* (4,700 alt., 103,000 pop. 1968, est.), State 76 branches (L) from State 96 (*see Tour 8b*) and proceeds southwest by way of Northern Avenue.

At 1.5 *m.* is the junction with a dirt road.

Right on this road to the PUEBLO MEMORIAL AIRPORT, 0.3 *m.*, where Frontier and Trans-Central Air Lines planes connect daily with Denver and other cities.

State 76 traverses rolling prairie country to BOGGS, 8.5 *m.*, lying in an uncultivated region of low monotonous hogbacks dotted with scrub cedar. On MULDOON HILL, 14 *m.*, was made the "discovery" of the Muldoon Stone Man by a certain Conant, a professed geologist. This giant figure, resembling a powerfully built man with unusually long arms and a rudimentary tail, was, according to Conant, the petrified body of a prehistoric man. P. T. Barnum, the famous showman, offered $20,000 for the find. Conant refused the offer, and the publicity resulting from the showman's interest attracted large crowds when the figure was exhibited in Pueblo. Scientists pronounced it authentic, heralding it as the missing link between man and ape, although skeptics, recalling the Cardiff Giant hoax perpetrated by Barnum 10 years before, suspected a partnership between the showman and the geologist. Nevertheless, the "Mysterious Muldoon" fascinated the public and was a money-maker until Conant and his son started East with their exhibit. There, Professor March of Yale, who had exploded the Cardiff hoax, pronounced the second giant a fraud. The promoters soon quarreled over the receipts, and one confessed that he had created the stone man and "planted" it to be "discovered" by Conant. Barnum's part in the affair was never definitely established.

At 21.2 *m.* is the junction with a dirt road.

Right on this road through sparsely settled country to a junction with another dirt road, 7 *m.*; R. here 9.5 *m.* to RED CREEK SPRINGS; in RED CREEK CANYON, 10.5 *m.*, Indian petroglyphs, chiefly animal figures, appear on the cliffs.

At 22.3 *m.* is the junction with a dirt road.

Left on this road to the THREE R RANCH, 3.5 *m.*, one of the largest in the region. In the near-by canyons branching from the St. Charles River are well-preserved Indian petroglyphs scratched on the rock walls. Some undoubtedly are prehistoric, the oldest perhaps dating from the time of the Mound Builders. Animals and reptiles are represented, as well as a scrawled design believed to be a map of the Wet Mountains. The dirt road continues to the junction with US 85 at CROW, 14 *m.* (*see Tour 12c*).

The highway descends Rock Creek Hill and crosses the foothills to GOODPASTURE, 23 *m.* Descending Beulah Hill, the route skirts MOUNT SIGNAL (L), 23.3 *m.*, a lookout used by Ute Indians and later by the Federal Government as a signal station during Indian raids, when messages were flashed to Pikes Peak and the Spanish Peaks. At the outbreak of the Civil War, Confederate sympathizers made this region their headquarters until dispersed by Federal troops.

At 23.5 *m.* is the junction with a dirt road. Right on this road is BEULAH, 1.5 *m.* (6,205 alt.). The town has several soda springs; near by are large marble deposits. Right from Beulah a foot trail ascends MIDDLE ST. CHARLES CREEK to BAVER-LI LODGE, 6 *m.*

State 76 ascends a steep grade along Squirrel Creek to the PINE CREST SILVER FOX FARM, 25 *m.*, at the junction with a dirt road. Left on this road to PUEBLO MOUNTAIN PARK (*outdoor fireplaces; tables; shelter*), 1.5 *m.* Southwest from the park 2.5 *m.* on a road to the BOY SCOUT CAMP BIRCH (*open*). Right from the camp a charted trail traverses the canyon, which must be scaled by a ladder.

The highway crosses the eastern boundary of San Isabel National Forest (*see Tour 8b*), 26.7 *m.*, to the PUEBLO MUNICIPAL CAMP-GROUND (*outdoor fireplaces; picnic facilities*), 28.1 *m.* This section of the route is known at Squirrel Creek Drive. Prominent against the skyline (L) is OVAL MOUNTAIN; its top is an almost perfect parabola, covered with a dense growth of pine and aspen.

At 28.8 *m.* is the junction with a dirt road. Left on this road to the beginning of the CASCADE TRAIL, 200 *ft.*, a foot trail leading to the Pueblo Community House (*see below*), 1.2 *m.* Along the way are many rustic bridges spanning Squirrel Creek. The trail terminates at a campground near the Community House.

The road ascends to the log PUEBLO COMMUNITY HOUSE (*meals*), 30.8 *m.*, and the DAVENPORT CAMPGROUND, 32.3 *m.*, at the junction with State 165 (*see Tour 12c*), and passes OPHIR CAMPGROUND (*fireplaces*), 34.8 *m.*

At 36 *m.* is the junction with a dirt road. Left on this road is OPHIR, 4.5 *m.* (9,800 alt.), a small gold-mining community. Along Ophir Creek are several beaver dams.

State 76 passes BAVER-LI LODGE, 36.5 *m.*, and loops outside the boundaries of San Isabel National Forest to BRASSEA RANCH, 41 *m.* Right from the ranch on a graveled road along South Hardscrabble Creek to the FLORENCE CAMPGROUND, 3 *m.*

The highway turns west to cross the western boundary of San Isabel National Forest, 41.5 *m.,* and skirts (R) the TOMPKINS CATTLE RANGE, 42 *m.,* formerly owned by a British syndicate, now the property of the Hatcher Cattle Company, operators of the Three R Ranch near Beulah (*see above*).

At 46.8 *m.* is the junction with State 96 (*See Tour 8b*).

I◆◆I◆◆I◆◆I◆◆I◆◆I◆◆I◆◆I◆◆I◆◆I◆◆I◆◆I◆◆I◆◆I◆◆I◆◆I◆◆I◆◆I◆◆I◆◆I◆◆I◆◆I◆◆I◆◆I◆◆I◆◆

Tour 9

(Garden City, Kans.)—Holly—Lamar—John Martin Reservoir—Las Animas—La Junta—Pueblo— Canon City— Salida— Monarch Pass— Gunnison—Montrose—Delta—Grand Junction—Fruita—(Thompsons, Utah) ; US 50.
Kansas Line to Utah Line, 483.9 *m.*

This is one of the major cross-State highways, reaching every form of municipal activity, recreation, and geographical diversity known to Colorado.

US 50 follows the Arkansas River from the plains into the mountains, ascends through wild and beautiful country to the top of the Continental Divide, descends into the valley of the Gunnison, a famed trout stream, which it follows into the high plateau country in the western part of the State. Monuments along the highway indicate that the extreme eastern section of this route follows the old Arkansas River branch of the Santa Fe Trail, established by Capt. William Becknell in 1821, as far as Bent's Fort, near Hadley, where it struck off southwest to Trinidad.

Section a. KANSAS LINE to PUEBLO; 152 m. US 50

In this section the plains slope down into the irrigated agricultural lands of the Arkansas Valley, one of the richest and most intensively cultivated sections of Colorado. Occasionally the highway swings away from the river bottom and crosses desolate prairie country for short distances. US 50 crosses the Kansas Line, 0 *m.,* 69 miles west of Garden City, Kans.

HOLLY, 4.5 *m.* (3,400 alt., 1,165 pop.) is a center for farm products, stock raising and feeding. Holly Sugar Corp., sugar-beet processor, started in a small factory here in 1905; today it operates 10 in five states.

The *Chieftain* is a weekly newspaper. The Holly Community Fair has a Fat Stock Show and the Holly Saddle Club Rodeo.

The highway crosses the ARKANSAS RIVER, 10.2 *m.*, the greatest western affluent of the Missouri-Mississippi River system. Rising near Leadville and flowing 2,000 miles through Kansas, Oklahoma, and Arkansas, it drains an area of 188,000 square miles. The river was known to early Spanish and French explorers as Rio Napesta or Rio Napestle, said by some to be derived from the Osage Ne Shutsa, or Red Water. It was later named for the Arkansas Indians who once lived along its lower reaches.

The route passes GRANADA (Sp. pomegranate), 15 *m.* (3,479 alt., 352 pop.), a trading center, once the terminus of the Santa Fe Railway.

During World War II the Federal Government detained 10,000 citizens of Japanese birth and descent from the Pacific Coast in a Relocation Center near Granada.

In this area is the district known as BIG TIMBERS, a name given by the Cheyenne to a vast grove of cottonwoods that once extended 30 miles along the Arkansas.

William Bent had a trading post at Big Timbers in 1844, and the trader Thorpe established another in 1846. "Buffalo were plentiful and Indians gathered there in force," wrote a visitor of that period. "A big camp of Cheyennes had pitched their lodges near the log houses of the traders; two miles below, on the north side of the river, was the Arapaho village; on the south bank, opposite the trading houses, were the camps of the Kiowas and Prairie Apaches, while farther down on the south side the northern bands of Comanche had gone into winter camp. At night, when the soldier societies were giving dances the drums could be heard beating in the camps all night long. In the daytime the trading houses were crowded with Indians bringing in their robes to trade."

LAMAR, 32.5 *m.* (3,622 alt., 8,500 pop.), seat of Prowers County, was named for L. Q. C. Lamar, Secretary of the Interior, 1885–1888. It is on the Santa Fe Ry., highways US 287, US 385, State 8, 59, 186, besides US 50, and is served by Frontier Airlines and Continental Buses. Lamar is publicized as "the Goose Capital of America." It profits from the farm and livestock production of the county, which averages an annual income of $12,000,000. About 45,000 hd. of cattle and 73,000 sheep are raised or fed annually, and feed lots are increasing.

The monument, Madonna of the Trail, is located at Main St. and the Santa Fe tracks. LAMAR COMMUNITY COLLEGE, founded 1937, reorganized 1953, occupies a newly acquired campus of 64 acres and has lately erected a new dormitory-student union complex. The college is recognized for its livestock judging teams and athletics, especially wrestling; its curriculum includes vocational training in machine shorthand, automobile repairing, business management and cosmetology. Here also is located the Melvin School for the Mentally Retarded. A new Community Building was erected by community cooperation. The *Tri-State Daily News* is published here.

At 41 *m.* is the junction with a dirt road.

Left on this road along high bluffs overlooking the rivers, to the SITE OF BENT'S SECOND FORT, 0.5 *m.*, built of stone in 1853 by William Bent after abandonment of a larger fort upstream (*see Tour 9A*). In 1859 he leased this fort to the Federal Government. First named Fort Fauntleroy for a colonel of the old First Dragoons and later Fort Wise in honor of the Governor of Virginia, it was again renamed during the Civil War in honor of General Lyon, the first Union general to fall in the war. In 1866 the river began cutting away the bank and a new Fort Lyon was built 20 miles upstream, two miles below the mouth of the Purgatoire.

At 54 *m.* is a junction with a dirt road. Left on this road across the Arkansas River to CADDOA, 3 *m.*

Caddoa is located near the JOHN MARTIN DAM, which holds back the flood waters of the Arkansas River in the huge JOHN MARTIN RESERVOIR, largest in Colorado. The project was originally called Caddoa, and the name was changed in June, 1940, to honor John A. Martin, long a member of the House of Representatives. The dam, 58 *m.* upstream from the Kansas line, is made of concrete and earth and 150 ft. tall. Work began in 1939 and ended in 1948. The reservoir covers almost 18,400 acres at maximum pool level, regulating flood waters from a drainage area of 18,915 *sq. m.* Total storage capacity (3,870 ft. above sea level) is 645,500 acre-ft. About 278,500 acre-ft. of this is reserved for flood control, the remaining 367,000 acre-ft. is for irrigation and supply storage. The dam and reservoir were built by the Corps of Engineers of the U. S. Army. The total Federal cost was approx. $15,-000,000. The usefulness of the installation has been proved numerous times, especially in May, 1955, when it halted waters that had inundated 30,000 acres downstream from Pueblo.

Below the Dam, and reached from HASTY, on US 50, is LAKE CITY, 75 acres, 12 ft. deep, developed by the Corps of Engineers for recreation. There are picnic tables, fireplaces, and sanitary facilities.

At 64 *m.* is a junction with a graveled road.

Left on this road to FORT LYON, 1.7 *m.*, 1934 VETERANS ADMINISTRATION HOSPITAL, 681 beds, for mentally ill patients. A new Chapel, costing $186,000, was erected in 1963. The landscaped grounds cover 1,140 acres.

On the reservation is the cabin in which Kit Carson died on May 23, 1868. Christopher (Kit) Carson, born in Kentucky December 24, 1809, spent his boyhood in Missouri. While working as a saddler's apprentice, he became enamoured of the life of trappers and traders, and in 1826 joined a caravan to Santa Fe. On this trip he demonstrated his skill in amateur surgery by amputating a wounded arm in which gangrene had developed. From Santa Fe, Carson went to Taos, N. M., where he served in various expeditions as saddler, wrangler, cook, teamster, and trapper. He is said to have killed his first Indian in a fight with the Apache in 1829, but always retained a deep sympathy for the redmen. In 1835, at a rendezvous of trappers in Green River Valley in northwestern Colorado, Carson fought a duel over an Arapaho woman with a Canadian trapper, Captain Shunan, a great bully of the camps, and seriously wounded his adversary. Carson then married the woman with the customary Indian rites. Waa-nibe, or Alice, as he rechristened her, bore him one child, a girl, but soon died. The daughter, Adeline, was sent East but was brought back by Carson when she was fourteen; the next year she married.

The Scout's second marriage, with Making-Out-The-Road, a Cheyenne, did not turn out well. An indulgent husband, Carson was nearly ruined by her extravagance. When he remonstrated, she drove him from their lodge at Bent's Fort, flinging his belongings after him.

His third wife was Maria Josefa Jaramillo, a beautiful Spanish girl of considerable wealth and position, sister-in-law of Charles Bent, Governor of New Mexico, who was killed during an Indian uprising in Taos. Josefa herself barely escaped with her life, and as Carson was serving as a guide at the time, it was almost two years before they were reunited. Although Josefa bore Carson eight children and brought him rich lands as her dowry, she never succeeded in domesticating him. He continued to follow the long trails, served as guide and companion to Lieutenant John C. Frémont on almost all of his expeditions, made several trips to Washington with dispatches, and for a short time was commander at Fort Garland (*see Tour 11b*). At the outbreak of the Civil War he was Indian Agent at Taos, but resigned to become a colonel in the Union Army.

After the war Carson was again appointed Indian Agent, and in 1865 was chosen mediator-in-chief for the tribes of the Southwest. Ill health forced him to relinquish this post in 1867, but a year later he was persuaded to accompany a delegation of Ute to Washington. While there, he was honored by high officials but was ill during his entire stay. Soon after his return to his home here, his wife died and Carson followed her a month later, dying peacefully while smoking his pipe after the evening meal. He was buried here at the fort beside Josefa; later their remains were removed to Taos, N. M., as Carson had requested.

US 50 follows the Arkansas River to LAS ANIMAS, 70 *m.* (4,100 alt., 3,500 pop.), seat of Bent County and named for Las Animas or Purgatoire River, which flows into the Arkansas River nearby. Founded in 1869 across the Arkansas from Fort Lyon, the first site of Las Animas was abandoned when the Kansas Pacific Railroad built its line six miles to the west in 1873. In 1874 the surrounding area was the scene of immense roundups of cattle and was noted for large shipments of buffalo meat. The Prairie Cattle Company, an English corporation, grazed more than 50,000 cattle here during the early 1880's. The last great roundup occurred in 1916.

Las Animas is a supply center not only for the farming-ranching enterprises of Bent County, but also has goods needed by sportsmen and vacationists that converge on the John Martin Reservoir, 6 *m.* east, Lake Hasty, Blue Lake, and Setchfield Lake. The last three are regularly stocked with trout, white bass, walleyed pike, perch, channel cat and other varieties. The city has runway facilities for small and medium-sized aircraft, and is on the line of the Santa Fe and two continental bus lines. A new main and nurses wing were built by the Bent County Memorial Hospital in 1962. There are two weekly newspapers, the Bent County Democrat and the Las Animas Leader.

A new KIT CARSON MUSEUM was opened in 1961 by the Pioneer Historical Society of Bent County.

At this point on November 15, 1806, Lieutenant Zebulon M. Pike first sighted the peak that was to bear his name.

Right from Las Animas on a dirt road is BOGGSVILLE, 2 *m.*, on the Purgatoire River. Here the first successful experiment in irrigation in this region was made by Thomas O. Boggs in 1866. He was joined by J. W. Prowers and Robert Bent, son of William Bent, who placed 1,000 acres of land under cultivation. Prowers is credited with bringing the first herd of cattle into this country in 1861, driving in 100 head from Missouri.

The highway crosses a large overpass and traverses fertile farm country growing alfalfa, corn, melons, onions, and sugar beets.

At 80 *m.* is a junction with a dirt road.

Right on this road 4 *m.* to the SITE OF BENTS FORT (*see Tour 9A*).

LA JUNTA (Sp. The Junction) pronounced Hunta, 89.5 *m.* (4,100 alt., 8,926 pop., 1960; 12,000 est., 1968), seat of Otero County, named for Miguel Otero, Spanish settler. This is the State's major cattle auction center, disposing of approx. 300,000 hd. annually, sales averaging $26,000,000. It is hq of the Colorado Division of the Santa Fe Ry., one of its largest employers. There are canning and packing plants. OTERO JUNIOR COLLEGE, home of the Otero Players, has up to 500 students.

Of special interest is the KOSHARE INDIAN KIVA, home of the Koshare Indian Dancers, an organization of Explorer Scouts, which give dances Saturday nights in summer in a stockade seating 1,200. (*Adults, $2; students, $1*). Here also is the Museum of Indian Arts and Crafts, with murals by Valino Hererra, Indian artist. (*free*). The Colorado Boys Ranch, north of La Junta, occupies the site of a former Air Force base.

Left from La Junta on a rough dirt road to HIGBEE, 19.1 *m.*
Right from Higbee 1 *m.* on a dirt road to the DINOSAUR TRACKS, discovered in December 1935 along the banks of the Purgatoire River. These tracks were imprinted in the rock floor of the river by Tyrannosaurus Rex, one of the fiercest of ancient reptiles. Eighteen tracks appear in a straight line. From the three-toed footprints, 3 inches deep, 11 inches wide, and 15 inches long, and from the 50-inch stride, it is estimated that the monster was some 50 feet long, 20 feet high, and weighed about 40 tons. A short distance from these tracks have been found the footprints of Triceratops, ancestors of the rhinoceros.

SWINK, 94.8 *m.* (4,118 alt., 420 pop.), was named for George W. Swink, developer of the Rocky Ford melons and State senator.

ROCKY FORD, 100.7 *m.* (4,178 alt., 5,350 pop.), was named for the ford on the stony bed of the Arkansas River, where pioneers crossed. It is famous for the Rocky Ford melons, which George W. Swink began growing here. In 1878 he invited neighbors to Watermelon Day, giving free melons; this has continued to the present, associated with the Arkansas Valley Fair (third week in August); more than 10,000 watermelons are given away. The Watermelon Derby (racing) began in 1957, and the Watermelon Sweepstakes Relay in 1962.

The American Crystal Sugar Co. employs 550 in the beet sugar season. Other industries produce seed cleaning machinery, lanolin and soured wool, frozen onions and bell peppers, beet pulp for feed, fertilizers. The seed industry is one of the largest in the nation, and the area is noted for its immense zinnia fields, blooming from mid-July to mid-September. Popcorn is a wholesale item. Cattle feeding in Otero County often accomodates 25,000 head. The *Rocky Ford Daily Gazette* is its newspaper.

MANZANOLA (Sp. apple orchard), 110 *m.* (4,250 alt.), is the center of a large apple, melon, and vegetable growing district. The route crosses the APISHAPA RIVER (Ind. stinking water), 115 *m.,* once called Quarreling Creek by the Cheyenne because, so a story runs, a party of Cheyenne here quarreled violently about the selection of a new chief, but they did not come to blows.

West of the river the highway passes FOWLER, 118 *m.* (4,300 alt., 1,300 pop.) where a road across the Arkansas connects US 50 and State 96. It is a shipping point for livestock and poultry, and traverses a stretch of barren prairie to ORCHARD PARK, 130 *m.* (4,000 alt., 300 pop.), a community possessing neither orchards nor parks. On the low bluffs along the north bank of the Arkansas River (R), known as Pawnee Hills, Cheyenne and Arapaho defeated a large Pawnee war party in 1833.

In spring and early summer, stretches of prairie land here are carpeted with squirrel-tail grass (or wild barley), porcupine grass, and several kinds of bunch and brome grasses. One variety of the latter, known as rattlesnake grass, grows close to the ground and dies before the dry season. When walked upon, it gives forth a rustling sound. Brightening the landscape in midsummer are the tall bee plant, with clusters of purplish-pink flowers, the purple and golden pea, and the handsome yellow evening star. In August and September the bushy butterweed, sunflowers, and sneeze weed grow profusely along irrigation ditches and railroad embankments.

Near the junction of the Huerfano and Arkansas Rivers, 132 *m.,* is the SITE OF AUTOBEES RANCH, built by Charles Autobees, a French trader and trapper in the 1840's and 1850's. It served as headquarters for frontiersmen, and in 1861 became the seat of Huerfano County, which embraced practically all the territory of southeastern Colorado.

The route traverses irrigated farm lands growing zinnias, bright with bloom in the fall months; flowers of different shades are planted in widely separated fields so that the colors do not mix during pollination.

On the SITE OF OLD FORT REYNOLDS (R), 144 *m.,* an Army post during the Civil War and Indian wars, is a dump where discarded weapons, cooking utensils, uniform buttons, and other relics of old life at the post are occasionally found.

The highway crosses the ST. CHARLES RIVER, 145 *m.,* a small tributary of the Arkansas, rising in the Wet Mountains. An early map shows the river as Rio Don Carlos, said to have been named for Don

Carlos Beaubien, French trader, who played an important part in the early history of this section. Some authorities assert that the name was handed down from the colony of San Carlos de los Jupes, a village of Comanche settled on the stream by Governor Anza of New Mexico in 1787. The mountain tribe of the Comanche, known as the Jupe, appeared before Governor Anza, and their leader Paruanarimuco proposed that the Spaniards aid them in establishing themselves in a fixed on the Rio Napestle (Arkansas River). The exact site of the settlement is unknown, although it was described as being on the "Rio Napestle near a spring with good land." This attempt to settle the nomadic Comanche failed when the Indians suddenly abandoned their villages. The reason for their abrupt exodus appears in the report of Fernando de la Concha, who succeeded Anza as Governor of New Mexico: "This nation, like almost all the gentiles, is full of superstitions. At the moment any person of estimation dies in any suitable spot where they have set their rancherias, they take them up and change the site, even going to a distance and a place ordinarily lacking everything necessary for subsistence in their manner."

The highway descends to SALT CREEK, 150.5 *m.* (4,500 alt.), typical of the Spanish-American communities found on the outskirts of almost all southern Colorado towns. Two- and three-room abode houses, most of them with sod roofs and floors of hard-packed earth, line the road; olive-skinned people pass along the dusty street, usually inconspicuous in faded work clothes, but on gala occasions they bedazzle with the startling colors of their holiday garb. The social life of the community revolves around the church with its holidays and fiestas. The easy tempo of life in the village sharply contrasts with the hum of the steel plant beyond Salt Creek.

In PUEBLO, 152 *m.* (4,700 alt., 103,000 pop. 1967 est.), are the junctions with US 85, State 96, State 76, and Interstate 25.

Section b. *PUEBLO to MONTROSE; 232.4 m. US 50*

This section of US 50 follows the Arkansas River Valley to cross the Continental Divide at Monarch Pass. One of the great natural entrances to the Rocky Mountains, the Arkansas was followed by many early explorers, including Pike and Frémont. Among the more spectacular sights is the Royal Gorge, or the Grand Canyon of the Arkansas.

Branching west from US 85 at the northern city limits of PUEBLO, 0 *m.,* US 50 traverses a wide plain of rolling grasslands scantily covered with grama grass and Russian thistles. Blue in the distance are Pikes Peak and the Wet Mountains.

At 14.9 *m.* is the junction with a dirt road.

Right on this road is STONE CITY, 6.5 *m.* (5,200 alt.); the Limestone Quarries here, one of the three largest in the State, furnished building stone for the Pueblo County Courthouse. Near the stone pits is the PETRIFIED SKELETON OF A DINOSAUR, known as Tyrannosaurus Rex.

The highway leaves the flat prairies and crosses a region of low rolling hills spotted with a growth of cedar and pine.

An abandoned plant and empty cement-block cottages mark the SITE OF CONCRETE, 22 *m.*, founded by the Portland Cement Company before it shifted operations to PORTLAND, 24.3 *m.*, where the Ideal Cement Co. has the largest mineral plant in Fremont County.

At 27.5 *m.* is the junction with State 115.

Right on this highway is PENROSE, 5 *m.* (5,200 alt., 90 pop.), center of the 4,000-acre Beaver Park farming district devoted to fruit-raising and general farming.

Apple orchards border the road for many miles east of FLORENCE, 30 *m.* (5,187 alt., 3,000 pop.), which began as a coal town and later became the center of considerable oil development. Oil was early found bubbling to the surface of Oil Creek, 3 miles west of town. In 1862 A. M. Cassedy drilled in the canyon and struck oil at 50 feet; hauled by ox cart to Pueblo, Santa Fe, and Denver, it sold at $1.25 to $2.85 a gallon; its price soared to $5 a gallon during Indian wars. Florence manufactures fiberboard, pipe and fittings, and wood products. Jesse Frazier, who opened the first coal mines here, also planted the first apple orchard, bringing his seedlings from Missouri; some of his trees still stand. Florence celebrates an annual Pioneer Day. The Fremont County Airport, between Florence and Canon City, has a 5,400 ft. runway and chartered service. The *Citizen* is its weekly newspaper.

CANON CITY, 38.4 *m.* (5,343 alt., 9,621 pop. 1967, est.), seat of Fremont County, incor. 1872, is the gate to the Royal Gorge. East Canon (1,300 pop. est.) is a separate incorporated community.

The site of Canon City, at the mouth of the Grand Canyon of the Arkansas, was a favorite camping ground for the Ute long before the coming of white men. Lieutenant Zebulon Pike and his party camped here in December 1806, departing a few days later to explore the head-waters of the Arkansas, which he believed to be the Red River. He returned on January 5, 1807, and here celebrated his 28th birthday. A blockhouse was built and nine days later, leaving two of his men and much baggage at the post, Pike set out with his party to cross "the great white mountain" (Sangre de Cristo) into the San Luis Valley, where he and his men were taken prisoners by the Spanish.

The town flourished with the influx of gold seekers in 1859–60. Joaquin Miller, the poet, served as judge, mayor, and minister in early days. He once attempted to change the name of the town to Oreodelphia, but was overruled by the miners, who protested they could neither write nor pronounce the word, stoutly insisting "the place is a canyon, and it's goin' to be called Canon City." In 1868 Canon City was offered the choice of the State penitentiary or the State university; it chose the former because it was an established institution and seemed likely to be the better attended; Boulder then spoke for the university. Apple Blossom Week is celebrated annually in Canon City.

Canon City is a trading center for Fremont County, which raises about 20,000 cattle, as well as sheep and hogs, annually, and produces a great variety of nonmetallic minerals, including barite, cement, dolomite, gypsum, silicon, graphite, uranium and petroleum.

Tourism brings large income; recreation sites in the Royal Gorge area comprise 104,365 acres, and in 1967 475,646 persons visited Royal Gorge Bridge. Canon City owns two parks of 640 acres each—Red Canyon Park and Temple Canyon Park.

The FREMONT COUNTY COURT HOUSE has a distinguished modern design and is built of pink Colorado granite and sheathed with copper. The MUNICIPAL MUSEUM, in the Municipal Building, 612 River St., has a collection of guns, antlers, Indian relics and mounted big game made by Dall DeWeese, land developer and explorer. Other collections include four mounted buffalo killed by poachers in 1897 and considered the last of great herds. Here and elsewhere are large murals painted by Robert W. Amick. Near the Museum is the cabin built in 1860 by Anson Rudd, first sheriff, later lieutenant governor of the Territory of Jefferson. It is now a museum of period furniture (*8 to 5 p.m. daily; 1 to 5 p.m. Sunday, free*). The FINE ARTS GALLERY of the Fine Arts Assn., 426 Main St., has permanent and loan exhibits. The ROBISON MANSION, an example of pioneer opulence, is filled with Victorian furniture (*adults $1, children 75¢*). Special events are the Blossom Festival in May, the Trail Ride in June, and the Royal Gorge Round-up and Rodeo in July. The *Daily Canon City Record,* the *Weekly Record* and the *Canon City Sun,* weekly, are its newspapers.

COLLEGE OF THE CANONS offers the first two years of college instruction an extension of Southern Colorado State College of Pueblo.

On the western outskirts the COLORADO STATE PENITENTIARY, founded 1876, covers approx. 5,000 acres. It has nearly 2,000 inmates and 464 employees (1967). Part of its funds come from farm products and livestock, and from canned goods, clothing, bedding, soap, and road signs, which are sold to other State institutions. The per capita cost of operation is the lowest of State institutions, $1,672 in 1963. Capital punishment is legal and lethal gas has displaced the rope.

The new COLORADO WOMEN'S CORRECTIONAL INSTITUTION was dedicated by Governor John Love on March 14, 1968. It cost $1,200,000 and stresses rehabilitation. It has a 20-acre site, can house 90 inmates, and has a staff of 37 women. The plant has a hospital, an auditorium-chapel seating 240, a kitchen equipped for instruction, a sewing unit with 32 machines, and opportunities for physical training and games. Typing and courses in high school subjects are available. The inmates may engage in needlework, sketching, basketball, square dancing, and hear radio through earphones in their cells, but there are "five soundproof meditation rooms in the basement for inmates with disciplinary problems." In 1968 there were 58 inmates, 70 per cent white. The common crime was passing bad checks. The operating budget for the fiscal year was $350,953.

At 41.5 *m.* is the junction with SKYLINE DRIVE, marked by an entrance gate built of stones from every State in the Union.

At 47 *m.* is the junction with a road to BUCKSKIN JOE, a pioneer mining village of houses assembled from elsewhere, with costumes to match (admission fee).

Continue on this road to a parking space on the rim of the ROYAL GORGE, or Grand Canyon of the Arkansas, 4.5 *m.,* the most accessible and for that reason perhaps the best known of the great river canyons of Colorado. At this point the red granite walls rise sheerly more than 1,000 feet above the foaming torrent in the narrow gorge. Sunlight brings out a variety of colors in the rock strata bands. Geologists agree that the canyon was caused by an uplift through which the river cut its way. As proof, they point to the fact that the rock strata run parallel on either side of the gorge.

The main line of the Denver & Rio Grande Western Railroad runs through the bottom of the Royal Gorge. The story of how men put steel through this canyon, which Lieutenant John C. Frémont declared to be impassible, is epic. Wide enough to accommodate only one right-of-way, the gorge was the scene of bitter struggle between the Denver & Rio Grande and the Atchison, Topeka & Santa Fe lines from 1876 to 1879. By July 1875 the Denver & Rio Grande had built as far west as Canon City but evidenced no immediate intention of proceeding. Impatient at the delay, Canon City residents organized the Canon City & San Juan Railroad and made surveys, which they filed with the Secretary of the Interior. Aroused, the Santa Fe sent a crew of workers by team from Pueblo to the mouth of the canon, and the Denver & Rio Grande dispatched a crew from Canon City. The latter won the race by half an hour and were grading a right-of-way when their rivals reached the scene, precipitating a war celebrated in railroad annals. Men of one camp laid rails by day and tore up those of their rivals by night. Guns were recklessly brandished, but no life was lost. Finally the quarrel was transferred to the courts. Then followed a compromise, and control of the right-of-way was awarded the Denver & Rio Grande. The cost of the struggle was roughly estimated at $500,000.

ROYAL GORGE PARK and the famous Bridge Area are located at the south end of the road. Just beyond the Main Gate there is a large space for parking. To the left a narrow-gauge Rio Grande locomotive is on exhibition. To the right is the miniature Royal Gorge & Silver Rock R.R., offering a mile-long ride. The great SUSPENSION BRIDGE is directly ahead. It is 1,055 ft. above the Arkansas River; its total length, exclusive of approaches, is 1,260 ft.; the main span is 880 ft. There are 5 ft. guard rails. The bridge was completed December 8, 1929, on the 123d anniversary of the discovery of the gorge by Zebulon Pike, and cost $200,000. Visitors may walk or drive across the bridge: speed limit is 10 mph. As *Touraide* (Sonoco) says: "It doesn't go anywhere but about 400,000 persons a year walk or ride over it anyway. There is enough wire in the bridge to reach from Colorado Springs to New York City and continue halfway to London."

An aerial tramway half a mile long, suspended above the gorge from rim to rim, began operations in 1969.

To the right of the bridge on the north rim is the Visitors Center, with a postoffice where mail is cancelled "Royal Gorge, Colorado." To the left is the INCLINE RAILWAY, which descends to the bottom of the canyon at a 45° angle for 1,550 ft. On the south rim of the gorge are Point Sublime, for viewing and taking pictures; Cliff Terrace Cafe (May to October) and picnic areas (no overnight camping).

The entrance fee, paid at the main gates, is $1.25 for adults, 50¢

for children, 7 through 11. This includes park facilities and bridge. The Incline Railway costs $1.25 for adults, 50¢ for children, 7 through 11. A combination ticket for both gets a 25¢ reduction for adults.

Circling north over high tablelands, US 50 descends a dry creek bed to PARKDALE, 50.4 m. (5,800 alt.), at the western extremity of the gorge, and follows the brawling Arkansas to TEXAS CREEK, 69.5 m. (6,210 alt.), at the junction with State 69 (see Tour 11B).

A shipping point for livestock and farm produce, COTOPAXI (Sp. shining pile), 71.5 m. (6,718 alt., 238 pop.), saw some mining activity in the late 1880's. Much of the first ore mined near here, a zinc compound, was shipped to refineries in Swansea, Wales.

West of COALDALE, 75.5 m. (7,550 alt.), formerly a coal camp but now supported by the mining of gypsum, the mountains and canyons are colored with sparkling quartz, granite, and delicately colored marble. Among the many rare and beautiful stones is travertine, with its curiously worm-eaten appearance, which has been used in the construction of many buildings in the United States, including the Department of Commerce Building, Washington, D. C.

SALIDA (Sp. gateway) 95.1 m. (7,050 alt., 5,000 pop. est.), seat of Chaffee County, was founded by the Denver & Rio Grande Western in 1880. It is the hub of a popular trout-fishing, hunting and skiing area and its Hot Mineral Waters have been known since Indian days. The waters, with temperatures of 145° to 185°, are cooled to 80° for bathing. A Frontier Museum is located in the Pool Bldg.

The Salida Airport, with a 7,000-ft. runway, is used by visitors to the Winter Ski Area, to which it provides free car service. The State's largest fish hatchery near Salida specializes in mountain trout. Salida has two newspapers, the daily *Mountain Mail* and the *Weekly Record*. It is served by the Denver & Rio Grande Western and Continental Trailways. The White Water Amateur Boat Races, on a 26-mile course to COTOPAXI, are a June feature; the Heart of the Rockies Rodeo is held in fall.

Between Salida and PONCHA JUNCTION, 99.1 m., US 50 and US 285 (see Tour 15b) are united, crossing a branch of the Arkansas known as the Little Arkansas.

West of Poncha Junction the route leaves the valley and ascends the Continental Divide through country heavily timbered with spruce, fir, and long-needled ponderosa pine, crossing the eastern boundary of SAN ISABEL NATIONAL FOREST, 106.4 m., created in 1905 by President Theodore Roosevelt; it includes 1,103,837 acres of Federal land.

Bordering the highway on the north and centering on SHAVANO PEAK (14,179 alt.), is the SHAVANO PEAK PRIMITIVE AREA; no highways, resorts, or developments are permitted within its confines. Shavano, named for a Ute chief, is believed to be a modified spelling of the Ute Che-wa-no, or blue flower. On its slopes, marked by slow-melting snows in deep fissures, a figure with outstretched arms, known as the ANGEL OF SHAVANO, is seen in spring and early summer. The angel, according to legend, appeared on the mountain when Shavano, who had been schooled by the Holy Friars of Santa Fe, prayed for the soul of his dying friend, George Beckwith, a member of the Gunnison expedition. The Mt. Shavano Trout Rearing unit is located here.

US 50 passes through GARFIELD, which is exploiting Ski Town. MONARCH, 113.7 m. (10,000 alt.). The Monarch winter sports area starts 1.8 m. east of Monarch Crest on US 50. It has 4 ski runs and a 3,200 ft. chair lift, and can handle 2,100 skiers per hour.

A bronze tablet in a granite slab marks the summit of MONARCH PASS (11,386 alt.), 118.4 m., on the crest of the Continental Divide. From the top of the pass, one of the highest in the Rocky Mountains crossed by an automobile highway, are visible the long rough outline of the Sangre de Cristo Range (L), the towering gray-domed peaks of the Collegiate Range (R), the colorful Ruby Range to the northwest (R), and the jagged peaks of the San Juans, more than 100 miles to the south-west (L). Twelve peaks seen from this vantage point exceed 14,000 feet in altitude; more than a score rise above 13,000 feet. At 127.1 m. is the junction with two dirt roads leading to (1) WAUNITA HOT SPRINGS, 8 m., and (2) WHITEPINE, 5 m., a ghost town.

The route follows Tomichi Creek (Ind., hot water), to SARGENTS, 134.5 m. (8,500 alt.). The highway descends into Tomichi Valley. At PARLIN, 153.4 m. a road parallels Quartz Creek to OHIO, 8.6 m., former mining camp. PIT-KIN, 14.6 m. (9,200 alt.) originally called Quartzville, was renamed for Gov. V. F. Pitkin. The annual Alpine Tunnel Days are three days at Pitkin early in August, with tours of the old rail tunnel, rides and auctions. QUARTZ, 21 m. is an abandoned mining camp.

At 159.4 m. on US 50 a dirt road, left, leads to CHANCE, 7 m. and IRIS, 10 m., old gold camps. The road runs along Gold Belt Basin Creek and joins US 50 at Gunnison.

GUNNISON, 165.4 m. (7,703 alt., 6,100 pop. est.), seat of Gunni-son County, at the junction of US 50 (State 6 plus State 114) and State 135, is the gateway to a vast recreation area with facilities for hunting, fishing, camping and skiing. It is at the door of Gunnison National Forest (1,660,050 acres), Blue Mesa Lake Recreational Area, and numerous trout and salmon streams. Its banks help finance the extensive ranch interests of the county, which annually produces 20,000 feeder calves and 3,500 yearlings, and large herds of sheep. In 1965 the Gun-nison County Pioneer and Historical Society opened its new museum at the east entrance to Gunnison on US 50 (hours 1–5, free). Craner Ski Hill, a community project, was opened 1965, 2 miles north.

WESTERN STATE COLLEGE OF COLORADO, opened 1911 as a normal school, expanded to four-years in 1920. It is a liberal arts college with a professional school of education and has given the Ed. S. degree since 1956. Among its well-equipped laboratories is a model classroom for observing teaching. Its Museum has valuable relics of Cliff Dweller, Basket Maker and other ancient Indian cultures. The LESLIE J. SAVAGE LIBRARY contains more than 108,000 vols., 21,000 pamphlets, western

Americana, Gunnison County newspapers, and the Clarence T. Hurst collection of archaeological and geological books. WSC has a campus of 230 acres and enrolled 2,577 in 1968.

The Gunnison Stockgrowers Association, founded 1894, started the annual event, Cattlemen's Days, in July, 1905. Since 1947 it has joined the Colorado State University in experimental projects. In 1967 the University leased a ranch on Ohio Creek for research. Gunnison County produces high altitude feeders. Stock on the upper Tomichi calved at 8,000 ft., summered up to 12,000 ft. altitude.

Gunnison County Airport is served by Frontier Airlines and Western State Aviation. Continental Trailways provides a bus service.

John W. Gunnison (1812–1853), a native of New Hampshire and a graduate in civil engineering from U. S. Military Academy, West Point, served as a 2nd lieutenant in the Seminole War in Florida. In 1849 he explored the valley of the Great Salt Lake, Utah, and wrote a report on the Mormon settlement. He advanced in rank to captain. In May, 1853, Secy. Jefferson Davis of the War Department ordered him to survey a railroad route westward through the Colorado Rockies. He started from St. Louis in June with entourage of 19 wagons and made camp near Bent's Old Fort late in July. He moved via Sangre de Christo Pass, Fort Massachusetts in the San Luis Valley, along the present Gunnison River, near the sites of Montrose, Delta, and Grand Junction, and by October reached the Sevier River in Utah. In his journal Capt. Gunnison noted that his exploration opened a new mail and military road to Taos, by way of Fort Massachusetts, a road for the southern state and emigrants to California, a military road to Utah and a railroad route to the western frontier.

On October 26, 1853, Indians of the Pah Vants tribe attacked Gunnison's camp with arrows, killing Capt. Gunnison and all but four of his expedition. Gunnison was buried at Fillmore, Utah. A monument marks the scene of his death. A great national forest, a city, a county, a river, a valley, a mountain, and streets and avenues, have been named for him.

The CURICANTI UNIT of the COLORADO RIVER STORAGE PROJECT comprises three dams that control the waters of the Gunnison River between Gunnison and Montrose. BLUE MESA DAM, completed in 1965, was the first major dam constructed by the Bureau of Reclamation after the original Uncompahgre Project of 1912. It has 3,080,000 cu. yds. of earth and rock, 1,600 ft. width at base and 30 ft. width at top, rises 342 ft. above streambed and is 800 ft. long at crest. Its power plant has two generators with a capacity of 60,000 kilowatts. It forms Blue Mesa Reservoir, with a capacity of 940,800 acre-ft., a shore line of 96 m., covering 14.3 sq. m., the largest lake in Colorado when full. It is stocked with millions of trout and kokanee salmon. Center Point is the main National Park Service boat ramp. Another ramp is at Iola.

Its released waters move down to MORROW POINT DAM. Begun in 1963 by the Bureau of Reclamation, the first thin arch, concrete double curvature dam. Double curvature means the dam curves from left to right and from bottom to top, the dome or cupola type. The dam is 469 ft. high, 740 ft. long, 52 ft. wide at the base, and contains 360,000 cu. yds. of concrete. The power plant is in an underground room excavated in hard rock, 50 ft. wide, 202 ft. long, with an arched roof 65 to 134 ft. high. The reservoir has a capacity of 117,000 acre-ft., covers 1.3 sq. m., and has a shoreline of 24 m. The power plant can produce 120,000 kilowatts. The water will move down to CRYSTAL DAM, almost at the head of the Black Canyon. This will be 219 ft. high, 760 ft. long, with a power plant of 28,000 kilowatts. The reservoir will extend 6.8 m. upstream, nearly to Morrow Point. The cost of the three dams is expected to reach $100,000,000, much of which the Bureau expends locally.

In IOLA, 177.4 m. (7,450 alt.), is the junction with State 149 (see Tour 21).

The highway crosses barren hills to CEBOLLA (Sp. onion), 184.4 m. (7,326 alt.), named for the fields of wild onions along the banks of Cebolla Creek. Ascending through a canyon lined with jagged stone spires, the road enters the mesa lands of western Colorado. The high escarpment of BLACK MESA, dark with pine and fir, merges with the distant Grand Mesa.

SAPINERO, 191.4 m. (7,255 alt.), a resourt town named for a Ute chief, is at the junction with State 92 (see Tour 9C).

The route descends through Blue Creek Canyon, ascends to the resort town of CIMARRON, 213.4 m. (6,896 alt.), and reaches CERRO SUMMIT (Sp. ridge), 217.6 m., overlooking Uncompahgre Valley, 40 miles long and 12 miles wide, with an average elevation of 5,500 feet. The bottom lands grow hay, beans, and truck garden crops, while peach, pear, apple, and cherry orchards cover the tops of many small mesas that rise several hundred feet above the valley.

Winding gradually through hills spotted with gnarled cedar and piñon, the highway passes the west portal of the GUNNISON DIVERSION TUNNEL, 225.6 m., constructed by the U. S. Reclamation Service at a cost of $2,905,000 as part of the Uncompahgre Reclamation Project, and opened by President Taft in 1909. The horseshoe-shaped bore, 5.8 miles long, was said at the time of its completion to be the longest irrigation tunnel in the world; it diverts 1,300 cubic feet of water a second from the Gunnison River under Vernal Mesa to the Uncompahgre Valley.

MONTROSE, 232.4 m. (5,820 alt., approx. 6,800 pop.), seat of Montrose County, deals in fruit, farm crops, sheep, wool, and minerals (uranium and vanadium). It attributes 32 per cent of its income to tourism, and a large share to the payrolls of the Bureau of Reclamation, which builds the three dams of the Gunnison River. It is hq of the Curecanti unit of the Colorado River Storage Project and hq of the Curecanti Recreation Area of the National Park Service, which controls the National Monument of the Black Canyon of the Gunnison, 12 m. away. (Visitors drive 6 m. east on US 50 and 5 m. north on State 347.) Frontier Airlines and Continental Trailways serve Montrose; the Denver & Rio Grande Western runs a freight service. A new private educational development is COLORADO WESTERN COLLEGE OF MONTROSE, which aims to combine technical sciences with the liberal arts in a four-year course. The Montrose Daily Press is the city's newspaper.

Montrose has the RCA Rodeo in early summer and the County Fair and Race Meet in August, the latter including the Little Britches Rodeo. The area is a center for hunting, fishing, camping, hiking and skiing.

Fishing licenses may be had at 334 S. 10th St., Montrose 81401. US 50 has a junction with US 550 and State 19.

The UTE INDIAN MUSEUM, 4 *m.* south of Montrose, was presented to the State Historical Society in 1945 by the Uncompahgre chapter of the D. A. R. The surrounding Chipeta Park was once the farm of Ute Chief Ouray and his wife Chipeta. A monument to Ouray (d. 1880) was erected here in 1926 by the State. Chipeta (d. 1924) is buried here, so is her brother, Chief John McCook (d. 1937). Ouray maintained peace with the whites. The photographic collection of Tom McKee in the museum is historically valuable.

Section c.   MONTROSE *to* UTAH LINE, *99.5 m.* US *50*

West of MONTROSE, 0 *m.,* the highway follows the Uncompahgre River to CHIPETA, 15.9 *m.,* named for the wife of Chief Ouray (*see Tour 18*).

DELTA, 22 *m.* (4,961 alt., 4,100 pop. est.), seat of Delta County, at the confluence of the Uncompahgre and Gunnison Rivers, is the shipping point for huge crops of apples, peaches and cherries raised in the county. The first settler was Antoine Robidoux, a French trapper from St. Louis, who built a fort in 1830.

Delta has a major plant of the Holly Sugar Corp. (*open to visitors*). It also has a Skyland Food plant, and a 500,000-ton elevator for malt barley built by the Coors Brewing Co. of Golden. Sweitzer Lake State Park, 1 *m.* southeast, is a recreation site. The contiguous area also profits from the Paonia Reservoir on the North Fork of the Gunnison, which holds 21,000 acre-ft. of water, and a reservoir on Smith Fork. Its newspaper is the *Delta County Independent,* a biweekly. Principal events are the Deltarado Days in August and the Apple Show in September.

Southwest of Delta the route follows the lower Gunnison. To the south is the Uncompahgre Plateau; northward, the aspen-fringed slopes rise to the crest of Grand Mesa.

At WHITEWATER, 54.5 *m.* (4,665 alt.), is the junction with the Lands End Road.

Right on this road (*open all winter*) to the winter sports area at LANDS END, Grand Mesa, 24 *m.* (*see Tour 5E*).

In GRAND JUNCTION, 65.5 *m.* (4,587 alt., 22,735 pop.), are junctions with US 24, US 6, Interstate 70, and a road to the Colorado National Monument (*see Tour 9D*).

West of Grand Junction the broad valley of the Colorado is extensively cultivated. Small garden tracts border the highway for several miles. Across the river peaches grow in the Redlands, where the green masses of orchards crowd against the carmine cliffs. The road passes from a cultivated area into a region of pasture lands where dairy farming is the chief occupation.

FRUITA, 79.5 *m.* (4,498 alt., 1,875 pop.) is a trading center of the lower Grand Valley. West of Fruita the refinery of the American Gilsonite Co. employs 200. The Mesa County Fair, together with the

Cowpunchers' Reunion, established in 1911 by ranchers of the area, is held here annually in September. The rodeo events are restricted to local cowpunchers, and no professionals take part.

Fruita is at the western junction with the Colorado National Monument road (*see Tour 9D*).

The route west of Fruita traverses a region devoted to the raising of sugar beets; fields are irrigated with water diverted from the Grand Valley dam north of Palisade. The highway crosses SALT WASH and LITTLE SALT, two streams that rise at the base of the Book Cliff Mountains, 20 miles to the north. Cloudbursts occasionally send walls of water rushing down the arroyos to ravage the countryside.

LOMA (Sp. hillock), 84.5 *m.* (4,515 alt.), lies near the heart of the territory irrigated by the Grand Valley Diversion Project.

MACK, 87.5 *m.* (5,540 alt.), a shipping point for sheep grazed on the dryland to the west, was formerly the eastern terminal of the Uintah Railroad, a narrow-gauge line (abandoned 1939) that hauled gilsonite from the Uintah Basin of Utah. Gilsonite, or Uintahite, is a hard black hydrocarbon used in the manufacture of paints, varnishes, roofing material, and rubber substitutes.

The highway swings westward, traversing a rough elevated outcrop covered with sage and sparse juniper growth, broken by numerous arroyos.

US 50 crosses the Utah line, 99.5 *m.*, 45 miles east of Thompsons, Utah.

Tour 9 A

US 50 to junction with State 194—Bent's Old Fort National Historic Site, 15 *m.*

BENT'S OLD FORT, since 1959 a National Historic Site administered by the National Park Service, is located on the north bank of the Arkansas River, 15 *m.* west of Las Animas and 8 *m.* east of La Junta, on the old Santa Fe Trail. When US 50 and State 6 cross the Arkansas to Las Animas, State 194 proceeds due west on the north bank to Bent's Old Fort, and as far as North La Junta. The Superintendent in charge of the site has his address as Box 581, La Junta, Colo., 81050.

The builders of the fort, Charles, Robert, George, and William Bent, and their partner, Ceran St. Vrain, played leading roles in the early development of trade in the West. The Bents were four of seven sons of Silas Bent, presiding judge of the St. Louis Court of Common

Pleas. William, who could speak Siouan fluently, was named Wa-Si-Cha-Chis-Chil-La (Little White Man) by the Sioux, for he was only 15 years old when he first came into the territory in 1823 as an employee of the American Fur Company.

In 1826 the Bents built their first stockade, farther up the Arkansas River, midway between Pueblo and Canon City. Two years later, while encamped near the mouth of the Purgatoire, they were visited by a party of Cheyenne, who declared the first post to be too far from the buffalo range for the Indians to frequent, and suggested that a new fort be built on this spot.

Although construction began that year, completion was delayed by Charles, who insisted that it should be built of adobe instead of logs. He went to Taos, engaged a number of Mexican workmen to make and lay the brick, and sent a wagonload of Mexican wool to mix with the clay as a binder.

Fort William, later known as Fort Bent, was 180 feet long and 135 feet wide, the walls 15 feet high and 4 feet thick. At its southwest and northwest corners were bastions, 30 feet high and 10 feet in diameter, with loopholes for muskets and openings for cannon. The second-story walls of the bastions were hung with sabers, heavy lances with long sharp blades, and muskets for use in case of an attempt to scale the walls. To prevent such attempts at night, the tops of the walls were thickly planted with cacti, which grew so luxuriantly that they overhung the sides.

Stores, warehouses, and living quarters opened into a graveled patio, in the center of which a brass cannon was mounted to impress the Indians. The rooms around the walls of the court were roofed with poles covered with grass and brush, overlaid with clay and a covering of gravel. The walls projected four feet above the roofs, which served as a promenade. The floors of the rooms were of hard-packed earth.

The east and main gateway was fitted with two large plank doors, reinforced and fireproofed with sheet iron studded with nails. The west or rear gate, opening into the corral, was constructed similarly, as was the south gate facing the river. A square watch tower was surmounted with a belfry, topped with a flagstaff. On the western side of the fort, outside the main walls, was a corral as wide as the fort, to hold large herds of cattle or horses. The corral walls were eight feet high and three feet wide at the top. An adobe house stood two hundred yards to the southwest of the fort; ice cut from the river in winter was stored in it to insure a fresh meat supply in summer.

The fort was a rendezvous of trappers, traders, plainsmen, Indians, Mexicans, adventurers, and Government troops on occasion. Trading began with the opening of the gates at sunrise. The Indians, whose tents were pitched around the fort, were soon passing in and out, at times filling the courtyard. While traders and clerks were busy at their work, patrols walked the battlements with loaded muskets, and guards stood in bastions with burning matches to light their carronades. At sunset the

Indians returned to their tents, and the great gates were swung shut for the night. Vigilance at Fort Bent was never for a moment relaxed.

In 1835 troops commanded by Col. Henry Dodge met near Bent's Fort with chiefs of several tribes to assure protection on the Santa Fe Trail. In 1840 the Cheyenne, Comanche and other tribes held a peace council 3 m. below the Fort and exchanged gifts bought from William Bent. In 1846 the Fort became hq for the Upper Platte and Arkansas Indian Agency. When war with Mexico came in May, 1846, Gen. Stephen Watts Kearny stopped at the Fort with 1,650 dragoons and Missouri volunteers for two summer months, then moved on to take Santa Fe and New Mexico. The U. S. Government found the Fort a convenient base for Army Quartermaster stores and teamsters.

Bill Williams, Dick Wootton, and other noted trappers made the post a rendezvous; Kit Carson was employed by Bent as a hunter from 1831 until 1842, when he joined Frémont's first expedition into the Rocky Mountains. Frémont used the fort as a base of supplies in 1845; Gen. Sterling Price, en route to Mexico in 1847–48, traveled by way of Bent's Fort and enlisted William Bent to guide him to Taos. From this brief association with the Army, William retained the honorary title of colonel.

William Bent married Owl Woman, daughter of White Thunder, a Cheyenne medicine man. Owl Woman died at the birth of a daughter, Julia, and William married her sister, Yellow Woman. After the Mexican War, Charles Bent, who had married Inezita Jaramillo, sister of the wife of Kit Carson, was appointed first Territorial Governor of New Mexico. On January 19, 1847, while visiting his family in Taos, he was killed by Mexican and Pueblo Indian rebels.

After his brother's death, William Bent continued the business of Bent & St. Vrain. Just when St. Vrain withdrew from the firm is not known, but he was a partner as late as 1850. With the lessening demand for beaver pelts and the decimation of the buffalo, trading became less profitable each year. Bent attempted to sell the fort to the Federal Government, but negotiations were so slow that in 1852, after loading his goods on 20 large wagons, each drawn by six yoke of oxen, he blew up the fort and moved five miles down the river to Short Timber Creek. Some of his men were sent with goods to trade with the Indians on the Platte; others he sent to a point on the Arkansas where Fort Lyon now stands. In the spring of 1853 Bent established still another fort forty miles down the river (*see Tour 9a*).

In 1859 William Bent was appointed United States Indian Agent for the Cheyenne and Arapaho but resigned the following year. He had entered into a contract to haul Federal Government supplies about the time he abandoned his fort here in 1852 and continued in that business until 1862. When hostilities with the Plains Indians became serious in 1864, Bent was employed to visit the various camps in an attempt to localize the trouble. But with troops roving the country, attacking Indians wherever found, it proved impossible to control the tribes. The Sand

Creek Massacre (*see Tour 8a*) in the fall of 1864 put an end to the old life on the upper Arkansas; within a few years the Indians of the region were forced onto a reservation in Oklahoma. In his last years Bent was separated from the people among whom he had married and lived peacefully for 40 years. The old trader died at the home of his daughter, Mary, near the Purgatoire River, May 19, 1869.

〖✦

Tour 9B

Gunnison—Crested Butte—Kebler Pass—Paonia—Hotchkiss; 82 *m.,* State 135.

The Denver & Rio Grande Western R. R. parallels the route between Gunnison and Crested Butte, and between Somerset and Hotchkiss; no service between Crested Butte and Somerset during winter.

In the country through which this highway passes sleep many old mining towns; each has its white-haired veteran who spins tales of wealth suddenly gained and often as quickly lost, of gold camps that sprang up overnight and boomed feverishly for a few years, only to be deserted for new bonanzas. When the spring sun warms the blood of these ancients, they pack their frugal stores on the backs of burros and with their dogs again start hunting the yellow metal.

State 135 branches north from US 50 (*see Tour 9*) in GUNNISON, 0 *m.* (7,703 alt., 4,050 pop.) (*see Tour 9b*), and follows the Gunnison River through flat park lands to the junction with a dirt road, 3.8 *m.*

Left on this road, which follows Ohio Creek through a fertile valley growing timothy hay as winter feed for Hereford cattle, is BALDWIN, 14.5 *m.* (8,500 alt.), supported by coal mining and stock raising.
Left from Baldwin 2 *m.* to the CASTLE CREEK RANGER STATION; along the creek brightly colored sandstone has been weathered into minarets, towers, and spires.

The highway crosses the southern boundary of GUNNISON NATIONAL FOREST, 7.8 *m.,* a tract of 1,660,050 acres of Federal, State, municipal, and private land. Established in 1905 by President Theodore Roosevelt, the forest was named for Captain John W. Gunnison. By 1968 the Government had equipped 34 campgrounds of 470 units, some suitable for trailers, and 5 picnic areas. There are 56 lakes in the forest. Open ranges here provide good pasturage for livestock; the many streams are annually stocked with rainbow, native, eastern brook, and Loch Leven trout; in the more inaccessible regions are elk, mule deer, black and brown bear, and mountain sheep.

The road ascends the Gunnison River, a famed trout stream, to ALMONT, 11 m. (8,000 alt.), a fishing resort. Here the East and Taylor Rivers unite to form the Gunnison.

Right from Almont on a dirt road to TAYLOR PARK (*camp grounds*), 5 m., a high meadowland fringed with groves of aspen, fir, and spruce.

TAYLOR DAM AND RESERVOIR, 19 m., is an important Federal irrigation project completed in 1937.

Right 10 m. from the dam on a rough mountain road (*drive carefully*), is TINCUP (*cabins and general store*), once a booming gold camp, now practically deserted except for summer visitors. The camp, first known as Virginia City, was rechristened by Fred Lottes, a prospector, who used a tincup to wash gravel. There were two smelters here in 1880, and when the town was incorporated in 1882, it claimed a population of 1,200. Tincup was notorious for the high mortality rate among its peace officers. CROSS MOUNTAIN (12,200 alt.), southwest of the town, is a miniature Mount of the Holy Cross (*see Tour 5c*); its snowy cross melts much later in the season than that on the larger mountain.

At 22 m. is the junction with a dirt road. Right on this road to the rocky valley of CEMENT CREEK, and through wild country to the southern side of ITALIAN MOUNTAIN, 14 m., 13,350 ft.

CRESTED BUTTE, 28.5 m. (8,885 alt.) began as a gold camp in the 1880's when more than $350,000 worth of nuggets came from nearby Washington Gulch. It is now a highly popular ski resort, equipped with a Telecar gondola, with a vertical rise of 2,000 ft.; a T-bar, a J-bar, and more than 24 m. of ski trails. Skiing from Thanksgiving to Easter. Lodges, inns and chalets, some open all year, provide food and lodging, and cocktail rooms. A ski school has classes for young and adult. The town has sports and curio shops, also reminders of its mining past in bars, Old Town Hall, mine shafts. Coal Creek runs through the town. While average mean temperature of Gunnison County is 38.5°, snowfall in Crested Butte Ski Area averages 200 in. Visitors may use Frontier Airlines to Gunnison; Colorado Springs is 168 m., Denver 201 m. away. Lift rates (1969), $5.50 a day for adults, $4 for half day; single gondola ride, $2.50. T- and J-bars, $3.75 a day.

Right from Crested Butte on a dirt road overlooking the East River, to the few remaining cabins of GOTHIC, 7.3 m., an early mining camp in a magnificent valley. Here is the ROCKY MOUNTAIN BIOLOGICAL LABORATORY, offering courses in biology, parasitology, field botany, and field zoology. The laboratory was organized for use by independent investigators, and by graduate and advanced undergraduate students in biology. The elevation (8,000–14,000 alt.) makes for great variety in plant and animal life. The broad meadows are covered in summer with Indian paintbrush, columbine, harebell, and wild roses.

Left 5.5 m. from Gothic on a dirt road and foot trail through a virgin forest to EMERALD LAKE (*fishing*), in a region designated by the U. S. Forest Service as a Primitive Area.

State 135 ascends through green uplands and rises above timberline to alpine meadows where many sheep are pastured in summer.

At 35.0 m. is the junction with a dirt road.

Right on this road is IRWIN, 1 *m.*, the first gold camp in the region, established in 1868.

1. Left from Irwin 0.5 *m.* on a forest road to LAKE IRWIN (*good hunting and fishing*), at the foot of RUBY PEAK (12,749 alt.).

2. Right from Irwin 4 *m.* on a foot trail to the summit of SCARP RIDGE. REDWELL and PEELER BASINS, dotted with small lakes in a setting of flowers, grasses, and evergreen trees, lie (R) below the ridge, while giant peaks tower above it.

The highway ascends steadily through luxuriant growths of flowers, grasses, and shrubs, crossing a high mesa to KEBLER PASS, 36 *m.* (10,000 alt.), with a view (L) of MOUNT BECKWITH (12,371 alt.), named for a lieutenant in Captain John W. Gunnison's exploring party. Southwest of Mount Beckwith is GUNNISON PEAK (12,714 alt.); right of the highway is rock-ribbed MARCELLINA PEAK (11,349 alt.), its sides scarred by glaciers.

The highway crosses the western boundary of Gunnison National Forest, 49.4 *m.* West of BARDINE, 58.1 *m.*, great veins of coal are exposed along the road; Grand Mesa, largest flat-topped mountain in Colorado, looms on the right. Following the North Fork of the Gunnison, State 135 enters a country of productive fruit farms growing giant Elberta peaches, apples, apricots, and pears. Sugar beets, potatoes, alfalfa, and truck crops are also grown.

At 72.4 *m.* is the junction with State 187.

Left on this graveled highway is PAONIA, 2 *m.* (5,674 alt., 1,250 pop.), chief supply center for this horticultural and agricultural area; extensive coal mining is also carried on. Paonia derives its name from the peony common in the region in early days.

Southwest of Paonia the highway crosses a strip of farming country to the junction with State 92, 13.5 *m.*, 1.3 miles northwest of Crawford (*see Tour 9C*).

HOTCHKISS, 82 *m.* (5,369 alt., 625 pop.), is at the junction with State 92 (*see Tour 9C*).

I⟨⟩I⟨⟩I⟨⟩I⟨⟩I⟨⟩I⟨⟩I⟨⟩I⟨⟩I⟨⟩I⟨⟩I⟨⟩I⟨⟩I⟨⟩I⟨⟩I⟨⟩I⟨⟩I⟨⟩I⟨⟩I⟨⟩I⟨⟩I⟨⟩I⟨⟩I⟨⟩I⟨⟩I⟨⟩I⟨⟩

Tour 9C

Sapinero—Black Canyon of the Gunnison—Hotchkiss—Delta; 83.9 *m.*, State 92.

The route is paralleled by the Denver & Rio Grande Western R. R. between Hotchkiss and Delta. It traverses an old Ute hunting ground where deer, elk, and bear are still found.

State 92 branches northwest from US 50 in SAPINERO, 0 *m.*
(7,255 alt.) and follows the old Black Mesa Indian trail, ascending the
slopes of the Black Mesa by easy stages. Now and again there is a
glimpse of the Black Canyon of the Gunnison. At 6 *m.* is the junction
with a dirt road.

Left on this road is CURECANTI, 1 *m.* (7,500 alt.), named for a Ute who,
with his twin, Kanneatches, for many years directed the Ute Bear Dance, a
spring festival.

The highway traverses the edge of the Black Canyon, presenting a
breath-taking view of the 2,000-foot chasm cut through granite by the
river. The road doubles back through groves of aspen and spruce, and
across meadowlands where cattle find excellent pasturage.

MAHER, 43 *m.* (6,882 alt.), is a trading point for farmers and
ranchers.

At 46.5 *m.* is the junction with a graded dirt road.

Left on this road to the BLACK CANYON OF THE GUNNISON NA-
TIONAL MONUMENT, 11 *m.,* established by President Hoover on March 2,
1933. It includes 10 miles of the most picturesque portion of the 50-mile gorge,
the deepest in Colorado; in places it narrows to 10 feet; its walls rise a sheer
3,000 feet at their highest point.
The first white men to see and explore the Gunnison River were a party of
Spaniards under Don Juan Maria de Rivera, who set out from Santa Fe in
1765 to prospect for gold in the mountains to the north. Upon touching the
Gunnison near the western end of the Black Canyon, the expedition carved
a cross on a tree near the river. Again in the summer of 1776 the river
was visited by a smaller expedition led by the priests, Francisco Escalante
and Antacio Dominguez, in search of a new route to the Spanish missions in
California. Escalante called it the Rio de San Xavier, a name it bore for many
years.
The Black Canyon was first noted in some detail in 1853 by Captain John W.
Gunnison, who had been appointed by Jefferson Davis, then Secretary of War,
to conduct a survey for the purpose of finding a practicable route for a transcontinental railroad. Gunnison followed the river that bears his name until the
stream lost itself in the dark depths here, where he was forced to turn back.
The highway reaches one of the wildest and most rugged sections of the
canyon near the center of the monument (*camp and picnic grounds; spring
water*), 14.2 *m.;* trails lead to many points of interest along the canyon rim.
Here the walls of the gorge rise 2,400 feet above the narrow canyon floor,
150 to 300 feet wide. Towers, pinnacles, spires, and other fantastic rock formations create a magnificent scene. At intervals narrow side gorges break the
walls, the largest being Red Rock Canyon, which enters from the south.
Sunshine brings out the striking color of the Black Canyon, cut through
a rock mass consisting chiefly of granite, with a crystalline complex of gneiss
and schists, and occasional dikes of permatite. In the granite and granitic
gneiss are whites, pinks, reds, and grays; the schists are predominantly black,
although blue occasionally occurs. Seams and large flakes of mica are found
along the canyon rim, together with veins of feldspar and quartz. The folds,
veins, and seams of the canyon walls vary in thickness, texture, and direction;
some are horizontal, others vertical, but most of them are curved and bent.
After autumn frosts the Black Canyon is bright with color. Against a background of dark pine and spruce are splashed the flaming red of scrub oak and
mountain mahogany, the bright green of the holly-like Oregon grape, and the
vivid lemon-yellow of aspens and willows. Occasionally, elk, bear, and mountain

lion range the canyon rim; along the water courses, beaver, muskrat, and mink are numerous.

In the winter of 1881, Byron H. Bryant, engineer for the Denver & Rio Grande Western Railroad, led a small party through the canyon in search of a feasible rail route; except for detours at two narrow places, they followed the bottom of the gorge for its entire distance, being the first to do so.

In 1901 a party of five volunteered to explore the canyon to determine whether the waters of the Gunnison might be diverted by a tunnel from the Black Canyon to the Uncompahgre Valley for irrigation purposes. Having spent three weeks traveling 14 miles, they turned back, but in August of that year A. L. Fellows of the U. S. Reclamation Service, and W. W. Torrence of Montrose, a member of the first party, reported after a perilous trip through the canyon that the Gunnison River waters could be so diverted by a tunnel through Vernal Mesa; the project was completed in 1909.

South of the junction US 92 descends into a farming district growing hay, grains, and potatoes.

HOTCHKISS, 60.5 m. (5,369 alt., 625 pop.), was named for G. L. Hotchkiss, who with Samuel Wade planted the first orchard in Delta County in the early 1880's. In this prosperous fruit and farming community is held the annual Delta County Fair each fall.

Hotchkiss is at the junction with State 133.

The highway traverses a region where peach, cherry, and apple culture and dairy farming are the chief sources of income. The North Fork of the Gunnison River provides irrigation.

Southeast of AUSTIN, 75.4 m. (5,070 alt.), a shipping point for fruit and dairy products, the route passes many small farms growing strawberries, raspberries, currants, sweet potatoes, and celery. Honey from the bee hives along the road is an important product.

At 80.9 m. is the junction with State 65 (see Tour 5E), which unites with State 92 into DELTA, 85 m. (4,961 alt., 4,100 pop. est.) (see Tour 9c), at the junction with US 50 (see Tour 9c) and State 348.

 I⟨◦I⟨◦I⟨◦I⟨◦I⟨◦I⟨◦I⟨◦I⟨◦I⟨◦I⟨◦I⟨◦I⟨◦I⟨◦I⟨◦I⟨◦I⟨◦I⟨◦I⟨◦I⟨◦I⟨◦I⟨◦I⟨◦I⟨◦I⟨◦I⟨◦I⟨◦

Tour 9D

Grand Junction—Colorado National Monument—Fruita; 30.9 m., US 50 and Monument Highway.

This tour leads through Colorado National Monument, by way of Rimrock Drive, a region of haunting beauty of a type unusual to Colorado. Here also are numerous dinosaur beds filled with fossilized remains.

In GRAND JUNCTION, 0 m. (4,587 alt., 22,735 pop.). US 50 continues northwest, parallel with the Colorado River and the right of way of the Denver & Rio Grande Western Ry. Another road crosses the river, sluggish except in spring. South of the river the road crosses a level plain inclosed with huge cliffs, the pasture ground of large bands of sheep guarded by overall-clad herders and their alert, shaggy dogs.

In the DINOSAURS BEDS, 4 *m.,* which extend more than a hundred miles along the banks of the Colorado River, bones and incomplete skeletons of the giant prehistoric saurians have been found in great numbers. One specimen of a 90-foot brontosaur, 13 feet high, removed from the beds in 1902, is in the Field Museum, Chicago. Many gastroliths, or gizzard stones—round, smooth, highly polished stones that formed part of the digestive system of the dinosaurs, have been unearthed. This region was once a torrid zone. Petrified bamboo stalks, ferns, and fossilized palm leaves have been uncovered in the same geologic stratum that yielded the dinosaur remains.

The highway crosses the eastern boundary of COLORADO NATIONAL MONUMENT, 4.8 *m.,* an area of 28 sq. mi. created in 1911; it is seamed with canyons, honeycombed with caves and filled with magnificent monoliths. It was established after long agitation by John Otto, a solitary settler in Monument Canyon, who built roads and trails. It is administered by the National Park Service, with Superintendent's hq at 334 So. 10th St., Montrose, 81401. A Ranger Station is at the east entrance on US 50.

Left from the shelter house on a rough dirt road into NO THOROUGHFARE CANYON to the foot of THE DEVIL'S KITCHEN (L), 0.5 *m.,* a huge sandstone formation named for its resemblance to a cluster of old-fashioned square chimneys. Across the canyon (R) is the UMBRELLA ROCK, a stone toadstool about 30 feet high.

The highway passes the mouth of No Thoroughfare Canyon and begins a steep ascent, known here as The Trail of the Serpent Drive, to COLD SHIVERS POINT, 7.5 *m.,* on the brink of a 1,000-foot precipice overlooking COLUMBUS CANYON, a tributary to Red Canyon (*see below*).

At 7.7 *m.* is the junction with a dirt road.

Left on this road is GLADE PARK, 6.3 *m.* (6,496 alt., 150 pop.), a store and post office.

1. Right from Glade Park a dirt road winds through a scenic region to rejoin the main road, 5.2 *m.*

2. West from Glade Park the road crosses a level section of Piñon Mesa to (R) ELA NATURAL BRIDGE, 7.2 *m.,* here the waters of Trail Canyon Creek have tunneled through the soft sandstone to form a red rock arch. At 8.5 *m.* is the junction with a semicircular drive leading past MIRACLE ROCK, 10.2 *m.,* a colossal boulder 80 feet high and weighing 12,000 tons, balanced on a narrow point of the underlying stratum.

South of Cold Shivers Point the route winds along RIMROCK DRIVE, on the edge of RED CANYON. The drive reaches the upper end of UTE CANYON (R), 12 *m.,* and skirts the rim of the gorge for several miles, overlooking cavernous depths hemmed in by sculptured walls. In May, June, and July, this section of the drive is bright with wildflowers—cacti, yucca, wild geraniums, and Indian pinks; scrub pine and cedar predominate on the mesa top.

At 16 *m.* is the western junction with the Glade Park Road (*see above*).

The highway skirts the edge of MONUMENT CANYON, with nothing to be seen from the road but the canyon floor 1,000 feet below; miles of this highway have been hewn from solid rock. Weird formations of red sandstone rise from the sagebrush-sprinkled valley floor. The road passes above the SQUAW'S FINGERS (R), 18.4 *m.,* a formation resembling the fingers of a hand.

At 18.5 *m.* is the junction with a trail.

Right down this trail to the COKE OVENS, 50 *yds.,* a row of great red and yellow sandstone masses resembling kilns or beehives.

Along the drive appear (R) CLEOPATRA'S COUCH, 19.7 *m.,* and MONOLITH PARADE and KISSING COUPLE, 19.9 *m.* INDEPENDENCE MONUMENT (R), 21.4 *m.,* the largest monolith in the park, juts abruptly from the flat canyon floor to a height of 1,000 feet.

At 23 *m.* is the junction with a circular drive.

Right on this road to VISITOR CENTER, 0.1 *m.,* a modern four-room sandstone building in landscaped grounds. Nearby is the SADDLEHORN camp and picnic area, with shelter.
Proceeding along the rim of Monument Canyon, the road overlooks PIPE ORGAN and the PRAYING HANDS, 0.4 *m.*
At 0.5 *m.* is a footpath.
Right here 200 *yards* to the KEYHOLE, a projecting part of the canyon wall which terminates in a natural bridge; from the top of the bridge is an excellent view of Monument Canyon and its scattered formations.

The highway descends to Fruita Canyon, passing through two tunnels that enable the road to cross over itself. Beyond DOUBLE BALANCED ROCK (R), 25 *m.,* the road crosses the western boundary of Colorado National Monument, 27.4 *m.* Vast dinosaur beds here (R) contain fossilized pink snail shells. Although these were fresh-water animals, the formation in which they are found is believed to have been laid down by a salt sea.

In FRUITA, 30.9 *m.* (4,512 alt., 1,870 pop.) (*see Tour 9c*), is the junction with US 50 (*see Tour 9c*).

Tour 10

La Junta—Thatcher—Trinidad; 81.5 *m.*, US 350.

US 350 is a section of the National Old Trails Highway, a transcontinental route between New York City and Los Angeles. Between La Junta and Thatcher the route is virtually that of the Military Branch of the old Santa Fe Trail that ran from Bent's Fort (*see Tour 9A*) to Taos, New Mexico. In the summer of 1846, during the war with Mexico, United States forces under command of Colonel Stephen W. Kearney, known as Kearney's Army of the West, traveled it from Bent's Fort to the Hole-in-the-Rock.

In LA JUNTA, 0 *m.* (4,100 alt., 12,000 pop. est. 1968), US 350 branches southwest from US 50 (*see Tour 9a*), traversing arid prairie country; sagebrush, cacti, yucca, and mesquite cover a somber land, the habitat of prairie dogs, jack rabbits, and lizards.

TIMPAS, 17 *m.* (4,200 alt., 80 pop.), consists of a few weather-beaten houses, a station, and general store. Far in the distance (R) rise the Spanish Peaks, the Wet Mountains, and Pikes Peak. South of Timpas a 20-mile belt has been ravaged by floods; deep gorges slash the prairies, and once-rich grazing land has been ruined. Only a few stunted cedars, sagebrush, and cane cacti relieve the desolate scene. The cane cactus, a giant in regions farther south, grows to a height of three or four feet here; during June it bears red and yellow blossoms.

At 44 *m.* is the junction with a dirt road.

Right on this road 0.5 *m.* to the HOLE-IN-THE-ROCK; although dry since 1929, this was one of the few watering places available to early trappers and traders traveling from Bent's Fort to Santa Fe. The trail, used by ox teams and horses, and also for cattle herds, crossed from the Arkansas to Timpas Creek and followed that stream to the point where it turned west.

In THATCHER, 45.5 *m.* (5,398 alt.,), named for M. D. Thatcher, southeastern Colorado banker and business man, are the HELIUM WELLS AND PLANT. The wells have been capped since the Federal Government started operations at its own plant in Amarillo, Tex.

South of Thatcher the prairie is broken by a low line of hills, their slopes matted with buffalo and gramma grasses, nesting places of the melodious black-and-white lark bunting, Colorado's State bird, and the yellow-breasted lark.

TYRONE, 54 *m.* (5,544 alt.,), is a station on the railroad.

Right from Tyrone on a dirt road to HOLE-IN-THE-PRAIRIE, 0.5 *m.*, a series of miniature lakes in a natural bowl, a watering place on the old Santa

Fe Trail and the Chisholm Trail from Texas. Vast northbound herds of longhorns, pack and wagon trains, painted Indian war parties, and troops of cavalry rested here, or met and clashed for possession of the water. In the days of the Chisholm Trail as many as two thousand head of cattle were watered here at one time. Deep-cut depressions left by old wagon wheels are visible along the sides of the little lakes. Many old cow-country ballads were sung by punchers driving their herds north. Among the songs still popular in this region is "The Old Chisholm Trail," which ends with the cowboy's lament:

I went to the boss to draw my roll;   6 1-2
He figgered me out nine dollars in the hole.
So I'll sell my outfit as fast as I can,
And I won't punch cows for no damn man.
With my knees in the saddle and my seat in the sky,
I'll quit punching cows in the sweet bye-and-bye.

At 59.5 *m.* is the junction with a dirt road.

Left on this road to PURGATOIRE CANYON, 23 *m.*, its walls eroded into grotesque shapes. Fossils dug from the cliffs and river bed belong to the age of giant reptiles, and hieroglyphics carved on the rocks have been identified as the work of prehistoric Indians.

The highway traverses a vast sagebrush-and-mesquite plain, frequented by desert horned larks and sage hens, dotted with prairie dog "towns." These colonies, honeycombing large areas, are identified by hundreds of mounds of earth dug from the burrows. The favorite pose of the furry little animal is to sit erect on the edge of a mound, tiny forepaws uplifted. When alarmed, he shakes his bushy tail and, with a ludicrous flirt of hind legs, dives from sight. Although called a dog, probably from its shrill bark, the animal is a rodent of the marmot family. During the early 1890's enterprising ranchers killed, dressed and shipped prairie dogs to eastern markets as "mountain squirrel." For several years they appeared on hotel menus in New York and Philadelphia; not until a buyer came west to contract for larger shipments was the hoax discovered.

The comical little burrowing owl, also known as the "Billy" owl, occupies many of the abandoned holes and lives on good terms with the prairie dog; the popular belief that these two share their underground quarters with rattlesnakes has no basis in fact.

South of EARL, 63.5 *m.* (5,673 alt.), a shipping and supply center, is Sunflower Valley, a prosperous farming district. Sheltered by cottonwood groves, farmhouses appear among rolling green fields of sugar beets, alfalfa, and beans. This area is notable for its pinto beans; as high as 2,500 pounds have been raised on an acre.

At 65.5 *m.* is the junction with a dirt road.

Right on this road is HOEHNE, 5.5 *m.* (5,705 alt., 320 pop.), named for Bill Hoehne, a German who settled here in 1865. The ditch he built from the Purgatoire River that year was the first extensive irrigation project in this region. The original 60 acres irrigated from the ditch are still watered from the same channel.

Left from Hoehne 7 *m.* on a dirt road to the old DeBusk Farm, laid out by Sam DeBusk, who in 1882 filed the first petition for adjudication of water rights in Las Animas County. Crossing this farm is the HATCHER DITCH, later known as the Lewelling-McCormick Consolidated Ditch, the oldest irrigation project in continuous operation in Colorado. John Hatcher, Indian fighter and plainsman, worked for Kit Carson, the Bent brothers, Jim Beckwourth, St. Vrain, and others of the time. He was sent to this district in 1846 by the Bents and St. Vrain to establish a farm, but was driven out when Indians killed his cattle and burned his crops.

South of Hoehne, the long winding trenches on both sides of the highway represent Colorado's incessant activity to prevent the destruction of rich lands by erosion.

At 74.5 *m.* is the junction with US 160 (*see Tour 11a*), which unites with US 350 as far as TRINIDAD, 81.5 *m.* (6,025 alt., 10,735 pop.) (*see Trinidad*).

In Trinidad is the junction with US 85 (*see Tour 12c*), US 160 (*see Tour 11a*), and State 12 (*see Tour 11A*).

❧❧❧❧❧❧❧❧❧❧❧❧❧❧❧❧❧❧❧❧❧❧❧❧❧❧❧❧❧

Tour 11

(Johnson, Kans.)—Springfield—Trinidad—Walsenburg—La Veta Pass —Alamosa—Pagosa Springs—Durango—Cortez—(Monticello, Utah) ; US 160.
Kansas Line to Utah Line, 540.4 *m.*

Atchison, Topeka & Santa Fe Ry. parallels route between Springfield and Pritchett; Colorado & Southern Ry. between Branson and junction with US 350; Denver & Rio Grande Western R.R. between Trinidad and South Fork; Rio Grande Southern R.R. between Durango and Mancos.
Accommodations limited between Kansas Line and Trinidad.

US 160, most southerly of trans-State highways, crosses two great mountain ranges and passes such notable points of interest as the Great Sand Dunes National Monument, the old Spanish settlements of the San Luis Valley, the Ute Reservation, and the cliff dwellings in Mesa Verde National Park and Hovenweep National Monument.

Section a. KANSAS LINE to WALSENBURG; 222 m. US 160

Crossing a dry-land farming area, this section of the route traverses a once-prosperous mining region now devoted to cattle raising and agriculture. The region was the habitat of the bison, chief food supply of an Indian race that left traces of its primitive culture in the form of petroglyphs, arrowheads, and other artifacts on the broad plains and mesas.

The highway crosses the KANSAS LINE, 0 *m.*, 18 miles west of Johnson City, Kans. and proceeds through barren plains broken by occasional arroyos and buttes to Bartlett, 6 *m.*, in Baca County. This is a part of that section loosely known as the Dust Bowl, which includes portions of southeastern Colorado, southwestern Kansas, and northern Oklahoma and Texas; it is frequently clouded by heavy spring dust storms. These storms are of recent origin, caused by the plowing up of the protective grass mat to plant wheat during World War I. Wind erosion was augmented by the long drought of the early 1930's. For several years almost no rain fell in the summer, and in the winter the fields lay dry and bare without their usual covering of snow.

Great dust storms here are at once magnificent and terrifying. They move forward in sky-high walls, black and ominous, and plunge the land into darkness. Sand sifts into houses and automobiles, even into intricate working parts of fine machinery. Often these storms cover vast areas. That which harried Colorado, Oklahoma, Kansas, New Mexico, and Texas on May 12, 1934, carried dust eastward across the United States to fall on ships far out at sea.

Scores of families were driven out by drought and wind. The dust piled up in drifted ridges, buried fences and idle machinery, swirled high about sun-warped buildings. But the wheat farmers of the ravaged Colorado plains are a hardy stubborn breed; most of them stayed on, believing that droughts occur in cycles. During the worst periods nothing could be grown; the air was hardly to be breathed. Even travel was sometimes precarious, for when the storms descended, cars were marooned on the highway, their drivers forced to wait until visibility returned. The wind that scoured the land to the raw subsoil drew from these men and women a grudging and bitter humor.

"Part of my farm blew off into Kansas yesterday, so I guess I'll have to pay taxes there, too," said one. "The wind that blew south Wednesday passed over my place came back yesterday and dropped some of the land it took away," said another. They told stories of "black snow" storms so dark they couldn't see to lace their shoes. A drop of water fell on a man, said one of his neighbors, "and we had to throw two buckets of dust in his face to revive him." A stranger driving through the region stopped at a farm house to remark at a cloud in the blazing sky. "Think it'll rain?" he inquired. "Hope so," said the farmer, "not so much for my sake as the children's. I've seen rain."

Since 1937 increasing moisture has fallen in the dust bowl, and many farmers are convinced that the drought is ended. However, Baca County has needed emergency tillage funds from the FHA. In cooperation with engineers and experts of the Department of Agriculture, the farmers are fighting to reclaim their land; three-fourths of Baca County, which constitutes the southeastern corner of Colorado, is now organized in soil erosion districts under the auspices of the State Soil Conservation Board with an integrated program for returning the land to grass. Planting of sorghums and other wind-resistant crops, contour farming, basin listing, and furrowing are being used in an effort to lessen wind damage, and considerable success has attended these efforts.

TWO BUTTES, 20.7 *m.* (4,075 alt.), was founded in 1909 by the builders of a reservoir north of the village.

Right from Two Buttes on a zigzag dirt road are the TWO BUTTES, 20 *m.*, for which the town is named. At their base TWO BUTTES LAKE (*boating and fishing*) has been created by the damming of Two Buttes Creek, its water used to irrigate adjoining territory.

West and south of Two Buttes the highway crosses almost level prairie land to SPRINGFIELD, 43.6 *m.* (4,365 alt., 2,000 pop.), seat of Baca County, settled by residents of Springfield, Mo., who named it for their home. Large fields west of Springfield are planted to winter wheat, and during midsummer small hills of threshed grain, bright yellow in the sun, are seen along the road, waiting to be trucked to market. Many here are "suitcase" farmers, residents of other districts, who appear in September and October to sow their wheat and return the following June and July to harvest the crop.

Baca County produces almost all of the broomcorn grown in the State, having some 30,000 acres of it under cultivation in 1938. Natural gas and petroleum account for more than $1,000,000 annually in value of mineral production in the county. New pipeline facilities were completed in 1965.

PRITCHETT, 59.8 *m.* (3,900 alt., 247 pop.), is the center of a large farming and dairying district. Only a mound of stones beside the road marks the SITE OF JOYCOY, 62.7 *m.;* the origin of its curious name is not known. West of Joycoy the highway traverses a country dotted with prairie dog towns and broken by sandstone bluffs and mesas covered with a scant growth of piñon and juniper. These singular rock outcroppings provide nesting places for the swift-flying prairie falcon, most splendid of Colorado's small birds of prey, which hides its brick-red eggs on the ledges and in the numerous potholes in the cliffs.

KIM, 96.3 *m.* (5,680 alt.), named for Kipling's boy hero, was founded by Olin D. Simpson in 1918 when he established here on a corner of his homestead a store and a post office. The large stone COMMUNITY BUILDING, with gymnasium, was completed under the Work Projects Administration.

1. Left (southeast) from Kim on a dirt road to CARRIZO MOUNTAIN, 18 *m.;* at the eastern foot of this large butte, 20 *m.,* is the SITE OF CARRIZO SPRINGS, which flourished in the 1880's when the copper mines to the south were in operation. The site is commonly known today as The Tubs, because the big wooden tanks that still stand here are used by stockmen.

2. Right from Kim on another road to POTATO BUTTE, 21.8 *m.,* jutting up from the surrounding prairie land; on the cliffs an ancient people carved petroglyphs.

Visible (L), 105 *m.,* are the steep slopes of Mesa de Maya (*see below*), covered with juniper and piñon. West of TOBE, 112 *m.* (5,500 alt.), a combined filling station and post office, the road crosses CHACUACO CÁNYON, 120.5 *m.,* a fissure created by torrents from Mesa de Maya, which in places have cut several hundred feet through sedimentary strata to red bedrock, sculpturing mesas, chasms, towers, and other fantastic formations.

While US 160 now proceeds west to Beshoar Junction, State 389 moves south—toward the New Mexico line.

BRANSON, 138.5 *m.* (6,000 alt., 237 pop.), was first settled by Spanish-Americans from New Mexico, who brought in small flocks of sheep, cattle, and chickens, and built their houses of sun-dried brick along small streams and springs. Descendants of the pioneers still occupy these dwellings. Lack of moisture, overgrazing, and farming of submarginal lands have transformed this country into practically desert land.

1. Left from Branson on a graded dirt road to TOLLGATE CANYON, 1.5*m.,* on the New Mexico State Line. In the days when few trails crossed the mountains, Bill Metcalf, an early settler, erected a tollgate here between two tall pillar-like stones on each side of the road. In the narrow canyon the traveler could neither proceed nor turn around with his ox team, and was glad to pay a 75¢ toll. Metcalf also established a profitable saloon near his tollgate. Metcalf was not the only man to make the most of what nature offered along the old highway. A desperado known as Black Jack stationed dummy men with wooden guns along the road to assist in his holdups.

One of the trails used by Colonel Charles Goodnight in driving cattle from Texas into Colorado entered the State through Tollgate Canyon and followed Trinchera Creek to the Purgatoire and the Hole-in-the-Prairie (*see Tour 10*).

2. Left from Branson on a graded road to MESA DE MAYA, 16 *m.,* named, according to one story, by a Spanish explorer who found mayflowers abundant on the slopes and draws of the great tableland. Petroglyphs, easily accessible by trail, are chiseled in the cliffs; arrowheads, stone axes, and other relics have been found near by. Abundant buffalo grass once covered the mesa top, and grama grass grew waist high in the draws and valleys, making ideal pasturage for the longhorn steers brought by cattlemen into the area during the 1870's.

West from Branson, the route traverses a cattle-grazing territory. To the south (L) is a long low escarpment, known as PIÑON RIDGE, which extends more than 30 miles westward. Above the ridge are NIGGER and HARDESTY MESAS, which give way in turn to the higher tablelands of JOHNSON and RATON MESAS.

TRINCHERA, 149.6 *m.* (7,567 alt.), a Spanish-American settlement, is a shipping point for cattle.

BARELA, 162.5 *m.* (5,739 alt.), was named by Casimiro Barela, known as the "Perpetual Senator," who served Las Animas County as its representative for 40 years (1876–1916). He owned extensive properties in Las Animas County, New Mexico, Old Mexico, and a coffee plantation in South America. His home at Rivera, near Barela, was maintained with all the pomp and state of a feudal lord.

Left from Barela on a dirt road, which follows San Francisco Creek Valley through foothills heavily overgrown with scrub oak, cedar, and a scattering of piñons, to CORTESE'S RANCH, 3 *m.*, and DUTTO'S RANCH, 5 *m.*

South from Dutto's Ranch 7 *m.* by trail to a GOAT RANCH. More than 6,000 goats are pastured annually in Las Animas County, and the home manufacture of goat-milk cheese is a leading industry; the cheese is shipped to domestic and foreign markets. Ascending the steep side of RATON MESA (Sp. mouse), the road crosses and recrosses SAN FRANCISCO CREEK (*good fishing*). Scrub oak increases in size, willows give way to aspens and cedars, piñons to pines and firs. This isolated section has many wild flowers, ferns, and shrubbery not found elsewhere in the State. Brown bears, coyotes, timber wolves, skunks, badger, deer, grouse, and pheasants are encountered on the mesa. The luxuriant grasses on the SUMMIT OF RATON MESA (9,450 alt.), 10 *m.*, fatten large herds of white-faced Herefords. Kanyatche, a chief of the Southern Ute, led his tribesmen on successful hunts over Raton Mesa. The territory was contested by the Comanche, who placed their dead in tree-tops along San Francisco Creek. Hunters, fishermen, and cowboys occasionally come upon these relics.

The highway passes through a region of deep arroyos cut by summer freshets to a junction with State 206, 171.8 *m.*

Left on this dirt road over Frijole Hill and through fields of beans, where prairie lands have been plowed in contour lines designed to retain moisture, to C. C. C. CAMP BUILDINGS, 7 *m.*

At 8 *m.* is TRINIDAD (*see Trinidad*).

BESHOAR JUNCTION, 176.5 *m.*, is at the junction with US 350 (*see Tour 10*), which unites with US 160 for 7 miles.

Huge slag piles at the eastern entrance to EL MORO, 179.8 *m.* (5,841 alt., 206 pop.), are refuse from coke ovens operated in the 1880's when coal from the district was converted into coke for use in the Pueblo smelters and steel works; the ovens were abandoned early in 1900. El Moro was a one-time rival of Trinidad.

SAN RAFAEL HOSPITAL, 181.5 *m.*, a large gray stone building, Trinidad's only hospital, is operated by the Catholic Sisters of Charity.

TRINIDAD, 183.5 *m.* (6,025 alt., 10,735 pop.) (*see Trinidad*), is at the junction with US 85 (*see Tour 12c*), US 360 (*see Tour 10*), and State 12 (*see Tour 11A*).

US 160 is united with US 85 as far as WALSENBURG, 222 *m.* (6,200 alt., 6,000 pop.) (*see Tour 12c*).

Section b.   WALSENBURG to ALAMOSA; 75 m. US 160

This section of the route crosses the Sangre de Cristo Range and traverses the San Luis Valley, largest of the four great mountain parks in Colorado. Politically and economically, the valley is part of Colorado, but culturally the southern extremity is an integral part of New Mexico. Shut off on all sides from the rest of the State by mountains, the valley developed almost as a minor principality. A large proportion of the inhabitants are descendants of early Spanish settlers, who retain many of their old customs and manners of living.

West of WALSENBURG, 0 *m.,* the highway passes through a region of dry grass-covered hills. In scattered park-like valleys crops of vegetables, hay, and grains are grown; some cattle are pastured on the slopes, but primarily this is an industrial district, its life centering around the coal mines that normally employ hundreds of workers.

Dominating the landscape are (L) EAST SPANISH PEAK (12,683 alt.) and WEST SPANISH PEAK (13,623 alt.), twin mountains standing well away from the Culebra Range, of which they are a part. Because of their isolated position, the Spanish Peaks served as landmarks for early explorers and fur traders, and their imposing bulks were regarded with superstitious awe by the Indians (*see Tour 12c*).

West of the Junction with State 111 (*see Tour 11C*), 15.1 *m.,* the route traverses foothill country near the southern edge of the Sangre de Cristo Range; forest growth becomes heavier as the road ascends by long curves to OJO HOT SPRINGS, 21.8 *m.* (*cabins, bathing*). The highway makes a sharp half-circle at MULESHOE, 26.2 *m.,* ascends by twists and loops to LA VETA PASS (9,378 alt.), 29.1 *m.,* a low, heavily-timbered saddle between the Sangre de Cristo and Culebra Ranges, then descends through foothills into the SAN LUIS VALLEY, a stretch of level prairie 125 miles long, with an average width of 50 miles. Once disputed by the Ute and Comanche, it was finally captured by the former. Irrigation canals are constructed in straight lines for long distances across the flat terrain. The valley was one of the first sections in Colorado penetrated by the Spanish, and many residents today are of that origin. The first recorded Spanish expedition northward along the Rio Grande into Colorado was that of Juan Maria Rivera in 1761. In 1779 the military expedition of Bautiste de Anza, pursuing the Comanche chief Cuerno Verde (*see Tour 12c*), traversed the valley from south to north and named several streams in the valley—among them, the Conejos and La Jara.

The first white man to enter from the east, it is believed, was James Purcell, a Kentucky trader, who was forced into the mountains here by hostile Indians in 1803. Lieutenant Zebulon M. Pike's expedition entered by way of Mosca Pass in 1807, and proceeded southward to the Conejos River (*see Tour 15c*); 40 years later Frémont crossed the valley in search of a route for a transcontinental railroad.

Settlement began about 1850 with the establishment of several small villages on Mexican land grants. Population rapidly increased after gold discoveries in 1870.

West of La Veta Pass, US 160 crosses a section of the 240,000-acre TRINCHERA RANCH, largest private estate in Colorado. The ranch is a fragment of the 1,038,000-acre Sangre de Cristo Grant given by the Mexican Government to Stephen Louis Lee and Narciso Beaubien in 1843. When the grant was made, Beaubien was 13 years old. He and Lee were killed four years later during the Pueblo Indian revolt in New Mexico that cost the life of the New Mexico Territorial Governor, Charles Bent (*see Tour 9A*). Beaubien's share of the grant passed to his father, Charles Beaubien, owner of a considerable part of the Maxwell Grant near Trinidad (*see Tour 12c*), and Lee's half was sold to the father for $100. After the elder Beaubien's death virtually all of the Sangre de Cristo Grant was purchased by William Gilpin, first Territorial Governor of Colorado, and his associates. In 1937 the Trinchera Ranch was bought by Mrs. Ruth McCormick Simms of Sante Fe, New Mexico, at a reported price of $500,000. Herds of cattle and sheep are grazed here, and the ranch has more than 6,000 acres of hay lands.

RUSSELL, 35.9 *m.* (9,105 alt.), a small mountain community clustered about a post office and general store, was founded as a placer-mining camp in the 1860's.

At 48.1 *m.* is the junction with an unimproved dirt road.

Left on this road to the unmarked SITE OF FORT MASSACHUSETTS, 6 *m.*, the first United States settlement in the San Luis Valley, and, so far as known, the first military post established by the U. S. Army in Colorado. Founded in 1852 to protect immigrants in the valley from Indians, the fort lay in a swampy hollow surrounded by foothills; soldiers not killed by the Indians were sickened by stagnant waters. The post was abandoned in 1858, and what was left of its garrison was removed to Fort Garland (*see below*).

FORT GARLAND, 50 *m.* (7,996 alt.), is a drowsy little farming town on the flat and arid eastern floor of the valley. Most of its buildings are of adobe; constructed of bricks about twelve inches long, six inches wide, and three inches thick, they are typical of such structures throughout the San Luis Valley. A mixture of adobe clay and water, into which straw has been worked for reinforcement, is molded by hand into bricks and dried in the sun. Adobe of a thinner consistency is used as mortar. In early days foundations were of stone bonded with this mortar; modern adobe structures are usually built on concrete foundations. Beams hewn from long logs are laid across the tops of the walls; usually they project two or three feet on each side, and the roofs consist of boards laid across the beams and thickly covered with adobe mud. The Spanish call the projecting timbers *vagas,* and on them string long ropes of red peppers, which add a touch of color to the gray walls.

Interiors are finished with adobe plaster. Contemporary buildings are usually brightened with stucco and whitewash; original settlers were usually content with hard-beaten earth as floor, but newer dwellings have wooden flooring. Undecorated, modest, in design, adobe houses usually have but one room. Sometimes window sills and door jams are painted a brilliant blue, a custom originating in the Spanish belief that the devil abhors this color, sacred to the Virgin Mary, and will not enter where it appears.

Named for Brigadier General John Garland, a fort was built here in 1858 when Fort Massachusetts was abandoned. The post was maintained until 1883 when the command was removed to Fort Lewis in the San Juan Basin. The fort was rather a threatening gesture to check the Ute, a refuge and social center for settlers, than an actual base for military operations.

James Baker, Lieutenant Colonel Albert Pfeiffer (*see below*), and Tom Tobin, noted frontier figures, lived here from time to time; Kit Carson commanded the post in 1866–67. In this vicinity Tobin killed the last of the Espinosas, fanatic assassins (*see Tour 5b*), and to prove it and claim the reward offered by the Territorial Legislature, cut off the man's head. As the legislature was not in session at the time, Tobin kept the trophy pickled in alcohol. A physician, so it is said, stole the head and departed for Pueblo. Discovering his loss, Tobin set out in pursuit and recovered it, for the doctor had dropped and broken the jar containing it. Tobin proceeded to Pueblo, where "a most unusual situation confronted him, because for the first and last time in the history of that city there was neither whisky nor alcohol enough to re-pickle the head." A supply train soon arrived with "strong waters," and Tobin claimed his reward.

OLD FORT GARLAND, on the southern edge of town, consists of a series of long low adobe buildings about a central plaza, or parade ground, shaded by huge cottonwood trees. The highway cuts across the old parade grounds, a portion of the old adobe walls having been destroyed to provide a right-of-way. In the center of the plaza are an old cannon and a tall flagpole.

In the STATE MUSEUM are preserved guns and other relics.

Trinchera Creek is the principal water supply for Smith Reservoir, 703 acres, and Mountain Home Reservoir, 639 acres, near Fort Garland.

Left from Fort Garland on State 159, across a tableland, to SAN LUIS (7,596 alt., 750 pop.), 15.5 m., seat of Costilla County, one of the oldest communities in Colorado. The town lies at the center of the Sangre de Christo Grant (*see above*). The first successful attempt to found a town on the grant was made in 1851 when six Spanish families settled north of the present town. Their adobe houses were built around a square, both for protection against Indians and promotion of social life. The outer walls were without openings, and all doors and windows faced the square, in which wells were dug. The surrounding land was divided into ranches. A tract of 860 acres, reserved as a town common in accord with the system then in vogue in Mexico, has been retained. The Ute made numerous raids on the colony, stealing livestock and supplies, until the establishment of Fort Massachusetts (*see above*).

San Luis has changed little since its early days. The inhabitants have preserved their culture, social life, foods, and dress, drawing inspiration from Spain and New Mexico.

Although the county seat, San Luis has not been incorporated. The population of Costilla County was estimated at 4,100 in 1964.

The Americans of Spanish descent are a religious people, most of them being of the Roman Catholic faith. Some belong to the Society of the Penitentes (*see Tour 11B*). Adobe churches, highly ornamented, are the dominating buildings in all old valley towns. The stone CHURCH OF THE MOST PRECIOUS BLOOD, erected in the early 1860's, still stands here. A general store, established in the same year by the Gallegos family, later kept by D. Salazar and known as the SALAZAR STORE, is said to be the oldest continuously operated business enterprise in Colorado.

At San Luis a short road, State 152, leads to Chama, San Pablo and San Francisco. About 10 m. is the SANCHEZ RESERVOIR, 3,151 acres, 103,155 acre-ft., largest in Costilla County.

West of Fort Garland, US 160 traverses the heart of the San Luis Valley, carpeted with sage and greasewood, a silvery plant that grows prolifically throughout the arid regions of the Southwest. Much of this area, splotched with alkali, is unfit for cultivation. North of the highway loom the overpowering bulks of MOUNT BLANCA (14,363 alt.) and OLD BALDY (14,125 alt.), rising abruptly from the level plain at the southern edge of the Sangre de Cristo Range. Visible from all parts of the San Luis Valley, these jagged peaks are among the highest in Colorado; they are, in reality, one mountain connected by a high saddle, and on many maps are shown as one. Geologists believe that a higher summit was torn away ages ago, either by glaciers or by volcanic action, leaving the two lesser stumps.

BLANCA, 54.5 m. (7,870 alt.), a community of adobe and stucco buildings, was born of a land drawing held in August 1908. People throughout the country bought small tracts of land here when offered a chance to draw for larger tracts. On the morning of the lottery hundreds of persons were encamped along Ute Creek. Difficulties in obtaining water rights and the generally unproductive soil prevented growth of the town.

What is called the shortest main line railroad is the Southern San Luis Valley R. R., with 1.3 m. of track, which connects with the Denver & Rio Grande W. at Blanca.

The highway crosses the sluggish RIO GRANDE, 74.6 m., more properly the Rio Grande Del Norte (Sp. Great River of the North). Rising above Creede and flowing in a southeasterly direction through the San Luis Valley, the stream marked the boundary between Texas and Mexico in 1836-48, and later marked the eastern limits of the territory obtained from Mexico after the Mexican War of 1848.

ALAMOSA (Sp. poplar grove), 75 m. (7,544 alt., 7,500 pop. est.), is the seat of Alamosa County, which has large crops of potatoes, vegetables, hay and barley, except for occasional drought. The city is a shipping center, served by the Denver & Rio Grande Western Ry., Continental Trailways, and Frontier and Silver State airlines. Its water supply comes from deep artesian wells, and natural gas is piped from the southwestern border. The city was founded 1878 when Garland City, former terminus of the D. & R. G. W. Ry., moved to this site. Stores, churches and houses were moved on flatcars. The townsmen suppressed a rowdy element by promptly hanging cattle rustlers and desperadoes on a poplar tree. Its newspaper is the *Alamosa Valley Courier*.

ADAMS STATE COLLEGE, estab. 1921, and named for Governor William H. Adams, is a liberal arts college with emphasis on training teachers and enrolls approx. 2,500, with a similar number using its state-wide extension service. It has 97 acres south of the Rio Grande, where the Education-Social Studies Bldg. and the Leon Memorial Bldg. (musical and recital groups) are recent additions in a program that will add a student union, and a library-reading resources center, each costing $2,000,000. The Planetarium and Observatory are open to visitors. The

Education Bldg. has a museum for anthropology and complete television equipment. The Fred J. Plachy Field House stands on 47 acres north of the Rio Grande.

One of the nation's most scenic highways is that used by the Alamosa-Durango section of the Denver & Rio Grande Western Ry., built 1879–1881, dying of lack of business, 1968. Trucks, using the fine concrete roads, took over its freight; passengers favored the skies. This narrow-gauge line of 199.5 *m.* ran south from Alamosa to Antonita parallel with US 285; crossed and recrossed the Colorado-New Mexico border and moved through the Combres Pass, 10,022 ft. above sea level. It passed through the Kit Carson National Forest, touched Chama, Monarco and Dulce, N. Mex., the last the town of the Jicarilla Apache Indian Reservation. It then moved north to Durango. In 1950 the regular passenger service was discontinued and only special trains were run to please tourists. In 1968 the D. & R. G. W. asked the Interstate Commerce Commission to abandon the section, on the ground that it incurred an annual loss of $500,000. Civic organizations endeavored to save the line for touring purposes.

Alamosa is at the junction with State 17 (*see Tour 11C*) and US 285. The latter joins US 160 as far as Monte Vista, 17 *m.,* then turns north to Saguacha.

Section c. ALAMOSA to UTAH LINE; 243.4 m. US 160

Proceeding through an agricultural belt into mountain country, this section of the tour descends into a region of sagebrush plateaus broken by mesas and many canyons. The route passes centers of a prehistoric culture and the last home of the once-powerful Ute, traverses grazing country where the customs of early cattle days are practically unchanged, and crosses desolate areas where the scattered inhabitants live in a more primitive manner than the ancient Cliff Dwellers.

West of ALAMOSA, 0 *m.,* US 160 traverses the intensively cultivated floor of the San Luis Valley. Almost all farms are under irrigation. The chief crop is potatoes, although many acres are sown to wheat, barley, oats, lettuce, cauliflower, alfalfa, and field peas. Pea-fed hogs from the San Luis Valley command top prices on the Pacific Coast. Potatoes are of high quality, and yields range from 400 to 700 bushels an acre. The long low buildings frequently seen from the road, built partly underground, are potato cellars.

At 16 *m.* is the junction with a road to HOMELAKE.

Right on this road to the MONTE VISTA GOLDEN AGE CENTER, a State-supported institution for the Colorado aged, which gives preference to veterans and closely-related dependents; to assistant cases on welfare roles, and to independent individuals at fixed fee. The appropriation is approx. $275,000 a year. About 130–150 persons can be accommodated. The present organization dates from 1958. Previously the State Soldiers & Sailors Home was located here.

MONTE VISTA (Sp. mountain view), 17.5 *m.* (7,500 alt., 4,000 pop. est.), lies in the center of the San Luis Valley at the intersection of US 160 (the Apache Trail) and State 15. Founded 1887 it has been a home-rule city since 1922 with a council-manager government. In a highly irrigated area served by reservoirs of the Rio Grande, the mountains and deep wells, it is a superior potato producing country and annually ships 10,000 carloads of Red McClures, as well as russets and other varieties. It also ships Moravian barley, for malting; lambs and wool, processes meat from the beef-cattle and sheep ranches, makes potato starch and flakes, farm machinery, and stores wool and lumber. The city is served by Continental Trailways, Interstate trucklines, the freight section of the Denver & Rio Grande Western. It has a minicipal airport 5 *m.* east near US 160. The *Monte Vista Journal* is its weekly newspaper. It has the hq of the Rio Grande National Forest.

The city also is a focal point for vacationers, since hunting, fishing, boating, camping, and skiing are available, as well as trips to old forts and mining towns. It is one of the few places in the State where deeds provide for the forfeiture of land if intoxicating liquor is sold on the premises.

The Ski-Hi Stampede, a three-day rodeo, founded 1919, is held annually late in July or early in August. Events include riding broncos and wild cattle, bareback riding, bulldogging, roping, lassoing of running animals, intricate tricks with one or more lariats, and trick riding by horsemen who swing under the neck and belly of their mounts—a feat learned from the Indians who used such tactics in warfare. Indians are sometimes brought from the reservations to perform their dances and ceremonials. Visual color is not lacking on the rodeo grounds; the sun blazes down upon the brilliant silk shirts, scarfs, and huge hats of the riders, and the elaborate trappings of the horses. The intercollegiate Top o' the Nation Rodeo of Adams State College takes place here.

Monte Vista is at the northwestern junction with US 285 (*see Tour 15b*).

Left from Monte Vista on an unnumbered country road to the PICTURE ROCKS, 10 *m.* (*private property; apply to owner of the Monte Vista Garage*). These cliffs lining Rock Creek have been carved and painted with petroglyphs or pictographs. Until 1935 these were believed to be the work of contemporary Indians, but in that year prospectors seeking gold stumbled upon a human skeleton and a well-preserved fragment of pottery. Archeologists now believe that the designs were the work of a people closely akin to those who lived on Mesa Verde (*see Mesa Verde National Park*).

West of Monte Vista the highway traverses the level irrigated valley, its prosperous farms watered by a series of canals established by a co-operative association. Almost all the area is subirrigated; water is run through ditches about 300 feet apart, which raises the water table to within two feet of the surface and provides a continuously even supply. In all directions the green valley is fringed with the hazy blue-and-white of distant mountains. To the west are the jagged San Juans; to the east, the Sangre de Cristos.

DEL NORTE, 31.2 *m.* (7,874 alt., 2,100 pop. est.) seat of Rio Grande County, founded in 1860, was a convenient rendezvous for freighters who formerly hauled supplies from the eastern slopes to the mines in the San Juan district. The settlement was built of stone, and many of the business structures of that day still stand. Vigilantes were active here for a time in early days.

The *Del Norte Prospector* is its newspaper. The city is engaged in shipping and food processing, the county producing large crops of potatoes, barley, lettuce, and wool from approx. 85,000 sheep.

The road proceeds across dry sage flats, broken at intervals by narrow water courses fringed with willows and cottonwoods. Here and there abruptly rise rough tors, formed by the breaking of underlying granite strata during the volcanic period when the San Juan Mountains were created.

SOUTH FORK, 46 *m.* (8,250 alt.), is at the confluence of the Rio Grande and South Fork River.

At 47 *m.* is the junction with State 149 (*see Tour 21*).

US 160 crosses the eastern boundary of RIO GRANDE NATIONAL FOREST, 47.4 *m.,* with 1,798,839 acres of United States government land that almost entirely cover the eastern slope of the San Juans. There are few roads, but the forest is crisscrossed by trails, and camp and picnic grounds are numerous. The highway follows the South Fork River along a canyon darkened by lofty varicolored cliffs. The mountains are a natural setting for year-round sports; the slopes are so smooth that the construction of ski runs is unnecessary. In winter, dark green spruce stands out against the snow, and ice formed by freezing mists sparkles on trees, rocks, and canyon walls.

The route crosses the Continental Divide through WOLF CREEK PASS (10,850 alt.), 66 *m.,* the boundary between the Rio Grande and the San Juan National Forests. Descending sharply through Wolf Creek Canyon, the highway follows the SAN JUAN RIVER to WOLF CREEK CAMP GROUND, 74.5 *m.* The U. S. Bureau of Reclamation has been building the San Juan-Chama Project in Archuleta and Mineral Counties. It will take 110,000 acre-ft. of water from the upper tributaries of the San Juan River and by means of a tunnel through the Continental Divide provide irrigation for 39,300 acres in the Rio Grande Basin. Rising on the left is TREASURE MOUNTAIN (11,800 alt.), where, according to legend, a party of storm-bound Frenchmen cached much bullion about 1750. They never returned, and the gold was never found.

PAGOSA SPRINGS (Ind. healing water), 89 *m.* (7,077 alt., 1,500 pop.), seat of Archuleta County, was named for its hot mineral springs, the largest of which is called Great Pagosa. They were discovered in 1859 when an expedition of the U.S. Topographical Engineer Corps under Captain J. N. Macomb explored the region. A military post, established here in 1878 and named for Colonel Lewis, remained until

1882, when the garrison was removed to a point on La Plata River near Durango (*see below*).

The mile-square area surrounding the principal springs was designated by the Federal Government as a townsite and platted in 1880; lots were sold from the land office of the district. The extensive timber resources of the area brought in several sawmills, and for a period Pagosa Springs was the center of the largest lumber-producing region in Colorado.

The medicinal springs attracted many health-seekers, and with the decline of lumbering the town prospered as a spa. Until hotels were built, visitors occupied tents and cabins along the creek. Today the spring waters, with an average temperature of 153 degrees, are used to heat the town's courthouse, schools, and several business buildings.

The medicinal value of the springs was known to the Indians, and possession of them was long disputed by the Ute and Navaho. The two tribes at length agreed to settle the matter by a duel between a representative of each tribe. The champion selected by the Ute was Lieutenant-Colonel Albert Pfeiffer, Indian scout and aide of Kit Carson, who had been adopted by the tribe. Pfeiffer's stipulation that he be allowed to name the weapons was agreed upon, and he chose bowie knives. Story has it that as the two men rushed at each other, Pfeiffer hurled his knife at the Navaho, killing him instantly, and the springs became the undisputed property of the Ute.

Albert Henry Pfeiffer, born in Scotland in 1822, came to America in 1844, joined a freighting outfit at St. Louis, and worked his way to Santa Fe, New Mexico, where he was appointed captain of the mounted militia in 1859. His wife, a Spanish girl, was slain by Indians four years later. A life-long friend of Kit Carson, he served several years in the latter's regiment, operating in what was known as the Navaho country, and in 1865 was appointed lieutenant colonel for gallant and meritorious service. Having served as Indian agent in New Mexico, he took up a homestead near Granger, Colorado, where he was adopted into the Ute tribe, receiving the name of "Tata" Pfeiffer.

West of Pagosa Springs, US 160 follows the abandoned grade of the Denver & Rio Grande Western Railroad. The highway winds across a series of barren hills where weather stumps and a sparse growth of grass are all that remain of a once-dense forest.

At 91.4 *m.* is the junction with a graveled road.

Right on this road across the southern boundary of the San Juan National Forest, 3.4 *m.*, and upward through mountain forest to DUTTON CREEK, 3.5 *m.*, MARTINEZ CREEK, 5.5 *m.*, and O'NEIL CREEK, 13.5 *m.*, all good trout streams. North of GORDON CREEK, 13.6 *m.*, the road swings west to the PIEDRA CAMP GROUND (*free; information at Bridge Ranger Station*), 16 *m.*, on the PIEDRA RIVER, also noted for its fishing.

At WILLIAMS CREEK, 18 *m.*, the road turns again northwest, following the trout stream to the junction with a dirt road, 21 *m.*; R. here 3 *m.*, along Williams Creek, to the edge of the SAN JUAN PRIMITIVE AREA, at the foot of the Continental Divide. Mullins Dam on Williams Creek provides a reservoir excellent for fishing.

The route passes DYKE, 101.5 *m.* (6,081 alt.), a rural community, and crosses another boundary of the San Juan National Forest, 103.5 *m.,* to a junction with State 151, 105.3 *m.*

Left on this road is ARBOLES, 18 *m.* (6,005 alt).

At CHIMNEY ROCK FILLING STATION, 107.8 *m.,* is a foot trail.

Left on this trail of CHIMNEY ROCK, 1.5 *m.* (*approximately 1½ hours each way*), a formation standing on a high mesa that contains architectural remains believed to date back more than 1,000 years. These ruins are important as they indicate the limits of the territory inhabited by the prehistoric people of the Southwest. A pueblo chamber, 200 feet long and 80 feet wide, the only one excavated, is in a fair state of preservation. In the vicinity are approximately 100 mounds believed to cover other structures containing stone relics of archeological importance. Remains of signal fires indicate the manner in which these tribes communicated with each other.

US 160 crosses the RIO PIEDRA (Sp. stone river), 111.5 *m.,* a clear stream named, it is believed, by the Escalante expedition in 1776. At its headwaters lies untouched wilderness, one of the popular packtrip regions of the State. There are no roads, and horse trails are few and difficult to follow. The country at the source of the Piedra has been set aside as a primitive area in which no commercial development is permitted. Box canyons, dead-end chasms, are a peculiarity of the region. Waters fall into the upper ends of these gorges in roaring cataracts and foam across the stony floors between sheer granite walls to emerge in the foothills. Wild game is abundant; bear are seen in numbers, although the grizzly, most ferocious of the species, has disappeared. Deer, elk, and antelope are also found; as few fishermen penetrate this high country, fishing is exceptionally good.

The road winds up and down foothills that form the divide between the drainage basins of the Piedra and Los Pinos. The hills are covered with rich stands of pine interspersed with aspen. The San Juan is the only forest in the State in which the aspen is not native; all have been planted in reforestation operations.

The route crosses the southwest boundary of the San Juan National Forest, 129.3 *m.,* to BAYFIELD, 131.5 *m.* (6,500 alt., 322 pop.), in a grove of cottonwoods and willows on Los Pinos River.

North from Bayfield 12 *m.* on a paved road to VALLECITO LAKE, the second largest lake in Colorado. It is impounded by a dam 125 ft. tall, has a surface area of 2,730 acres and can hold 120,900 acre-ft. of water. A popular vacation area, it is surrounded by motels, lodges, and cabins; trailer parks and picnic areas, and supply stores. Well stocked with native, rainbow and German brown trout, northern and walleye pike, and kokanee salmon, the lake and tributary streams afford capital fishing. Riding and pack trips can be arranged, and boats and fishing tackle are available.

GEM VILLAGE, near Bayfield, is known for its rock curios.
At 147.2 *m.* is the junction with US 550 (*see Tour 18*).
CARON MOUNTAIN (L), 148.8 *m.* (7,834 alt.), has been
the object of observation by scientists because of frequent landslides, explained by erosion that undermined the anchorage of shale on a stratum
of sandstone.
DURANGO, 151.6 *m.* (6,512 alt., 11,600 pop. est.) seat of La
Plata County, is the center of the San Juan basin, a busy shipping point
for the products of cattle ranges and irrigated farms, and key to a
large area for outdoor sports. It attracts hunters, fishermen, campers,
skiers, and people interested in prehistoric cliff dwellings and Indian
culture. It has the benefits of highways US 160 (east-west) and US
550 (north-south); on the Apache Trail 37 *m.* from Mesa Verde National Park, and 84 *m.* from Four Corners, where the boundaries of
Colorado, New Mexico, Utah and Arizona meet. About 8 *m.* south is
the northern line of the Southern Ute Indian Reservation, and off US
160 on State 172 is Ignacio, hq of the reservation.
Durango has a modernized retail business section of 14 blocks and its
retail sales volume annually exceeds $35,000,000. A modern airport, 14
m. southeast of the city, is served by Frontier Airlines; other transportation includes major trucking lines and Denver & Rio Grande Western
freight service to Alamosa. The city has 44 hotels and motels to accomo-
date the tourists who annually expend some $15,000,000 in the area.
The farm crops of the San Juan basin include wheat, oats, barley
(especially malt barley) pinto beans, alfalfa, potatoes; apricots, peaches,
cherries; the products of aviaries, dairying and poultry raising. Timber
operators in the San Juan National Forest process lumber and wood
products worth more than $3,000,000 annually. There is some oil and
natural gas in the county, and 30 major operators maintain offices in
Durango. The Durango *Herald* publishes daily except Saturday.
On US 550 near Durango is located a large trout hatchery, with a
capacity of 10,000,000 annually.
The town was founded in 1880 by the Denver & Rio Grande Railroad, which avoided Animas City (*see Tour 18*) when building through
this region and established its own town here to profit from the business
created by the building of the road.
The first mail was carried in by anyone who happened to be coming
this way, and was dumped into a cracker box in a store, where those
expecting letters were at liberty to rummage. Water, hauled from springs
several miles away, sold at 40¢ a barrel. Court was held in a large room
over a general store, and on one occasion when the jury in a murder
trial was out, the spectators cleared the floor and had a dance. When
the jurors returned, the judge ordered silence while the verdict of guilty
was pronounced, after which the dance was resumed.
FORT LEWIS COLLEGE, a State-supported liberal arts college,
occupies a mesa above the city close to the towering San Juan Mountains.
It became a 4-year institution in 1962, and had moved to Durango a
decade before from the Fort Lewis site near Hesperus. It enrolls more

than 1,200 students and has a faculty of 80. A CENTER OF SOUTHWEST STUDIES has been established. Fort Lewis College cooperates with Colorado State University in an engineering program of three years at Fort Lewis, two at CSU. The college is actively engaged in completing a building program. A library-classroom building and six residence halls were opened in 1967 and a student center in 1968. A life-sciences section and eight new dormitories also were authorized. The College has special facilities for American Indian students and instruction for teaching aides and dormitory supervisors of the Bureau of Indian Affairs.

The SILVERTON TRAIN, a registered historic landmark, offers a unique daily experience to tourists and railroad buffs. A narrow-gauge (3 ft.) road, it was established in 1882 as a branch of the Denver & Rio Grande to serve the Silverton mining camp. In the 1950 decade, when it was the last of the narrow-gauge lines, it acquired importance as an antique unlocking the scenic wonders of San Juan National Forest and the canyons of the Rio de las Animas. The train makes the Durango-Silverton round trip daily from June to October, covering 45 miles through woods of aspen and ponderosa pine, past high cliffs and waterfalls, climbing hills and crossing trestles; if the riders are numerous a second section follows one hour after the first. (*For reservations address Agent, Rio Grande Depot, Durango, 81301; adults, $6.50; children 11 or younger, $4.50*)

The train departs from RIO GRANDE-LAND, the pioneer business section of Durango, located adjacent to the Rio Grande Railroad Depot, restored as a monument to pioneer railroading. Here also are the General Palmer House, a modern motor hotel in Victorian decor, the Grande Palace, a turn-of-the-century type restaurant, and several similar establishments.

West of Durango the highway traverses the flat cultivated valley into low rolling hills. On the west the granite LA PLATA MOUNTAINS are a saw-tooth edge against the horizon, sloping southward to fade into the high plateau country of Mesa Verde. Much of this country is good grazing land, and cowhands are occasionally seen rounding up cattle. In early days the native Ute were regarded as nuisances by cattlemen, who viewed "trespassing" Indians with suspicion, particularly when stock was missing. While searching for a horse, so runs the story, a rancher met and questioned a Ute who said that he was headed for the reservation. "You just come from the timber?" The Ute nodded. "Seen anything of a bell horse?" The Ute grunted and nodded. "Hobbled?" Another nod. "A light bay with U-X brand on the left shoulder?" Again the Indian nodded. "Well, he's mine," the rancher declared. "Where'd you run across him?" "No see um," the Ute responded.

Northeast of Durango on a paved road, 14 *m.*, is LEMON RESERVOIR of the Florida River section of the Colorado River Storage Project. The dam built by the U. S. Bureau of Reclamation, is an earthfill structure of 284 ft. high, 1,360 ft. long at the crest, with a maximum width at the base of 1,170 ft. tapering to 30 ft. at the top. The reservoir is one-half *m.* wide, 3 *m.* long, covers 600 acres, and has water capacity of 40,000 acre-ft. It was completed in 1963. Irrigation is its principal function.

The Bureau of Reclamation in 1963 rebuilt the Florida Farmers Diversion Dam, 7 *m.* east of Durango. It enlarged the Florida Farmers Ditch and the Florida Canal, in the Florida Mesa area nearby. All help irrigate this area.

At 159.5 *m* is the junction with State 140.

Left on this road to the former site of Fort Lewis College, originally a military post, later a State institution. The post, established in 1880, was garrisoned with troops moved from Fort Garland (*see above*) to protect the first white settlers in this region. After the Ute had been confined to reservations in 1892, the garrison was withdrawn, and the buildings at Fort Lewis utilized as an Indian school. For a time the Indian children could not understand and did not take kindly to "white-man schooling." They started fires that destroyed many buildings, including the barracks and most of officers' row. The 6,300-acre grounds included in the military reservation and the remaining buildings were turned over to the State by the Federal government in 1910 as part of the land grant college system, with the proviso that "Indian pupils shall at all times be admitted to such school, free of charge for tuition, and on terms of equality with white pupils." The State maintained a junior college here as a branch of Colorado A. & M. at Fort Collins (now Colorado State University). Fort Lewis College was moved to Durango in the 1950s.

Passing HESPERUS, 164.5 *m.* (8,113 alt.), a farm village, the route crosses the southern boundary of Montezuma National Forest, 169.3 *m.,* and ascends into higher plateau country to the crest of the divide between the watersheds of the Rio Mancos and Animas River. To the west is SLEEPING UTE MOUNTAIN; according to Indian legend, the Ute of this region were once a tribe of giants as large as this prostrate form. One year, departing to hunt in the north, they left a lone brave to guard their possessions. The faithful sentinel remained at his post day after day, year after year, for centuries. Finally, he stretched out on the ground and slept. His tribe, whose return he had vainly awaited, had offended the Great Spirit, it seems, and as punishment they had been reduced in stature to that of ordinary mortals. Only the faithful watcher, fast asleep, was spared. When, after many ages, the Ute returned home, they found him recumbent upon the ground, and here he still sleeps.

MANCOS, 182.5 *m.* (7,035 alt., 1,000 pop.), a shipping point for stock, is also an outfitting place for tourists, miners, and prospectors bound for La Plata Mountains, noted for their silver lodes. Much mining was done above timberline, lending support to the old prospectors' maxim: "A good silver mine is above timberline ten times out of nine."

West of Mancos the highway traverses what is known as the purple sage country, a broad level plateau. The sweep of purple and gray, accented by flashes of bright green, where juniper or scrub cedar has found root, lends the region an indescribable beauty.

At 190.1 *m.* is the junction with State 146, leading into Mesa Verde National Park. At 198.5 *m.* is the junction with State 145, which runs north to Telluride.

CORTEZ, 200.5 *m.* (6,200 alt., 8,000 pop. 1967 est.), seat of Montezuma County, is expanding because of profits from new enterprises, the county's oil production, principally at Aneth and Cache oil fields, and tourist business. Exploitation of the numerous natural formations and prehistoric Indian relics in the southwestern corner of Colorado is bringing thousands of visitors annually. Frontier Airlines provides daily flights at the County Airport, 5 *m.* south, and Continental Trailways maintains a daily schedule.

This is Four Corners country. The FOUR CORNERS MUSEUM, in the basement of the City Hall, displays dinosaur relics, Indian skeletons and artifacts. The Four Corners Boat Club holds races on July 4 on Lake Narraguinnep, the reservoir 15 *m.* north of town.

State 145 (off US 160), leads north 12 *m.* to DOLORES (830 pop.), and the beautiful Dolores River Valley; 3 *m.* farther is STONER, a new ski area.

Northwest on US 160 are sage-covered plateau and meager grazing fields for cattle and sheep.

YELLOW JACKET, 215.6 *m.* (7,035 alt.), chiefly a general store and post office, was named for a near-by canyon, the walls of which are plastered with numberless yellow jacket nests.

ACKMEN, 218.9 *m.* (7,000 alt.), is a trading post for Indians and tourists. Stock raising is the principal occupation of the surrounding country, which is slashed with dry arroyos and rocky canyons.

Left from Ackmen on a dirt road to RUIN CANYON (*inquire directions locally*), 6 *m.,* site of one of the many groups of prehistoric ruins of southwestern Colorado. Here in what at first apears to be a mound of quarried stones are discernible the crumbling walls of a 22-room pueblo.

Northwest of CAHONE, 225.8 *m.,* is DOVE CREEK, 235 *m.* (6,600 alt.), a frontier town resembling a movie set with its false front frame structures—one bearing in faded two-foot letters Dove Creek Opera House. In new buildings are tractors and farm implements displayed for sale. Development of the area was slow until the completion of the new highway in 1936. Farmers from the Dust Bowl in eastern Colorado, western Oklahoma, and Texas, have come in and grubbed sagebrush from the rich productive soil; the area is experiencing a small boom.

In his younger days Zane Grey, writer of western fiction, lived for a time in Dove Creek, and much of his novel *Riders of the Purple Sage* is said to have been written here. There are several elderly townsfolk who identify themselves with characters in the book.

US 160 crosses the UTAH LINE, 243.4 *m.,* 10 miles east of Monticello, Utah.

ᏆᏟᎭ

Cities and Towns

ᏆᏟᎭ

Colorado Dept. of Public Relations

STONE FACADE, CENTRAL CITY OPERA HOUSE (1874)

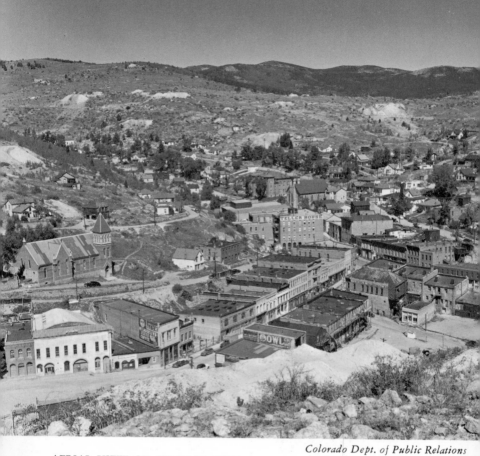

AERIAL VIEW OF CENTRAL CITY

TWO VIEWS OF THE BROADMOOR HOTEL, WITH NEW ADDITION

The Broadmoor, Colorado Springs

FORMAL DINING ROOM, BROADMOOR HOTEL

VICTORIAN PARLOR, TELLER HOUSE, CENTRAL CITY

SILVERTON IN THE SAN JUAN MOUNTAINS

Charles N. Bell Photo, Ouray

MAIN STREET IN ESTES PARK VILLAGE

Yale Camera Exchange, Denver

HOUSES AND SHACKS IN COLORADO GHOST TOWN

GHOST TOWN FOUND BY MODERN MOTOR CARS

CLOUD EFFECTS IN THE ROCKIES

Tour 11 A

Trinidad—Stonewall—Junction US 160; 66.3 *m.*, State 12. Two-lane paved road between Trinidad and La Veta.

Limited accommodations.

This tour traverses the picturesque Stonewall country and affords an opportunity for study of Spanish-American communal life. In the region around Stonewall Gap and Monument Lake are summer houses of many Trinidad residents; trout fishing is good; there is small game hunting in season in all sections outside San Isabel National Forest.

In TRINIDAD, 0 *m.* (6,025 alt., 10,800 pop.) (*see Trinidad*), State 12 proceeds westward by way of Robinson Hill. The road passes between low chalk bluffs wooded with cedar; the Purgatoire River (*see Tour 12c*) lies (L) just beyond a narrow strip of cultivated land.

JANSEN, 2.5 *m.* (6,085 alt., 30 pop.), a farm community settled in the 1860's, derives its income from garden truck and sugar beets.

West of Jansen the highway follows the northern bank of the Purgatoire River through higher foothill country, covered with a thick growth of juniper and piñon; numerous small farms and truck gardens dot the narrow valley.

At 4.8 *m.* is the junction with a dirt road.

Left on this road across the Purgatoire; on the hills above the road is (L) PIEDMONT, a former coal camp. Old weather-beaten houses are occupied by a few Spanish-American families.

SOPRIS, 0.7 *m.* (6,166 alt., 300 pop.), a small coal town founded by E. R. Sopris, pioneer, was originally known as the Sopris Coal Camp, and was at one time the largest producer in Las Animas County. Adobe huts along the road, built during the late 1870's, are occupied by Spanish-American coal miners.

At 6.8 *m.* is the junction with another dirt road.

Right on this road is COKEDALE, 1 *m.* (6,350 alt.), founded in 1906 by the American Smelting and Refining Company on land belonging to Sam Thor; incorporated 1948. Manufactures have ceased.

TIJERAS PLAZA (Sp. scissors), 9.5 *m.*, a small community of adobe huts occupied by Italian and Spanish-American coal miners, was so named because early settlers left the roof poles of their houses projecting beyond the walls in a "V" shape suggestive of scissor blades. A large adobe church (L), dedicated to the Child Jesus of Atocha, was erected in 1874 and is interesting for its unrelieved severity of design.

The thick walls are pierced by narrow windows and surmounted with a simple wooden spire crowned with a white cross. An adobe building (R) on a low hill, survival of an experiment of early Spaniards in communal housing, is divided into cubicles, the compartment doorways facing the road. Each apartment was occupied by a member of the family. When a son married, he built his one-room house against the wall of the family dwelling and thus had to erect only three walls instead of four. As the family's children grew up and established their own households, the size of such apartment buildings increased correspondingly. At the western edge of town is (R) an old graveyard, where several piles of small stones, some surmounted with wooden crosses, mark resting places on which coffins were temporarily placed while pallbearers rested.

At 10.9 m. is the junction with a dirt road.

Left on this road across the Purgatoire, is VALDEZ, 0.5 m. (6,000 alt.) ; the FREDERICK MINE here, with some 30 miles of underground tunnels, is one of the largest coal mines in southern Colorado. East of the Camp several hills of black slag have been burning for years, having been ignited by spontaneous combustion.

SEGUNDO, 12.3 m. (6,220 alt.), on the banks of the Purgatoire, has many dwellings and store buildings constructed of crudely fashioned red clay brick; window frames and doorways are painted bright blue, a color that inhabitants believe keeps the devil away. In the fall, strings of small dried pumpkins and red peppers hang from porch beams.

Right from Segundo on a dirt road to the ghost town of PRIMERO, 1 m., a flourishing coal camp with a population of 2,000 in 1902. Until 1925, when the town was abandoned, it produced more than 68,000 tons of coal a month. Most of the buildings have been torn down for salvage; only the walls of a church and the concrete bases of the mine tipple remain.

SAN JUAN PLAZA, 12.8 m., and ZARCILLO PLAZA (Sp. earring), 13.8 m., are family communities; the latter was named for two large rock formations in ZARCILLO CANYON, 14.3 m.

VELESQUEZ, 15.1 m., and MEDINAS PLAZA, 16.2 m., are likewise family communities; in the latter is GUADALUPE CHURCH (inquire at Velesquez for key), built sometime before 1872 and dedicated to Our Lady of Guadalupe. Three generations of the Medinas family live in this settlement.

The highway traverses Purgatoire Valley through luxuriant fields of alfalfa to CORDOVA PLAZA, 17.8 m., another family community ruled by the white-haired grandfather. It is virtually self-supporting; even the weaving of cloth was done by the women at one time. The MOUNT CARMEL CHURCH (open), built of adobe in 1872, is kept spotlessly clean; linens embroidered by the women of the family cover the altar. A priest comes from Trinidad each Christmas and again on July 16 when the founding of the church is celebrated. On the northern outskirts of the settlement, in an old MEXICAN CEMETERY (L), is a Penitente cross, constructed of poles eight inches in diameter and eight feet long, marking the spot where a Cristo fell while carrying a cross during one of the Good Friday rites of this cult (*see Tour 11B*).

West of Cordova Plaza the road winds between foothills into a valley largely devoted to stock raising. The wide meadows provide excellent pasturage during summer; alfalfa grown in the irrigated sections is cured for winter feeding.

WESTON, 19.6 *m.* (6,976 alt.), a hamlet built of wood instead of adobe and named for Sam Weston, pioneer settler, is the center of an extensive lumbering and farming area.

West from Weston is the STONEWALL, a long gray rock barrier stretching across the valley like an enormous dam. Beyond is a striking view of the Culebra range; granite crags and deep fissures sweep down sharply to the forests below. The highest peak in this section of the range is CULEBRA (14,069 alt.), noted for its double peak. To the left of Culebra is RED PEAK (13,600 alt.), prominent with its red sandstone cap.

STONEWALL, 30.1 *m.* (7,640 alt.), a resort town, was established in 1867 by Juan Guitterez, who grazed cattle in the valley. During the 1880's the settlement was the scene of many cattle and timber wars, during which grazing and lumbering interests bitterly fought homesteaders. A park here (*free campgrounds; cottage*) is maintained by the City of Trinidad.

Left from Stonewall on a dirt road across the Middle Fork of the Purgatoire and through high meadow lands to DULING'S LODGE, 1 *m.* (*meals, rooms, saddle horses*).
Right from the lodge 5 *m.* on wagon road to the junction with a foot trail; R. here 2 *m.* to LOST LAKE (*trout*). Far above timberline, its rocky shores fringed with alpine vegetation, kinnikinnick, creeping phlox, and stunted grass, the cold blue waters have never been fathomed.

The road passes through STONEWALL GAP, 30.4 *m.,* a natural opening in the dike that juts up at intervals across the United States from Mexico to Canada. According to geologists, the Stonewall was thrown up by the volcanic action that created the Sangre de Cristo Range, at which time great masses of lava were forced up through crevices in the granite understrata; only in this vicinity does it attain any considerable height; here the eastern face of the wall rises abruptly more than 250 feet high. On the steep dirt slope on the western side, trees, shrubs, and grasses find a precarious foothold. Waters of the Middle Fork of the Purgatoire River pour through the gap.

At 35.8 *m.* is the junction with State 152, also known as the Whisky Creek Pass Road.

Left on this dirt road over numerous switchbacks to the SUMMIT OF THE CULEBRA RANGE, 12 *m.* The road ascends Culebra Mountain through dense forests of aspen, fir, pine, and spruce. Turbulent Whisky Creek is crossed, recrossed, and finally lost as the highway climbs above timberline to the base of the gray granite crags of Culebra's precipitous peaks, reaching an altitude of 12,270 feet. This road was completed in 1937 as a Work Progress Administration project.

At 36 *m.* is the junction with a dirt road. Right on this road to MONU-MENT LAKE 0.5 *m.,* named for a monolith rising from its center. Trinidad and Las Animas County maintain a game preserve here for deer and buffalo.

The highway passes CITY HOUSE, 38.4 *m.,* a pumping station for the Trinidad Waterworks, ascends over hairpin curves to NORTH LAKE, 39.1 *m.,* part of the Trinidad water system, and crosses the eastern boundary of San Isabel National Forest, 45.1 *m.* (*see Tour 8b*). From CUCHARAS PASS (9,994 alt.), 46.5 *m.,* is a wide view of the towering Sangre de Cristo Range to the north and west, and the massive Spanish Peaks to the northeast. At the northern boundary of San Isabel National Forest, 54 *m.,* is a view of the huge walls that radiate from the Spanish Peaks like spokes of a wheel. One known as the DEVIL'S STAIR STEPS approaches the highway at this point. State 12 follows the widening valley of Cucharas Creek.

LA VETA (Sp. vein), 63.5 *m.* (7,024 alt., 782 pop.), a trading center, was incorporated 1886. According to an old Aztec legend, the valley in which La Veta lies, at the foot of the Spanish Peaks, was once a Paradise on earth, where no man suffered pain or cold, or was ever unhappy. This blissful state continued until the first Spanish arrived, when the gods of Huajotolla, as the Spanish Peaks were known to the early Indians, became angry and made the valley as other parts of earth.

La Veta is a center for registered Hereford cattle. The museum of the Francisco Fort, erected about 1863, is a tourist attraction.

At 66.3 *m.* is the junction with US 160 (*see Tour 11b*), 10 miles west of Walsenburg (6,200 alt., 6,000 pop.) (*see Tour 12c*).

ꜩꜩꜩꜩꜩꜩꜩꜩꜩꜩꜩꜩꜩꜩꜩꜩꜩꜩꜩꜩꜩꜩꜩꜩꜩꜩꜩꜩ

Tour 11B

Walsenburg—Westcliffe—Texas Creek (Junction US 50) ; 85 *m.,* State 69.

This route traverses a region once the stronghold of the Ute, whose trails crisscrossed mountains and valleys where game was abundant and sheltered parks provided excellent winter camp grounds. Spanish explorers followed these trails into the wilderness to build forts and search for treasure. This is a country of ever-changing mountain and river vistas, with high forests of spruce and pine, and numerous clear streams well-stocked with trout.

In WALSENBURG, 0 *m.* (6,200 alt., 6,182 pop.) (*see Tour 12c*),

State 69 branches northwest from US 160 (*see Tour 11*) and passes through extensive bituminous coal fields.

BADITO, 18 *m.* (6,387 alt.), on the Huerfano River, is at the entrance to the Huerfano Valley.

Left from Badito on a ⁻dirt road paralleling Oak Creek, to the crumbling ruin of an old SPANISH FORT, 7 *m.* The faint triangular outline of the walls crowns a hill overlooking Oak Creek and commands a good view of the valley where the old Taos Trail wound from Badito south to Sangre de Cristo Pass. The fort was built between 1819–20 at the order of Don Facundo Melagres, Spanish Governor of New Mexico, to guard the pass against American invasion. An encounter occurred a few months after the fort was constructed, when six members of the garrison were killed by an attacking party of white men reputedly disguised as Indians. The fort was abandoned after a treaty with the United States fixed the boundary along the Arkansas River.

State 69 crosses rough hilly country, skirting the southern edge of the Wet Mountains. The most prominent peak in this range is GREEN-HORN MOUNTAIN (12,334 alt.), named for the Comanche chieftain, Cuerno Verde (*see Tour 12c*).

FARISITA, 21.2 *m.* (6,700 alt.), was once known as Talpa, but the postmaster, John Farris, renamed it for his daughter, Jeanette, called "La Farisita" (the little Farris lady) by the Mexican inhabitants. FORT TALPA, an adobe outpost established by the Spaniards about 1820, still stands next to the general store.

A *morada* (meeting house) of *Los Hermanos Penitentes,* or the Penitent Brothers, appears among the trees across the river. While many members of this cult, all men, live in the Huerfano Valley, there is no general organization of supreme authority, each local society being independent. The chief officer, *hermano mayor* (elder brother), has absolute authority, and as a rule holds office for life.

Their grim practices, brought to New Mexico in 1598 by Don Juan de Onate, spread rapidly, although practiced secretly through fear of excommunication. In 1886 the Catholic Church attempted to abolish the flagellation ceremonies, but they still survive, a somber mixture of Christianity and Indian paganism.

During Holy Week their Passion Play is enacted up and down the Huerfano Valley, as in many other Southern Colorado communities, much as it was in the sixteenth century. The secret ceremonies start in the *morada,* where the freshly whitewashed adobe walls, it is said, are often splotched with blood after the flagellation rites have been concluded. Witnesses have testified that the brothers kneel before a *sangrador* (blood-letter), who gouges crosses on their bare backs with a piece of jagged glass. These wounds are kept open and bleeding, often by rubbing salt into them, until Easter. The Penitent Brothers whip themselves all Holy Thursday afternoon and night, chanting dismally as lashes of soapweed swish through the air.

Before dawn on Good Friday twelve chanting marchers leave the *morada* to the accompaniment of a wailing *pito* (flute) and march toward a secret *Calvario* in some mountain fastness; here the final ritual is enacted. Outsiders are not permitted to witness these proceedings; often deputy sheriffs are enlisted to insure privacy. Leading the procession are two men bearing lanterns to guide the bare, frozen, and bleeding feet of a brother clothed in flapping cotton drawers, with a black bag resembling a hangman's cap over his head. He stumbles along blindly, lashing his naked back and shoulders with a soapweed whip.

Behind him, similarly dressed, follows the *Cristo* elected to play the role because of his godly life. He staggers along under a huge wooden cross often five times his own weight. Trailing the *Cristo,* the other brothers continue to lash themselves with razor-sharp soapweed and cactus whips. Men have been known to tie the skull of a cow to a rope hooked with barbs into the muscles of their back, and drag the burden over the steep hills until the hooks are torn free.

Upon reaching the *Calvario* the procession halts. The *Cristo* is tied with ropes to the cross he has been carrying; the cross is then raised by attendants wearing headbands of thorns. Until half a century ago the man was nailed to the cross, but this is no longer done. Throughout this day-long ceremony the brothers continue to lash themselves until in pain or religious fervor they fall exhausted, or deliberately throw themselves into beds of cacti to increase suffering in penance for their sins.

At dusk the haggard and tortured brothers return to the *morada,* where others of the faith are waiting. As psalms are sung, the twelve candles burning on the altar are extinguished until only one remains lighted. The *amatrada,* a noise-making machine made with a flat piece of wood that rotates against a toothed wheel, is set in motion; chains are dragged across the floor and rattled; the *pito* shrills loudly in this pandemonium, which is a command to the dead to arise. Abruptly there is silence as the *hermano mayor* lifts his arms and chants a prayer for the dead. Singing is resumed, and the candles, one by one, are relighted. The brothers then kneel in a last prayer, and the grim ceremonies are concluded for another year.

GARDNER CONE (L), 23.3 *m.,* an old landmark, is recognizable by its squat shape and prismatic coloring. To the north (R) the hills are dark with groves of piñon pine. This conifer differs from others of the species in that its seeds are large and edible; the gathering and marketing of piñon nuts provides a regular source of income for the Spanish-American folk of this district. The pungent smell of burning piñon wood comes from the chimneys of the small adobe houses that dot the slopes.

GARDNER, 28 *m.* (7,002 alt.), typical of the old Southwest, retains the spirit of the frontier; many of its business buildings and houses are of adobe. Gardner, named for Herbert Gardner, a farmer instrumental in introducing cantaloupe into the Rocky Ford region (*see Tour 9a*), is the chief outfitting point for excursions into the Sangre de Cristo Range to the south and west. This is one of the few sections of Colorado where Spanish holidays are celebrated almost as they were one hundred years ago. Among the festivals are *El Dia Santiago* (St. James' Day) and *El Dia de Santa Ana* (St. Ann's Day). St. James' Day, better known as *Gallo* (Sp. cock) Day, is celebrated on July 25; the day is devoted to rodeo and racing events, the night to dancing. In former years a cock was buried in the sand, with only his head showing; riders galloped by, leaning from their saddles, as they attempted the difficult feat of plucking the bird from the sand by his head. A gunny sack is now substituted for the rooster, although the old practice survives in some small villages. St. Ann's Day is celebrated on July 26 by the women; open house is held throughout the community; and women go on horseback to visit their friends.

Left from Gardner on State 150 is MALACHITE, 6 *m.* (7,600 alt.).

Right from Malachite 1 *m.* on a dirt road to TOM SHARP'S POST, a log trading station built in 1870. It contains the table and chairs used by Sharp in entertaining his friend Ouray, chief of the Uncompahgre Ute (*see Tour 11D*). Sharp, born in Hannibal, Missouri, served in the Confederate Army and later came West as a prospector and railroad worker. Later, he settled near Gardner, constructed the trading post, and built a large red adobe house, still standing west of the post, furnishing it with goods brought by ox teams from Missouri. Sharp, who died in 1929, was among the first to bring thoroughbred horses into the West. His place was long known as Buzzard Roost Ranch because a large number of these birds roosted in the cottonwoods along the stream. An old Ute Indian trail, which can still be followed on horseback over the Sangre de Cristo Mountains, ran through Sharp's ranch, thence to Badito and Greenhorn Mountain.

Southwest of Malachite on State 150 is REDWING, 8 *m.* (7,800 alt.) and a dude ranch, HACIENDA DEL MONTE 10 *m.*, at the gateway to the HUERFANO PARK REGION, a mountain-rimmed valley known to the Indians as "the land where the grass is always green." In this forested area are numerous deer, elk, mountain sheep, beaver, and game fowl, and more than 15 miles of excellent fishing streams.

West of Gardner, State 69 follows winding Big Muddy Creek through wild and broken country to the top of PROMONTORY DIVIDE (9,000 alt.), 47 *m.*, separating the upper drainage basins of the Huerfano and Arkansas Rivers, affording a view (L) of the SANGRE DE CRISTO MOUNTAINS (Sp. Blood of Christ), named, so one story goes, by the Spanish explorer Valverde. One morning he broke camp in the Purgatoire Valley just as the sun was rising, led his band over a small hill, suddenly reined in his horse, and bowed his head in wonder at the prospect before him. Every snow-capped peak was bathed in a deep red glow against a bank of dark clouds. From Valverde's lips burst a fervent "Sangre de Cristo!" The Sangre de Cristo Mountains, extending in an unbroken chain from Salida southward to Santa Fe, N. M., are among the youngest mountains in the Rockies. Many of the great upthrusts have never been named or measured; eight rise more than 14,000 feet.

Directly west of Promontory Divide are the lofty peaks known as the CRESTONE NEEDLES, a group of almost unscalable points that challenge skilled climbers. Only foot and pack trails penetrate this region, which is being developed by the Forest Service as one of the great recreational areas of the State. Fishing is good in the many lakes and streams, and game is plentiful. In the valleys numerous stock ranches still range their herds much as they did when this was frontier country.

The mountains include Crestone Needle, 14,191 ft., Crestone Peak, 14,294 ft., Kit Carson Peak, 14,165 ft. and Humboldt Peak, 14,064 ft. On the west slope is the village of CRESTONE, reached by a road from MOFFAT, on State 17.

Here the Ute clashed with their ancient enemies, the Comanche, and adventurous Spanish soldiers and monks sought the gold of legendary mines in the hills. In January 1807, Zebulon Pike and his small party almost lost their lives in the snow fields on the high elevations when crossing Medano Pass into the San Luis Valley, where they were later captured by the Spanish. French and American trappers, the Mountain Men, followed mountain trails here to trap beaver. Silver Cliff, Rosita, Querida, and other mining towns of the region, many now vanished, contributed a colorful chapter to Colorado history when silver was king.

North of Promontory Divide State 69 descends into Wet Mountain Valley, drained by Grape Creek, which flows into the Arkansas River near Canon City. Most of the place names of this region are English, for the Spanish did not colonize the valley to any extent. The country differs from that along the Big Muddy; productive farms extend from the highway to the base of the mountains; luxuriant stands of alfalfa and fields of lettuce, celery, and potatoes, for which the valley is noted, surround well-kept houses flanked with barns and silo.

At 58 m. is the junction with a dirt road.

Left on this road through the San Isabel National Forest to the HENDRICK RANCH, 7 m., nearest automobile approach to Marble Mountain (see below) and its mysterious caves in the heart of the Sangre de Cristo Range.

West of the ranch (inquire here for directions and guides) a trail ascends 4 m. through a canyon to the MARBLE MOUNTAIN CAVES. In the marble formation are embedded numerous prehistoric plant and animal fossils, including those of the crinoid, a sea lily that moved about in pursuit of its food.

Seven caves have been discovered in this vicinity—among others, the BRIDAL CAVE, 300 feet deep; WOODMAN CAVE, 68 feet deep and shaped like a gallon jug; and MARBLE CAVE, never fully explored. The Forest Service has done little to publicize or develop the caverns, and warns against exploration without competent guides. Old Spanish legends refer to the Marble Cave as La caverna del Oro (the cave of gold) and have it that the Conquistadores entered it from another opening on the western or San Luis side of the range and worked rich mines in its depths. According to another tale, the fabulously rich Three Steps Mine of the Spanish was near the cave.

The blast of wind from the mouth of Marble Cave is very cold and so strong that it will extinguish a lantern or even a carbide light if unprotected by a reflector. A large Maltese cross is painted on a large rock at the entrance.

The cave was discovered in 1920 by Forest Ranger Paul Gilbert, who thus describes it: "I first heard of Marble Cave in 1919 from a Mexican woman who at the time was 105 years of age—she died at the age of 110. The woman stated that the Spanish obtained gold from it, that if one were to descend to a sufficient depth, a set of oak doors would be found, which forced open, would disclose a tunnel leading to the source of the gold. She said that when she was a child her people used to take a blanket, wrap it around a heavy stone, and throw it down the shaft. In a short time the blanket would be blown back, minus the rock, by the strong winds that come from the hole." Following the woman's directions, Gilbert found Marble Cave the next spring. The cavern is rather a volcanic fissure than a cave. It is entered by a vent; at 90 feet is a circular shaft 20 feet in diameter. Gilbert failed to interest anyone in further exploration until 1929, when a party of ten from the Colorado Mountain Club and Ranger Truman of Westcliffe undertook the most extensive exploration yet made.

The party descended far down the shaft without finding bottom. At 70 feet, on a small offset, they discovered the remains of a crude ladder that scientists in the party judged to be at least 200 years old. At approximately 300 feet was found a hand-forged hammer, believed to be of seventeenth century manufacture. Two of the party made their way down the shaft to a depth of some 500 feet, at which level, according to Gilbert, "the hole was little more than a cold and muddy shaft-like cave with dangerous loose rock in the walls. Upon returning from the Marble Cave, the party discovered, some thousand feet below on the side of the mountain, the remains of an old log and stone fort the purpose of which is a matter of conjecture."

North of the junction State 69 traverses a farming region originally developed by German colonists. In 1870, after a committee appointed by a group of Germans living in Chicago had selected Wet Mountain Valley as a site for colonization, several hundred settlers came here to take up homesteads on a cooperative basis, each member paying $250 into the general fund. Most of the newcomers were artisans and laborers, not farmers; they knew nothing of irrigation or of growing conditions at this altitude. Early crops were failures, money and supplies ran low, and finally the group broke up. Many drifted away to Pueblo, Canon City, and Denver. Those who remained, however, prospered in time, and today the valley is one of the richest agricultural districts in the State. In 1870 a number of Mormon families from Utah settled on Taylor Creek, a tributary of the Grape, adjacent to the land taken up by the Germans.

WESTCLIFFE, 61 *m.* (7,800 alt., 300 pop.), seat of Custer County, was founded in 1885 by Dr. J. W. Bell, a large landowner, who named it for his birthplace, Westcliffe-on-the-Sea, England. The white frame HOPE EVANGELICAL LUTHERAN CHURCH here was built by German colonists in 1872. Here State 96 comes in from Pueblo.

The *Wet Mountain Tribune,* a weekly newspaper, is published here. The Wet Mountain Valley Fair and the Westcliffe Stampede are well-attended annual events.

At 62 *m.* is the junction with a dirt road. Right on this road to the DEWEESE RESERVOIR, 6.3 *m.,* 2763 acre-ft., is fed by Grape Creek and its principal tributaries.

North of the junction the highway pursues an up-and-down course across hills spotted with piñon and cedar. Passing HILLSIDE, 73.6 *m.* (7,473 alt.), State 69 follows Texas Creek to TEXAS CREEK, 85 *m.* (6,198 alt.), at the junction with US 50 (*see Tour 9*).

Tour 11C

Alamosa—Mosca—Great Sand Dunes National Monument; 38 *m.*, State 17, State 150.

A dirt road leaves US 160 (State 10) 5 *m.* west of Blanca and joins US 150. A bathing suit is the best costume for sand skiing, but the wearer should guard against sunburn.

The Great Sand Dunes, established as a national monument by President Hoover in 1932, cover an area of 57 square miles along the western base of the Sangre de Cristo Range, between Mosca Pass on the south and the Crestone Needles on the north. Rising more than 1,500 feet, these changing mounds are large enough to cover cities. The area is administered by the National Park Service. The address of the Superintendent is Box 60, Alamosa, Colo., 81101.

In ALAMOSA, 0 *m.* (7,544 alt., 6,750 pop.), State 17 proceeds north while US 285 turns west to join US 160.

MOSCA (Sp. fly), 13.7 *m.* (7,562 alt.), was named for Mosca Pass.

At 14.5 *m.* is the junction with State 150, which moves east and northeast 31 *m.*, being joined en route by the road from US 160. The view includes the Sangre de Cristo range, with Sierra Blanca Peak (14,363 alt.). The road reaches Dunes Outpost, Entrance Station, Visitor Center, Picnic Area, and Campground at the foot of the GREAT SAND DUNES—naked, barren, and mysterious, encroaching upon the mountains beyond.

The dunes rise so abruptly and so surprisingly in this corner of the San Luis Valley that they seem to have been scooped up by a giant's hand. One explanation of their presence is that the sands once constituted the bed of a great inland sea and were blown by the prevailing winds against the western wall of the Sangre de Cristos, where they piled higher and higher through the ages. Others ascribe them to the wear and tear on the sandstone of the so-called Santa Fe formation in this region, augmented by sand blown in from the valley.

The sand of the dunes, for the most part, is of extremely fine grain. Under a magnifying glass the particles appear white, red, pink, green, gray, and of mixed hues, which accounts for the dunes' remarkable coloring. To a hiker on the smooth slopes, the sand masses are tawny, but from a distance—they are visible for 70 miles—the colors change constantly with the light; in the glare of the sun they are creamy white, but shadows bring out chocolate and purple tones, and the setting sun paints them a brilliant red. By moonlight, the shadowed and whispering ridges present a cold, eerie, and forbidding appearance; on such nights the legends of the dunes are told anew, in appropriate setting. The only vegetation on the dunes are long coarse grasses and sunflowers that grow in the shallows between hillocks.

At the end of the road a river runs down from the base of the mountains at certain seasons of the year, skirting the dunes, only to sink suddenly from view in a dry expanse. A few miles to the west the river reappears at INDIAN SPRINGS, once a water hole for game. When the river is dry, no bed marks its course.

The best view of the dunes is obtained by walking across a half mile of sandy waste and climbing upward along the slopes; it is not advisable, however, to penetrate far into them alone, or without water, as there is danger of becoming lost. The dunes are never static; a constant breeze stirs the surface, and the hiker may be walking through an ankle-deep sandstorm while his head is in clear air. When the wind is blowing strong, or sliding occurs on the steep lee sides of the dunes, weird moaning sounds are heard. When persons slide down the long slopes between the hummocks, a deep rumbling sound sometimes reverberates through the sand and is audible a quarter of a mile away. Informal skiing tournaments are held on the slopes; sweeping down from one of the higher crests provides a thrill said to be unsurpassed by the snow sport. During electrical storms the air above the dunes becomes so charged that a man's hair "stands on end."

The first white men to look upon the Great Sand Dunes undoubtedly were Spanish explorers who came northward up the Rio Grande. Lieutenant Zebulon Pike marveled when he crossed the Sangre de Cristos and came upon the sea of sand in 1807. Travelers, artists, geologists, and naturalists from many countries have since viewed this phenomenon. As the ridges and summits shift under constant wind pressure, skeletons of Indians and perhaps of whites have been exposed. That this place held a fascination for the Indians is proved by the number of arrowheads and other artifacts found in the vicinity.

One of the strangest legends about the dunes is that of the webfooted horses. On bright moonlight nights, or just before sunrise, so it is said, large horses can be seen against the horizon, manes blowing in the wind, heads uplifted in challenge. In place of hoofs, they have great webbed feet that enable them to race over the sands with ease. There is some truth in this, for bands of wild horses do roam the edges of the dunes. They have developed broad hoofs and usually are able to outdistance ordinary steeds in racing across the sands. The only other animals that frequent the dunes are coyotes, foxes, and an occasional skunk.

Other stories concern the mysterious disappearance of sheepherders and their flocks, presumably in the trackless wastes of the ever-shifting hills. Many of these disappearances can be explained by the fact that sheepherders formerly used Mosca Pass, which crosses the high Sangre de Cristos above the dunes, in taking their flocks to summer pasture. No doubt many flocks were sold or kept permanently on the other side of the mountains, and thus "were never seen again." One spring, Peter

Hansen, an early rancher in the San Luis Valley, ordered his herders to different parts of the range. The most difficult assignment, that of moving sheep past the dunes, was given to an old Mexican herder who set out with 1,000 sheep and a pack train. Two men accompanied him to the foot of Mosca Pass, from which point he went on alone. When weeks had passed with no word of him, Hansen instituted a search. As far as could be determined, the Mexican never reached the other side of the pass, and nothing was ever heard of him.

At the time the San Luis Valley was being settled, rough and dangerous Mosca Pass was much used as a freight route. A long wagon train reached the bottom of the pass one night and halted at the edge of the dunes. Arena Creek, which feeds both Head Lake and San Luis Lake, was flowing across the waste, and the wagons were drawn up together beside it; the mules hobbled and turned out to graze, and the teamsters rolled up in their blankets a short distance away. Next morning both mules and wagons had vanished, and were never found. It is probable that the train dropped into quicksands that occasionally form here, but many persons still credit the disappearance to the supernatural.

Told and retold around campfires is the story of the Mystery Family of the Dunes. Years ago the Martinez family—father, mother, and a small son—lived on a homestead near the sands. One day the boy, dazed and unable to speak, stumbled into a ranch house some miles from his home. Neighbors found the mother and father dead in their cabin, but the cause of their death could not be ascertained. A farmer provided a home for the lad, who took a hand tending sheep. When he was out one day, a dust storm arose. When he did not return, a search was made, but the boy and his flock had disappeared.

Archeologists have unearthed campsites of prehistoric hunters, finding the so-called Folsom spear points dating 10,000 years ago. The San Luis Valley was inhabited chiefly by Ute Indians, but Comanche, Cheyenne, and Arapaho tribes are known to have reached the area.

❧❧❧❧❧❧❧❧❧❧❧❧❧❧❧❧❧❧❧❧❧❧❧❧❧❧❧❧❧❧❧❧❧❧

Tour 11D

Southern Ute Indian Reservation—Ignacio—US 160, US 550, State 151, State 172.

To reach the Southern Ute Indian Reservation, and subsequently the Ute Mountain Indian Reservation, tribal lands of the two tribes recognized by the Consolidate Ute Agency in Ignacio, the best connecting roads have junctions with the east-west artery, US 160, from Pagosa Springs west to Cortez. State 151 leaves US 160 17 *m.* west of Pagosa Springs; and goes southwest 20 *m.* to Arboles on the New Mexican boundary, where the San Juan River forms the Navaho Reservoir. Here and at the adjoining Allison it meets State 172 coming down from a junction with US 160 9 *m.* west to Bayfield. A county road leaves US 160 at Bayfield for Ignacio on US 172. From Durango the driver takes US 550 south to junction with US 160, 5 *m.,* and proceeds east 3 *m.* to junction with State 172.

Both reservations extend along the border of New Mexico. The Ute Mountain lands lie west and south of Mesa Verde National Park and extend as far as Four Corners, where Utah, Arizona, Colorado and New Mexico meet. About 1,700 of the 4,300 Indians of Colorado (est.) live in the Southern Ute Reservation. Ignacio (6,432 alt.) has around 600 pop. It was named for a Ute chief. It trades in farm products and does a lively business in articles of Indian make, some of which the Ute obtain by trading with their southern neighbors, the Navajos.

The Bureau of Indian Affairs of the Dept. of the Interior has a dormitory at Ignacio for over 200 Ute and Navajo children enrolled in nearby public schools. Financial aid is given. A welfare program is supported by the Bureau in both reservations. Both Ute tribes assist their youth with scholarships for higher education. An adult education program is conducted at Towaoc. The Government arranges for training in vocational schools and employment afterward. Both the Southern Ute and the Mountain Ute aid the schooling of their young people. Tribal income from natural resources, principally oil and gas, in 1962 gave each member of the Southern Ute tribe $700 and the Mountain Ute $1,575, in monthly payments.

The town's weekly newspaper is the *Ignacio Chieftain.*

The Ute are slowly increasing in number. They have retained their tribal unity, although some intermarriage with other tribes has taken place and a few Navajo and Pueblo Indians have migrated to the reservation. For the most part, these are not enrolled in the tribe; in cases of intermarriage, however, the children are regarded as Ute.

The old command of the tribes by the chief and his council of elders has been replaced among the Southern Ute, who elect the council by popular vote. The Southern Ute constitution provides for internal self-government through this council, which maintains law and order, establishes rules for judicial procedure, and governs the disposition of tribal lands.

Although many Old Ute customs are fast disappearing, their language has persisted with little apparent change. All younger Indians speak both Ute and English, and most can speak Mexican-Spanish. Like other Indians, the Ute employ sign language, and depend on frequent and expressive gestures to make themselves understood.

Most of the Southern Ute live in frame or adobe houses. Floors, doors, windows, and some kind of heating apparatus are usually found in their winter dwellings. As farmers, they are most inclined to establish permanent dwellings than the pastoral Mountain Ute, although they still use temporary summer houses of poles covered with branches of oak, cottonwood, birch, or willow. Tepees are made of canvas laid over a circular structure of 12 to 14 poles, and have only two openings—a flap for a doorway, and a flap at the apex, through which escapes the smoke from the fireplace in the center of the tepee. Food is cooked on stoves with modern utensils. The only native food much used is a bread made of Indian corn pounded to a heavy paste, but even this is being displaced by white wheat bread.

Southern Ute families have an average of 40 acres on which to raise alfalfa, wheat, and oats. The majority have gardens and occasionally a milk cow. Modern farming methods and equipment are the rule rather than the exception.

The Ute tribes never possessed great skill in the handicrafts, and such arts as they had are largely disappearing. One remaining handicraft of importance is leather work, in which the tribe excels. Excellent buckskin leather is made by scraping hair from hides with a knife or sharp bone; sheep brains are then rubbed into it and allowed to remain until it dries in the sun; manipulation with the hands, or pounding with rocks, renders the buckskin soft and pliable.

Weaving of willow baskets is another of their remaining arts. Their medicine and wedding baskets are similar in shape to a wooden chopping bowl. The names of the two baskets are used interchangeably, although some Ute declare that the wedding basket differs from the medicine basket in that it is slightly larger and has a touch of yellow in its design. The wedding basket is still used to serve ceremonial cornmeal mush to bride and groom. A heavy stalk is used for the inner framework of the baskets; around this are woven lighter willow strands, obtained by splitting a willow reed and removing the pith. The reeds are laid away in a damp place for a time, and during the weaving process are kept pliable by moistening with saliva. The practice of holding the strands between the lips results in chronic sores around the mouth. Ute baskets possess great strength and are cream-colored, the natural color of the willows, but red and black commercial dyes are generally used in their ornamentation. Woven willow jugs are coated with piñon pitch to render them watertight.

The Ute do no fabric weaving, no pottery or metal work, but make belts, hat bands, purses, dolls, moccasins, and arm bands, all intricately embellished with beads. Some magnificent war bonnets are fashioned by sewing eagle feathers to cotton caps. Twelve feathers are always used, and beadwork and weasel tails are additional decorations. Feather fans, used in the ceremonial dances, are manufactured. Some work is still done with porcupine quills, although this is almost a forgotten art.

The Ute have two ceremonial dances, the Bear Dance and Sun Dance, both of which last several days. According to agency officials, the dances are fast losing their original significance and esteem.

At 4.1 m. is the junction with State 172, which the route now follows. At 5.4 m. is the junction with a dirt road.

Left on this road to (R) the SUN DANCE FIELD, 2.2 *m.;* admission fees are used to feed Indians who come to witness the Sun Dance held in mid-July. This religious rite is performed by men, who abstain from food and water throughout the ceremony, which lasts from three to five days. Fasting, it is believed, bestows upon the dancers a supernatural power drawn from the sun.

The dance is held in a circular corral about 150 feet in diameter, constructed of cedar, piñon, or cottonwood branches woven between poles set in the earth. In the center stands a tall pole, topped with a bundle of twigs arranged to resemble a sheaf of wheat. Small resting places for the participants are partitioned off with boughs, and each has a small pathway before it. Facing the pole at all times, the dancers move forward and backward along their individual paths, but not simultaneously. Each carries an eagle-bone whistle upon which he blows when not chanting. Dangling from wrists, ankles, elbows, ears, are feathers, silver objects, animal teeth, and beads. Now and again a dancer lingers a moment at the pole, gesticulating and bowing, at which time he is said to be communing with the sun. No words are spoken, and no instructions given. The rhythm of the dance produces in the dancers a kind of auto-intoxication; each dances until he has acquired supernatural power, which is evidenced by his falling into a faint.

At 7.5 *m.* is the junction with the Agency Road. Left on this road to the AGENCY HEADQUARTERS, 0.3 *m.,* where the Federal Government maintains a co-educational boarding school and hospital for the Indians. The hospital is well staffed and equipped, and field nurses are employed. The school supplements academic studies with courses in manual training, domestic science, and instruction in Indian arts and crafts. Athletic events, farm extension work, and demonstration projects arouse considerable interest.

Here is the BEAR DANCE FIELD, an inclosure similar to that used for the Sun Dance (*see above*), except that it has no center pole. The dance, held annually late in May or early in June, was formerly held in March to celebrate the emergence of the bear from hibernation; because it later came to interfere with spring farm work, the date of observance was changed. When the Ute were nomads, the dance was a meeting place and provided opportunity for courtship.

Women participate in the Bear Dance and select their partners; it is believed that a man who does not dance when invited will be harmed by the bear when alone in the woods. In the inclosure the men form a line facing the east entrance; the women form another line facing the musicians at the west. Music is provided by an "orchestra" seated around a sheet of tin laid over two logs or a pit. With two notched sticks, one pressed against the resonator and rubbed with the other, a rhythmic and not unpleasant humming sound is produced on this instrument, the *morache.* Children do not participate, but white men are allowed to join the dance, the usual fee being 10¢ to a young woman partner, or 25¢ to an old squaw, in addition to the regular admission fee.

Right from Agency Headquarters on a road that crosses Pine River to the junction with a dirt road, 0.2 *m.*

1. Right here through a cemetery to the GRAVE OF CHIEF OURAY, 200 *yds.,* indicated by a small marker placed on the boundary between the Protestant and Roman Catholic sections in order to satisfy both sects on the reservation. Another chief, Capote, is buried here, but his grave is without a marker, and only one or two Ute know its site.

Ouray, best known of Ute chiefs, was the son of a Ute father and an Apache mother. Born in 1820 in a tepee near the present town of Ignacio (*see below*), he was adopted into the Uncompahgre Ute tribe and became its outstanding figure. Ruling at a time when the great mining districts were being opened, Ouray had frequent contacts with the whites. Perhaps realizing the futility of resisting encroachment, Ouray always counseled peace and undoubtedly prevented many bloody clashes. One of his acts of friendship was to persuade the rebellious Northern Ute to return the women and children taken captive in the massacre at White River Agency in 1878 (*see Tour 17*). Unable to preserve any desirable part of his people's domain, largely because of the massacre, Ouray died a broken man in 1883. His body was smuggled away by Buckskin Charley, another Ute chief, and buried in a secret cave. Not until 1924 were the Ute induced to disinter the body and bring it here to the Agency cemetery, where it was reburied with great ceremony.

❦❦❦❦❦❦❦❦❦❦❦❦❦❦❦❦❦❦❦❦❦❦❦❦❦❦❦❦❦❦❦❦

Tour 11E

Pleasant View—Hovenweep National Monument—Yucca House National Monument—US 160 from Cortez and connections. South from Cortez US 164 and US 666 are combined, this route also using State 108 and 799. At 21 *m.* from Cortez US 164 branches west to Four Corners and Arizona; US 666 continues south, crosses the border of New Mexico to Shiprock, N. M. 41 *m.* from Cortez.

According to the National Park Service Hovenweep is isolated. There are no paved roads in the vicinity. Approach roads are fair if it is not storming or has not been storming. There are no accommodations, stores, or service stations in or near the monument, and no wood is available for building camp-fires in the campground.

The best approach to Hovenweep is from Pleasant View, Colo., 18 miles north of Cortez on US 160. Turn west in Pleasant View at the Hovenweep directional sign and follow the graded road 27.2 miles to Square Tower Group, Utah. There are three other routes, which are not recommended: State 146, which leaves US 666 three miles south of Cortez and approaches Hovenweep via McElmo Canyon, is rough and longer. A dirt road approaches Hovenweep from Aneth, Utah. A graded road leads to Hovenweep from the west, leaving Utah 47 midway between Blanding and Bluff, but it is generally impassable, except for 4-wheel-drive vehicles, during and following storms.

HOVENWEEP NATIONAL MONUMENT is an impressive area of ruined masonry—pueblos, cliff dwellings, and towers with multiple rooms—built and inhabited by pre-Columbian Indians between about 400 and 1300 A.D. Six large groups lived on what is today the Utah-Colorado line near the southwestern part of Colorado. The Hovenweep National Monument, established 1923, has 345 acres in Montezuma County, Colorado, and 160 acres in Utah. A smaller site, YUCCA HOUSE NATIONAL MONUMENT, established 1919, occupies 9.6 acres on the eastern slope of Sleeping Ute Mountain (9,884 alt.), near Cortez. The latter has not been fully excavated and is not open to the public. Two of the groups at Hovenweep are in Hackberry and Keely Canyons in Colorado.

The KEELY CANYON GROUP, 3.5 *m.*, includes five large buildings set on the rim of a canyon spur and clustered about its base. Other smaller structures are scattered along the canyon walls. After centuries of weathering, the ruins still evidence fine masonry.

The HACKBERRY CANYON GROUP, 5 *m.*, is distinguished by the HORSESHOE HOUSE, a ruin formed by two concentric walls, a curved outer wall on the north, about four feet from a curved inner wall and connected with it by partitions. The compartments between these partitions are well preserved.

The ruins of Hovenweep (Ind. deserted canyon) are of special interest to archeologists for their fine state of preservation and for certain architectural features found in no other buildings of this culture, chiefly the multiple chambers in some of the towers. Nothing comparable to this construction has been noted in other dwellings of an approximate period, or in modern pueblos.

West of the junction with the Keely Canyon turn-off, the dirt road from McElmo crosses the Utah Line, 28.5 *m.*, 42 miles east of Bluff, Utah. The RUIN CANYON GROUP of the monument lies just across the line; to the south is the Square Tower Group of 19 buildings centered about Hovenweep Castle, which has walls 66 feet long and 22 feet high.

YUCCA HOUSE NATIONAL MONUMENT, still inaccessible, was created to preserve what archeologists believe are the remains of a prehistoric village. Huge mounds of dirt cover the ruins, the two most conspicuous being Upper House and Lower House. Little preparatory excavation has been done so far, but buildings constructed of fossiliferous limestone, probably taken from an outcrop along the base of Mesa Verde, have been uncovered. Preliminary work reveals that the inhabitants had a highly developed artistic skill, using exceptional patterns both in pottery and weaving.

US 164 from Cortez crosses the boundary of the big Ute Mountain Indian Reservation, 10.8 *m.*, a barren stretch of grassland. The Ute Mountain, or Weminuche, Ute, are distinguished from the Southern Ute by the fact that their tribal land is held in common. The Southern Ute are mostly farmers, but this branch of the tribe remains a nomadic people, living in tents and driving sheep across the sage. Occasionally, as the highway winds cross this forbidding land, a Navaho hogan, or conical mud hut, is seen. Usually the only opening in this primitive habitation is a doorway covered with a canvas flap. Except for the few educated in Government schools, these Indians speak little English, although most of them can converse in broken Spanish. They object to being photographed, and visitors attempting to photograph a child, especially a boy, often have their cameras smashed. Trading with the Indians is almost impossible, as they invariably raise prices to strangers. To a greater extent than the Southern Ute, the Weminuche cling to old customs; they still do most of their cooking over a campfire and preserve meat by cutting it into strips, salting it, and drying it in the sun.

The Ute Mountain Ute elect their chief and have organized cattle associations.

The Ute Indian Museum, which deals with the customs of the Utes of all groups, is located 4 *m.* south of Montrose on US 550.

At 11.6 *m.* is the junction with a graveled road. Right on this road to TOWAOC (toy-yak), 3 *m.*, headquarters for the Ute Mountain reservation, consisting of the agency buildings, a hospital, and the UTE MOUNTAIN SCHOOL (open), attended by day students.

At 20 *m.* US 164 turns west, while US 666 continues south. US 164 proceeds to FOUR CORNERS MONUMENT, a solitary spot in the desert marking the point where the boundaries of Colorado, Utah, New Mexico and Arizona meet, and then crosses into Arizona.

Right on this road to the MANCOS CREEK TRADING POST, 2 *m.*, where the Ute sell Indian jewelry and souvenirs.

US 666 crosses the New Mexico Line, 27 *m.*, 18 miles north of Shiprock, N. M.

I❖I❖I❖I❖I❖I❖I❖I❖I❖I❖I❖I❖I❖I❖I❖I❖I❖I❖I❖I❖I❖I❖I❖I❖I❖I❖I❖I❖

Tour 12

(Cheyenne, Wyo.) — Greeley — Brighton — Denver — Littleton — Castle Rock — Palmer Lake — Colorado Springs — Pueblo — Walsenburg — Trinidad — Raton Pass — (Raton, N. M.) ; US 85.
Interstate 25 runs from Cheyenne to Denver west of US 85. The two highways merge at Denver.
Wyoming Line to New Mexico Line, 312 *m.*

US 85, the most heavily traveled north and south highway in Colorado, skirts the Rockies for its entire distance, passing through the most populous cities of the State and traversing rich irrigated areas. Only at Palmer Lake does it enter the higher foothills. Historically, it is of less interest than the routes followed by explorers and pioneers.

Section a. WYOMING LINE to DENVER; 93 m. US 85

This section traverses arid and sparsely settled hill country which gradually merges with fertile farm lands watered by the State's first and largest irrigation system.

Crossing the Wyoming Line, 0 *m.*, 10 miles south of Cheyenne, US 85 traverses broken grassland, a continuation of the Wyoming plains country, a region of high wind-swept hills, picturesque in its desolation. To the west the peaks of the Rockies rise in glittering contrast. This area is chiefly used for cattle grazing.

NUNN, 21.6 *m.* (5,186 alt.), a farming center, was named for "Bob" Nunn, who forestalled an accident on the Union Pacific Railroad by flagging a train in time to prevent its running into a collapsed culvert.

The highway crosses the northern boundary of the Weld County irrigated area at PIERCE, 26 *m.* (5,041 alt.), and traverses miles of sugar beet fields to AULT, 30 *m.* (4,940 alt.), at the junction with State 14 (*see Tour 2*).

EATON, 33.5 *m.* (4,750 alt., 1,300 pop.), in the Cache la Poudre Valley, was founded in 1881 by Governor B. H. Eaton, who established the flour mill and grain elevator still operating here. The town's greatest development followed the introduction of sugar beets. Surrounding farms produce a diversity of crops, and there is considerable livestock feeding.

Left from Eaton on a dirt road to the GREAT WESTERN BEET SUGAR FACTORY 0.5 *m.,* the town's largest industrial plant, with a daily beet-slicing capacity of several thousand tons. East of GALETOWN, 7 *m.,* the road crosses dry hill country through great sand drifts piled up by dust storms to CORNISH, 16 *m.* (6,708 alt.), a farming hamlet in Crow Creek Valley.

Here, between 10,000 and 20,000 years ago, was the homeland of a prehistoric people (*see The People*). Little is known about these ancient hunters whose arrowheads and other artifacts have been uncovered here as high winds have swept away the topsoil. Collecting these articles became a popular local pastime, and George Bowman, local school teacher, and Oscar Shirk, a member of the school board, arranged an exhibit of artifacts, sponsored by the local grade school. The first Stone Age Fair, as it was called, was held July 10–15, 1934, at which were displayed 25,000 artifacts of the Yuma and the Folsom man, as anthropologists have named the prehistoric peoples of the Southwest. The fair attracted 5,000 visitors; 20,000 attended the fair in 1935, and again in 1936, when archeologists throughout the West contributed exhibits; lectures were given by a staff headed by Dr. Frank H. H. Roberts, archeological authority of the Smithsonian Institution. The fair is now an annual event, August 6–9. The Cornish collection is said to be one of the largest of its kind in the world.

In GREELEY, 41 *m.* (4,637 alt., 83,300 pop.) (*see Greeley*), is the junction with US 34 (*see Tour 3*).

South of Greeley the highway traverses the valley of the South Platte, richest agricultural section in eastern Colorado, to EVANS, 44.5 *m.* (4,647 alt., 1,600 pop.), founded in 1869 by promoters of the Denver Pacific Railroad, headed by Governor John M. Evans. For a time the terminus of the railroad which was to connect Denver with the Union Pacific R. R. at Cheyenne, it was a busy loading point for wagon trains hauling supplies to numerous mining camps. In 1879 Evans was chosen for settlement by the St. Louis Western Colony, established by parishioners of the Reformed Presbyterian (Covenanter) Church. That same year the railroad was extended to Denver, the county seat was removed to Greeley, and Evans' boom period was over.

The route crosses the SOUTH PLATTE RIVER, 45.5 *m.,* which has a drainage basin of approximately 24,000 square miles and contains the oldest extensively cultivated and irrigated area in the State. The stream has been called Dry River, Sand River, Silver River, and "the river that is upside down." The Mallet brothers, French trappers who penetrated Colorado as far as the present site of Julesburg, named it the Riviere la Platte (shallow), a translation of the Spanish Rio Chato, given it by Juan de Saldiver. According to Washington Irving, the river was once designated as the Ne-braska by the Otoe Indians.

LA SALLE, 46.5 *m.* (4,700 alt., 1,085 pop.) an irrigated agricultural center, is a junction point on the Union Pacific Railroad.

GILCREST, 52.5 *m.* (4,752 alt., 400 pop.), is at the junction with a dirt road.

Right on this road to ST. VRAINS, 3 *m.*, a substation of the Public Service Company of Colorado.
Right from St. Vrains 0.2 *m.* to the SITE OF FORT ST. VRAIN, indicated by a granite marker. Fort St. Vrain, the first and largest of the South Platte trading posts, the third largest in the Rocky Mountain West, was exceeded in size and importance only by Fort Laramie on the North Platte and Fort Bent on the Arkansas (*see Tour 9A*). This post was established in 1838 by William Bent and Ceran St. Vrain, agents of the American Fur Company, to compete with Fort Lupton and Fort Vasquez (*see below*) of the Rocky Mountain Fur Company. Built of adobe, the fort was 125 feet long and 100 feet wide, with walls 2 feet thick and 14 feet high. Half way between Fort Bent and Fort Laramie, it was a popular rendezvous of traders, emigrants, and adventurers. Kit Carson spent several months here, and Lieutenant John C. Frémont visited the post in 1842 and again in 1843. The post was abandoned in 1844 when the American Fur Company and Lancaster P. Lupton agreed to give up their competing South Platte Valley posts.

The Atomic Energy Commission in 1968 announced plans for building a high temperature, gas-cooled reactor facility near Platteville in cooperation with the Public Service Co. of Colorado. The reactor, scheduled to begin operation (criticality) in 1971, will have a capacity of 330,000 kwe. Called the FORT ST. VRAIN NUCLEAR GENERATING STATION, it is described by the AEC as "the second and largest of its type to be built in this country, and its planned net thermal efficiency of about 40 percent will be the highest for any nuclear power plant in the U. S."

South of Gilcrest the road is bordered with irrigated fields of alfalfa, sugar beets, potatoes, and garden truck. Throughout this area ringnecked pheasants, native to China, known locally as "stubble ducks," are seen in the fields and along the highway. The long-tailed males are brilliantly colored, with iridescent orange, red, and bronze plumage. The birds were introduced into Colorado in 1894 by W. F. Kendrick of Denver, who later released 100 pairs in Weld and Larimer Counties; from these have sprung the present stock. Protected for many years, the birds multiplied rapidly, to the annoyance of farmers.

PLATTEVILLE, 58 *m.* (4,820 alt., 650 pop.), is the center of a large irrigated farm area; dairying is an important occupation. The town was founded by the Platte River Land Company in 1871.

Right from Platteville on a graveled road is MEAD, 10.5 *m.* (5,280 alt.), another of the many towns that sprang to life with the sugar beet industry.

FORT VASQUEZ STATE MUSEUM, 59.5 *m.*, is built on the site of the original post destroyed by Indians in 1842. The fort then stood on the bank of the South Platte, but the stream now runs five miles farther west. The large court of the reconstructed fort, 125 feet long and 100 feet wide, is surrounded by heavy adobe walls pierced with loopholes. At each corner are towers for riflemen; footpaths extend along the top of the walls.

Louis Vasquez and Andrew Sublette, who built the fort in 1836, conducted the fur-trading post for four years as agents of the Rocky Mountain Fur Company; in 1840 it was sold to Locke and Randolph; two years later Indians captured and looted it. Although never completely rebuilt, the fort was used as a base by troops during the Indian wars of the 1860's. Directly south of the fort is the OLD WELD COUNTY COURTHOUSE, some fifteen feet square, built of hewn logs.

IONE, 63 m., (4,858 alt.), is a scattered farm settlement. When a Union Pacific official arrived in 1890 he asked who owned the land west of the contemplated station site. "I own it," answered W. A. Davis, a local resident. "To the north?" the official queried. "I own it," Davis repeated. And so it was for all points of the compass, which is said to have led to the naming of the town. Ione once had a ghost; as the phantom habitually took midnight rambles along the tracks, the railroad ran "ghost trains" from surrounding towns; the specter in the end proved to be two frolicsome cowboys in sheets.

Right from Ione to the unmarked and approximate SITE OF FORT JACKSON, 3 m., least known of the Platte Valley fur posts, founded by Peter Sarpy and Henry Fraeb in 1833, for Platte, Chouteau & Company of St. Louis. According to company records, the post shipped furs valued at $10,000 in one season. The post, bought by St. Vrain in 1838, was later abandoned.

South of Ione the serpentine course of the South Platte River (R) is marked by cottonwood trees. A fieldstone monument (R) marks the SITE OF FORT LUPTON, 65 m., on a farm whose dairy barn is built around some of the original adobe walls. This fur trading post, founded in 1836 by Lancaster P. Lupton, formerly a lieutenant in the Army under Colonel Henry Dodge, was the first permanent settlement in northern Colorado. At times hundreds of Indians gathered here for a council, and the air pulsed day and night with the rumble of ceremonial drums. The fort was never attacked, but numerous battles between enemy tribesmen were fought nearby. John C. Frémont, Kit Carson, and Francis Parkman visited the fort, which was abandoned in 1844.

Surrounded by immense beet fields is a three-story red brick GREAT WESTERN BEET SUGAR FACTORY, 66.4 m.

FORT LUPTON, 67 m. (4,906 alt., 2,194 pop.), was founded about 1872; free lots were offered to home builders, and an acre of ground to anyone putting up a hotel, blacksmith shop, or saloon. The town is a trading center for a rich farming country. A beet sugar factory, a vegetable cannery, and a condensed milk plant are the principal industrial enterprises. Fort Lupton celebrates Tomato Day annually in August.

BRIGHTON, 74 m. (4,979 alt., 7,400 pop.), seat of Adams County, was originally named Hughes Station for General Bela M. Hughes, promoter of the Denver Pacific and other railroads. Platted as a town in 1889 by D. F. Carmichael, it was named for the birthplace of his wife in Massachusetts. The town is one of the largest sugar beet centers in the State. The first Independence Day celebration in this State was held here when Major Stephen Long camped here in 1820.

HENDERSON, 80 *m.*, 1 *m.* west of US 85 on State 22 or 124th Ave. of suburban Denver. Since World War II this area has been developing as residential contiguous with Denver proper.

DENVER, 93 *m.*

Section b. DENVER *to* PUEBLO *; 115 m.* US 85, *Interstate 25*

US 85 becomes the Santa Fe Drive in Denver as it proceeds south. Parallel with the Drive are the Sante Fe railroad tracks, and west of the Drive runs the South Platte River.

ENGLEWOOD (5,306 alt., 37,400 pop., 1967) established 1875 and incorporated 1903, is located just across the southern line of Denver. It has more than doubled its population in twenty years and is the largest city in Arapahoe County. A group of gold seekers made a digging here in 1858 and then went on to the site of Denver. In recent years Englewood has attracted numerous industries, chiefly in metals, but it still retains its fame as Carnation City, exploiting the Colorado Carnation, an award-winning product. According to the *Colorado Year Book* Englewood produces 20,000,000 of these blooms a year, with Arapahoe County producing 40,000,000, about half of the Colorado output. The ARAPAHOE COUNTY AIRPORT is located near Englewood. In 1968 the "world's largest shopping center" was opened with 100 stores, and 70 more in preparation. Retail sales exceed $120,000,000 annually. The Englewood Public Library, the Swedish Memorial Hospital, the Continental National Bank, and the Englewood High School are among structures with new, modern facilities.

The FEDERAL CORRECTIONAL INSTITUTION, in Bear Creek Valley, was opened in 1940. It has 640 acres, of which 460 are cultivated. It has about 450 youths averaging 18 years of age, teaches general and vocational courses, and grows and processes much of the food it consumes.

West of Englewood and the Sante Fe Drive is the suburban community of SHERIDAN, named for General Philip H. Sheridan. US 287 and State 88 run in a straight north-south line along Federal Blvd. in Denver to Sheridan, where there is a junction with the east-west US 285.

FORT LOGAN MILITARY RESERVATION and the community of Fort Logan have been annexed by Denver. Here are located the FORT LOGAN NATIONAL CEMETERY and the FORT LOGAN MENTAL HEALTH CENTER OF THE STATE OF COLORADO. The institution was opened in 1961 and gives psychiatric and medical treatment, educates students in psychological medicine, and provides facilities for research. It is financed by the General Assembly, which appropriates about $4,000,000 annually.

Fort Logan was established Oct. 20, 1887, by General Philip H. Sheridan, at which time the Federal Government discontinued posts at

Forts Garland, Crawford, Lewis, Lyon, and Uncompahgre. For a long time it was headquarters of the Second Engineers, USA.

LORETTO HEIGHTS COLLEGE occupies a campus of 157 acres on Loretto Heights in Denver.

LITTLETON, 9.9 m. (5,362 alt., 21,000 pop. 1968, est.) on the South Platte, seat of Arapahoe County, has approx. 50 industries including the Martin Marietta Corp., maker of the Titan rocket. It has 5 shopping centers, 5 country clubs, 14 parks, a public library and one branch library. Arapahoe Junior College is located at 5900 S. Curtice St. The Centennial Turf Club has races from June to October. There is an hourly bus service to downtown Denver.

WOLHURST (R), 12.6 m., is a large country estate; its white mansion with bright green roof was built by Senator E. O. Wolcott, and later was the home of Thomas F. Walsh, bonanza king.

At 20.9 m. is the junction with a dirt road.

Right on this road is LOUVIERS, 0.8 m. (5,800 alt.), a Du Pont powder town. Across the river the DU PONT POWDER PLANT was built in 1907 for production of explosives used in mines.

The highway traverses broken hill country, most of it belonging to the Diamond K Ranch, last of the great cattle holdings in this section, and skirts SEDALIA, 24.1 m. (6,000 alt.). Neighboring creek bottoms were favorite camping grounds of the Plains Indians, particularly the Arapaho. After the town had been founded, Indians continued to frequent the region, occasionally raiding isolated farms and ranches. One of the first sawmills in Colorado was set up in the pine stands on Plum Creek here in 1859 by D. C. Oakes and supplied lumber for the then raw town of Denver.

1. Right from Sedalia on State 105 is an alternate route to PALMER LAKE (see below), 24.1 m.

2. Right from Sedalia on graveled State 67, an alternate route to Colorado Springs, through rolling country to the mouth of JARRE CANYON, 5.1 m. The road crosses the eastern boundary of Pike National Forest (see Tour 5b), 7.3 m., to a junction with a dirt forest road, 10 m.
Left here 10 m. to DEVIL'S HEAD, a jutting mass of rock, crowned with a Forest Service fire lookout station.
State 67 passes PINE CREEK (store and cabins), 13.3 m., swings in a wide circle to bring Mount Evans (R) into full view, and descends into the valley of the South Fork of the South Platte, which is crossed several times. The route passes a picnic ground, 23.6 m., and the cabin resort of SNOW WATER SPRINGS, 26 m. DECKERS, 27.3 m. (6,250 alt.), a summer resort (cabins), is popular with anglers. Here the highway ascends along West Creek, a tributary of the South Platte, to camp grounds, 34.5 m., and the junction with a graveled road, 36.2 m.
Right here 21 m. to FLORISSANT, at the junction with US 24 (see Tour 5b).
State 67 continues south, crossing a boundary of Pike National Forest, 39.9 m., to WOODLAND PARK, 49.9 m., at the junction with US 24 (see Tour 5b), 18 miles northwest of Colorado Springs (see Colorado Springs).

The highway crosses broken foothills to CASTLE ROCK, 31.2 *m.* (6,000 alt., 1,300 pop.), seat of Douglas County, named for the high outcrop of salmon-colored stone seen by Major Long's party in 1820. US 85 joins US 87 and Interstate 25 at Castle Rock, site of the Continental Divide Raceways and an annual rodeo. Four railroads and several bus lines meet here; the Denver-Douglas Airport, outside of town, was completed 1963.

South of LARKSPUR, 42.2 *m.* (6,580 alt.), the road ascends the divide separating the drainage basins of the South Platte and Arkansas Rivers. Here the route, winding through pine-clad hills, approaches the mountains. This area is subject to sudden violent storms.

PALMER LAKE, 50.1 *m.* (7,237 alt., 1,000 pop.), built around a spring-fed lake at the top of the divide, was one of the first resort towns in Colorado; many residents of the larger cities still have summer houses here. When the Denver & Rio Grande Railroad reached the town in 1872, it was known as Weisport, but in 1889 it was renamed for General William J. Palmer, builder of the road, who did much to publicize the resort. During the 1870's columbines grew profusely in the vicinity, and travelers spoke so often of the beauty of the flower that it was made the State flower in 1889. Each year, the Sunday before Christmas, the ancient ceremony of hunting and burning the Yule log is held at Palmer Lake.

South of Palmer Lake the highway passes (L) ELEPHANT ROCK, 51.7 *m.,* a mass of curiously eroded sandstone.

At 53.5 *m.* is the junction with State 50, a graveled road.

Right on State 50 is MONUMENT, 0.5 *m.* (6,895 alt.), founded in 1859 and named for the stone formation west of the town.

Left from Monument a graveled road, known as the Mount Herman Road, crosses the eastern boundary of Pike National Forest (*see Tour 5b*), 1.5 *m.,* and passes (L) the MONUMENT NURSERY (*open*), 2.8 *m.,* maintained by the U. S. Forest Service. Approximately 5,500,000 pine, spruce, and cedar seedlings are planted here each year, and are transplanted when they are from two to four years old. Early pine tree growth is slow, as evidenced by the fact that seedlings several years old resemble small tomato plants.

Ascending a high ridge west of the nursery, the road reaches (R) the great MOUNT HERMAN BURN, 7.4 *m.,* which has been entirely reforested from the Monument Nursery. Here 10,000 acres of forest were burned in 1879, but young and hardy evergreens are now growing between the stumps.

Mount Herman Road continues to WOODLAND PARK, 19 *m.,* at the junction with US 24 (*see Tour 5b*).

Left on State 50 to BLACK FOREST, a recreation center.

Some distance south of the junction with State 50 begins the 17,900-acre reservation of the UNITED STATES AIR FORCE ACADEMY, which extends south to within 5 *m.* of the city limits of Colorado Springs (*see Colorado Springs*).

US 85 now parallels Monument Creek. At 65.3 *m.* is the junction with an oiled road.

Right on this road is WOODMEN, 3 *m.,* a small community built around the MODERN WOODMEN OF AMERICA SANITARIUM (*open 8:30–11, 1–4 daily;*

guides). The Modern Woodmen of America is a fraternal society with thousands of members who carry insurance underwritten by the order. Tubercular patients are cared for here in 180 individual tent-cottages, painted red, white, and green, the colors of the order. The community has its own post office; water, sewer, heating, and refrigeration systems; store, laundry, dairy, blacksmith shop, carpenter shop, and auditorium.

In COLORADO SPRINGS, 71.8 *m.* (5,900 alt., 118,000 pop. 1968 est.), is the junction with US 24 and State 94. At 73.7 *m.* is the junction with Cheyenne Boulevard.

Right here through a suburban district to Cheyenne Mountain Junior and Senior High School, noted for folk dancing and dramatics in its courses.
The route follows Cheyenne Canyon to a toll gate 3.7 *m.* The waters of South Cheyenne Creek break over ledges of a narrow gorge in a series of cascades known as SEVEN FALLS, 4.5 *m.;* a stairway of 295 steps leads to the top of the falls. On INSPIRATION POINT, 200 yards southeast, is the FORMER SITE OF HELEN HUNT JACKSON'S GRAVE. Before the body was removed to Evergreen Cemetery in Colorado Springs in 1894, hundreds visited this spot. It was the custom to leave a stone on the grave, and the cairn reached great proportions.

At 73.9 *m.* is the junction with Broadmoor Road.

Right on this road to the BROADMOOR HOTEL, 2.3 *m.* (*see Colorado Springs*).
From the hotel follow the signs to Cheyenne Mountain Highway and proceed to CHEYENNE MOUNTAIN ZOO, which can be reached by a miniature cog railway. It was established in 1921 when a Hindu rajah contributed an elephant named Tessie. In the zoo are camels, lions, leopards, kangaroos, elephants, and zebras, 36 species of snakes, and 52 of birds; back from the road are parks of buffalo, elk, and deer.
South of the gardens the road, electrically lighted, passes between two great masses of granite known as HELL'S GATE, 5.2 *m.,* and makes a stiff zigzag climb up the face of Cheyenne Mountain to (L) the WILL ROGERS SHRINE OF THE SUN MEMORIAL, 6.3 *m.,* on a knoll about 200 yards from the highway, reached by a side drive. The tower of rose-pink local granite, 100 feet high, resembles a medieval donjon keep, erected by the late Spencer Penrose in memory of the noted journalist and actor. No wood or nails were used in construction of the tower, which contains 15,000,000 pounds of steel reinforcement. In one of four rooms in the tower, reached by a spiral staircase is a bust of Will Rogers by Jo Davidson. The interior walls are adorned with frescoes of western American life by Randall Davey, of Santa Fe, N. M. The tower is surmounted with an observation balcony that affords a good view of Colorado Springs and the plains. A sodium mercury light, visible at night for 125 miles, is intended to burn perpetually; the entire memorial is floodlighted after dark.
From the SUMMIT of CHEYENNE MOUNTAIN, 10 *m.,* is a wide view of mountains, foothills, and plains.

At 74.8 *m.* is the junction with State 115.

Right here to the MYRON STRATTON HOME (*open 9–5 daily*), 0.8 *m.,* built in 1913, eleven years after the death of Winfield Scott Stratton, mining millionaire and philanthropist, who founded the home in memory of his father.
The greater part of his fortune, approximately $4,000,000, was willed to this institution, established to care for those physically incapable of earning a livelihood. On the 5,000-acre estate in a 98-acre landscaped tract on which stand a hospital, administration building, community house, dormitories for

boys and girls, and housekeeping cottages for aged married couples. About 100 adults and 85 children ranging from 5 to 20 years of age, reside here. To be eligible for admission, a child's parents must have lived in El Paso County for six years; aged persons must have lived in the county for five years, and must have been residents of the State for 10 years. Children are offered an education through senior high school.

On the grounds is the bronze WINFIELD SCOTT STRATTON STATUE, erected as a memorial by Colorado Springs citizens. Born in Indiana in 1848, Stratton was a carpenter and contractor in several parts of the Middle West before coming to Colorado Springs in 1872. He prospected throughout Colorado for many years, but not until 1891 did he make his rich strike at Cripple Creek (*see Tour 5B*). After his first strike, it is said, he sent a $1,000 check to a friend who had once given him a dollar when he was hungry. He gave a coachman an equal amount for averting a runaway, and on another occasion bestowed a bicycle upon every laundry girl in Colorado Springs. Stratton died in Colorado Springs in 1902.

The highway crosses FOUNTAIN CREEK, 77.5 *m.*, named Fontaine qui Bouille (fountain that boils) by early French fur traders, because of the bubbling mineral springs at Manitou Springs that feed it. At 78.5 *m.* is the junction with a dirt road.

Left on this road to the FOUNTAIN VALLEY SCHOOL FOR BOYS, 4 *m.*, a private boarding school for youths between 16 and 18 years old; it attracts students from many States. Several of the interior walls are decorated with murals by Boardman Robinson.

FOUNTAIN, 84.9 *m.* (5,500 alt., 2,500 pop.), one of the oldest settlements in central Colorado, is the only town of importance between Colorado Springs and Pueblo. Once its only trade was with surrounding ranches, but today it is an important shipping point for alfalfa and sugar beets grown in the irrigated section of the valley. On May 14, 1889, a car loaded with dynamite broke lose in the railroad yards at Colorado Springs and rolled down the tracks, exploding at the Fountain depot; four persons were killed, and the village was almost leveled by the blast.

South of Fountain the route crosses windy arid country, in places almost devoid of vegetation, to BUTTES, 92.9 *m.*, a railroad station named for the conical hills in the vicinity. South of the railroad station in WIGWAM, 96.4 *m.*, are (L) the remains of a STAGE STATION CORRAL. The extensive forests of piñon that once covered the hills southwest of PIÑON, 102.6 *m.*, were long ago cut down by charcoal burners who supplied fuel for Pueblo steel mills. When oil was struck near Florence and Canon City in the 1870's, oil was piped to refineries here. Near EDEN, 109.2 *m.*, a train of four cars was caught in a flood in 1893 and washed downstream for three miles. Many passengers were drowned; one of the cars, buried in quicksands, was never found. South of Eden the highway traverses a desolate region spotted with yucca and sagebrush. The Wet Mountains (R) are a dark shadow against the western horizon; smoke from the Pueblo mills rises directly ahead.

In PUEBLO, 115 *m.* (4,700 alt., 103,000 pop. 1968 est.), are junctions with US 50 (*see Tour 9*), State 96 (*see Tour 8*), and State 76 (see *Tour 8A*). Interstate 25 parallels US 85 and US 87.

Section c. PUEBLO *to* NEW MEXICO LINE; *104 m.* US 85

South of Pueblo, US 85 passes through a region touched with the romance and legends of early Spanish occupation. The Spanish-American people, representing a large proportion of the population of this section, retain many of their old traditions and customs. There are few towns of importance.

In PUEBLO, 0 *m.,* the highway proceeds south by Lake Avenue, skirting (R) the tree-fringed shore of LAKE MINNEQUA, a municipal playground. The blast furnaces and high smokestacks of steel mills are visible at this point. On the open prairie slag dumps parallel the road for some distance. At night the molten dross, tipped along the dump by ladles carried on railroad cars, lights the sky with a red glare. The countryside is windy, arid, and desolate, broken by abrupt small hills and rocky outcroppings.

CROW, 27 *m.* (5,100 alt.), occupies the site of one of the first ranches in southeastern Colorado. Alex Hicklin, the founder, came with Kearney's Army of the West in 1846 and remained to marry the daughter of Charles Bent, then Governor of New Mexico. As a wedding present from his father-in-law, Hicklin received a large tract of land on the Greenhorn River; for years his ranchhouse stood alone in this region. Hicklin dug one of the first irrigation ditches in Colorado to water his fields. One of the old adobe buildings of the Hicklin Ranch, now used as a cow barn (R), stands just south of the general store.

At 28.5 *m.* is the junction with State 165.

Right on State 165 to COLORADO CITY, 2 *m.*
RYE, 4.8 *m.* (6,700 alt., 250 pop.), is a farm village and summer resort.
Left (straight ahead) at Rye on a graveled road to the junction with a dirt road, 0.5 *m.*
Right here to RYE PARK, 1 *m.*
The graveled road becomes a wagon trail, 2 *m.,* and continues to the base of GREENHORN MOUNTAIN, 5 *m.*
State 165 proceeds northwest of Rye to the junction with a dirt road, 8.3 *m.*
Left here 1 *m.* to CAMP CROCKET, a summer camp for boys maintained by the Pueblo Y.M.C.A.
State 165 traverses the deep CANYON OF THE MUDDY, its walls fantastically carved and honeycombed with caves, and descends by a series of serpentine curves to the junction with a dirt road, 13.1 *m.*
Left here 3 *m.* to MARION LAKE (*trout*).
State 165 crosses the St. Charles River below ST. CHARLES DAM, 13.8 *m.,* which impounds the waters of LAKE ISABEL (*boating and swimming*), in the heart of the St. Charles Recreational Area (*cabins, stables, boat houses, ski course, community camp*), developed by the C.C.C.
SAN ISABEL CITY, 14.1 *m.,* was once known as Willow Creek. The road crosses GREENHILL DIVIDE, 17.1 *m.,* and descends through Davenport Gulch, where unusually large aspen trees are found, to the junction with State 76 (*see Tour 8A*), 20.5 *m.*

US 85 crosses GREENHORN CREEK, 28.6 *m.,* where a monument commemorates the battle in which Cuerno Verde (Sp. Greenhorn), a Comanche war chief, was killed by Governor Anza of New Mexico in 1779. The name "greenhorn" was bestowed upon the chieftain because bull elk or deer are bold when their new antlers are growing and still "green." Cuerno Verde was the fiercest of all Comanche chiefs of his time and so troublesome to the Spanish that Anza determined in 1778 to end his power, following him through the lower San Luis Valley and across the Sangre de Cristos, finally overtaking him here at Greenhorn Creek. In the battle that followed the Indian leader was killed, with four of his sub-chiefs, his high priest, his eldest son, and 32 followers.

GREENHORN, 30 m. (6,200 alt.), was a pioneer stagecoach station. A white frame house (R), south of the general store, was at one time the GREENHORN INN (*open*), frequented by Kit Carson and other notables of the frontier. In a Zoo (*open*) are animals native to this region.

The highway crosses the HUERFANO RIVER (Sp. orphan), 41.2 m.; HUERFANO BUTTE (L), an almost perfect cone of volcanic rock, long a landmark, was so named because it stands isolated.

WALSENBURG, 51 m. (6,200 alt., 6,182 pop.), seat of Huerfano County, was originally a small Spanish village known as La Plaza de los Leones (Sp. square of the lions), named for a prominent Spanish family. In the seventeenth century the Conquistadores visited this region in search of gold. Later, Spanish-American farmers and American traders and trappers settled along the Cuchara River and its tributary creek. Much of the land was held by titled *hacendados* under the seal of the governor of Santa Fe; but increasing numbers of Americans finally dealt a death blow to the rule of the landed gentry.

Walsenburg is the junction for State 10 (Navajo Trail) from the east and US 160 going west. It is near segments of San Isobel National Forest. The county raises livestock (some Herefords) and feed crops; coal mining has ceased. Attractions for tourists include fishing and hunting; Harold Lathrop State Park, and Martin and Horseshoe Lakes, are 9 m. west; Orlando and Cucharas Reservoirs are northeast. The new Huerfano Memorial Hospital has been built in Walsenburg.

The highway follows the foothills to AGUILAR, 69 m. (6,700 alt., 750 pop.), on the APISHAPA RIVER (Ind. stinking water), so named because its waters are stagnant during certain seasons. Southwest (R) of Aguilar, across several miles of broken hill country, are the SPAN-ISH PEAKS, which the Indians and the Spanish called Huajatolla, or breasts of the world. They were held in awe by the Ute Indians, who believed them to be the home of fearsome gods. In 1811 a traveler from Mexico reported that gaping fissures from which fumes arose indicated a recent earthquake in these mountains.

Many stories have been told of gold discoveries here. "Many years ago," according to an Indian legend recorded in the Mexico City archives, "before the first white man stepped ashore, even before the alliance of the three kingdoms, Alcolhua, Aztec and Tepance, gold was already an eagerly sought article. But it was not coined in those days, nor was it used in barter; it was offered to the deities only, and with it the shrines of Huitzilopochtli were decked. The bulk of it was taken to the cities of Mexico, Tezcuco, and Tlacopan. But when Nezhuatcoyotl reigned in splendor at Tezcuco, the gods of the Mountain Huajatolla became envious of the magnificence of his court, and they placed demons on the double mountain and forbade all men further approach."

Three monks and other followers of Coronado were left behind when the explorer returned to Mexico after his fruitless search for the mythical cities of Quivira, according to another legend. Two of the monks endeavored to teach the natives the doctrines of Christianity, and both died as martyrs. The third, Juan de la Cruz, so the story goes, overcame the evil spirits of the twin mountain and gained access to their hidden treasures. Indians of the Pecos region reported that their people were compelled by torture to enter subterranean passages here and bring forth the gold; when these slaves had served their purpose, all were killed. Juan de la Cruz, with his followers and a number of pack animals heavily laden with treasure, left the demon-haunted region at last, bound for the city of Mexico, but they never reached their destination. Gold nuggets that might possibly have been part of their treasure were found in 1811 by a Mexican traveler scattered along an ancient trail some distance south of the double mountain, far from any mine or mineral-bearing lodes. If fabulously rich mines once existed here on the Spanish Peaks, all traces have been obliterated by rock slides.

At 75.8 *m.* is the junction with a side road.

Right on this road to LUDLOW, 1 *m.,* where a monument commemorates the strikers and their families who lost their lives in the so-called "Battle of Ludlow" during the Colorado coal strike of 1913–14. The strike was called on September 23, 1913, after mine operators had refused demands for an eight-hour day, a check weighman, the right to trade in other than company-owned stores, a 10 per cent increase in wages, and recognition of the United Mine Workers of America. Here striking miners and their families, union officials, organizers, and sympathizers established a tent colony. At the request of county officials of Las Animas and Huerfano Counties, Governor Elias M. Ammons sent units of the Colorado National Guard to the scene and declared martial law. Ill feeling grew until a conflict was precipitated between striking miners and the militia. During hostilities several strikers were killed; on April 20, 1914, the tents were burned, causing the deaths of two women and 11 children, probably from suffocation. The monument stands on the site of the "tent dugout" where the women and children died. The "Ludlow Massacre" was heatedly debated; while the strike was lost, the issue aroused public opinion and brought about improvement of working conditions and civil liberties in the coal camps.

Skirting the foothills, the road follows the general route of the old Goodnight cattle trail, leading south to New Mexico and Texas. FISHERS PEAK, named for Captain Fisher, a German artillery officer in General Kearney's Army of the West during the Mexican War, looms in the foreground. To the west, the peaks of the CULEBRA RANGE (Sp. snake) of the Sangre de Cristo Mountains (*see Tour 11B*), snow-covered most of the year, rise in purple and silver splendor.

Turning west, US 85 enters the PURGATOIRE VALLEY. In 1594–96 a band of Conquistadores, believed to have been in search of the fabulous Seven Cities of Cibola, or the village of Quivira, left Mexico on an ill-fated trek northward. A quarrel arose between Francisco Bonilla and Juan Hermana, leaders of the expedition; the former was slain and Hermana assumed command. A priest accompanying the expedition refused to continue under the leadership of a murderer, and turned back with a handful of followers. Hermana and his men went on, and nothing was heard of them until a second expedition, following much the same route, came upon the bones of Hermana and his followers along the banks of the Purgatoire River. The expedition apparently had been massacred by Indians. As no priest accompanied the party, the men died without administration of the last rites of the Church, and their souls were presumably wandering forever in purgatory. The Spaniards therefore named the stream El Rio de las Animas Perdidas en Purgatorio (*the river of the souls lost in purgatory*), a title shortened and subsequently corrupted, with the result that the names of Las Animas, Purgatoire, and Picketwire, the cowboy version of Purgatoire, are used interchangeably.

Until recently throughout this valley, and even now in some communities, festivals were held to celebrate episodes in the early history of the region. Along the upper Purgatoire River the pageant of Los Comanches, held by settlers who made their way here from Taos, celebrated the victory of the New Mexicans over the Comanche Indians. Young men formed into two groups, representing the New Mexicans and the Indians, the former in military dress, the latter painted and feathered, and engaged in a spirited battle in which the Indians were always defeated.

Old World marriage customs are followed by Spanish-Americans in this vicinity. Courtship and marriage are attended with little sentiment. When a young man decides that the time has come, his parents are the first to know of his intentions. They escort him to the family of the girl of his choice and make formal application for her hand. She is consulted, and if her answer is favorable, a time is arranged when the two can meet and agree upon the wedding date. The bans are announced in church on three consecutive Sundays or Holy Days. Weddings are invariably gay, and as lavish as the parents of the bridegroom can afford. The offering to the priest is made by the best man, *valedor,* who also usually presents the bride with her wedding bouquet. After the ceremony the couple, their families, and their guests engage in feasting, singing, and dancing, sometimes lasting for several days.

In TRINIDAD, 89.5 *m.* (5,999 alt., 10,800 pop.) (*see Trinidad*), are junctions with US 160 (*see Tour 11*), US 350 (*see Tour 10*), and State 12 (*see Tour 11A*).

1. Right from Trinidad a road winds northwest to SIMPSON'S REST, 0.5 *m.*, a small hill containing the rock-bound crypt of George S. Simpson, pioneer. Simpson once sought refuge from an Indian war party here, hiding in the caves that honeycombed the crest; he was buried here in 1885.

2. Left from Trinidad on a wagon road across grassy prairies to MARSH'S MINE, 3 *m.*, now in part abandoned, at the foot of Fishers Peak (9,586 alt.).

Right from the mine a trail strikes upward through the foothills to FIRST SPRING, 2 *m.*, where icy mountain water bubbles from among the rocks, and wood violets grow profusely. From here can be seen a stretch of the Purgatoire Valley, the Spanish Peaks, and a wide sweep of the Sangre de Cristos. The trail ascends through heavy oak brush where grouse are often flushed from the undergrowth. A small lake, edged with iris in spring, is passed, and the trail turns steeply through loose gravel to the SUMMIT OF FISHERS PEAK, 9 *m.* (*the trip by foot or horseback requires a full day*). On the summit a surveyor's marker indicates the northeastern corner of the MAXWELL LAND GRANT, a large tract granted to Guadalupe Miranda and Charles Beaubien by Governor Armijo of New Mexico in 1843. When formal ownership was given, a magistrate took the grantees by the hand and "walked with them, caused them to throw earth, pull up weeds, and show other evidences of possession." After the acquisition of New Mexico by the United States in 1848, the Congress confirmed the owners' title to some 1,700,000 acres. Title soon passed to Beaubien's son-in-law, Lucien B. Maxwell, western trader and scout. Maxwell later sold out to an English syndicate, the Maxwell Land Grant Company, for more than $1,000,000. Squatters, pioneer farmers, and ranchers settled on the grant and in 1888 they resisted attempts of agents to dispossess them. Captain Richard D. Russell, who had taken up a homestead in the Stonewall Valley in 1871 and made many improvements, including a large lake for irrigation purposes, was ordered after 16 years of settlement to pay for his homestead or move off. United States marshals arrived and put up at a small hotel in Stonewall. Settlers burned the hotel in an effort to rid the country of the "varmits" who were annoying them, an act that precipitated hostilities between Government agents and Stonewall settlers, who barricaded themselves in their houses. Captain Russell was slain during a fight on August 28, 1888. His widow later purchased their homestead from the Maxwell Land Grant Company.

The highway traverses a foothill area and winds over the route of the Mountain or Military Branch of the Santa Fe Trail to STARK-VILLE, 92.3 *m.* (6,500 alt.), an old Mexican settlement. Many Spanish-American people still occupy adobe houses in the Lower Plaza. Sitting in the shade on warm days strumming their guitars, they sing "La Cucaracha," "La Paloma," "Rancho Grande," or other native songs in exchange for a glass of beer.

MORLEY, 100 *m.* (7,200 alt.) was once a model road camp of neat cement houses surrounded by attractive gardens; mining has ceased.

WOOTTON, 101.2 *m.* (7,534 alt.), stands on the SITE OF THE OLD WOOTTON TOLL GATE, where, in 1865, Richens L. ("Uncle Dick") Wootton, a frontier scout with a good eye for business, built a road over Raton Pass and collected tolls, often at the point of a gun. He divided his patrons into five groups—stage companies, freighters, military authorities, Mexicans, and Indians. The last were usually allowed to pass free, at which "Mexicans" invariably but futilely protested. Entries in an account book show the following charges: "two wagons, $3; three horsemen, 75¢; one meal, 75¢; hay and meat, $5.50; for blanket of Mexican, $1.75; for knife, 50¢; for whiskey, 40¢, and for one candle, 10¢."

Wootton was one of the great figures of the mountain frontier. As a youth, he had trapped beaver with the Mountain Men and later served in the Mexican War. Times becoming dull, he established a buffalo farm near Pueblo, capturing buffalo calves and pasturing them with his cattle. During the gold rush to California he started overland with 9,000 sheep, and notwithstanding Indians and bad weather, succeeded in bringing 8,900 of them safely to Sacramento. In 1858, as the Pikes Peak gold rush gained momentum, Wootton opened the first saloon and general store in Denver; soon tiring of a merchant's life, he returned to southern Colorado to build his toll road. When the railroad entered the country in 1878, he sold his rights and retired.

From Wootton, by easy grades, the road climbs to RATON PASS (8,560 alt.), named by the Spanish for the small rock rats found here. The pass, originally on an old Indian trail that followed Raton Creek to the summit of Raton Range, was later used by the Mountain Branch of the Sante Fe Trail, which replaced the Cimarron Branch when the latter was abandoned because of its dangerous desert stretches. In 1718 and 1719 expeditions sent north by the governor of New Mexico to check the advance of the French, probably used the pass, as did La Lande, a French Creole from Kaskaskia, Ill., and James Purcell, of Bradstown, Ky., in 1803 and 1804. As early as 1846 much traffic between the Missouri River and Sante Fe passed this way, and the volume increased after the Mexican War. There had been little vehicular traffic until the supply trains and artillery of Kearney's Army of the West passed this way in August 1846.

The coming of the railroad was marked by a two-year controversy between the Denver & Rio Grande and Santa Fe Railroads. In February 1878, the Rio Grande sent a construction crew to the pass on a train from Pueblo, to begin work extending the line from El Moro. A few hours later the Santa Fe chartered a special train for its working crew. They reached El Moro at 11 o'clock at night, and were immediately sent into the mountains, where the Rio Grande crew found them on their arrival the next morning. After some conflict a compromise was reached; the Rio Grande gave up its designs on Raton Pass and the Santa Fe agreed not to contest the right-of-way through the Royal Gorge (*see Tour 9b*).

At 104 *m.* US 85, US 87 and Interstate 25 cross the New Mexico Line, 11 miles north of Raton, New Mexico.

Tour 13

(Cheyenne, Wyo.)—Fort Collins—Loveland—Longmont—Lafayette—
Denver; US 87 and Interstate 25.
Wyoming Line to Denver, 98.8 *m.*

The route of US 87 runs from Cheyenne to Denver several miles
west of US 85. It is also the route of Interstate 25, which now carries
the bulk of traffic between the two cities.

Between the Wyoming Line and Denver the highway skirts the Front
Range of the Rocky Mountains, traversing in turn a dry range country,
the irrigated valleys of the Cache la Poudre and South Platte Rivers,
and the northern Colorado coal fields.

US 87 crosses the Wyoming Line, 0 *m.,* 13 miles south of Cheyenne,
Wyoming.

This region is the southern extremity of the Wyoming highlands, with
brown rolling hills broken occasionally by rocky outcroppings weathered
into fantastic shapes. Herds of white-faced cattle graze along the highway, which passes a group of WARREN RANCH BUILDINGS, 0.6 *m.,* a
part of the estate of Senator Francis E. Warren of Wyoming (1844–
1929), one of the most important ranch properties in the West, lying
both in Colorado and Wyoming.

At 3.3 *m.* is the junction with a dirt road.

Left on this road to the NATURAL FORT (*open on application to foreman
of Warren Ranch*), 1.5 *m.,* an exceptionally large outcrop of gray sandstone
characteristic of the region. Rain and almost constant winds have carved
in it a deep recess, 30 feet wide and 80 feet long, protected on all sides by
massive walls, forming a natural corral. The eastern slope is protected by rough
broken terrain; on the west are heavy growths of underbrush along the creek.
The natural breastworks on both the northern and southern sides of the formation have been leveled by souvenir hunters.

Here, in 1831, a battle was fought between the Crow and the Blackfeet,
both driven from their usual hunting grounds by a long drought that sent
the buffalo southward from the Yellowstone country. The Crow, led by their
famous mulatto chief, Jim Beckwourth, and aided by a number of white trappers, inflicted a crushing defeat upon their ancient enemies. Tales are told
of many other Indian battles here; of freighters seeking protection; of
immigrant trains "holed-up" to avoid Indians and white outlaws; of fierce
battles fought until the gray walls were stained crimson; and of bandit gangs
who hid their loot in its recesses and defied the law.

The road traverses a sparsely settled region to WELLINGTON,
22.3 *m.* (5,201 alt., 635 pop.), a supply point for the surrounding agricultural territory. The town experienced a brief oil boom in 1924. There
is a junction here with southbound State 1.

The highway crosses BOX ELDER VALLEY, one of the first agricultural districts in the State. Many of the frame farmhouses along the route were built in the 1880's. The rich bottom lands produce large crops of sugar beets, hay, and grains; on the higher levels pasturing and turkey raising are important sources of income.

At 27.8 *m.* is the junction with a dirt road.

Right on this rough road to the LINDENMEIR SITE, 22.9 *m.*, where valuable archeological discoveries have been made. The area is licensed for digging, and unauthorized searching is forbidden. Investigations have been conducted since 1935 by the Smithsonian Institution. Artifacts were first uncovered in 1926, chiefly spear- and arrow-heads, believed to be 20,000 years old by archeologists. It is hoped to find remains of the prehistoric Folsom Man (*see The People*), who achieved great skill in fashioning stone implements of war.

CACHE LA POUDRE, 30.2 *m.,* enlarged for the storage of water diverted from the Cache la Poudre River, contains at its maximum 400,-000,000 cubic feet of water, almost all of which is used for irrigating the valley. The discovery in 1919 that red clover produced heavy crops in the alkali soil, led to the reclamation of much marshy and alkalized land previously uncultivated.

At 30.5 *m.* is the junction with a graveled road.

Left on this road to a CHERRY CANNING FACTORY, 0.6 *m.* The juice, known locally as cherry cider, is also marketed. During the season wayside stands sell the juice by the drink and in gallon lots.
A GREAT WESTERN BEET SUGAR FACTORY is located here.

At 31.7 *m.* is the junction with US 287 (*see Tour 13A*), which unites with US 87 for 1.8 miles.

The route crosses the EATON DITCH, 32.6 *m.,* an irrigation canal with the second oldest legally established water right in the State. The water laws of Colorado differ materially from those of Eastern States in that riparian rights are not recognized; based upon the principle of appropriation, rights depend upon the date of application of the water to beneficial use. The Eaton Ditch dates from April 1, 1864. On the southern side of the ditch (L) are the fields of INVERNESS FARM, laid out by Phillips Lariviere in 1860, the first patented land in the Fort Collins district. The highway crosses the CACHE LA POUDRE RIVER, 33.2 *m.,* just above the dam that furnishes power for (L) the FORT COLLINS MUNICIPAL LIGHT PLANT. This river once ran high but now so much water is diverted for irrigation that the level is often low.

FORT COLLINS, 33.5 *m.* (4,984 alt., 39,000 pop.) (*see Fort Collins*). Interstate 25 follows US 87 in a straight line down the Valley Highway to Denver. At Fort Collins US 287 comes down from Wyoming (*see Tour 13A*). The places named below are served by US 287 and connect with Interstate 25 by means of State roads, 4 to 7 *m.* long. They are Loveland, State 16; Campion, State 60; Berthoud, State 56; Longmont, State 119; Lafayette, State 7.

Thousands of sheep are shipped in each fall to be fattened in the Fort Collins winter-feeding district. A center of extensive winter feeding as early as 1880, it has received in recent years many thousand head from the semiarid ranges of Colorado, Wyoming, Texas, and Utah. The lambs, ranging from five to seven months old, are bought by the feeder at market prices, unloaded at the "docks," placed in yards and fed for a period ranging from three to five months. The process of fattening is gradual. The animals are usually started on "third cutting" alfalfa, which approximates the diet to which they have been accustomed. This is followed with richer foods, including ensilage, cottonseed meal, beet pulp, molasses, and corn.

The feeder as a rule cannot contract in advance for feed needed during the season. Wet snows, rain, and cold weather often bring loss of weight and many deaths among the lambs. Transportation charges from the range to the feeding lots, as well as the cost of subsequent shipping to Missouri River points, are included in the price the feeder pays for his stock. The letters FPR that appear after lamb quotations mean "freight paid to the river." After the fattened stock reaches the river yards, the feeder's profit or loss depends upon the market.

HORSETOOTH RESERVOIR, named after a peak in the foothills, supplies some of the water to the city of Fort Collins. The dam is 170 ft. tall, covers 1,610 acres, and holds 151,700 acre-ft.

South and west of Horsetooth looms the northern section of the Front Range of the Rocky Mountains. On clear days the mountains appear to be but a short distance away, although they are separated from the highway by 20 miles of plains and foothills. FOSSIL CREEK, 38.1 *m.*, is a tiny trickle of water, along whose banks have been found many fossilized remains of small prehistoric fish. The highway traverses the Loveland cherry-growing district; straight rows of small green trees stretch for miles in every direction.

LOVELAND, 46 *m.* (4,982 alt., 15,000 pop. est.), is at the junction with US 34 (*see Tour 3*).

BOYD LAKE, east of Loveland, a reservoir, covers 2,022 acres and can hold 44,018 acre-ft. of water.

South of Loveland orchards give way to the fields of sugar beets, grain, and hay that surround CAMPION, 49.6 *m.* The CAMPION ACADEMY is a parochial boarding school maintained by the Seventh Day Adventist Church.

Left from Campion on State 60, a graveled road, is JOHNSTOWN, 9.4 *m.* (4,820 alt., 767 pop.), and MILLIKEN, 13 *m.* (4,760 alt., 483 pop.), adjoining towns largely supported by THE GREAT WESTERN BEET SUGAR REFINERY. This plant receives molasses from all company factories for the final extraction of sugar crystals. In 1954 it added a plant to extract from factory solutions monosodium glutamate, used to intensify flavors of foods; also liquid protein concentrate (LPC) and potash fertilizer.

BERTHOUD, 53 *m.* (5,240 alt., 1,400 pop.), named for Captain Edward L. Berthoud, Civil War officer and pioneer railroad construction engineer, is the oldest community in the Little Thompson Valley; the surrounding country produces sugar beets, potatoes, and grains.

Carter Lake, west of Berthoud, has the highest dam in Colorado— 285 ft., earthen fill. The reservoir covers 1,140 acres.

Right on State 56 to the BERTHOUD OIL FIELD, 3 *m.*, where a few wells on the western slope of a long hogback are producing.

The route passes through an intensively cultivated hill country dominated (R) by the great mass of Longs Peak. The farms are comparatively old, and most of the frame houses are surrounded by tall cottonwoods.

At 62.4 *m.* is the junction with State 66 (*see Tour 4*).

LONGMONT, 63.9 *m.* (5,000 alt., 17,000 pop. est.), was founded 1870 by the Chicago-Colorado Colony Company, which purchased virgin land, divided it into small tracts, and induced farmers to settle here. The town's name is a combination of the name of the discoverer of Longs Peak, Major Stephen H. Long, and the French term for mountain. The community is the center of a prosperous sugar beet area, and its largest industries are the Great Western Sugar Beet Co., Amphenol, Inc., Gould National Batteries, Inc., and International Business Machines, the last employing 475. The Denver Air Traffic Center of the FHA controls commercial air traffic in a 5-state area and employs 400. The St. Vrain Memorial Bldg. has large auditorium facilities and a Pioneer Museum. The city provides free porch lighting.

SUNSET PARK, one of four municipal recreational grounds, contains a free swimming pool and 9-hole golf course. At 4th and Kimbark Sts. stands the FIRST ORE MILL, brought into Boulder County in 1859 and used in the workings at Gold Hill (*see Tour 6*). This crude mortar-type mill consists of a granite block with a large cavity to hold the ore and an outlet for the pulverized rock.

At 64.6 *m.* is the junction with the Burlington road.

Right on this road to the junction with an unmarked dirt road, 5 *m.;* L here 0.1 *m.* to the RYSSBY SCHOOL, a modern building on the site of the log cabin school of the old Ryssby settlement. The RYSSBY LUTHERAN CHURCH, 1 *m.*, a small graystone structure built in 1882, is the only remaining landmark of a colony founded in 1872 by a group from Ryssby parish in the province of Smaland, Sweden. These settlers had little money; crop after crop failed, first because there was no water, and again because there was too much, and finally because of a grasshopper plague. Largely due to the influence of the church through the years of trial, the Swedish colonists remained closely knit, retaining the language, dress, and customs of the Old Country.

Christmas was a gala occasion here, and for a week in advance there was much butchering, baking, and brewing. On Christmas Eve the scrubbed floors were strewn with pine needles, pine boughs were hung in the windows, and hand-dipped candles provided light. The tree was decorated with paper birds, butterflies, and flowers, and strung with popcorn and cranberries. *Kaffe Kalas* was served in the evening. This meal, starting with *fruit suppa,* a soup made of raisins, prunes, apples, and tapioca, was followed by a variety of sausages, cheese, and coffee. Church services were held early the next morning with the colonists in new finery. Then came a bountiful Christmas dinner of sausages, spareribs, *lut fisk* (a white fish with sauce), head cheese, many kinds of bread, *pan kaka* (a sort of custard), wines, and ale.

In later years the Swedish group has been absorbed into neighboring American communities, and the festivals have been abandoned. The church is open only one day a year, for the Mid-year Festival on the Sunday nearest June 24, when Swedish services are held. The Ryssby Record Book, dating from January 3, 1878, and written in Swedish, has been presented to the State Historical Society, Denver.

At 71.5 *m.* is the junction with a dirt road.

Left on this road is ERIE, 3 *m.* (5,000 alt.), near the center of a productive lignite coal field. Here is the State Mine, with more than 20 miles of underground workings. The New Morrison and the Puritan are also large producers.

LAFAYETTE, 75.9 *m.* (5,237 alt., 2,850 pop.), is a coal town reflecting the declining prosperity of that industry. During a strike of miners in 1927, Lafayette was the center of agitation in the northern field, and strikers and strike-breakers clashed frequently here.

Left from Lafayette on an unimproved road to SERENE, 5 *m.*, another coal camp clustered about the COLUMBINE MINE (*visitors admitted only by pass from Denver office*). During the labor strike of 1927, this mine, which supplied coal to the Burlington Railroad, remained in operation, although it was picketed daily. On November 21, 1927, pickets were met by State police, who forbade trespassing on company property. In the dispute that ensued, the police fired into the crowd, killing five persons and seriously wounding many others.

The tragedy was followed by a reorganization of the company, during which Miss Josephine Roche, later Assistant Secretary of the Treasury, obtained control. A new labor policy was adopted with the recognition of the United Mine Workers of America. The company's policy, directed by Miss Roche and her advisers, enabled the union to gain a foothold in the Colorado fields, which are now completely organized.

At 77.5 *m.* is the junction with a paved highway.

Right on this road is LOUISVILLE, 2.5 *m.* (5,350 alt., 1,681 pop.), a coal town similar in appearance to Lafayette.

Left from Louisville to the MONARCH MINE, 4 *m.*, still a producer despite the fact that a part of its workings was destroyed in 1936 by an explosion that killed eight persons.

The highway traverses a rich agricultural district; the Front Range of the Rockies rises beyond the rolling foothills.

At 78.4 *m.* is the junction with a dirt road.

BROOMFIELD, 81 *m.* (5,420 alt., 6,600 pop. 1967, est.) was named for broom corn originally grown here. Today it is an expanding part of the Denver metropolitan area. Land has been donated for a junior college. The MAMIE DOWD EISENHOWER PUBLIC LIBRARY contains books once owned by John Dowd of Denver, father of Mrs. Eisenhower. Jefferson County Airport for light planes is 1 *m.* from city. The *Star-Builder* is its weekly newspaper.

WESTMINSTER, 89 *m.* (5,280 alt., 18,700 pop. 1967, est.) on the Denver-Boulder Turnpike, is a rapidly expanding town in the Denver metropolitan area. It has a new Civic Center and Westminster Plaza Shopping Center. The new Standley Lake will furnish its water supply.

THORNTON, a new city north of Denver, is located on US 87, between 88th Ave. and 104th Ave., 2 *m.* west of US 85. It began as a housing development in 1954, named for Dan Thornton, former governor; incorporated as a second-class city in 1956, and in 1957 voted a bond issue to move its administrative offices from a quonset hut into a Municipal Building. It has approx. 15,000 people. Most of its citizens are employed in the Denver metropolitan area of which Thornton is a part.

Immediately north of Thornton is a real estate development called NORTHGLENN, covering 2,600 acres. In 1960 the area was farmland. In June, 1969, it was incorporated, with about 23,000 people and 5,000 dwellings.

DENVER, 98.8 *m.*

Tour 13*A*

(Laramie, Wyoming)—Virginia Dale—Fort Collins; US 287, State 123.
Wyoming Line to Fort Collins, 39.5 *m.*

Part of this route is used by one of the Circle Tours out of Fort Collins.

US 287 skirts the base of the Front Range of the Rockies and follows the routes of the old Overland Stage and the Fort Collins-Fort Laramie Stage lines through stark arid hill country, which gives way to fertile irrigated farm lands as the highway approaches Fort Collins.

The route crosses the Wyoming Line, 0 *m.*, 27 miles south of Laramie, Wyoming, and traverses a region of rolling foothills broken by grotesque masses of sandstone.

On the BISHOP RANCH, 3.8 *m.*, founded by Thomas Bishop in 1873 and still occupied by his descendants, stands (L) a log building, one of the original structures. The VIRGINIA DALE MONUMENT (L), 4.5 *m.*, which bears a bronze tablet pointing the way to the old Virginia Dale Station on the Overland Stage route, is at the junction with a dirt road.

Left on this road to the old VIRGINIA DALE STAGE STATION (*open*), 0.9 *m.* The original station house, 20 feet by 60 feet, was built of hand-hewn logs.

Its great rock chimney is well-preserved, and the original andirons are to be seen. In the logs at the northeastern corner are numerous bullet holes. Under the house is a walled-in cellar, into which livestock were driven in times of Indian trouble. The wells that served the station are still used, but the stage barns that stood 200 feet south of the house have been dismantled.

The Virginia Dale Station, established in 1862 when the Overland Stage was forced by Indian depredations in Wyoming to operate through northern Colorado, was named for the wife of Joseph Slade, division manager of the line, who killed Jules Beni, his predecessor (*see Tour 1A*). Although the exact spot where Beni was kidnapped and slain is unknown, it was probably somewhere between Virginia Dale and Fort Laramie, Wyo. Slade remained as division manager for more than a year, but his violence—he was fond of shooting canned goods off grocery shelves—necessitated his discharge.

Construction of the railroad in 1867 put an end to the stage routes and the station was sold.

East of the station is LOOKOUT MOUNTAIN, 0.2 *m.*, from the crest of which Indian smoke signals rose in the old days; and nearby is ROBBERS' ROOST, a high hill with a bowl-shaped depression that served outlaws as a natural fortress.

VIRGINIA DALE, 5.1 *m.* (6,977 alt.), took the name of the old station and often is confused with it. South of Virginia Dale the highway traverses rolling country, crosses several creeks that are dry ravines most of the year, and penetrates more rugged country. STEAMBOAT ROCK (L), long a landmark, resembles an old-fashioned steamer with two funnels. The "funnels" were used by Indians as a lookout and a point for signal fires.

The SPRING HILLS RANCH, 17.3 *m.*, is at the junction with a dirt road.

Right on this road 1.9 *m.*, to one of two commercially developed North American alabaster beds; the other is on Owl Creek (*see below*).

The FORKS, 18.5 *m.*, also known as the Forks Hotel, was built in 1874 to accommodate workers in great lumbering operations, then a major industry in this section.

Right from the Forks on a graveled road through a region of steep hills to a junction with a marked dirt road, 2 *m.*
Right here 32 *m.* to Alabaster Quarries.
Left (straight ahead) the graveled road crosses the North Fork of the Cache la Poudre River on an old steel and frame bridge and continues to the almost-deserted town of LIVERMORE, 2.5 *m.* (5,733 alt.); the telephone exchange (L) is the only occupied building. Livermore was named jointly for the two earliest settlers in this country, Adolph Livernash and Stephen Moore. In 1863, when the first cabins were erected, Livermore embraced the entire district from Laporte west to the Continental Divide and from the southern boundary of Larimer County to the Colorado-Wyoming boundary.
At LOG CABIN, 16 *m.*, a post office and a rural supply center, the road forks.
Right from Log Cabin on a road that winds through a mountainous region to the old FLYING W RANCH, 21 *m.;* here is (R) a fire-warden station. The PARVIN RESERVOIR AND GAME PRESERVE (*open*), 23 *m.*, lies on South Lone Pine Creek, which feeds the reservoir, a propagation lake for trout. RED FEATHER LAKES VILLAGE, 23.6 *m.* (8,300 alt.), is a summer

resort. Of the nine natural lakes that make up the Red Feather Group, Twin Lakes and Dowdy Lake are unlicensed and open to fishermen.

Left from Log Cabin the road traverses rich cattle-grazing country, a region of comparatively low hills, broken by jutting cliffs carved into fantastic forms by wind and rain. Crossing Elkhorn Creek, tributary of the Cache la Poudre, the road reaches the ELKHORN SILVER FOX RANCH, 5.4 *m.*, where, in open pens on the southern hill slope, foxes are bred and raised (*see Tour 7b*). At 7.1 *m.* is the MANHATTAN RANGER STATION.

At 20.7 *m.* is the junction with a foot trail.

Left on this trail 3 *m.* to a PIÑON GROVE, one of the most northerly growths of this tree in America. The age of some of the piñons has been fixed at 4,000 years, approximating that of the largest California redwoods. A few trees here are four feet in diameter—about 18 inches greater than that of any other known piñons.

At 22.3 *m.* is the junction with a narrow dirt road.

Right on this road to the RUINS OF BONNAR SPRINGS STAGE STATION, 3.5 *m.*, the outline of its foundations still visible. The road passes a massive bald rock and MUSGROVE CORRAL, 4 *m.*, a natural bowl-shaped inclosure on the North Fork of the Cache la Poudre, used as a corral and fortress by "Three-Finger" Musgrove, a bandit of early days.

US 287 penetrates the western mouth of OWL CANYON, twisting between limestone cliffs that wall in the narrow gorge. At the eastern mouth, 22.9 *m.*, is the OWL CANYON STORE.

INGLESIDE, 25.2 *m.* (5,400 alt.), founded in the early part of the century, occupies land owned by the Great Western Sugar Company, which quarries limestone nearby for use in beet-sugar manufacture.

HOOK AND MOORE CANYON, 28 *m.*, a narrow valley between two hogbacks carved out by glaciers during the Ice Age, was once the property of H. M. Hook and James Moore, who harvested and sold hay to the U. S. Army, the Overland Stage stations, and local markets. Hook later became the first mayor of Cheyenne, Wyo. The great green stone (R), known as BIG ROCK, is believed to have been carried into the canyon by the ice mass.

On the southern limit of TED'S PLACE, 30.6 *m.*, are a number of log cabins built by forgotten pioneers.

Ted's Place is at the junction with State 14 (*see Tour 2*), which unites with US 287 for 8.9 miles.

ROCKY RIDGE (L), 30.9 *m.*, is an old Indian battleground where arrowheads are occasionally found.

At 31.4 *m.* is the junction with a graveled road.

Right on this road, an alternate route to Fort Collins, into RIST CANYON, 1.2 *m.* The EARLY TRAPPERS MONUMENT (L), 2.2 *m.*, in the grounds of a roadside country house, marks the approximate site where, in 1836, a party of French trappers were caught in a snowstorm and lightened their overloaded wagons. They cached their surplus supplies, including a great store of powder, hoping that it would not be discovered by a large party of Indians following them. Upon their return in the spring the food and supplies were found intact—the origin of the name Cache la Poudre (Fr. hiding place of powder).

Opposite (R) is the SAMUEL BINGHAM FARM, settled in 1860. Bingham's name was given to the steep hill over which the road leaves Pleasant Valley, as the district is locally known. Passing (L) CLAYMORE LAKE (*good fishing*), 3.4 *m.*, the road turns south to FORT COLLINS, 7.5 *m.* (*see below*).

South of the junction US 287 passes (L) the ANTOINE JANIS MONUMENT, 33.8 *m.*, a stone marker at the entrance to a narrow lane leading to the site where Antoine Janis, first white settler in Larimer County, established his home in 1854; the original cabin stands in the library grounds at Fort Collins.

LAPORTE (Fr. the gate), 34.6 *m.* (5,063 alt.), a rural supply center, came into existence as the permanent camp of a band of Canadian-French hunters and trappers. In 1860, when a town company was organized, the village took the name of Colona, which was later changed to Laporte. As headquarters of the mountain division of the Overland Stage Company, the town flourished and at one time aspired to be the capital of the Territory.

Left from Laporte to the BOETTCHER PLANT of the Ideal Cement Company. Limestone deposits owned by the company are sufficient to operate the plant at capacity for more than 100 years.

US 287 crosses rich agricultural land to the junction with State 1 (*see Tour 13*), 37.7 *m.,* which unites with US 287 as far as FORT COLLINS, 39.5 *m.* (4,984 alt., 25,027 pop).

In Fort Collins are junctions with US 87 (*see Tour 13*), State 14 (*see Tour 2*) and Interstate 25.

❧❧❧❧❧❧❧❧❧❧❧❧❧❧❧❧❧❧❧❧❧❧❧❧❧❧❧❧❧❧❧❧❧

Tour 14

(Laramie, Wyo.)—Walden—Rand—Junction US 40 (Granby); State 127 and State 125.
Wyoming Line to Junction US 40, 80.3 *m.*

This route follows the North Platte River southward across North Park, a circular sloping valley walled in by lofty mountains. From an altitude of 7,700 feet near the Wyoming border, the park, approximately 40 miles in diameter, rises gradually to 8,700 feet at its southern extremity. The upper slopes are covered with sagebrush and scrub oak, but on the well-watered bottomlands grows wild hay. The park has always been a grazing ground, and certain place names, such as Bull Pen and Cow Lodge, are literal translations of Indian names given them when the region was dark with slow-moving buffalo herds. Their presence brought trappers and hide hunters, who named the park Buffalo Pasture, although it was also known as New Park, to distinguish it from South Park. Later, when Middle Park became well known, the name was changed to North Park. Hunters were followed by prospectors, who found gold, coal, and other minerals in the surrounding mountains.

Lieutenant John C. Frémont, who visited North Park in 1844, said of it: "The valley narrowed as we ascended and presently descended into a gorge, through which the river passed as through a gate—a beautiful circular valley of thirty miles in diameter, walled in all around with snowy mountains, rich with water, and with grass, fringed with pine on the mountain sides below the snow and a paradise to all grazing animals." Although the park's reputation as a natural game land has led to considerable exploitation, there is still good fishing and much small game.

State 127, traversing the northern end of the Medicine Bow Mountains, crosses the Wyoming Line, 0 *m.,* 27 miles southwest of Laramie, Wyoming. Near the line the clear lazy North Platte River winds across the valley in a series of intricate loops. The wild beauty of mountains here accounts for the ancient belief that the hills were the abode of spirits. The route passes KINGS CANYON, 5.6 *m.,* a shipping point on the Laramie, North Park & Western Railroad, and winds through a gap. In spring the landscape is a tapestry of greens and blues; in late summer and fall it becomes a field of matted gold. A log blockhouse (L), 9 *m.,* built in 1876 by James O. Pinkham, a pioneer, was used as a refuge during numerous Indian uprisings. Pinkham panned gold in near-by hills, and his tales of rich placers brought other settlers into the valley.

At 9.5 *m.* is the junction with State 125, which the route now follows.

COWDREY, 14 *m.* (8,000 alt.), a village of log houses, is an outfitting point for fishermen on their way to the North Platte and its tributary, the Michigan. South of Cowdrey the road follows the Middle Fork of the North Platte, which supplies COWDREY LAKE. Above the green valley rise monoliths of rose granite, resembling grotesque sand dunes.

BROWNLEE LOADING STATION, 20.2 *m.,* is a shipping point for products of the North McCallum Oil Field.

Left from the station on an improved road to NORTH McCALLUM, 3 *m.,* a recently developed oil field, its chief claim to distinction being an ICE CREAM WELL. Here at a depth of 5,000 feet drillers struck a mixture of oil and carbon dioxide gas having a temperature of 136° below zero. Even on the hottest summer day the machinery, pipe lines, and derrick are covered with a thick coating of pale yellow frost resembling lemon sherbet; it has been found impossible to reduce the gas to dry ice.

The highway crosses the MICHIGAN RIVER, 28.8 *m.,* a tributary of the North Platte, where (R) a small gray building houses machinery to regulate the flow of water for irrigation purposes. Water measurement is of much importance along the North Platte because it is an interstate stream over which Colorado and Wyoming have engaged in extensive litigation.

WALDEN, 23.5 *m.* (8,300 alt., 850 pop.), is at the junction with State 14 (*see Tour 2*).

RAND, 49 *m.* (8,900 alt.), named for J. A. Rand, a frontier scout, is a starting point for fishing trips along the Illinois River and tributary streams.

Left from Rand 20 *m.* to the SITE OF TELLER, accessible only by pack horse. This town was founded after a silver strike in 1879, and within a year its population exceeded 2,000. Lack of transportation prevented profitable development, and the mines were soon abandoned. Timbers of collapsed houses mark the site.

The highway traverses rolling sagebrush-covered foothills, crosses the northern boundary of Routt National Forest, 54 *m.* (*see Tour 7b*), and climbs the Rabbit Ears Mountains by way of WILLOW CREEK PASS, 59 *m.*, a densely forested rocky gorge at the boundary between the Routt and Arapaho National Forests. The timbered slopes at these altitudes abound in bird life. The three-toed woodpecker, the ruby-crowned kinglet, and the purple finch are perhaps less in evidence than the noisy Rocky Mountain jay. This friendly but mischievous bird is dubbed the "camp robber" for its habit of pilfering small articles left in the open. In its nests have been found rings, keys, silver coins, even watches.

South of the pass the route winds through Willow Creek Valley, hemmed in by towered hills. The GILSONITE RANGER STATION, 62.9 *m.*, is summer headquarters of the rangers. At intervals are seen traces of abandoned corduroy roads, relics of early logging days. The highway crosses the southern boundary of Arapaho National Forest.

At 80.3 *m.* is the junction with US 40 (*see Tour 7b*), 3.6 miles west of Granby (7,935 alt., 600 pop.) (*see Tour 7b*).

I◦◦I◦◦I◦◦I◦◦I◦◦I◦◦I◦◦I◦◦I◦◦I◦◦I◦◦I◦◦I◦◦I◦◦I◦◦I◦◦I◦◦I◦◦I◦◦I◦◦I◦◦I◦◦I◦◦I◦◦I◦◦I◦◦

Tour 15

Denver—Morrison—Platte Canyon—Kenosha Pass—South Park—Junction US 24 (Buena Vista)—Salida—Poncha Pass—Saguache—Monte Vista—Alamosa—Antonito—Cumbres Pass—(Chama, N. M.) ; US 285.
Denver to New Mexico Line, 315.9 *m.*

The northern section of this tour leads through rugged, thinly populated country roughly paralleling the Continental Divide, a popular recreational area, with many camp sites and streams well-stocked with trout. The highway crosses South Park and the San Luis Valley. Much of the area, once rich mining country, retains some of the color of the boom days. The southern portion of the route traverses a region devoted to ranching and agriculture, and dotted with Spanish-American settlements.

Section a. DENVER *to* JUNCTION US *24; 122.4 m.* US *285*

Through rolling foothills dotted with farms, the road winds up through the Denver Mountain Parks Game Preserve, crosses Kenosha Pass into South Park, then climbs Trout Creek Pass to descend into the Arkansas Valley.

In DENVER, 0 *m.* (5,280 alt., 493,837 pop.) (*see Denver*), US 285 proceeds west by way of Alameda Avenue, striking directly toward the foothills of the Front Range through a suburban district of small farms and country houses, passing the green fairways and white-columned buildings of the GREEN GABLE COUNTRY CLUB (*private*), 7.4 *m.*

MORRISON, 14.7 *m.* (5,669 alt., 500 pop.), a resort at the mouth of Bear Creek Canyon, is one of the principal entrances to the Denver Mountain Parks System. The site was homesteaded by George Morrison in 1870. The town was laid out two years later "in one of the most romantic spots in Colorado," so ran an item in the *Rocky Mountain News* at the time, "where a beautiful mountain stream runs a sawmill, a plant for the manufacture of plaster of paris, and furnishes abundant water for irrigation." Golden near by was greatly disturbed for the moment, fearing the new town would become a dangerous rival. In the town is a STATE FISH HATCHERY (*open 9–5 daily*).

Morrison is at the junction with State 74 (*see Tour 15A*).

Left from Morrison to the MOUNT VIEW GIRLS' SCHOOL, 3 *m.*, a State institution for juvenile offenders. A new gymnasium costing $200,000 has been erected.

Southwest of Morrison the highway crosses the high ridge separating Bear and Turkey Creeks. The great red sandstone spires jutting through masses of evergreens are similar to those in the Park of the Red Rocks (*see Tour 15A*). The road ascends Turkey Creek Canyon, winding along tree-crowned slopes high above the brawling stream. In the canyon are numerous summer houses, ranging from one-room cabins to elaborate log and stone lodges.

TINY TOWN, 20.3 *m.*, a summer settlement, was named for a miniature city on the bank of the creek. Here, built to scale, one inch to a foot, are stores, dwellings, a filling station, a church facing a park, a broadcasting station with aerial towers, a large terra-cotta office building, a railroad station, and an old-fashioned river steamboat on a diminutive pond. Five mines dot the surrounding hillsides; near by are an ore mill and supply house. The miniature city, built by George E. Turner of

Denver as an attraction for children, has been twice destroyed by flood and once by fire, and promptly reconstructed.

At 22.6 *m.* is the junction with State 124.

Left on this road is PHILLIPSBURG, 3.5 *m.*, a scattered settlement, formerly a supply town. Of the original buildings only a log house and a clapboard general store remain.

Right from Phillipsburg 5.5 *m.* on a country road to the SITE OF HILL CITY, once a prosperous mining town and the first sizable settlement in the Deer Creek section, having been established in 1895. Much prospecting had been done in the Deer Creek region as early as 1888.

Right from the site 3 *m.* on a country road is the junction with an old wagon road (*ascent must be made on foot*); R. here 0.3 *m.* to the SAMPSON MINE, on the southeast slope of Sampson Mountain, once the largest and richest in the region. The mine is reputed to have been discovered in 1874 by a Negro minister named Sampson, who worked it successfully until its sale in 1880. Rich in gold and silver, it continued operations until 1900.

South of Tiny Town the highway ascends by easy grades to the ridge separating Turkey and Elk Creeks. From the rim of the broad valley the higher mountain ranges are visible. The principal peaks in the Park Range, from north to south, are MOUNT CAMERON (14,233 alt.), MOUNT LINCOLN (14,284 alt.), and MOUNT BROSS (14,170 alt.).

At the bottom of the canyon is SHAFFERS CROSSING, 36.2 *m.* (7,938 alt., 14 pop.), a summer resort and supply town. The old Denver-Leadville Stage Line forded Elk Creek here. Previously, the isolated country along Elk Creek had been a rendezvous of robbers and other desperadoes.

The road traverses a wooded ridge separating Elk and Deer Creek Valleys and ascends CROW HILL, 38.3 *m.,* from which can be seen traces of the old stage road at the bottom of the ravine; the highway crosses the northern boundary of Pike National Forest (*see Tour 5b*), 47.8 *m.,* to the North Fork of the South Platte (*good fishing*).

In BAILEY, 47.9 *m.* (6,000 alt.), the highway crosses an abandoned narrow-gauge roadbed of the Colorado & Southern Railroad. When begun in 1873 as the Denver, South Park & Pacific Railroad, it was an ambitious venture; plans were made to lay track to the Pacific Coast. Construction was hampered by the panic of 1873, but the delay was fortunate, for the Platte Canyon route was found to be more feasible than that originally planned up Bear Creek. By 1880 the line had been extended almost to Leadville, then at the height of its great boom.

Travel and shipping rates were exorbitant; passengers were charged 10¢ a mile from Denver to the terminus; freight rates ran as high as $29 per ton, more than charged for goods shipped from New York to California by way of Cape Horn. Furthermore, stage accommodations at the terminus being limited, travelers and their luggage were frequently shipped back to Denver to await another train. The lucrative enterprise was bought by the Union Pacific Railroad, backed by the millions of Jay Gould, and stockholders in the original company received $248 for every dollar invested. The Union Pacific extended the line to Leadville late in 1880, and a maze of branch lines was constructed. By 1886 capital stock had increased to $6,235,400. The collapse of the Leadville boom brought disaster to investors, and in 1889 the line was sold under foreclosure. Union Pacific interests bought it back and reorganized it as the Denver, Leadville & Gunnison Railroad, but this project also failed, and when the panic of 1893 again forced the line into receivership, it became part of the Colorado & Southern System.

West of Bailey the highway pursues a winding course through dense forest of spruce and lodgepole pines, home of the pine squirrel, or chick-aree, cousin of the eastern red squirrel. This squirrel builds not one but many nests of grass and moss amid the branches of the pines. Only a few are occupied; the others are apparently constructed for the fun of doing it. Seeds of spruce and pine constitute their diet; cone scales stripped away and dropped to the ground often form mounds several feet high.

Passing SHAWNEE, 53.4 m. (8,125 alt.), a resort on a wooded slope, the road follows the river to SANTA MARIA CAMP CASSELS 57.9 m., a camp for girls, established to give two-week summer vacations to four groups of 160 girls, selected by charitable agencies among under-privileged Denver families. Much of the foodstuff used at the camp is grown on the terraced and cultivated hillsides. On a hill across the river looms the 75-ton CHRIST OF THE ROCKIES, dedicated in 1934, modeled in cream-white glazed porcelain, 52 feet from base to top, flood-lighted at night. A life-size figure of the dead Christ, guarded by two angels, reclines in the crypt at the base of the statue.

The road follows the narrow canyon of the Platte and ascends to KENOSHA PASS, 67.1 m., a broad grassy saddleback between two comparatively low mountains, the divide between the North and South Forks of the South Platte. Since early days the pass has been an important route to South Park. The Leadville Stage Line used it, as did the railroad later.

From a broad curve of the highway is a magnificent view of the treeless, almost-level expanse of SOUTH PARK, which stretches away 40 miles to the south and west. Rimming the valley are snow-capped mountains, their lower slopes blanketed with pine forests, which terminate abruptly at the valley floor, leading geologists to believe that the park was once the bed of an ancient sea. Innumerable streams, tributaries of the South Fork of the South Platte, weave a network of silver through green haylands; the park is dotted with lakes.

The SOUTH PARK MARKER (R), 65.7 m., erected by the State Historical Society, recounts briefly the history of the park. One of the first white men to enter the valley, James Purcell, a Kentucky trader, told Lieutenant Zebulon Pike that he had found traces of gold here in 1803—apparently the first report of gold in this section that was to prove one of the richest placer-mining regions of the State. Pike entered the park with his party in 1806; in 1844, Lieutenant John C. Frémont crossed the basin on his way to California, reporting it alive with "buffalo and other game." Bison and antelope made it a hunters' paradise for the Ute and the plains tribes, as well as for the Mountain Men, who knew it as Bayou Salado because of its salt marshes. George Frederick Ruxton, a young Englishman who visited the Rocky Mountains in 1847, met hunters and trappers here. In his *Life in the Far West* he described the process of "making meat," or butchering, as the Mountain Men practiced it. Dead buffalo were turned upon their bellies, supported by their out-spread legs, and by transverse cuts at the neck and along the spine the skin was stripped away. The shoulders were then severed, ribs chopped off, and the coveted back fat skinned from the spin. The tongue and entrails (*boudin*), choice portions, were removed last. Much was eaten during the process—liver and entrails, often raw—but most of it was "jerked," or cured by drying in the sun. In the form of sticks of almost wooden consistency, it was easily carried and became savory with cooking. Indian wives of the Mountain Men were expert in preparing pemican, a concoction of dried meat, blood, melted fat, berries, and certain roots, a nutritious and portable foodstuff.

Prospectors working southwest in 1859 from the overcrowded Gilpin County gold fields (*see Tour 6*) found "color" along the streams in the northern section of the park, founding the camps of Hamilton and Tarryall (*see below*) and Fairplay (*see Tour 16*). Other goldseekers, among them H. A. W. Tabor, came in from the east by way of Ute Pass; his wife Augusta, one of the really remarkable pioneer women, found the park "gorgeously beautiful." Tabor and his party attempted to guide themselves by Frémont's published maps and letters, but without success; they finally tossed a stick in the air and proceeded in the direction to which it pointed when it fell—a course that took them westward to the Arkansas River, along which they made their way to California Gulch (*see Tour 5b and Leadville*). Most of the placer mines in the park were short-lived, and within a few years only one or two camps remained. Gradually South Park filled up with cattlemen. The now-abandoned Denver & South Park Railroad entered it in 1879. At this time most of it is broken up into large ranches; wild hay for winter feed is cut in the lush meadows. South Park is noted for its fine trout fishing; although many of the streams are overfished, some of the largest trout taken annually in Colorado are caught here.

At 67.6 *m.* is the junction with a dirt road.

Left on this road through rough and uninhabited country to LOST PARK, 17 *m.*, surrounded on three sides by swamps, one of the most primitive areas in the State. Fishing is good; deer, elk, black and brown bear, and mountain lion are numerous. It was here that the last wild buffalo in Colorado, perhaps the last in the country, were killed in 1897, fifteen years after the enactment of the law forbidding the shooting of bison. The hides of the animals, three adults and a calf, were hidden in the hills, but were discovered and confiscated by the authorities. In 1928 they were mounted and sold to the Canon City Municipal Museum (*see Tour 9b*).

The highway descends across broad meadowlands to JEFFERSON, 72 *m.* (9,500 alt.), a shipping point for cattle and timber.

Left from Jefferson on State 77, a graveled road, to 700-acre TARRYALL LAKE, 16 *m.*, used by the State Game and Fish Department as a spawning place for trout. NORTH TARRYALL PEAK (11,400 alt.), 5 miles northwest, is the highest of a series of peaks along the route.

The road follows Tarryall Creek through a rugged canyon to TARRYALL, 30 *m.* (10,254 alt.), a diminutive offspring of the original camp that lay farther up the creek (*see below*).

At 41.5 *m.* is LAKE GEORGE (*see Tour 5b*), at the junction with US 24 (*see Tour 5b*).

The road crosses Tarryall Creek, 76.8 *m.*, where a granite marker points (R) to the SITES OF TARRYALL AND HAMILTON, true ghost towns.

Right along Tarryall Creek 2 *m.* to the TARRYALL DIGGINGS (*accessible only on foot*), which extended west along the creek to the base of the mountains. During the 1860's both banks of the creek were lined with tents and cabins of miners. The rival camps of Hamilton and Tarryall were separated only by the creek, but refused to merge. Gold was plentiful; life, hard and exciting. Saloons and dance halls lined the crowded streets. A private mint was established at Tarryall in 1861 by John Parsons, who minted $2.50 and $5 gold coins. Gold deposits were discovered here in 1859 by prospectors from Central City who found all the good lodes there staked out. At first Tarryall Creek proved a disappointment, but pay dirt was struck just as they were preparing to leave. "Let us tarry all," said a miner, so the story goes, and thus the creek and camp were named.

Word of the strike brought a general rush into South Park. The chief pay streak at Tarryall was the course of an old creek channel where the gravel was filled with scales of gold as large as watermelon seeds. Mining declined in the early 1870's, and population of the camps dwindled rapidly. When the railroad was extended into the park in 1879 the remaining inhabitants moved to Como (*see below*).

Still visible at the site of Tarryall is a deep pit known as WHISKEY HOLE, a placer claim worked one winter by 150 miners who spent most of their earnings for whisky. During boom days men who desired a drink and had no money were permitted to pan gold on the premises to pay for their liquor.

At 78 *m.* is the junction with a dirt road.

Right on this road is COMO, 0.8 *m.* (9,796 alt.), a mining and railroad town that prospered during the 1880's and 1890's. The railroad shops here were destroyed by fire in 1909 and never rebuilt. In an explosion in the King Cole Mine 16 miners were killed.

FAIRPLAY, 88.4 *m.* (9,953 alt., 400 pop. est.), is the seat of Park County at a junction with State 9. The Progressive Mine & Smelter, a community enterprise, was formed to process ores of the area.

ANTERO RESERVOIR, covering 4,102 acres, is at the base of a triangle formed by State 9 on the east, US 285 on the west and US 24 on the south. The highways meet at ANTERO JUNCTION.

Section b. JUNCTION US 24 to ALAMOSA; 122 m. US 285

This section of the route follows the Arkansas River downstream to Salida and then crosses Poncha Pass into the great flat expanse known as the San Luis Valley, one of the most productive agricultural regions of the State. High mountains rise on every hand, and the scenery is richly varied.

US 285 branches south from US 24, 0 *m.* (*see Tour 5b*), 2 miles south of Buena Vista (*see Tour 5b*). Beyond the sheltered and cultivated fields of the Arkansas Valley are the majestic peaks of the COLLEGIATE RANGE; the northernmost is MOUNT HARVARD (14,399 alt.); almost due west is MOUNT YALE (14,172 alt.); straight ahead is MOUNT PRINCETON (14,177 alt.). Rimming the valley to the east are the lower mountains of the Park Range.

SALIDA, 23 *m.* (7,050 alt.), is at the junction with US 50, which unites with US 285 as far as PONCHA JUNCTION, 25.5 *m.* (*see Tour 9b*).

PONCHA SPRINGS (Sp. mild), 27.5 *m.* (7,500 alt., 206 pop.), is built along a mountain slope from which bubble 99 mineral springs. Their waters, varying in temperature from 90 to 185 degrees, contain salts similar to those at Hot Springs, Ark.

The route ascends through heavily forested foothills to PONCHA PASS (9,010 alt.), 35.4 *m.*, chief northern entrance to the San Luis Valley, one of the lowest mountain traverses in the State, usually open throughout the winter. Indians and the Mountain Men used this pass over which Otto Mears constructed a toll road in 1875.

Otto Mears, highway and railroad builder, was born in Russia in 1841 and came to San Francisco with his parents in 1854. At the outbreak of the Civil War he joined the First California Volunteers, serving for a time with Kit Carson in the Indian campaign. After his discharge he explored New Mexico and Arizona Territories, then settled at Conejos (*see below*) in the San Luis Valley. With Major Lafayette Head he built a sawmill and a grist mill. As iron was scarce, everything in the mills except the saw and grinding stones was of wood. Rawhide thongs and pegs were used in place of nails; stones for the grist mill were of lava rock found near the town.

Mears brought one of the first mowers and steam threshers into the San Luis Valley in 1867, but Mexicans refused to have their wheat threshed by the machine, claiming it stole much of their grain. To reach a market for his flour that sold as high as $20 a hundred pounds, Mears constructed a road over Poncha Pass to the Arkansas Valley, the beginning of the Mears system of toll roads that comprised about 300 miles in the San Luis Valley. Several roads were later utilized as railroad beds, notably the route over Marshall Pass.

Mears was a presidential elector from Colorado in 1876. Always active in Indian affairs, he had charge of the removal of the Ute to their new reservation in Utah. Later he was appointed one of five commissioners to make a new treaty with the Indians for 11,000,000 acres of land now included in Montrose, Delta, and Mesa Counties. The Ute complained that the Federal Government had not kept its promises in the past and demanded cash. Mears paid them $2 each, and they signed the treaty. Charges of bribery filed against him were dismissed when he explained to Secretary of the Interior Kirkwood that the Ute preferred the small cash payment to the uncertain payment of interest on $1,800,-000. The $2,800 he spent for the purpose was refunded. Mears constructed a section of the Denver & Rio Grande Southern Railroad, later becoming its president. He died at Pasadena, Calif., in 1931; his portrait in stained glass occupies a window in the State capitol dome.

South of Poncha Pass the highway runs between (L) San Isabel National Forest (see Tour 8b) and Cochetopa National Forest (see Tour 9b); slopes as heavily wooded with spruce, pine, aspen, and cedar.

ROUND HILL, 37.7 m. (8,677 alt.), a railroad repair siding and water station, was named for the mountain east of town. Local legend has it that an old miner once buried a donkey skin filled with gold on this hill, and innumerable holes pitting the slopes bear testimony to the industry of the credulous. South of Round Hill the highway roughly parallels the Sangre de Cristo Range (L) to VILLAGROVE, 50.4 m. (7,952 alt.), a ranch center, typical of the villages of the more remote parts of Colorado.

Except for occasional upthrusts of rock, the SAN LUIS VALLEY, once the bed of an inland sea, is level. Broad expanses are covered with chico and greasewood, broken frequently by well-cultivated green fields. Potatoes grown on rich irrigated lands are the chief money crop of the valley. The Rocky Mountains and Mexico were the original habitat of the Colorado potato beetle, ever the pest of potato growers. Living almost exclusively on the sandbur, which is related to the potato, the beetle was happy to add "spuds" to its menu. Soon the pests swarmed eastward, to the consternation of growers. During the 1870's the rose-breasted grosbeak, closely related to the cardinal, developed a liking for the beetle, devouring them in such great numbers that it became known as the "potato-bug bird," and its appearance in the fields was welcomed.

At 51 m. is the junction with State 17.

Left on this road is MINERAL HOT SPRINGS, 5.3 m. (7,767 alt.), a resort with a cottage camp and outdoor swimming pool.
MOFFAT, 12 m. (7,564 alt.), a shipping point for an extensive cattle-raising district, is at the junction with an unmarked road.
Left on this improved country road is CRESTONE, 13 m. (7,500 alt.), on the site of an old Indian campground where numerous arrow and spear heads, and stone tools have been found. It is named for the CRESTONE NEEDLE (14,191 alt.), the high serrated spike of the Sangre de Cristos that lies to the southwest. Most of the country around Crestone once belonged to William Gilpin, first Territorial Governor of Colorado, whose holdings were acquired from the Bacas (see Tour 11b) and included 100,000 acres, chiefly grazing land. This great domain has since been broken up, either by purchase or by squatters.
South of Moffat, State 17 continues its straight course across dry and dusty flats to HOOPER, 29 m., MOSCA, 35 m., at the junction with State 150, and ALAMOSA, 48 m.

US 285 turns southwest, crossing a bleak area where sheep and cattle are pastured. The Sangre de Cristos to the east and the Cochetopa Hills to the northwest alone break the monotonous level of the valley.

SAGUACHE (pronounced sa-wátch; Ind. blue earth), 69.7 m. (7,697 alt., 750 pop.), county seat and center for lumber and meat processing, was founded by Nathan Russel in 1866 when excited throngs of prospectors rushed into the valley seeking gold. Among them were a number of Germans mustered out of military service at Fort Garland, who named one of the streets "Sauerkraut Avenue." They were soon followed by ranchers, who settled permanently. Today, ranching almost entirely supports the town, one of the few in Colorado where cowboys in high-heeled boots, blue denim jeans, and ten-gallon hats are seen on the streets.

During early days Saguache, then headquarters of the Ute Agency, led a riotous existence; almost every other building was a saloon. The town won the county seat from Milton by a margin of six votes, said to have been cast by the oxen of a local farmer. Old-timers still talk of the race held here on July 4, 1879, when Red Buck, a local horse, was beaten by Little Casino, a "foreigner." Red Buck was the favorite, never having lost a race, and Little Casino's owner, a traveler from Kansas, had difficulty covering all the bets offered at tremendous odds. The Kansan rode away with practically the entire wealth of the community, including the buffalo robes and ponies of the Indians.

Right from Saguache on State 114, used as an alternate route between the Western Slope and Pueblo during winter months when Monarch Pass (*see Tour 9b*) is closed. The highway follows the Saguache River, well stocked with trout. The bluish earth frequently exposed along the road, probably colored by copper content, caused this region to be called "blue earth" by the Indians.

The route crosses the Continental Divide over NORTH PASS (10,149 alt.) to a junction with US 50 (*see Tour 9b*), 61.5 m. The older road uses Cochetopa Pass.

South of Saguache, US 285 is known as the Gunbarrel Road for its singularly straight course.

MONTE VISTA, 105 m. (7,500 alt., 4,000 pop.), is at the junction with US 160 (*see Tour 11*), which is united with US 285 for 17 miles (*see Tour 11c*).

In ALAMOSA, 122 m. (7,544 alt., 6,750 pop.), is the western junction with US 160 (*see Tour 11*).

Section c. ALAMOSA to the NEW MEXICO LINE; 71.5 m.
US 285

South of ALAMOSA, 0 m., the route traverses the lower portion of San Luis Valley, a level barren region covered with sagebrush, greasewood, and mesquite, and whitened by alkali. Distant blue mountains encircle the valley, populated largely by people of Spanish descent whose customs have changed little since early days. Many Spanish families settled along the river bottoms here in the early 1850's.

At 3.5 *m.* is the junction with a graveled road.

Right on this road to the junction with another graveled road, 3.5 *m.;* R. here 0.5 *m.* to the SAN LUIS VALLEY FARMS PROJECT of the Farm Security Administration. During 1938–39 the Administration here resettled 84 families whose submarginal farm lands in eastern Colorado had been purchased by the Federal Government under the land-use program. Identical six-room houses and other buildings have been built on the farm units, the majority occupied under a 40-year lease and purchase contract. An extensive irrigation system was built. Potatoes are the chief cash crop.

The rambling, one-story, white frame COMMUNITY HOUSE contains an auditorium, school rooms, kitchen, dining room, and office.

LA JARA (Sp. rock rose), 15 *m.* (7,600 alt., 750 pop.), is the center of a large truck-farming area growing peas, lettuce, and cauliflower. Cattle, sheep and hog raising are important here. The THOMAS MEDICAL CLINIC is a recent addition. The *La Jara Gazette* is a weekly newspaper. The La Jara Reservoir, 14,052 acre-ft., is part of an irrigation system.

Left from La Jara on graveled State 136 is SANFORD, 4.5 *m.* (7,560 alt., 700 pop.), colonized in 1880 by Mormons from Salt Lake City, who first established a settlement called Ephraim on low swampy ground at the confluence of the Rio Grande and Conejos River. Unhealthful conditions caused them to move to the present site in 1885.

Left from Sanford 5 *m.* on an unimproved country road to the State-owned SITE OF PIKES STOCKADE, marked by a peculiarly shaped rock standing in a grove of trees on the bank of the Conejos River. In the winter of 1806–07, Lieutenant Zebulon Pike entered San Luis Valley over the Sangre de Cristos by way of Mosca Pass while searching for the source of the Red River. Noting the Great Sand Dunes at the foot of the pass (*see Tour 11C*), he proceeded to the banks of the Rio Grande (Rio Grande del Norte), which he believed to be the Red River. In February 1807 he built a stockade here to serve as a winter base for his explorations. It was constructed of cottonwood poles set on end to form a wall, and was protected by a moat spanned by a drawbridge. Here, unaware that he had overstepped the vague boundary between the United States and Mexico, Pike raised the Stars and Stripes. When Spanish officials became aware of this, an armed force of 100 was sent to the fort, ostensibly to offer protection against the Indians, but in reality to arrest the explorer for trespass. On the morning of February 26, 1807, so Pike recorded in his journal, he invited two Spanish lieutenants into his stockade where, after breakfast, the commanding officer said: "Sir, the Governor of Mexico, being informed you had missed your route, ordered me to offer you, in his name, mules, horses, money, or whatever you stand in need of, to conduct you to the head of Red River . . ."

This was Pike's first intimation that he was on the Rio Grande del Norte. The commander further stated that the Governor should be visited and acquainted with Pike's business on the frontier. Pike immediately surrendered the fort and lowered his flag. "I was induced to consent to the measure," Pike wrote, "by conviction that the officer had positive orders to bring me in, and I had no orders to commit hostilities." Pike added that as he had innocently violated Spanish territory, "it would appear better to show a will to come to an explanation than to be anyway constrained."

Pike and his party were conducted to Santa Fe, where he was closely questioned and many of his credentials taken. Later, he was sent to Chihuahua, Mexico, and subsequently released on his promise not to return again to Mexico.

ROMEO, 21.8 *m.* (8,360 alt.), is a farm hamlet with a general store, grain elevator, and potato exchange.

Left from Romeo on State 142 is MANASSA, 3 *m.* (7,700 alt., 1,000 pop.), founded in 1878 by Mormon colonists from Alabama and Georgia, who are said to have so named it because they believed that the Spanish-Indian settlers they met in the area were direct descendants of Manasseh, eldest son of Joseph.

The town is best known as the birthplace of William Harrison (Jack) Dempsey, former world's heavyweight boxing champion (1919–1926), whom sports writers christened "the Manassa Mauler." The JACK DEMPSEY HOUSE (*visitors admitted*), a one-story adobe and clapboard structure west of the high school, was Dempsey's home between the ages of eight and seventeen. The house in which Dempsey was born, which stood on a near-by lot, was burned many years ago. During his early youth Dempsey roamed over western Colorado and eastern Utah working in mines and on railroads; he began his career as a professional fighter in the mining camps.

South of Romeo the countryside is well cultivated, and good crops are grown under irrigation.

At 28 *m.* is the junction with an unimproved country road.

Right on this road is CONEJOS, 1 *m.* (7,880 alt.), seat of Conejos County; founded in 1854, it is one of the oldest towns in Colorado, but is not incorporated. With its squat dwellings and dusty streets it retains perhaps more of the old Spanish atmosphere than any other village founded at a contemporary date. Young men and women with flashing eyes and indolent grace, plodding old women, and older men with patient faces, wrinkled like parchment, move through the little community, intent upon affairs that have little in common with the life of the *gringos,* many of whom have absorbed some of the "live for today" attitude of their Latin neighbors.

South of the courthouse is the CHURCH OF OUR LADY OF GUADALUPE, established in 1856 by Padre Juan Vigil. The adobe building of typical Spanish design, although damaged by several fires, has not been greatly altered. North of the courthouse is the long, low, adobe MAJOR LAFAYETTE HEAD HOUSE. Long prominent in the San Luis Valley, Head served in the legislatures of both Colorado and New Mexico. When Colorado became a State in 1876, he was elected its first lieutenant-governor.

North, across the river, is the SITE OF GUADALUPE, the original settlement in this vicinity. According to legend, this settlement was founded because a mule in the pack train of a Spanish traveler balked here. The animal was bearing a small image of the Virgin of Guadalupe, and when threats, beatings, and cajolings failed to budge him, the traveler decided that the image was in some way concerned and vowed to erect a church upon the spot. The mule, apparently satisfied, moved on. As good as his word, the traveler returned with some of his countrymen, and a church and settlement were reared to bear witness to the miracle. Major Head fortified the town against the threat of the Tabeguache Ute who claimed this territory, and the fort was attacked soon after its completion in 1855 by a large force under Chief Kanakache, who carried a shield of buffalo hide so thick that it deflected bullets. During the fight Kanakache lowered his shield for a moment and was severely wounded by Major Head. The Ute withdrew, and did not again attack the settlement. Guadalupe was finally abandoned because of the threat of floods. Cloudbursts have obliterated all traces of the early town.

ANTONITO, 28.5 *m.* (7,888 alt., 1,060 pop.), is economically the most important of the small valley towns. Although still colored by Spanish influence, it is a modern village; up-to-date business houses line the main street, and long sheds for the storage of potatoes and other vegetables adjoin the railroad station. Situated at the junction of two lines of the Denver & Rio Grande Western Railroad, one south to Santa Fe, New Mexico, and the other—narrow-gauge—west to Durango, Antonito is the chief shipping point for a large agricultural region.

US 285 continues south and crosses the border of New Mexico, 5 *m.* beyond Antonito. State 17 leaves US 285 at Antonito and proceeds west.

The highway crosses the Conejos River to ascend the eastern slope of the SAN JUAN MOUNTAINS, one of Colorado's last frontiers. Along their densely forested crests are almost inaccessible areas where snow lies unmelted most of the year. A few cattlemen and sheepmen live in this inhospitable land. The highway ascends to CUMBRES PASS (Sp. peaks), 66 *m.* (10,003 alt.), a narrow gap in the San Juan Range; Indians used this pass, and early Spanish explorers came north through it in the sixteenth and seventeenth centuries.

State 17 crosses the New Mexico Line, 71.5 *m.,* 9 miles north of Chama, New Mexico.

IC❖IC❖IC❖IC❖IC❖IC❖IC❖IC❖IC❖IC❖IC❖IC❖IC❖IC❖IC❖IC❖IC❖IC❖IC❖IC❖IC❖IC❖IC❖IC❖IC❖IC❖

Tour 15*A*

Morrison—Park of the Red Rocks—Evergreen—Echo Lake—Summit of Mount Evans—Idaho Springs; 55.7 *m.,* State 74, State 103.

This tour leads through the Denver Mountain Parks, a chain of 27 recreational areas of 13,500 acres, connected by highways radiating south and west from Denver. A charter amendment empowering the city to acquire and maintain these parks, condemn land in other counties for park purposes, and build and maintain roads outside the city limits, was adopted in 1912. The parks contain lodges, shelter houses, outdoor fireplaces, water supplies, and sanitary conveniences. Park rules forbid the picking of flowers, the removal or destruction of trees and shrubbery, the mutilation of property, and the building of fires except in designated spots. The parks are patrolled to enforce these regulations.

State 74 branches west (R) from US 285 (*see Tour 15*) in MOR-RISON, 0 *m.* (*see Tour 15a*), 14.7 miles southwest of Denver.

At 0.5 *m.* a road, right, leads to the most famous of the Denver parks, the Park of the Red Rocks, which contains in its more than 600 acres the accoustically perfect Amphitheater. Here public-spirited citizens have taken advantage of the natural conformations to install 10,000 seats on a mountainside facing huge rocks of red-tinctured sandstone that form the walls of a stage. In the opinion of musicians and architects no spot on the continent gives greater auditory satisfaction than "Red Rocks," whether the program comprises full orchestra and a large chorus, or the individual performance of a virtuoso such as Heifetz. From dawn to dusk the play of light on the surroundings adds visual enchantment to the experience. Its most impressive moments come during the sunrise services on Easter morning.

The stone formations of the Park belong to the Cambrian period and consist chiefly of quartzitic sandstone, with some shale, limestone, and flat-pebble conglomerates. The varied strata were formed by silt deposits on the bed of a sea. A violent upheaval caused the sea to recede; rock strata were thurst upward at a sharp angle, leaving the ends exposed. Erosive forces have carved them into strange shapes. Many varieties of shells, teeth of curious fish, and plants are found preserved in the stone. Among the important discoveries in this vicinity was the thigh bone, 9 feet long and 28 inches in diameter, of an Atlantosaurus.

At 0.4 *m.* is the junction with a side road.

Right here to the SOUTH PICNIC GROUNDS, 0.2 *m.*, at the base of PARK CAVE ROCK.

The main road winds between Park Cave Rock and FROG ROCK and circles PICNIC ROCK, 0.9 *m.*, to the RED ROCKS PUEBLO 1.3 *m.*, resembling an Indian pueblo in design. It houses a museum of Indian art. At the rear of the building are picnic tables and benches. From the parking space (L) is a broad view of the chief formations in the park. These monoliths are, from left to right, PICNIC ROCK, ROCK OF THE NINE PARTS, named for its many visible strata, the TITANIC AND THE ICEBERG, so called for its resemblance to the ill-fated liner and the cause of its destruction, and SHIP ROCK.

At the Pueblo is the junction with a side road.

Left here through the deep crevice between Ship Rock and the Rock of the Nine Parts to the SOUTH ENTRANCE of the park and a junction with State 74, 1.4 *m.*

The main road passes between the ROCK OF THE SEVEN LADDERS and CREATION ROCH 1.5 *m.*, to the junction with a side road 2.3 *m.*

Right here to the NORTH ENTRANCE of the park, 1.1 *m.*, and the junction with the West Alameda Parkway, an alternative route to Denver, 9.4 *m.*

On the main road is the junction with another side road, 2.4 *m.*

Right here 0.3 *m.* to the NORTH PICNIC GROUNDS, situated in rugged surroundings.

The main road passes through a tunnel, 2.6 *m.*, through which is revealed a view of MOUNT MORRISON (7,880 alt.). The road skirts towering formations to a parking space at the base of CREATION ROCK, 3.4 *m.*, its summit reached by a series of steps.

At the parking space is the junction with a footpath.

Left here to the AMPHITHEATER.

State 74 ascends Bear Creek Canyon, winding along high above the stream between towering pine-clad slopes dotted with numerous summer houses, to IDLEDALE, 3 *m.* (6,426 alt.), formerly known as Starbuck, a supply point for occupants of near-by cottages.

Left from Idledale 0.2 *m.* to LITTLE PARK, a 400-acre wooded track with shelter houses, tables, and fireplaces, part of the Denver Mountain Parks System.

CORWINA PARK (*picnic facilities*), 6 *m.,* a 298-acre tract, is a section of the Denver Mountain Parks.

KITTREDGE, 7.3 *m.* (6,825 alt.), is a resort at the head of a small valley.

Left from Kittredge on a side road to PENSE PARK, 4.5 *m.,* a 320-acre area in the Denver Mountain Parks System, on the divide between Bear and Turkey Creeks.

The highway continues up Bear Creek Canyon to EVERGREEN, 9.5 *m.* (7,037 alt.), the center of a region of hotels, resorts, and summer residences. The town is built along the narrow tree-fringed canyon, and the highway constitutes its only street.

Left from Evergreen on State 73 to CUB CREEK PARK, 0.8 *m.,* 549 acres in a region of primitive grandeur. The road winds through wooded slopes to a junction with US 285 (*see Tour 15a*), 8 *m.*

The road skirts EVERGREEN LAKE, 9.7 *m.,* to DEDISEE PARK, 9.9 *m.,* its 400 sloping acres part of the Denver Mountain Parks System, and ascends steadily to BERGEN PARK, 15 *m.,* a 40-acre track on the site of the home built by T. C. Bergen in 1859. Later he built a small hotel, where meals were never higher than 50¢. In 1961 the CECIL H. GREEN GEOPHYSICAL OBSERVATORY of the Colorado School of Mines was built here.

Hagan's Clock Manor, a large collection of clocks, is open daily except Mondays, May-Oct. *Adults $1, children 35¢.*

Right from Bergen Park to FILLIUS PARK, 0.5 *m.,* a 69-acre plot in the Denver Mountain Parks; leaving the park, 0.9 *m.,* the road winds between wooded slopes to the junction with US 40, 2.7 *m.* The Game Preserve has herds of buffalo and elk.

The highway passes FORSBURG PARK (*picnic facilities*), 19.6 *m.,* crosses the eastern boundary of Arapaho National Forest (*see Tour 7b*), 25.8 *m.,* traverses SQUAW PASS (9,807 alt.), and skirts a shoulder of SQUAW MOUNTAIN (11,733 alt.). West of Squaw Mountain, State 74 passes CHIEF MOUNTAIN (11,709 alt.), 29.5 *m.,* and WARRIOR MOUNTAIN (11,260 alt.), 30 *m.,* and crosses the eastern boundary of ECHO LAKE PARK, 33.4 *m.*

From ECHO LAKE (10,605 alt.), 33.6 *m.,* set in a natural park, numerous trails lead along the surrounding slopes; at the lower end of the lake are picnic and campgrounds.

Left from Echo Lake on a graded road to SUMMIT LAKE PARK, 8.7 *m.,* a 160-acre area about SUMMIT LAKE, a snow-fed body of water in a glacial cirque on the slope of Mount Evans. In a series of hairpin curves the road winds upward to the SUMMIT OF MOUNT EVANS (14,259 alt.), 13.2 *m.,* the highest automobile road in the United States. The last few yards are made on foot. The peak was originally named Mount Rosalie by Albert Bierstadt, German painter, in honor of his wife; Bierstadt and Fitz-Hugh

Ludlow climbed the mountain in 1863. On the second trip to the region he began painting his *Storm in the Rocky Mountains,* in which the peak appears. In 1870 the mountain was renamed for John Evans, second Territorial Governor of Colorado (1862–65).

On the crest of Mount Evans stands the COSMIC RAY LABORATORY of the University of Denver, the highest laboratory in the world, built in 1936 for the furtherance of scientific study of the cosmic ray; it is also used for meteorological observation and experiments in biochemistry. Carl Anderson, R. A. Millikan, and A. H. Compton, three Americans who received the Nobel Prize in physics, made studies here. The laboratory is a conical structure; flat side walls were eliminated to enable the building to withstand a wind velocity of 150 miles an hour. It consists of two rooms, each 20 by 24 feet, one equipped as a laboratory, the other as living quarters for six observers. The building was constructed in Denver, cut into sections, and transported by truck to the mountain. Protection against lightning is afforded by metal strips on walls, roof, and floor, which are connected with buried ground wires.

At Echo Lake is the junction with State 103, which the tour now follows. At 48.8 *m.* is the junction with a foot trail.

Left on this trail up Chicago Creek Canyon to LOWER CHICAGO LAKE, 4.2 *m.,* and UPPER CHICAGO LAKE, 4.5 *m.,* walled in on three sides by precipitous cliffs. The cliff (L) can be scaled by experienced climbers, the climb ending at Summit Lake.

The highway continues down the granite-walled corridor of Chicago Creek Canyon to IDAHO SPRINGS, 55.7 *m.* (*see Tour 7b*), at the junction with US 40 (*see Tour 7b*).

❧❧❧❧❧❧❧❧❧❧❧❧❧❧❧❧❧❧❧❧❧❧❧❧❧❧❧❧❧❧

Tour 16

Junction. US 40 (Kremmling)—Breckenridge—Hoosier Pass—Alma—Fairplay—Junction US 24 (Hartsel) ; 89.7 *m.,* State 9.

State 9 branches southeast from US 40, 0 *m.,* 2.8 miles south of Kremmling (7,322 alt., 850 pop.).

The road follows the Valley of the Blue River with the Gore Mountains on the west and the Williams Fork Mts. and Arapaho National Forest on the east. At 13 *m.* is the 309-ft. high dam of Green Mountain Reservoir, 2,125 acres. The power plant generates 21,600 kw. Across the lake is HEENEY, a resort village.

DILLON 37.3 *m.* (9,000 ft.), is a new town replacing the original, now under the Dillon Reservoir; it is served also by US 6 (*see Tour 1b.*).

BRECKENRIDGE, 46.8 *m.* (9,603 alt., 500 pop.), was at one

time the center of a group of gold camps claiming a population of 8,000. The first gold was panned in the Blue River in 1859 by prospectors who fortified a blockhouse and built 50 miles of flumes and ditches for placer mining; lode mining followed.

In the 1880s Breckenridge was served by the Denver, South Park & Pacific Railroad, a narrow gauge line that crossed the Divide via Boreas Pass and later recrossed via Fremont Pass to reach Leadville. The ties were removed in 1939 and a solid dirt road now uses the old roadbed, giving views of the Valley of the Blue River and Peak 8. A double chair-lift moves up Peak 8 to the ski slopes, which cover 12 miles. In 1936 the local woman's club contended that the Breckenridge area had not been made officially a part of Colorado. They asked the State to let it act as a free and independent kingdom for three days a year. The Ullr Dag Winter Festival is named for a Nordic deity who protects skiers. The first church, near the Courthouse, was built in 1880 by Father Dyer, who found the Warrior's Mark Mine on Boreas Pass, where the ghost town of Dyersville now stands.

Bayard Taylor, author and correspondent of the New York *Tribune,* rode into camp in 1865 "over ditches, heaps of stone and gravel, and all the usual debris of gulch-mining." He found the town's one long street lined with log houses and covered wagons. Taylor was a guest at a hotel kept by Alex Sutherland, who, "taking the bugle with which he blew the signal for the immortal Light Brigade charge at Balaklava, made the notes of 'Peas upon the Trencher' ring out over the shanties of Brecken-ridge."

The road crosses the northern boundary of ARAPAHO NA-TIONAL FOREST, 48.3 *m.,* a preserve embracing 984,630 acres of Federal land.

HOOSIER PASS, 57.8 *m.* (11,542 alt.), usually kept open during winter although ice and snow make motoring difficult, slits the high barrier of the Park Range, which includes some of the loftiest peaks in Colorado. To the west are the glittering summits of MOUNT BROSS (14,170 alt.), MOUNT DEMOCRAT (14,142 alt.), MOUNT LINCOLN (14,284 alt.), the highest peak in the range, and MOUNT CAMERON (14,233 alt.). The pass marks the boundary between Arapaho and Pike National Forests.

In a mountain-shadowed hollow at the western edge of South Park is ALMA, 65.6 *m.* (10,300 alt.), one of the earliest gold camps in the region, still the center of a rich lode-mining district. Almost destroyed by fire in 1937, the town has been rebuilt.

According to old-timers, an attractive dance-hall girl appeared in Alma during the early boom days and became a great camp favorite. One young admirer fashioned a pair of silver heels for her slippers. Dancing through riotous nights in her slippers, she became known as Silver Heels, and in time her real name was forgotten. When the camp was ravaged by smallpox, and the women were removed to the com-parative safety of Fairplay (*see below*), Silver Heels refused to leave. She stayed to nurse the stricken and comfort the dying. Her work done, she vanished. Some years later a richly gowned woman, always heavily veiled, visited the town to walk among the graves of the plague victims. Her visits, repeated annually for several years, aroused much comment and speculation. Although her identity was never disclosed, the miners were certain that she was Silver Heels returning to mourn her friends; and her reason for wearing the veil was to conceal pock marks that marred her former beauty. MOUNT SILVERHEELS (13,825 alt.), northwest of Alma, was named in honor of the "Angel of Mercy of South Park."

Right from Alma on a dirt road to the approximate SITE OF BUCKSKIN JOE, 2 m., a mining camp named in 1859 for Joseph Higginbottom, "Buckskin Joe," who first discovered gold in the vicinity. For a time it was the seat of Park County. Late in 1860 the town was officially rechristened Laurette for two sisters, Laura and Jeanette Dodge, the only women in camp, but it continued to be known by its first name. The camp owed its few years of prosperity to the Phillips Lode, a thick iron-gold deposit at the grass roots, opened and worked like a stone quarry. It is said to have been discovered when Harris, a hunter, shot at a deer and found that the bullet, missing the deer, had plowed through grass and sand to uncover rich gold-bearing quartz. So much gold was taken from the mine that Harris is reported to have stored it in his cabin in pots and pans, even in a pair of old boots. Later he took in a partner, Stancil, and together they built three dance houses and a theater in which a Negro minstrel company played continuously. Soon the camp had a newspaper, a band, several quartz mills, and a population of more than 1,000. H. A. W. Tabor (see Leadville) established a store here early in the 1860's, and purchased a number of claims, all of which proved worthless. By 1865 the camp was almost deserted, and in 1866 the county seat was removed to Fairplay. Nothing remains to mark the site, now private property.

In 1861 "Father" Dyer, known throughout the region as the "Snowshoe Itinerant," arrived to preach on street corners. A man of fifty, Dyer had spent many years as a miner and preacher in Minnesota and Wisconsin. In spite of his years he carried mail from Buckskin Joe to Cache Creek a distance of 40 miles, and to other distant mining camps, stopping to preach wherever men would listen. Within two months he traveled more than 500 miles, his collections totalling $43.

At 65.7 m. is the junction with a dirt road. Right on this road to the NEW LONDON MINE, 1.5 m., once one of the most productive gold mines in the United States. The route continues over MOSQUITO PASS (13,188 alt.), 8.9 m., a high traverse of the Park Range, once known as the "highway of frozen death"; hundreds perished along it in the late 1870's, during the mad rush to the booming camp of LEADVILLE, 15.2 m. (see Leadville).

West of Alma the route skirts (R) CHINAMAN'S GULCH, a deep ravine along the South Fork of the South Platte, so named because many Chinese, imported in the early days to pan gold, were quartered here. Huge gold dredges have heaped up unsightly mounds through which the shallow river winds its muddy course.

FAIRPLAY, 71.3 m. (9,964 alt., 400 pop.), is another of the State's old mining towns. A group of prospectors, affronted because miners drove them from the rich placers at Tarryall (see Tour 15a), settled here in 1859 and named their camp Fairplay in disparagement of their rivals.

Near the center of town a monument (L), erected in 1930, marks the grave of PRUNES, a 63-year-old burro. Brought into South Park in

1867, Prunes is said to have worked in every mine in the Fairplay-Alma district. Robert Sherwood, an old-time miner, who died in 1931 at the age of 82, was buried at the rear of the monument as he had requested.

The burro, the butt of endless gibes, often called "the Rocky Mountain Canary" and "the Colorado Mocking Bird" for its raucous bray, played an important part in the exploration, conquest, and settlement of the West. Although occasionally perverse, the burro was strong, sure-footed, and willing, and if given his head, could extricate himself from almost any predicament. His nose ever found water and the trail of man or beast; his huge ears were extraordinarily keen; he required little food and could abstain from water for astonishingly long periods. Companionable, nursing no grudges, and apparently enjoying human society, the burro was half-brother to the prospector, who regarded him warmly and cursed him roundly. Thousands of these shaggy little animals were brought into the State during mining days.

For years the huge gold mine tailings were worked over by a dredge, which earned $6,000 a week until 1950, when the operation no longer paid. Fairplay has organized the Progressive Mine & Smelter Corp. to process ores of that area.

In midsummer Fairplay is at the start of the annual Pack Burro Race over Mosquito Pass to Leadville, 22 *m.*

SOUTH PARK CITY in Fairplay is a restoration of a pioneer town.

At 72 *m.* is the junction with US 285 (*see Tour 15a*).

South of the junction the highway traverses rolling grassland studded with occasional clumps of pines and aspens, and broken by hills. Crossing a tributary of the South Fork of the South Platte, 76.5 *m.,* the road reaches GARO PARK, 80 *m.* This is good cattle country, and much of the State's hay crop is cut on its broad smooth meadows.

At 88.7 *m.* is the junction of US 24 (*see Tour 5b*), 1 mile west of HARTSEL (8,875 alt.) (*see Tour 5b*).

ⅠⅭ♦

Tour 17

(Green River, Wyo.)—Craig—Meeker—Rifle; State 13 and State 789. Wyoming Line to Rifle, 130.8 *m.*

This route cuts across the northern part of Colorado's western plateau country, a region of rolling sage-covered hills, walled in on the east by the Elkhead Mountains. Almost all of it is occupied by large ranches.

At 18 *m.,* Fortification Hall. The road crosses Fortification Creek as it comes from the Elkhead Mts., most of which are in ROUTT NATIONAL FOREST, 1,144,813 acres. The highway roughly parallels the old wagon trail from Fort Steel near Laramie, Wyo., to the White River Indian Agency at Meeker.

State 13 crosses the Wyoming Line, 0 *m.,* 865 miles south of Green River, Wyoming and traverses a sage-covered plateau to CRAIG, 38 *m.* (6,185 alt., 5,000 pop.) (*see Tour 7c*), at the junction with US 40 (*see Tour 7c*).

The road follows the narrow, fertile valley of the Yampa River, a slash of green across the gray aridity of the plateau. Where the highway crosses the river, a large bird refuge has been established. Ascending the southern slope of the valley, the highway enters barren hills, descends into a deep canyon, and again ascends the plateau.

At 55.8 *m.* is a junction with a dirt road.

Left on this road through uncultivated hill country to a junction with a side road, 10.9 *m.;* R. here 0.6 *m.* across open prairie to the THORNBURG MONUMENT, a granite shaft erected in memory of Major T. T. Thornburg and those of his command slain in a battle here with the Ute.

In September 1879 the Ute rose against Nathan C. Meeker, in command of the White River Agency (*see below*). When the news reached Fort Rawlins, Major Thornburg was ordered to the scene with three troops of cavalry, a company of light infantry, and a large supply train. On the second day, fearing that his advance was being delayed by foot soldiers, Thornburg stationed his infantry at Old Fortification and pushed on with his cavalry force of 160 men. Twice the expedition was met by delegations of Ute, headed by subchief Captain Jack, who gave assurance that there was no trouble. Near the site of the present town of Thornburg the troops ran into an ambush laid by the Ute, who were massed on the bluffs above Red Canyon. A scout's last-minute discovery of the hidden warriors averted another Custer Massacre. During the first few minutes of disorganized fighting, 15 white men, including Thornburg, were killed, and 35 wounded. The surviving troops fell back and made a barricade of the supply train. The Indians surrounded this position and a siege, marked by desultory fighting, ensued.

Early the first night, Rankin, a scout, slipped through the lines to summon help and rode 165 miles to Fort Rawlins in 28 hours. Another scout reached Captain Dodge and his troop of Negro cavalry in Middle Park. Dodge arrived first, on the third day of the battle, and although he had only 40 men, broke through the Indian lines without losing a man. The siege continued three days until the full fighting force at Fort Rawlins arrived under the command of General Wesley Merritt, when the Ute dispersed and took to the hills. More than half of Thornburg's command had been killed or wounded. The Major's body was sent to Rawlins for interment; other dead were buried in a common grave.

The dirt road continues through brown hills and windswept flats to the southern junction with State 13, 27.2 *m.* (*see below*).

The road traverses rough hill country to the rim of a broad shallow valley overlooking the ILES DOME OIL FIELD.

ILES GROVE, 60.7 *m.,* is a dense growth of western cottonwoods, the "tree claim" of Thomas H. Iles, an early settler. Iles settled in northwestern Colorado in 1874 and acquired vast holdings by purchasing the homestead titles of Civil War soldiers. The homestead law then permitted the patenting of a claim by the annual planting of a specified number of trees. Iles acquired title to this part of his domain by planting all trees in this single grove. A gray granite monument on the edge of the grove honors the pioneer. ILES MOUNTAIN (R), 63 *m.*, an old landmark, has alternating bands of red and white sandstone.

AXIAL, 65.4 *m.* (6,400 alt.), is a small coal-mining center; rich coal deposits of this region remain undeveloped for lack of railroad facilities. The principal vein, 92 feet thick, was well known in early days; it is said the Ute used the coal to such an extent that freight wagons, caught in storms, sought shelter in the cave that the Indians had dug.

The route follows a narrow valley walled in by low hills, passes several coal mines, and crosses the divide between the Yampa and White River basins.

At 8.5 *m.* is the southern junction with the Thornburg Road. At 8.6 *m.* is the junction with State 132.

Left on this graveled highway is BUFORD, 22 *m.* (7,000 alt.), a supply town and starting point for pack trips into the wild country along the South Fork of the White River. Nearby is BEAVER CREEK RESERVOIR.

Right from Buford on a Forest Service highway to the junction with a graveled road, 2 *m.* Right here to SOUTH FORK CAMPGROUND, 11.2 *m.*

Right from the campground 100 *yds.* on a foot trail along the western bank of the South Fork to the junction with a side trail; R. here 0.5 *m.* to a massive limestone and chalk cliff containing SPRING CAVE. Along the intricate subterranean passages, filled with stalactites and stalagmites, runs a spring-fed stream.

South of the junction the Forest Service road skirts (L) the Flat Top Country and proceeds to NEW CASTLE, 30 *m.* (*see Tour 5c*), at the junction with US 6 and US 24.

State 132 continues east from Buford in WHITE RIVER NATIONAL FOREST to the RIPPLE CREEK CAMPGROUND, 39 *m.*

From the campground a dirt road leads (R) southeast to TRAPPERS LAKE, 11 *m.* (10,500 alt.), a sportsman's rendezvous. This region, in the heart of the White River National Forest (*see Tour 5c*), is one of the finest recreational areas in the State; deer and elk are plentiful; lakes and streams provide good trout fishing.

Left from Trappers Lake a foot and horse trail leads past Little Trappers Lake to the DEVIL'S CAUSEWAY, 5.5 *m.*, a high narrow basalt ridge, and descends through forested lowlands to YAMPA, 20 *m.* (*see Tour 7b*).

MEEKER, 87.5 *m.* (6,240 alt., 1,655 pop.), seat of Rio Blanco County, in the ranching area of the White River Valley, was named for Nathan C. Meeker (*see Greeley*), Indian agent, who was killed in the Ute uprising at the White River Agency in 1879 (*see below*); a military headquarters was established here four years after the outbreak. The courthouse occupies the center of a park once the parade ground of the old post. At the northern end of the park are three log cabins used as barracks. In the MEEKER HOTEL, Theodore Roosevelt's headquarters on one of his western hunting trips, are specimens of animal life in the White River region.

The highway follows the White River Valley to the MEEKER MONUMENT, 90.7 *m.*, an uncut pink granite slab, marking the approximate SITE OF THE OLD WHITE RIVER AGENCY and the SCENE OF THE

Mining, Milling, Farming

CF & I Steel Corp.

START OF A NEW BASIC OXYGEN FURNACE AT CF & I STEEL, PUEBLO

U. S. Forest Service

MINING IN THE PAST: CRIPPLE CREEK, 1900

MINING IN THE PAST: SLUICE MINING

Colorado Visitors Bureau

MINING LANDSCAPE, CRIPPLE CREEK

FRYER HILL, LEADVILLE, 1883

American Metal Climax, Inc.

MODERN MINING MACHINERY, CLIMAX MOLYBDENUM CO.

Public Service Co. of Colorado

FORT SAINT VRAIN NUCLEAR GENERATING STATION
NEAR PLATTEVILLE

PLANT FOR PROCESSING MOLYBDENUM ORE, NEAR BERTHOUD PASS

Climax Molybdenum Company

GOLD NUGGETS OF TODAY: INSPECTING SUGAR BEETS

Holly Sugar Corporation

SUGAR BEETS TOPPED BY MACHINE NEAR MONTROSE

HILLS OF SUGAR BEETS AT HOLLY SUGAR PLANT, DELTA

Holly Sugar Corporation

Holly Sugar Corporation

FIELD OF SUGAR BEETS READY FOR TOPPING

MEEKER MASSACRE. The agency buildings stood in a field about five miles west of the monument; no road leads to the site, nor is there any marker.

On September 20, 1879, Nathan C. Meeker and ten of his employees at the agency were slain in a revolt of the Ute. Meeker, long prominent in Colorado affairs, had cooperated with Horace Greeley in establishing the Union Colony at Greeley in 1870. His appointment as Indian Agent proved unfortunate. The Ute, who lived by hunting and fishing, chafed at his unrelenting efforts to convert them to a sedentary life. In addition, they were sullen because money and goods promised by the Federal Government by treaty were long overdue. Meeker's tactless methods offended leaders of the tribe; his final and fatal mistake was to plow a channel for an irrigation ditch across the racetrack where the Ute exercised their horses.

Council fires burned in the Northern Ute camp, wizards made red medicine and cried for blood, and the throbbing of drums came down from the hills. Meeker appealed for military aid, but negotiations with the Ute chiefs led nowhere; even the influence of Ouray, great chief of the Southern Ute, always friendly to the white men, was checkmated by the hostility of chiefs Colorow, Captain Jack, and Douglas.

Major Thornburg's force, moving to support the agency, was all but annihilated by the Ute in Red Canyon (*see above*). Then the Indians, blaming Meeker for the advance of the troops, swept down upon the station, burned it to the ground, and killed all men at the post. Meeker's wife, their daughter Josephine, and another woman and her children, were spared because a chief argued correctly that they were valuable hostages. Chief Douglas, who claimed Josephine Meeker as his personal captive, got drunk following the massacre and sang "Swing Low, Sweet Chariot" over the body of her father as it lay stripped and mutilated. Douglas asked the girl if she did not think he had a fine voice.

Having killed the agent and defeated Major Thornburg, the Ute sued for peace. Release of the hostages was accomplished a month later (*see Tour 5E*). Extremely lenient terms were granted the Ute, and neither the chiefs who led the uprising nor the actual slayers of Meeker and his people were punished.

Meeker and Rangely are two prosperous towns of Rio Blanco County, and while Rangely profits chiefly from the oil and gas production that makes the county the second largest in output of minerals in the State, Meeker trades in meat, honey, stone and gravel, and lumber. The County Hospital is in Meeker. Its weekly newspaper is the *Meeker Herald*. Meeker has a Meeker Massacre Pageant and Rodeo in July and the County Fair in August.

Right from the Meeker Monument on State 64 through a region of low hills matted with sage and scrub growth, and broken by occasional outcroppings of shale and sandstone. To the south spreads the wide and shallow JOSEPHINE BASIN, across which Josephine Meeker attempted to flee during the massacre at the agency.

At 7 *m.* is the junction with a graveled road.

Left here is a curving drive known as the SCENERY GULCH DETOUR, lined with fantastic formations of clay and shale strata ribbed with sandstone. Here and there the elements have cut monoliths away from the cliffs; these dolmans, capped with standstone crowns, resemble great idols standing before the scattered ruins of ancient temples; the curious coloring of clay and stone adds to the weird air of unreality. The drive rejoins State 64, 15 *m.*

West of the junction (L) rise rugged cliffs and mountains of mahogany-colored oil shale. Characteristic of the region are the great veins of sand asphaltum, formed by the solidification of oil in the earth.

WHITE RIVER, 18.2 *m.,* an old cow town, was once known as White River City; nothing remains but the schoolhouse.

The highway passes near the BATTLEFIELD OF THE SECOND UTE WAR (R), 43 *m.,* where the Ute made a last stand for their ancient rights and privileges. After the Meeker Massacre the Northern Ute were removed from the White River region into Utah, but in 1887 a band of fighting men under Colorow, most implacable of the Ute war chiefs, determined to return to Colorado to reclaim their old hunting grounds. They advanced through a deserted country-side, the terrified settlers having fled eastward. A military force from Fort Laramie, Wyo., augmented by cattlemen, met the Unite below the broken hills. The fight was short but savage. Many Indians were slain, and the routed forces were sent back to Utah under military escort. Colorow died on the reservation in 1888.

At 54.6 *m.* is the junction with State 139.

Left on this unimproved dirt road, which swings away from the valley of the White River, to the ROAN CLIFFS RANGE. The route skirts the base of a curious double mesa known as TWIN BUTTES (4,608 alt.), 33 *m.,* and ascends the pass by many switchbacks. From the top of DOUGLAS PASS (8,000 alt.), 36 *m.,* is a spectacular view of the entire region. Far to the north lies the green ribbon of the White River Valley; on both sides and directly ahead break serrated waves of hills, cliffs, and shadowed ravines. Descending, the highway enters BROWN'S CANYON, 45 *m.,* a long and rugged valley offering magnificent vistas. The BOOKCLIFFS RANGE, 55 *m.,* while not so high as the Utah section of this chain, is scenically superb. Sweeping out of the mountain country, State 139 passes (L) the GARMESA NATURAL GAS FIELDS, 62 *m.,* traverses a narrow belt of stark desert land, and crosses a highland farming section to LOMA, 68 *m.,* at the junction with US 50 (*see Tour 9c*).

State 64 proceeds west, to RANGELY, 55.4 *m.* (5,200 alt., 2,000 pop.), a supply town founded in 1880 as a trading post, and crosses the White River, 56.4 *m.;* swinging away from the fertile strip along the stream, it enters a semiarid grazing and stock raising district. The area contains much undeveloped mineral wealth; valuable deposits of gilsonite have been found near Rangely; the flats are dotted with oil wells.

RANGELY COLLEGE, a tax-supported two-year college is under the jurisdiction of Mesa Junior College District. Rangely has an annual Rodeo and Oil Progress Week. The *Times* is its weekly newspaper.

South of the junction, State 13, following a comparatively level course, is lined with rolling sage-covered hills. Sheep raising is the principal source of revenue, but cattlemen still control the ranges to the west.

At 127.4 *m.* is a junction with a side road. Left on this dirt road to RIFLE MOUNTAIN PARK (*cabins*), 15 *m.* Here are GLEN RULAC FALLS, two cascades on East Rifle Creek, the upper fall having a drop of 150 feet; the lower operates a hydroelectric plant. The mineral springs in the park contain varying amounts of carbonate and sulphate of lime. From the park a motor road connects with a dirt road to NEW CASTLE, 40 *m.* (*see Tour 5c*).

In RIFLE, 130.8 (5,345 alt., 3,000 pop.) (*see Tour 5c*), is the junction with US 24, Interstate 70.

ᗤᗤᗤᗤᗤᗤᗤᗤᗤᗤᗤᗤᗤᗤᗤᗤᗤᗤᗤᗤᗤᗤᗤᗤᗤᗤᗤᗤᗤ

Tour 18

Montrose—Ouray—Red Mountain Pass—Silverton—Durango—(Aztec, N. M.) ; US 550.
Montrose to New Mexico Line, 132 *m.*

Multilane road, sometimes temporarily closed following severe storms ; during winter months inquire locally for conditions.
Denver & Rio Grande R.R. parallels route between Montrose and Ouray, and between Silverton and New Mexico Line.
Good accommodations.

US 550 passes through a region of exceptionally high mountains from which came ores that wrote a dramatic page in Colorado's history. Between Montrose and Ridgway the highway closely parallels the route followed by Padres Escalante and Dominguez, who came north from Mexico in 1776 seeking a short way to the California missions. Many places in this region were named by Escalante, one of the first to note the ancient Cliff Dweller ruins that dot southwestern Colorado.

The San Juan Mountains, among the highest and most rugged in the State, are new mountains, geologically speaking ; their gray granite has been little touched by erosion. Their summits are jagged, cut, and broken by deep crevasses and sharp pinnacles. In this range fourteen peaks rise 14,000 or more feet above sea level. A tourist starting south on this highway asked a guide, pointing to the formidable wall of the San Juans, "How do we get through them?" "We don't go through 'em," drawled the guide, "we jes' go right over 'em."

US 550 branches south from US 50 (*see Tour 9c*) in MONTROSE, 0 *m.* (5,820 alt., 6,800 pop.) (*see Tour 9c*), which is also at the junction with State 90 (*see Tour 19*).

Highly productive farms cover this part of the Uncompahgre Valley and the terraces that slope to the south and west toward the higher plateaus. The lower levels are covered with sage ; on the bluffs are pine and scrub oak, which flames brightly in the fall.

OURAY-CHIPETA PARK, 4 *m.,* is the burial place of Chipeta, wife of the great Ute chief Ouray, who for many years endeavored to keep peace between his people and the whites. In 1859 Ouray chose Chipeta, a Tabeguache Ute girl, for his wife. The great tragedy of their lives was the loss of their seven-year-old son, who was abducted by the Kiowa. Before his death in 1881, Ouray, embittered by friction with the whites, asked his people never to reveal the site of his grave. The secret was kept until the death of Chipeta in 1924, when the remains of Ouray were discovered and reinterred in the cemetery of the Ute Reservation at Ignacio (*see Tour 11D*).

At 8 *m.* is the approximate SITE OF FORT CRAWFORD, a military post built in 1880 and garrisoned by a troop of cavalry detailed to restrain the Ute. The entire valley was part of the Ute reservation until 1881 when it was opened to settlement. Most of the garrison was withdrawn from Fort Crawford in 1884.

COLONA, 12.6 *m.* (6,387 alt.), a farming village at the southern edge of the valley, is the center of a partly developed coal field in which veins 30 feet thick have been found. South of Colona the Uncompahgre Valley narrows to a long rocky gulch; the underlying granite formation rises in great cliffs broken at intervals by smaller side gulches.

RIDGWAY, 27 *m.* (6,770 alt.), is at the junction with State 62 (*see Tour 20*).

The route traverses a broad grassy valley between forested hills to UNCOMPAHGRE HOT SPRINGS, 29 *m.*, with a flow of 300 gallons a minute. The temperature of the water is 132 degrees; iron oxide is responsible for its reddish color. The springs were included in a four-mile-square area known as the Hot Springs Reservation that the Ute retained for several years after their removal to Utah. The highway skirts the base of BALDY PEAK (10,612 alt.), an irregular mass of granite, and ascends through a well-populated valley.

PORTLAND, 33 *m.* (7,233 alt.), formerly a mining center, was founded in 1883 on the assumption that the Denver & Rio Grande Southern Railroad, then building toward Ouray, would not attempt the final climb through the steep canyon, thus making Portland its terminus and eventually the county seat. But General William J. Palmer, builder of the road, with characteristic disregard for mountains, drove the line through to Ouray.

The road crosses a section of the Uncompahgre National Forest (*see Tour 19*), 34.3 *m.*, and enters a deep canyon. RADIUM SPRINGS PARK, 36.8 *m.*, contains camp grounds, kitchens, goldfish ponds, and an outdoor warm-water swimming pool. The park is at the junction with HORSETHIEF TRAIL, over which early day outlaws drove stolen horses into Utah and brought back cattle stolen on Utah ranges. Modern rustlers rely for escape on the speed of their trucks. The trail is one of the few routes across the San Juan Mountains, in which deep ravines and treacherous snowdrifts combine to make crossings dangerous.

Left on this trail (*horses, guides, can be hired at Ouray; persons unfamiliar with country should obtain guides, as trail is poorly marked and easily confused with numerous sheep trails*) on a hard ride upward toward the crest of the San Juan range. In spring and summer the route is bright with mountain flowers; Ouray appears (R) cupped in the granite mountains. As the trail leaves the forest country, the Uncompahgre Valley is spread out below, and at times the huge mass of Grand Mesa (*see Tour 5E*) is visible through the blue haze to the north.

The BRIDGE OF HEAVEN, 4 *m.*, is a narrow hogback rising nearly 2,000 feet above the floor of the canyon, on each side. East of the bridge the trail ascends to a grassy level known as AMERICAN FLATS, 7 *m.*, on the south shoulder of WILDHORSE PEAK (13,268 alt.), and at the junction with another trail.

Right here down Bear Creek to the junction with US 550, 18 *m.*, 3 miles south of Ouray (*see below*).

From American Flats, Horsethief Trail descends eastward through a country of pine and spruce to LAKE CITY, 26 *m.* (*see Tour 21*).

OURAY, 37 *m.* (7,706 alt., 800 pop.), seat of Ouray County, named for the great Ute chief, lies pocketed in a pear-shaped valley, with WHITE HOUSE MOUNTAIN (13,493 alt.) on the west, HAYDEN MOUNTAIN (13,100 alt.) on the south, and CASCADE MOUNTAIN (12,100 alt.) to the northwest. To the east, extending upward to the crest of the range, is a great natural amphitheater, part of the Ouray State Game Refuge. Densely wooded, but with many small parks, it is easily accessible on foot. Years ago the area was stocked with elk. Ouray profits from mining, especially in the northwestern part of the county. In 1966 the county produced gold, silver, copper, lead and zinc valued at $2,287,982.

Ouray was founded in 1875 when rich silver lodes were discovered in the surrounding hills, and was incorporated the next year. A train of six wagons brought type and presses from Canon City to print the Ouray *Times,* the first newspaper in the Uncompahgre region. Early church services were held in an uncompleted saloon, with boxes of liquor and beer kegs as seats. The camp boomed through the 1880's, but with the collapse of silver prices it languished until 1896 when Thomas F. Walsh discovered gold here. The mining of gold, silver, lead, and zinc is still the chief industry, but farming and stock raising have grown in importance.

Relics of Ouray's glamorous past are the BEAUMONT HOTEL, 5th Ave. and Main St., a rambling, ornate, three-story, white-brick structure built in 1886, and the CITY HALL, 6th Ave. between Main and Fourth Sts., with its gilded dome. A small area at the northern edge of town, once the red-light, is now a cottage camp.

At the southwest corner of town are two large NATURAL HOT SPRINGS, the waters of which are piped to the outdoor swimming pool in Radium Park. Sanitariums have been built over other hot springs. Rotary Park, north of town, is a campground owned by the city. Amphitheater Campground, in Uncompahagre Forest, is maintained by the Forest Service.

1. Right from Ouray on a trail to the TOP OF TWIN PEAKS, 4 *m.* (*time, 3 hrs. up; 1½ hrs. down*), a steady but not difficult climb, one of the best hikes in the vicinity, offering many good views of the surrounding mountains, particularly of MOUNT SNEFFELS (14,143 alt.) to the west.

2. Right on a marked road, branching from Main Street just outside the city limits, to the junction with another dirt road, 0.3 *m.*

Left here 6 *m.* to the CAMP BIRD MILL (*open weekdays on application*), a rambling high-eaved frame building, housing machinery for processing ore from the Camp Bird Mine.

Left from the mill on a dirt road (*narrow; inquire at office for schedule of traffic*) to the CAMP BIRD MINE, 2 *m.* (*open 9–4 weekdays on application*).

The Camp Bird Mine, from which Thomas Walsh made his fortune, was originally a silver claim; its first owner did not suspect that much of the ore contained gold. While prospecting in 1896, Walsh made the discovery and bought the properties for $20,000. He first reworked the dumps, obtaining immediate rewards. Between 1896 and 1902 the mine annually yielded between $3,000,000 and $4,000,000 of ore, sometimes at the rate of $5,000 a day. In 1902, Walsh sold the Camp Bird to a British syndicate for $5,200,000. The mine is still profitably operated by the Federal Resources Corp.

Thomas F. Walsh, an Irish-born carpenter, came to America when 19 years old, and for a time worked in the construction of bridges for the Colorado Central Railroad near Golden. He tried his luck mining at Del Norte and Central City, and in 1876, at Deadwood, S. D. Returning to Colorado, he married Carrie Bell Reed in Leadville in 1879, kept a boarding house, and began acquiring mining properties. Walsh suffered financial reverses in the silver crash of the early 1890's, having lost most of his fortune when he came to Ouray in 1895. With the development of the Camp Bird Mine, he moved to Washington, D. C. In 1900 he was appointed one of the national commissioners to the Paris Exposition, and a few years later joined King Leopold of Belgium in mining enterprises in the Congo. He died at Washington in 1909. Evalyn Walsh McLean of Washington, D. C., his daughter, told the story of the family in her *Father Struck it Rich* (1936).

West of the junction with the Camp Bird Road, the marked dirt road continues to BOX CANYON PARK, 0.5 *m.*, the starting point for two short trails to BOX CANYON.

1. Left on one trail to a HIGH BRIDGE, 200 *ft.*, a flume across the narrow canyon. Above this bridge Canyon Creek plunges downward through a dark narrow gash cut into solid granite. Just below the bridge the racing water disappears into an underground passage.

2. Right from the park on the second trail to the BOTTOM OF BOX CANYON, 350 *ft.*, where the waters of the creek emerge in a fall that turns them boiling white.

South of Ouray, US 550 begins an immediate and steep ascent, twisting along the wall of Uncompahgre Canyon by means of sharp switchbacks. This section of the road directly overlooks Ouray. Once a heavy truck lost a wheel here; it bounced down the mountainside and crashed through the roof of a house in town.

This section of US 550 is known as the MILLION DOLLAR HIGHWAY because of the gold-bearing gravels with which it is surfaced. Their value was not discovered until the road had been completed. The highway continues to twist and turn up the black rock walls, following one of many toll roads built by Otto Mears (*see Tour 15b*) in the early 1880's. Before it was opened, all ores were packed out of the district by mule train for as much as $80 a ton. Mears' project made it profitable to work low-grade ores and increased mining activities throughout the Ouray-Silverton-Telluride district.

During the late 1870's a typical freight outfit on these roads consisted of three spans of mules and two heavy wagons. The teamster, or "skinner," had to be an expert driver; he rode the left wheel mule and drove with a jerk line to the bridle of the left leader. Brakes were of utmost importance, and each wagon was equipped with heavy brake blocks; to increase leverage, the brake arms were long wooden poles, from the top of which a rope ran to the teamster's saddle. Toll rates varied with the length and character of the road, ranging from $1 to $5 a team.

To the west is the quadrangular bulk of WHITE HOUSE MOUNTAIN (13,493 alt.), its even, white strata, formed of Mississippi limestone, known locally as Leadville limestone, distinguishing it from the darker surrounding mountains of volcanic rock. The highway passes through a short tunnel, 39 m., driven through granite and wide enough for two cars to pass. Framed in its south portal is the regular pyramidal mass of MOUNT ABRAM (12,800 alt.), its bald top snow-covered most of the year. This area lies in the UNCOMPAHGRE NATIONAL FOREST area, comprising 957,003 acres in seven counties, in much of which hunting is forbidden and no further development is permitted. The road reaches the top of the switchbacks, 39.3 m.; commanding the eastern skyline is ENGINEER MOUNTAIN (13,195 alt.). At BEAR CREEK FALLS, 39.4 m., where a small stream drops 227 feet in silvery mist, is the bronze OTTO MEARS MEMORIAL TABLET, set in quartz.

IRONTON PARK, 43.1 m., is a level grassy valley surrounded by wooded hills; from a small bridge in the center of the park can be seen the abandoned SARATOBE MINE, with mill, a great silver bonanza before 1900.

The route passes IRONTON, 45 m. (9,790 alt.), the remains of a once-thriving silver camp, and ascends the steep slopes of the San Juan Range. Several high peaks (L) are colored a brilliant red by iron pyrites in the igneous rock—RED MOUNTAIN NO. 1 (12,500 alt.), RED MOUNTAIN No. 2 (12,200 alt.), and RED MOUNTAIN NO. 3 (12,870 alt.). Grouped about the now-deserted CAMP OF RED MOUNTAIN, 48.1 m., are many old mines. Ore deposits were found here in 1881, and mining activity increased steadily until 1893. The largest mines, Yankee Girl and the Guston, which together produced approximately $6,000,000, continued to operate until 1896. US 550 rises in tortuous twists and turns to the top of RED MOUNTAIN PASS, 49.8 m. (11,018 alt.), marked by a granite-bronze monument commemorating the first highway use of the pass in 1882. The pass forms the boundary between the Uncompahgre and SAN JUAN NATIONAL FORESTS, the latter the second largest in the State with 1,849,612 acres, second only to White River National Forest. Almost every evergreen and broadleaf tree common to Colorado can be found among the twenty-three varieties in the forest.

The highway follows the west side of narrow Mineral Creek Valley, passing an outcrop of a dark red and black rock, originally granite but later melted by volcanic fire and thrown up here in lustrous, almost glassy, form. SULTAN MOUNTAIN (13,341 alt.) and BEAR

MOUNTAIN (12,955 alt.) are marked by glacial cirques—great chasms cut into the granite by creeping masses of ice.

At 56.4 *m.* is (L) a junction with a trail over which supplies are carried to mines in the high reaches of the Red Mountains. Frequently the old and the new in mining transportation can be seen together here. Supplies brought to this point by trucks are unloaded and repacked on burros. Packing is an art; the load must be properly balanced and securely tied. Often a burro is almost hidden by its bulging load. When mules are used, they are usually hitched tandem and led by a driver; burros are driven from the rear of the single-file pack train. In early days haulage rates averaged $2.50 a hundred pounds for 10 miles.

The route descends through heavily forested hills scarred with snow slides. With the first warm days of spring the drifts on the upper slopes plunge down the mountain, crushing everything in their paths. So punctual are these annual slides that in several gulches they form the basis of climatological calculations; the crash of falling earth and snow is the signal for resumption of mining and prospecting activities.

The road crosses the eastern boundary of San Juan National Forest, 58.3 *m.,* to the North Star Sultan Mine, 59.8 *m.,* which has produced more than $8,000,000 worth of ore.

Left on a side road to SILVERTON (99,318 alt., 850 pop.), seat of San Juan County, mining center and tourist attraction. In 1966 the county produced $4,554,802 worth of zinc, lead, silver, copper, gold, uranium. Silverton retains its frontier look, and the Bent Elbow saloon stages daily gun fights in summer, when the Denver & Rio Grande Western brings tourists from Durango in its antique coaches. Silverton has been developing a ski center.

Originally called Baker's Park, for Captain Charles Baker, the first prospector in the region, the town was rechristened Silverton, according to local tradition, by a mine operator who remarked: "We may not have gold here, but we have silver by the ton." With a population of 2,153 in 1910, Silverton was a supply center from which narrow-gauge lines served surrounding mines that annually produced $2,000,000 worth of ore.

Left from Silverton on a highway that winds almost to the top of the high San Juans. HOWARDSVILLE, 5.4 *m.* (9,670 alt.), inhabited by workers employed in the Shenandoah Dives and the Sunnyside Mines, was once the seat of San Juan County; the diminutive log cabin that served as the courthouse still stands.

EUREKA, 8.7 *m.* (9,800 alt.,), is a cluster of frame houses, a two-story boarding house and store building, and the frame buildings of the SUNNYSIDE MILL.

US 550 follows the South Fork of the Animas River and then ascends by a long switchback to higher elevations. The river flows through a gorge 2,000 feet deep, too narrow for both railroad and highway to follow its tortuous course. Deer, elk, a few black bear, and small game are found in this primitive region, and the numerous mountain streams afford excellent trout fishing. San Juan County is one of the few counties in the United States that does not have an acre of tillable soil. Along the route are many examples of volcanic action. Quartzite, a glistening white metamorphic rock, is the most common; the bright red Molas formation is a characteristic shale of soft composition.

The highway skirts MOLAS LAKE, 65.3 *m.* (10,488 alt.), one of many trout-stocked lakes in the vicinity, and crosses a flat divide to descend into Lime Creek Valley. To the west are the HERMOSA CLIFFS, jagged bluffs serving as footstools for the rugged La Platas, barren gray mountains seen at intervals through breaks in the foothills. The walls close in to form LIME CREEK CANYON, 73.3 *m.,* a spectacular gash 2,000 feet deep. Much of the road through this section was blasted from solid rock. Near the southern end of the canyon is LIME CREEK BURN, the result of a forest fire in 1879 which destroyed 26,000 acres of forest.

The huge steel siphon that arches over the highway, 80.9 *m.,* is a section of the 15-mile pipe-line and canal that brings water from the upper reaches of Cascade Creek to Electra Lake (*see below*). On COLUMBINE LAKE (R), 83 *m.* is a campground and the COLUMBINE RANGER STATION, a group of white frame buildings in a grove of pines. South of CASTLE ROCK, 85.3 *m.,* named for its rock turrets and battlements, the road traverses a broad mountain valley used as pasture for cattle.

At 88.6 *m.* is a junction with an unimproved road.

Left on this road to ELECTRA LAKE (*private*) 1.5 *m.;* three miles long and one mile wide, the lake is broken by a large wooded island that forms an almost perfect green circle in the center of the blue water. Electra Lake was created by damming the Animas River to supply electric power for Durango and the surrounding San Juan Basin.

US 550 skirts (R) the edge of the Hermosa Cliffs, behind which loom the saw-toothed Needle Mountains, and traverses a series of flat grassy benches.

At 95.7 *m.* is the junction with a graveled road.

Left here to the SITE OF BAKER BRIDGE, 0.5 *m.,* a short-lived settlement on the eastern bank of the Animas River; founded in 1861 by the Charles Baker expedition, it was the first mining camp in southwestern Colorado. Baker, who had done some prospecting in the Animas Valley in 1859 and 1860, returned the following year with a party of more than 100 men, women, and children. Selecting this spot, the gold seekers laid out their townsite and began building log huts. Little gold was found, Indians were unfriendly, and during the winter the expedition suffered great hardships. When news of the Civil War came in July, the party disbanded, leaving most of the houses unfinished. Baker went to Missouri and joined the Confederate Army. After the war he returned to this region and was slain by Indians in 1868 while panning gold at the mouth of the San Juan River.

PINKERTON SPRINGS, 96.5 *m.,* is a summer resort (*hot springs; swimming pool; cabins; lodge*) hidden in the densely forested Animas Valley. To the south, broad fields are dotted with haystacks and substantial farm buildings. Large crops of apples and other fruits are grown in the district.

TRIMBLE HOT SPRINGS, 101.6 *m.,* built around a group of natural hot springs, has a night club, bathhouses, and lodging accommodations; adjoining is a swimming pool.

ANIMAS CITY, 108.6 *m.,* absorbed by Durango, came into being with the signing of the Brunot Treaty of 1873, under which the Ute relinquished their rights to the San Juan mining district; by 1876 the settlement had 30 cabins, a school, and the usual array of mining camp saloons. In spite of the treaty, conflict continued between the whites and the Indians. After the Meeker Massacre in 1879 (*see Tour 17*), when a general uprising was feared, Fort Flagler, a log stockade, was built here; fires were kept burning all night on surrounding mountains; in the fall of that year 600 soldiers under the command of General Buell were quartered here and remained until the Indian troubles subsided.

Animas City lost the majority of its inhabitants in 1880 when the Denver & Rio Grande Railroad extended its lines westward from the San Luis Valley, avoided the camp, and laid out a new town named Durango, two miles south.

A State Fish Hatchery (*open daily*), 109.4 *m.,* consists of two large buildings with troughs for hatching and several pools where the fingerlings are kept until large enough to be placed in the streams (*see Tour 5b*).

DURANGO, 110.1 *m.* (6,505 alt., 11,600 pop.) (*see Tour 11c*), is at the junction with US 160, which unites with US 550 for 5.3 miles (*see Tour 11c*).

The route traverses a dry, hilly region covered with scrub oak and juniper, and crosses Florida Mesa into the cultivated lands of the Animas Valley. This valley was once the home of an ancient people, but the ruins here are unimportant archeologically in comparison with those found farther south in Aztec Ruins National Monument, N. M. The Navaho of the region will not eat fish from the Animas River, and the reason, according to legend, is that the Navaho once battled Cliff Dwellers here and threw their bodies into the river, where the dead Cliff Dwellers turned to fish.

At BONDAD STATION (Sp. goodness), 126.6 *m.,* the highway crosses the Florida River, named by Escalante, a tributary of the Animas.

US 550 crosses the New Mexico Line, 132 *m.,* 16 miles north of Aztec, New Mexico.

Tour 19

Montrose—Nucla—Uravan—Paradox—(Moab, Utah) ; State 90.
Montrose to Utah Line, 93.8 *m.*

Graded road to Naturita, difficult in wet weather. Winter travel not recommended; inquire conditions locally.
Accommodations extremely limited.

Although the old West has largely vanished, a glimpse of what remains is found along this route in the mesa lands and sagebrush country
of southwestern Colorado. This rough untamed land, peopled by a few
courageous settlers, is the habitat of deer, elk, mountain lion, and small
game.

West of MONTROSE, 0 *m.* (5,820 alt., 6,800 pop.) (*see Tour
9c*), State 90 crosses the fertile Uncompahgre Valley, an alkali and
sagebrush waste reclaimed by water brought from the Gunnison River
through the 6-mile Gunnison Diversion Tunnel (*see Tour 9c*). The
valley is narrow, and prosperous farms occupy the hillsides. To the
north is the great tree-covered Grand Mesa (*see Tour 5E*), a mass of
green during summer and of red in autumn when frost has touched the
scrub oak.

The route ascends SPRING MESA (6,900 alt.), the first of a
series of terraces that rise to the top of the Uncompahgre Plateau. This
area is irrigated, much of it planted with apple orchards and alfalfa.

Alfalfa was introduced in the Clear Creek Valley in 1867 with seed
brought from Mexico. After the establishment of the Colorado Experiment Station in 1888, a study was made of the crop and interest in it
became general. Most of the State's alfalfa is grown under irrigation;
the seed is sowed on smooth level ground crossed by laterals to facilitate
a flood type of irrigation. As a rule, the laterals separate tracts of approximately one-twentieth of an acre, arranged so that water from one
can be drained into a lower adjoining section. One flooding before each
cutting is adequate, and three cuttings a year are not unusual. One planting produces hay for three years.

Alfalfa provides feed for livestock and poultry, brings cash in the
market, and completes a crop rotation that replaces nitrogen in the soil.
Alfalfa has the highest poundage of digestible matter of any hay but the
native wild variety. Much of it is processed into alfalfa meal.

West of the valley the highway ascends steadily through a rough,
sparsely settled region in which scrub cedar has crowded out all other
vegetation. Far to the north are the jagged La Plata Mountains, rising

14,000 feet to rocky snow-covered summits. On higher levels the thinning cedar gives way to sage.

The route ascends the UNCOMPAHGRE PLATEAU (10,000 alt.), covered with vast untouched stands of timber, and crosses the eastern boundary of UNCOMPAHGRE NATIONAL FOREST, 20.6 *m.*, created in 1905 by President Theodore Roosevelt. It embraces 957,003 acres owned by the U.S. Government. Twenty-three varieties of trees are found in its wooded areas, the predominant tree being the Engelmann spruce. Wild game is still plentiful in this old hunting ground of the Ute as animals wander in from the Ouray State Game Preserve, a 53,120-acre area within the forest near Ouray (*see Tour 18*).

SILESCA RANGER STATION (L), 21.4 *m.*, a log cabin, the first habitation house on the route west of Spring Creek Valley, is occupied only in summer. At IRON SPRINGS CAMPGROUNDS (L), 24.1 *m.* (*cleared camping spaces; fireplaces, sanitary facilities*), are springs containing iron salts as the principal element.

West of the springs, great aspens, some 100 feet high and 18 inches in diameter, border the highway. Here live brilliant-hued broad-tailed hummingbirds, violet-green swallows, and the red-naped sapsucker. Stretches of scrub oak appear as the lower levels of the plateau are reached. The distant valleys are great seas of blue, topped with the jagged white La Platas. The road follows the canyon of the SAN MIGUEL RIVER, fringed with cottonwoods and willows. Here and there through breaks in the red rock canyon walls appear (R) La Sal Mountains, 100 miles distant in Utah.

The highway passes under the wooden flume of the 20-mile COLORADO CO-OPERATIVE DITCH, 32.5 *m.*, which diverts water from the upper valley of the San Miguel to the fields of First Park Mesa, site of the socialistic Nucla Colony (*see below*). The ditch crosses a broad level plateau intensively developed as a fruit and vegetable growing area. This region was desolate until settlers succeeded in bringing water to the land and grubbed out scrub oak and sagebrush, to plant apples, grapes, peaches, and potatoes. Sheep and cattle raising are important sources of income.

At 49.1 *m.* is the junction with an improved road.

Right on this road is NUCLA, 5.1 *m.* (7,000 alt., 900 pop.), a compact town of neat frame bungalows, center of a cooperative community. In the small grassy park shaded by poplars, school children eat their lunches and townsfolk pasture their cows. Most business enterprises in Nuclas were once conducted as a cooperative venture; today, only the irrigation ditch remains as community property. The ditch was constructed almost entirely by hand. To avoid the cost of blasting through solid rock, a large part of it originally consisted of wooden flumes built along the edge of the canyon.

Coal is mined from the Nucla strip mine operated by the Peabody Coal Co.

NATURITA, 54.1 *m.* (5,427 alt.), is a scattered village of small false-front buildings.

At 56.5 *m.* is the junction with State 141.

Right on this graded road to URAVAN, 13 *m.* (4,995 alt.), a mill operated by the U. S. Vanadium Company (*open weekdays*). The name is a combination of the first syllables of uranium and vanadium, found with a carnotite, a yellow viscous ore mined here. This radioactive ore, one of the first of its kind to be discovered in the world, was used in the discovery of radium. Carnotite was first mined here in 1881 for small amounts of gold found with it. In 1898, after the Smithsonian Institution had found that the ore contained uranium, several tons were shipped by two French scientists, Poulot and Voilleque, to the School of Mines in Paris, where they were delivered to Madame Curie and used by her in experiments that resulted in the extraction of radium. The ore was named for M. Carnot, inspector-general of mines in France. Between 1898 and 1928 ores taken from this region accounted for almost one half of the world production of radium. The production of uranium concentrates is regulated, but a new vanadium material has been developed and found most useful as an alloying agent by the steel industry. U. S. Vanadium Co. is a subsidiary of Union Carbide Corp.

Between Uravan and Gateway State 141 moves past the U. S. ATOMIC ENERGY RESERVE.

West of the junction State 90 crosses the San Miguel Valley and ascends the dun-colored slopes of Long Park, passing the concrete foundations of abandoned coke ovens, 58.6 *m.* During the boom days of carnotite mining the mill and general offices of the Standard Chemical Company, original developers of the region, were established here.

The highway traverses the eastern portion of PARADOX VALLEY, an uninhabited sagebrush waste, walled in by massive red cliffs on the north and by rolling hills on the south. The valley was so named because the Dolores River crosses it at right angles, an unusual phenomenon. The "strike" or direction of the valley is northwest and southeast, but the Dolores River enters it on the south and runs in a northeasterly direction to leave the valley through a great gap in the cliffs to the north.

At 74.1 *m.* is the junction with an unimproved dirt road.

Right on this road, across red sage-covered gumbo, to a SALT MINE (*open daily*), 2.5 *m.* Paradox Valley was apparently once the bed of a dead sea, similar to the Great Salt Lake. As the water evaporated beds of salt were deposited, which in course of time were covered with successive layers of soil and rock. From a 5,100-foot well, brine is pumped for processing of vanadium. The brine is run to settling ponds, where the water is evaporated. Both brine and solid salt are used in vanadium operations at Uravan (*see above*). A mechanic and his helper, who operate the pumps, are the only inhabitants of this section of East Paradox Valley.

BEDROCK, 76.6 *m.* (4,983 alt.), is a community on the Dolores River.

Left from Bedrock by trail to the little-known DOLORES CANYON, 1 *m.* Ranchers sometime act as guides through this rugged area, but the trip should be attempted only by experienced mountain climbers. At MULEBEND, 10 *m.,* the stream turns east for half a mile, abruptly reverses its course, and returns to within a few hundred feet of the bend.

West of Bedrock the route traverses a cliff-protected section of the valley, devoted to wintering of livestock. A few areas along the river are irrigated and produce small crops, but cattle raising is the chief occupation.

At 82.4 *m.* is the junction with an improved road.

Right on this road is PARADOX, 1 *m.* (5,180 alt.), where food and supplies can be obtained.

The highway turns south, re-enters the sagebrush, and twists up the side of NYSWONGER MESA (6,983 alt.), its table-top a mass of scrub oak and cedar. To the north the downward sweep of Paradox Valley appears as a purple lake damned by sheer red cliffs, while to the west the monotonous vista of the mesa lands is broken by the distant jagged upthrust of La Sal Mountains in Utah.

State 90 crosses the Utah Line, 93.8 *m.,* 16 miles east of La Sal, Utah.

Tour 20

Junction US 550—Ridgway—Placerville—Telluride—Lizard Head Pass—Rico—Dolores—Junction US 160 (Cortez); 109 *m.,* State 62, State 145.

Narrow road with many sharp twists and steep grades; dangerous in wet weather; winter travel inadvisable.
Good accommodations at Telluride and Dolores.

The highway passes through a sparsely settled region of wild grandeur. On every side rise jagged peaks, snow-covered and flanked with dense forests filled with game and crisscrossed by fishing streams. In this section are many mines, once as rich as any in the State; only a few are now being operated.

State 62 branches southwest from US 550 (*see Tour 18*), 0 *m.,* 27 miles south of Montrose (5,820 alt., 6,800 pop.) (*see Tour 9c*).

RIDGWAY, 0.3 *m.* (6,770 alt.), a scattering of frame cottages, is overshadowed by smoke-blackened railroad shops. Good hunting and fishing in the vicinity attract many sportsmen. The town was named for A. G. Ridgway, one of General W. J. Palmer's associates in the construction of the Denver & Rio Grande Western. The Ouray County Fair opens on Labor Day.

West of Ridgway the highway crosses rolling hills toward the Uncompahgre Plateau; wide expanses of brown grassland are relieved by patches of sagebrush, silver-gray in the sunlight and purple in the shadows.

DALLAS DIVIDE, 10.2 *m.*, a flag station on the railroad, is situated on the crest of the UNCOMPAHGRE PLATEAU, its higher regions covered with dense pine forests interspersed with sage flats. This is a country of magnificent distances. To the left rise the forbidding La Plata Range, with many summits rising 14,000 feet or more. Throughout practically the entire year these mountains are snow-covered.

The route descends the western slope of the Uncompahgre Plateau through groves of quaking aspens. Nipped by frost, the foliage burns like fire against the somber background of the changeless pines. The aspen, seldom achieving timber size, is of value as a nurse tree, covering burns and sheltering slow-growing evergreens. According to a Ute legend, the continuous quivering of aspen leaves, even when there is no appreciable breeze, is due to the Great Spirit who once visited earth during a full moon. All living things awaited him, trembling with anticipation—all save the proud aspen, which stood still, refusing to pay homage. The deity, angered, decreed that in the future its leaves should tremble whenever eye looked upon them.

SAW PIT, 19.4 *m.* (7,500 alt.), often serves as a base for sportsmen. The country to the south, habitat of deer, elk, and mountain lion, is one of the big-game regions in the State. The road descends into the valley of the SAN MIGUEL RIVER (*good fly fishing*). With the decline of mining operations, which polluted the water, fish again abound in the crystal-clear stream.

At 23.3 *m.* is the junction with State 145, which the route now follows (L) southeast.

PLACERVILLE, 23.9 *m.* (7,523 alt.), was originally a mining camp. When the placer mines played out, it became a shipping center for cattle and sheep, and today is one of the principal loading points in western Colorado.

Southeast from Placerville, State 145 follows a devious course through San Miguel Canyon, its red walls formed of intricately eroded rock strata. The meandering river channel is fringed with cottonwoods and beaded with small dark pools where trout abound.

At 29.8 *m.* is a junction with a dirt road.

Right here is VANADIUM, 0.4 *m.* (7,650 alt.), with store and post office flanked by several buildings. The large green frame mill was formerly operated by the U. S. Vanadium Company.

East of Vanadium the valley of the San Miguel strikes through low, round, sage-covered hills, their forests long since cut away. The road crosses the northern boundary of Uncompahgre National Forest, 32.4 *m.*

At 35.9 *m.* State 145 turns south, but a short spur runs east 4 *m.* to TELLURIDE (8,500 alt., 700 pop. est.) seat of San Miguel County, a National Historical Landmark, famous as the City of Gold. Well-known mines brought their rich ores to Telluride. Mining still continues; in 1966 the county produced vanadium, zinc, lead, uranium ore, copper, silver and gold valued at nearly $17,000,000, with most of it coming from the Idarado mine in the Pandora Basin, 2 *m*. east, where the Bridal Veil Falls, 365 ft., and the Ingram Falls, are tourist attractions.

In 1875 John Fallon staked out the Sheridan, Emerald, Ausboro, and Ajax claims here. His associate, White, staked out extensions on these claims but allowed his claims to lapse through failure to perform the $100 assessment work required by law. Later, the celebrated Smuggler was struck on one of these claims, uncovering a vein that assayed $1,200 a ton. This rich strike caused a rush to Telluride, named for the tellurous ores of the district, and soon the surrounding mountain sides were pitted with prospect holes. New veins were uncovered and the region enjoyed a wild prosperity. Transportation was facilitated in 1890 by the construction of the Rio Grande Southern Railroad. At the peak of the boom, with the Smuggler, Alta, Liberty Bell, Tomboy, Black Bear, and other mines pouring forth treasure, Telluride was one of the liveliest gold camps in Colorado. Its population exceeded 5,000; an opera house was built. Among the camp's prominent figures was George Costigan, Sr., a Virginia lawyer, who operated the Liberty Bell Mine and served as district judge. His sons, George Jr., author of numerous legal text books, and Edward P., United States Senator (1931–37), spent their early years here. Telluride's decline began in the 1890's, but many mines were worked for another decade. By 1909 the Telluride district had produced more than $60,000,000 in precious metals. Since the early 1930's a few gold mines have been reopened, and the town profits from summer tourists and trade with surrounding farms and ranches.

The Sheridan Opera House, built 1891, has its original stage settings and houses the Potted Players, who give summer performances. A motion picture, *The Unsinkable Molly Brown,* dealing with one of Colorado's eccentric pioneers, was filmed here in 1963. Many of the late Victorian structures are carefully preserved in Telluride.

South of the junction the highway winds upward through heavy stands of yellow pine and Engelmann spruce into the SAN MIGUEL MOUNTAINS, a low spur of La Platas. Beautiful at any season, the San Miguels are at their best when blanketed with mid-winter snows. Along the route are dumps of many mines, few of them operating. Here and there an abandoned shaft house, its timbers rotting and roof near collapse, pushes its head through the forest fast reclaiming the land.

OPHIR, 44.1 *m.,* is on the main route of State 145. The area is suitable for summer sports and is being developed for the tourist trade.

North of Ophir are the OPHIR NEEDLES (12,100 alt.), masses of gray granite peaks almost triangular in shape.

The road continues its winding course through foothills; below the highway, half way down the mountain, is the OPHIR LOOP, remarkable engineering feat in the construction of the Rio Grande Southern Railroad. In order to route the railroad past Ophir Station and eliminate excessive grades, the tracks were laid in the shape of a great horseshoe, a section of which is supported on high wooden trestles. In their course the rails almost overlap themselves.

SAN BERNARDO MOUNTAIN (11,845 alt.), 45.8 *m.,* a sheer

point of granite rises (R) far above the timberline; it is sometimes called the Matterhorn for its resemblance to the famous Swiss peak.

TROUT LAKE, 47 m. (9,750 alt.), is a magnificent expanse of azure nestling in a valley between heavily forested hills, a favorite camping spot for fishermen. Small supplies can be obtained from neighboring ranchers, and boats are available.

LIZARD HEAD PASS, 49.1 m., on the crest of the San Miguel Mountains, lies between (R) BLACK FACE MOUNTAIN (12,100 alt.) and (L) SHEEP MOUNTAIN (13,200 alt.). At the top of the pass the railroad is covered for almost a quarter of a mile by a frame shed, built to keep snow from blocking the tracks. Snowfall in southwestern Colorado is exceptionally heavy, and in addition to snowsheds, constant use of plows is necessary to maintain train schedules.

The highway descends the slopes of the San Miguels, along which stark peaks reach at the sky in a long procession. The few habitations here are lone ranch houses. Occasionally a cowboy, who might be from the pages of a Zane Grey novel, is met; less often an old prospector, weather-beaten as the towns, plods along a dim trail in his perpetual search of El Dorado. The hills of western Colorado are peopled with men whose dreams are of the untouched treasure stores that will—some day—produce a stream of gold for them.

RICO (Sp. rich), 62.1 m. (8,900 alt.), a string of false-front frame buildings along a rutted street, is one of the last outposts of the Old West. As late as the 1920's horse thieves were active in the region and often were pursued by posses in automobiles and on motorcycles.

The earliest explorations in the region were made by the Spanish, who made no discovery of treasure. Padre Escalante, who made a brave attempt to find a route between the Santa Fe and California missions, left a record of his visit and was responsible for naming many peaks and rivers in Colorado. Trappers penetrated this region from the east in 1832–33, and one party wintered in the Rio Dolores valley to take beaver and other fur-bearing animals along the banks of the stream. The first gold discoveries were made in 1866, when Sheldon Shafer and Joe Fearheiler, prospectors bound for Montana, made valuable finds near the present town of Rico. Other gold seekers were driven away by Indians and the settlement was abandoned. Working of the mines began in 1878 when the Ute signed a treaty surrendering their claims. While some gold and silver are still mined, lead, zinc, and copper are of equal importance. Rico's peak population of 6,000 dwindled to 300 in 1920. The Rico Argentine mine is one of two principal mines and obtains gold, silver, lead, zinc, and some pyrite.

South of Rico the route follows an old Ute trail along the banks of the Dolores River flanked by low hills heavily wooded with aspen. Here is unfenced grazing country, and care should be exercised in driving, for sheep frequently block the highway.

STONER, 82.8 m., a post office and flag station, with a Cottage Camp and a Ranger Station is now a winter sports center. South of

Stoner the road traverses a broad fertile valley carpeted with fields of alfalfa. The channel of the Dolores River is screened by a wall of cottonwoods.

DOLORES, 99 *m.* (6, 957 alt.) is in the heart of a rich grazing district; the main street is flanked with parkways.

At 109 *m.* is the junction with US 160 (*see Tour 11c*), 2 miles east of CORTEZ (6,198 alt., 8,000 pop.) (*see Tour 11c*). Ten miles west of Dolores on State 147 is a junction with US 160 proceeding northwest.

((

Tour 21

Iola—(Junction US 50)—Lake City—Slumgullion Pass—Spring Creek Pass—Creede—Wheeler National Monument—Junction US 160 (South Fork) ; 123 *m.,* State 149.

State 149, a back-country road, traverses a rugged region where game and fish abound. The landscape is a succession of high mountains, plateaus, rocky defiles, and broad valleys growing forage crops. Ore veins in the surrounding hills have yielded fortunes in gold and silver, and during the late 1890's this district was among the richest in the State. Today cattle and sheep grazing are the chief support of the scattered population.

In IOLA, 0 *m.* (7,450 alt.) (*see Tour 9c*), State 149 branches south from US 50 (*see Tour 9*) and crosses the fertile valley of the Gunnison, rich in grasses and dotted with ranches. From the summit of NINE MILE HILL, 9 *m.,* are vistas of green fields and mountain ranges.

At 10.5 *m.* is the junction with an unimproved road.

Right on this road to the SITE OF SPENCER, 1.5 *m.,* an abandoned mining camp surrounded by scarred and pitted hills. The only buildings in use are school and two ranch houses. Well known mines in this district were the Headlight, the Old Lott, and the Anaconda, now marked by collapsing shaft houses.

The road descends into the well-watered, cottonwood-shaded valley of the Cebolla, traversing rolling acres of hay fields to a junction with a dirt road, 16.4 *m.*

Left on this road is POWDERHORN, 1.5 *m.* (8,056 alt.) (*cabins and hotels*), a trading center; here are the CEBOLLA HOT SPRINGS and CARBONATE SPRINGS, known to the Ute for their healing properties.

The highway ascends SAPINERO MESA, its steep slopes covered with dense growths of sage, dark-green juniper, and scrub oak. The road follows Indian Creek Valley to the broader valley of the LAKE FORK OF THE GUNNISON, a prosperous ranching country, and at THE GATE, 28.6 m., passes between the towering granite portals of a richly colored gorge. The cliffs wall in the highway, the river, and an abandoned branch line of the Denver & Rio Grande Western Railroad between Gunnison and Lake City. Approaching the Continental Divide, the route parallels the eastern border of the Uncompahgre National Forest to YOUMAN, 34.7 m. The towering rugged summits, a northern extension of the San Juans, lift snow-white caps against fleecy clouds that hang almost constantly on the horizon. To the west is UNCOMPAHGRE PEAK (14,306 alt.); southwest is MATTERHORN PEAK (13,585 alt.); farther southwest, WETTERHORN PEAK (14,017 alt.), seamed with gorges and ravines. The streams here, remote from the main-traveled highway, are well stocked with trout.

This region became known to white men through the explorations of Lieutenant John C. Frémont in 1848 (see The People), but until 1873 remained in possession of the Ute. A few prospectors found "color" here and precipitated a gold rush. The old story of the white men and the Indians were reenacted as the Ute were forced out and the district was thrown open for settlement. Crude roads were built and dozens of mining camps established. A highway between Lake City (see below) and Saguache (see Tour 15b) was the principal outlet until the Denver & Rio Grande Western Railroad completed its branch line from Gunnison to Lake City in 1889.

LAKE CITY, 45.7 m. (8,500 alt.), is the seat of Hinsdale County, larger in extent than Rhode Island. In 1967 Colorado Municipalities, a State publication, reported 75 residents in Lake City. In 1963 Lake City had 14 children and two teachers in the primary and high schools. In 1964 the county had 200 people. Split by the Continental Divide, much of Hinsdale County is isolated from Lake City throughout winter. The settlement here was one of the first in western Colorado. Optimistic settlers built far in excess of their needs, and today many buildings are abandoned. Upon completion of the railroad the town was a shipping point for gold and silver ores from near-by mines, including the immensely rich Hidden Treasure and Golden Fleece. During the 1890's agriculture and cattle raising became the chief occupations. Although mining activities have revived since the late 1920's, the collapsing structures of mines and mills still splotch the hillsides.

1. Left from Lake City on a trail to CANNIBAL PLATEAU, 5 m., the scene of a gruesome episode in Colorado's history. In December 1873, a party of men from Utah, bound on a prospecting trip through the San Juan Mountains, reached the encampment of Ouray, chief of the Ute, who urged them to remain until spring. The majority accepted, but six men, Packer, Bell, Humphreys, Swan, Noon, and Miller, pushed on. Six weeks later Packer appeared alone at the old Los Piños Agency, 75 miles from Lake City, and declared that after a few days'

travel from Ouray's camp he had become lame and his companions had deserted him, forcing him to subsist on roots and small game. His appearance and actions belied his story. His first demand was for whisky, not food. Claiming to be without funds, he, appeared in Saguache several days later with considerable money, which he spent drinking and gambling.

Meanwhile, an Indian had come to the agency with strips of flesh picked up along Packer's trail. They proved to be strips cut from a human body. Suspicion against Packer mounted and he was arrested. That spring a photographer for *Harper's Weekly,* crossing the plateau, stumbled upon the remains of five men, their skulls crushed; strips of flesh were missing from several of the bodies. Exactly what happened is not known. Packer claimed that starvation had made his companions insane, and that he had killed Bell in self defense. Subsequently he discovered that the other four had been slain, apparently by Bell. Packer's story was not believed and he was charged with murder. As there was no prison at the agency, he was chained to a rock, from which he managed to escape. Recaptured in Wyoming in 1883, he was tried for murder in Lake City and sentenced to be hanged. An apocryphal story, widely believed, has it that in sentencing Packer the judge said: "Packer, you so-and-so, you have eaten half the Democrats in Hinsdale County." In fact, the judge was far more eloquent. Addressing Packer, he exclaimed, "In 1873, you, in the company with five companions, passed through this beautiful mountain valley where stands the town of Lake City. . . . You and your victims had a weary march, and when the shadows of the mountains fell upon your little party and the night drew her sable curtain around you, your unsuspecting victims lay down on the ground and were soon lost in the sleep of the weary; and then, thus sweetly unconscious of danger from any quarter, and particularly from you, their trusted companion, you cruelly and brutally slew them all. . . . To other sickening details of your crime I will not refer. . . . I sentence you to be hanged by the neck until you are dead, dead, dead, and may God have mercy on your soul."

But Packer was not to hang; he was granted a new trial on a technicality and sentenced to 40 years for manslaughter. A few years later, he was paroled and died in Denver in 1906. During his incarceration Packer was brought to Denver as a witness in another case, and was interviewed by a newspaper reporter. "I thought when I was told about having to come to Denver and testify," he said, "that maybe the people would kind of shrink from me after all the things that have been said, but there was nothing of the kind. They seemed like they wanted to see me." His greatest enjoyment came from a visit to a theater. "And what I liked about it most was that it wasn't anything vulgar, like some of these plays that I read about. There was skirt dancing in it, and all that, but not one of those girls lifted her feet higher than that (Packer indicated about one foot and a half above the ground)."

2. Right from Lake City on another trail to CRYSTAL LAKE, 5 *m.* (12,000 alt.), at the foot of CRYSTAL PEAK (12,923 alt.) ; trout are plentiful in the lake and in numerous springs that feed it.

South of Lake City the route winds through a country of canyons and mountains, its streams walled in by high and jagged cliffs. This almost uninhabited region is one of the few remaining primitive areas in Colorado accessible by highway.

At 48.2 *m.* is the junction with an unimproved road.

Left on this road to LAKE SAN CRISTOBAL (*cabins and inn*), 1.3 *m.,* a favored spot for fishing and hunting. The lake covers about three square miles and contains many small wooded islands. The mountain slopes, blanketed with aspens, scrub oak, and pines, are mosaics of brilliant red, yellow, and green in the fall.

The highway crosses the western boundary of the Gunnison National Forest, 53.7 *m.,* and ascends to the top of SLUMGULLION PASS (11,000 alt.), 54.4 *m.,* where early prospectors stopped to rest and prepare their slumgullion stew, a concoction of meat and vegetables. Here is a fine view of snowy peaks stretching four ways to the horizon. The pass, first used as an ore trail in 1879, is blocked by snow in winter.

Penetrating wild mountain country, the road crosses the Continental Divide at SPRING CREEK PASS, 66 *m.* (10,901 alt.) ; here is clearly seen (R) the RIO GRANDE PYRAMID (13,827 alt.), almost perpetually snow-covered. At its base lies the Rio Grande Reservoir, which impounds water for irrigation.

Passing the boundary between the Gunnison and the Rio Grande National Forests, 66.3 *m.,* the route crosses SOUTH FORK CREEK, 72.4 *m.* Just off the highway (R) are SOUTH FALLS (*free camping*), about 100 feet high, with three separate drops. In its downward plunge are numerous churning pools, haunts of rainbow trout.

South of the falls State 149 traverses a lofty forested mesa; resorts and dude ranches appear at intervals; hunting and fishing are exceptionally good.

At 87 *m.* is the junction with a dirt road.

Left on this road to ANTELOPE SPRINGS, 0.5 *m.* (8,957 alt.), once a relay station on the stagecoach route between Del Norte (*see Tour 11b*) and Silverton (*see Tour 18*). Passengers and mail were carried over this rough rocky way to the booming camps of the San Juan district. Upon completion of the railroad in 1882 the stage line was abandoned.

Left from Antelope Springs on a trail to a natural swimming pool, 0.7 *m.,* fed by the waters of a warm spring. This section was favored hunting country of the Ute and early miners, for deer and elk came in numbers to a salt lick near by.

The route follows the canyon to SEVEN MILE BRIDGE, 93.4 *m.,* at the junction with a county road.

Right on this road to SPAR CITY, 7.8 *m.,* a relic of the early 1880's. A contemporary of Creede (*see below*), the settlement was much smaller and lacked the gay life of the other camp. The one-time population of 200 were employed in the Denver Tunnel Mine.

Northeast of ANTLERS PARK (*free campground*), 94 *m.,* is CREEDE, 100.2 *m.* (8,854 alt., 500 pop.), seat of Mineral County, the shadow of a once populous mining camp which, springing up overnight, sat perched on stilts and high foundations above the brawling waters of the Rio Grande. Twice almost destroyed by fire, the town has few old landmarks remaining. General stores, a post office, and unpainted frame houses constitute Creede today. But turbines in one of the old mills high up the gorge supply electricity for lamps along the single street, which burn twenty-four hours a day.

The town, one of the later mining camps, was founded by Nicholas C. Creede, a discouraged prospector, who in 1890 stumbled upon "color" when he stopped to eat lunch. His silver bonanza, christened the Holy Moses, then the Amethyst, made the fortune of each successive owner. With the discovery of the King Solomon, another treasure trove, hundreds stampeded to the area. The first flimsy camp, known as Jim Town, grew so rapidly that at one time 200 carpenters were engaged in building houses. Other rich strikes emblazoned the name of Creede on the roster of great bonanza camps along with Central City, Leadville, Aspen, and Cripple Creek.

Gold, silver, and zinc were the basis of prosperity, and during the boom years the district led the State in the production of silver. Population had climbed to 8,000 by 1893. Six-shooters were local life insurance policies; gambling houses and saloons ran day and night. Along the streets moved many dissolute and colorful characters—among them, "Soapy" Smith, silver-tongued bunco artist, who demonstrated over and over again that the hand is quicker than the eye by selling cakes of soap wrapped in dollar bills—always retaining the bills.

To Creede came Cy Warman to found its first newspaper, *The Candle,* still published, and to celebrate the attractions of the camp in the poem, "And There is No Night in Creede," now known throughout the West.

> Here's a land where all are equal—
>   Of high or lowly birth—
> A land where men make millions,
>   Dug from the dreary earth.
> Here meek and mild-eyed burros
>   On mineral mountains feed.
> It's day all day in the daytime,
>   And there is no night in Creede.
> The cliffs are solid silver,
>   With wond'rous wealth untold,
> And the beds of the running rivers
>   Are lined with the purest gold.
> While the world is filled with sorrow,
>   And hearts must break and bleed—
> It's day all day in the daytime,
>   And there is no night in Creede.

10

Warman, who grew up with a passion to run a locomotive, came to Colorado in 1880 and worked many years for the Denver & Rio Grande Railroad. Embarking upon his journalistic career at Creede, he contributed to magazines and wrote several volumes of short stories and poetry.

Several camps in the vicinity of Creede eventually merged with it. North Creede became a residential section; Weaver City, at the junction of Nelson and West Willow Creeks, named for the many Weaver families living there, is today a straggling line of abandoned log cabins.

The mines closed down with the decline of silver prices after 1893, although the ore bodies were far from exhausted. Since the late 1920's Creede has stirred with new life. Approximately 500,000 pounds of silver ore were shipped weekly from the mines here in 1939. Mineral County produced 148,034 troy ownces of silver in 1966.

FORD'S SALOON was built by Bob Ford, reputed slayer of Jesse James, Missouri desperado. On the eve of opening a new dance hall, June 10, 1892, after one of Creede's fires, a miner named O'Kelly, who claimed that the saloon owner had persecuted his parents years before, shot and killed Ford. Later Ford's body was removed to Missouri. O'Kelly served a short prison term at Canon City.

Left from Creede on a winding horseback trail by way of MAMMOTH MOUNTAIN (11,650 alt.) to WHEELER MONUMENT, an area of remarkable sandstone formations, originally set aside by President Theodore Roosevelt in 1908 and now incorporated in Rio Grande National Forest. Monoliths carved by erosive forces stand in the canyon like chimeras before castellated lines of soaring cliffs. Such descriptive titles as "The Temple" and "The Cathedral" have been given the configurations. The site was known to Indians for centuries; the Ute called the formations the "sand stones." Tribal renegades used the locality as a hideout. Probably the first white man to visit here was Lieutenant John C. Frémont while in search of a feasible transcontinental railroad route.

Passing through the Monument, the trail continues to WAGON WHEEL GAP, 34 m. (see below).

WASON, 102.8 m. (8,567 alt.), primarily a resort (dude ranches, cabins), once Creede's bitter rival, was founded in 1892 by M. H. Wason, who had used the land as a cattle range. At the confluence of the Rio Grande and Willow Creek, the camp with its wide streets and substantial buildings enjoyed the natural advantage of a level meadow site. The Wason Miner was the first newspaper published in the district. In a futile attempt to promote his town as the seat of Mineral County, Wason once sponsored a huge Fourth of July celebration, with bands, fireworks, dancing, drinking, and free lunches. A courthouse built by him stood empty in the center of the town until, according to local historians, a group of men came by night and removed it piecemeal to Creede.

South of Wason the highway enters the narrow canyon of the Rio Grande and winds between high brightly-colored walls along the banks of the clear mountain stream, fringed with willows and cottonwoods, its waters golden from amber-colored sands. At intervals the canyon widens into small wooded parks, excellent camp and picnic grounds.

WAGON WHEEL GAP, 109.1 m. (8,500 alt.), is a rural resort where many wealthy Coloradoans maintain summer houses. Several mineral springs known to the Indians have been developed here. Numerous streams offer good trout fishing.

State 149 passes through the Gap, a narrow, highly-colored gorge barely accommodating highway and river, named for a discarded wheel found beside an old trail in 1873. The wheel presumably was dropped by a party of prospectors led by Charles Baker, who, ordered by the Ute to leave camp near what is now Animas City, obeyed with such alacrity that their supplies and equipment were scattered along the trail. In summer months this region is carpeted with white mountain daisies, goldenrod, purple asters, and fragile star flowers.

The AMERICAN LEGION CAMP, 118 m., a resort maintained by the

Legion Post of Monte Vista, contains a rustic community house; the camp is sometimes rented to other than post members.

MASONIC PARK, 118.3 *m.,* reached by a rustic bridge (R), lies between pine-forested slopes and the river. The administration building, housing the park office and recreational hall, is surrounded by cabins owned by members of the Southwestern Masonic Association.

The highway crosses the eastern boundary of the Rio Grande National Forest, 120.3 *m.,* and descends the narrow canyon between hills covered with piñon, cedar, and pine, to the junction with US 160 (*see Tour 11*), 122 *m.,* 1 mile west of South Fork (8,250 alt.) (*see Tour 11c*).

Rocky Mountain National Park

Administration: Rocky Mountain National Park is administered by the National Park Service, Dept. of the Interior. The address of the Superintendent is Estes Park, Colo., 80517.

Seasons: Parts of the Park are open the year around, but camping and hiking is best from May to September. Lectures and guided tours end on Labor Day. Winter activities, chiefly skiing at Hidden Valley, are open December through April, unless blocked by snow.

Highways and Transporation: US 34 reaches both gateways, at Estes Park Village and Granby. US 36 is a direct route from Denver, 65 *m.* The major air, bus and railroad terminals are at Denver, and Cheyenne, Wyo., 91 *m.* In summer the Colorado Transporation Co. makes connections with air, bus, and rail lines at Denver and bus and rail lines at Greeley and Granby. In winter it provides service to Hidden Valley. *Write the company at 3455 Ringsby Court, Denver, 80216.*

Fees: Can be paid at entrances or at Park hq and apply to visitors aged 16 and over. The Golden Eagle Passport (annual) applies to all Federal areas and costs $7. It also may be obtained by mail from the Bureau of Outdoor Recreation, Box 7763, Washington, D. C., 20044. Persons accompanying the holder in an automobile may enter free. Visitors entering in bus pay 50¢ a day. Visitors staying overnight and using a private motor car pay $1. At Hidden Valley all-day tows cost $4.50 for adults, $3.00 for children; all needed equipment can be bought or rented, and ski instruction is available. *For details address Rocky Mountain Park Co., 601 Broadway, Denver, 80203.* Horse rentals, June 1–Sept. 30, are as follows: $4.50 for 2 hrs., $6 for half day, $10 for all day with a minimum of 6 in all-day party; breakfast ride, $7.50, plus 3% sales tax on food. Address Hi Country Stables, Box 1111, Estes Park, 80517. Climbs with guides, including Longs Peak, vary from $20 to $60 for one person, $10 to $15 for each additional person, depending on routes taken. *Consult Hubert Cretton, Box 769, Estes Park, 80517.* Cretton conducts a climbing school all summer in Estes Park.

Accommodations: There are 12 campgrounds, open from mid-May through September, with fireplaces, running water (June 1–Sept. 10) and comfort stations of varying types. No reservations are taken; sites are allotted on first-come, first-served basis. Camp tenders are present to assist. Camping is limited to 14 days per year; camping in the Back Country needs a special permit. Timber Creek and Moraine Park are the only campgrounds with sites for trailers, but trailers may use other areas that have no facilities No camping along roads. Firewood is sold at Estes Park. Groceries are available at Estes Park, Grand Lake, and Allenspark. Estes Park and Grand Lake have churches, postoffices, drug stores, laundromats, medical services. Two campgrounds operated by the U. S. Forest Service are on State 7, 17 *m.* south of Estes Park, and on Devils Gulch Road, 8 *m.* northeast of Estes Park. Visitors should have tents, sleeping bags, cooking utensils, and be prepared for cool nights. Bathing in Streams and lakes is prohibited. Dogs not allowed on trails.

Fishing: The Colorado State fishing laws apply, with additions. Waters are open the year around. Bear Lake and Black Canyon Creek are closed to fishing. Hours for fishing, 4 a.m. to 9 p.m. Worms may be brought but not dug in the Park. Bag: west of Continental Divide, 10 fish, May 20–Oct. 31; 6 fish rest of year; 10 brook trout (char) if under 8 in. long. License: Resident fishing only, $6; nonresident season fishing, $10; nonresident 10-day, $5. A juvenile under 15 needs no license if his bag is one-half that of adult.

ROCKY MOUNTAIN NATIONAL PARK, lying on both sides of the Continental Divide, here a 35-mile chain of giant peaks, contains within its 405 square miles a remarkable grouping of mountain scenery and upland meadows, split and gouged by gulches and canyons, dotted with glacial lakes, altogether forming a bold and colorful scene described by Albert Bierstadt, German landscape artist, as America's finest composition for the painter. The park's charm lies less in any one of its features than in the great variety of country within so small an area. It is a workshop and playground alike for the naturalist, the photographer, the hiker, the sportsman, and the vacationist with no special hobby.

As early as 1865 campers pitched their tents in this region; by 1874 there was a stage line between Estes Park and Longmont by way of North St. Vrain Canyon. Joel Estes, the first settler, for whom Estes Park was named, built a cabin on Fish Creek in 1860. Two or three families followed, and Estes moved his family from the park, complaining of "too many people." Word of the park spread rapidly, and many notable visitors came: among them, the Earl of Dunraven, yachtsman, hunter, explorer, author, and war correspondent for the London *Daily Telegraph* in Abyssinia (1867) and later in the Franco-Prussian War. Succeeding to the title in 1871, he came to hunt and fish in the Rockies, bought 6,000 acres in Estes Park, and constructed a lodge, where he entertained English nobility and American frontiersmen. Dunraven later fought in the Boer War; selling his property here in 1904, he returned to Ireland where he served in the senate of the Irish Free State until just before his death in 1926, at the age of 85.

Much of the popularity of this country must be credited to the late Enos Mills, who spent his life climbing peaks, exploring canyons, making friends with the wildlife, and writing books glowingly describing the grandeur of the region. He was one of the first to campaign to have it set aside as a national park. The closing years of Mills' life, ironically, were embittered by his success, for he quarreled constantly with the park authorities.

Rocky Mountain National Park, created by act of Congress January 26, 1915, includes much of the Front Range of the Rockies, the eastern slopes of which are rugged, with many sharp rises and cliffs. Within the park are 65 peaks more than 10,000 feet high, and 16 rising more than 12,000. A profusion of wild flowers carpets the high mountain meadows. Hundreds of streams on both sides of the Divide are well stocked with fish, and there are many lakes ranging in size from tiny crystal pools to Grand Lake. Longs Peak (14,256 alt.) dominates the park. A stark mass of red-gray granite with a sheer 2,000-foot face to the northeast, this perpetually snow-capped mountain is a popular goal for climbers.

Heavy forest, its character changing with the altitude, covers much of the park, its beauty marred only where forest fires have left scars; the forests west of the Divide are denser. At lower elevations grow Douglas fir, Colorado blue spruce, lodgepole pine, ponderosa pine, and aspen. On the higher levels are thick groves of Engelmann spruce, limber pine, Alpine fir, Arctic willow, and black birch. At approximately 11,000 feet a few straggling trees, twisted and bent by wind and ice, mark the upper limit of the forest.

More than 700 kinds of wild flowers brighten forest and valley floors. The columbine, the State flower, blooms here all summer—on the lower levels in June; on the higher, in September. Mariposa lilies, phlox, Indian paint brush, asters, and marigolds are found in abundance. In the high marshy regions are a few bog orchids.

Deer, elk, and Rocky Mountain or bighorn sheep are numerous. During summer they retreat to the heights and are seldom glimpsed. Colder weather drives them to lower levels, and they graze along the edges of the highway. The park still has a few bear and mountain lion—usually not seen—and there are numerous smaller animals. Aspen groves near streams are sources of food and building material for beavers. Woodchucks, squirrels, and chipmunks are so tame that they allow close approach. The chipmunk, an impudent little member of the squirrel family, can often be induced to eat from the hand. Within the park 283 species of birds have been noted. The bluebird, wren, hermit thrush, hummingbird, and white-crowned sparrow are summer visitors; the ouzel, Rocky Mountain jay, chickadee, woodpecker, and magpie are familiar year-round residents. Higher up live the rosy finch and the ptarmigan, its color changing to snow white in winter.

The climate of the park is mild for such great altitudes; the air is light and dry, and cloudy days are rare in summer. During the day the sun is frequently hot, but nights are always cool. Short mid-day showers are frequent, but there is no rainy season. Snowfall in the lower parks is light, but on the ranges it piles up in deep banks, ideal for winter sports.

PARK TOUR 1

Estes Park Village—Horseshoe Park—Hidden Valley—Milner Pass— (Grand Lake) ; 48.9 m., US 34 and Trail Ridge Road.

Milner Pass is usually blocked by snow in mid-winter.
Numerous campgrounds; good accommodations at Estes Park Village and Grand Lake Village.

Crossing Rocky Mountain National Park, the Trail Ridge Road (US 34) is one of the finest examples of mountain highway engineering in America. Unlike other roads that ascend mountain ranges by way of

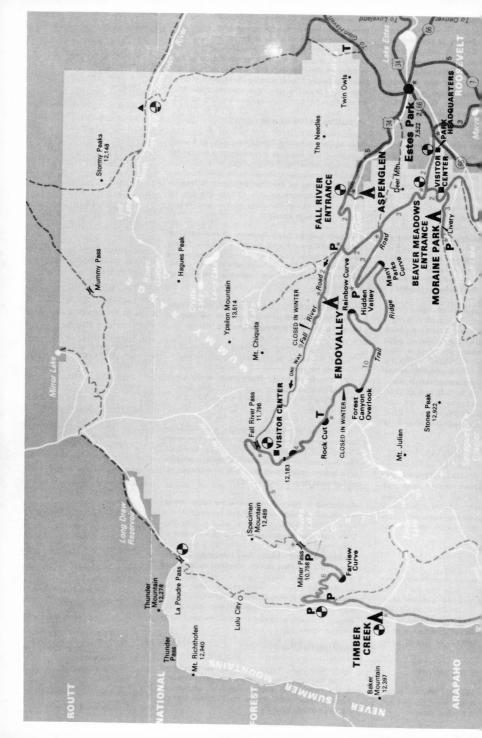

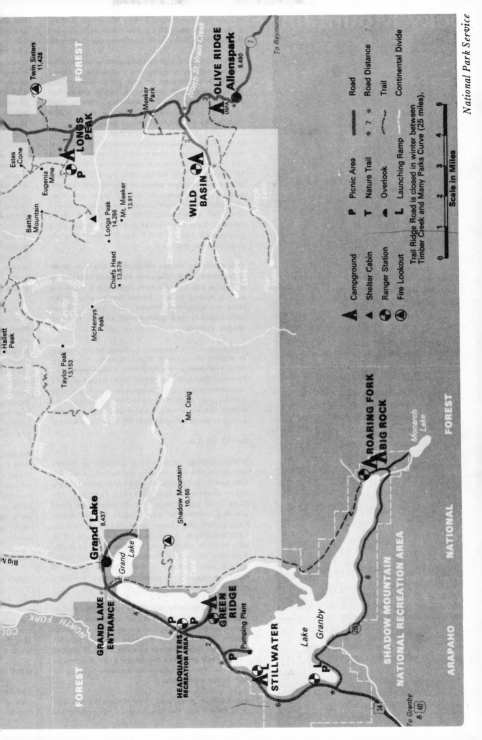

National Park Service

valleys and canyons, the trail makes its way upward to Milner Pass along the ridge tops, roughly following an old Ute trail. Much of the route is above timberline, affording magnificent views of great mountains, and rivers and valleys thousands of feet below.

ESTES PARK VILLAGE, 0 *m.* (7,500 alt., 1,518 pop.), lies in the narrow western neck of Estes Park (*see Tour 4*), almost surrounded by Rocky Mountain National Park. On all sides are densely forested hills, their slopes and craggy summits dotted with cabins and hotels. Although inhabited the year around, the village lives by its summer trade. Cars and parties on horseback or on foot throng the main street. Riding and hiking clothes are the fashion; fishing, camping, mountain climbing, and trail trips are engrossing topics of conversation. The village, and Estes Park itself, are commonly confused with Rocky Mountain National Park because so many visitors make the village, near-by hotels, dude ranches, and camps their headquarters.

ESTES PARK AERIAL TRAMWAY on Moraine Park Road, two blocks south of the village, rises to the top of Prospect Mtn., 8,896 ft.

Estes Park Village is at the junction with State 66, which enters the Park and connects with a road leading to Bear Lake (*see Park Tour 3*).

US 34 proceeds west by way of Fall River; few Colorado streams are more beautiful, and few spots more inviting than its valley. Passing a STATE FISH HATCHERY (*open 8–5 daily*), 3.6 *m.,* the highway moves past several public campgrounds to the FALL RIVER ENTRANCE TO ROCKY MOUNTAIN NATIONAL PARK, 4 *m.* Inside the gate, set in a deep aspen grove, is the BIG HORN RANGER STATION, housing rangers and their fire-fighting equipment. Within the park US 34 is known and marked as the Trail Ridge Road; dense growths of pine flank the highway.

HORSESHOE PARK, 5.5 *m.,* a high flat grassland where wild flowers bloom in profusion, was named for the shape of the valley. According to geologists, the valley once was the bed of a great lake, which accounts for the lack of forest here.

At 6 *m.* is the junction with the Fall River Road (*see Park Tour 2*).

West of the junction, the Trail Ridge Road, swinging left, ascends the side of a lateral moraine. Underfoot is a mass of gravel and smoothed spheroid rocks; the slopes are grass-covered, and the high inner banks of the highway have been sodded. During spring and summer the landscape is bright with wild flowers. The route crosses Hidden Valley Creek, trickling down the mountain through thickets of pine and willow herb, to DEER RIDGE, 8.9 *m.* (8,920 alt.), affording a wide view of the central and eastern portions of the park. Horseshoe Park and the broad grassland of Estes Park are spread at the foot of great mountains. Longs Peak, with its sheer granite face, lies to the south. Close at hand is the MUMMY RANGE, so called because its barren peaks suggest the form of a recumbent giant. Three of the peaks tower more than 13,000 feet. The mass of YPSILON MOUNTAIN (13,507 alt.), with its clearly defined "Y," is the most striking; to the north is MOUNT FAIR-CHILD (13,502 alt.); farther north, HAGUE'S PEAK (13,562 alt.). Deer Ridge is at the junction with a road from Moraine Park (*see Park Tour 3*).

West of Deer Ridge the highway follows Hidden Valley Creek through a timbered area. Evidence of the work of beavers appears, 10.8 *m.*, where aspens have been felled for use in construction of dams. Beavers sometimes draw logs along the ground for short distances, but, where possible, drop trees directly into the water and strip off the branches. The dams, chinked with mud, are so strongly built that men seeking to clear watercourses have been forced to use dynamite. Beavers use branches and mud in constructing their dome-shaped houses, about 40 of which appear in the valley. The beavers are extremely tame, and pay little heed to onlookers.

MANY PARKS CURVE, 12.9 *m.*, one of many overlooking spaces provided along Trail Ridge Road, presents a broad view of the mountains, forests, and valleys of the eastern part of the park. A populous colony of chipmunks, tiny squirrel-like animals with long bushy tails and five black-and-white stripes along their dun backs, inhabit the rocks and crannies near by. Impelled alike by curiosity and desire for food, they play along the rock retaining wall, close to visitors, a few being bold enough to take food from out-stretched hands.

HIDDEN VALLEY is a center for winter sports from December through April. Skiing, skating and snowshoeing are practiced. There are a lounge, and restrooms. A glacier-formed ridge separates the Valley from Horseshoe Park.

The road swings around Many Parks Curve to reveal (R) the gaunt bare peaks of the Mummy Range. They are, from south to north: Mount Chapin (12,458 alt.), Mount Chiquita (13,052 alt.), Ypsilon Mountain (13,507 alt.), Mount Fairchild (13,502 alt.), Hagues Peak (13,562 alt.), and Mummy Mountain (13,413 alt.); all lie east of the Continental Divide.

The highway climbs steadily, passing timberline several times within a short distance. Timberline varies considerably, being much lower on shaded than on sunlit slopes. The road reaches a point two miles above sea level (10,560 alt.), 16.6 *m.*, and at Rainbow Curve Overlook 17.2 *m.*, is an extensive view of the entire Mummy Range to the north. To the east lie the foothills of the main range, through which the highway enters the park; extending to the horizon are the plains stretching away like a vast blue sea.

TIMBERLINE (11,436 alt.), 19.3 *m.*, offers a view (L) of Stones Peak. Far to the south the granite cap of Longs Peak, highest in the park, is clearly distinguishable among its stalwart neighbors. Above timberline the road crosses a grassland dotted with bluebells and alpine flowers.

TOMBSTONE RIDGE (12,121 alt.), 22.3 *m.*, a jagged knife-like edge of dark purplish-red granite, thrusts up through the high meadow. West of the ridge is another overlook, with a view across Forest Canyon to the GORGE LAKES, tiny blue dots in the canyon. At the ROCK CUT a trail leads to the ROGER TOLL MEMORIAL.

From a long overlook, 24.6 *m.*, on the edge of a 500-foot precipice, ICEBERG LAKE (11,500 alt.) is seen below, held in a glacial cirque. The lake is fed by melting snowbanks, and during most of the summer great cakes of ice bob on its surface.

Ascending to the highest point on Trail Ridge Road (12,183 alt.), 25.1 *m.*, the highway offers a continuous view of great mountains, a succession of blue and purple masses. The rugged Gore Range (L), almost 60 miles distant, named for Sir George Gore, an Irishman who spent much of his life in the mountain country, has been only partly explored. Ahead are the bulks of the Never Summer Mountains, named for their perpetually snow-covered peaks. The jagged sawtooth outline of this range marks the western boundary of Rocky Mountain National Park for eight miles; within this distance are six peaks rising more than 12,000 feet. The principal summits are, from north to south: BAKER MOUNTAIN (12,406 alt.), MOUNT NIMBUS (12,730 alt.), RED MOUNTAIN (11,505 alt.), MOUNT CUMULUS (12,724 alt.), HOWARD MOUNTAIN (12,814 alt.), MOUNT CIRRUS (12,804 alt.), LEAD MOUNTAIN (12,532 alt.), MOUNT RICHTHOFEN (12,953 alt.), named for a German nobleman who planned a great summer resort in the Colorado mountains, and THUNDER MOUNTAIN (11,700 alt.). All but Red Mountain and Baker Mountain form part of the Continental Divide.

At the junction with the Fall River Road, 26.7 *m.*, is a view of mountains and distant plains. Directly ahead, through a notch in Specimen Mountain, looms the pyramidal peak of Mount Richthofen. In the background is the bleak, blue-and-white sky-line of the Never Summers; to the northwest are Clarks Peak and the distant Wyoming mountains. At the intersection is the ALPINE VISITORS CENTER of Fall River Pass, with exhibits revealing the geological evolution of the park. The first display shows the park as part of the ocean floor before the great upheaval; the second, the smooth rolling mountains after the upheaval; the park during the Ice Age is then shown; the final chart portrays its appearance after the recession of the ice masses, leaving the jagged canyons and moraines much as they are today. Other exhibits illustrate the life story of plants and animals of the high country.

North of the parking area the highway continues for some distance above timberline, then descends into the timber, prominent among the trees is the Engelmann spruce with its dark green foliage. Because of heavy rainfall the trees are taller and more thickly set here than elsewhere.

The highway crosses the Continental Divide at MILNER PASS (10,759 alt.), 31.1 *m.*, over which a transcontinental railroad was projected. At the top of the pass is POUDRE LAKE, the source of Cache la Poudre Creek, which flows east from the pass toward the Mississippi.

Poudre Lake is at the junction with a foot trail.

Right on this trail through dense forests to a fork, 0.5 *m.*, presenting a view of the CACHE LA POUDRE RIVER (R) winding through open grassland. Above timberline the trail ends, 1.1 *m.*, near the CRATER, an open jagged pit. Some of the blue and green crystal rock formations and glinting black obsidian here are as soft as beeswax; varicolored basalts and geodes contribute to the prismatic effects in the sunlight.

Crater is at the junction with a steep trail that ascends by way of the eastern ridge to the top of SPECIMEN MOUNTAIN (12,482 alt.), formed almost entirely of dark volcanic materials, the habitat of numerous species of wild animal life, including the shy bighorn sheep.

West of Poudre Lake the highway winds down a canyon between smooth hills covered by heavy forests. From an overlook at Far View Curve, 33.4 *m.*, the North Fork of the Colorado River can be seen flowing southward through beaver ponds. After curves the road reaches a Ranger Station and picnic areas. Farther south there are a Ranger Station and campgrounds where Timber Creek enters the Colorado River. The new PUBLIC INFORMATION BUILDING is located approximately 8 miles south of Timber Creek. The highway proceeds to the entrance of GRAND LAKE, and the SHADOW MOUNTAIN RECREATION AREA, 29 sq. m., also managed by the National Park Service.

The town of Grand Lake, on the north shore of the lake, (350 pop.) is a fishing center. The lake is the largest natural lake in Colorado. Granby Dam, 5½ *m.* northeast of Granby, Colo., stores water in LAKE GRANBY, capacity 539,080 acre-ft. From here water is pumped into SHADOW MOUNTAIN LAKE, capacity 18,400 acre-ft. Its outlet is Grand Lake, which sends water under the Continental Divide via the Alva B. Adams tunnel 13.1 *m.* long, part of the Colorado-Big Thompson Project, Bureau of Reclamation. There are campgrounds near the towns of Green Ridge and Stillwater.

Trail Ridge Road becomes US 34 (*see Tour 3*) at the western boundary of Rocky Mountain National Park, 48.9 *m.*, 17.6 miles north of Granby (7,935 alt., 600 pop.) (*see Tour 7*).

PARK TOUR 2

Estes Park—Aspenglen—Roaring River Trail—Fall River Pass—Junction Trail Ridge Road ; 11.9 *m.*, Fall River Road.

From Estes Park US 34 runs northwest 5 *m.* to the Fall River Entrance of Rocky Mountain National Park. A short road crosses the river to the ASPENGLEN campground. The highway continues through Horseshoe Park. At 2 *m.* is the junction with the Old Fall River Road.

At 1 *m.* is the junction with a trail.

Right on this trail 0.5 *m.* to a point where a break in the forest reveals Horseshoe Park (*see Park Tour 1*). At 1.7 *m.* the trail branches; L. here to YPSILON LAKE (10,600 alt.), 5 *m.*, walled in by high and precipitous rocks at the foot of Ypsilon Mountain; from the high stony rim a thin waterfall tumbles into the blue lake.

The right branch continues by easy grades along the bank of Roaring River through a dense stand of lodgepole pine. On the left are a number of cascades and strange rock formations. Beavers have dammed the stream at frequent intervals. As timberline is approached, the trees are dwarfed and twisted.

A Ranger Patrol Cabin of the Park Service stands on the shore of LAWN LAKE, 6.5 *m.,* (10,950 alt.), a cobalt-blue pool in a glacial cirque, with only a few trees to relieve its stark surroundings.

Here is the starting point for a number of hard climbs to near-by points of interest, but there are no marked trails. One leads to CRYSTAL LAKE, lying at the foot of Fairchild Peak to the south, the source of Roaring River, which flows into Lawn Lake.

On the north face of Hague Peak is ROWE GLACIER, formerly Hallets Glacier, an ice mass three-quarters of a mile wide, a third of a mile long, and of uncharted depth. The hike is difficult and should be attempted only by experienced climbers accompanied by guides.

The road crosses ROARING RIVER, 0.8 *m.,* a tributary of Fall River, which cascades from the heights (R).

Right on a marked trail to HORSESHOE FALLS, 0.6 *m.,* where Roaring River cascades 200 feet into Fall River Canyon through a cloud of rainbow-tinted mist; the spray from the falls has created a spot of unusual greenery much favored by picnic parties.

West of Roaring River the highway enters a thick aspen grove fringed on all sides by stands of ponderosa, or western yellow pine; these trees are often seven feet in circumference and attain an average height of 60 feet.

At 2 *m.* is the junction with a side road.

Left on this road to ENDOVALLEY CAMPGROUND, 0.2 *m.* (*free; fireplaces, sanitary facilities*).

The Fall River Road, an attractive drive, follows Fall River through its steep and narrow canyon; grades are steep. In the dense forests that blanket the hills are hidden lakes, waterfalls, streams, and picnic grounds. Along the route, reached by short trails branching from the main highway, are places of exceptional beauty.

The road begins a steep and steady ascent (*second or low gear*), and as greater altitudes are reached, a change in vegetation occurs. Engelmann spruce, with heavy dark-green needles and rough ruddy bark, and slender lodgepole pine grow in dense stands along the route. At intervals, through a break in the trees, are glimpses of high mountains overshadowing the canyon.

As the highway crosses CHIQUITA CREEK, 2.9 *m.,* there is a good view (L) of HANGING VALLEY. Geologists believe that ages ago this canyon and Fall River Canyon were on one level; but the Fall River Glacier, pushing down the main gorge, gouged it out so deep that the side canyon was left high up on the wall. Across the creek are pot holes, pits in granite rock, ground out by the swirling waters of the glacier.

The knoll in the center of the valley, 3 *m.,* is a *roche moutonée,* or sheeps-back, a hard rock ledge that defied the glacier to do more than polish its surface. Thick-standing lodgepole pines wall in the road; the almost solid mass of foliage completely shades the highway, and the air is chill even when the sun is overhead.

CHASM FALLS PARKING SPACE, 3.6 *m.,* overlooking Chasm Falls, is reached by a series of steep switchbacks affording constantly changing views of Horseshoe Park and the forested lower canyon.

Left from the parking space to CHASM FALLS, 50 *yds.,* where the sparkling waters of Fall River cascade 50 feet across tumbled rocks through a cloud of silvery mist. On all sides are giant pines and Englemann spruce.

A matted growth of wild raspberries, huckleberries, and willow shrubs renders the mountain slopes here almost impassable except by established trails. The forest has been slashed by numerous snow slides which carried away trees, underbrush, and everything in their way as they came crashing down draws and gulches to pile up in Fall River canyon, sometimes blocking stream and road. The highway ascends through a region of fantastic rock formations.

The highway reaches an altitude of two miles above sea level, 8.3 *m.,* passing timberline (11,300 alt.), 9.5 *m.* Here at first hand is the mute story of one of nature's enduring conflicts. In their struggle to survive at this altitude trees are bent into grotesque shapes; frequently all limbs point in one direction; trunks are occasionally twisted in a complete circle. Beyond these last outposts of the forest is nothing but rock and grassland. In summer this grassland is the pasture of deer, elk, and bighorn sheep frequently seen at a distance, but in winter it is buried under heavy snows; drifts often pile up to a depth of 30 feet, forcing animals to pasture in the valleys.

At 11.9 *m.* is the junction with Trail Ridge Road (*see Park Tour 1*).

PARK TOUR 3

Estes Park Village—Moraine Park—Glacier Basin Campground—Bierstadt Lake; 11.1 *m.,* Bear Lake Road.

This tour traverses a section of the Big Thompson Valley, presenting ever changing vistas of the Continental Divide. At times the clear stream paralleling the road is lined with fisherman; others wade out to cast flies into deep pools.

From Estes Park follow Route 66 2 *m.* to PARK HEADQUARTERS and INFORMATION STATION. Continue .3 *m.* through BEAVER MEADOWS ENTRANCE STATION and turn left .1 *m.* at Bear Lake Road Jctn. Then

1 *m.* farther to MORAINE PARK VISITOR CENTER (L) and MORAINE PARK CAMPGROUND (R).

Moraine Park is an open valley on the Big Thompson River, with camp-grounds, a picnic area, and a livery. To the south is a great moraine of rock and debris carried down the valley by glaciers. This 2,500-acre park is cov-ered with a thick matting of grass, a favorite pasture for deer and elk during the fall, when snow drives them from the higher ranges. In these months it is not unusual to come upon herds of these animals along the road.

Bear Lake Road winds through Tuxedo Park and along Mill Creek (L) to Hallowell Park, 5.6 *m.,* another open grassland, once the path-way of glacial masses.

At 6.9 *m.* is the junction.

Left on this road 0.1 *m.* to the GLACIER BASIN, with campgrounds and Ranger Station, where park naturalists lecture on local flora and fauna.

The highway remains well up on the hillsides among thick lodgepole pine and aspen. From the curves and occasional open places the great peaks of the park are sighted, dominated by Longs Peak, which stands well apart from the main range to the south. In front of Longs Peak and slightly to the east is MT. LADY WASHINGTON (13,269 alt.); to the east (L) of the highway are the TWIN SISTERS (11,436 and 11,438 alt.), outside the park.

At 9 *m.* is the junction with a marked trail.

Right on this trail on a stiff zigzag climb to the top of a moraine, 1.1 *m.;* here the trail descends through a forest of lodgepole pine to BIERSTADT LAKE, 1.3 *m.,* named for Albert Bierstadt, the painter, and turns northwest (L) along abandoned Mill Creek Road. It reaches the summit of a ridge, 3.1 *m.,* from which appears (R) CUB LAKE, a tiny body of water far below.

The Bear Lake Road ascends steadily; green forests mantle the hills in all directions; tiny lakes and pools dot parks and valleys; numerous streams, like silver threads, appear and disappear in the changing vista.

BEAR LAKE (8,700 alt.), 11.1 *m.,* is hemmed in by towering sum-mits, but its beauty is marred by the effects of a fire that swept the slopes many years ago. Here is the BEAR LAKE RANGER STATION, the starting point for hiking or horseback trips to Loch Vale (*see Trail Tour 2*), Fern Lake (*see Trail Tour 3*), and Grand Lake (*see Trail Tour 4*).

TRAIL TOUR 1

Longs Peak Campground—Chasm Lake—Mills Moraine—Keyhole—Summit of Longs Peak; 7.4 *m.,* Longs Peak Trail.

Longs Peak Campground to Boulder Field: on foot 3½ hrs.; on horseback, 1¾ hrs.; Boulder Field to Summit: on foot only, 2½ hrs.

Climb beyond Boulder Field is difficult and dangerous in places; guide service advisable.

The summit of Longs Peak (14,256 alt.), the highest in Rocky Mountain National Park, is the goal of hundreds who visit the park each summer. Parties are organized throughout the summer.

This principal trail to the summit of Longs Peak starts at LONGS PEAK CAMPGROUND, 0 *m.*, reached by a side road branching west from State 7 (*see Tour 4*), 8.8 miles south of Estes Park Village (*see Tour 3 and Park Tour 1*). Some climbers drive to the campground and remain overnight to start up the trail at dawn.

West of the campground the grade is easy; few of the higher peaks are visible; as heavy forest shades the trail, this part of the trip is usually chilly until the sun is well up.

The trail makes a switchback near ALPINE BROOK, 0.9 *m.*, and climbs from the valley. The many small brooks here, all cold and pure, have their headwaters in the high recesses of Longs Peak. The trail crosses LARKSPUR CREEK, 1.6 *m.*, which tumbles down a timbered valley from the north, and Alpine Brook, 2.4 *m.*, spanned by a log bridge.

At 2.6 *m.* is the junction with another trail.

Left on this trail to CHASM LAKE (*shelter cabin*), 2 *m.*, a wind-riffled pool magnificently set in Chasm Gorge at the foot of the sheer 2,000-foot northern face of Longs Peak. East from the lake is a broad view of foothills and timbered slopes as they drop away to the plains.

The trail ascends sharply to the crest of a high lateral moraine, 3 *m.*, known locally as MILLS MORAINE, for Enos Mills, naturalist and author, who did much to publicize the park. The trail continues along the top of the moraine to GRANITE PASS, 4.5 *m.*; winding through this rocky cleft, it ascends above timberline to the lower edge of the BOULDER FIELD, 5.5 *m.*, a mass of broken fragments of dark-red granite.

At the end of the horse trail (11,200 alt.), 6.4 *m.*, formerly stood a Government-supervised lodge. Movement of the moraine under the lodge cracked the structure, rendering it dangerous.

Left from the Boulder Field, the CABLE COURSE, known also as the North Face Route (*for experienced mountaineers only*), an alternate route to the summit, ascends the sheer northeastern face of the peak. Climbers make the ascent over ledges and perilous declivities, guided and aided by a stout cable. This route offers a half mile of strenuous and exciting climbing.

The safest route from Boulder Field to the summit is through the KEYHOLE (*storm shelter*), a great notch in the face of the mountain at the upper extremity of Boulder Field. Once through the Keyhole, the trail follows THE LEDGE, a narrow rock shelf, traverses an ice-filled gully, known as THE TROUGH, and crosses THE NARROWS, a thin and difficult ledge. Finally, The HOME STRETCH, a steep incline, leads to the

SUMMIT OF LONGS PEAK (14,256 alt.), 4.7 *m.* Those making the climb record their names in a register here.

The view from the top of Longs Peak is spectacular. More than 2,000 feet below, Chasm Lake, fed by melting snows, appears as a Lilliputian pond in its craggy setting. Rising from the lake's northern shore is MOUNT LADY WASHINGTON (13,269 alt.). Southwest from the peak is the little-explored WILD BASIN, at the headwaters of the St. Vrain River. To the west the great peaks of the Continental Divide rise in bold relief, while to the east is the vista of foothills and plains, stretching away in blue haze to the horizon.

TRAIL TOUR 2

Bear Lake—Lake Mills—Glacier Gorge—Loch Vale; 2.6 *m.,* Loch Vale Trail.

This trail to one of the most beautiful lakes in Rock Mountain National Park starts at the GLACIER GORGE PARKING AREA, 0 *m.,* 1 mile north of the Bear Lake Ranger Station (*see Park Tour 3*), and follows the valley of GLACIER CREEK in a southwesterly direction.

The trail winds through a rugged fire-swept region where gaunt white tree trunks stand as ghostly reminders that one careless moment can destroy a century-old forest. Peaks visible here, from right to left, are: Flattop, Hallett, Otis, Taylor, Thatchtop, and Chiefs Head; all are part of the Continental Divide and rise above 12,000 feet. At 1 *m.* is a fine view of the MUMMY RANGE (*see Park Tour 1*) to the northwest. To the east spreads out the great glacial valley of Moraine Park (*see Park Tour 3*). The trail passes ALBERTA FALLS (L), 1.6 *m.,* a small cascade on Glacier Creek, a glittering fan of water dropping from the lip of a stone ledge above.

At 2.1 *m.* is the junction with the Glacier Gorge Trail.

Left on this trail across a branch of Glacier Creek and up a steep ridge; the route is marked by several cairns, small heaps of stone piled at regular intervals to serve as guide posts.

LAKE MILLS, 0.4 *m.,* mirrors in its clear waters a scene of wild beauty. South of the lake opens the great rift of GLACIER GORGE, gouged out by ancient ice floes. Walled in by Longs Peak (L) and Thatchtop and McHenrys Peak (R), the gorge lies between high jutting cliffs, broken and torn, crowned with fantastic battlements. JEWEL LAKE adjoins Lake Mills on the south.

Left, on a pathway along the southern edge of Lake Mills to BLACK LAKE, 3.1 *m.,* lying at the upper end of the canyon, set high in the shadow of McHenrys Peak, and fed by melting ice from year-round snowbanks.

At the junction with the Glacier Gorge Trail is an impressive view of the west face of Longs Peak (*see Trail Tour 1*) and the Keyhole through which one trail leads to the summit. The grade becomes steeper, necessitating several switchbacks. Along this stretch the outlet of The Loch (*see below*) cascades downward through heavy pine forest.

The trail ends at THE LOCH, 2.6 *m.,* a shining body of water, jade green and placid, lying in the center of Loch Vale, a glacier-watered valley about three miles long, surrounded by heavy forests and honey-colored cliffs that rise to breath-taking heights. The open glades are tapestries of wild flowers; here columbine grows in profusion. To the south (L) is the sloping cone of THATCHTOP MOUNTAIN (12,800 alt.), and beyond rears the bulk of TAYLOR PEAK (13,150 alt.), slashed by the white ribbon of TAYLOR GLACIER. In the center of Loch Vale is CATHEDRAL WALL; and to the extreme right is OTIS PEAK (12,478 alt.). Between Taylor and Otis Peaks, and right of Cathedral Wall, ANDREWS GLACIER, another ice mass, moves down a steep-walled gorge; its slowly melting waters join Icy Brook from Taylor Glacier above The Loch; the brook connects the three lakes in Loch Vale.

TRAIL TOUR 3

Bear Lake Ranger Station—Bierstadt Moraine—Odessa Lake—Fern Lake; 5.2 m., Fern Lake Trail.

Time: on foot, 4 hrs.; on horseback, 2 hrs.

Branching southwest from BEAR LAKE RANGER STATION, 0 m. (see Park Tour 3), this trail skirts the northern shore of Bear Lake and turns (R) in a steep climb, with several switchbacks, to the top of BIERSTADT MORAINE. Masses of aspen and small pine saplings grow among the rotting white trunks of trees destroyed long ago by fire.

At 0.5 m. is a junction with a side trail.

Right on this trail to BIERSTADT LAKE, 4 m. (see Park Tour 3).

The trail enters dense forest; at intervals stand Engelmann spruce, frequently mistaken for Colorado blue spruce, which it somewhat resembles in its form and its bluish-silver coloring. The latter, however, grows in moist river valleys and foothill canyons at altitudes of less than 8,600 feet.

At 1 m. is the junction (L) with the Flattop Trail (see Trail Tour 4).

Above timberline, 1.5 m., marked by a fringe of dwarfed and deformed trees, stretches a rocky open meadow, along which the descending trail winds through spruce and aromatic balsam fir. The curiously elongated mountains, known as the Mummy Range (see Park Tour 1), appear to the north. The trail crosses a mass of shattered rock dislodged from the upper cliffs; a log footbridge spans the eastern outlet of Two Rivers Lake. Winding through heavy timber for half a mile, the trail reaches the shore of TWO RIVERS LAKE, 2.8 m., little more than a pool. Passing LAKE HELENE, 3 m., another small pool, the trail crosses the valley in two switchbacks and descends into a wooded valley.

At 3.5 m. is the junction with a side trail.

Left on this trail to ODESSA LAKE, 0.2 *m.,* above timberline, its blue surface reflecting the grandeur of the encircling peaks. This lake and its companion, Fern Lake (*see below*), lie in the heart of a country of spectacular canyons that gash the eastern slope of the Continental Divide.

The trail parallels Fern Creek to FERN LAKE, 5.2 *m.,* smaller than Odessa, in a setting of spruce and pine.

TRAIL TOUR 4

Bear Lake—Flattop Mountain—Tyndall Glacier—Grand Lake; 16.5 *m.,* Flattop Trail.

Time: on foot, 1 day; on horseback, 6 hrs.

This partly improved trail, which follows a route laid out years ago by the Indians, is the shortest route across Rocky Mountain National Park from east to west.

Branching west from FERN LAKE TRAIL (*see Trail Tour 3*), 0 *m.,* 1 mile north of Bear Lake (*see Trail Tour* 3), Flattop Trail crosses a narrow forest burn and ascends the steep but even slopes of BIER-STADT MORAINE. From a long switchback, 1.3 *m.,* overlooking (L) Dream Lake, is a view to the south (L) of HALLETT PEAK (12,725 alt.), a barren stone mass flanked by the white expanse of Tyndall Glacier; to the north (R) looms Flattop Mountain. The trail pursues a winding course through heavy timber, emerging briefly into a clearing with a view of the north face of Longs Peak (*see Trail Tour 1*); here is (R) a trail marker.

The ascent to timberline, 2.5 *m.,* is rapid. As the forest thins, the trail crosses a grassy meadow dotted with high mountain shrubs. The trail, marked by cairns, swings to the edge of a deep glacial gorge walled in by sheer cliffs that drop away to the green waters of Emerald Lake far below; at the head of the gorge lies Tyndall Glacier (*see below*).

North of the gorge is an almost continuous rise to the SUMMIT OF FLATTOP MOUNTAIN (12,300 alt.). The trail, still marked by cairns, is noteworthy for its fine views of mountains and lakes. To the east are the rolling foothills around Estes Park; to the south, the spire of Longs Peak; to the southwest, the jagged peaks of the Gore Range in a purple haze; to the west and north, the Never Summer Mountains and the Mummy Range.

The trail reaches the head of TYNDALL GLACIER (12,200 alt.), 4.5 *m.,* where ice of unknown depth spreads along the shattered mountain walls.

Left from the glacier a poorly marked trail crosses broken rocky slopes along the southern edge of the gorge to the SUMMIT OF HALLETT PEAK (12,725 alt.).

At 5 *m.*, the highest point on the trail, is the junction with the Toha-hutu Creek Trail.

Right on this circuitous route, which leads through a wild region, to GRAND LAKE VILLAGE, 17 *m.* (*see Tour 3*).

The zigzag trail descends abruptly, 6 *m.*, to cross grassy meadows of the highlands; thick willow growths give way to towering pines. A sign, 7.3 *m.*, points the way across a stream to a SHELTER CABIN (*not open to public*).

The trail proceeds dense forests along the valley of the North Inlet of Grand Lake to a junction with a side trail, 8.9 *m.*

Left on this trail, which crosses a swampy meadowland, fords a tributary of the North Inlet, and passes an unnamed lake, 1.2 *m.*, to LAKE NOKONI (*fishing*), 2.4 *m.*, just below timberline.

At 9.5 *m.* is a junction with a side trail.

Left on this trail to LAKE NANITA, 2 *m.*, another excellent fishing spot.

Flattop Trail continues down the valley of the North Inlet, passing (L) CASCADE FALLS, 12 *m.* At 14.9 *m.* is the junction (L) with a secondary road, which the route now follows, crossing the boundary of the Rocky Mountain National Park, 16 *m.*

The trail terminates at GRAND LAKE VILLAGE, 16.5 *m.* (8,369 alt., 350 pop.).

Grand Lake since 1952 has been part of the Colorado-Big Thompson Project of the U. S. Bureau of Reclamation. Its waters supply the Alva B. Adams Tunnel, 9 ft. 9 in. in diameter, 13.1 *m.* long through the Continental Divide, to a point 4.5 *m.* southwest of Estes Park. Grand Lake also gets water from Shadow Mountain Lake and Lake Granby, two units of the Shadow Mountain Lake Recreation Area created by dams erected as part of the Colorado-Big Thompson Project.

Mesa Verde National Park

Season: May 15 to Oct. 15. Interpretative services, June 15 through Labor Day. Oct. 15 to mid-May: snack bar and groceries available.

Administration: National Park Service, U. S. Dept. of the Interior. Address of Superintendent is Mesa Verde National Park, Colorado, 81330.

Entrance and Highways: Enter from US 160, 8 *m.* west of Mancos, or 10 *m.* east of Cortez. Park headquarters is 21 *m.* from entrance. The Morfield Campground is 6 *m.* from the entrance; the Navajo Hill Visitor Center 14 *m.* Visitors are urged to go first to the Center during the summer and to Chapin Mesa Museum the rest of the year for planning their trips with the help of attendants. There are scheduled flights to Durango and Cortez, bus service from Durango. Railroads stop at Grand Junction, Colo., and Gallup, N. M. Rent-a-car service is available at airline and rail terminals.

Accommodations: Far View Lodge at Navajo Hill operates motel and cabins during summer; address the Mesa Verde Co. for reservations. Morfield Campground, for tent and trailer camping, April 1 to Nov. 1, supplies at Morfield Village store. No utility hookup for trailers. Summer camping limited to 14 days, June 1 to September 7.

Special Attractions: Arts and crafts of Indians shown at Chapin Mesa Museum. Trips through ruins guided by Rangers scheduled in summer; in winter they go only to Spruce Tree House. Campfire lectures, June to September. Horseback riding, June–September, write MV Pack & Saddle Horse Co. Religious services Sunday morning and evening at Campfire Circle, Park hq, and Morfield Village.

Services: Mail should be sent to General Delivery, Mesa Verde National Park or to Far View Lodge if a guest there. Messages are received at Far View Lodge, Navajo Hill Visitor Center, or Far View Terrace. Telephones at Far View Terrace and Chapin Mesa Museum parking area. Bus transportation to ruins by Far View Lodge. Service stations at Morfield Village and Navajo Hill Museums and gift shops at Morfield Village and Far View Terrace. Showers and laundry at Morfield Village and Plaza Area.

Regulations: Visitors must let wildlife alone. Firearms must be declared on entering Park and cannot be used. Pets must be restrained. Do not disturb wildflowers, fossils, or prehistoric objects. Do not throw cigarettes, matches, from car; in times of emergency smoking in vehicles is prohibited.

The MESA VERDE NATIONAL PARK includes 50,275 acres of canyons and mesa lands set aside by the Congress in 1906 for the preservation of its many ancient cliff dwellings and surface pueblos. Mesa Verde (Sp. green table) is itself a great mound of earth and rock about 15 miles long and 8 miles wide; on the north it rises abruptly 2,000 feet above Montezuma Valley. South of this rim is a sloping expanse cut by deep and almost parallel canyons caused by heavy spring rains running off into the Mancos River. The mesa terminates at the south in a series of bluffs more than 1,000 feet high. Along the walls of the canyons are found the most spectacular cliff dwellings.

The first recorded observation of the Mesa Verde region was made by Padre Escalante in 1776 while seeking a short route from New Mexico to the Spanish missions in California. Escalante noted the crumbling ruins throughout this area; although he did not climb the great mesa, he bestowed upon it its descriptive name.

One of the earliest archeological explorations was made by W. H. Jackson under the auspices of the Federal Government in 1874, but he and his party did not discover any of the larger ruins. In a dramatic discovery in 1888, Richard Wetherill and Charlie Mason, two cattlemen who had come on horseback to Sun Point, looked across a deep canyon and saw with amazement the great structure of Cliff Palace nestled in a cave high on the opposite wall. Word of this discovery inspired Baron Gustav Nordenskiold's exploration in 1891. Nordenskiold investigated many of the ruins, including Spruce Tree House, and assembled a large collection of Indian pottery and artifacts which he sent to Sweden. Although intended for the Royal Museum at Stockholm, the collection remained in warehouses until 1938 when it was removed to a museum at Helsinki, Finland. Subsequent explorations, most of them conducted by the late Dr. J. Walter Fewkes, once chief of the Bureau of American Ethnology, established many facts about the vanished race of "little people" who constructed the immense and beautiful dwellings in great crevices along the canyon walls. As yet, only relatively few of the several hundred known cliff dwellings and pueblos in the park have been excavated.

The original occupants of the natural caves on Mesa Verde, it is believed, were primitive Mongoloid hunters who used them as temporary shelters after their migration from Asia to Alaska by way of the Aleutian Islands some ten to twelve thousand years ago. The race made slow progress for several thousand years, and not until they learned to grow maize and other plants did any great change occur.

The Basket Makers are the earliest people known to have permanently settled on Mesa Verde, as early as 500 B.C. These long-headed people constructed circular subterranean rooms both in the caves and on the mesa tops. In time rectangular lines supplanted circular forms; the one-room units were enlarged and joined to others.

About 1000 A.D. an alien people absorbed or supplanted the Basket Makers. These were Pueblo Indians who eventually built the stone cliff houses that are their monuments. They first lived on top of the mesa, then built their stone houses along the face of cliffs almost impossible to ascend. It is believed they built under the cliffs for protection against marauding bands. They used sandstone blocks broken from rock sheets on the mesa top. Although they had no metal they made stone instruments that were most effective. Their men were 5 ft. 6 in. to 5 ft. 9 in. tall. Their infants were strapped to boards that flattened their heads.

The Pueblo were able farmers; they grew corn on the dry mesa tops, and beans, squash, and cotton on the moister canyon floors. They gathered the prickly pear, removed the spines, and ate the flesh raw or roasted. They shot and ate wild turkey; they also domesticated the turkey which was raised primarily for its plumage for use in making feather blankets, clothing, and personal ornaments. They wove cloth from cotton and yucca fibers.

The men were hunters and weavers; looms have been found in the ceremonial rooms forbidden to women. From the bows, arrows, spears, stone balls, and axes that have been uncovered, and from the fortified entrances to the cliff houses, it is evident that these people could and did fight when forced to.

The women were the millers, bakers, and pottery makers of the communities, and apparently assisted in constructing the buildings. The clay found between sandstone strata was fashioned into excellent pottery. Walls were coated with puddled earth plastered on with rocks and hands; fingerprints of workers still remain on many of the walls. Occasionally a white paint, made of powdered gypsum mixed with water, was applied with grass or cedar bark brushes. The Cliff Dwellers had no written language, but pictographs on the stone walls, baskets, and pottery reveal a high artistic sense.

Archeologists have deduced that the Cliff Dwellers were undone by sand and drought. Corn, the staple of their diet, was ground to meal with instruments made of the prevailing soft sandstone of the mesa country. As this stone wears with rubbing, much sand found its way into the meal and gradually wore down teeth to the gums, as evidenced in almost all skeletons discovered. Bad teeth doubtless caused gastric disorders and severe attacks of rheumatism; after the age of 30, so scientists believe, the Cliff Dwellers suffered constant ill health.

The Cliff Dwellers, it has been definitely established, occupied Mesa Verde and the surrounding country into the thirteenth century. Probably the great drought between 1276 and 1299 drove them from Mesa Verde, and their fate remains something of a mystery. They may have been absorbed by other Pueblo communities in the Southwest; they may have been decimated by more warlike Indians; some anthropologists believe that the present New Mexico and Arizona tribes are descendants of the prehistoric people who left fascinating evidences of their culture here on Mesa Verde.

MESA VERDE PARK TOUR 1

Junction US 160—Point Lookout—Park Point—Far View Ruins—Park Headquarters—Spruce Tree House; 20 m., Park Road.

The entrance to Mesa Verde National Park is located on US 160, 8 m. west of Mancos and 10 m. east of Cortez, at an elevation of 6,964 ft. The visitor sees, first, POINT LOOKOUT, a promotory, 8,428 ft., 2.2 m., beyond which is the MANCOS VALLEY OVERLOOK, with remarkable views. At 4 *m.* is the head of MORFIELD CANYON. The Knife Edge, a great bulwark of rock created by erosion, overlooks Montezuma Valley at the left, 5.5 *m.* At 6 *m.* right, is MORFIELD CAMPGROUND and Village. Here is room for tent and trailer camping (*April-November*). Fuel and carry-out food may be obtained at the village store; gas station.

The highway, though at a great height, is well protected and safe for the careful driver. Here are wide views of the valley, its mountainous background revealed at almost every turn.

Prater Canyon, 6.3 *m.,* contains numerous ruins, the majority of the pueblo type.

At 10 *m.* is the junction with a graveled road.

Right on this road to PARK POINT (8,575 alt.), 0.9 *m.,* highest elevation in Mesa Verde National Park, and offering the finest lookout. On clear days parts of four States can be seen. In the foreground, 2,000 feet below, is the green lake-dotted Montezuma Valley; beyond, to the north, rise the great shafts of the Rico Mountains. Westward, 80 miles away, are the Blue Mountains and La Sals of Utah; and southwest, a distance of 115 miles, the Black Mesa in Arizona. Here is probably the finest view of Shiprock, 40 miles to the south of the Navaho Reservation, New Mexico; rising abruptly from the middle of a great plain to a height of 1,860 feet, this great bulk of igneous rock presents a startling illusion of an old ship under full head of sail. Shiprock is best seen in the evening or early morning. Park Point overlooks the whole of Mesa Verde, affording an extensive view of the canyons that cut southward to the Mancos River.

At 14 *m.* the Park highway reaches NAVAJO HILL VISITOR CENTER (*open 8–7:30, mid-June to Labor Day*). The Mesa Verde Company operates Far View Lodge at Navajo Hill, with motel units, restaurant; summer reservations advisable.

At 15.4 *m.* is the junction with an improved road.

Left on this road to the FAR VIEW GROUP of ruins, 0.2 *m.,* also known as the Mummy Lake Group for the reservoir-like depression on the slope above them. Mummy Lake was not used as a reservoir by the Pueblo, but drainage ditches leading into it indicate that early cowmen attempted to store water here for their stock. The Far View ruins are closely grouped, probably for protection. Although surface structures, they are of the same culture as the cliff dwellings, but pottery found in them shows them to be of earlier construction.

FAR VIEW HOUSE, first of the group excavated, has an exceptionally large central *kiva,* 32 feet in diameter, around which are grouped smaller ones. The large *kiva,* it has been suggested, was a central meeting place for the several clans that lived here—a plan sometimes adopted in pueblos having large *kivas.* Far View House was originally three stories high at the north end and one story high at the south. Around the *kivas* were living and storage room. The walled court at the south was used for religious dances and festivals.

One hundred feet southeast of the structure is a CLIFF DWELLERS CEMETERY, also used as a rubbish heap, for the Pueblo interred their dead in piles of refuse; the bodies were almost always buried in a flexed position, often wrapped in turkey-feather blankets or a shroud of reeds, and surrounded with pottery. Several skeletons and pieces of pottery have been found here.

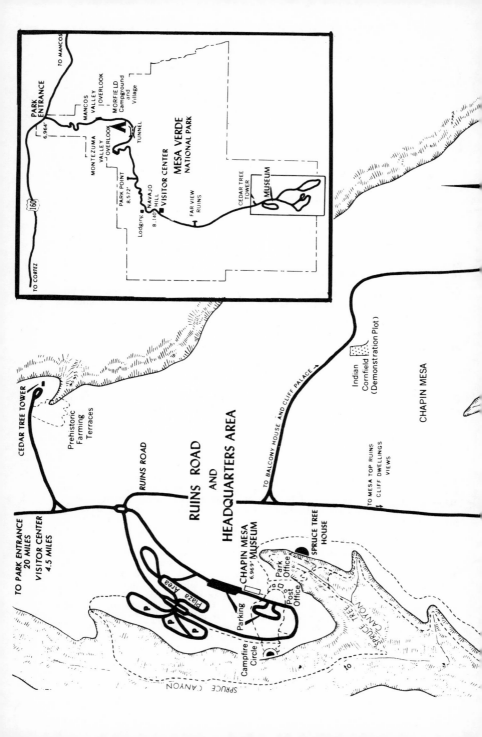

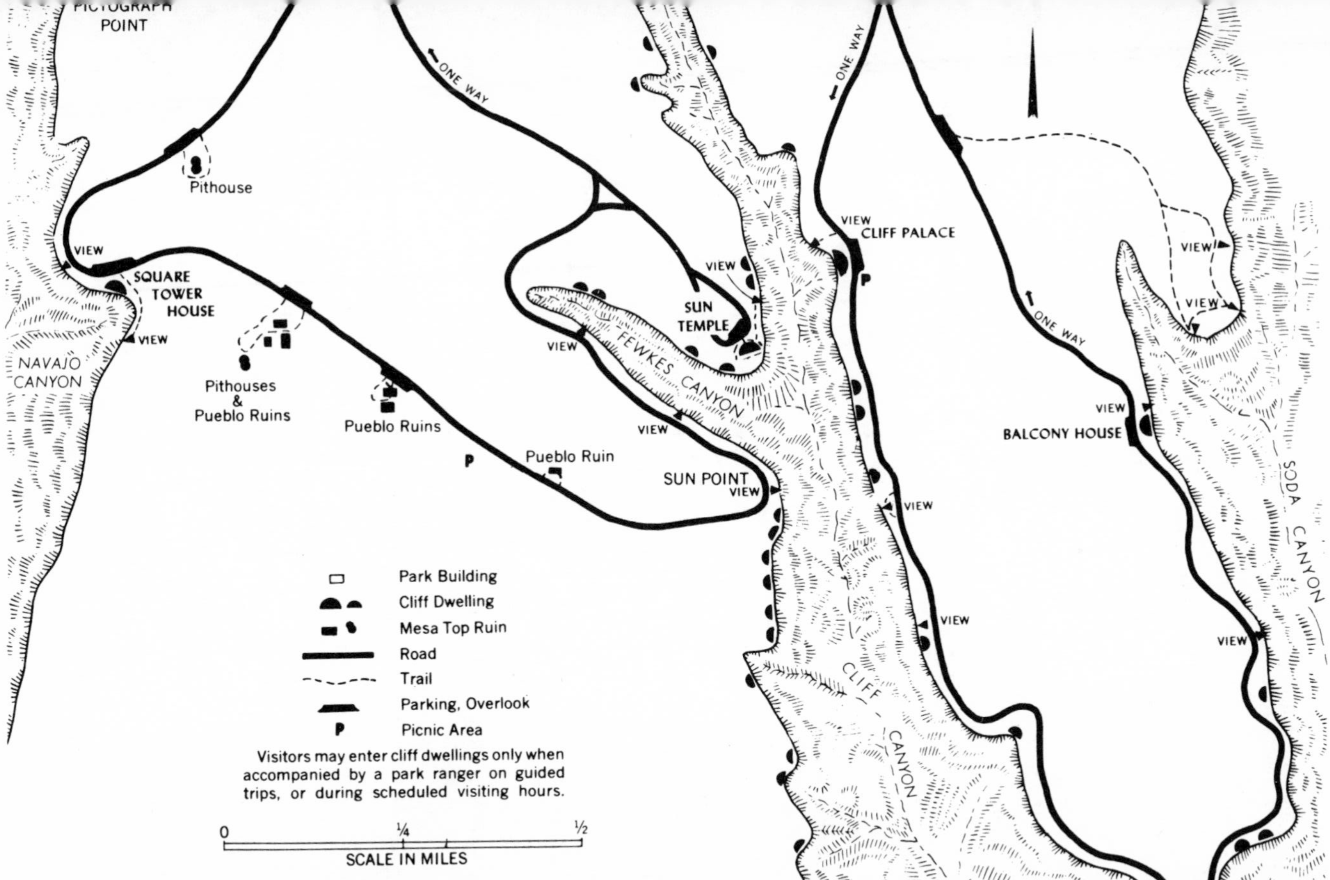

PICTOGRAPH POINT
ONE WAY
ONE WAY
ONE WAY
Pithouse
VIEW
SQUARE TOWER HOUSE
VIEW
NAVAJO CANYON
Pithouses & Pueblo Ruins
Pueblo Ruins
P
Pueblo Ruin
VIEW
FEWKES CANYON
VIEW
SUN TEMPLE
VIEW
SUN POINT
VIEW
CLIFF PALACE
VIEW
P
VIEW
VIEW
CLIFF CANYON
VIEW
BALCONY HOUSE
VIEW
VIEW
VIEW
SODA CANYON
Park Building
Cliff Dwelling
Mesa Top Ruin
Road
Trail
Parking, Overlook
Picnic Area
Visitors may enter cliff dwellings only when accompanied by a park ranger on guided trips, or during scheduled visiting hours.
0
1/4
1/2
SCALE IN MILES

National Park Service

In the partly excavated ruin of FAR VIEW TOWER, 200 feet north of Far View House evidences of later or secondary construction have been found. Three *kivas* have been excavated.

One of the oldest houses in the group is MEGALITHIC HOUSE, 100 yards north of Far View Tower, containing a *kiva* surrounded by rectangular rooms; the house may have been constructed earlier than the larger pueblos, as suggested by pottery findings. Crumbled walls and lack of debris indicate that parts of the house were torn down for use in other buildings. The foundations of some walls were built of stones three feet long and eight to ten inches wide, but the house itself was constructed of smaller stones.

PIPE SHRINE HOUSE, 200 feet south of Far View House, is believed to have been built earlier than Far View but later than other buildings of the group. The house, similar in design to Far View, was excavated in 1922. Eleven long clay pipes were found in one of the *kivas,* indicating that tobacco or a similar plant was used in religious ceremonies. Bowls and jars have also been found here.

ONE CLAN HOUSE, 0.3 miles southeast of Far View on the rim of Soda Canyon, contains a single large deep *kiva;* only one clan is believed to have lived here.

South of the junction the highway traverses more open country. Most of the Mesa Verde ruins lie to the south where the land was more suitable for farming, being less encumbered with scrub oak.

At 18.5 *m.* is the junction with an improved road.

Left on this road to CEDAR TREE TOWER, 0.6 *m.,* hidden in the timber on the rim of Soda Canyon. This ruin, 12 feet high, is similar in age and type to Far View Tower. Connected by tunnels with the base of the tower, which is of excellent masonry and massive character, are two subterranean chambers; one a *kiva,* the other a small square room. In the solid rock floor of the tower is a circular hole known as the *sipapu,* believed to be symbolic of the entrance to the underworld; the term is of Hopi origin.

From Cedar Tree Tower a trail (*hazardous*) descends the canyon 100 yards to PAINTED KIVA, a cliff dwelling, its walls highly decorated with pictographs and symbols, probably of religious significance.

The highway follows a spur of Chapin Mesa to PARK HEADQUARTERS, 20 *m.,* starting point for motor trips (*only under supervision of official guides*) to the major ruins on Chapin Mesa and supervised pack trips to the little known ruins along Wildhorse and Wetherill Mesas to the west.

In the CHAPIN MESA MUSEUM (*8–7:30 in summer, 8–5 rest of year*) are exhibited Cliff Dweller and Basket Maker materials, as well as examples of arts and crafts of modern Southwestern Indians, all arranged in chronological order. A series of miniature caves with wax figures picture the five phases of Mesa Verde culture. One room has been set aside for exhibits of the geology, flora, and fauna of the park. The museum has a reference library on the archeology and natural history of this region (*apply to museum assistant; books not to be removed from reading room*). Nearby are the PARK OFFICE and the POSTOFFICE.

Each evening during the season members of the park staff, and often visiting scientists, lecture informally on the archeology of the Mesa Verde region at the CAMPFIRE CIRCLE. After the talks Navaho Indians employed in the park dance for a small fee.

Left from the Park Headquarters on a foot trail across Spruce Tree Canyon to SPRUCE TREE HOUSE (ranger on duty), 300 yds., in view of the headquarters buildings. This house, 216 feet long and approximately 89 feet wide, one of the largest in the park, was a village in itself. An estimated population of 200 inhabited its 122 rooms; eight were kivas, and fourteen apparently were storage rooms. The walls here, as in few cliff dwellings, were raised to the top of the cave, which served as a roof for the higher chambers. The masonry work is exceptionally fine and well preserved; stones were smoothed and laid with great care; some of the walls were plastered with red mortar, a color also used for paintings and decorations. The village had a "street," a court opening from the front to the back of the cave, near the center. As few of the rooms had fireplaces, it is assumed that most of the cooking was done in small courts and passageways. Roofs of two of the eight kivas have been restored on the pattern of those found in fairly good condition at Square Tower House (see Park Tour 1). Visitors can descend by ladders into the chambers.

The kivas, typical of those found throughout Mesa Verde, ranged from twelve to fifteen feet in diameter; those in the surface structures were slightly larger. A narrow ledge or banquette, about three feet above the floor and broader on the south side, ran around the ceremonial room; its use has not been definitely established. The head-high roof, rising from the banquette, supported by six stone buttresses or pilasters, was made of horizontal beams covered with bark and earth. On the south side of each kiva a horizontal shaft near the floor let in fresh air, and an almost vertical one permitted the escape of smoke. The fire was made in a small pit in the center of the chamber and protected from the stream of fresh air by a deflector. Between the fire pit and ventilators was a small sipapu. Although all native woods were used in construction—piñon, juniper, and Douglas fir—only four kinds were burned on the sacred fires within the kivas—three-leaf sumac, rabbitbrush, greasewood, and gray saltbush.

The Cliff Dwellers, according to a Ute legend, once were animals living inside the earth; they climbed to the upper world on a giant corn stalk made to grow by the Life Force and the Rain. Upon reaching the surface they assumed the form of human beings; afterwards they celebrated their deliverance in underground kivas, clothing themselves in skins and masks to resemble their ancestors. The Cliff Dwellers, so the Ute say, finally began building their kivas above ground, which displeased the gods, who withheld rain and caused a great drought at Mesa Verde.

From tree rings in the twenty-three roof beams found in Spruce Tree House, it has been adduced that the village was constructed between 1230 and 1274 A. D. A spruce tree found growing upon the ruin, and for which it was named, was cut down by Baron Nordenskiold and proved to be 307 years old. The ruin could not have been occupied much before the great drought began, but the stone door sills here were worn smooth by the countless feet that passed over them.

MESA VERDE PARK TOUR 2

(Park Headquarters)—Square Tower House—Sun Point—Fire Temple —Sun Temple—Park Contact Station; Park Road, 5.5 m.

Motor caravans of private cars from Park Headquarters daily in season; guides. First trip, 8 a. m., returning 11:15 a. m.; second trip (Square Tower House not entered), at 10 a. m., returning 11:15 a. m.

The route branches east from the road to Park headquarters and swings south to the major excavated ruins on the western branch of Chapin Mesa.

At 0.3 *m.* is the junction (L) with an improved road (*see Mesa Verde Park Tour 3*).

EARTH LODGE A, 1.6 *m.,* on the flat top of the mesa (L), is a good example of the Late Basket Maker pit house, a type of structure abandoned with the development of the art of masonry. The mud-and-pole roof of this building once stood as high as a man's head; there remains only the underground part of the structure, a pit 30 inches deep and 18 feet in diameter, protected by a modern shingle roof. As no side entrance has been found, it was probably entered by a ladder through the roof. The pits of such houses are believed to have been the forerunner of the sunken *kivas* of succeeding cultures.

The road continues southwestward to the rim of CHAPIN MESA, 2 *m.*

Right here 500 *ft.* on a foot trail along the rim of Navaho Canyon to a point of descent down the cliff and northward along its face, following an old Cliff Dweller trail, to Square Tower House, 0.2 *m.* Approximately 138 feet long, it was built compactly in a great shallow cave. One entrance is through a narrow stone passageway aptly termed "Fat Man's Misery," the easier entrance is below. The tree-ring chronology developed by Dr. A. E. Douglass, director of the Steward Observatory, University of Arizona, sets the date of construction of Square Tower House somewhere between 1204 and 1246 A. D., making it one of the latest cliff houses in the park. The ruin is named for its square stone tower, 35 feet high, set on a boulder in an angle at the eastern end of the cave; the tower has only three masonry walls, the cliff supplying the fourth. The upper floors of the tower have disappeared, but the walls still bear the original red and white clay plaster. In an extreme angle of the cliff at the eastern end of the cave, several rooms, known as the Crow's Nest, are supported high above the main ruin on logs set in notches cut in the rock. There were no streets or courts here as in Spruce Tree House, the only open spaces being those surrounding the six *kivas,* which are among the best preserved yet found.

KIVA B, the largest, is 16 feet 9 inches in diameter and has half its original roof in place. KIVA A, somewhat smaller, has the usual fireplace and *sipapu,* as well as two slight depressions in the stone floor that may have been made by the end of the ladder. This kiva was finished with many layers of brown plaster. Above some of the *kivas,* on the face of the cliff, are petroglyphs, probably of religious significance.

North of Square Tower House the foot trail continues along the side of the canyon to LITTLE LONG HOUSE, 0.4 *m.,* an unexcavated ruin plainly evidencing the condition in which archeologists have found the cliff dwellings after several hundred years of neglect and exposure to the elements.

Right from Little Long House a precipitous trail ascends the canyon to the highway, 0.8 *m.* Visitors can make the ascent either by ladder or by a rope dangling over the cliff.

The highway turns southeastward to cross Chapin Mesa to SUN POINT (R), 3.2 *m.,* a bare rock promontory overlooking Cliff Canyon and a number of the larger ruins. From this point Richard Wetherill and Charlie Mason, while hunting stray cows in 1888, looked across the canyon and saw the great structure they named Cliff Palace (*see Mesa Verde Park Tour 3*).

Across FEWKES CANYON (L), which cuts westward into Chapin Mesa, are Fire Temple, New Fire House, Oak Tree House, and Mummy House, all cliff dwellings (*see below*). The highway winds northward around Fewkes Canyon, always near the edge of the mesa, to a parking space, 3.6 *m.*, with a good view of the ruins opposite. At 3.7 *m.* is the junction with a foot trail.

Right on this trail through Fewkes Canyon to FIRE TEMPLE, formerly known as Painted House, 400 *yds.*, one of the two excavated structures in the park believed to have been used wholly for religious purposes (*see below*), being a temple of the fire cult. The ruin consists of two massive buildings flanking a 50-foot court, entirely filling the shallow cave in which it is built. Walls of the rooms are plastered inside and out with red and white clay. In the lower middle room of the west building are a number of red symbols and figures, some of mountain sheep, others of wild animals. A head-high masonry wall built against the back of the cave along the court is decorated with the zigzag line and markings that appear on the pottery of the Cliff Dwellers. In the center of the court a round-walled pit contains a quantity of ashes. As far as can be determined, Fire Temple was never used as a habitation.

East of Fire Temple the trail continues to NEW FIRE HOUSE, 500 *yds.*, built in two caves, one above the other, connected by a ladder and footholds in the cliff. The lower cave has several *kivas* and is believed to have been a habitation, but evidence indicates that the upper rooms were used chiefly for storage. In one granary a well-preserved skeleton, mortuary offerings, and three grinding stones were found.

East along the trail from New Fire House to OAK TREE HOUSE, 700 *yds.*, believed to be one of the oldest of the cliff dwellings, not yet completely excavated. Its construction has been placed between 1112 and 1184 A. D. One of its seven uncovered *kivas* shows evidence of other than religious use, for almost its entire floor was covered with a series of grinding bins.

MUMMY HOUSE, 900 *yds.*, east of Oak Tree House, was so named when the mummy of a dwarf, now in the Park Headquarters Museum, was found here.

At 3.8 *m.* on the highway is the junction with a graveled road.

Right on this road to SUN TEMPLE, 0.3 *m.*, on the mesa top, the other excavated structure on Mesa Verde believed to have been designed exclusively for religious purposes. The mound that covered Sun Temple was excavated by Dr. Fewkes in 1915, revealing one of the most unusual buildings found in the Southwest. Its general plan is that of a letter "D," with the straight side toward the south. Part of the building appears to have been an annex. Two concentric walls surround an open courtyard containing two *kivas;* a third is set among the rooms of the annex. The space between the peripheral walls, narrow except at the western end, is partitioned into small oblong chambers.

The sun symbol, for which the temple was named, is placed horizontally in a little shrine on the outer side of the wall at the western corner. This little sandstone slab, with a shallow depression a foot or more in diameter and closely resembling a conventionalized sun with rays, is a natural geologic formation, rare but not unique in this region. The stone bears no artificial marking except two small holes drilled in a line running due East and West.

The building itself, unlike most sacred edifices, is not oriented to the cardinal points of the compass; adapted to topography, it faces a little East of South. It is of note that the massive walls, both interior and exterior, are not of solid masonry, but consist of stone facings with earth fill between. This type of construction, it has been suggested, was used to satisfy the requirement that ceremonial rooms be "in the earth," for Sun Temple was built on solid rock where excavation was impossible.

While the absence of roof timbers and beams makes its almost impossible to date Sun Temple, it is believed to be one of the later structures. From the crumbled remains it appears that the walls were at least six feet higher than their present level, but there are indications that the building never was completed. It may have been abandoned when the prolonged drought caused the Cliff Dwellers to migrate southward. The masonry and pottery are typical of the classic period of Pueblo culture. Details of the religious ceremonies of the Cliff Dwellers are not known, but it is assumed by archeologists that they were similar to those of modern Pueblo Indians. Bringing rain for crops undoubtedly was one of their most sacred rites, and probably like modern Pueblo, they deified the earth, sun, cardinal directions, various mountains, maize, and the spirits of their ancestors. There is no indication of barbarism in their religion, and certainly Sun Temple was never used for human sacrifice.

North of Sun Temple junction the highway swings westward to join itself, 4.5 *m.* (*see above*), 1 mile south of the Contact Station.

The tour is completed at headquarters with a visit to the Park Museum (*see above*), conducted by park officials who explain how they have been able to reconstruct the early civilization of the Basket Makers and Cliff Dwellers from a study of their remains.

MESA VERDE PARK TOUR 3

(Park Headquarters)—Junction with Mesa Verde Park Tour 2—Cliff Palace—Balcony House—Junction with Mesa Verde Park Tour 2; Park Road, 6.1 *m.*

Motor caravans of private cars from Park Headquarters daily in season; guides. First trip, 1:30 p. m., returning 4:15 p. m.; second trip (*tour of Cliff Palace omitted*), 3 p. m. returning 4:30 p.m.

This tour leads to the two major ruins on the eastern tongue of Chapin Mesa, between Cliff Canyon and Soda Canyon.

The route branches east from the junction with Mesa Verde Park Tour 2, 0 *m.* (*see Mesa Verde Park Tour 2*), 0.3 miles south of the Contact Station (*see Mesa Verde Park Tour 1*).

At an EXPERIMENTAL STATION, 1 *m.*, park naturalists have demonstrated that grain can be grown on the semiarid mesa top without irrigation. Corn was one of the principal crops of the Pueblo peoples.

The highway reaches the CLIFF PALACE PARKING SPACE, 1.8 *m.*

Right from the parking space by foot trail to a high point, 200 *ft.*, overlooking the ruin; north from here into the canyon and southeast to CLIFF PALACE, 0.2 *m.*, the largest known cliff dwelling. This great structure, which once had an estimated population of more than 400, lies in a cave 300 feet long and 100 feet high, just under the mesa rim. Built between 1073 and 1273, it was one of the earliest of the Mesa Verde cliff houses. From an architectural standpoint, Cliff Palace is especially interesting. Its builders, faced with an outward sloping cave floor, were forced to use terraces, with the result that there are six distinct floor levels. Building space was limited, and as many as three additional stories were imposed on the original one-story houses. Yet few of the structures were built up to the top of the great cave. The twenty-two *kivas* were made by walling in the necessary space as the terracing progressed and by filling in around the walls; very little excavation was required. The *kivas*, for the most part, are of the typical Mesa Verde pattern, but two are square, with rounded corners, and have no banquettes or pilasters. The size of the population made it necessary to have a large number of storage rooms; many are fine examples of masonry. Thin slabs of stone were used to partition off bins, and all chinks were well mortared to keep out the rodents that must have infested the cave.

A feature of the ruin is the round, tapering, stone tower just south of the cave center, its exact purpose unknown. The stones used here, rounded to produce the smooth circular effect of the building, were laid with great care. When it was excavated, a beautiful stone hammer was found. In another four-story tower some of the finest Cliff Dweller paintings have been uncovered, bright red designs on a white background. The white paint was obtained by mixing finely ground gypsum with water; the red, by mixing water and hematite, or red ochre.

South of the ruin the trail continues 200 feet along the canyon wall, then upward by ladders to the rim of the mesa, 0.4 m.

The highway circles to the eastern side of the mesa, following the rim, to the junction with another trail, 3.8 m.

Right on this trail into Soda Cáanyon and south to BALCONY HOUSE, 0.3 m.; the last 25 feet of the climb into the cave is by ladder. From a standpoint of defense against enemies, which must have been an impelling motive in its construction, Balcony House is perhaps better situated than any of the park ruins. The cave is virtually inaccessible; its only approach is by several narrow ledges. At the south entrance, guarded by a narrow cleft, the builders erected a stone wall with a tunnel passable only on hands and knees.

Balcony House takes its name from an unusual architectural feature. At the north end of the ruin, where a supporting wall was built on a lower ledge to brace the building above, the floor beams of the upper rooms project two feet beyond the outer wall. These ends were covered with split poles and clay to form a balcony that permitted communication between the upper rooms. The ruins of twenty rooms and two *kivas* at Balcony House, believed to have been built between 1190 and 1272, are among the best preserved in the park; several ceilings are still intact.

North of the junction with the trail the highway circles back to join itself, 4.6 m., 1.5 miles south of the junction with Mesa Verde Park Tour 2 (*see above*).

PART IV

Appendices

Chronology

1541 Coronado may have crossed southeastern corner of present Colorado on return march to Mexico.

1598 Juan de Onate, hunting for gold, comes from Mexico as far north as San Luis Valley.

1601 Onate's second expedition penetrates as far north as present site of Denver.

1682 La Salle appropriates for France all of Colorado east of the Rocky Mountains.

1706 Juan de Uribarri formally claims possession of southeastern Colorado in name of Philip V of Spain.

1719–20 Valverde leads Spanish military expedition from Santa Fe as far north as Pikes Peak.

1761 Juan Maria Rivera leads Spanish expedition in search of gold and silver; said to have been first white men to visit Gunnison Valley.

1763 Treaty of Fontainebleau between France and England reveals that France has ceded all territory west of Mississippi to Spain.

1776 Friars Silvestre Velez de Escalante and Francisco Antasio Dominguez, seeking route from Santa Fe to California missions, traverse what is now western Colorado as far north as White River; discover and name Mesa Verde.

1800 Spain retrocedes Louisiana Territory to France in exchange for Duchy of Tuscany, Italy.

1803 United States acquires part of Colorado by Louisiana Purchase.

1806 Lieut. Zebulon M. Pike, sent to explore southwestern boundary of Louisiana Purchase, reaches headwaters of Arkansas River.

1807 Pike crosses Sangre de Cristo Mountains to Conejos River.

1819 United States and Spain agree to fix southwestern boundary of Louisiana Purchase in this region at Arkansas River, thence northward along Continental Divide.

1820 Maj. Stephen H. Long is sent to explore new boundary. Dr. Edwin James, historian of expedition, leads first recorded ascent of Pikes Peak.

1825 Opening of era of fur traders, trappers, and Mountain Men—Bent brothers, Ceran St. Vrain, Louis Vasquez, Kit Carson, Jim Baker, James Bridger, Thomas Fitzpatrick, "Uncle Dick" Wootton, and Jim Beckwourth—who establish posts in Arkansas and South Platte Valleys.

1826 First headquarters of Bent brothers is established about twenty miles west of present site of Pueblo.

1832 Bent's Fort, one of most important trading posts in the West, is built by the Bents and St. Vrain near present site of La Junta.

1836 Texas becomes independent republic and claims narrow strip of mountain territory extending northward through Colorado to 42nd parallel.

1842 October, James P. Beckwourth establishes trading post and begins settlement of Fort Pueblo—Lieut. John C. Frémont undertakes first of his five exploration trips into Rocky Mountains.

1846 Gen. Stephen W. Kearney leads Army of the West along Santa Fe Trail through southeastern Colorado en route to conquest of New Mexico during Mexican War.

1848 By Treaty of Guadalupe Hidalgo, Mexico cedes to United States most of that part of Colorado not acquired by Louisiana Purchase; property rights of former Mexican citizens in this area are guaranteed.

1850 Federal Government purchases Texas' claims in Colorado.

1852 First permanent white settlement in Colorado is founded at Conejos in San Luis Valley; irrigation is begun; Fort Massachusetts established in valley to protect settlers from Indians.

1853 Capt. John W. Gunnison leads exploring party across southern and western Colorado. Frémont's last expedition, seeking feasible railroad route through mountains, largely follows Gunnison's route.

1854 Indians massacre inhabitants of Fort Pueblo on Christmas Day.

1858 Green Russell's discovery of small placer gold deposits near confluence of the South Platte River and Cherry Creek, precipitates Pike's Peak gold rush. Montana City, St. Charles, Auraria, and Denver City are founded on present site of Denver. November 6, two hundred men meet here to organize County of Arapahoe, Kansas Territory.

1859 Gold is found by George A. Jackson along Chicago Creek on present site of Idaho Springs. March 9, first stagecoach with mail for Cherry Creek settlements leaves Leavenworth, Kansas. April 23, first newspaper in Pikes Peak region, *Rocky Mountain News,* is published. May 6, John Gregory makes famous gold-lode strike on North Clear Creek, stimulating rush of prospectors, who establish camps of Blackhawk, Central City, and Nevadaville. October 3, O. J. Goldrick opens first school, at Auraria. Jefferson Territory is organized without sanction of Congress to govern gold camps;

officers are elected. Prospectors spread through mountains and found camps at Boulder, Colorado City, Gold Hill, Hamilton, Tarryall, and Pueblo.

1860 Rich placer discoveries cause stampede of miners to California Gulch on present site of Leadville. First schoolhouse is built, at Boulder. Region continues to be administered variously by Jefferson Territory officials, Arapahoe County officials, and Miners' and Peoples' Courts.

1861 Congress establishes Colorado Territory with boundaries of present State; William Gilpin is appointed first Territorial governor. July, supreme court is organized and Congressional delegates chosen. September, first assembly meets, creates 17 counties, authorizes university, and selects Colorado City as Territorial capital. Manufacture of mining machinery begins. Population, 25,371.

1862 Colorado troops aid in defeating Gen. Henry H. Sibley's Confederate Army at La Golrieta Pass, New Mexico. Second Territorial Legislature meets for few days at Colorado City, adjourns to Denver, and selects Golden as new capital. First tax-supported schools are established, and first oil well drilled near Florence. John Evans succeeds Gilpin as governor.

1863 Telegraph line links Denver with East: ten words to New York, $9.10. Plains Indians raid wagon trains and outlying ranches.

1864 Sand Creek Massacre stirs Indians to fresh violence and overland trails are often closed. Colorado Seminary (now University of Denver) is chartered; Sisters of Loreto open academy in Denver. Fort Sedgwick is established near Julesburg. Placer mining operations decline with exhaustion of richest deposits.

1865 Indian attacks along trails reach highest intensity; food is sometimes scarce; potatoes bring $15 a bushel; Fort Morgan established as protection against Indians.

1867 Denver is chosen as Territorial capital. Troops freed at close of Civil War gradually overcome hostile Indians.

1868 Nathaniel Hill erects Colorado's first smelter at Blackhawk, inaugurating era of hard-rock mining. Cheyenne Indians disastrously defeated at Beecher Island near present site of Wray.

1870 Denver & Pacific R. R. is constructed to connect Denver with Union Pacific at Cheyenne, Wyo.; the Kansas Pacific enters Colorado from Missouri River. Union Colony is established by Horace Greeley and Nathan C. Meeker at Greeley, and digs first large irrigation canal. Population, 39,864.

1871 Colorado Springs is founded by Gen. William J. Palmer and associates. Denver & Rio Grande R. R. is built southward from Denver.

1872 Blackhawk and Central City are connected with Denver by railroad; Denver & Rio Grande reaches Pueblo. Agricultural settlements established throughout South Platte Valley.

1873 Gold and silver discoveries in San Juan Mountains attract miners to southwestern Colorado; Ute are dispossessed of territory held by treaty with Federal Government.

1874   Colorado College is founded at Colorado Springs; legislature appropriates $15,000 for University of Colorado at Boulder, on condition that equal sum is raised by that city. W. H. Jackson of Hayden Survey notes ruins of ancient cliff dwellings along canyon of Mancos River.

1875   Lead carbonate ores, rich in silver, are found near present site of Leadville.

1875   Constitutional Convention of 38 members holds first meeting, Dec. 20.

1876   Colorado is admitted to Union as thirty-eighth State; John L. Routt is elected first governor.

1877   University of Colorado opens classes at Boulder, with two teachers and 44 students. State Board of Agriculture is created.

1878   Leadville is incorporated; rich silver strikes on Iron, Carbonate, and Fryer hills soon make it one of world's greatest mining camps. Central City opera house opens. First telephones are installed in Denver.

1879   Colorado College of Agriculture and Mechanic Arts offers instruction at Fort Collins. Nathan C. Meeker, Indian Agent on White River, and several employees are slain in Ute uprising.

1880   Denver & Rio Grande lays tracks to Leadville. Great Ute chief, Ouray, dies. Dry land farming undertaken extensively in eastern Colorado. Population, 194,327.

1881   Ute tribes are removed from western Colorado; Grand Junction is founded. Small quantities of carnotite is mined in western Colorado along with gold; later, this mineral is used in discovery of radium. Sept. 5, Tabor Opera House opens in Denver.

1882   Steel is milled in Pueblo from Colorado ores.

1883   Narrow-gauge line of Denver & Rio Grande is completed from Gunnison to Grand Junction. First electric lights are installed in Denver.

1886   Denver Union Stockyards are established, becoming largest receiving market for sheep in country.

1888   Band of Ute from Utah under Colorow make last Indian raid into Colorado; they are defeated and returned to their reservation. Union Colony at Greeley completes 900,000-acre irrigation project.

1890   Passage of Sherman Silver Purchase Act raises the price of silver to more than $1.00 an ounce. New rich silver strikes are made along Rio Grande; Creede is founded. July 4, cornerstone of State Capitol at Denver is laid. Oct. 3, first building of State Normal School (now Colorado State College) at Greeley is occupied. Population, 413, 249.

1891   Robert Womack's discoveries open great gold field of Cripple Creek. First national forest reserve in State is set aside. Pikes Peak cog railroad begins operation.

1893   National panic brings great distress to Colorado; repeal of Sherman Act strikes silver mining a paralyzing blow and adds to already acute unemployment problems. November 2, Colorado is second State to extend suffrage to women.

1894 State Capitol is completed at cost of $2,500,000.

1899 First beet sugar refinery is built at Grand Junction.

1900 Gold production reaches peak of more than $20,000,000 annually at Cripple Creek, the second richest gold camp in world. Population, 539,700.

1902 Constitutional amendment bestows "home-rule" upon towns of 2,000 population or more. Beet sugar refinery is built at Fort Collins.

1903–1904 Mine, mill, and smelter workers strike in many camps for higher wages and better working conditions; at Cripple Creek, strike results in much property damage and loss of life; all strike objectives in gold field are lost. Uncompahgre irrigation project, first of Federal Government reclamation projects in Colorado, is authorized. Mining of tungsten begins.

1906 U. S. mint, Denver, issues first coins. June 29, Mesa Verde National Park is created by Congress.

1907 With Ben B. Lindsey as judge, Denver Juvenile Court opens.

1908 July 7, Denver Municipal Auditorium, seating 12,500, is completed in time for Democratic National Convention. Aug. 1, Colorado Day is first celebrated, marking thirty-second anniversary of State's admittance to Union. Colorado Museum of Natural History, Denver, is opened.

1909 Colorado attains first rank among States in irrigated area, with almost 3,000,000 acres under irrigation. Western State Teachers College opens at Gunnison, now Western State College.

1910 First airplane flight in Denver. Population, 799,024.

1914 Strike of coal miners in southern fields is climaxed by "Battle of Ludlow" near Trinidad; several women and children die during hostilities between miners and militia.

1915 Workmen's compensation measures are passed; State Industrial Commission is created. Jan. 12, Rocky Mountain National Park is created by Congress.

1916 Colorado adopts prohibition; Emily Griffith Opportunity School is opened at Denver.

1917 Colorado reaches maximum mineral production—more than $80,000,000.

1918 More than 125,000 Colorado citizens register for World War draft. State attains maximum coal production—12,500,000 tons.

1920 First Music Week is observed in Denver. Population, 939,629.

1921 Pueblo suffers disastrous flood; scores are drowned and property losses amount to $20,000,000.

1922 Moffat Tunnel Improvement District is created by legislature for construction of 6.4-mile bore under Continental Divide to provide better rail connections between Eastern and Western Slopes. First commercial radio license in Colorado is issued.

1924 April 26, Colorado is second State to ratify child labor amendment to Federal constitution.

1925 Federal Reserve branch bank is established at Denver. Adams State

Teachers College at Alamosa, now Adams State College, and junior colleges at Grand Junction and Trinidad open.

1926 Denver established as air-mail post office on U. A. L. route between Pueblo and Cheyenne.

1927 Helium gas deposits are found near Thatcher. Moffat Tunnel is completed at a cost of $18,000,000.

1930 Depression increases number of unemployed. Population, 1,035,791.

1931 Cooperative credit unions are approved by legislature. Tobacco is grown commercially on small scale.

1932-37 Prolonged drought and high winds cause tremendous damage through soil erosion in southeastern Colorado.

1932 Central City's opera house is restored by Opera House Association, and first annual theatrical festival is held in July.

1934 More than $3,000,000,000 in gold bullion is transferred from San Francisco and stored in Denver mint.

1935 Dotsero Cut-off is completed, placing Denver on direct transcontinental railroad route through Moffat Tunnel.

1936 Monthly old-age pensions of $45 are authorized by amendment to State constitution.

1937 Technical school and bombing field of U. S. Army Air Corps established at Lowry field near Denver.

Governors of Colorado since 1939. 1939–1943, Ralph L. Carr, Republican. 1943–1947, John C. Vivian, R. 1947–1950, W. Lee Knous, Democrat. 1950–1951, Walter W. Johnson, D. 1951–1955, Dan Thornton, R. 1955–1957, Edwin C. Johnson, D. 1957–1963, Stephen L. R. McNichols, D. 1963–1970, John A. Love, R.

Colorado national election vote since 1939. 1940. Roosevelt, D., 265,554; Wilkie, R., 279,576. 1944. Roosevelt, D., 234,331; Dewey, R., 268,731. 1948. Truman, D., 267,288; Dewey, R., 239,714. 1952. Eisenhower, R., 379,782; Stevenson, D., 245,506. 1956. Eisenhower, R., 394,782; Stevenson, D., 263,997. 1960. Kennedy, D., 330,629; Nixon, R., 402,242. 1964. Johnson, D., 476,024; Goldwater, R., 296,167. 1968. Nixon, R., 408,146; Humphrey, D., 335,715; Wallace, Ind., 60,447.

Colorado in World War II, et. seq. 1940–1948. From November, 1940, to December, 1946, the Selective Service System of Colorado inducted 73,664 men. The largest number, 25,960, was indicted in 1942. The Colorado National Guard put 2,424 officers and men into the service by February, 1941. When the State boards began to operate Brig. General H. H. Richardson was named director. Originally men aged 20 to 44 were called up for 18 months; in December, 1941, this was extended to duration of the war and 6 months thereafter, and all men from 18 to 64 were registered. The number of men enlisted in all categories was 138,832. The U. S. War Department reported 2,736 fatalities.

The tremendous impact of the war on Colorado life is effectively summarized by Leroy R. Hafen in *Colorado and Its People*. One out of every 8 men in Colorado was in some form of the service. The war loan quota assigned to the State was $474,379,000; Colorado raised $700,683,980, a percentage of 145.8.

Great sums poured into Colorado for construction of camps and airfields, and for manufacture of munitions and military equipment. The Rocky Mountain Arsenal on a 20,000-acre military reservation northeast of Denver became the major chemical warfare plant in 1942, with a Government expenditure of $62,000,000. It was designed to manufacture incendiary bombs, and a whole line of gases, including mustard, tear gas, Lewisite and toxic smoke. The Denver Ordnance Plant, 8 miles west of the city, had an appropriation of $122,249,880 for all purposes and by 1943 had 265 buildings and 19,500 employees. Henry J. Kaiser received a large contract for shells and the Thompson Pipe & Steel Co. added shipbuilding to Colorado Industries, producing landing barges.

Military installations, camps and airfields were located chiefly in the eastern part of the State. Lowry Field had been dedicated in 1938 as a technical school for the Army Air Corps and had more than 64,000 acres for bombing practice.

The Air Corps also took over Fort Logan. Buckley Field was opened on 2,210 acres east of Lowry. The Army Air Corps established its photographic division at Peterson Field, Colorado Springs. Another air base was opened 6 miles east of Pueblo. The Pueblo Ordnance Depot, near North Avondale, had 1,200 storage magazines and more than 20,000 acres. The British RAF was allotted a field at La Junta. The largest camp was Camp Carson, 6 miles south of Colorado Springs, which had 60,000 acres and accommodated up to 40,000 men.

Colorado also had a Japanese Relocation Center near Granada, a village in Prowers County on the Kansas border, where slightly more than 10,000 of Japanese birth or descent were detained until the war ended.

Colorado in the Korean War, 1950–51. The Department of Military Affairs of the State of Colorado reported that 48,000 Colorado men served during this war, including 35 National Guard units and 2,225 National Guard personnel. Total dead was 297.

1963. The Veterans Administration Regional Office, Denver, reported disbursements of $77,510,869 to Colorado veterans during fiscal 1963. The 16,757 living veterans of World War II received $14,553,422 and dependents of 4,080 deceased veterans received $4,008,461. The 2,340 living veterans of World War I received $3,474,750 and dependents of 4,328 deceased veterans received $3,150,663. The largest amount expended in one year was $78,662,851 in 1949, peak year of the veterans education program. Total compensation for other wars during 1917–1963 was $140,175,000.

1966. Mineral production was valued at $352,000,000, a record; the previous high was $346,200,000 in 1961. Record volume was reported for iron ore, molybdenum, sand and gravel, stone and tin. Metals accounted for 43% of value, fuels 42%, nonmetals, 15%.

1969. Jefferson City was incorporated out of suburbs west of Denver and in November changed its name to Lakewood. It became one of Colorado's largest cities.

Selective Reading List

Adams, Andy. *Log of a Cowboy*. Houghton Mifflin, 1903.

Alter, J. C. *James Bridger, Trapper, Frontiersman, Scout, and Guide*. Shepard Book Co., 1925.

Ashton, Ruth. *Plants of the Rocky Mountain National Park*. Washington, Government Printing Office, 1933.

Baker, J. H., and Hafen, LeRoy. *History of Colorado*. State Historical Society of Colorado, 1927.

Bancroft, H. H. *History of Nevada, Colorado, and Wyoming*. San Francisco, 1890.

Bayly, Charles. *The Glory That Was Gold*. University of Denver, 1932.

Beckwourth, James P. (ed. T. D. Bonner). *Life and Adventures of James P. Beckwourth*. (1856) Knopf, 1931.

Bennet, Horace. *Bright Yellow Gold*. J. C. Winston, 1935.

Borland, Hal. *Rocky Mountain Tipi Tales*. Doubleday Doran, 1924.

Bradley, G. D. *The Story of the Pony Express*. A. C. McClurg, 1930.

Breakenridge, Wm. *Helldorado*. Houghton Mifflin, 1928.

Cather, Willa S. *Song of the Lark*. Houghton Mifflin, 1915.

Chittenden, H. M. *The American Fur Trade of the Far West*. Press of the Pioneers, 1936.

Cody, Colonel W. *An Autobiography of Buffalo Bill*. Cosmopolitan Book Co., 1910.

Coleman, Rufus A. (ed). *The Golden West in Story and Verse*. Harper, 1932.

Collier, Wm. R., and Westrate, Edwin. *Dave Cook of the Rockies*. Rufus Rockwell Wilson, 1936.

Conrad, Howard L. "Uncle Dick" Wootton. Dibble & Co., 1890.

Cooper, Courtney Riley. *Cross-Cut*. Little, Brown, 1921. *High Country*. Little, Brown, 1926.

Davidson, L. J., and Postwick, P. *The Literature of the Rocky Mountain West*. Caxton Printers, 1939.

Davis, Carlyle Channing. *Olden Times in Colorado*. Phillips Pub. Co., 1916.

Davis, Clyde Brion. *The Anointed*. Farrar & Rinehart, 1937.

Davis, Herman S. (ed.). *Reminiscences of General William H. Larimer and of his son Wm. H. H. Larimer*. Lancaster, Pa., 1918.

Dier, Mrs. Caroline (Lawrence). *Lady of the Gardens*. Hollywood, Hollycrofters, 1932.

Duffus, R. L. *The Santa Fe Trail*. Longmans Green, 1930.

Ellis, Anne. *Life of an Ordinary Woman*. Houghton Mifflin, 1929.

National Parks and Monuments

COLORADO-UTAH VISITORS CENTER, DINOSAUR NATIONAL MONUMENT

CHIPPING DINOSAUR BONES OUT OF SOLID ROCK, DINOSAUR NATIONAL MONUMENT

MOUNT OF THE HOLY CROSS

Cooper & Cooper, Denver

EXPLORING BROOK AND DUNES, GREAT SAND DUNES NATIONAL MONUMENT

ENTRANCE ROAD, GREAT SAND DUNES NATIONAL MONUMENT

BLACK CANYON OF THE GUNNISON

ODESSA LAKE, ROCKY MOUNTAIN NATIONAL PARK

SNOWY WEATHER, ECHO PARK

SHADOW MOUNTAIN NATIONAL RECREATION AREA

TOURIST HALT ON TRAIL RIDGE ROAD

FLOWERS OF THE YUCCA BACCATA
National Park Service

PRICKLY PEAR CACTUS,
MESA VERDE NATIONAL PARK
National Park Ser

CUT THROAT CASTLE, HOVENWEEP NATIONAL MONUMENT

CASCADE CREEK MEADOWS, ROCKY MOUNTAIN NATIONAL PARK

WHERE FIRE SWEPT; GLADES BURN AREA, LA PLATA MOUNTAINS

Ellis, M. & H. J. *The Amphibia and Reptilia of Colorado.* University of Colorado, 1913.

Farnham, Thomas Jefferson. *Travels in the Great Western Prairies; 1841,* reprinted in Thwaites' *Early Western Travels,* 1906.

Ferril, Thomas Hornsby. *High Passage.* Yale University Press, 1926. *Westering.* Yale University Press, 1934.

Fewkes, J. W. *Prehistoric Villages.* Government Printing Office, 1919.

Fewkes, J. W. *Antiquities of the Mesa Verde National Park.* Government Printing Office, 1911.

Field, Eugene. *The Tribune Primer.* Denver, 1882. *Little Book of Western Verse.* Scribners, 1889.

Fowler, Gene. *Timberline.* Covici, 1933 *Return to Yesterday.* Random House, 1937.

Gandy, L. C. *The Tabors.* Press of the Pioneers, 1934.

Gardiner, D. K. *Golden Lady.* Doubleday, 1936. *Snow Water.* Doubleday, 1939.

Garland, Hamlin. *They of the High Trails.* Harper, 1916.

George, R. D. *Geology and Natural Resources of Colorado.* University of Colorado, 1927.

Gillmore, Francis, and Wetherell, L. W. *Traders to the Navajos.* Houghton Mifflin, 1934.

Greeley, Horace. *An Overland Journey from New York to San Francisco in the Summer of 1859.* Saxton, Barker & Co., 1860.

Gregg, Josiah. *Commerce of the Prairies, the Journal of a Santa Fe Trader; 1884,* reprinted in Thwaites' *Early Western Travels.*

Grinnell, G. B. *Bent's Old Fort and its Builders.* Kansas State Historical Society Collections, v. 15, 1919–1922. *The Fighting Cheyenne.* Scribners, 1915.

Hafen, LeRoy. *Colorado, the Story of a Western Commonwealth.* Peerless Publishing Co., 1933.

Hafen, LeRoy, and Ghent, W. I. *Broken Hand.* Old West Pub. Co., 1931.

Hart, H. M. *Recollections and Reflections.* Smith-Brooks Co., 1917.

Hart, John Lathrop. *Fourteen Thousand Feet.* Colo. Mountain Club, 1931.

Henderson, Junius. *Extinct and Existing Glaciers in Colorado.* University of Colorado, 1910. "The Prehistoric Peoples of Colorado" in *Colorado: Short Studies of its Past and Present.* 1927.

Hough, Emerson. *The Story of the Cowboy.* Appleton, 1897.

Howbert, Irving. *Memoirs of a Lifetime in the Pike's Peak Region.* Putnam's, 1925.

Howlett, Rev. W. J. *Life of the Right Reverend Joseph P. Machebeuf.* Franklin Press, 1908.

Irwin, W. H. *Youth Rides West.* Knopf, 1925.

Jackson, Helen Hunt. *Bits of Travel at Home.* Roberts Bros., 1878. *Nelly's Silver Mine.* 1878. *A Century of Dishonor.* 1885. *Colorado Springs.* Roberts Bros., 1883.

Jackson, Wm. M., and Driggs, H. D. *Rocky Mountain Adventures with a Camera.* World Book Co., 1929.

Jocknock, David. *Early Days on the Western Slope*. Carson-Harper Co., 1913.

John, Wm. M. *Seven Women*. Sears, 1929.

Karsner, David. *Silver Dollar*. Covici, 1932.

Kingery, Elinor Eppich. *Climber's Guide to the High Peaks*. Colorado Mountain Club, 1931.

Lambe, P. O. *Sign of the Buffalo Skull*. Frederick Stokes, 1932.

McKeehan, Irene. "Colorado in Literature" in *Colorado: Short Studies of its Past and Present*. University of Colorado, 1927.

McLean, E. W. *Father Struck it Rich*. Little, Brown, 1936.

Mills, Enos. *Bird Memories of the Rockies*. Houghton Mifflin, 1931. *Rocky Mountain National Park*. Doubleday Page, 1924.

Mumey, N. *Life of Jim Baker*. World Press, 1931.

Nusbaum, Deric. *With Deric in Mesa Verde*. Putnam's, 1926.

Parkman, Francis. *The Oregon Trail*. Putnam's, 1849, and later.

Raine, Wm. McLeod. *Colorado*. Doubleday, 1928.

Ramaley, Francis. *Colorado Plant Life*. University of Colorado, 1927.

Ramaley, Francis. *Wild Flowers and Trees of Colorado*. A. A. Greenman, 1909.

Renaud, E. B. "The Indians of Colorado" in *Colorado: Short Studies of its Past and Present*. University of Colorado, 1927.

Richards, Clarice. *A Tenderfoot Bride*. Revell, 1920.

Sabin, E. L. *Kit Carson Days*. A. C. McClurg, 1914.

Sinclair, Upton. *Mountain City*. Boni, 1930.

Smedley, Agnes. *Daughter of Earth*. Coward-McCann, 1929.

Smiley, Jerome C. *History of Denver*. Denver *Times,* 1901.

Steinel, A. T. *History of Agriculture in Colorado*. Fort Collins, 1926.

Sublette, Clifford M. *Golden Chimney*. Little, Brown, 1931.

Sykes, H. W. *Second Hoeing*. Putnam's, 1935.

Taylor, Bayard. *Colorado: A Summer Trip*. Putnam's, 1867.

Toll, Roger. *The Mountain Peaks of Colorado*. Colorado Mountain Club, 1923.

Vestal, Stanley. *Dobe Walls*. Houghton Mifflin, 1929. *Kit Carson*. Houghton Mifflin, 1928.

Vickers, W. B. (ed.) *History of the Arkansas Valley. History of Clear Creek and Boulder Valleys*. O. L. Baskins & Co., 1880–81.

Villard, H. *Past and Present of the Pike's Peak Region*. Princeton University Press, 1932.

Walsh, Richard, and Salsbury, M. S. *The Making of Buffalo Bill*. Bobbs Merrill, 1928.

Warren, E. R. *The Mammals of Colorado*. Putnam's, 1901.

Warman, Cy. *Last Spike and Other Railroad Stories*. Scribner's, 1906.

Waters, Frank. *Midas of the Rockies*. Covici Friede, 1937.

Webb, Walter P. *The Great Plains*. Ginn and Co., 1931.

Wharton, J. E. *History of the City of Denver from the Earliest Settlement to the Present Time*. Byers & Bailey, 1866.

White, S. E. *The Long Rifle*. Doubleday Doran, 1932.

Willard, James F., and Goodykoontz, C. B. "Experiments in Colorado Colonization" and "Union Colony at Greeley, Colorado," in *University of Colorado Historical Collections*. University of Colorado.

Willison, George F. *Here They Dug the Gold*. Brentano's, 1931.

Wissler, Clark. *North American Indians of the Plains*. American Museum of Natural History, 1920.

Wyer, Malcolm Glenn (ed). "Art in Denver" in The *Outlook*. Denver Public Library, 1928.

RECENT BOOKS OF COLORADO INTEREST

Bancroft, Caroline. *Colorful Colorado, Its Dramatic History*. Swallow, 1959.

Bromfield, Louis. *Colorado*. Harper, 1947.

Casewit, Curtis W. and Dick Pownall. *The Mountaineering Handbook; an Invitation to Climbing*. Lippincott, 1968.

Carver, Jack, *et al. Colorado, Land of Legend*. Caravon Press, 1959.

Costigan. *Papers of Edward Prentiss Costigan*. Boulder, 1941.

Eblen, Jack Ericson. *The First and Second United States Empires; Governors & Territorial Government, 1794–1912*. Univ. of Pittsburgh Press, 1968.

Ferril, Thomas Hornsby. *Trial by Time*, Harper, 1944. *I Hate Thursday*, Harper, 1946. *New and Selected Poems*, Harper, 1952. *Words for Denver and Other Poems*, Morrow, 1966.

Florin, Lambert. *Ghost Town Trails*. Superior, Seattle, 1963.

Freeman, Orville L. and Michael Frome. *The National Forests of America*. Putnam, 1968.

Frondsen, Maude Lindstrom. *Sixty and Three on the C.* Johnson, 1960.

Goldwater, Barry Morris. *An Odyssey of the Green and Colorado Rivers*. Phoenix, 1941.

Hafen, Leroy R. *Colorado and Its People*. 4 vols. Lewis Historical Publishing Co., 1948.

Hafen, Leroy R. *The Indians of Colorado*. State Historical Society of Colorado, 1952.

Hafen, Leroy R. and Ann. *Our State, Colorado; A History of Progress*. Old West Publishing Co., 1966.

Hunt, Inez, and Wanetta Draper. *To Colorado's Restless Ghosts*. Sage Books, 1960.

Jett, Stephen C. Kenneth Brower, ed. *Navajo Wildlands*. The Sierra Club.

Johnson, Samuel W. *Autobiography*. Big Mountain Press, 1960.

Kent, Ruth. *Colorado Vacations: An Intimate Guide*. Knopf, 1939.

Lavender, David. *The Rockies*. Harper & Row, 1968.

Leckerby, Charles Harrison. *The Tread of Pioneers*. Pilot Press, 1945.

Morgan, Dale L. and Harris, Eleanor, eds. *The Rocky Mountain Journals of William Marshall Anderson*. The Huntington Library, 1967.

Ormes, Robert M. *Guides to the Colorado Mountains*. (Colorado Mountain Club). Sage Books, 1952.

Parkhill, Forbes. Donna Madixxa Goes West. (Novel about Mrs. William B. Daniels of Denver). The Pruett Press, 1968. *The Law Goes West*. Sage Books, 1956.

Reinhardt, Richard. *Out West on the Overland Train*. American West Pub. Co., 1967.

Stanley, Percy. *Colorado, the Centennial State*. 1941.

Stegner, Wallace, ed. *The Exploration of the Colorado River, by John Wesley Powell*. Chicago, 1957.

Terrill, John Upton. *The Man Who Rediscovered America: John Wesley Powell*. Weybright & Talley, 1969. *The Six Turnings; Major Changes in the American West*. Arthur H. Clarke Co., 1968.

Taylor, J. Golden, ed. and Stegner, Wallace, intro. *Great Western Short Stories*. American West Pub. Co., 1967.

Taylor, Ralph C. *Colorado South of the Border*. Sage Books, 1963.

Towne, Mary E. *Colorado Calls*. Big Mountain Press, 1958.

Ullman, James Ramsey. *Down the Colorado With Major Powell*. Houghton Mifflin, 1967.

Watkins, T. H., et al.; foreword by Wallace Stegner. *The Grand Colorado; the Story of a River and its Canyons*. Photos by Philip Hydel. American West Publishing Co., 1969.

Williams, Brad. and Pepper, Choral. *The Mysterious West*. World, 1967.

Woodbury, David Oakes. *The Colorado Conquest*. Dodd Mead, 1941.

Wyman, Leland Clifton. *Navaho Sandpainting*. The Huckell Collection, Taylor Museum, Colorado Springs Fine Art Center, 1960. *The Windways of the Navaho*, same publisher, 1962.

MAP OF
COLORADO
IN SECTIONS

Index to State Map Sections

LEGEND

35 INTERSTATE	
50 U. S. HIGHWAY	FORT
87 STATE HIGHWAY	BATTLEFIELD
--- OLD TRAIL ROUTE	NATIONAL PARK OR MONUMENT
-- STATE BOUNDARY	NATIONAL OR STATE FOREST
CAPITAL	
COUNTY SEAT	RESERVATION
TOWN	
POINT OF INTEREST	ELEVATION
HISTORICAL	WATER FEATURE

SECTIONAL DIVISION OF STATE MAP

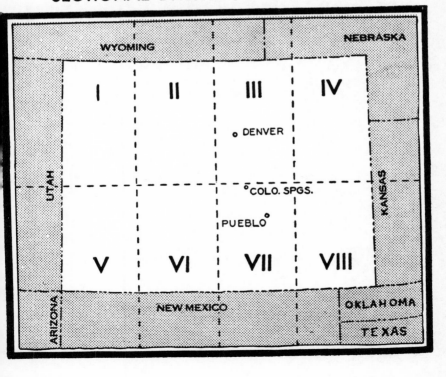

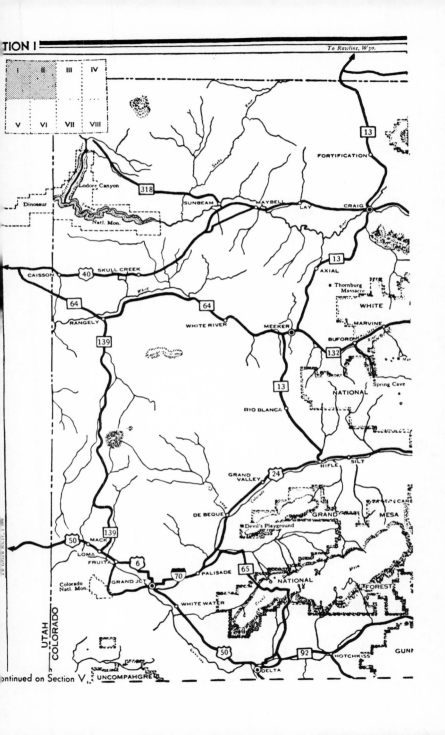

To Rawlins, Wyo.

| I | II | III | IV |
| V | VI | VII | VIII |

13

FORTIFICATION

Lodore Canyon   318

Dinosaur   SUNBEAM   MAYBELL   LAY   CRAIG

Natl. Mon.

CAISSON   40   SKULL CREEK   13   AXIAL

Thornburg Massacre   WHITE

64   64   MARVINE

RANGELY   WHITE RIVER   MEEKER   BUFORD

139   132   Spring Cave

13   NATIONAL

RIO BLANCA

RIFLE   SILT

GRAND VALLEY   24

DE BEQUE   GRAND   CARE   MESA

Devil's Playground

50   MACK   139   65

LOMA   6   PALISADE   NATIONAL   FOREST

FRUITA   70

Colorado Natl. Mon.   GRAND JCT.

WHITE WATER

50   92   HOTCHKISS   GUN

ontinued on Section V   UNCOMPAHGRE   DELTA

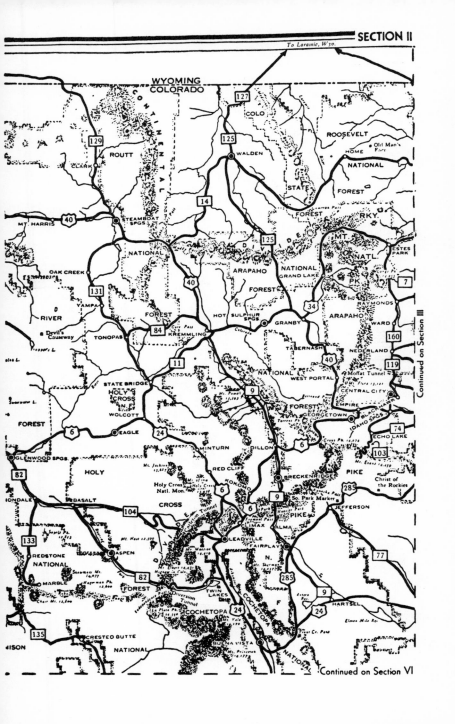

Continued on Section III

Continued on Section VI

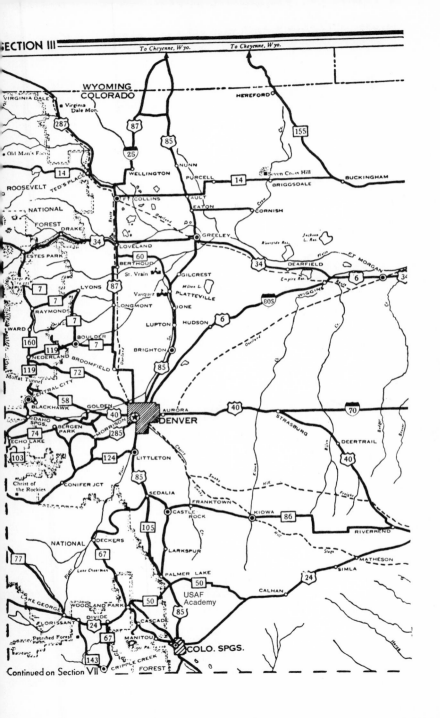

To Cheyenne, Wyo.   To Cheyenne, Wyo.

WYOMING
COLORADO

VIRGINIA DALE
Virginia
Dale Mon.

287

Old Man's Face

87

85

155

25

14

WELLINGTON   NUNN   HEREFORD

PURCELL   Seven Cross Hill   BUCKINGHAM

ROOSEVELT   TED'S PLACE   14   AULT   BRIGGSDALE

NATIONAL   FT COLLINS   EATON   CORNISH

FOREST   DRAKE

34   LOVELAND   GREELEY   DEARFIELD   FT MORGAN

ESTES PARK   60   BERTHOUD   34   6   3

7   St. Vrain   OGILCREST   Empire Res.

LYONS   87   Vasquez   PLATTEVILLE   Milton L.   WIGGINS

7   RAYMONDS   LONGMONT   IONE   805

WARD   LUPTON   HUDSON   6

160   BOULDER   7

119   NEDERLAND   BRIGHTON   85

119   BROOMFIELD

Moffat Tunnel   72

CENTRAL CITY   70

58   BLACKHAWK   GOLDEN   AURORA   40   STRASBURG   70

IDAHO SPGS.   40   DENVER

74   BERGEN PARK   285   MORRISON

ECHO LAKE   DEERTRAIL

103   124   LITTLETON   40

Christ of the Rockies   CONIFER JCT   85   SEDALIA

FRANKTOWN   KIOWA   86   RIVERBEND

CASTLE ROCK

NATIONAL   DECKERS   105   LARKSPUR   MATHESON

77   67   SIMLA

PALMER LAKE   24

50   CALHAN

LAKE GEORGE   50   USAF Academy

WOODLAND PARK   85

FLORISSANT   DIVIDE   24   CASCADE

Petrified Forest   67   MANITOU

143   COLO. SPGS.

CRIPPLE CREEK   FOREST

Continued on Section VII

SECTION IV

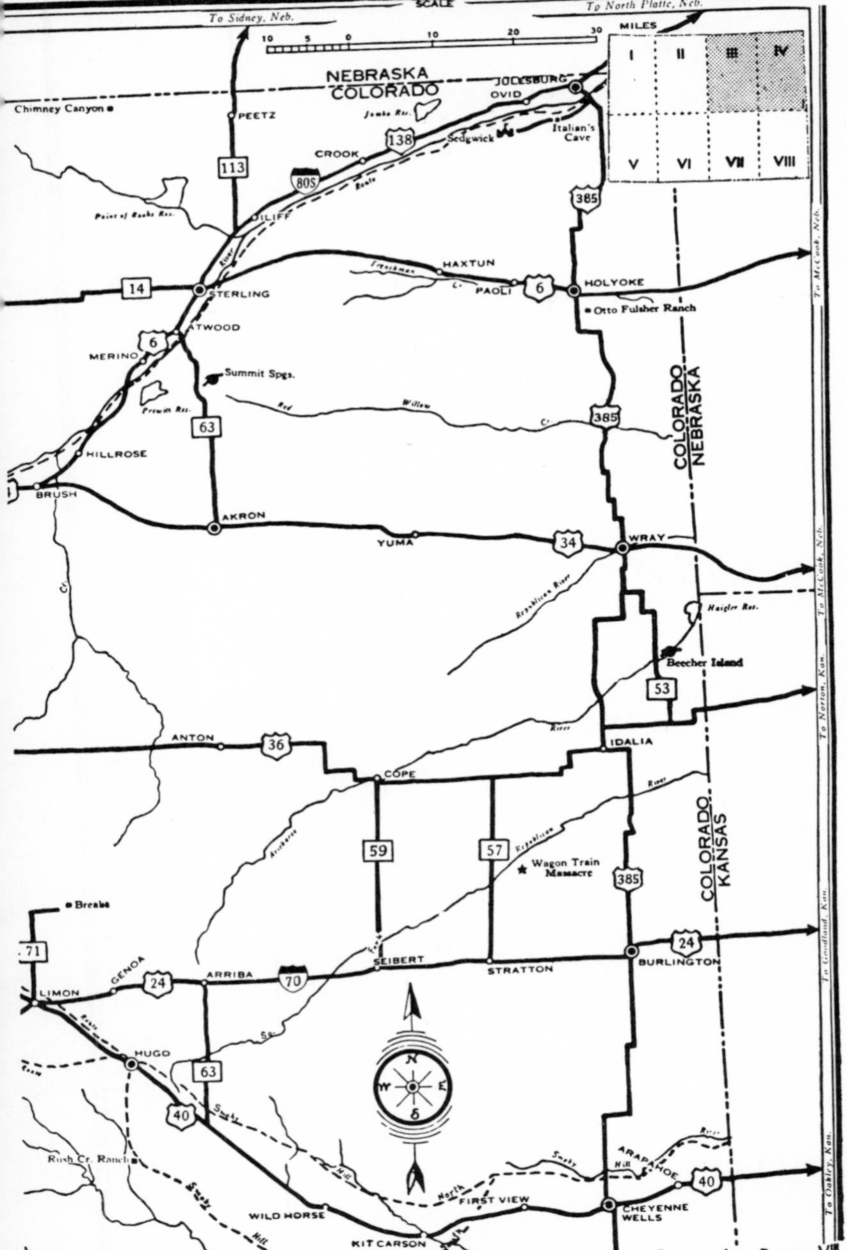

Continued on Section VIII

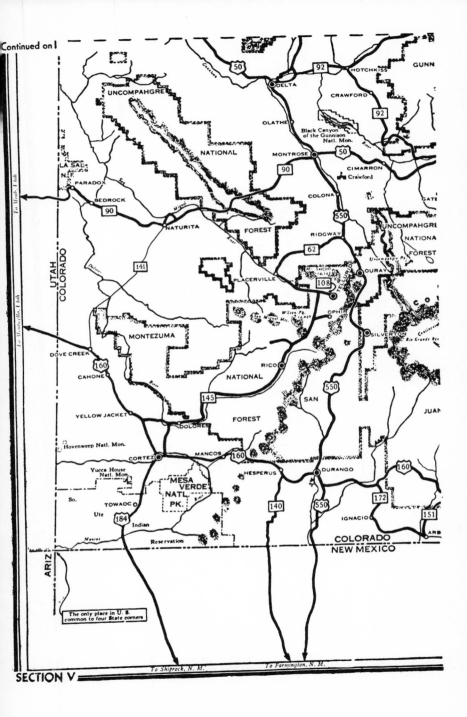

Continued on I

SECTION V

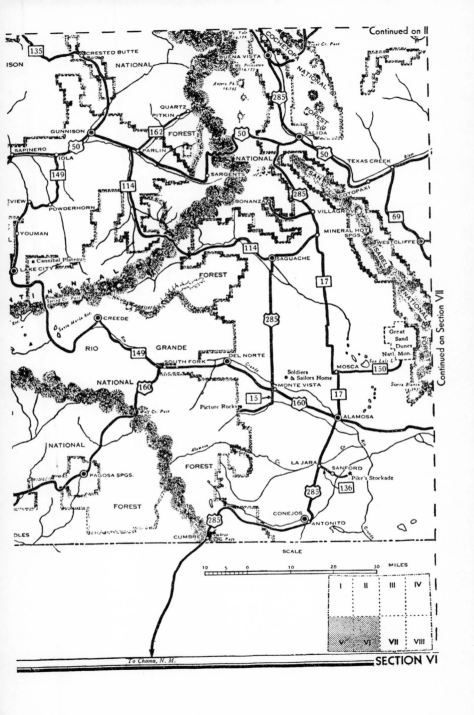

Continued on Section VII

ISON

135   CRESTED BUTTE

NATIONAL

Mt. Yale 14,170

BUENA VISTA

COCHETOPA

NATIONAL

Great Cr. Pass

Mt. Princeton 14,179

Antero Pk. 14,245

285

QUARTZ

PITKIN

FOREST

GUNNISON

162

50

SALIDA

SAPINERO   50

IOLA

PARLIN

NATIONAL

SARGENTS

TEXAS CREEK

SAN

149

114

POWDERHORN

285

COTOPAXI

VIEW

YOUMAN

BONANZA

VILLAGRO

69

WESTCLIFFE

MINERAL HOT SPGS.

Cannibal Plateau

LAKE CITY

114

SAGUACHE

ISABEL

NENTAL

FOREST

17

NATIONAL

CREEDE

285

Great Sand Dunes Natl. Mon.

RIO   GRANDE

149   SOUTH FORK

DEL NORTE

MOSCA

San Luis L.

150

NATIONAL

160

Soldiers & Sailors Home

MONTE VISTA

Sierra Blanca 14,363

15

160

17

Picture Rocks

ALAMOSA

NATIONAL

PAGOSA SPGS.

FOREST

Alamosa

LA JARA

SANFORD

FOREST

Pike's Stockade

285   136

CONEJOS

DLES

285   ANTONITO

CUMBRES

SCALE

10   5   0   10   20   30   MILES

I	II	III	IV
V	VI	VII	VIII

To Chama, N. M.

SECTION VI

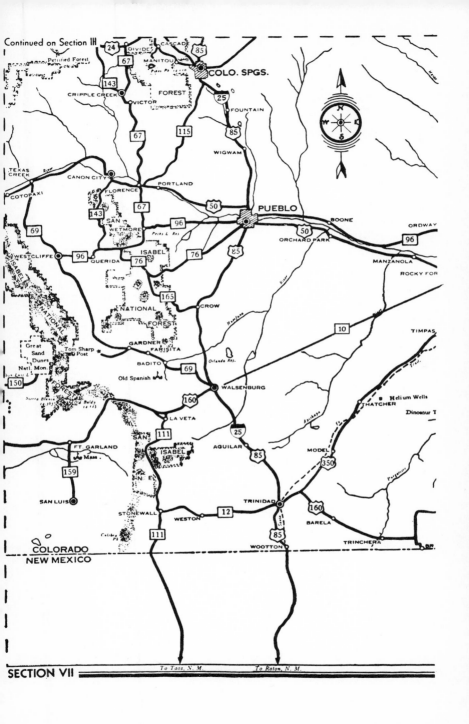

Continued on Section III

SECTION VII

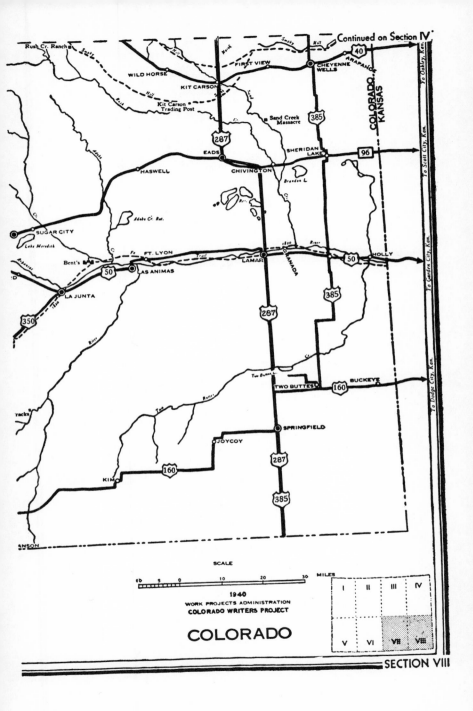

Continued on Section IV

Rush Cr. Ranch

WILD HORSE

FIRST VIEW

To Oatley, Kan.

CHEYENNE
WELLS

ARAPAHOE

40

KIT CARSON

Kit Carson
Trading Post

Sand Creek
Massacre

385

COLORADO
KANSAS

287

EADS

SHERIDAN
LAKE

96

To Scott City, Kan.

HASWELL

CHIVINGTON

Brandon L.

SUGAR CITY

Lake Meredith

FT. LYON

Trail

River

HOLLY

Bent's

50

LAMAR

CANADA

50

LAS ANIMAS

LA JUNTA

385

350

287

To Garden City, Kan.

Two Buttes Cr.

BUCKEYE

TWO BUTTES

160

SPRINGFIELD

JOYCOY

287

KIM

160

To Dodge City, Kan.

385

ANSON

SCALE

10   5   0   10   20   30

MILES

1940
WORK PROJECTS ADMINISTRATION
COLORADO WRITERS PROJECT

COLORADO

I	II	III	IV
V	VI	VII	VIII

SECTION VIII

Index